ENTREPRENEURSHIP

NINTH EDITION

ROBERT D. HISRICH, PhD

Garvin Professor of Global Entrepreneurship
Director, Walker Center for Global Entrepreneurship
Thunderbird School of Global Management

MICHAEL P. PETERS, PhD

Professor Emeritus
Carroll School of Management
Boston College

DEAN A. SHEPHERD, PhD

Randall L. Tobias Chair in Entrepreneurial Leadership and
Professor of Entrepreneurship
Kelley School of Business
Indiana University

McGraw-Hill Irwin

D1471662

The McGraw-Hill Companies

ENTREPRENEURSHIP, NINTH EDITION
International Edition 2013

Exclusive rights by McGraw-Hill Education (Asia), for manufacture and export. This book cannot be re-exported from the country to which it is sold by McGraw-Hill. This International Edition is not to be sold or purchased in North America and contains content that is different from its North American version.

Published by McGraw-Hill, a business unit of The McGraw-Hill Companies, Inc., 1221 Avenue of the Americas, New York, NY 10020. Copyright © 2013 by The McGraw-Hill Companies, Inc. Previous editions © 2010, 2008, and 2005. All rights reserved. No part of this publication may be reproduced or distributed in any form or by any means, or stored in a database or retrieval system, without the prior written consent of The McGraw-Hill Companies, Inc., including, but not limited to, in any network or other electronic storage or transmission, or broadcast for distance learning.

Some ancillaries, including electronic and print components, may not be available to customers outside the United States.

10 09 08 07 06 05 04 03 02 01
20 15 14 13 12
CTP SLP

When ordering this title, use ISBN 978-007-132631-5 or MHID 007-132631-6

Printed in Singapore

www.mhhe.com

To our wives,
Tina, Debbie, and Suzie,
and children,
Kary, Katy, Kelly, Christa, Kimberly, Jack, and Meg,
and grandchildren,
Rachel, Andrew, Sarah, and Jack,
for their supportive entrepreneurial spirit

ABOUT THE AUTHORS

ROBERT D. HISRICH

Robert D. Hisrich is the Garvin Professor of Global Entrepreneurship and Director of the Walker Center for Global Entrepreneurship at Thunderbird School of Global Management. He holds a B.A. from DePauw University and an M.B.A. and a doctorate from the University of Cincinnati.

Professor Hisrich's research pursuits are focused on entrepreneurship and venture creation: entrepreneurial ethics, corporate entrepreneurship, women and minority entrepreneurs, venture financing, and global venture creation. He teaches courses and seminars in these areas, as well as in marketing management and product planning and development. His interest in global management and entrepreneurship resulted in two Fulbright Fellowships in Budapest, Hungary, honorary degrees from Chuvash State University (Russia) and University of Miskolc (Hungary), and being a visiting faculty member in universities in Austria, Australia, Ireland, and Slovenia. Professor Hisrich serves on the editorial boards of several prominent journals in entrepreneurial scholarship, is on several boards of directors, and is author or coauthor of over 300 research articles appearing in such journals as *Journal of Marketing, Journal of Marketing Research, Journal of Business Venturing, Journal of Small Business Finance, Small Business Economics, Journal of Developmental Entrepreneurship,* and *Entrepreneurship Theory and Practice.* Professor Hisrich has authored or coauthored 28 books or their editions, including *Marketing: A Practical Management Approach, How to Fix and Prevent the 13 Biggest Problems That Derail Business, International Entrepreneurship: Starting, Developing and Managing a Global Venture,* and *Technology Entrepreneurship: Value Creation, Protection, and Capture.*

MICHAEL P. PETERS

Michael P. Peters is Professor Emeritus, Marketing Department, Carroll School of Management, Boston College. He has his Ph.D. from the University of Massachusetts, Amherst, and his M.B.A. and B.S. from Northeastern University. Presently retired from full-time teaching, Professor Peters has been a visiting professor at the American College of Greece's Graduate School of Business, in Athens, Greece. There he developed an entrepreneurship and business planning component in its M.B.A. program. In addition, he continues to write, lecture, serve on numerous boards, and assist in the management of a family business. Besides his passion for assisting American entrepreneurs in new ventures he has consulted and conducted seminars and workshops worldwide related to entrepreneurship, international and domestic decision making for new product development, market planning, and market strategy. He has published over thirty articles in such journals as the *Journal of Business Research, Journal of Marketing, Journal of Marketing Research, Journal of International Business Studies, Columbia Journal of World Business, Journal of Business Venturing,* and the *Sloan Management Review.* He has co-authored three texts, *Marketing a New Product: Its Planning, Development and Control; Marketing Decisions for New and Mature Products;* and *Entrepreneurship,* now in its 9th edition. He was Department Chair and Director of the Small Business Institute at Boston College for more than 16 years. He loves photography, tennis, golf, and kayaking on Cape Cod Bay.

DEAN A. SHEPHERD

Dean A. Shepherd is the Randall L. Tobias Chair in Entrepreneurial Leadership at the Kelley School of Business, Indiana University. Dean received his doctorate and M.B.A. from Bond University (Australia). His research is in the field of entrepreneurial leadership; he investigates both the decision making involved in leveraging cognitive and other resources to act on opportunities and the processes of learning from experimentation, in ways that ultimately lead to high levels of individual and organizational performance. Dean has published, or has accepted for publication, over 100 papers primarily in the top entrepreneurship, general management, strategic management, operations management, and psychology journals.

PREFACE

Starting and operating a new business involves considerable risk and effort to overcome the inertia against creating something new. In creating and growing a new venture, the entrepreneur assumes the responsibility and risks for its development and survival and enjoys the corresponding rewards. This risk is compounded for entrepreneurs who go international or in fact are born global. The fact that consumers, businesspeople, and government officials from every part of the world are interested in entrepreneurship is evident from the increasing research on the subject, the large number of courses and seminars on the topic, the more than 2 million new enterprises started each year (despite a 70 percent failure rate), the significant coverage and focus by the media, and the realization that this is an important aspect of the economics of developed, developing, and even controlled economies.

Who is the focus of all this attention? Who is willing to accept all the risks and put forth the effort necessary to create a new venture? It may be a man or a woman, someone from an upper-class or lower-class background, a technologist or someone lacking technological sophistication, a college graduate, or a high school dropout. The person may be an inventor, manager, nurse, salesperson, engineer, student, teacher, homemaker, or retiree. It is always someone able to juggle work, family, and civic responsibilities while meeting payroll.

To provide an understanding of this person and the process of creating and growing a new venture on an international basis, this ninth edition of *Entrepreneurship* is divided into five major sections.

Part 1—The Entrepreneurial Perspective introduces the entrepreneur and the entrepreneurial process from both a historical and a research perspective. The role and nature of entrepreneurship as a mechanism for creating new ventures and affecting economic development are presented, along with career aspects and the future direction of entrepreneurship. The characteristics and background of entrepreneurs are discussed, as well as some methods for individual self-assessment. Following the presentation of corporate entrepreneurship, this part concludes with a discussion of strategies for generating and exploiting new entries.

Part 2—From Idea to the Opportunity focuses on the aspects of creativity and innovation and all the elements in the entrepreneurial process that are a part of creating the new venture. Focus is on the various sources of ideas as well as trends occurring through this decade. Specific attention is also paid to various creative problem-solving technologies, identifying domestic and international opportunities, creating an opportunity analysis plan, and protecting the idea developed, as well as other legal concerns in forming and launching the venture.

Part 3—From the Opportunity to the Business Plan focuses on the all-important business plan. First, the overall business plan and its various aspects are presented. Then, a chapter is devoted to each of the major components of the business plan: the marketing plan, the financial plan, and the organizational plan.

Part 4—From the Business Plan to Funding the Venture focuses on one of the most difficult aspects of creating and establishing a new venture—raising capital. First the aspects of debt versus equity and internal versus external funding are discussed. After a discussion of the alternative sources of capital (self, family and friends, suppliers and trade credit, government grants and programs, private placements, and commercial banks) specific attention is given to three financing mechanisms: informal risk capital, venture capital, and going public.

Part 5—From Funding the Venture to Launching, Growing, and Ending the New Venture presents material related to establishing, developing, and ending the venture. Particular attention is paid to developing an entrepreneurial strategy, establishing strategies for growth, managing the new venture during growth, early operations, expansion, and accessing external resources for growth. Managerial skills that are important to the successful performance and growth of a new venture are included in this part, which also addresses methods for ending the venture. Specific topics examined include mergers and acquisitions, franchising, joint ventures, and human and financial resources needed for growth.

To make *Entrepreneurship,* ninth edition, as meaningful as possible to the student, each chapter begins with chapter learning objectives and a profile of an entrepreneur whose career is especially relevant to the chapter material. Numerous business examples occur throughout each chapter along with important Web sites to assist the reader in getting started. Boxed summaries of articles in the news ("As Seen in *Business News*") that illustrate the chapter discussion and Ethics boxes discussing ethical issues are found in all the chapters. Each chapter concludes with research tasks, class discussion questions, and selected readings for further research and study.

At the end of the book is a selection of Cases that can be used along with any chapter, as well as a listing of other appropriate cases on a chapter by chapter basis.

Many people—students, business executives, entrepreneurs, professors, and publishing staff—have made this book possible. Of great assistance were the detailed and thoughtful comments of our reviewers:

Ted Khoury
Oregon State University

Craig Watters
Syracuse University

Howard Van Auken
Iowa State University

Daniel Bochsler
University of Texas, Dallas

Robert Garrett
Oregon State University

Special thanks go to Carol Pacelli for preparing the manuscript so competently and to Tracy Droessler, David Kralik, Rebecca Knowles, and Katie Nehlsen for providing research material, editorial assistance, and case development for this edition. Also thanks to our editors—Anke Weekes, brand manager, and Laura Hurst Spell, managing developmental editor. We are deeply indebted to our spouses, Tina, Debbie, and Suzie, whose support and understanding helped bring this effort to fruition. It is to future entrepreneurs—our children Kary, Katy, Kelly, Christa, Kimberly, Jack, and Meg and grandchildren Rachel, Andrew, Sarah, and Jack—and the new generation they represent—that this book is particularly dedicated. May you always beg forgiveness rather than ask permission.

Robert D. Hisrich
Michael P. Peters
Dean A. Shepherd

CONTENTS IN BRIEF

CONTENTS

15   SUCCESSION PLANNING AND STRATEGIES FOR HARVESTING AND ENDING THE VENTURE   416

PART 6   CASES   441

1

THE ENTREPRENEURIAL PERSPECTIVE

1

ENTREPRENEURSHIP AND THE ENTREPRENEURIAL MIND-SET

1

To introduce the concept of entrepreneurship and explain the process of entrepreneurial action.

2

To describe how structural similarities enable entrepreneurs to make creative mental leaps.

3

To highlight bricolage as a source of entrepreneurs' resourcefulness.

4

To introduce effectuation as a way expert entrepreneurs sometimes think.

5

To develop the notion that entrepreneurs cognitively adapt.

6

To introduce sustainable entrepreneurship as a means of sustaining the natural environment and communities and developing gains for others.

OPENING PROFILE

EWING MARION KAUFFMAN

Born on a farm in Garden City, Missouri, Ewing Marion Kauffman moved to Kansas City with his family when he was eight years old. A critical event in his life occurred several years later when Kauffman was diagnosed with a leakage of the heart. His prescription was one year of complete bed rest; he was not even allowed to sit up.

www.kauffman.org

Kauffman's mother, a college graduate, came up with a solution to keep the active 11-year-old boy lying in bed—reading. According to Kauffman, he "sure read! Because nothing else would do, I read as many as 40 to 50 books every month. When you read that much, you read anything. So I read the biographies of all the presidents, the frontiersmen, and I read the Bible twice and that's pretty rough reading."

Another important early childhood experience centered on door-to-door sales. Since his family did not have a lot of money, Kauffman would sell 36 dozen eggs collected from the farm or fish he and his father had caught, cleaned, and dressed. His mother was very encouraging during these formative school years, telling young Ewing each day, "There may be some who have more money in their pockets, but Ewing, there is nobody better than you."

During his youth, Kauffman worked as a laundry delivery person and was a Boy Scout. In addition to passing all the requirements to become an Eagle Scout and a Sea Scout, he sold twice as many tickets to the Boy Scout Roundup as anyone else in Kansas City, an accomplishment that enabled him to attend, for free, a two-week scout summer camp that his parents would not otherwise have been able to afford. According to Kauffman, "This experience gave me some of the sales techniques which came into play when subsequently I went into the pharmaceutical business."

Kauffman went to junior college from 8 to 12 in the morning and then walked two miles to the laundry where he worked until 7 p.m. Upon graduation, he went to work at the laundry full time for Mr. R. A. Long, who would eventually become one of his role models. His job as route foreman involved managing 18 to 20 route drivers, where he would set up sales contests, such as challenging the other drivers to get more customers on a particular route than he could obtain. Ewing says, "I got practice in selling and that proved to be beneficial later in life." R. A. Long made money not only at the

3

laundry business but also on patents, one of which was a form fit for the collar of a shirt that would hold the shape of the shirt. He showed his young protégé that one could make money with brains as well as brawn. Kauffman commented, "He was quite a man and had quite an influence on my life."

Kauffman's sales ability was also useful during his stint in the Navy, which he joined shortly after Pearl Harbor on January 11, 1942. When designated as an apprentice seaman, a position that paid $21 per month, he responded, "I'm better than an apprentice seaman, because I have been a Sea Scout. I've sailed ships and I've ridden in whale boats." His selling ability convinced the Navy that he should instead start as a seaman first class, with a $54 monthly salary. Kauffman was assigned to the admiral's staff, where he became an outstanding signalman (a seaman who transmitted messages from ship to ship), in part because he was able to read messages better than anyone else due to his previous intensive reading. With his admiral's encouragement, Kauffman took a correspondence navigator's course and was given a deck commission and made a navigation officer.

After the war was over in 1947, Ewing Kauffman began his career as a pharmaceutical salesperson after performing better on an aptitude test than 50 other applicants. The job involved selling supplies of vitamin and liver shots to doctors. Working on straight commission, without expenses or benefits, he was earning pay higher than the president's salary by the end of the second year; the president promptly cut the commission. Eventually, when Kauffman was made Midwest sales manager, he made 3 percent of everything his salespeople sold and continued to make more money than the president. When his territory was cut, he eventually quit and in 1950 started his own company—Marion Laboratories. (Marion is his middle name.)

When reflecting on founding the new company, Ewing Kauffman commented, "It was easier than it sounds because I had doctors whom I had been selling office supplies to for several years. Before I made the break, I went to three of them and said, 'I'm thinking of starting my own company. May I count on you to give me your orders if I can give you the same quality and service?' These three were my biggest accounts and each one of them agreed because they liked me and were happy to do business with me."

Marion Laboratories started by marketing injectable products that were manufactured by another company under Marion's label. The company expanded to other accounts and other products and then developed its first prescription item, Vicam, a vitamin product. The second pharmaceutical product it developed, oyster shell calcium, also sold well.

To expand the company, Kauffman borrowed $5,000 from the Commerce Trust Company. He repaid the loan, and the company continued to grow. After several years, outside investors could buy $1,000 worth of common stock if they loaned the company $1,000 to be paid back in five years at $1,250, without any intermittent interest. This initial $1,000 investment, if held until 1993, would have been worth $21 million.

Marion Laboratories continued to grow and reached over $1 billion per year in sales, due primarily to the relationship between Ewing Kauffman and the people in the company, who were called associates, not employees. "They are all stockholders, they build this company, and they mean so much to us," said Kauffman. The concept of associates was also a part of the two basic philosophies of the company: Those who produce should share in the results or profits, and treat others as you would like to be treated.

The company went public through Smith Barney on August 16, 1965, at $21 per share. The stock jumped to $28 per share immediately and has never dropped below that level, sometimes selling at a 50 to 60 price/earnings multiple. The associates of the company were offered a profit-sharing plan, where each could own stock in the company. In 1968 Kauffman brought Major League Baseball back to Kansas City by purchasing the Kansas City Royals. This boosted the city's economic base, community profile, and civic pride. When Marion Laboratories merged with Merrill Dow in 1989, there were 3,400 associates, 300 of whom became millionaires as a result of the merger. The new company, Marion Merrill Dow, Inc., grew to 9,000 associates and sales of $4 billion in 1998 when it was acquired by Hoechst, a European pharmaceutical company. Hoechst Marion Roussel became a world leader in pharmaceutical-based health care involved in the discovery, development, manufacture, and sale of pharmaceutical products. In late 1999 the company was again merged with Aventis Pharma, a global pharmaceutical company focusing on human medicines (prescription pharmaceuticals and vaccines) and animal health. In 2002, Aventis's sales reached $16.634 billion, an increase of 11.6 percent from 2001, while earnings per share grew 27 percent from the previous year.

Ewing Marion Kauffman was an entrepreneur, a Major League Baseball team owner, and a philanthropist who believed his success was a direct result of one fundamental philosophy: Treat others as you would like to be treated. "It is the happiest principle by which to live and the most intelligent principle by which to do business and make money," he said.

Ewing Marion Kauffman's philosophies of associates, rewarding those who produce, and allowing decision making throughout the organization are the fundamental concepts underlying what is now called *corporate entrepreneurship* in a company. He went even further and illustrated his belief in entrepreneurship and the spirit of giving back when he established the Kauffman Foundation, which supports programs in two areas: youth development and entrepreneurship. Truly a remarkable entrepreneur, Mr. K, as he was affectionately called by his employees, will now produce many more successful "associate entrepreneurs."

Like Ewing Marion Kauffman, many other entrepreneurs and future entrepreneurs frequently ask themselves, "Am I really an entrepreneur? Do I have what it takes to be a success? Do I have sufficient background and experience to start and manage a new venture?" As enticing as the thought of starting and owning a business may be, the problems and pitfalls inherent to the process are as legendary as the success stories. The fact remains that more new business ventures fail than succeed. To be one of the few successful entrepreneurs requires more than just hard work and luck. It requires the ability to think in an environment of high uncertainty, be flexible, and learn from one's failures.

THE NATURE OF ENTREPRENEURSHIP

entrepreneurial opportunities Those situations in which new goods, services, raw materials, and organizing methods can be introduced and sold at greater than their cost of production

entrepreneurial action Action through the creation of new products/processes and/or the entry into new markets, which may occur through a newly created organization or within an established organization

entrepreneurial thinking Individuals' mental processes of overcoming ignorance to decide whether a signal represents an opportunity for someone and/or reducing doubt as to whether an opportunity for someone is also an opportunity for them specifically, and/or processing feedback from action steps taken

Entrepreneurship plays an important role in the creation and growth of businesses, as well as in the growth and prosperity of regions and nations. These large-scale outcomes can have quite humble beginnings; entrepreneurial actions begin at the nexus of a lucrative opportunity and an enterprising individual.[1] *Entrepreneurial opportunities* are "those situations in which new goods, services, raw materials, and organizing methods can be introduced and sold at greater than their cost of production."[2] For example, an entrepreneurial opportunity could stem from introducing an existing technological product used in one market to create a new market. Alternatively, an entrepreneurial opportunity could be creating a new technological product for an existing market or creating both a new product/service and a new market. The recurring theme is that an entrepreneurial opportunity represents something new. However, such possibilities require an enterprising individual or a group of enterprising individuals to recognize, evaluate, and exploit these situations as possible opportunities. Therefore, entrepreneurship requires action—*entrepreneurial action* through the creation of new products/processes and/or the entry into new markets, which may occur through a newly created organization or within an established organization.

Entrepreneurs act on what they believe is an opportunity. Because opportunities exist in (or create and/or generate) high uncertainty, entrepreneurs must use their judgment about whether or not to act. However, doubt can undermine entrepreneurial action. Therefore, a key to understanding entrepreneurial action is being able to assess the amount of uncertainty perceived to surround a potential opportunity and the individual's willingness to bear that uncertainty. The individual's prior knowledge can decrease the amount of uncertainty, and his or her motivation indicates a willingness to bear uncertainty.

As illustrated in Figure 1.1, the McMullen-Shepherd model explains how knowledge and motivation influence two stages of entrepreneurial action. Signals of changes in the environment that represent possible opportunities will be noticed by some individuals but not others. Individuals with knowledge of markets and/or technology are more capable of detecting changes in the external environment, and if they are also motivated, they will allocate further attention to processing this information. Others, however, will remain ignorant of the possibility. The result of Stage 1 is an individual's realization that an opportunity exists for someone. The individual then needs to determine whether it represents an opportunity for him or her (Stage 2). This involves assessing whether it is feasible to successfully exploit the opportunity given one's knowledge and whether it is desirable given one's motivation. In other words, does this opportunity for someone (third-person opportunity belief) represent an opportunity for me (first-person opportunity belief)? If the individual overcomes enough doubt to form (1) the belief that the situation represents an opportunity for someone in general, and then (2) the belief that the opportunity for someone is an opportunity for himself or herself personally, this individual may act.

Therefore, to be an entrepreneur is to act on the possibility that one has identified an opportunity worth pursuing.[3] It involves *entrepreneurial thinking*—individuals' mental processes of overcoming ignorance to decide whether a signal represents an opportunity for someone and/or reducing doubt as to whether an opportunity for someone is also an opportunity for them specifically, and/or processing feedback from action steps taken. To explain these processes more fully, we now turn to different forms of entrepreneurial thinking.

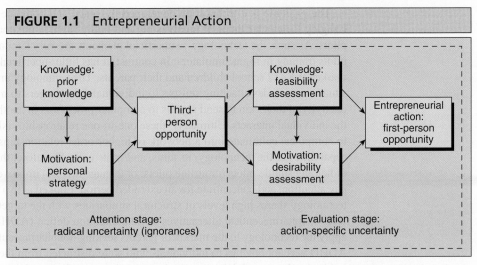

FIGURE 1.1   Entrepreneurial Action

Reprinted with permission from McMullen, J. and Shepherd, D. A. (2006). Entrepreneurial Action and the Role of Uncertainty in the Theory of the Entrepreneur. *Academy of Management Review*. 31: 132–142.

HOW ENTREPRENEURS THINK

Entrepreneurs think differently from nonentrepreneurs. Moreover, an entrepreneur in a particular situation may think differently from when faced with some other task or decision environment. Entrepreneurs must often make decisions in highly uncertain environments where the stakes are high, time pressures are immense, and there is considerable emotional investment. We all think differently in these strained environments than we do when the nature of a problem is well understood and we have time and rational procedures at hand to solve it. Given the nature of an entrepreneur's decision-making environment, he or she must sometimes (1) think structurally, (2) engage in bricolage, (3) effectuate, and (4) cognitively adapt.

Think Structurally

Forming opportunity beliefs often requires creative mental leaps. These creative mental leaps are launched from a source—one's existing knowledge. In the case of entrepreneurial opportunities, an example of a creative mental leap is from knowledge about existing markets to a new technology that could lead to products/services that satisfy that market. Alternatively, the creative mental leap could be from knowledge about a technology to a new market that could benefit from its introduction. Making these connections between a new product (or new service, new business model, or new technology) and a target market where it can be introduced is aided by the superficial and structural similarities between the source (e.g., the market) and the destination (e.g., technology). *Superficial similarities* exist when the basic (relatively easy to observe) elements of the technology resemble (match) the basic (relatively easy to observe) elements of the market. In contrast, *structural similarities* exist when the underlying mechanisms of the technology resemble (or match) the underlying mechanisms of the market. The entrepreneurial challenge often lies in making creative mental leaps based on *structural* similarities. This is best illustrated with an example based on a real case that Denis Gregoire from Syracuse University and me (Dean Shepherd from Indiana University) used as part of a study of entrepreneurial thinking.[4]

superficial similarities
Exist when the basic (relatively easy to observe) elements of the technology resemble (match) the basic (relatively easy to observe) elements of the market

structural similarities
Exist when the underlying mechanisms of the technology resemble (or match) the underlying mechanisms of the market

The example is a technology developed by space and computer engineers at NASA's Langley Research Center. It involves big and bulky flight simulators used by space shuttle pilots. As such, the technology's superficial elements are very similar to a market for airline pilots training in flight simulators. In contrast, it has little superficial similarity with a target market of K–12 school children and their parents. The technology underlying the superficial situations includes attaching sensors to individuals' forefingers to monitor the electric conductivity of their skin to send signals to computer processors in another machine with which the individual interacts. Ultimately, these one-to-one relationships (skin to sensor and sensor to computer) culminate into a network of higher order relationships that reflect the overall capabilities of the technology, its aims, and/or its uses. Therefore, the technology is capable of helping shuttle pilots (or airline pilots, or teenage drivers) improve their abilities to focus, pay attention, and concentrate for an extended period. Looked at in a new light, however, the technology shares high levels of structural similarities with the target market of parents who seek nonpharmaceutical alternatives to treat attention deficit (ADHD). This opportunity to apply the technology to the market of parents seeking nonpharmaceutical alternatives to treat ADHD was not obvious to individuals who were distracted from the deeper structural similarities by the superficial mismatch between the technology and the new market.

Thus, individuals who can see or create structural matches between a technology and a target market, especially in the presence of superficial mismatches, are more likely to recognize entrepreneurial opportunities. Knowledge specific to a technology and/or a market can facilitate this ability,[5] and the good news is that this skill can also be enhanced through practice and training.

Bricolage

bricolage Entrepreneurs making do by applying combinations of the resources at hand to new problems and opportunities

Entrepreneurs often lack resources. As a result, they either seek resources from others to provide the "slack" necessary to experiment and generate entrepreneurial opportunities, or they engage in bricolage. By *bricolage* we mean that some entrepreneurs make "do by applying combinations of the resources at hand to new problems and opportunities."[6] This involves taking existing resources (those at hand) and experimenting, tinkering, repackaging, and/or reframing them so they can be used in a way for which they were not originally designed or conceived.[7] From this process of "making do," entrepreneurs can create opportunities. Baker and Nelson (2005: 341–42) offer the following example of bricolage.

Tim Grayson was a farmer whose land was crisscrossed by abandoned coal mines. He knew that the tunnels—a nuisance to farmers because of their tendency to collapse, causing mammoth sinkholes in fields—also contained large quantities of methane. Methane is another nuisance, a toxic greenhouse gas that poisons miners and persists in abandoned mines for generations. Grayson and a partner drilled a hole from Grayson's property to an abandoned mine shaft, then acquired a used diesel generator from a local factory and crudely retrofitted it to burn methane. During the conversion process, Grayson was repeatedly blown off his feet when the odorless, colorless gas exploded. His bricolage produced electricity, most of which he sold to the local utility company using scavenged switchgear. Because Grayson's generator also produced considerable waste heat, he built a greenhouse for hydroponic tomatoes, which he heated with water from the generator's cooling system. He also used electricity generated during off-peak hours to power special lamps to speed plant growth. With the availability of a greenhouse full of trenches of nutrient-rich water that were heated "for free," Grayson realized he might be able to raise tilapia, a tropical delicacy increasingly popular in the United States. He introduced the fish to the waters that bathed the tomato roots and used the fish waste as fertilizer. Finally, with abundant methane still at hand, Tim began selling excess methane to a natural gas company. As you can see from this example, bricolage is a resourceful way of thinking and behaving that represents an important source of entrepreneurial opportunities.

Effectuation

As potential business leaders you are trained to think rationally and perhaps admonished if you do not. This admonishment might be appropriate given the nature of the task, but it appears that there is an alternate way of thinking that entrepreneurs sometimes use, especially when thinking about opportunities. Professor Saras Sarasvathy (from Darden, University of Virginia) has found that entrepreneurs do not always think through a problem in a way that starts with a desired outcome and focuses on the means to generate that outcome. Such a process is referred to as a *causal process*. But, entrepreneurs sometimes use an *effectuation process,* which means they take what they have (who they are, what they know, and whom they know) and select among possible outcomes. Professor Saras is a great cook, so it is not surprising that her examples of these thought processes revolve around cooking.

causal process   A process that starts with a desired outcome and focuses on the means to generate that outcome

effectuation process   A process that starts with what one has (who they are, what they know, and whom they know) and selects among possible outcomes

Imagine a chef assigned the task of cooking dinner. There are two ways the task can be organized. In the first, the host or client picks out a menu in advance. All the chef needs to do is list the ingredients needed, shop for them, and then actually cook the meal. This is a process of causation. It begins with a given menu and focuses on selecting between effective ways to prepare the meal.

In the second case, the host asks the chef to look through the cupboards in the kitchen for possible ingredients and utensils and then cook a meal. Here, the chef has to imagine possible menus based on the given ingredients and utensils, select the menu, and then prepare the meal. This is a process of effectuation. It begins with given ingredients and utensils and focuses on preparing one of many possible desirable meals with them.[8]

Sarasvathy's Thought Experiment #1: Curry in a Hurry

In this example I [Sarasvathy] trace the process for building an imaginary Indian restaurant, "Curry in a Hurry." Two cases, one using causation and the other effectuation, are examined. For the purposes of this illustration, the example chosen is a typical causation process that underlies many economic theories today—theories in which it is argued that artifacts such as firms are inevitable outcomes, given the preference orderings of economic actors and certain simple assumptions of rationality (implying causal reasoning) in their choice behavior. The causation process used in the example here is typified by and embodied in the procedures stated by Philip Kotler in his *Marketing Management* (1991: 63, 263), a book that in its many editions is considered a classic and is widely used as a textbook in MBA programs around the world.

Kotler defines a market as follows: "A market consists of all the potential customers sharing a particular need or want who might be willing and able to engage in exchange to satisfy that need or want" (1991: 63). Given a product or a service, Kotler suggests the following procedure for bringing the product/service to market (note that Kotler assumes the market exists):

1. Analyze long-run opportunities in the market.
2. Research and select target markets.
3. Identify segmentation variables and segment the market.
4. Develop profiles of resulting segments.
5. Evaluate the attractiveness of each segment.
6. Select the target segment(s).
7. Identify possible positioning concepts for each target segment.
8. Select, develop, and communicate the chosen positioning concept.
9. Design marketing strategies.

10. Plan marketing programs.

11. Organize, implement, and control marketing effort.

This process is commonly known in marketing as the STP—segmentation, targeting, and positioning—process.

Curry in a Hurry is a restaurant with a new twist—say, an Indian restaurant with a fast food section. The current paradigm using causation processes indicates that, to implement this idea, the entrepreneur should start with a universe of all potential customers. Let us imagine that she wants to build her restaurant in Pittsburgh, Pennsylvania, USA, which will then become the initial universe or market for Curry in a Hurry. Assuming that the percentage of the population of Pittsburgh that totally abhors Indian food is negligible, the entrepreneur can start the STP process.

Several relevant segmentation variables, such as demographics, residential neighborhoods, ethnic origin, marital status, income level, and patterns of eating out, could be used. On the basis of these, the entrepreneur could send out questionnaires to selected neighborhoods and organize focus groups at, say, the two major universities in Pittsburgh. Analyzing responses to the questionnaires and focus groups, she could arrive at a target segment—for example, wealthy families, both Indian and others, who eat out at least twice a week. That would help her determine her menu choices, decor, hours, and other operational details. She could then design marketing and sales campaigns to induce her target segment to try her restaurant. She could also visit other Indian and fast food restaurants and find some method of surveying them and then develop plausible demand forecasts for her planned restaurant.

In any case, the process would involve considerable amounts of time and analytical effort. It would also require resources both for research and, thereafter, for implementing the marketing strategies. In summary, the current paradigm suggests that we proceed inward to specifics from a larger, general universe—that is, to an optimal target segment from a predetermined market. In terms of Curry in a Hurry, this could mean something like a progression from the entire city of Pittsburgh to Fox Chapel (an affluent residential neighborhood) to the Joneses (specific customer profile of a wealthy family), as it were.

Instead, if our imaginary entrepreneur were to use processes of effectuation to build her restaurant, she would have to proceed in the opposite direction (note that effectuation is suggested here as a viable and descriptively valid alternative to the STP process—not as a normatively superior one). For example, instead of starting with the assumption of an existing market and investing money and other resources to design the best possible restaurant for the given market, she would begin by examining the particular set of means or causes available to her. Assuming she has extremely limited monetary resources—say $20,000—she should think creatively to bring the idea to market with as close to zero resources as possible. She could do this by convincing an established restaurateur to become a strategic partner or by doing just enough market research to convince a financier to invest the money needed to start the restaurant. Another method of effectuation would be to convince a local Indian restaurant or a local fast food restaurant to allow her to put up a counter where she would actually sell a selection of Indian fast food. Selecting a menu and honing other such details would be seat-of-the-pants and tentative, perhaps a process of satisficing.[9]

Several other courses of effectuation can be imagined. Perhaps the course the entrepreneur actually pursues is to contact one or two of her friends or relatives who work downtown and bring them and their office colleagues some of her food to taste. If the people in the office like her food, she might get a lunch delivery service going. Over time, she might develop enough of a customer base to start a restaurant or else, after a few weeks of trying to build the lunch business, she might discover that the people who said they enjoyed her food did not really enjoy it so much as they did her quirky personality and conversation, particularly her rather unusual life perceptions. Our imaginary entrepreneur might now decide to give up the lunch business and start writing a book, going on the lecture circuit and eventually building a business in the motivational consulting industry!

Given the exact same starting point—but with a different set of contingencies—the entrepreneur might end up building one of a variety of businesses. To take a quick tour of some possibilities, consider the following: Whoever first buys the food from our imaginary Curry in a Hurry entrepreneur becomes, by definition, the first target customer. By continually listening to the customer and building an ever-increasing network of customers and strategic partners, the entrepreneur can then identify a workable segment profile. For example, if the first customers who actually buy the food and come back for more are working women of varied ethnic origin, this becomes her target segment. Depending on what the first customer really wants, she can start defining her market. If the customer is really interested in the food, the entrepreneur can start targeting all working women in the geographic location, or she can think in terms of locating more outlets in areas with working women of similar profiles—a "Women in a Hurry" franchise?

Or, if the customer is interested primarily in the idea of ethnic or exotic entertainment, rather than merely in food, the entrepreneur might develop other products, such as catering services, party planning, and so on—"Curry Favors"? Perhaps, if the customers buy food from her because they actually enjoy learning about new cultures, she might offer lectures and classes, maybe beginning with Indian cooking and moving on to cultural aspects, including concerts and ancient history and philosophy, and the profound idea that food is a vehicle of cultural exploration—"School of Curry"? Or maybe what really interests them is theme tours and other travel options to India and the Far East—"Curryland Travels"?

In a nutshell, in using effectuation processes to build her firm, the entrepreneur can build several different types of firms in completely disparate industries. This means that the original idea (or set of causes) does not imply any one single strategic universe for the firm (or effect). Instead, the process of effectuation allows the entrepreneur to create one or more several possible effects irrespective of the generalized end goal with which she started. The process not only enables the realization of several possible effects (although generally one or only a few are actually realized in the implementation) but it also allows a decision maker to change his or her goals and even to shape and construct them over time, making use of contingencies as they arise.[10]

Our use of direct quotes from Sarasvathy on effectuation is not to make the case that it is superior to thought processes that involve causation; rather, it represents a way that entrepreneurs sometimes think. Effectuation helps entrepreneurs think in an environment of high uncertainty. Indeed organizations today operate in complex and dynamic environments that are increasingly characterized by rapid, substantial, and discontinuous change.[11] Given the nature of this type of environment, most managers of firms need to take on an entrepreneurial mind-set so that their firms can successfully adapt to environmental changes.[12] This *entrepreneurial mind-set* involves the ability to rapidly sense, act, and mobilize, even under uncertain conditions.[13] In developing an entrepreneurial mind-set, individuals must attempt to make sense of opportunities in the context of changing goals, constantly questioning the "dominant logic" in the context of a changing environment and revisiting "deceptively simple questions" about what is thought to be true about markets and the firm. For example, effective entrepreneurs are thought to continuously "rethink current strategic actions, organization structure, communications systems, corporate culture, asset deployment, investment strategies, in short every aspect of a firm's operation and long-term health."[14]

To be good at these tasks individuals must develop a *cognitive adaptability*. Mike Haynie, a retired major of the U.S. Air Force and now professor at Syracuse University, and me (Dean Shepherd from Indiana University) have developed a number of models of cognitive adaptability and a survey for capturing it, to which we now turn.[15]

Cognitive Adaptability

Cognitive adaptability describes the extent to which entrepreneurs are dynamic, flexible, self-regulating, and engaged in the process of generating multiple decision frameworks focused on sensing and processing changes in their environments and then acting on them. Decision frameworks are organized on knowledge about people and situations that are used to help someone make sense of what is going on.[16] Cognitive adaptability is

entrepreneurial mind-set
Involves the ability to rapidly sense, act, and mobilize, even under uncertain conditions

cognitive adaptability
Describes the extent to which entrepreneurs are dynamic, flexible, self-regulating, and engaged in the process of generating multiple decision frameworks focused on sensing and processing changes in their environments and then acting on them

WHAT ME WORRY? HOW SMART ENTREPRENEURS HARNESS THE POWER OF PARANOIA

Depending on whom you're talking to, paranoia is: (1) a psychotic disorder characterized by delusions of persecution, (2) an irrational distrust of others, or (3) a key trait in entrepreneurial success.

Sound crazy? Not according to Andrew S. Grove, president and CEO of Intel Corp. in Santa Clara, California, and author of *Only the Paranoid Survive* (Doubleday/Currency). The title of Grove's book comes from an oft-repeated quote that has become the mantra of the chip king's rise to the top of the technology business.

"I have no idea when I first said this," Grove writes, "but the fact remains that, when it comes to business, I believe in the value of paranoia." To those who suffer from clinical delusions of persecution, of course, paranoia is neither a joke nor a help. However, in a business context, the practice of voluntarily being highly concerned about potential threats to your company has something of a following.

"If you're not a little bit paranoid, you're complacent," says Dave Lakhani, an entrepreneur in Boise, Idaho, who offers marketing consulting to small businesses. "And complacency is what leads people into missed opportunities and business failure."

PICK YOUR PARANOIA

Being paranoid, according to Grove, is a matter of remembering that others want the success you have, paying attention to the details of your business, and watching for the trouble that inevitably awaits. That basically means he is paranoid about everything. "I worry about products getting screwed up, and I worry about products getting introduced prematurely," Grove writes. "I worry about factories not performing well, and I worry about having too many factories."

For Grove, as for most advocates of paranoia, being paranoid primarily consists of two things. The first is not resting on your laurels. Grove calls it a "guardian attitude" that he attempts to nurture in himself and in Intel's employees to fend off threats from outside the company. Paranoia in business is also typically defined as paying very close attention to the fine points. "You need to be detail-oriented about the most important things in your business," says Lakhani. "That means not only making sure

you're working in your business but that you're there every day, paying attention to your customers."

As an example of paranoia's value in practice, Lakhani recalls when sales began slowly slumping at a retail store he once owned. He could have dismissed it as a mere blip. Instead, he worried and watched until he spotted a concrete cause. "It turned out one of my employees had developed a negative attitude, and it was affecting my business," Lakhani says. "As soon as I let him go, sales went back up."

The main focuses of most entrepreneurs' paranoia, however, are not so much everyday internal details as major competitive threats and missed opportunities. Situations in which competition and opportunity are both at high levels are called "strategic inflection points" by Grove, and it is during these times, typically when technology is changing, that his paranoia is sharpest.

Paranoia is frequently a welcome presence at major client presentations for Katharine Paine, founder and CEO of The Delahaye Group Inc. In the past, twinges of seemingly unfounded worry have caused Paine to personally attend sales pitches where she learned of serious problems with the way her firm was doing business, she says. The head of the 50-person Portsmouth, New Hampshire, marketing evaluation research firm traces her paranoid style to childhood days spent pretending to be an Indian tracking quarry through the forest. When she makes mental checklists about things that could go wrong or opportunities that could be missed, she's always keeping an eye out for the business equivalent of a bent twig. "If you are paranoid enough, if you're good enough at picking up all those clues, you don't have to just react," says Paine, "you get to proact and be slightly ahead of the curve."

PARANOID PARAMETERS

There is, of course, such a thing as being too paranoid. "There are times when it doesn't make any sense," acknowledges Lakhani. Focusing on details to the point of spending $500 in accounting fees to find a $5 error is one example of misplaced paranoia. Worrying obsessively about what every competitor is doing or what every potential customer is thinking is also a warning sign, he says. Lack of balance with interests outside the business may be another. "If your whole life is focused around your work, and that's the only thing you're thinking about 24 hours a day, that becomes detrimental," Lakhani says.

For Paine, failing to act is a sign that you're going past beneficial paranoia and into hurtful fear. "Fear for most of us results in inaction—absolute death for an entrepreneur," she says. "If we feared the loss of a paycheck or feared entering a new market, none of our businesses would have gotten off the ground."

All this may be especially true for small-business owners. While paranoia may be appropriate for heads of far-flung enterprises, some say entrepreneurs are already too paranoid. It's all too easy for entrepreneurs to take their desire for independence and self-determination and turn it into trouble, says Robert Barbato, director of the Small Business Institute at the Rochester Institute of Technology in Rochester, New York. Typically, entrepreneurs take the attitude that "nobody cares as much about this business as I do" and exaggerate it to the point of hurtful paranoia toward employees and even customers, he says. "They're seeing ghosts where ghosts don't exist," warns Barbato.

That's especially risky when it comes to dealing with employees. Most people—not just entrepreneurs—do their work for the sense of accomplishment, not because they are plotting to steal their employer's success, Barbato says. He acknowledges this may be a difficult concept for competition-crazed entrepreneurs—especially those who have never themselves been employees—to understand. "People who own their own business are not necessarily used to moving up the ranks," Barbato notes. Entrepreneurs must learn to trust and delegate if their businesses are to grow.

PRACTICAL PARANOIA

No matter how useful it is, paranoia may be too loaded a label for some entrepreneurs. If so, critical evaluation or critical analysis are the preferred terms of Stephen Markowitz, director of governmental and political relations of the Small Business Association of Delaware Valley, a 5,000-member trade group. The distinction is more than name-deep. "When I say 'critically evaluate,' that means look at everything," Markowitz explains. "If you're totally paranoid, the danger is not being able to critically evaluate everything."

For example, Markowitz says a small retailer threatened by the impending arrival of a superstore in the market would be better served by critically evaluating the potential for benefit as well as harm, instead of merely worrying about it. "If you're paranoid," he says, "you're not going to critically evaluate how it might help you."

Whatever name it goes by, few entrepreneurs are likely to stop worrying anytime soon. In fact, experience tends to make them more confirmed in their paranoia as they go along. Paine recalls the time a formless fear led her to insist on going to a client meeting where no trouble was expected. She lost the account anyway. "The good news is, my paranoia kicked in," she says. "The bad news is, it was too late. That made me much more paranoid in the future."

ADVICE TO AN ENTREPRENEUR

A friend who has just become an entrepreneur has read the above article and comes to you for advice:

1. I worry about my business; does that mean that I am paranoid?
2. What are the benefits of paranoia and what are the costs?
3. How do I know I have the right level of paranoia to effectively run the business and not put me in the hospital with a stomach ulcer?
4. Won't forcing myself to be more paranoid take the fun out of being an entrepreneur?

Source: Reprinted with permission of Entrepreneur Media, Inc., "How Smart Entrepreneurs Harness the Power of Paranoia," by Mark Henricks, March 1997, *Entrepreneur* magazine: www.entrepreneur.com.

reflected in an entrepreneur's metacognitive awareness, that is, the ability to reflect upon, understand, and control one's thinking and learning.[17] Specifically, metacognition describes a higher-order cognitive process that serves to organize what individuals know and recognize about themselves, tasks, situations, and their environments to promote effective and *adaptable* cognitive functioning in the face of feedback from complex and dynamic environments.[18]

How cognitively adaptable are you? Try the survey in Table 1.1 and compare yourself to some of your classmates. A higher score means that you are more metacognitively aware,

TABLE 1.1 Mike Haynie's "Measure of Adaptive Cognition"

How Cognitively Flexible Are You? On a scale of 1 to 10, where 1 is "not very much like me," and 10 is "very much like me," how do you rate yourself on the following statements?

Goal Orientation

I often define goals for myself.	Not very much—1 2 3 4 5 6 7 8 9 10—Very much like me like me
I understand how accomplishment of a task relates to my goals.	Not very much—1 2 3 4 5 6 7 8 9 10—Very much like me like me
I set specific goals before I begin a task.	Not very much—1 2 3 4 5 6 7 8 9 10—Very much like me like me
I ask myself how well I've accomplished my goals once I've finished.	Not very much—1 2 3 4 5 6 7 8 9 10—Very much like me like me
When performing a task, I frequently assess my progress against my objectives.	Not very much—1 2 3 4 5 6 7 8 9 10—Very much like me like me

Metacognitive Knowledge

I think of several ways to solve a problem and choose the best one.	Not very much—1 2 3 4 5 6 7 8 9 10—Very much like me like me
I challenge my own assumptions about a task before I begin.	Not very much—1 2 3 4 5 6 7 8 9 10—Very much like me like me
I think about how others may react to my actions.	Not very much—1 2 3 4 5 6 7 8 9 10—Very much like me like me
I find myself automatically employing strategies that have worked in the past.	Not very much—1 2 3 4 5 6 7 8 9 10—Very much like me like me
I perform best when I already have knowledge of the task.	Not very much—1 2 3 4 5 6 7 8 9 10—Very much like me like me
I create my own examples to make information more meaningful.	Not very much—1 2 3 4 5 6 7 8 9 10—Very much like me like me
I try to use strategies that have worked in the past.	Not very much—1 2 3 4 5 6 7 8 9 10—Very much like me like me
I ask myself questions about the task before I begin.	Not very much—1 2 3 4 5 6 7 8 9 10—Very much like me like me
I try to translate new information into my own words.	Not very much—1 2 3 4 5 6 7 8 9 10—Very much like me like me
I try to break problems down into smaller components.	Not very much—1 2 3 4 5 6 7 8 9 10—Very much like me like me
I focus on the meaning and significance of new information.	Not very much—1 2 3 4 5 6 7 8 9 10—Very much like me like me

Metacognitive Experience

I think about what I really need to accomplish before I begin a task.	Not very much—1 2 3 4 5 6 7 8 9 10—Very much like me like me
I use different strategies depending on the situation.	Not very much—1 2 3 4 5 6 7 8 9 10—Very much like me like me
I organize my time to best accomplish my goals.	Not very much—1 2 3 4 5 6 7 8 9 10—Very much like me like me

I am good at organizing information.	Not very much—1 2 3 4 5 6 7 8 9 10—Very much like me like me
I know what kind of information is most important to consider when faced with a problem.	Not very much—1 2 3 4 5 6 7 8 9 10—Very much like me like me
I consciously focus my attention on important information.	Not very much—1 2 3 4 5 6 7 8 9 10—Very much like me like me
My "gut" tells me when a given strategy I use will be most effective.	Not very much—1 2 3 4 5 6 7 8 9 10—Very much like me like me
I depend on my intuition to help me formulate strategies.	Not very much—1 2 3 4 5 6 7 8 9 10—Very much like me like me

Metacognitive Choice

I ask myself if I have considered all the options when solving a problem.	Not very much—1 2 3 4 5 6 7 8 9 10—Very much like me like me
I ask myself if there was an easier way to do things after I finish a task.	Not very much—1 2 3 4 5 6 7 8 9 10—Very much like me like me
I ask myself if I have considered all the options after I solve a problem.	Not very much—1 2 3 4 5 6 7 8 9 10—Very much like me like me
I re-evaluate my assumptions when I get confused.	Not very much—1 2 3 4 5 6 7 8 9 10—Very much like me like me
I ask myself if I have learned as much as I could have after I finish the task.	Not very much—1 2 3 4 5 6 7 8 9 10—Very much like me like me

Monitoring

I periodically review to help me understand important relationships.	Not very much—1 2 3 4 5 6 7 8 9 10—Very much like me like me
I stop and go back over information that is not clear.	Not very much—1 2 3 4 5 6 7 8 9 10—Very much like me like me
I am aware of what strategies I use when engaged in a given task.	Not very much—1 2 3 4 5 6 7 8 9 10—Very much like me like me
I find myself analyzing the usefulness of a given strategy while engaged in a given task.	Not very much—1 2 3 4 5 6 7 8 9 10—Very much like me like me
I find myself pausing regularly to check my comprehension of the problem or situation at hand.	Not very much—1 2 3 4 5 6 7 8 9 10—Very much like me like me
I ask myself questions about how well I am doing while I am performing a novel task. I stop and re-read when I get confused.	Not very much—1 2 3 4 5 6 7 8 9 10—Very much like me like me

Result—A higher score means that you are more aware of the way that you think about how you make decisions and are therefore more likely to be cognitively flexible.

Source: Reprinted with permission from M. Haynie and D. Shepherd, "A Measure of Adaptive Cognition for Entrepreneurship Research," *Entrepreneurship, Theory and Practice* 33, no. 3 (2009), pp. 695–714.

and this in turn helps provide cognitive adaptability. Regardless of your score, the good news is that you can learn to be more cognitively adaptable. This ability will serve you well in most new tasks, but particularly when pursuing a new entry and managing a firm in an uncertain environment. Put simply, it requires us to "think about thinking which requires, and helps provide, knowledge and control over our thinking and learning activities—it requires us to be self-aware, to think aloud, to reflect, to be strategic, to plan, to have a plan in mind, to know what to know, to self-monitor.[19] We can achieve this by asking ourselves a series of questions that relate to (1) comprehension, (2) connection, (3) strategy, and (4) reflection.[20]

comprehension questions
Questions designed to increase entrepreneurs' understanding of the nature of the environment

1. *Comprehension questions* are designed to increase entrepreneurs' understanding of the nature of the environment before they begin to address an entrepreneurial challenge, whether it be a change in the environment or the assessment of a potential opportunity. Understanding arises from recognition that a problem or opportunity exists, the nature of that situation, and its implications. In general, the questions that stimulate individuals to think about comprehension include: What is the problem all about? What is the question? What are the meanings of the key concepts? Specific to entrepreneurs, the questions are more likely to include: What is this market all about? What is this technology all about? What do we want to achieve by creating this new firm? What are the key elements to effectively pursuing this opportunity?

connection tasks Tasks designed to stimulate entrepreneurs to think about the current situation in terms of similarities to and differences from situations previously faced and solved

2. *Connection tasks* are designed to stimulate entrepreneurs to think about the current situation in terms of similarities to and differences from situations previously faced and solved. In other words, these tasks prompt the entrepreneur to tap into his or her knowledge and experience without overgeneralizing. Generally, connection tasks focus on questions like: How is this problem similar to problems I have already solved? Why? How is this problem different from what I have already solved? Why? Specific to entrepreneurs, the questions are more likely to include: How is this new environment similar to others in which I have operated? How is it different? How is this new organization similar to the established organizations I have managed? How is it different?

strategic tasks Tasks designed to stimulate entrepreneurs to think about which strategies are appropriate for solving the problem (and why) or pursuing the opportunity (and how)

3. *Strategic tasks* are designed to stimulate entrepreneurs to think about which strategies are appropriate for solving the problem (and why) or pursuing the opportunity (and how). These tasks prompt them to think about the what, why, and how of their approach to the situation. Generally, these questions include: What strategy/tactic/principle can I use to solve this problem? Why is this strategy/tactic/principle the most appropriate one? How can I organize the information to solve the problem? How can I implement the plan? Specific to entrepreneurs, the questions are likely to include: What changes to strategic position, organizational structure, and culture will help us manage our newness? How can the implementation of this strategy be made feasible?

reflection tasks Tasks designed to stimulate entrepreneurs to think about their understanding and feelings as they progress through the entrepreneurial process

4. *Reflection tasks* are designed to stimulate entrepreneurs to think about their understanding and feelings as they progress through the entrepreneurial process. These tasks prompt entrepreneurs to generate their own feedback (create a feedback loop in their solution process) to provide the opportunity to change. Generally, reflection questions include: What am I doing? Does it make sense? What difficulties am I facing? How do I feel? How can I verify the solution? Can I use another approach for solving the task? Specific to the entrepreneurial context, entrepreneurs might ask: What difficulties will we have in convincing our stakeholders? Is there a better way to implement our strategy? How will we know success if we see it?

Entrepreneurs who are able to increase cognitive adaptability have an improved ability to (1) adapt to new situations—i.e., it provides a basis by which a person's prior experience and knowledge affect learning or problem solving in a new situation; (2) be creative—i.e., it can lead to original and adaptive ideas, solutions, or insights; and (3) communicate one's reasoning behind a particular response.[21] We hope that this section of the book has not only provided you a deeper understanding of how entrepreneurs can think and act with great flexibility, but also an awareness of some techniques for incorporating cognitive adaptability in your life.

We have discussed how entrepreneurs make decisions in uncertain environments and how one might develop an ability to be more cognitively flexible. It is important to note that entrepreneurs not only think but they also intend to act.

THE INTENTION TO ACT ENTREPRENEURIALLY

Entrepreneurial action is most often intentional. Entrepreneurs intend to pursue certain opportunities, enter new markets, and offer new products—and this is rarely the process of unintentional behavior. Intentions capture the motivational factors that influence a behavior; they are indications of how hard people are willing to try, of how much of an effort they are planning to exert to perform the behavior. As a general rule, the stronger the intention to engage in a behavior, the more likely should be its performance.[22] Individuals have stronger intentions to act when taking action is perceived to be *feasible* and *desirable*. *Entrepreneurial intentions* can be explained in the same way.

entrepreneurial intentions The motivational factors that influence individuals to pursue entrepreneurial outcomes

The perception of feasibility has much to do with an entrepreneur's self-efficacy. *Entrepreneurial self-efficacy* refers to the conviction that one can successfully execute the behavior required; people who believe they have the capacity to perform (high self-efficacy) tend to perform well. Thus, it reflects the perception of a personal capability to do a particular job or set of tasks. High self-efficacy leads to increased initiative and persistence and thus improved performance; low self-efficacy reduces effort and thus performance. Indeed, people with high self-efficacy think differently and behave differently than people with low self-efficacy.[23] Self-efficacy affects the person's choice of action and the amount of effort exerted. Entrepreneurship scholars have found that self-efficacy is positively associated with the creation of a new independent organization.[24]

entrepreneurial self-efficacy The conviction that one can successfully execute the entrepreneurial process

Not only must an individual perceive entrepreneurial action as feasible for entrepreneurial intention to be high, the individual must also perceive this course of action as desirable. *Perceived desirability* refers to an individual's attitude toward entrepreneurial action—the degree to which he or she has a favorable or unfavorable evaluation of the potential entrepreneurial outcomes.[25] For example, creative actions are not likely to emerge unless they produce personal rewards that are perceived as relatively more desirable than more familiar behaviors.[26]

perceived desirability The degree to which an individual has a favorable or unfavorable evaluation of the potential entrepreneurial outcomes

Therefore, the higher the perceived desirability and feasibility, the stronger the intention to act entrepreneurially. We next investigate the background characteristics of entrepreneurs to understand why some individuals are more likely to engage in entrepreneurship than other individuals. That is, we examine how background characteristics provide an indication of whether certain individuals are more or less likely to perceive entrepreneurial action as feasible and/or desirable and therefore whether they are more or less likely to intend to be entrepreneurs.

ENTREPRENEUR BACKGROUND AND CHARACTERISTICS
Education

Although some may feel that entrepreneurs are less educated than the general population, research findings indicate that this is clearly not the case. Education is important in the upbringing of the entrepreneur. Its importance is reflected not only in the level of education obtained but also in the fact that it continues to play a major role in helping entrepreneurs cope with the problems they confront. Although a formal education is not necessary for starting a new business—as is reflected in the success of such high school dropouts as Andrew Carnegie, William Durant, Henry Ford, and William Lear—it does provide a good background, particularly when it is related to the field of the venture. For example, entrepreneurs have cited an educational need in the areas of finance, strategic planning, marketing (particularly distribution), and management. The ability to communicate clearly with both the written and the spoken word is also important in any entrepreneurial activity.

Even general education is valuable because it facilitates the integration and accumulation of new knowledge, providing individuals with a larger opportunity set (i.e., a broader base of knowledge casts a wider net for the discovery or generation of potential opportunities), and assists entrepreneurs in adapting to new situations.[27] The general education (and experiences) of an entrepreneur can provide knowledge, skills, and problem-solving abilities that are transferable across many different situations. Indeed, it has been found that while education has a positive influence on the chance that a person will discover new opportunities, it does not necessarily determine whether he will create a new business to exploit the discovered opportunity.[28] To the extent that individuals believe that their education has made entrepreneurial action more feasible, they are more likely to become entrepreneurs.

Age

The relationship of age to the entrepreneurial career process also has been carefully researched.[29] In evaluating these results, it is important to differentiate between entrepreneurial age (the age of the entrepreneur reflected in his or her experience) and chronological age (years since birth). As discussed in the next section, entrepreneurial experience is one of the best predictors of success, particularly when the new venture is in the same field as the previous business experience.

In terms of chronological age, most entrepreneurs initiate their entrepreneurial careers between the ages of 22 and 45. A career can be initiated before or after these ages, as long as the entrepreneur has the necessary experience and financial support, and the high energy level needed to launch and manage a new venture successfully. Also, there are milestone ages every five years (25, 30, 35, 40, and 45) when an individual is more inclined to start an entrepreneurial career. As one entrepreneur succinctly stated, "I felt it was now or never in terms of starting a new venture when I approached 30." Generally, male entrepreneurs tend to start their first significant venture in their early 30s, while women entrepreneurs tend to do so in their middle 30s. However, an entrepreneurial career is quite popular later in life when the children have left home, there are fewer financial concerns, and individuals start to think about what they would really like to do with the rest of their lives.[30]

Work History

work history The past
work experience of an
individual

Work history can influence the decision to launch a new entrepreneurial venture, but it also plays a role in the growth and eventual success of the new venture. While dissatisfaction with various aspects of one's job—such as a lack of challenge or promotional opportunities, as well as frustration and boredom—often motivates the launching of a new venture, previous technical and industry experience is important once the decision to launch has been made. Experience in the following areas is particularly important: financing, product or service development, manufacturing, and the development of distribution channels.

As the venture becomes established and starts growing, managerial experience and skills become increasingly important. Although most ventures start with few (if any) employees, as the number of employees increases, the entrepreneur's managerial skills come more and more into play. In addition, entrepreneurial experiences, such as the start-up process, making decisions under high levels of uncertainty, building a culture from "scratch," raising venture capital, and managing high growth, are also important. Most entrepreneurs indicate that their most significant venture was not their first one. Throughout their entrepreneurial careers, they are exposed to many new venture opportunities and gather ideas for many more new ventures.

Finally, previous start-up experience can provide entrepreneurs with expertise in running an independent business as well as benchmarks for judging the relevance of information, which can lead to an understanding of the "real" value of new entry opportunities, speed up the business creation process, and enhance performance.[31] Previous start-up experience is a relatively good predictor of starting subsequent businesses.[32] To the extent that start-up experience provides entrepreneurs with a greater belief in their ability to successfully achieve entrepreneurial outcomes, this increased perceived feasibility will strengthen entrepreneurial intentions.

ROLE MODELS AND SUPPORT SYSTEMS

role models Individuals whose example an entrepreneur can aspire to and copy

One of the most important factors influencing entrepreneurs in their career path is their choice of a *role model*.[33] Role models can be parents, brothers or sisters, other relatives, or other entrepreneurs. Successful entrepreneurs frequently are viewed as catalysts by potential entrepreneurs. As one entrepreneur succinctly stated, "After evaluating Ted and his success as an entrepreneur, I knew I was much smarter and could do a better job. So I started my own business." In this way, role models can provide important signals that entrepreneurship is feasible for them.

Role models can also serve in a supportive capacity as mentors during and after the launch of a new venture. An entrepreneur needs a strong support and advisory system in every phase of the new venture. This support system is perhaps most crucial during the start-up phase, as it provides information, advice, and guidance on such matters as organizational structure, obtaining needed financial resources, and marketing. Since entrepreneurship is a social role embedded in a social context, it is important that an entrepreneur establish connections and eventually networks early in the new venture formation process.

As initial contacts and connections expand, they form a network with similar properties prevalent in a social network—density (the extensiveness of ties between the two individuals) and centrality (the total distance of the entrepreneur to all other individuals and the total number of individuals in the network). The strength of the ties between the entrepreneur and any individual in the network is dependent upon the frequency, level, and reciprocity of the relationship. The more frequent, in-depth, and mutually beneficial a relationship, the stronger and more durable the network between the entrepreneur and the individual.[34] Although most networks are not formally organized, an informal network for moral and professional support still greatly benefits the entrepreneur.

Moral-Support Network

moral-support network
Individuals who give
psychological support to
an entrepreneur

It is important for each entrepreneur to establish a *moral-support network* of family and friends—a cheering squad. This cheering squad plays a critical role during the many difficult and lonely times that occur throughout the entrepreneurial process. Most entrepreneurs indicate that their spouses are their biggest supporters and allow them to devote the excessive amounts of time necessary to the new venture.

Friends also play key roles in a moral-support network. Not only can friends provide advice that is often more honest than that received from other sources, but they also provide encouragement, understanding, and even assistance. Entrepreneurs can confide in friends without fear of criticism. Finally, relatives (children, parents, grandparents, aunts, and uncles) also can be strong sources of moral support, particularly if they are also entrepreneurs. As one entrepreneur stated, "The total family support I received was the key to my success. Having an understanding cheering squad giving me encouragement allowed me to persist through the many difficulties and problems."

Professional-Support Network

In addition to encouragement, the entrepreneur needs advice and counsel throughout the establishment of the new venture. This advice can be obtained from a mentor, business associates, trade associations, or personal affiliations—all members of a *professional-support network*.

*professional-support
network*   Individuals
who help the entrepreneur
in business activities

Most entrepreneurs indicate that they have mentors. How does one find a mentor? This task sounds much more difficult than it really is. Since a mentor is a coach, a sounding board, and an advocate—someone with whom the entrepreneur can share both problems and successes—the individual selected needs to be an expert in the field. An entrepreneur can start the "mentor-finding process" by preparing a list of experts in various fields—such as in the fundamental business activities of finance, marketing, accounting, law, or management—who can provide the practical "how-to" advice needed. From this list, an individual who can offer the most assistance should be identified and contacted. If the selected individual is willing to act as a mentor, he or she should be periodically apprised of the progress of the business so that a relationship can gradually develop.

Another good source of advice can be cultivated by establishing a network of business associates. This group can be composed of self-employed individuals who have experienced starting a business; clients or buyers of the venture's product or service; experts such as consultants, lawyers, or accountants; and the venture's suppliers. Clients or buyers are a particularly important group to cultivate. This group represents the source of revenue to the venture and is the best provider of word-of-mouth advertising. There is nothing better than word-of-mouth advertising from satisfied customers to help establish a winning business reputation and promote goodwill.

Suppliers are another important component in a professional-support network. A new venture needs to establish a solid track record with suppliers to build a good relationship and to ensure the adequate availability of materials and other supplies. Suppliers also can provide good information on the nature of trends, as well as competition, in the industry.

In addition to mentors and business associates, trade associations can offer an excellent professional-support network. Trade association members can help keep the new venture competitive. Trade associations keep up with new developments and can provide overall industry data.

Finally, personal affiliations of the entrepreneur also can be a valuable part of a professional-support network. Affiliations developed with individuals through shared hobbies, participation in sporting events, clubs, civic involvements, and school alumni groups are excellent potential sources of referrals, advice, and information. Each entrepreneur needs to establish both moral- and professional-support networks. These contacts provide confidence, support, advice, and information. As one entrepreneur stated, "In your own business, you are all alone. There is a definite need to establish support groups to share problems with and to obtain information and overall support for the new venture."

Therefore, it is important to recognize that entrepreneurial activity is embedded in networks of interpersonal relationships. These networks are defined by a set of actors (individuals and organizations) and a set of linkages between them, and they provide individuals access to a variety of resources necessary for entrepreneurial outcomes.[35] These resources may assist in efforts to discover and exploit opportunities, as well as in the creation of new independent organizations.[36] The trust embedded in some of these networks provides potential entrepreneurs the opportunity to access highly valuable resources. For example, business networks are composed of independent firms linked by common interests, friendship, and trust and are particularly important in facilitating the transfer of difficult-to-codify, knowledge-intensive skills that are expensive to obtain in other ways.[37] These networks also create opportunities for exchanging goods and services that are difficult to enforce through contractual arrangements, which facilitates the pursuit of opportunities.[38] To the extent that a network provides an individual greater belief in his or her ability to access resources critical to the successful achievement of entrepreneurial outcomes, this increased perceived feasibility will strengthen entrepreneurial intentions. This can include intentions for sustainable entrepreneurship.

SUSTAINABLE ENTREPRENEURSHIP

sustainable entrepreneurship Entrepreneurship focused on preserving nature, life support, and community (sustainability) in the pursuit of perceived opportunities to bring future products, processes, and services into existence for gain (entrepreneurial action) where gain is broadly construed to include economic and noneconomic benefits to individuals, the economy, and society (development)

Sustainable development is perhaps the most important issue of our time, and entrepreneurship can have a positive impact on this issue. That is, entrepreneurial action can help us both sustain and develop. Specifically, *sustainable entrepreneurship* is focused on preserving nature, life support, and community (sustainability) in the pursuit of perceived opportunities to bring future products, processes, and services into existence for gain (entrepreneurial action) where gain is broadly construed to include economic and noneconomic benefits to individuals, the economy, and society (development).[39]

Based on the McMullen-Shepherd model, we know that entrepreneurial action is driven by knowledge and motivation. Those with greater knowledge of the natural environment— the physical world, including the earth, biodiversity, and ecosystems[40]—are more likely to notice changes in that environment that form opportunity beliefs than those with less knowledge. However, we cannot underestimate the role of entrepreneurial knowledge of markets, technologies, and/or opportunity exploitation; without entrepreneurial knowledge, opportunities for sustainable development are unlikely to become a reality.

For entrepreneurial actions that preserve nature to be considered sustainable entrepreneurship, they must also develop gains for the entrepreneur, others, and/or society. It has long been accepted that entrepreneurs can generate economic wealth for themselves, but their impact on development can be far greater. They can generate gains for others that are economic, environmental, and social, including employment opportunities, improved access to quality/valuable goods, and revenues for the government(s). The environmental gain generated for others could be reduced air pollution, improved air quality, improved drinking-water quality, and other enhanced living conditions. The social gains include improved child survival rates, longer life expectancy, superior education, equal opportunity, and so on. For example, individuals who were knowledgeable about cooking practices in

 ETHICS

COMPANY'S CODE OF ETHICS

The financial scandals of 2002 [and 2008] have already led to increased action by legislators and associations, and many companies are beginning to develop a code of ethics for all employees.

There are a number of advantages to implementing a code of ethics. The more your employees are aware of proper conduct, the more likely they are to do the right thing. They'll better understand their responsibilities and expectations and assume the appropriate level of accountability when identifying and managing business risks. A code of ethics is more than just a formal document outlining related policies. It's about integrating positive values throughout an organization. Here are some key components to an effective program:

Leaders Set the Example: Employees often model their own behavior after executives, managers, and others who've succeeded in the company. Therefore, everyone at every level must adhere to the firm's guidelines. What seems like a small action—discussing confidential financial information with a colleague, for instance—can have a ripple effect throughout all staff. If the members of senior management do not follow the highest ethical standards at all times, they shouldn't be surprised when those who report to them fail to do so.

Ethics Is a Core Value: Companies known for their ethical business practices make ethics a key element of their corporate culture. Conducting yourself with integrity is considered as important as bottom-line results. Ethical standards are applied any time a decision is made or an action is taken, not just during controversial situations. A recent survey by our company found that more organizations are taking ethics into account when hiring employees. Fifty-eight percent of chief financial officers polled said the qualities that impress them most about applicants, aside from ability and willingness to do the job, are honesty and integrity. That's a substantial increase from only 32 percent in 1997.

Employees Feel Safe to Share Concerns: The work environment must be one in which people feel they can deliver bad news to management without fear of repercussions. In an ethics-driven company, staff members can report any type of wrongdoing—whether it is false information on an expense report or major financial fraud—and feel confident they will not suffer negative career consequences. Once supervisors are made aware of a potential problem, they need to take immediate action. Failure to follow through on even minor issues can undermine the success of an ethics program.

Having a code of ethics will not prevent every crisis, but it will ensure that staff members have a clear understanding of expectations. Collaborate with employees on defining the rules, and make sure everyone is aware of the requirements. Then take steps to instill core values throughout the organization. With regular reinforcement, ethics will guide every decision your team makes and become a central element in the way your company conducts business.

Source: From Max Messmer, "Does Your Company Have a Code of Ethics?" *Strategic Finance*, April 2003. Excerpted with permission from Strategic Finance published by the Institute of Management Accountants, Montvale, NJ.

developing countries were able to recognize opportunities for hybrid stoves that substantially reduced particle pollutants in households but were consistent with traditional recipes.[41] It is not just the natural environment that can be sustained, though; communities also need to be preserved. Indeed, knowledge of indigenous groups' cultures has led to the pursuit of opportunities that serve to sustain these cultures.

We recognize that our explanation of sustainable entrepreneurship could be considered highly idealistic. However, it is consistent with thinking of entrepreneurial action as a tool (e.g., a hammer) that can be used for good (e.g., to build a community center) or for bad (e.g., as a weapon for harming others). We do believe, however, that there are many people in the world today who are motivated to use the tool of entrepreneurial action to sustain the natural environment and communities and develop gains for others. Perhaps you are one of these people.

IN REVIEW

SUMMARY

Entrepreneurship involves action. Before action individuals use their knowledge and motivation to overcome ignorance to form a belief that there exists an opportunity for someone. They then need to determine if this opportunity for someone matches their knowledge and motivation—is it an opportunity for them? Individuals engaging in the entrepreneurial task think differently from those engaged in other tasks, such as managerial tasks. The process requires that the individual and the firm have an entrepreneurial mind-set. We started our discussion of this mind-set with the concepts of thinking structurally and effectually, which challenges traditional notions of the way that entrepreneurs think about their tasks.

By thinking structurally and not being distracted by superficial features, entrepreneurs are able to identify opportunities by making connections between a technology and a market that may not be obvious. Furthermore, although entrepreneurs think about some tasks in a causal way, they also are likely to think about some tasks effectually (and some entrepreneurs more so than other entrepreneurs). Rather than starting with the desired outcome in mind and then focusing on the means to achieving that outcome, entrepreneurs sometimes approach tasks by looking at what they have—their means—and selecting among possible outcomes. Who is to say whether the "causal chef" who starts with a menu or the "effectual chef" who starts with what is in the cupboard produces the best meal? But we can say that some expert entrepreneurs think effectually about opportunities. Thinking effectually helps entrepreneurs make decisions in uncertain environments. Entrepreneurs are often situated in resource-scarce environments but are able to make do with (and recombine) the resources they have at hand to create opportunities.

The external environment can also have an impact on performance and therefore the entrepreneur needs to be able to adapt to changes in the environment. In this chapter we introduced the notion of cognitive flexibility and emphasized that it is something that can be measured and learned. By asking questions related to comprehension, connection, strategy, and reflection, entrepreneurs can maintain an awareness of their thought process and in doing so develop greater cognitive adaptability.

Individuals become entrepreneurs because they intend to do so. The stronger the intention to be an entrepreneur, the more likely it is that it will happen. Intentions become stronger as individuals perceive an entrepreneurial career as feasible and desirable. These perceptions of feasibility and desirability are influenced by one's background and characteristics, such as education, personal values, age and work history, role models and support systems, and networks.

The outcome of entrepreneurial action can be economic gain for the entrepreneur and his or her family. But this may not be the only motivation for the intention to be an entrepreneur. Some individuals exploit opportunities that sustain (the natural environment and/or communities) and generate gains for others. We call this process sustainable entrepreneurship.

RESEARCH TASKS

1. Speak to people from five different countries and ask what entrepreneurship means to them and how their national culture helps and/or hinders entrepreneurship.

2. Ask an entrepreneur about his business today and ask him to describe the decisions and series of events that led the business from start-up to its current form. Would you classify this process as causal, effectual, or both?

3. Ask two entrepreneurs and five students (not in this class) to fill out the Haynie-Shepherd "Measure of Adaptive Cognition" (see Table 1.1). How do you rate relative to the entrepreneurs? Relative to your fellow students?

4. When conducting a homework exercise for another class (especially a case analysis), ask yourself comprehension questions, connection questions, strategy questions, and reflection questions. What impact did this have on the outcome of the task?

5. What impact does entrepreneurship have on your natural environment? What impact does it have on sustaining local communities? Use data to back up your arguments.

CLASS DISCUSSION

1. List the content that you believe is necessary for an entrepreneurship course. Be prepared to justify your answer.

2. Do you really think that entrepreneurs think effectually? What about yourself—do you sometimes think effectually? In what ways is it good? Then why are we taught in business classes to always think causally? Are there particular problems or tasks in which thinking causally is likely to be superior to effectuation? When might effectuation be superior to causal thinking?

3. To be cognitively flexible seems to require that the entrepreneur continually question himself or herself. Doesn't that create doubt that can be seen by employees and financiers such that success actually becomes more difficult to achieve? Besides, although flexibility is a good thing, if the firm keeps changing based on minor changes in the environment, the buyers are going to become confused about the nature of the firm. Is adaptation always a good thing?

4. Do you believe that sustainable development should be part of an entrepreneurship course, or did the textbook authors just include a section on it to be "politically correct"?

5. Provide some examples of the mental leaps that entrepreneurs have taken.

6. What excites you about being an entrepreneur? What are your major concerns?

SELECTED READINGS

Baker, Ted; and Reed Nelson. (2005). Something from Nothing: Resource Construction through Entrepreneurial Bricolage. *Administrative Science Quarterly,* vol. 50, no. 3, pp. 329–66.

In this article the authors studied 29 firms and demonstrated that entrepreneurs differ in their responses to severe resource constraints. Some entrepreneurs were able to render unique services by recombining elements at hand for new purposes that challenged institutional definitions and limits. They introduce the concept of bricolage to explain many of these behaviors of creating something from nothing by exploiting physical, social, or institutional inputs that other firms rejected or ignored. Central to the study's contribution is the notion that companies engaging in bricolage refuse to enact the limitations imposed by dominant definitions of resource environments; rather they create their opportunities. (from journal's abstract)

Baron, Robert. (1998). Cognitive Mechanisms in Entrepreneurship: Why and When Entrepreneurs Think Differently Than Other People. *Journal of Business Venturing,* vol. 13, no. 4, pp. 275–95.

In this conceptual article, the author presents information on a study that examined the possible differences in the thinking of entrepreneurs and other people. This paper offers a number of implications of a cognitive perspective for entrepreneurship research.

Busenitz, Lowell; and Jay Barney. (1997). Differences between Entrepreneurs and Managers in Large Organizations: Biases and Heuristics in Strategic Decision Making. *Journal of Business Venturing,* vol. 12, no. 1, pp. 9–30.

In this article the authors explore the differences in the decision-making processes between entrepreneurs and managers in large organizations. In particular they focus on a number of biases, such as the overconfidence bias, but also point out some benefits from the use of biases and heuristics.

Davidsson, Per; and Benson Honig. (2003). The Role of Social and Human Capital among Nascent Entrepreneurs. *Journal of Business Venturing,* vol. 18, pp. 301–31.

This study examines nascent entrepreneurship by comparing individuals engaged in nascent activities with a control group and finds that social capital is a robust predictor for nascent entrepreneurs, as well as for advancing through the start-up process. With regard to outcomes like first sale or showing a profit, only one aspect of social capital, viz., being a member of a business network, had a statistically significant positive effect. The study supports human capital in predicting entry into nascent entrepreneurship, but only weakly for carrying the start-up process toward successful completion.

Gaglio, Connie Marie; and Jerome Katz. (2001). The Psychological Basis of Opportunity Identification: Entrepreneurial Alertness. *Small Business Economics,* vol. 16, pp. 95–111.

In this article the authors describe a model of entrepreneurial alertness and propose a research agenda for understanding opportunity identification. They investigate the origin of the entrepreneurial alertness concept and the notion of the psychological schema of alertness.

Gregoire, Denis; and Dean A. Shepherd. (In press). Technology Market Combinations and the Identification of Entrepreneurial Opportunities. *Academy of Management Journal,* http://www.aom.pace.edu/amj/inpress.

Integrating theoretical work on the nature of entrepreneurial opportunities with cognitive science research on the use of similarity comparisons in making creative mental leaps, the authors develop a model of opportunity identification that examines the independent effects of an opportunity idea's similarity characteristics and the interaction of these characteristics with an individual's knowledge and motivation. They test this model with an experiment where they asked entrepreneurs to form beliefs about opportunity ideas for technology transfer. They found that the superficial and structural similarities of technology-market combinations impact the formation of opportunity beliefs, and that individual differences in prior knowledge and entrepreneurial intent moderate these relationships. (from journal's abstract)

Haynie, J. Michael; Dean A. Shepherd; Elaine Mosakowski; and Christopher Earley. (2010). A Situated Metacognitive Model of the Entrepreneurial Mindset. *Journal of Business Venturing,* vol. 25, issue 2, pp. 217–29.

The authors develop a framework to investigate the foundations of an "entrepreneurial mindset"—described by scholars as the ability to sense, act, and mobilize under uncertain conditions. They focus on metacognitive processes that enable the entrepreneur to think beyond or reorganize existing knowledge structures and heuristics, promoting adaptable cognitions in the face of novel and uncertain decision contexts. They integrate disparate streams of literature from social and cognitive psychology toward a model that specifies entrepreneurial metacognition as situated in the entrepreneurial environment. They posit that foundations of an entrepreneurial mindset are metacognitive in nature, and subsequently detail how, and with what consequence, entrepreneurs formulate and inform "higher-order" cognitive strategies in the pursuit of entrepreneurial ends. (from journal's abstract)

Haynie, J. Michael; and Dean A. Shepherd. (2011). Toward a Theory of Discontinuous Career Transition: Investigating Career Transitions Necessitated by Traumatic Life-Events. *Journal of Applied Psychology,* vol. 96, pp. 501–24.

Career researchers have focused on the mechanisms related to career progression. Although less studied, situations in which traumatic life events necessitate a discontinuous career transition are becoming increasingly prevalent. Employing a multiple case study method, the authors offer a deeper understanding of such transitions by studying an extreme case: soldiers and Marines disabled by wartime combat. Their study highlights obstacles to future employment that are counterintuitive and stem from the discontinuous and traumatic nature of job loss. Effective management of this type of transitioning appears to stem from efforts positioned to formulate a coherent narrative of the traumatic experience and thus reconstruct foundational assumptions about the world, humanity, and self. These foundational assumptions form the basis for enacting future-oriented career strategies, such that progress toward establishing a new career path is greatest for those who can orientate themselves away from the past (trauma), away from the present (obstacles to a new career), and toward an envisioned future career positioned to confer meaning and purpose through work. (from journal's abstract)

Hitt, Michael; Barbara Keats; and Samuel DeMarie. (1998). Navigating in the New Competitive Landscape: Building Strategic Flexibility and Competitive Advantage in the 21st Century. *Academy of Management Executive,* vol. 12, pp. 22–43.

The article cites the importance of building strategic flexibility and a competitive advantage for organizations to survive in the face of emerging technical revolution and increasing globalization. The nature of the forces in the new competitive landscape requires a continuous rethinking of current strategic actions, organization structure, communication systems, corporate culture, asset deployment, and investment strategies—in short, every aspect of a firm's operation and long-term health.

Hmieleski, Keith; and Andrew Corbett. (2006). Proclivity for Improvisation as a Predictor of Entrepreneurial Intentions. *Journal of Small Business Management,* vol. 44, pp. 45–63.

This study examines the relationship between improvisation and entrepreneurial intentions and finds that entrepreneurial intentions are associated with measures of personality, motivation, cognitive style, social models, and improvisation. The strongest relationship is found between entrepreneurial intentions and improvisation.

Ireland, R. Duane; and Michael Hitt. (1999). Achieving and Maintaining Strategic Competitiveness in the 21st Century: The Role of Strategic Leadership. *Academy of Management Executive,* vol. 13, pp. 43–55.

In this article the authors acknowledge that effective strategic leadership practices can help firms enhance performance while competing in turbulent and unpredictable environments. They then describe six components of effective strategic leadership. When the activities called for by these components are completed successfully, the firm's strategic leadership practices can become a source of competitive advantage. In turn, use of this advantage can contribute significantly to achieving strategic competitiveness and earning above-average returns in the next century.

Keh, Hean; Maw Der Foo; and Boon Chong Lim. (2002). Opportunity Evaluation under Risky Conditions: The Cognitive Processes of Entrepreneurs. *Entrepreneurship: Theory and Practice,* vol. 27, pp. 125–48.

This study uses a cognitive approach to examine opportunity evaluation, as the perception of opportunity is essentially a cognitive phenomenon. The authors present a model that consists of four independent variables (overconfidence, belief in the law of small numbers, planning fallacy, and illusion of control), a mediating variable (risk perception), two control variables (demographics and risk propensity), and the dependent variable (opportunity evaluation). They find that illusion of control and belief in the law of small numbers are related to how entrepreneurs evaluate opportunities. Their results also indicate that risk perception mediates opportunity evaluation.

Krueger, Norris. (2000). The Cognitive Infrastructure of Opportunity Emergence. *Entrepreneurship: Theory and Practice,* vol. 24, pp. 5–23.

In this article the author argues that seeing a prospective course of action as a credible opportunity reflects an intentions-driven process driven by known critical antecedents. On the basis of well-developed theory and robust empirical evidence, he proposes an intentions-based model of the cognitive infrastructure that supports or inhibits how individuals perceive opportunities. The author also shows the practical diagnostic power this model offers to managers.

Kuemmerle, Walter. (May 2002). A Test for the Fainthearted. *Harvard Business Review,* pp. 122–27.

Starting a business is rarely a dignified affair. The article discusses what really makes an entrepreneur; what characteristics set successful entrepreneurs apart, enabling them to start ventures against all odds and keep them alive even in the worst of times; and finally, whether, if you don't possess those characteristics, they can be developed.

McGrath, Rita; and Ian MacMillan. (2000). *The Entrepreneurial Mindset: Strategies for Continuously Creating Opportunity in an Age of Uncertainty.* Cambridge, MA: Harvard Business School Press.

In this book the authors provide tips on how to achieve an entrepreneurial mindset. For example, they discuss the need to focus beyond incremental improvements to entrepreneurial actions, assess a business's current performance to establish the entrepreneurial framework, and formulate challenging goals by using the components of the entrepreneurial framework.

McMullen, Jeffery S.; and Dean Shepherd. (2006). Entrepreneurial Action and the Role of Uncertainty in the Theory of the Entrepreneur. *Academy of Management Review,* vol. 31, pp. 132–52.

By considering the amount of uncertainty perceived and the willingness to bear uncertainty concomitantly, the authors provide a conceptual model of entrepreneurial action that allows for examination of entrepreneurial action at the individual level of analysis while remaining consistent with a rich legacy of system-level theories of the entrepreneur. This model not only exposes limitations of existing theories of entrepreneurial action but also contributes to a deeper understanding of important conceptual issues, such as the nature of opportunity and the potential for philosophical reconciliation among entrepreneurship scholars.

Mitchell, Ron; Lowell Busenitz; Theresa Lant; Patricia McDougall; Eric Morse; and Brock Smith. (2002). Toward a Theory of Entrepreneurial Cognition: Rethinking the People Side of Entrepreneurship Research. *Entrepreneurship: Theory and Practice,* vol. 27, no. 2, pp. 93–105.

In this article the authors reexamine "the people side of entrepreneurship" by summarizing the state of play within the entrepreneurial cognition research stream, and by integrating the five articles accepted for publication in a special issue focusing on this ongoing narrative. The authors propose that the constructs, variables, and proposed relationships under development within the cognitive perspective offer research concepts and techniques that are well suited to the analysis of problems that require better explanations of the distinctly human contributions to entrepreneurship.

Sarasvathy, Saras. (2001). Causation and Effectuation: Toward a Theoretical Shift from Economic Inevitability to Entrepreneurial Contingency. *Academy of Management Review,* vol. 26, no. 2, pp. 243–64.

In this article, the author argues that an explanation for the creation of artifacts such as firms/organizations and markets requires the notion of effectuation. Causation rests on a logic of prediction, effectuation on the logic of control. The author illustrates effectuation through business examples and realistic thought experiments, examines its connections with existing theories and empirical evidence, and offers a list of testable propositions for future empirical work.

Sarasvathy, Saras. (2006). *Effectuation: Elements of Entrepreneurial Expertise.* Cheltenham, UK: Edward Elgar Publishers.

This book gives the history of the development of effectuation and provides provocative new applications and future research directions.

Sarasvathy, Saras. www.effectuation.org.

This Web site provides an up-to-date collection of works on effectuation.

Shepherd, Dean A.; and Holger Patzelt. (2011). Sustainable Entrepreneurship: Entrepreneurial Action Linking "What is to be Sustained" with "What is to be Developed." *Entrepreneurship: Theory and Practice,* vol. 1, pp. 137–63.

Informed by the sustainable development and entrepreneurship literatures, the authors offer the following definition: Sustainable entrepreneurship is focused on the preservation of nature, life support, and community in the pursuit of perceived opportunities to bring into existence future products, processes, and services for gain, where gain is broadly construed to include economic and noneconomic gains to individuals, the economy, and society. (from journal's abstract)

END NOTES

1. S. Venkataraman, "The Distinctive Domain of Entrepreneurship Research: An Editor's Perspective," in J. Katz and R. Brockhaus (eds.), *Advances in Entrepreneurship, Firm Emergence, and Growth* 3 (1997), pp. 119–38 (Greenwich, CT: JAI Press).
2. Scott Shane and S. Venkataraman, "The Promise of Entrepreneurship as a Field of Research," *The Academy of Management Review* 25, no. 1 (January 2000), pp. 217–26.
3. J. S. McMullen and D. A. Shepherd, "Entrepreneurial Action and the Role of Uncertainty in the Theory of the Entrepreneur," *The Academy of Management Review* 31, no. 1 (2006), pp. 132–52.
4. Denis Grégoire and Dean A. Shepherd, "Technology Market Combinations and the Identification of Entrepreneurial Opportunities," *Academy of Management Journal* (in press), http://www.aom.pace.edu/amj/inpress.
5. D. A. Grégoire, P. S. Barr, and D. A. Shepherd, "Cognitive Processes of Opportunity Recognition: The Role of Structural Alignment," *Organization Science* 21, no. 2 (2010), pp. 413–31.
6. T. Baker and R. E. Nelson, "Creating Something from Nothing: Resource Construction through Entrepreneurial Bricolage," *Administrative Science Quarterly* 50, no. 3 (2005), p. 329.

7. J. M. Senyard, T. Baker, and P. R. Steffens, "Entrepreneurial Bricolage and Firm Performance: Moderating Effects of Firm Change and Innovativeness," Presentation at 2010 Annual Meeting of the Academy of Management, Montreal, Canada. (2010).

8. S. Sarasvathy, "Causation and Effectuation: Toward a Theoretical Shift from Economic Inevitability to Entrepreneurial Contingency," *Academy of Management Review* 26 (2001), p. 245.

9. H. A. Simon, "Theories of Decision Making in Economics and Behavioral Science," *American Economic Review* 49 (1959), pp. 253–83.

10. Sarasvathy, "Causation and Effectuation," pp. 245–47.

11. M. A. Hitt, "The New Frontier: Transformation of Management for the New Millennium," *Organizational Dynamics* 28, no. 3 (2000), pp. 7–17.

12. R. D. Ireland, M. A. Hitt, and D. G. Sirmon, "A Model of Strategic Entrepreneurship: The Construct and Its Dimensions," *Journal of Management* 29 (2003), pp. 963–90; and Rita McGrath and Ian MacMillan, *The Entrepreneurial Mindset: Strategies for Continuously Creating Opportunity in an Age of Uncertainty* (Cambridge, MA: Harvard Business School Press, 2000).

13. Ireland, Hitt, and Sirmon, "A Model of Strategic Entrepreneurship."

14. M. A. Hitt, B. W. Keats, and S. M. DeMarie, "Navigating in the New Competitive Landscape: Building Strategic Flexibility and Competitive Advantage in the 21st Century," *Academy of Management Executive* 12 (1998), pp. 22–43 (from page 26).

15. M. Haynie, D. A. Shepherd, E. Mosakowski, and C. Earley, "A Situated Metacognitive Model of the Entrepreneurial Mindset," *Journal of Business Venturing* (2009); and M. Haynie and D. A. Shepherd, "A Measure of Adaptive Cognition for Entrepreneurship Research," *Entrepreneurship: Theory and Practice* (2009).

16. Haynie and Shepherd, "A Measure of Adaptive Cognition for Entrepreneurship Research."

17. G. Schraw and R. Dennison, "Assessing Metacognitive Awareness," *Contemporary Educational Psychology* 19 (1994), pp. 460–75.

18. A. Brown, "Metacognition and Other Mechanisms," in F. E. Weinert and R. H. Kluwe (eds.), *Metacognition, Motivation, and Understanding* (Hillsdale, NJ: Lawrence Erlbaum Associates, 1987).

19. E. Guterman, "Toward a Dynamic Assessment of Reading: Applying Metacognitive Awareness Guiding to Reading Assessment Tasks," *Journal of Research in Reading* 25, no. 3 (2002), pp. 283–98.

20. Z. R. Mevarech and B. Kramarski, "The Effects of Metacognitive Training versus Worked-out Examples on Students' Mathematical Reasoning," *British Journal of Educational Psychology* 73, no. 4 (2003), pp. 449–71; and D. Shepherd, M. Haynie, and J. McMullen (working paper), "Teaching Management Students Metacognitive Awareness: Enhancing Inductive Teaching Methods and Developing Cognitive Adaptability."

21. Mevarech and Kramarski, "The Effects of Metacognitive Training."

22. J. Ajzen, "The Theory of Planned Behavior," *Organizational Behavior and Human Decision Processes* 50 (1991), pp. 179–211.

23. A. Bandura, *Self-Efficacy: The Exercise of Control* (New York: W. H. Freeman, 1997); and D. A. Shepherd and N. Krueger, "An Intentions-Based Model of Entrepreneurial Teams' Social Cognition," Special Issue on Cognition and Information Processing, *Entrepreneurship: Theory and Practice* 27 (2002), pp. 167–85.

24. N. F. J. Krueger and D. V. Brazael, "Entrepreneurial Potential and Potential Entrepreneurs," *Entrepreneurship: Theory and Practice* 18 (1994), pp. 91–104.

25. Shepherd and Krueger, "An Intentions-Based Model."

26. C. M. Ford and D. A. Gioia, *Creativity in Organizations: Ivory Tower Visions and Real World Voices* (Newbury Park, CA: Sage, 1995).

27. See J. Gimeno, T. Folta, A. Cooper, and C. Woo, "Survival of the Fittest? Entrepreneurial Human Capital and the Persistence of Underperforming Firms," *Administrative Science Quarterly* 42 (1997), pp. 750–83.

28. P. Davidsson and B. Honig, "The Role of Social and Human Capital among Nascent Entrepreneurs," *Journal of Business Venturing* 18 (2003), pp. 301–31. D. R. DeTienne, D. A. Shepherd, and J. O. De Castro, "The Fallacy of 'Only the Strong Survive': The Effects of Extrinsic Motivation on the Persistence Decisions for Under-Performing Firms," *Journal of Business Venturing* 23 (2008), pp. 528–46.

29. Much of this information is based on research findings in Robert C. Ronstadt, "Initial Venture Goals, Age, and the Decision to Start an Entrepreneurial Career," *Proceedings of the 43rd Annual Meeting of the Academy of Management,* August 1983, p. 472; and Robert C. Ronstadt, "The Decision Not to Become an Entrepreneur," *Proceedings, 1983 Conference on Entrepreneurship,* April 1983, pp. 192–212. See also M. Lévesque, D. A. Shepherd, and E. J. Douglas, "Employment or Self-Employment: A Dynamic Utility-Maximizing Model," *Journal of Business Venturing* 17 (2002), pp. 189–210.

30. See also Lévesque, Shepherd, and Douglas, "Employment or Self-Employment."

31. A. C. Cooper, T. B. Folta, and C. Woo, "Entrepreneurial Information Search," *Journal of Business Venturing* 10 (1995), pp. 107–20; and M. Wright, K. Robbie, and C. Ennew, "Venture Capitalists and Serial Entrepreneurs," *Journal of Business Venturing* 12, no. 3 (1997), pp. 227–49.

32. Davidsson and Honig, "The Role of Social and Human Capital."

33. The influence of role models on career choice is discussed in E. Almquist and S. Angrist, "Role Model Influences on College Women's Career Aspirations," *Merrill-Palmer Quarterly* 17 (July 1971), pp. 263–97; J. Strake and C. Granger, "Same-Sex and Opposite-Sex Teacher Model Influences on Science Career Commitment among High School Students," *Journal of Educational Psychology* 70 (April 1978), pp. 180–86; Alan L. Carsrud, Connie Marie Gaglio, and Kenneth W. Olm, "Entrepreneurs-Mentors, Networks, and Successful New Venture Development: An Exploratory Study," *Proceedings, 1986 Conference on Entrepreneurship,* April 1986, pp. 29–35; and Howard Aldrich, Ben Rosen, and William Woodward, "The Impact of Social Networks on Business Foundings and Profit: A Longitudinal Study," *Proceedings, 1987 Conference on Entrepreneurship,* April 1987, pp. 154–68.

34. A thoughtful development of the network concept can be found in Howard Aldrich and Catherine Zimmer, "Entrepreneurship through Social Networks," in *The Art and Science of Entrepreneurship* (Cambridge, MA: Ballinger, 1986), pp. 3–24.

35. H. Hoang and B. Antoncic, "Network-Based Research in Entrepreneurship: A Critical Review," *Journal of Business Venturing* 18 (2003), pp. 165–88.

36. S. Birley, "The Role of Networks in the Entrepreneurial Process," *Journal of Business Venturing* 1 (1985), pp. 107–17; A. Cooper and W. Dunkelberg, "Entrepreneurship and Paths to Business Ownership," *Strategic Management Journal* 7 (1986), pp. 53–68; and B. Johannisson, "Networking and Entrepreneurial Growth," in D. Sexton and H. Landström (eds.), *The Blackwell Handbook of Entrepreneurship* (Oxford, MA: Blackwell, 2000), pp. 26–44.

37. A. Larson, "Network Dyads in Entrepreneurial Settings: A Study of the Governance of Exchange Relationships," *Administrative Science Quarterly* 37 (1992), pp. 76–104; W. Powell, "Neither Market nor Hierarchy: Network Forms of Organization," in B. Staw and L. Cummings (eds.), *Research in Organizational Behavior* (Greenwich, CT: JAI Press, 1990); and B. Uzzi, "The Sources and Consequences of Embeddedness for the Economic Performance of Organizations: The Network Effect," *American Sociological Review* 61 (1996), pp. 674–98.

38. Uzzi, "The Sources and Consequences of Embeddedness."

39. Dean A. Shepherd and Holger Patzelt, "Sustainable Entrepreneurship: Entrepreneurial Action Linking 'What is to be Sustained' with 'What is to be Developed,'" *Entrepreneurship: Theory and Practice* 1 (2011), pp. 137–63.

40. T. M. Parris and R. W. Kates, "Characterizing and Measuring Sustainable Development," *Annual Review of Environment and Resources* 28, no. 1 (2003), pp. 559–86.

41. C. K. Prahalad, *The Fortune at the Bottom of the Pyramid: Eradicating Poverty through Profits* (Wharton: 2010).

2

CORPORATE ENTREPRENEURSHIP

1

To understand the causes of interest in corporate entrepreneurship.

2

To introduce the "entrepreneurial" mode of managing firms and distinguish it from the traditional mode.

3

To provide a scale for capturing the extent to which management adopts entrepreneurial or traditional behaviors.

4

To discuss how established firms can develop an entrepreneurial culture and the challenges of doing so.

5

To acknowledge that projects fail and people feel bad about it, and to introduce the dual process model for maximizing learning from failure experiences.

OPENING PROFILE

ROBERT MONDAVI

Robert G. Mondavi, the son of poor Italian immigrants, began making wine in California in 1943 when his family purchased the Charles Krug Winery in Napa Valley, where he served as a general manager. In 1966, at the age of 54, after a severe dispute over control of the family-owned winery, Robert Mondavi used his personal savings and loans from friends to start the flagship Robert Mondavi Winery in Napa Valley with his eldest son, Michael Mondavi. Robert's vision was to create wines in California that could successfully compete with the greatest wines of the world. As a result, Robert Mondavi Winery became the first in California to produce and market premium wines that were expected to compete with premium wines from France, Spain, Italy, and Germany.

www.mondavi.com

To achieve this objective Robert believed that he needed to build a Robert Mondavi brand in the premium wine market segment. This resulted in the initial production of a limited quantity of premium wines using the best grapes, which brought the highest prices in the market and had the highest profit margins per bottle. However, he soon realized that this strategy, while establishing the brand, did not allow the company to generate enough cash flow to expand the business. To solve this problem Robert decided to produce less expensive wines that he could sell in higher volumes. He dedicated time and effort to finding the best vineyards in Napa Valley for the company's production of grapes. In addition, he signed long-term contracts with growers in Napa Valley and worked closely with each grower to improve grape quality.

Robert Mondavi built a state-of-the-art winery that became a premium wine-making facility as well as conveying a unique sense of Mondavi wines to the visitors. Soon the new winery became a place where the best practices in the production of premium wines were developed, eventually establishing the standard in the wine industry. Robert Mondavi was the first winemaker to assemble experts with various backgrounds in the fields of viticulture and wine-making to give advice on the new wines. He also developed new technology that allowed special handling of grapes and the cold fermentation of white wines. Furthermore, Mondavi's company created process innovations, such as steel fermentation tanks, vacuum corking of bottles, and aging of wines in new French oak barrels. Dedicated to growing vines naturally, Robert

Mondavi introduced a natural farming and conservation program that allowed enhanced grape quality, environmental protection, and worker health. Moreover, from the very beginning, the company promoted the presentation of wine as part of a sociable way of everyday living. Robert Mondavi Winery was one of the first wineries to present concerts, art exhibitions, and culinary programs.

In his book, Robert Mondavi describes his search for innovation:

> From the outset, I wanted my winery to draw inspiration and methods from the traditional Old World chateaux of France and Italy, but I also wanted to become a model of state-of-the-art technology, a pioneer in research and a gathering place for the finest minds in our industry. I wanted our winery to be a haven of creativity, innovation, excitement, and that unbelievable energy you find in a start-up venture when everyone is committed, heart and soul, to a common cause and a common quest.

In 1972 Mondavi's hard work and dedication to his venture were formally recognized when the Los Angeles Times Vintners Tasting Event selected the 1969 Robert Mondavi Winery Cabernet Sauvignon as the top wine produced in California.

Despite Robert Mondavi's relentless efforts, things did not always go smoothly. A noticeable improvement in the quality and reputation of the Robert Mondavi wines during the 1970s did not spark the interest of reputable five-star restaurants and top wine shops across the country. So, for over a decade, Mondavi traveled throughout the country and abroad, promoting Napa Valley wines and the Robert Mondavi brand name. Often, while dining alone on business trips, Mondavi offered restaurant employees the opportunity to taste his wine. Slowly, Mondavi got his wines on the wine lists of the top five-star restaurants in the United States. By the end of the 1970s, restaurant owners, famous wine connoisseurs, and industry critics were eager to be introduced to Robert Mondavi products. Recognizing the increased popularity of his wines, Mondavi began slowly raising the prices of his wines to the price level of comparable French wines. Subsequently, the company expanded its capacity to produce 500,000 cases of premium wines annually.

About this time Robert Mondavi started building a portfolio of premium wine brands to satisfy the needs of consumers in various price and quality segments of the domestic wine market. As a result, from the late 1970s until the 1980s Robert Mondavi diversified its portfolio through acquisition and further growth of the Woodbridge, Byron, and Coastal brands of California wine. Most of these acquisitions were financed through long-term debt.

In the early 1990s Robert Mondavi faced financial difficulties as a result of the rapid expansion; the increased competition; and a *phylloxera* infestation of several of the company's vineyards, which necessitated replanting. After contemplating the matter for several years, Robert Mondavi decided to raise enough capital to continue expansion of his company while maintaining family control of the company. On June 10, 1993, Robert Mondavi issued 3.7 million shares of stock at $13.50 a share and began trading on the NASDAQ as MOND. The initial public offering (IPO) raised approximately $49.95 million, bringing the company's market capitalization to $213.3 million.

The IPO was structured with two classes of stock: Class A common stock issued to the Mondavi family, and Class B common stock offered to the public. Class A shares carried ten votes per share, and Class B shares carried one vote per share. This structure allowed the Mondavi family to retain 90 percent ownership of the company and, subsequently, to preserve control over the company's destiny. Robert Mondavi stock was trading at $8 a share a few days after the initial offering and at $6.50 a share six months later, slashing the company's value, and the Mondavi family's wealth, by half.

One factor affecting the price decrease in the stock was the difficulty that the investment community and analysts had in valuing Robert Mondavi due to a lack of information on the wine industry. There were only two other publicly traded wine companies, both in low-end wine categories. To help solve this problem, Robert Mondavi began educating investors, trying to convince them that it is possible to build a strong, globally recognized business selling premium wines. As part of his knowledge-building and awareness-creation campaign, Robert sent teams to New York, Boston, and Chicago, who brought wine presentations, receptions, and tastings to the investors. According to Robert Mondavi, "Well, we had to mount an effective campaign and take it right to them, and not just explain our approach but put our wines right in their hands! Let them taste, in their own mouths, our expertise and commitment to excellence."

At the same time the company was continuing its innovating efforts, creating in 1994 a revolutionary, capsule-free, flange-top bottle design, which became widely accepted in the industry.

In the mid-1990s, the company started engaging in various multinational partnerships on a 50:50 basis: Its partnership with the Baron Philippe de Rothschild of Chateau Mouton Rothschild in Bordeaux, France, resulted in the creation of *Opus One* wine in 1979; with the Frescobaldi family of Tuscany, Italy, Mondavi launched *Luce, Lucente,* and *Danzante* wines in 1995; with the Eduardo Chadwick family of Chile, it introduced *Caliterra* wines in 1996; and with Australia's largest premium producer, Southcorp, it began producing and marketing new wines from Australia and California in 2001.

Today, the company continues to pursue its goals around the world with its unique cultural and innovative spirit and its consistent growth strategy, reaching revenue of over $441 million in 2002. The company produces 20 unique and separate labels representing more than 80 individual wines from California, Italy, Chile, and France and sells its wines in more than 80 countries. Some of the popular Robert Mondavi fine wine labels such as Robert Mondavi Winery, Robert Mondavi Coastal Private Selection, and Woodbridge Winery have gained enormous popularity among wine lovers in the United States as well as the rest of the world. The company remains a close family business.

Recognized as the global representative of California wines, Robert Mondavi has been a major force in leading the U.S. wine industry into the modern era and has devoted his life to creating a fine wine culture in America. Through hard work and a constant striving for excellence, he has achieved his goal of causing California wines to be viewed as some of the great wines of the world.

CAUSES FOR INTEREST IN CORPORATE ENTREPRENEURSHIP

Interest in entrepreneurship within established businesses has intensified due to a variety of events occurring on social, cultural, and business levels. On a social level, there is an increasing interest in "doing your own thing" and doing it on one's own terms. Individuals who believe strongly in their own talents frequently desire to create something of their own. They want responsibility and have a strong need for individual expression and freedom in their work environment. When this freedom is not there, frustration can cause that individual to become less productive or even leave the organization to achieve self-actualization elsewhere. This new search for meaning, and the impatience involved, has recently caused more discontent in structured organizations than ever before. When meaning is not provided within the organization, individuals often search for an institution that will provide it.

Corporate entrepreneurship is one method of stimulating, and then capitalizing on, individuals in an organization who think that something can be done differently and better. Most people think of Xerox as a large, bureaucratic Fortune 100 company. Although, in part, this may be true of the $23 billion giant company, Xerox has done something unique in trying to ensure that its creative employees do not leave like Steve Jobs did to form Apple Computer, Inc. In 1989, Xerox set up Xerox Technology Ventures (XTV) for the purpose of generating profits by investing in the promising technologies of the company, many of which would have otherwise been overlooked.[1] Xerox wanted to avoid mistakes of the past by having "a system to prevent technology from leaking out of the company," according to Robert V. Adams, president of XTV.

The fund has supported numerous start-ups thus far, similar to Quad Mark, the brainchild of Dennis Stemmle, a Xerox employee of 25 years. Stemmle's idea was to make a battery-operated, plain paper copier that would fit in a briefcase along with a laptop computer. Although Xerox's operating committee did not approve the idea for 10 years, it was finally funded by XTV and Taiwan's Advanced Scientific Corporation. As is the case with all the companies funded by XTV, the founder and key employees of a company own 20 percent of it. This provides an incentive for employees like Dennis Stemmle to take the risk, leave Xerox, and form a technology-based venture.

XTV provides both financial and nonfinancial benefits to its parent, Xerox. The funded companies provide profits to the parent company as well as the founders and employees, and now Xerox managers pay closer attention to employees' ideas as well as internal technologies. Is XTV a success? Apparently so, if replication is any indication. The XTV concept contains an element of risk in that Xerox employees forming new ventures are not guaranteed a management position if the new venture fails. This makes XTV different from most entrepreneurial ventures in companies. This aspect of risk and no guaranteed employment is the basis for AT&T Ventures, a fund modeled on XTV.

What Xerox recognized is what hundreds of executives in other organizations are also becoming aware of: It is important to keep, or instill, the entrepreneurial spirit in an organization to innovate and grow. This realization has revolutionized management thinking. In a large organization, problems often occur that thwart creativity and innovation, particularly in activities not directly related to the organization's main mission. The growth and diversification that can result from flexibility and creativity are particularly critical since large, vertically integrated, diversified corporations are often more efficient in a competitive market than smaller firms.

corporate
entrepreneurship
Entrepreneurial action
within an established
organization

The resistance against flexibility, growth, and diversification can, in part, be overcome by developing a spirit of entrepreneurship within the existing organization, called *corporate entrepreneurship*. An increase in corporate entrepreneurship reflects an increase in social, cultural, and business pressures. Hypercompetition has forced companies to have an increased interest in such areas as new product development, diversification, increased productivity, and decreasing costs by methods such as reducing the company's labor force.

Corporate entrepreneurship is most strongly reflected in entrepreneurial activities as well as in top management orientations in organizations. These entrepreneurial endeavors consist of the following four key elements: new business venturing, innovativeness, self-renewal, and proactiveness.[2]

New business venturing (sometimes called corporate venturing) refers to the creation of a new business within an existing organization. These entrepreneurial activities consist of creating something new of value either by redefining the company's current products or services, developing new markets, or forming more formally autonomous or semiautonomous units or firms. Formations of new corporate ventures are the most salient manifestations of corporate entrepreneurship. Organizational innovativeness refers to product and service innovation, with an emphasis on development and innovation in technology. It includes new product development, product improvements, and new production methods and procedures.

Self-renewal is the transformation of an organization through the renewal of the key ideas on which it is built. It has strategic and organizational change connotations and includes a redefinition of the business concept, reorganization, and the introduction of systemwide changes to increase innovation. Proactiveness includes initiative and risk taking, as well as competitive aggressiveness and boldness, which are particularly reflected in the orientations and activities of top management. A proactive organization tends to take risks by conducting experiments; it also takes initiative and is bold and aggressive in pursuing opportunities. Organizations with this proactive spirit attempt to lead rather than follow competitors in such key business areas as the introduction of new products or services, operating technologies, and administrative techniques.

In the previous chapter we showed that acting entrepreneurially is something that people choose to do based on their perceptions of the desirability and feasibility of creating a new venture to pursue an opportunity. However, existing companies also can pursue opportunities, but this requires that the management of these firms create an environment that encourages employees to think and act entrepreneurially. Such an environment is one that helps people realize that entrepreneurial behavior within the firm is both personally desirable and feasible. This builds a strong entrepreneurial intention and, as discussed in the previous chapter, the general rule is that the stronger the intention to engage in entrepreneurial action, the more likely it will happen. To create such a culture requires a different orientation toward the management of the firm, to which we now turn.

MANAGERIAL VERSUS ENTREPRENEURIAL DECISION MAKING

Howard Stevenson, a professor at Harvard University, believes that entrepreneurship represents a mode of managing an existing firm that is distinct from the way existing firms are traditionally managed. Entrepreneurial management is distinct from traditional management in terms of eight dimensions: (1) strategic orientation, (2) commitment to opportunity, (3) commitment of resources, (4) control of resources, (5) management structure, (6) reward philosophy, (7) growth orientation, and (8) entrepreneurial culture.[3] The nature of the differences among these dimensions is represented in Table 2.1 and described in greater detail below.[4]

Strategic Orientation and Commitment to Opportunity

The first two factors that help distinguish more entrepreneurially managed firms from those that are more traditionally managed relate to strategic issues—strategic orientation

TABLE 2.1   Distinguishing Entrepreneurially from Traditionally Managed Firms

Entrepreneurial Focus	Conceptual Dimension	Administrative Focus
Driven by perception of opportunity	Strategic orientation	Driven by controlled resources
Revolutionary with short duration	Commitment to opportunity	Evolutionary with long duration
Many stages with minimal exposure	Commitment of resources	A single stage with complete commitment out of decision
Episodic use or rent of required resources	Control of resources	Ownership or employment of required resources
Flat with multiple informal networks	Management structure	Hierarchy
Based on value creation	Reward philosophy	Based on responsibility and seniority
Rapid growth is top priority; risk accepted to achieve growth	Growth orientation	Safe, slow, and steady
Promoting broad search for opportunities	Entrepreneurial culture	Opportunity search restricted by controlled resources; failure punished

Source: This table is taken from T. Brown, P. Davidsson, and J. Wiklund, "An Operationalization of Stevenson's Conceptualization of Entrepreneurship as Opportunity-Based Firm Behavior," *Strategic Management Journal* 22 (2001), p. 955.

and commitment to opportunity. An emphasis on strategy in developing a deeper understanding of entrepreneurship at the firm level is not surprising because both entrepreneurship and strategy have important implications for the performance of the firm.

strategic orientation
A focus on those factors that are inputs into the formulation of the firm's strategy

Strategic orientation refers to those factors that are inputs into the formulation of the firm's strategy. We can think of it as the philosophy of the firm that drives its decision about strategy; the way that it looks at the world and the way it looks at itself and these perceptions are the driving factors behind the firm's strategy. The strategy of entrepreneurial management is driven by the presence or generation of opportunities for new entry and is less concerned about the resources that may be required to pursue such opportunities. Acquiring and marshaling the necessary resources represents a secondary step for the entrepreneurially managed firm and perhaps part of the thinking about the implementation of discovered opportunities. Resources do not constrain the strategic thinking of an entrepreneurially managed firm. In contrast, the strategy of traditional management is to use the resources of the firm efficiently. Therefore, the type and the amount of resources that the firm has (or knows it can readily access) represent a key starting point for thinking strategically about the future of the firm. Only those opportunities that can be pursued effectively using existing resources are considered the appropriate domain of further strategic thinking.

Both entrepreneurship and strategy are more than simply thinking about the future of the firm, they are also concerned with the firm taking action. It is through its actions that a firm is judged, often by analysis of its financial and competitive performance. Entrepreneurially and traditionally managed firms can be distinguished in terms of their commitment to opportunity. More entrepreneurially managed firms have an *entrepreneurial*

entrepreneurial orientation toward opportunity
A commitment to taking action on potential opportunities

orientation toward opportunity in that they are committed to taking action on potential opportunities and therefore can pursue opportunities rapidly, making the most of windows of opportunity. They also are able to withdraw their resources from a particular opportunity and do so rapidly, such that if initial feedback from the pursuit of an opportunity provides information suggesting that it might not be the right opportunity for the firm, then management can "pull the plug," minimizing losses from the initial pursuit. In contrast, traditionally managed firms tend to place considerable emphasis on information; information is derived from data collection and analysis of that information to determine, say, the return on resources to be deployed. If the traditionally managed firm chooses to pursue the given opportunity, it would be with a much larger initial investment and the intention of remaining in that line of business for a considerable time.

Commitment of Resources and Control of Resources

entrepreneurial orientation toward commitment of resources A focus on how to minimize the resources that would be required in the pursuit of a particular opportunity

It is important to note that entrepreneurs still care about the resources they must commit to the pursuit of an opportunity, but they have an *entrepreneurial orientation toward the commitment of resources* that is focused on the opportunity. Thoughts of resources turn more to how the firm can minimize the resources that would be required in the pursuit of a particular opportunity. By minimizing the resources that the firm must invest to initially pursue an opportunity, the amount of resources at risk if the opportunity does not "pan out" is also minimized. For example, entrepreneurially managed firms may "test the waters" by committing small amounts of resources in a multistep manner with minimal (risk) exposure at each step. This small and incremental process of resource commitment provides the firm the flexibility to change direction rapidly as new information about the opportunity or the environment comes to light. Psychologically, these smaller sunk costs help stop entrepreneurially managed firms from becoming entrenched with a particular course of action, especially if that course of action turns out to be a losing one. In contrast, when traditionally managed firms decide to commit resources to an opportunity, they do so on a large scale. That is, rather than put a toe in to test the water, they make calculations based on the ambient temperature over the last week, the density of the water, and whether a pool cover has been used or not. If, based on that calculation, the water is theoretically deemed to be sufficiently warm, the traditional manager commits to that assessment with a full swan dive. Having made a large commitment of resources the firm often feels compelled to justify the initial decision to commit, and so the initial commitment gains momentum that maintains the status quo of continual resource commitment. Therefore, a traditionally managed firm uses in-depth analysis of available information to go for it or not—and if they do go for it, then the investment of resources is not easily reversed.

Over and above their commitment of resources, entrepreneurially and traditionally managed firms differ in their control of resources. Entrepreneurially managed firms are less concerned about the ownership of resources and more concerned about having access to others' resources, including financial capital, intellectual capital, skills, and competencies. Entrepreneurially managed firms operate from the standpoint, "Why do I need to control resources if I can access them from others?" Access to resources is possible to the extent that the opportunity allows the firm to effectively deploy others' resources for the benefit of the entrepreneurial firm and the owner of the invested resources. In contrast, traditionally managed firms focus on the ownership of resources and the accumulation of further resources. They believe that if they control their own resources then they are self-contained. For these firms, the control that comes with ownership means that resources can be deployed more effectively for the benefit of the firm.

entrepreneurial orientation toward control of resources A focus on how to access others' resources

entrepreneurial orientation toward management structure More organic focus—has few layers of bureaucracy between top management and the customer and typically has multiple informal networks

Management Structure and Reward Philosophy

An *entrepreneurial orientation toward management structure* is organic. That is, the organizational structure has few layers of bureaucracy between top management and the customer and typically has multiple informal communication channels. In this way,

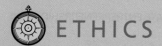

ETHICAL CONDUCT OF ENTREPRENEURS VERSUS MANAGERS

Understanding the factors that contribute to and influence the ethical conduct of managers and entrepreneurs is important for the future of the U.S. economic system as well as the economic system of the world. The significance of these factors becomes all the more salient when operating in a hypercompetitive global economy. In such an environment, competitors aggressively disrupt the status quo and seek to change the rules of competition. While current businesses impact the ethical standards used in present business dealings, emerging entrepreneurial companies set the ethical tone for the future economic system of the world.

Although the United States has strong laws, such as the Foreign Corrupt Practices Act of 1977, and promotes ethical behavior on the part of managers and entrepreneurs, the ethical attitudes of these groups are not well understood. How will managers and entrepreneurs react in certain situations? Will they have high ethical standards in their internal and external dealings? Will managers, because of their more bureaucratic environment, have higher ethical standards than entrepreneurs? Or, will entrepreneurs, because their business practices more closely reflect their personal values, have higher ethical attitudes than managers?

In one study, 165 entrepreneurs and 128 managers were surveyed using a detached measuring instrument containing binary, response questions, scenarios, and comprehensive demographic information.

Generally, entrepreneurs and managers differed only slightly in their views regarding the ethics of various activities and their ethical perceptions regarding others. There were few differences in the two groups regarding their evaluation of the ethical nature of 12 circumstances and 7 scenarios. The similarities in ethical attitudes between the two groups of decision makers seem to be one of the important findings, which can be explained by similar legal, cultural, and educational factors that affect the ethical attitudes of both groups. Some significant differences consistently indicate that entrepreneurs are more prone to hold ethical attitudes.

The findings indicate that managers need to sacrifice their personal values to those of the company more than entrepreneurs. Also, entrepreneurs consistently demonstrate higher ethical attitudes in the internal dealings of the company, such as not taking longer than necessary for a job and not using company resources for personal use. These findings are consistent with the theory of property where we would expect someone to be more ethical in dealing with his or her own property. This finding suggests that, through increased ownership, managers might be motivated to have more ethical dealings with their company's assets. Profit-sharing companies (managers and other key employees) can therefore perhaps reduce the possibilities of moral hazard and opportunistic behavior within the company through some type of managerial ownership. Likewise, long-term relationships with customers and the community in general have to be reflected in the property of the company through philanthropic acts and different liability accounts.

entrepreneurially managed firms are able to capture and communicate more information from the external environment and are sufficiently "fluid" to be able to take quick action based on that information.

In addition, entrepreneurially managed firms are more structured to make use of both their internal networks (for example, through informal communication channels at work) and external networks (with buyers, suppliers, and financial institutions), which provide information and other resources important in the discovery/generation and exploitation of opportunities. In contrast, the traditionally managed firm has a structure well suited for the internal efficiencies of allocating controlled resources. There is a formalized hierarchy with clear roles and responsibilities, highly routinized work, and layers of middle management to "manage" employees' use of the firm's resources. Traditionally managed firms have structures that are typically inwardly focused on efficiency rather than on detecting and rapidly acting on changes in the external environment.

Firms are organized not only by their structures but also by their reward philosophy. The entrepreneurially managed firm is focused on pursuing opportunities for new entry that represent new value for the firm (and hopefully for others, including society as a whole). It is not surprising then that entrepreneurially managed firms have an *entrepreneurial philosophy toward rewards* that compensates employees based on their contribution toward the discovery/generation and exploitation of opportunity. Given the organic structure described earlier, employees often have the freedom to experiment with potential opportunities and are rewarded accordingly. The traditionally managed firm rewards management and employees based on their responsibilities, where responsibilities are typically determined by the amount of resources (assets and/or people) that each manager or employee controls. Promotion is a reward that provides a manager control of even more resources and, therefore, further scope for rewards.

entrepreneurial philosophy toward rewards   One that compensates employees based on their contribution toward the discovery/generation and exploitation of opportunity

Growth Orientation and Entrepreneurial Culture

entrepreneurial orientation toward growth   A focus on rapid growth

In a firm that has an *entrepreneurial orientation toward growth* there is a great desire to expand the size of the firm at a rapid pace. Although traditionally managed firms may also desire to grow, they prefer growth to be slow and at a steady pace. That is, they prefer a pace of growth that is more "manageable" in that it does not "unsettle the firm" by putting at risk the resources that the firm controls and thus does not put at risk the jobs and power of top management.

culture   The environment of a particular organization

entrepreneurial orientation toward culture   A focus on encouraging employees to generate ideas, experiment, and engage in other tasks that might produce opportunities

Culture also distinguishes entrepreneurially and traditionally managed firms. A firm with an *entrepreneurial orientation toward culture* encourages employees to generate ideas, experiment, and engage in other tasks that might produce creative output. Such output is highly valued by entrepreneurial management because it is often the source of opportunities for new entries. Opportunities are the focus of the entrepreneurially managed firm.

In contrast, the traditionally managed firm begins with an assessment of the resources that it controls, and this is reflected in its organizational culture. So while a traditionally managed firm is still interested in ideas, it is mostly interested in ideas that revolve around currently controlled resources. With only ideas considered that relate to currently controlled resources, the scope of opportunities discovered and generated by a traditionally managed firm is limited.

It is unlikely that there are many firms that are "purely" entrepreneurially managed or purely traditionally managed; most firms fall somewhere in between. Table 2.2 presents a scale for determining how entrepreneurially managed a particular firm is. The higher the score, the more entrepreneurially managed the firm is.

Establishing a Culture for Corporate Entrepreneurship

How can the culture for corporate entrepreneurship be established in an organization? In establishing an entrepreneurial environment within an established organization, certain factors and leadership characteristics need to be present.[5] The overall characteristics of a good entrepreneurial environment are summarized in Table 2.3. The first of these is that the organization operates on the frontiers of technology. Since research and development are key sources for successful new product ideas, the firm must operate on the cutting edge of the industry's technology, encouraging and supporting new ideas instead of discouraging them, as frequently occurs in firms that require a rapid return on investment and a high sales volume.

TABLE 2.2   Scale to Capture How Entrepreneurially a Firm Is Managed

Strategic Orientation

As we define our strategies, our major concern is how to best utilize the sources we control.	1 2 3 4 5 6 7 8 9 10	We are not constrained by the resources at (or not at) hand.
We limit the opportunities we pursue on the basis of our current resources.	1 2 3 4 5 6 7 8 9 10	Our fundamental task is to pursue opportunities we perceive as valuable and then to acquire the resources to exploit them.
The resources we have significantly influence our business strategies.	1 2 3 4 5 6 7 8 9 10	Opportunities control our business strategies.

Resource Orientation

Since our objective is to use our resources, we will usually invest heavily and rapidly.	1 2 3 4 5 6 7 8 9 10	Since we do not need resources to commence the pursuit of an opportunity, our commitment of resources may be in stages.
We prefer to totally control and own the resources we use.	1 2 3 4 5 6 7 8 9 10	All we need from resources is the ability to use them.
We prefer to use only our own resources in our ventures.	1 2 3 4 5 6 7 8 9 10	We like to employ resources that we borrow or rent.
In exploiting opportunities, access to money is more important than just having the idea.	1 2 3 4 5 6 7 8 9 10	In exploiting opportunities, having the idea is more important than just having the money.

Management Structure

We prefer tight control of funds and operations by means of sophisticated control and information systems.	1 2 3 4 5 6 7 8 9 10	We prefer loose, informal control. There is a dependence on informal relations.
We strongly emphasize getting things done by following formal processes and procedures.	1 2 3 4 5 6 7 8 9 10	We strongly emphasize getting things done even if this means disregarding formal procedures.
We strongly emphasize holding to tried and true management principles and industry norms.	1 2 3 4 5 6 7 8 9 10	We strongly emphasize adapting freely to changing circumstances without much concern for past practices.
There is a strong insistence on a uniform management style throughout the firm.	1 2 3 4 5 6 7 8 9 10	Managers' operating styles are allowed to range freely from very formal to very informal.
There is a strong emphasis on getting line and staff personnel to adhere closely to their formal job descriptions.	1 2 3 4 5 6 7 8 9 10	There is a strong tendency to let the requirements of the situation and the personality of the individual dictate proper job behavior.

Reward Philosophy

Our employees are evaluated and compensated based on their responsibilities.	1 2 3 4 5 6 7 8 9 10	Our employees are evaluated and compensated based on the value they add to the firm.
Our employees are usually rewarded by promotion and annual raises.	1 2 3 4 5 6 7 8 9 10	We try to compensate our employees by devising ways that they can benefit from the increased value of the firm.
An employee's standing is based on the amount of responsibility s/he has.	1 2 3 4 5 6 7 8 9 10	An employee's standing is based on the value s/he adds.

	Growth Orientation	
Growth is not necessarily our top objective. Long-term survival may be at least as important.	1 2 3 4 5 6 7 8 9 10	It is generally known throughout the firm that growth is our top objective.
It is generally known throughout the firm that steady and sure growth is the best way to expand.	1 2 3 4 5 6 7 8 9 10	It is generally known throughout the firm that our intention is to grow as big and as fast as possible.
	Entrepreneurial Culture	
It is difficult to find a sufficient number of promising ideas to utilize all of our resources.	1 2 3 4 5 6 7 8 9 10	We have many more promising ideas than we have time and resources to pursue.
Changes in the society-at-large seldom lead to commercially promising ideas for our firm.	1 2 3 4 5 6 7 8 9 10	Changes in the society-at-large often give us ideas for new products and services.
It is difficult for our firm to find ideas that can be converted into profitable products/services.	1 2 3 4 5 6 7 8 9 10	We never experience a lack of ideas that we can convert into profitable products/services.

Source: This table is taken from T. Brown, P. Davidsson, and J. Wiklund, "An Operationalization of Stevenson's Conceptualization of Entrepreneurship as Opportunity-Based Firm Behavior," *Strategic Management Journal* 22 (2001), Appendix.

Second, experimentation—trial and error—is encouraged. Successful new products or services usually do not appear fully developed; instead, they evolve. It took time and some product failures before the first marketable computer appeared. A company wanting to establish an entrepreneurial spirit has to establish an environment that allows mistakes and failures in developing new and innovative products. This is in direct opposition to the established career and promotion system of the traditional organization. Yet without the opportunity to fail in an organization, few, if any, corporate entrepreneurial ventures will be developed. Almost every entrepreneur has experienced at least one failure in establishing a successful venture. The importance and the difficulty of learning from the experience are discussed in the last section of this chapter.

TABLE 2.3 Characteristics of an Entrepreneurial Environment

- Organization operates on frontiers of technology
- New ideas encouraged
- Trial and error encouraged
- Failures allowed
- No opportunity parameters
- Resources available and accessible
- Multidiscipline teamwork approach
- Long time horizon
- Volunteer program
- Appropriate reward system
- Sponsors and champions available
- Support of top management

Third, an organization should make sure that there are no initial organizational obstacles that inhibit creativity in new product development. Frequently in an organization, various "turfs" are protected, frustrating attempts by potential entrepreneurs to establish new ventures. In one Fortune 500 company, an attempt to establish an entrepreneurial environment ran into problems and eventually failed when the potential entrepreneurs were informed that a proposed new product and venture was not possible because it was in the domain of another division.

Fourth, the resources of the firm need to be available and easily accessible. As one corporate entrepreneur stated, "If my company really wants me to take the time, effort, and career risks to establish a new venture, then it needs to put money and people resources on the line." Often, insufficient funds are allocated not to creating something new, but instead to solving problems that have an immediate effect on the bottom line. Some companies—like Xerox, 3M, and AT&T—have recognized this problem and have established separate venture-capital areas for funding new internal as well as external ventures. Even when resources are available, all too often the reporting requirements become obstacles to obtaining them.

Fifth, a multidisciplined team approach needs to be encouraged. This open approach, with participation by needed individuals regardless of area, is the antithesis of the typical corporate organizational structure. An evaluation of successful cases of corporate entrepreneurship indicated that one key to success was the existence of "skunkworks" involving relevant people. Developing the needed teamwork for a new venture is further complicated by the fact that a team member's promotion and overall career within the corporation are based on his or her job performance in the current position, not on his or her contribution to the new venture being created.

Besides encouraging teamwork, the corporate environment must establish a long time horizon for evaluating the success of the overall program as well as the success of each individual venture. If a company is not willing to invest money without a guarantee of return for 5 to 10 years, it should not attempt to create an entrepreneurial environment. This patient attitude toward money in the corporate setting is no different from the investment/return time horizon used by venture capitalists and others when they invest in an entrepreneurial effort.

Sixth, the spirit of corporate entrepreneurship cannot be forced upon individuals; it must be on a volunteer basis. There is a difference between corporate thinking and entrepreneurial thinking (discussed earlier and summarized in Table 2.1), with certain individuals performing much better on one side of the continuum or the other. Most managers in a corporation are not capable of being successful corporate entrepreneurs. Those who do emerge from this self-selection process must be allowed the latitude to carry a project through to completion. This is not consistent with most corporate procedures for new product development, where different departments and individuals are involved in each stage of the development process. An individual willing to spend the excess hours and effort to create a new venture needs the opportunity and the accompanying reward of completing the project. A corporate entrepreneur falls in love with the newly created internal venture and will do almost anything to help ensure its success.

The seventh characteristic of a good entrepreneurial environment is a *reward system*. The corporate entrepreneur needs to be appropriately rewarded for all the energy, effort, and risk taking expended in the creation of the new venture. Rewards should be based on the attainment of established performance goals. An equity position in the new venture is one of the best rewards for motivating and eliciting the amount of activity and effort needed for success.

Eighth, a corporate environment favorable for corporate entrepreneurship has sponsors and champions throughout the organization who not only support the creative activity but also have the planning flexibility to establish new objectives and directions as needed. As one corporate entrepreneur stated, "For a new business venture to succeed, the corporate entrepreneur needs to be able to alter plans at will and not be concerned about how close they come to achieving the previously stated objectives." Corporate structures frequently measure managers on their ability to come close to objectives, regardless of the quality of performance reflected in this accomplishment.

Finally, and perhaps most important, the entrepreneurial activity must be wholeheartedly supported and embraced by top management, both by their physical presence and by making sure that the necessary personnel and financial resources are available. Without top management support, a successful entrepreneurial environment cannot be created.

Leadership Characteristics of Corporate Entrepreneurs

Within this overall corporate environment, certain individual characteristics have been identified that constitute a successful corporate entrepreneur. As summarized in Table 2.4, these include understanding the environment, being visionary and flexible, creating management options, encouraging teamwork, encouraging open discussion, building a coalition of supporters, and being persistent.

An entrepreneur needs to understand all aspects of the environment. Part of this ability is reflected in the individual's level of creativity, which generally decreases with age and education in most individuals. To establish a successful corporate venture, the individual must be creative and have a broad understanding of the internal and external environments of the corporation.

The person who is going to establish a successful new venture within the firm must also be a visionary leader—a person who dreams great dreams. Although there are many definitions of leadership, the one that best describes what is needed for corporate entrepreneurship is: "A leader is like a gardener. When you want a tomato, you take a seed, put it in fertile soil, and carefully water under tender care. You don't manufacture tomatoes; you grow them." Another good definition is that "leadership is the ability to dream great things and communicate these in such a way that people say yes to being a part of the dream." Martin Luther King, Jr., said, "I have a dream," and articulated that dream in such a way that thousands followed him in his efforts, in spite of overwhelming obstacles. To establish a successful new venture, the corporate entrepreneur must have a dream and overcome obstacles to achieving it by selling the dream to others.

The third necessary leadership characteristic is that the corporate entrepreneur must be flexible and create management options. A corporate entrepreneur does not "mind the store," but rather is open to and even encourages change. By challenging the beliefs and

TABLE 2.4   Leadership Characteristics of a Corporate Entrepreneur
• Understands the environment
• Is visionary and flexible
• Creates management options
• Encourages teamwork
• Encourages open discussion
• Builds a coalition of supporters
• Persists

assumptions of the corporation, a corporate entrepreneur has the opportunity to create something new in the organizational structure.

The corporate entrepreneur needs a fourth characteristic: the ability to encourage teamwork and use a multidisciplined approach. This also violates the organizational practices and structures taught in most business schools that are apparent in established organizational structures. In forming a new venture, putting together a variety of skills requires crossing established departmental structure and reporting systems. To minimize disruption, the corporate entrepreneur must be a good diplomat.

Open discussion must be encouraged to develop a good team for creating something new. Many corporate managers have forgotten the frank, open discussions and disagreements that were a part of their educational process. Instead, they spend time building protective barriers and insulating themselves in their corporate empires. A successful new venture within an established firm can be formed only when the team involved feels free to disagree and to critique an idea to reach the best solution. The degree of openness among the team members depends on the degree of openness of the corporate entrepreneur.

Openness leads also to the establishment of a strong coalition of supporters and encouragers. The corporate entrepreneur must encourage and affirm each team member, particularly during difficult times. This encouragement is very important, as the usual motivators of career paths and job security are not operational in establishing a new corporate venture. A good corporate entrepreneur makes everyone a hero.

Last, but not least, is persistence. Throughout the establishment of any new venture, frustration and obstacles will occur. Only through the corporate entrepreneur's persistence will a new venture be created and successful commercialization result.

ESTABLISHING CORPORATE ENTREPRENEURSHIP IN THE ORGANIZATION

Over and above the creation of an organizational culture and the leadership characteristics discussed so far, an organization wanting to establish a more entrepreneurial firm must implement a procedure for its creation. Although this can be done internally, frequently it is easier to use someone outside to facilitate the process. This is particularly true when the organization's environment is very traditional and has a record of little change and few new products being introduced.

top management commitment Managers in an organization strongly supporting corporate entrepreneurship

The first step in this process is to secure a commitment to corporate entrepreneurship in the organization by top, upper, and middle management levels. Without *top management commitment*, the organization will never be able to go through all the cultural changes necessary for implementation. Once the top management of the organization has been committed to corporate entrepreneurship for a sufficient period of time (at least three years), the concept can be introduced throughout the organization. This is accomplished most effectively through seminars, where the aspects of corporate entrepreneurship are introduced and strategies are developed to transform the organizational culture into an entrepreneurial one. General guidelines need to be established for corporate venture development. Once the initial framework is established and the concept embraced, corporate entrepreneurs need to be identified, selected, and trained. This training needs to focus on identifying viable opportunities and their markets and developing the appropriate business plan.

Second, ideas and general areas that top management is interested in supporting should be identified, along with the amount of risk money that is available to develop the concept further. Overall program expectations and the target results of each corporate venture should be established. As much as possible, these should specify the time frame, volume, and profitability requirements for the new venture, as well as the impact of the organization. Along with entrepreneurial training, a mentor/sponsor system needs to be established. Without sponsors or champions, there is little hope that the culture of the organization can be transformed into an entrepreneurial one.

Third, a company needs to use technology to make itself more flexible. Technology has been used successfully for the past decade by small companies that behave like big ones.[6] How else could a small firm like Value Quest Ltd. compete against very large money management firms, except through a state-of-the-art personal computer and access to large data banks? Similarly, large companies can use technology to make themselves responsive and flexible like smaller firms.

Fourth, the organization should be a group of interested managers who will train employees as well as share their experiences. The training sessions should be conducted one day per month for a specified period of time. Informational items about corporate entrepreneurship in general—and about the specifics of the company's activities in developing ideas into marketable products or services that are the basis of new business venture units—should be well publicized. This will require the entrepreneurial team to develop a business plan, obtain customer reaction and some initial intentions to buy, and learn how to coexist within the organizational structure.

Fifth, the organization needs to develop ways to get closer to its customers. This can be done by tapping the database, hiring from smaller rivals, and helping the retailer.

Sixth, an organization that wants to become more entrepreneurial must learn to be more productive with fewer resources. This has already occurred in many companies that have downsized. Top-heavy organizations are out of date in today's hypercompetitive environment. To accommodate the large cutbacks in middle management, much more control has to be given to subordinates at all levels in the organization. Not surprisingly, the span of control may become as high as 30-to-1 in divisions of such companies. The concept of "lean and mean" needs to exist if corporate entrepreneurship is to prevail.

Seventh, the organization needs to establish a strong support structure for corporate entrepreneurship. This is particularly important since corporate entrepreneurship is usually a secondary activity in the organization. Since entrepreneurial activities do not immediately affect the bottom line, they can be easily overlooked and may receive little funding and support. To be successful, these ventures require flexible, innovative behavior, with the corporate entrepreneurs having total authority over expenditures and access to sufficient funds. When the corporate entrepreneur has to justify expenses on a daily basis, it is really not a new internal venture but merely an operational extension of the funding source.

Eighth, support also must involve tying the rewards to the performance of the entrepreneurial unit. This encourages the team members to work harder and compete more effectively since they will benefit directly from their efforts. Because the corporate venture is a part of the larger organization and not a totally independent unit, the equity portion of the compensation is particularly difficult to handle.

Finally, the organization needs to implement an evaluation system that allows successful entrepreneurial units to expand and unsuccessful ones to be eliminated. The organization can establish constraints to ensure that this expansion does not run contrary to the corporate mission statement. Similarly, corporate ventures that fail to show sufficient viability should not be allowed to exist just because of vested interests.

Problems and Successful Efforts

Corporate entrepreneurship is not without its problems. One study found that new ventures started within a corporation performed worse than those started independently by

AS SEEN IN *BUSINESS NEWS*

HOT OR NOT?

DO YOU BELIEVE THIS DIGITAL FRIDGE TECHNOLOGY REPRESENTS AN OPPORTUNITY?

Why, oh why, must employees stop working just because they're having lunch or stoking up on caffeine? They won't if your lunchroom is equipped with the Multi-Media Refrigerator ($8,000) from LG Electronics (www.lgappliances.com). A 25.5-cubic-foot refrigerator with an Internet connection and built-in LCD, the digital fridge lets workers keep researching Web projects and reading e-mail while they munch. The fridge has a built-in TV, camera, and Web radio so you can stretch videoconferences through coffee breaks. Here's a morale booster: Alternate photos of your office manager with those pencil requisition training videos on its LCD.[a]

DO YOU BELIEVE THIS "SMALL WORLD" TECHNOLOGY REPRESENTS AN OPPORTUNITY?

Rick Snyder, CEO of Ardesta, a holding firm in Ann Arbor, Michigan, has a mantra: "Smaller, faster, better, cheaper." He's talking about "small tech," a term that describes nanotechnology, microtechnology, and micro-electromechanical systems (MEMS). Nanotechnology in particular has gotten a lot of coverage as big companies like Hewlett-Packard and Intel have begun to introduce nano into computing. It's hard to pinpoint exactly what small tech is because it has so many wide-ranging applications. "I would call it more of a revolution than an evolution," says Snyder. Nanotechnology, for example, deals with matter at an atomic and molecular level—that is, with matter often described as being less than the width of a human hair in size. It's appearing in everything from stainproof coating for fabrics to scratch-resistant coating for eyeglasses to miniscule computer chip circuits from HP Labs.

Research funding for small tech is enormous. Ardesta is devoted to investing in and helping launch various small tech ventures with an ultimate goal of bringing actual products to market. Many businesses in this fledgling technological area are small entrepreneurial start-ups and spin-offs from research institutions. Life sciences and materials manufacturing are two industries that will really feel the early effects of the growing small tech market. Eventually, though, small tech will touch just about everything. Snyder calls it pervasive and transparent.

Some applications are out already and operating in your business right under your nose. Microtech is built into inkjet cartridges and portable projectors. At SmallTimes.com, a clearinghouse for information on small technology, the section devoted to applications is an eye-opener: A recent visit to the site brought up articles on nanotech use in products such as tennis rackets and LCD monitors, among others.

There are a million microscopic reasons to get excited, but it's important to keep them all in perspective. Snyder sees an accelerating growth curve over the next five years as small tech makes its way into real-life markets. But you shouldn't expect companies to shout "nano" or "MEMS" in their product advertising. The way you'll know small tech has touched your business is when Snyder's mantra comes into play: "Smaller, faster, better, cheaper."[b]

[a]Source: Mike Hogan, "Employees Can Munch and Work on the Web at the Same Time with This Time-Saver," *Entrepreneur* (February 2003), pp. 18–22.
[b]Source: Reprinted with permission of Wright's Media, "Employees Can Munch and Work on the Web at the Same Time with This Time-Saver," by Mike Hogan, February 2003, *Entrepreneur*, pp. 18–22.

entrepreneurs.[7] The reasons cited were the corporation's difficulty in maintaining a long-term commitment, a lack of freedom to make autonomous decisions, and a constrained environment. Generally, independent, venture-capital-based start-ups by entrepreneurs tend to outperform corporate start-ups significantly. On average, not only did the independents become profitable twice as fast, but they ended up twice as profitable.[8]

These findings should not deter organizations from starting the process. There are numerous examples of companies that, having understood the environmental and entrepreneurial characteristics necessary, have adopted their own version of the implementation process to launch new ventures successfully. One of the best known of these firms is Minnesota Mining and Manufacturing (3M). Having had many entrepreneurial successes, 3M, in effect, allows employees to devote a percentage of their time to independent projects. This enables the divisions of the company to meet an important goal: to generate a significant percent of sales from new products introduced within the last five years. One of the most successful of these entrepreneurial activities was the development of Post-it Notes by entrepreneur Arthur Fry. This effort developed out of Fry's annoyance that pieces of paper marking his church hymnal constantly fell out while he was singing. As a 3M chemical engineer, Fry knew about the discovery by a scientist, Spencer Silver, of an adhesive with very low sticking power, which to the company was a poor product characteristic. However, this characteristic was perfect for Fry's problem; a marker with a light-sticking adhesive that would be easy to remove provided a good solution. Obtaining approval to commercialize the idea proved to be a monumental task until the samples distributed to secretaries within 3M, as well as to other companies, created such a demand that the company eventually began selling the product under the name Post-it.

Another firm committed to the concept of corporate entrepreneurship is Hewlett-Packard (HP). After failing to recognize the potential of Steven Wozniak's proposal for a personal computer (which was the basis for Apple Computer Inc.), Hewlett-Packard has taken steps to ensure that it will be recognized as a leader in innovation and not miss future opportunities. However, the entrepreneurial road at HP is not an easy one. Such was the case for Charles House, an engineer who went far beyond his entrepreneurial duty when he ignored an order from David Packard to stop working on a high-quality video monitor. The monitor, once developed, was used in NASA's manned moon landings and in heart transplants. Although projected to achieve sales of no more than 30 units, these large-screen displays have obtained good sales and profits.

IBM also decided that corporate entrepreneurship would help spur corporate growth. The company developed the independent business unit concept, in which each unit is a separate organization with its own mini-board of directors and autonomous decision-making authority on many manufacturing and marketing issues. The business units have developed such products as the automatic teller machine for banks, industrial robots, and the IBM personal computer. The latter business unit was given a blank check with a mandate to get IBM into the personal computer market. Corporate entrepreneur Philip Estridge led his group to develop and market the PCs, through both IBM's sales force and the retail market, breaking some of the most binding operational rules of IBM at that time.

These and other success stories indicate that the problems of corporate entrepreneurship are not insurmountable and that implementing corporate entrepreneurship can lead to new products, growth, and the development of an entirely new corporate environment and culture.

Learning from Failure

Entrepreneurial actions are shrouded in uncertainty because opportunities exist in (or create) such environments. They are essentially experiments with unknown outcomes. Whether it is a new project, new venture, or new business model, sometimes these entrepreneurial initiatives do not work out as expected—they fail to achieve their objectives and, as a result, are terminated. This represents an opportunity to learn. By learning why an entrepreneurial initiative failed, entrepreneurs can avoid such mistakes in the future and/or do a better job of managing the uncertainties associated with entrepreneurial action. While a common saying is that we learn more from our failures than our successes, doing so in practice can be quite difficult. In particular, such learning is made difficult when strong negative emotions are generated from the loss felt by the failure. The more important the entrepreneurial initiative is to an entrepreneur, the greater his or her negative emotional reaction to the loss of that initiative will be.[9] While these negative emotions can interfere with the learning process,[10] those individuals who can more quickly recover from the emotions of failure can more quickly and effectively learn from the experience and are often more motivated to try again.

dual process model of coping with negative emotions Involves oscillation between a loss orientation and a restoration orientation

Individuals who use a *dual process model of coping with negative emotions* or grief recovery can more quickly recover from the negative emotions generated by the failure of an entrepreneurial initiative. This dual process model requires oscillating (shifting back and forth) between two alternate approaches to loss. The first is a *loss orientation,* which involves focusing on the loss event to create an account of (i.e., a plausible story for) the failure. Entrepreneurs with a loss orientation might seek out friends, family, or psychologists to talk through the event and their negative emotions. As the individual gains a deeper understanding of the reasons underlying the failure, he or she is able to break the emotional bonds to the loss of the initiative. But by focusing on the failure event for an extended period, thoughts can shift to the emotions surrounding the failure event, making the current situation worse—escalating grief. This negative cycle can be broken by shifting to the second alternative—a *restoration orientation*. This orientation involves distracting oneself from thinking about the failure and focusing one's energy on addressing other (secondary) problems that have arisen as a result of the failure. The "distracting" reduces the short-term level of negative emotions and the proactiveness towards secondary problems helps reduce the "enormity" of the failure itself. However, without allocating attention to the events surrounding the failure, there is little opportunity to learn. Therefore, oscillation (moving backward and forward) between the two orientations means the entrepreneur can benefit from both orientations while minimizing the costs of maintaining either for too long.

loss orientation An approach to negative emotions that involves working through, and processing, some aspect of the loss experience and, as a result of this process, breaking emotional bonds to the object lost

restoration orientation An approach to negative emotions based on both avoidance and a proactiveness toward secondary sources of stress arising from a major loss

The dual process of learning from failure has a number of practical implications. First, knowledge that the feelings and reactions being experienced by the entrepreneur are normal for someone dealing with such a loss may help to reduce feelings of shame and embarrassment. This in turn might encourage the entrepreneur to articulate his or her feelings, possibly speeding the recovery process. Second, there are psychological and physiological outcomes caused by the feelings of loss. Realizing that these are "symptoms" can reduce secondary sources of stress and may also assist with the choice of treatment. Third, there is a process of recovery from failure to learn, which offers entrepreneurs some comfort that their current feelings of loss, sadness, and helplessness will eventually diminish. Fourth, the recovery and learning process can be enhanced by some degree of oscillation between a loss orientation and a restoration orientation. Finally, recovery from loss offers an opportunity to increase one's knowledge of entrepreneurship. This provides benefits to the individual and to society.

IN REVIEW

SUMMARY

Established firms can create environmental conditions to motivate individuals within their organizations to act entrepreneurially, that is, conditions that allow organizational members to perceive entrepreneurial outcomes as feasible and desirable. Within existing corporate structures, this entrepreneurial spirit and effort is called *corporate entrepreneurship*.

Corporate entrepreneurship requires an entrepreneurial management approach. To demonstrate this entrepreneurial approach, we contrasted entrepreneurially managed firms with traditionally managed firms on eight dimensions: (1) strategic orientation, (2) commitment to opportunity, (3) commitment of resources, (4) control of resources, (5) management structure, (6) reward philosophy, (7) growth orientation, and (8) entrepreneurial culture. Fortunately, three leading Swedish researchers developed a scale that enables us to assess firms in terms of where they fall on the scale between entrepreneurial and traditional management.

Organizations desiring an entrepreneurial culture need to encourage new ideas and experimental efforts, eliminate opportunity parameters, make resources available, promote a teamwork approach and voluntary corporate entrepreneurship, and enlist top management's support. The corporate entrepreneur also must have appropriate leadership characteristics. In addition to being creative, flexible, and visionary, the corporate entrepreneur must be able to work within the corporate structure. Corporate entrepreneurs need to encourage teamwork and work diplomatically across established structures. Open discussion and strong support of team members are also required. Finally, the corporate entrepreneur must be persistent to overcome the inevitable obstacles.

The process of establishing corporate entrepreneurship within an existing organization requires the commitment of management, particularly top management. The organization must carefully choose leaders, develop general guidelines for ventures, and delineate expectations before the entrepreneurial program begins. Training sessions are an important part of the process. As role models and entrepreneurial ventures are introduced, the organization must establish a strong organizational support system, along with a system of incentives and rewards to encourage team members. Finally, the organization should establish a system to expand successful ventures and eliminate unsuccessful ones.

It is important for individuals (and organizations) to learn from the projects that are terminated. However, learning from these failed projects is likely easier said than done. Those who invest their time and energy in the projects will feel bad when the project is terminated and these negative emotions can obstruct learning. The dual process of coping with negative emotions will help individuals recover more quickly and learn from their experiences.

RESEARCH TASKS

1. Interview three individuals employed within the research and development (R&D) departments of large, well-established companies. From the interview, gain an understanding of what the company does to foster corporate entrepreneurship, what it does to inhibit corporate entrepreneurship, and what it could be doing better toward further enhancing entrepreneurship throughout the whole organization.

2. Search the Internet for four accounts of successful corporate entrepreneurship. What key factors for success are common across all these accounts? Which are unique? If one company can foster an entrepreneurial culture within an existing firm, what stops another company from copying its process and taking away the initial advantage?

3. Request the participation of managers from two companies and then ask them to fill out an "entrepreneurial management" scale (see Table 2.2). Based on the scale, which firm is more entrepreneurially managed? Does this coincide with your "gut feel" about the businesses?

4. Interview three employees that have worked on projects that were terminated. Ask them how they felt about the project, how they felt after it was terminated, and how they feel today. How did they deal with the loss of the project?

CLASS DISCUSSION

1. Isn't "corporate entrepreneurship" an oxymoron? Do the characteristics of an established organization, such as its routines and structure, increase efficiency but at the same time kill any entrepreneurial spirit? Is there any way that a company can have the best of both worlds?

2. Is increasing the entrepreneurial orientation of a firm *always* a good thing? Or are there circumstances or environments in which the further pursuit of opportunities can diminish firm performance?

3. What does it mean to say that something is important to you? Who has lost something that was important to them? How did it feel? What did you do to recover from the loss?

SELECTED READINGS

Brown, Terence; Per Davidsson; and Johan Wiklund. (2001). An Operationalization of Stevenson's Conceptualization of Entrepreneurship as Opportunity-Based Firm Behavior. *Strategic Management Journal,* vol. 22, pp. 953–69.

This article describes a new instrument that was developed specifically for operationalizing Stevenson's conceptualization of entrepreneurial management. The instrument should open up opportunities for researchers to further evaluate entrepreneurship in existing firms.

Dess, Gregory; R. Duane Ireland; Shaker Zahra; Steven Floyd; Jay Janney; and Peter Lane. (2003). Emerging Issues in Corporate Entrepreneurship. *Journal of Management,* vol. 29, pp. 351–78.

In this article, the authors identify four major issues scholars can pursue to further our understanding about corporate entrepreneurship (CE). The issues explored include various forms of CE and their implications for organizational learning; the role of leadership and social exchange in the CE process; and key research opportunities relevant to CE in an international context. Throughout the article, the authors use the organizational learning theory as a means of integrating our discussion and highlighting the potential contributions of CE to knowledge creation and effective exploitation.

Ireland, R. Duane; Jeffrey G. Covin; and Don F. Kuratko. (2009). Conceptualizing Corporate Entrepreneurship Strategy. *Entrepreneurship: Theory and Practice,* vol. 33, pp. 19–46.

In this article the authors conceptualize the components of corporate entrepreneurship (CE) to include (1) the individual entrepreneurial cognitions of the organization's members and external environmental conditions that invite entrepreneurial activity; (2) the top management's entrepreneurial strategic vision for the firm, organizational architectures that encourage entrepreneurial processes and behavior, and the generic forms of entrepreneurial process that are reflected in entrepreneurial behavior; and (3) the organizational outcomes resulting from entrepreneurial actions, including the development of competitive capability and strategic repositioning.

Krueger, Norris. (2000). The Cognitive Infrastructure of Opportunity Emergence. *Entrepreneurship: Theory and Practice,* vol. 24, pp. 5–23.

In this article the author argues that seeing a prospective course of action as a credible opportunity reflects an intentions-driven process driven by known critical antecedents. On the basis of well-developed theory and robust empirical evidence, he proposes an intentions-based model of the cognitive infrastructure that supports or inhibits how individuals perceive opportunities. The author also shows the practical diagnostic power this model offers to managers.

Kuratko, Donald; R. Duane Ireland; Jeffrey Covin; and Jeffrey Hornsby. (2005). A Model of Middle-Level Managers' Entrepreneurial Behavior. *Entrepreneurship: Theory and Practice,* vol. 29, pp. 699–716.

In this article, the authors integrate knowledge about corporate entrepreneurship and middle-level managers' behaviors to develop and explore a conceptual model. The model depicts the organizational antecedents of middle-level managers' entrepreneurial behavior, the entrepreneurial actions describing that behavior, and outcomes of that behavior, as well as factors influencing its continuance.

Morris, Michael H.; Donald F. Kuratko; and Jeffrey G. Covin. (2010). *Corporate Entrepreneurship and Innovation: Entrepreneurial Development within Organizations.* Mason, OH: Thompson Publishing.

This book provides an extensive account of how to introduce entrepreneurial action within an existing organization. The goal of the book is to explain how to develop an entrepreneurial mindset and is organized around a three-phase model to examine (1) the nature of entrepreneurship within established organizations, (2) how to create an organizational environment that supports entrepreneurship, and (3) how to sustain entrepreneurship, and its performance benefits, over time.

Shepherd, Dean A. (2003). Learning from Business Failure: Propositions about the Grief Recovery Process for the Self-Employed. *Academy of Management Review,* vol., 28, pp. 318–29.

This article employs the psychological literature on grief to explore the emotion of business failure. It suggests that the loss of a business due to failure can cause the self-employed to feel grief, which is a negative emotional response interfering with the ability to learn from the events surrounding that loss. Recovering from grief involves dealing with the loss, avoiding thinking about the loss, or a dual process that iteratively combines these two approaches. A dual process provides the speediest path to grief recovery enabling the self-employed to learn more from the events surrounding the loss of the business owing to a lack of emotional interference. Those who have not yet completed this process continue to feel negative emotions and remain in the recovery process. But even in the presence of grief, a dual process minimizes emotional interference enhancing the ability of the self-employed to learn from the loss of a business. An improved ability to learn from business failure is important for individuals and society.

Shepherd, Dean A. (2009). *Lemons to Lemonade: Squeezing the Most out of Your Mistakes.* Wharton School Press.

Learn More from Failure, Learn It Faster . . . and Use Those Lessons to Achieve Breakthrough Success! We all fail. And we all want to learn from our failures. But learning from failure doesn't happen automatically. It requires very specific emotional and rational skills. You can learn those skills from this book. Drawing on leading-edge research with hundreds of failing and successful entrepreneurs, Dr. Dean A. Shepherd offers powerful strategies for managing the emotions generated by failure so failure becomes less devastating, learning happens faster, and you grow as much as possible from the experience. Shepherd shows how to clarify why you failed, so you can walk away with insights you can actually use . . . how to eliminate "secondary" stresses that aggravate failure or make it more likely . . . how to master the self-compassion you deserve in times of trouble . . . and a whole lot more. Failing will never be easy or desirable. But this book will make it less catastrophic, and more instructive, so you can get back to success and get there fast. Mourn your failure faster, so you can learn from it sooner. Learn how to "undo" your emotional ties to failure. Grow from the experience of failure. Absorb the lessons that don't fit with your preconceptions. Discover when to "pull the plug" on a failure in progress. Know when to move on, so failure won't last longer or feel worse than it has to. Stay committed to excellence, no matter what. Keep focused on success, even in environments where multiple failures are commonplace. (from abstract)

Shepherd, Dean A.; Holger Patzelt; and Marcus Wolfe. (2011). Moving Forward from Project Failure: Negative Emotions, Affective Commitment, and Learning from the Experience. *Academy of Management Journal,* vol. 54, pp. 1229–59.

Project failures are common. We theorized and found that although time heals wounds (reduces the negative emotions from project failure), it heals differently depending on the strength of individuals' specific coping orientations. Further, wounds are shallower for those who perceive that their organization normalizes failure. We conjointly consider learning from failure and affective commitment to an organization as determining how individuals move forward from project failure. Findings suggest that studies framing moving forward solely as learning from failure will likely overstate the benefits of a "loss orientation" and understate the benefits of both a "restoration" and an "oscillation orientation."

Shepherd, D. A.; Jeffrey G. Covin, and Donald F. Kuratko. (2009). Project Failure from Corporate Entrepreneurship: Managing the Grief Process. *Journal of Business Venturing,* vol. 24, pp. 588–600.

In this paper, the authors complement social cognitive theory with psychological theories on grief in their discussion of two approaches to grief management—grief regulation and grief normalization—that hold promise for enabling corporate entrepreneurs to cope with negative emotions induced by project failure. They propose that to the extent that organizational members have high self-efficacy for recovering from grief over project failure, or this coping self-efficacy can be built through the social support offered by the organizational environment, regulating rather than eliminating grief via normalization processes will explain superior learning and motivational outcomes.

Shepherd, Dean A.; and Melissa Cardon. (2009). Negative Emotional Reactions to Project Failure and the Self-Compassion to Learn from the Experience. *Journal of Management Studies,* vol. 46, pp. 923–49.

Project failure is likely to generate a negative emotional response for those involved in the project. But do all people feel the same way? And are some better able to regulate their emotions to learn from the failure experience? In this paper the authors develop an emotion framework of project failure that relies on self-determination to explain variance in the intensity of the negative emotions triggered by project failure and self-compassion to explain variance in learning from project failure. They discuss the implications of the model for research on entrepreneurial and innovative organizations, employees' psychological ownership, and personal engagement at work.

Shepherd, Dean; and Norris Krueger. (2002). An Intentions-Based Model of Entrepreneurial Teams' Social Cognition. *Entrepreneurship: Theory and Practice,* vol. 27, pp. 167–85.

In this article the authors present an intentions-based model of how to promote entrepreneurial thinking in the domain of corporate entrepreneurship. They emphasize the importance of perceptions of desirability and feasibility and that these perceptions are from the team as well as the individual perspective.

Stevenson, Howard; and J. Carlos Jarillo. (1990). A Paradigm of Entrepreneurship: Entrepreneurial Management. *Strategic Management Journal,* vol. 11 (Special Issue), pp. 17–27.

In this article the authors propose that the very concept of corporate entrepreneurship sounds to many entrepreneurship scholars like something of an oxymoron. They point out that there is no doubt that, of late, entrepreneurship in general has gained its status as a legitimate scholarly research subject, enjoying in addition much public interest. The authors offer a discussion of the concept of entrepreneurship within established firms.

END NOTES

1. For a discussion of XTV, see Larry Armstrong, "Nurturing an Employee's Brainchild," *BusinessWeek/Enterprise* (1993), p. 196.
2. For a discussion of corporate entrepreneurship elements and their measures, see G. T. Lumpkin and G. G. Dess, "Clarifying the Entrepreneurial Orientation Construct and Linking It to Performance," *Academy of Management Review* 12, no. 1 (1996), pp. 135–72; and B. Antoncic and R. D. Hisrich, "Intrapreneurship: Construct Refinement and Cross-Cultural Validation," *Journal of Business Venturing* 16, no. 61 (September 2001), pp. 495–527.
3. H. H. Stevenson and D. Gumpert, "The Heart of Entrepreneurship," *Harvard Business Review* 63, no. 2 (1985), pp. 85–94.
4. Based on T. Brown, P. Davidsson, and J. Wiklund, "An Operationalization of Stevenson's Conceptualization of Entrepreneurship as Opportunity-Based Firm Behavior," *Strategic Management Journal* 22 (2001), pp. 953–69 (table on page 955).
5. For a thorough discussion of the factors important in corporate entrepreneurship, see R. M. Kanter, *The Change Masters* (New York: Simon & Schuster, 1983); and G. Pinchot III, *Intrapreneuring* (New York: Harper & Row, 1985).
6. For a discussion of this aspect, see Peter Coy, "Start with Some High-Tech Magic . . . ," *BusinessWeek/Enterprise* (1993), pp. 24–25, 28, 32.
7. N. Fast, "Pitfalls of Corporate Venturing," *Research Management* (March 1981), pp. 21–24.
8. For complete information on the relative performance, see R. Biggadike, "The Risky Business of Diversification," *Harvard Business Review* (May–June 1979), pp. 103–11; L. E. Weiss, "Start-Up Business: A Comparison of Performances," *Sloan Management Review* (Fall 1981), pp. 37–53; and N. D. Fast and S. E. Pratt, "Individual Entrepreneurship and the Large Corporation," *Proceedings, Babson Research Conference,* April 1984, pp. 443–50.
9. D. A. Shepherd and M. Cardon, "Negative Emotional Reactions to Project Failure and the Self-Compassion to Learn from the Experience," *Journal of Management Studies* 46, no. 6 (September 2009), pp. 923–49.
10. D. A. Shepherd, "Learning from Business Failure: Propositions about the Grief Recovery Process for the Self-Employed," *Academy of Management Review* 28, no. 2 (2003), pp. 318–29.

3

ENTREPRENEURIAL STRATEGY: GENERATING AND EXPLOITING NEW ENTRIES

1
To understand that the essential act of entrepreneurship involves new entry.

2
To be able to think about how an entrepreneurial strategy can first generate, and then exploit over time, a new entry.

3
To understand how resources are involved in the generation of opportunities.

4
To be able to assess the attractiveness of a new entry opportunity.

5
To acknowledge that entrepreneurship involves making decisions under conditions of uncertainty.

6
To be able to assess the extent of first-mover advantages and weigh them against first-mover disadvantages.

7
To understand that risk is associated with newness, but there are strategies that the entrepreneur can use to reduce risk.

OPENING PROFILE

JUSTIN PARER

> Sorry it had taken so long to get back to you. I think in some way I have been avoiding this because I don't know if I actually know the answers to what you are asking. I think sometimes you justify afterwards why you did something.

This quote is from Justin Parer, an Australian entrepreneur, in response to my direct questions about the plan he followed for entrepreneurial success. His history indicates a series of steps and missteps that have emerged into a strategy of personal and business success—a strategy that may be more obvious to the objective observer taking a long-run perspective than to the actor who is immersed in the daily details of a pressurized situation and is making "intuitive" decisions.

Justin's first entrepreneurial venture failed. The story is not pretty. He started up a mobile pizza business when he was 18 years old. "The idea for the van was actually someone else's. I was working in a pizza shop as a delivery driver trying to decide what I wanted to do in my life. I had recently been thrown out of uni [university] for gross failing and was at a loose end. One of the other guys in the shop said, 'Why don't they sell pizzas outside night clubs?' The market at the time was being serviced by a number of very unhygienic hot dog vendors who operated out of questionable mobile huts." Eventually Justin's business failed because, among other things, the local council terminated permits for these types of mobile food businesses.

When asked about the failed business, Justin's first comment was that it was the best learning experience of his life. His second comment was that it was a great motivator. It provided motivation "to avoid that sick feeling that rips at your guts when you know things are not going well and you can't pay your bills," to "face reality," and where necessary to "cut your losses" and get out.

He went on to say: "I am not sure that straight after the failure I was that motivated to get back into it. I knew I enjoyed business and was frustrated that I couldn't make it work, but I felt more like a failure than a 'success waiting to happen.' My confidence was hurt and I was looking for a lot more security. How was I ever [going] to buy a house? Have a family? I had few options and no clear vision, so when the opportunity came along to go back to university, I grabbed it with both hands. With the pizza van failure I knew I could work like a dog and get nowhere. I needed to have an edge. University gave me options."

Justin's second attempt at university had no resemblance to his first attempt. He had become an exceptional student with a passion to learn and a passion to apply that knowledge. He majored in accounting and his first job out of university was with Ernst & Young (an accounting consulting firm). Accounting education and experience provided valuable knowledge about the inner workings of a business (with the auditing department) and the numbers reflecting the entrepreneurial decision-making process (in the business services and tax department). Over and above the opportunity to build important knowledge, Justin also chose accounting as the foundation from which to relaunch his entrepreneurial career because it gave him legitimacy with others in the business community (including potential stakeholders), helped him build a large network with influential people, and would act as an income "insurance policy" if his business failed.

One of Justin's accounting clients was a slipway (ship building and repair) business. From this work he was able to gain considerable industry-specific knowledge and an industry-specific network. This newly formed network provided early information about a business in the industry that might come on the market, and his new industry-specific knowledge meant that he could assess the value of this opportunity. He bought the business and is growing it while simultaneously improving its efficiency. The success of the business has even exceeded his own dreams for it at the time of purchase.

He has recently gone into partnership with his brother Warwick and purchased another business—a metal-working business. This business has considerable potential in its own right but has the added benefit of synergies with the slipway. This business is also on the path to success. When I think of the "ideal" entrepreneur, I think of Justin. Justin is an optimistic and charismatic entrepreneur who attacks his tasks and life with confidence and passion (with the possible exception of answering questions about his success). He has control over the money side of his businesses but also has the flexibility to allow his strategies to emerge.

NEW ENTRY

new entry Offering a new product to an established or new market, offering an established product to a new market, or creating a new organization

One of the essential acts of entrepreneurship is new entry. *New entry* refers to (1) offering a new product to an established or new market, (2) offering an established product to a new market, or (3) creating a new organization (regardless of whether the product or the market is new to competitors or customers).[1] Whether associated with a new product, a new market, and/or a new organization, "newness" is like a double-edged sword. On the one hand, newness represents something rare, which can help differentiate a firm from its competitors. On the other hand, newness creates a number of challenges for entrepreneurs. For example, newness can increase entrepreneurs' uncertainty over the value of a new product and place a greater strain on the resources necessary for successful exploitation.[2]

FIGURE 3.1   Entrepreneurial Strategy: The Generation and Exploitation of New Entry Opportunities

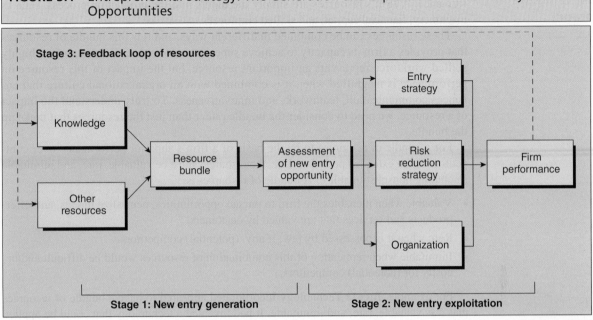

entrepreneurial strategy
The set of decisions, actions, and reactions that first generate, and then exploit over time, a new entry

Entrepreneurial strategy represents the set of decisions, actions, and reactions that first generate, and then exploit over time, a new entry in a way that maximizes the benefits of newness and minimizes its costs.

Figure 3.1 illustrates the important elements of an entrepreneurial strategy. An entrepreneurial strategy has three key stages: (1) the generation of a new entry opportunity, (2) the exploitation of a new entry opportunity, and (3) a feedback loop from the culmination of a new entry generation and exploitation back to stage 1. The generation of a new entry is the result of a combination of knowledge and other resources into a bundle that its creators hope will be valuable, rare, and difficult for others to imitate. If the decision is that the new entry is sufficiently attractive that it warrants exploitation, then firm performance is dependent upon the entry strategy; the risk reduction strategy; the way the firm is organized; and the competence of the entrepreneur, management team, and the firm.

Although the remainder of this chapter focuses on stages 1 and 2, we should not underestimate the importance of the feedback loop of stage 3 because an entrepreneur cannot rely on the generation and exploitation of only one new entry; rather, long-run performance is dependent upon the ability to generate and exploit numerous new entries. If the firm does rely on only one new entry, then as the life cycle for the product enters maturity and declines, so goes the life cycle of the organization.

GENERATION OF A NEW ENTRY OPPORTUNITY
Resources as a Source of Competitive Advantage

When a firm engages in a new entry, it is hoped that this new entry will provide the firm with a sustainable competitive advantage. Understanding where a sustainable competitive advantage comes from will provide some insight into how entrepreneurs can generate new entries that are likely to provide the basis for high firm performance over an extended

resources The inputs into the production process

period of time. *Resources* are the basic building blocks to a firm's functioning and performance. A firm's resources are simply the inputs into the production process, such as machinery, financial capital, and skilled employees.

These resources can be combined in different ways, and it is this bundle of resources that provides a firm its capacity to achieve superior performance. For example, a highly skilled workforce represents an important resource, but the impact of this resource on performance is magnified when it is combined with an organizational culture that enhances communication, teamwork, and innovativeness. To truly understand the impact of a resource, we need to consider the bundle rather than just the resources that make up the bundle.

For a bundle of resources to be the basis of a firm's superior performance over competitors for an extended period of time, the resources must be valuable, rare, and inimitable (including nonsubstitutable).[3] A bundle of resources is:[4]

- Valuable when it enables the firm to pursue opportunities, neutralize threats, and offer products and services that are valued by customers.
- Rare when it is possessed by few, if any, (potential) competitors.
- Inimitable when replication of this combination of resources would be difficult and/or costly for (potential) competitors.

For example, Breeze Technology Incorporated appeared to have a bundle of resources that was valuable, rare, and inimitable. It had invented a technology that could be applied to the ventilation of athletic shoes to reduce foot temperature. A ventilated athletic shoe is likely to be highly valued by customers because people have problems with their current athletic shoes—their feet get hot and sweaty, which in turn causes blisters, fungal infections, and odor. (I know my wife would be happy for me to wear shoes that reduced foot odor.) The product was also valuable to the newly formed management team of Breeze Technology because it provided the means of entering into a large and highly lucrative market.

This technology also appeared to be rare and inimitable. It was rare because others had failed to adequately ventilate people's feet. Some had attempted to blow air into the shoe and found that it only increased foot temperature. Current footwear attempted to passively ventilate feet, but the porous uppers on shoes were relatively ineffective at this task and also made the shoe vulnerable to water intrusion—that is, if you stepped into a puddle, your feet would get wet. Breeze Technology pumped air out of the shoe, which was a novel and unobvious approach to shoe ventilation.

Given that this technology was deemed likely to be valuable to customers, novel, and unobvious, it was provided a patent. The purpose of the patent is to protect the owner of the technology from people imitating the technology. Along with other intellectual property protection such as copyrights and trademarks, Breeze Technology had a new product that could be protected from competition (at least for a period of time). Therefore, Breeze Technology had a bundle of resources that was valuable, rare, and inimitable. The important questions are, then: (1) where does this valuable, rare, and difficult-to-imitate bundle of resources come from? and (2) how can it best be exploited?

entrepreneurial resource The ability to obtain, and then recombine, resources into a bundle that is valuable, rare, and inimitable

Creating a Resource Bundle That Is Valuable, Rare, and Inimitable

The ability to obtain, and then recombine, resources into a bundle that is valuable, rare, and inimitable represents an important *entrepreneurial resource*. Knowledge is the basis of this entrepreneurial resource, which in itself is valuable. This type of knowledge is built up over time through experience, and it resides in the mind of the entrepreneur and in the collective mind of management and employees. To a large extent such an experience is idiosyncratic—unique to the life of the individual—and therefore can be considered rare. Furthermore, it is typically difficult to communicate this knowledge to others, which makes it all the more difficult for (potential) competitors to replicate such knowledge.

Therefore, knowledge is important for generating a bundle of resources that will lead to the creation of a new venture with a long and prosperous life. Does this mean that only highly experienced managers and/or firms will typically generate these opportunities for new entry? On the contrary, the evidence suggests that it is the outsiders that come up with the most radical innovations. For example, the pioneers of mountain bikes were biking enthusiasts, and it was quite a considerable time before the industry giants, such as Schwinn and Huffy, reacted to the trend.[5]

It appears that the existing manufacturers of bikes had difficulty "thinking outside the box" or they had little incentive to do so. Notice that those who did invent the mountain bike were bike enthusiasts. They had knowledge about current technology and the problems that customers (themselves included) had with the current technology under certain circumstances. This knowledge was unique and based upon personal experience. It was this knowledge that provided the basis for their innovation.

Those wishing to generate an innovation need to look to the unique experiences and knowledge within themselves and their team. This sort of knowledge is unlikely to be learned in a textbook or in class, because then everyone would have it and what would be unique about that? Knowledge that is particularly relevant to the generation of new entries is that which is related to the market and technology.

market knowledge
Possession of information, technology, know-how, and skills that provide insight into a market and its customers

Market Knowledge

Market knowledge refers to the entrepreneur's possession of information, technology, know-how, and skills that provide insight into a market and its customers. Being knowledgeable about the market and customers enables the entrepreneur to gain a deeper understanding of the problems that customers have with the market's existing products. In essence the entrepreneur shares some of the same knowledge that customers have about the use and performance of products. From this shared knowledge, entrepreneurs are able to bring together resources in a way that provides a solution to customers' dissatisfaction.

In this case, the entrepreneur's market knowledge is deeper than the knowledge that could be gained through market research. Market research, such as surveys, has limited effectiveness because it is often difficult for customers to articulate the underlying problems they have with a product or service. Entrepreneurs who lack this intimate knowledge of the market, and of customers' attitudes and behaviors, are less likely to recognize or create attractive opportunities for new products and/or new markets.

The importance of this knowledge to the generation of a new entry is best illustrated by returning to the example of the invention of the mountain bike. These guys were bike enthusiasts and therefore were aware of the problems that they personally encountered, as well as the problems their friends encountered, in using bikes that relied on the current technology. It could be that these individuals were using their bikes in a way that was not anticipated by the bike manufacturers, such as taking them off-road and exploring rough terrain.

Market research would not likely have revealed this information about deficiencies in the current technology. It is difficult for people to articulate the need for something that does not exist. Besides, the manufacturers may have dismissed any information that they received. For example, "Of course the frame broke, this idiot was going 30 miles per hour down a stony hiking track." It was because these bike enthusiasts had an intimate knowledge of the market and customers' attitudes and behaviors that they were able to bring together resources in a way that provided a solution to customers' dissatisfaction—the mountain bike represented a solution and opened up a new market.

technological knowledge
Possession of information, technology, know-how, and skills that provide insight into ways to create new knowledge

Technological Knowledge   *Technological knowledge* is also a basis for generating new entry opportunities. Technological knowledge refers to the entrepreneur's possession of information, technology, know-how, and skills that provide insight into ways to create new knowledge. This technological knowledge might lead to a technology that is the basis for a new entry, even though its market applicability is unobvious.

For example, the laser was invented over 30 years ago and has led to many new entry opportunities. Those with expertise in laser technology are more able to adapt and improve the technology and in doing so open up a potentially attractive market. Laser technology has been adapted to navigation, precision measurement, music recording, and fiber optics. In surgery, laser technology has been used to repair detached retinas and reverse blindness. These new entries were derived from the knowledge of laser technology, and market applicability was often of only secondary consideration.[6]

Similarly, the initial reaction to the invention of the computer was that its market was rather limited. If we investigate the application of the computer to one industry, we can see the sort of new markets that have arisen from the further development of computer technology. Computers are used in the aviation industry to conduct aerodynamic research to find efficient aircraft designs; in the automation of the navigation and flying functions of pilots, such as the autopilot; in the radar system used by air traffic control; in flight simulators used by airlines to train pilots on new aircraft; and in the computer network system for ticketing and tracking baggage (although my bags still seem to get lost).[7]

Therefore, technological knowledge has led to technological advancement that in many ways has created new markets rather than generating a technology to satisfy an unmet market need. Often these technologies were created by people wanting to advance knowledge, without concern for commercial applicability. Other times, a technology has been invented for a specific and narrow purpose only to find out later that the technology has broader implications. For example, Tang, freeze-dried coffee, Velcro, and Teflon were all products invented for the space program but were found to have broader applications.

In sum, a resource bundle is the basis for a new entry. This resource bundle is created from the entrepreneur's market knowledge, technological knowledge, and other resources. The new entry has the potential of being a source of sustained superior firm performance if the resource bundle underlying the new entry is valuable, rare, and difficult for others to imitate.

Assessing the Attractiveness of a New Entry Opportunity

Having created a new resource combination, the entrepreneur needs to determine whether it is in fact valuable, rare, and inimitable by assessing whether the new product and/or the new market are sufficiently attractive to be worth exploiting and developing. This depends on the level of information on a new entry and the entrepreneur's willingness to make a decision without perfect information.

Information on a New Entry

Prior Knowledge and Information Search   The prior market and technological knowledge used to create the potential new entry can also be of benefit in assessing the attractiveness of a particular opportunity. More prior knowledge means that the entrepreneur starts from a position of less ignorance about the assessment task at hand. That is,

ELEVATOR PITCH FOR PROJECT ALABAMA

A wealthy friend has asked you to keep your eye out for attractive businesses in which she can invest. Your wealthy friend is very busy and you only want to introduce those businesses that are genuinely attractive. After hearing the following pitch, would you introduce Natalie and Enrico to your wealthy friend?

Entrepreneurs Natalie Chanin (41) and Enrico Marone-Cinzano (39), co-founders of Project Alabama in Florence, Alabama

Description Clothing company that largely uses recycled materials

Start-Up 2000 for $20,000

Sales Projecting $1.5 million in 2003

Helping Hands Heading to a party one night, Chanin hand-sewed a T-shirt and was hooked. With a costume design and fashion stylist background, Chanin joined forces with co-founder Marone-Cinzano, a businessman with experience in finance and marketing. She was unable to find a manufacturer in New York to do the handwork—her collection's resemblance to quilting inspired Chanin to return to her native Alabama and find "quilting circles" that could lend a hand (she now lives in both New York and Alabama, but spends most of her time in Alabama).

Recycled Goods Project Alabama's growth necessitates branching out to include new materials, but the core of the collection is made from recycled cotton jersey T-shirts. Retailing for $250 to $4,000, their target has always been high-end. "We made a conscious effort to contact those type of stores," explains Chanin. "Luckily, we had some of the world's best stores buy from the beginning, like Barneys New York and Browns in London."

Supplies Needed "Project Alabama consists of two components: the use of recycled materials and the quality of handwork," says Chanin, speaking proudly of the 120 women who subcontract stitchwork. "The kind of pride they have in each and every piece is rare."

Source: Reprinted with permission of Entrepreneur Media, Inc., "Natalie Chanin and Enrico Marone-Cinzano," by April Y. Pennington, February 2003, *Entrepreneur* magazine: www.entrepreneur.com.

less information needs to be collected to reach a threshold where the entrepreneur feels comfortable making a decision to exploit or not to exploit.

Knowledge can be increased by searching for information that will shed some light on the attractiveness of this new entry opportunity. Interestingly, the more knowledge the entrepreneur has, the more efficient the search process. For example, entrepreneurs who have a large knowledge base in a particular area will know where to look for information and will be able to quickly process this information into knowledge useful for the assessment.

The search process itself represents a dilemma for an entrepreneur. On the one hand, a longer search period allows the entrepreneur time to gain more information about whether this new entry does represent a resource bundle that is valuable, rare, and difficult for others to imitate. The more information the entrepreneur has, the more accurately she or he can assess whether sufficient customer demand for the product can be generated and whether the product can be protected from imitation by competitors.

However, there are costs associated with searching for this information—costs in both money and time. For example, rather than deciding to exploit a new product, an entrepreneur may decide to search for more information to make a more accurate assessment of whether this new product is an attractive one for her; but while this entrepreneur continues with her information search, the opportunity may cease to be available.

Window of Opportunity The dynamic nature of the viability of a particular new entry can be described in terms of a *window of opportunity*. When the window is open, the

window of opportunity
The period of time when the environment is favorable for entrepreneurs to exploit a particular new entry

environment is favorable for entrepreneurs to exploit a particular new product or to enter a new market with an existing product; but the window of opportunity may close, leaving the environment for exploitation unfavorable. An example of a window of opportunity closing is when another entrepreneur has entered the industry and erected substantial barriers to entry and to imitation. While more information is desirable, the time spent in collecting additional information increases the likelihood that the window of opportunity will close.

Comfort with Making a Decision under Uncertainty

The trade-off between more information and the likelihood that the window of opportunity will close provides a dilemma for entrepreneurs. This dilemma involves a choice of which error they prefer to commit: Do they prefer to commit an error of commission over an error of omission, or vice versa?[8] An *error of commission* occurs from the decision to pursue this new entry opportunity, only to find out later that the entrepreneur had overestimated his or her ability to create customer demand and/or to protect the technology from imitation by competitors. The costs to the entrepreneur were derived from acting on the perceived opportunity.

error of commission
Negative outcome from acting

An *error of omission* occurs from the decision not to act on the new entry opportunity, only to find out later that the entrepreneur had underestimated his or her ability to create customer demand and/or to protect the technology from imitation by competitors. In this case, the entrepreneur must live with the knowledge that he let an attractive opportunity slip through his fingers.

error of omission
Negative outcome from not acting

Decision to Exploit or Not to Exploit the New Entry

As illustrated in Figure 3.2, the decision to exploit or not to exploit the new entry opportunity depends on whether the entrepreneur has what she or he believes to be sufficient information to make a decision, and on whether the window is still open for this

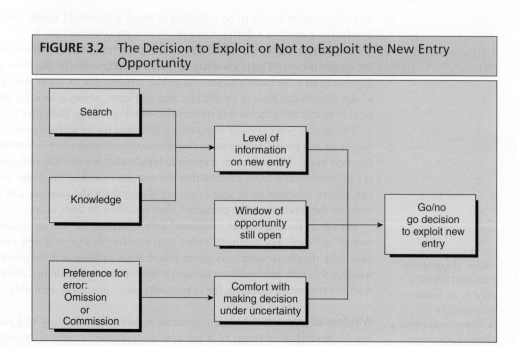

FIGURE 3.2   The Decision to Exploit or Not to Exploit the New Entry Opportunity

new entry opportunity. A determination by an entrepreneur that she has sufficient information depends on the stock of information (accumulated through search and from prior knowledge) and on the level of comfort that this entrepreneur has with making the decision without perfect information (which depends on a preference of one type of error over another).

assessment of a new entry's attractiveness
Determining whether the entrepreneur believes she or he can make the proposed new entry work

It is important to realize that the *assessment of a new entry's attractiveness* is less about whether this opportunity "really" exists or not and more about whether the entrepreneur believes he or she can make it work—that is, create the market demand, efficiently produce the product, build a reputation, and develop customer loyalty and other switching costs. Making it work depends, in part, on entrepreneurial strategies.

ENTRY STRATEGY FOR NEW ENTRY EXPLOITATION

The common catchphrase used by entrepreneurs when asked about their source of competitive advantage is, "Our competitive advantage comes from being first. We are the first movers." Whether they are the first to introduce a new product and/or the first to create a new market, these claims have some merit. Being first can result in a number of advantages that can enhance performance. These include:

- *First movers develop a cost advantage*. Being first to offer and sell a particular product to a specific market means that the first mover can begin movement down the "experience curve." The experience curve captures the idea that as a firm produces a greater volume of a particular product, the cost of producing each unit of that product goes down. Costs are reduced because the firm can spread its fixed costs over a greater number of units (economies of scale) as well as learn by trial and error over time (learning curve) to improve products and processes.[9]

- *First movers face less competitive rivalry*. Although first movers might initially have only a few customers, if they have correctly assessed the opportunity, the market will grow rapidly. Even though competitors will enter this growing market, the market share lost to new competitors will be more than compensated for by market growth. In fact, in the growth stage of the market, firms are more concerned with keeping up with demand than they are with taking actions, such as price cutting, to take market share from others.

- *First movers can secure important channels*. First movers have the opportunity to select and develop strong relationships with the most important suppliers and distribution channels. This may represent a barrier to those considering entry and may force those who do eventually enter to use inferior suppliers and distribution outlets.

- *First movers are better positioned to satisfy customers*. First movers have the chance to (1) select and secure the most attractive segments of a market, and (2) position themselves at the center of the market, providing an increased ability to recognize, and adapt to, changes in the market. In some cases, they may even (3) establish their product as the industry standard.

- *First movers gain expertise through participation*. First movers have the opportunity to (1) learn from the first generation of products and improve, for example, product design, manufacturing, and marketing; (2) monitor changes in the market that might be difficult or impossible to detect for those firms not participating in the market; and (3) build up their networks, which can provide early information about attractive opportunities. These learning opportunities may be available only to those participating in the market. In this case, knowledge is gained through learning-by-doing rather than through observing the practices of others (vicarious learning).

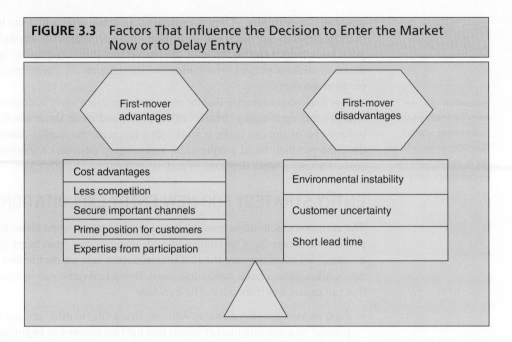

FIGURE 3.3 Factors That Influence the Decision to Enter the Market Now or to Delay Entry

First movers do not always prosper. Many first movers with new products in new markets have been surpassed by firms that entered later. For example, in the market for video recorders the first movers were Ampex and Sony, yet they were surpassed by JVC and Matsushita. Similarly, in the ballpoint pen market the first movers (Reynolds and Eversharp) disappeared, whereas later entrants (Parker and Bic) have been highly successful.

As illustrated by the scales in Figure 3.3, there are forces pushing toward first-mover advantages, but there are also environmental conditions that can push a first mover toward performance disadvantages. When considering whether to be one of the first to enter with a new product and/or into a new market, entrepreneurs must determine whether the first-mover advantages outweigh the first-mover disadvantages. Such an assessment depends on (1) the stability of the environment surrounding the entry, (2) the ability of the entrepreneur to educate customers, and (3) the ability of the entrepreneur to erect barriers to entry and imitation to extend the firm's lead time. We now explore each of these influences.

Environmental Instability and First-Mover (Dis)Advantages

The performance of a firm depends on the fit between its bundle of resources and the external environment. If there is a good fit between its resources and the external environment, then the firm will be rewarded with superior performance; however, if the fit is poor, then performance will also be poor. For example, if the entrepreneur offers a new product that has attributes that the market does not value, then there is a poor fit between the firm's current product offerings and the external environment and performance will be poor.

key success factors The requirements that any firm must meet to successfully compete in a particular industry

To obtain a good fit with the external environment, the entrepreneur must first determine the key success factors of the industry being targeted for entry. *Key success factors* are the requirements that any firm must meet to successfully compete in a particular industry. For example, maybe the key success factor of an industry is superior service, or reliability, or the lowest price, or having one's technology adopted as the industry standard.

However, the first mover will not know these key success factors in advance; rather, the entrepreneur must commit the firm's resources based upon his or her best guess of what these key success factors might be. If the guess is correct and the environment remains stable, then the firm has a chance of achieving success. However, if the environment changes, so too will the key success factors, and, as a result, the entrepreneur's prior commitment of resources will be less effective and may even reduce the firm's ability to recognize and adapt to the new environment.

emerging industries
Industries that have been newly formed and are growing

Environmental changes are highly likely in *emerging industries*. Emerging industries are those industries that have been newly formed. As such, the rules of the game have not yet been set. This means that the entrepreneur has considerable freedom in how he or she achieves success, including establishing the rules of the game for the industry such that the firm is at a competitive advantage. Until the rules of the game have been established and the industry has matured (aged), the environment of an emerging industry is often changing. Determining whether change will occur and the nature of that change is often difficult for entrepreneurs because they face considerable demand uncertainty and technological uncertainty. Even if the change is detected, it is difficult to respond effectively.

Demand Uncertainty   First movers have little information upon which to estimate the potential size of the market and how fast it will grow. Such *demand uncertainty* makes it difficult to estimate future demand, which has important implications for new venture performance as both overestimating and underestimating demand can negatively impact performance. By overestimating demand, the entrepreneur will suffer the costs associated with overcapacity (there was no need to build such a large factory, for instance) and will find that the market may be so small that it cannot sustain the entrepreneur's business. By underestimating market demand, the entrepreneur will suffer the costs of undercapacity, such as not being able to satisfy existing and new customers and losing them to competitors, or will face the additional costs of incrementally adding capacity.

demand uncertainty
Considerable difficulty in accurately estimating the potential size of the market, how fast it will grow, and the key dimensions along which it will grow

Demand uncertainty also makes it difficult to predict the key dimensions along which the market will grow. For example, customers' needs and tastes may change as the market matures. If the entrepreneur is unaware of these changes (or is incapable of adapting to them), then there is an opportunity for competitors to provide superior value to the customers. For example, as the personal computer industry matured, the key success factors changed from reputation for quality to being the low-cost provider. Dell was able to create a business model that enabled it to sell personal computers at a low price. Those that were late to adapt to the change in customer demand and continued to rely primarily on their reputation for quality were surpassed by Dell.

Entrepreneurs that delay entry have the opportunity to learn from the actions of first movers without the need of incurring the same costs. For example, Toyota delayed entry into the small-car market of the United States and was able to reduce demand uncertainty by surveying customers of the market leader (Volkswagen) and using this information to produce a product that better satisfied customers.[10] Therefore, followers have the advantage of more information about market demand. They also have more information about long-run customer preferences because the additional time before entry means that the market is more mature and customer preferences are more stable. Therefore, when demand is unstable and unpredictable, first-mover advantages may be outweighed by first-mover disadvantages and the entrepreneur should consider delaying entry.

Technological Uncertainty   First movers often must make a commitment to a new technology. There are a number of uncertainties surrounding a new technology, such as whether the technology will perform as expected and whether an alternate technology will be introduced that leapfrogs the current technology. If the technology does not perform as expected, the entrepreneur will incur a number of costs that will negatively impact performance, for example, damage to the entrepreneur's (and his or her firm's) reputation and also the additional R&D and production costs incurred by making necessary changes to the technology.

Even if the technology works as expected, there is the possibility that a superior technology might be introduced that provides later entrants a competitive advantage. For example, Docutel provided almost all the automatic teller machines in 1974. However, when technology became available that allowed customers to electronically transfer funds, companies such as Honeywell, IBM, and Burroughs were in a position to adopt the new technology and better satisfy customer demands. As a result, Docutel's market share dropped to 10 percent in just four years.[11]

technological uncertainty
Considerable difficulty in accurately assessing whether the technology will perform and whether alternate technologies will emerge and leapfrog over current technologies

Delayed entry provides entrepreneurs with the opportunity to reduce *technological uncertainty*. For example, they can reduce technological uncertainty by learning from the first mover's R&D program. This could involve activities such as reverse engineering the first mover's products. This provides a source of technological knowledge that can be used to imitate the first mover's product (unless there is intellectual property protection) or to improve upon the technology. Delayed entry also provides the opportunity to observe and learn from the actions (and mistakes) of the first mover. For example, a first mover may enter a particular market segment only to find out that there is insufficient demand to sustain the business. The later entrant can learn from this failure and can avoid market segments that have proved themselves to be unattractive. Therefore, when technological uncertainty is high, first-mover advantages may be outweighed by first-mover disadvantages and the entrepreneur should consider delaying entry.

Adaptation   Changes in market demand and technology do not necessarily mean that first movers cannot prosper. They do mean that the entrepreneur must adapt to the new environmental conditions. Such changes are difficult. The entrepreneur will likely find it difficult to move away from the people and systems that brought initial success and toward new configurations requiring changes to employees' roles and responsibilities as well as changes to systems. In other words, the organization has an inertia that represents a force for continuation that resists change. For example, Medtronics was the market leader in heart pacemakers but lost its position after it was slow to change from its existing technology to a new lithium-based technology. A new entrant, unconstrained by organizational inertia, was able to exploit and penalize Medtronics for its tardiness.[12]

In addition, the entrepreneurial attributes of persistence and determination, which are so beneficial when the new venture is on the "right course," can inhibit the ability of the entrepreneur to detect, and implement, change. For example, there is a tendency for entrepreneurs to escalate commitment; that is, when faced with a new technology, the entrepreneur commits more resources to his or her current technology and reinforces the initial strategic direction, rather than adopting the new technology and changing strategic direction,[13] which has the effect of accelerating the firm's demise. Therefore, adaptation to changes in the external environment is important for all firms (especially first movers) but is often a very difficult task to conduct in practice.

Customers' Uncertainty and First-Mover (Dis)Advantages

Whether introducing a new product into an established market or an established product into a new market, the entry involves an element of newness. Embedded in this newness is

***uncertainty for
customers*** Customers
may have considerable
difficulty in accurately
assessing whether the
new product or service
provides value for them

uncertainty for customers. They may be uncertain about how to use the product and whether it will perform as expected. Even if it does perform, they may wonder to what extent its performance provides benefits over and above the products that are currently being used. Customers, like most people, are uncertainty averse, which means that even if the potential benefits of the new product are superior to existing products, customers may still not switch from the old to the new because of the uncertainties described earlier. Therefore, offering a superior product is not sufficient to enable a first mover to make sales; the entrepreneur must also reduce customer uncertainties.

To do this, the entrepreneur can offer informational advertising that, for example, provides customers with information about how the product performs and articulates the product's benefits. The entrepreneur may even use comparison marketing to highlight how the product's benefits outweigh those of substitute products. If this approach works, customers will be more likely to switch to the firm's product. The "home shopping" channels on television provide numerous examples of this informational advertising. For example, an advertisement describes a set of plastic bags into which clothes (or other things) may be inserted, and the air within the bags evacuated (using a vacuum cleaner), which substantially reduces the volume of the clothes and allows more to be packed into a suitcase (so much so that the weight of the case exceeds one's ability to lift it, as I learned by experience).

However, providing customers with information on the performance of a new product does not always work. When the new product is highly innovative, as are the products that create a new market, the customers may lack a frame of reference for processing this information.[14] For example, products developed for the purpose of national defense and for other high-technology government purposes may provide an opportunity for new entry but require that customers be given a context for understanding their application. Teflon, developed for use in construction of the space shuttle, required customers to develop a new frame of reference before they could understand how it performed as a nonstick surface in frying pans and the benefits to them from this surface.[15] Therefore, entrepreneurs may be faced with the challenging task of creating a frame of reference within the potential customers before providing informational advertising.

Potential customers' uncertainty may also stem from the broader context in which the product is to be used. For example, even if the potential customers understand how the product performs, they are unlikely to purchase a product until they are convinced that the product is consistent with enabling products, systems, and knowledge. For example, a customer may know that a new software package provides more powerful spreadsheet functions and at a lower price but will remain reluctant to purchase the new product until she or he knows how long it will take to learn how to use the new software. In this circumstance, the entrepreneur can educate customers through demonstration and documentation on how to use the product. This could include an extensive tutorial as part of the software package as well as a free "help line."

Those that decide to enter later face a market that is more mature and one in which customers' uncertainties have already been substantially reduced by those who pioneered the market. In essence, by delaying entry into a market that requires considerable education, the entrepreneur may be able to receive a free ride on the investments made by the first movers.

However, it still may pay to be a first mover in this type of market if the educational effort can be used for the firm's advantage rather than to the advantage of the industry as a whole. For example, education may direct customer preferences in ways that will give the firm an advantage over potential customers (e.g., it may create an industry standard around the firm's products); it might enable the entrepreneur to build a reputation as "founder,"

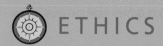

ETHICS

DO THE RIGHT THING

SMART ENTREPRENEURS ARE DOING WELL BY DOING GOOD

Charlie Wilson is trying to run an ethical business. He's made social responsibility part of the mission statement at his $1.6 million Houston-based salvage company, SeaRail International Inc. And he's made "self-actualization"—not wealth—his ultimate goal as an entrepreneur.

But don't mistake Wilson for some moralistic stick-in-the-mud. It's all about success. "Ethics is what's spearheading our growth," says Wilson. "It creates an element of trust, familiarity and predictability in the business. We're in an industry where a lot of people cut corners. I just don't think that's good for business. You don't get a good reputation doing things that way. And eventually, customers don't want to do business with you."

For years, ethics and business had a rocky marriage. Ask entrepreneurs to talk about ethics, and the responses ranged from scorn to ridicule. Here are folks who—by definition—like breaking the rules. Suggesting that entrepreneurs should follow a pre-defined set of edicts was about as popular as asking them to swear off electricity. But this may be changing. Whether people are hung over from the freewheeling '80s or reflective about the coming millennium, talk about values, integrity, and responsibility is not only becoming acceptable in the business community, it's almost required.

"This looks just like the quality movement of 20 years ago," says Frank Walker, chairman of Indianapolis-based Walker Information Inc., a research and consulting company that tracks customer satisfaction and business ethics. "Customers need a way to differentiate one firm from another." For years, the dominant point of differentiation has been quality. Now, says Walker, "Everyone can deliver quality, [so businesses] need to step up to a higher plane."

Are the nation's entrepreneurs ready to ascend to new heights of ethical literacy and compliance? Well, sort of. Although most entrepreneurs still aren't trying to unseat the likes of Socrates and Plato, many are giving considerable thought to improving their ethics, with hopes that doing good business will be good for business as well.

Source: Reprinted with permission of Entrepreneur Media, Inc., "Do the Right Thing," by Gayle Sato Stodder, August 1998, *Entrepreneur* magazine: www.entrepreneur.com.

encouraging customer loyalty; and it could benefit the company through the erection of other barriers to entry and imitation. We now explore the role of barriers to entry and imitation in influencing the performance of an entrepreneur's entry strategy.

Lead Time and First-Mover (Dis)Advantages

Being first to market might provide some initial advantages, but unless the entrepreneur can stop or retard potential competitors from entering the industry and offering similar products, the initial advantage will be quickly eroded, diminishing firm performance. Entry barriers provide the first mover (and nobody else) with the opportunity to operate in the industry for a grace period under conditions of limited competition (although the firm must still battle for customers with firms that offer substitute products). This grace period represents the first mover's lead time.

lead time The grace period in which the first mover operates in the industry under conditions of limited competition

The *lead time* gives the entrepreneur a period of limited competition to best prepare the firm for when competition does increase. This preparation could involve a concerted effort to influence the direction in which the market develops to the advantage of the first mover. For example, during the lead time the entrepreneur can use marketing to define quality in the minds of existing and potential customers—a definition of quality that is highly consistent with the entrepreneur's products.

Lead time can be extended if the first mover can erect barriers to entry. Important barriers to entry are derived from relationships with key stakeholders, which may dissuade entry by (potential) competitors. This can be done by:

Building customer loyalties. First movers need to establish their firms and their products in the minds of their customers and thus build customer loyalty. Such customer loyalty will make it more difficult and more costly for competitors to enter the market and take the first mover's customers. Loyalty is sometimes established when customers associate the industry with the first mover. For example, Japanese beer drinkers associated "super-dry beer" with the pioneer of a new form of beer, Asahi. This customer loyalty made it more difficult for others, including the dominant beer producer (Kirin), to enter the super-dry market and gain market share.

switching costs The costs that must be borne by customers if they are to stop purchasing from the current supplier and begin purchasing from another

Building switching costs. First movers need to develop *switching costs* in an effort to lock in existing customers. This is a mechanism by which customer loyalty is enhanced. Reward programs, such as frequent flyer points with a particular airline, establish for the customer a financial and/or emotional attachment to the first mover, which makes it costly for the customer to switch to a competitor.

Protecting product uniqueness. If the uniqueness of the product is a source of advantage over potential competitors, then first movers need to take actions to maintain that uniqueness. Intellectual property protection can take the form of patents, copyrights, trademarks, and trade secrets (detailed in Chapter 6).

Securing access to important sources of supply and distribution. First movers that are able to develop exclusive relationships with key sources of supply and/or key distribution channels will force potential entrants to use less attractive alternatives or even to develop their own. For example, Commercial Marine Products was the first to find an infestation of a special kind of seaweed in Tasmania, Australia. This seaweed is called *wakame* and is a staple food for Japanese and Koreans. Commerical Marine Products was able to obtain an exclusive license to manage and harvest this area of the Tasmanian coast, the only known location in Australia (and possibly the Southern Hemisphere) where wakame was growing. Being first meant that Commercial Marine Products was able to secure the only source of supply.

These barriers to entry can reduce the amount of competition faced by the first mover. Because competition typically puts downward pressure on prices and may increase marketing costs, it usually results in reduced profit margins and a drop in overall profitability. However, competition is not always bad; sometimes it can enhance the firm's performance. Competition within an industry can have a positive effect on industry growth. For example, competition among firms encourages them to become efficient and innovative to create even more value in their products for customers. Increases in customer value (whether from increases in product quality, lower prices, or both) will mean that more customers will enter the new market. New customers might be added by entering international markets.

Therefore, first movers need to keep in mind that they might win the battle by lowering the level of potential competition within an industry through the creation of barriers to entry but lose the war because insufficient customers are willing to substitute into the new industry. Under these conditions the first mover should consider allowing a number of competitors into the industry to share the pioneering costs and then working together to erect barriers to subsequent entry by potential competitors.

PROVIDE ADVICE TO AN ENTREPRENEUR ABOUT BEING MORE INNOVATIVE

When Neil Franklin began offering round-the-clock telephone customer service in 1998, customers loved it. The offering fit the strategic direction Franklin had in mind for Dataworkforce, his Dallas-based telecommunications-engineer staffing agency, so he invested in a phone system to route after-hours calls to his 10 employees' home and mobile phones. Today, Franklin, 38, has nearly 50 employees and continues to explore ways to improve Dataworkforce's service. Twenty-four-hour phone service has stayed, but other trials have not. One failure was developing individual Web sites for each customer. "We took it too far and spent $30,000, then abandoned it," Franklin recalls. A try at globally extending the brand by advertising in major world cities was also dropped. "It worked pretty well," Franklin says, "until you added up the cost."

Franklin's efforts are similar to an approach called a "portfolio of initiatives" strategy. The idea, according to Lowell Bryan, a principal in McKinsey & Co., the New York City consulting firm that developed it, is to always have a number of efforts under way to offer new products and services and attack new markets or otherwise implement strategies, and to actively manage these experiments so you don't miss an opportunity or overcommit to an unproven idea.

The portfolio of initiatives approach addresses a weakness of conventional business plans—that they make assumptions about uncertain future developments, such as market and technological trends, customer responses, sales, and competitor reactions. Bryan compares the portfolio of initiatives strategy to the ship convoys used in World War II to get supplies across oceans. By assembling groups of military and transport vessels and sending them in a mutually supportive group, planners could rely on at least some reaching their destination. In the same way, entrepreneurs with a portfolio of initiatives can expect some of them to pan out.

MAKING A PLAN

Three steps define the portfolio of initiatives approach. First, you search for initiatives in which you have or can readily acquire a familiarity advantage—meaning you know more than competitors about a business. You can gain familiarity advantage using low-cost pilot programs and experiments or by partnering with more knowledgeable allies. Avoid businesses in which you can't acquire a familiarity advantage, Bryan says.

After you identify familiarity-advantaged initiatives, begin investing in them using a disciplined, dynamic management approach. Pay attention to how initiatives relate to each other. They should be diverse enough that the failure of one won't endanger the others, but should also all fit into your overall strategic direction. Investments, represented by product development efforts, pilot programs, market tests, and the like, should start small and increase only as they prove themselves. Avoid overinvesting before initiatives have proved themselves. The third step is to pull the plug on initiatives that aren't working out, and step up investment in others. A portfolio of initiatives will work in any size company. Franklin pursues 20 to 30 at any time, knowing 90 percent won't pan out. "The main idea is to keep those initiatives running," he says. "If you don't, you're slowing down."

ADVICE TO AN ENTREPRENEUR

An entrepreneur who wants his firm to be more innovative has read the above article and comes to you for advice:

1. This whole idea of experimentation seems to make sense, but all these little failures can add up, and if there are enough of them, then this could lead to one big failure—the business going down the drain. How can I best get the advantages of experimentation in terms of innovation while also reducing the costs so that I don't run the risk of losing my business?

2. My employees, buyers, and suppliers like working for my company because we have a lot of wins. I am not sure how they will take it when our company begins to have a lot more failures (even if those failures are small)—it is a psychological thing. How can I handle this trade-off?

3. Even if everyone else accepts it, I am not sure how I will cope. When projects fail it hits me pretty hard emotionally. Is it just that I am not cut out for this type of approach?

Source: Reprinted with permission of Entrepreneur Media, Inc., "Worth a Try. Who Knows What's Going to Work? So Put as Many Ideas as You Can to the Test," by Mark Henricks, February 2003, *Entrepreneur* magazine: www.entrepreneur.com.

RISK REDUCTION STRATEGIES FOR NEW ENTRY EXPLOITATION

risk The probability, and magnitude, of downside loss

A new entry involves considerable risk for the entrepreneur and his or her firm. *Risk* here refers to the probability, and magnitude, of downside loss,[16] which could result in bankruptcy. The risk of downside loss is partly derived from the entrepreneur's uncertainties over market demand, technological development, and the actions of competitors. Strategies can be used to reduce some or all of these uncertainties and thereby reduce the risk of downside loss. Two such strategies are market scope and imitation.

Market Scope Strategies

scope A choice about which customer groups to serve and how to serve them

Scope is a choice by the entrepreneur about which customer groups to serve and how to serve them.[17] The choice of market scope ranges from a narrow- to a broad-scope strategy and depends on the type of risk the entrepreneur believes is more important to reduce.

Narrow-Scope Strategy
A narrow-scope strategy offers a small product range to a small number of customer groups to satisfy a particular need. The narrow scope can reduce the risk that the firm will face competition with larger, more established firms in a number of ways.

- A narrow-scope strategy focuses the firm on producing customized products, localized business operations, and high levels of product quality. Such outcomes provide the basis for differentiating the firm from larger competitors who are oriented more toward mass production and the advantages that are derived from that volume. A narrow-scope strategy of product differentiation reduces competition with the larger established firms and allows the entrepreneur to charge premium prices.

- By focusing on a specific group of customers, the entrepreneur can build up specialized expertise and knowledge that provide an advantage over companies that are competing more broadly. For instance, the entrepreneur pursuing a narrow-scope strategy is in the best position to offer superior product quality, given his or her intimate knowledge of the product attributes customers desire most.

- The high end of the market typically represents a highly profitable niche that is well suited to those firms that can produce customized products, localized business operations, and high levels of product quality. From the first point listed, we know that firms pursuing a narrow-scope strategy are more likely to offer products and services with these attributes than are larger firms that are more interested in volume.

However, a narrow-scope strategy does not always provide protection against competition. For example, the firm may offer a product that the entrepreneur believes is of superior quality, yet customers may not value the so-called product improvements or, if they do perceive those improvements, they may be unwilling to pay a premium price for them, preferring to stick with the products currently being offered by the larger firms. That is, the boundary between the market segment being targeted by the entrepreneur and that of the mass market is not sufficiently clear and thus provides little protection against competition.

Furthermore, if the market niche is attractive, there is an incentive for the larger and more established firms (and all firms) to develop products and operations targeted at this niche. For example, a larger, more mass market–oriented firm might create a subsidiary to compete in this attractive market segment.

Although a narrow-scope strategy can sometimes reduce the risks associated with competition, this scope strategy is vulnerable to another type of risk: the risk that market demand does not materialize as expected and/or changes over time. For example, a narrow-scope strategy focuses on a single customer group (or a small number of customer groups), but if the market changes and decreases substantially the size and attractiveness of that market segment, then the firm runs a considerable risk of downside loss. Having a narrow-scope strategy is like putting all your eggs in one basket. If that basket is fundamentally flawed, then all the eggs will be dropped and broken. A broad-scope strategy, on the other hand, provides a way of managing demand uncertainty and thereby reducing an aspect of the entrepreneur's risk.

Broad-Scope Strategy   A broad-scope strategy can be thought of as taking a "portfolio" approach to dealing with uncertainties about the attractiveness of different market segments. By offering a range of products across many different market segments, the entrepreneur can gain an understanding of the whole market by determining which products are the most profitable. Unsuccessful products (and market segments) can then be dropped and resources concentrated on those product markets that show the greatest promise. In essence, the entrepreneur can cope with market uncertainty by using a broad-scope strategy to learn about the market through a process of trial and error.[18]

The entrepreneur's ultimate strategy will emerge as a result of the information provided by this learning process. In contrast, a narrow-scope strategy requires the entrepreneur to have sufficient certainty about the market that he is willing to focus his resources on a small piece of the market, with few options to fall back on if the initial assessment about the product proves incorrect. Offering a range of products across a range of market segments means that a broad-scope strategy is opening the firm up to many different "fronts" of competition. The entrepreneur may need to compete with the more specialized firms within narrow market niches and simultaneously with volume producers in the mass market.

Therefore, a narrow-scope strategy offers a way of reducing some competition-related risks but increases the risks associated with market uncertainties. In contrast, a broad-scope strategy offers a way of reducing risks associated with market uncertainties but faces increased exposure to competition. The entrepreneur needs to choose the scope strategy that reduces the risk of greatest concern. For example, if the new entry is into an established market, then competitors are well entrenched and ready to defend their market shares. Also the market demand is more stable and market research can inform the entrepreneur on the attractiveness of the new product with a particular group of customers. In this situation, where the risk of competition is great and market uncertainties are minimal, a narrow-scope strategy is more effective at risk reduction.

However, if new entry involves the creation of a new market or entry into an emerging market, then competitors are more concerned with satisfying new customers entering the market than on stealing market share from others or retaliating against new entrants. Also there is typically considerable market uncertainty about which products are going to be winners and which are going to be losers. In this situation, a broad-scope strategy reduces the major risk, namely, risks associated with uncertainties over customer preferences.

Imitation Strategies

Why Do It?   Imitation is another strategy for minimizing the risk of downside loss associated with new entry. Imitation involves copying the practices of other firms, whether those other firms are in the industry being entered or from related industries. This idea of using *imitation strategies* to improve firm performance at first appears inconsistent with the argument at the start of the chapter that superior performance arises from the qualities of being valuable, rare, and inimitable. An imitation strategy cannot be rare or inimitable.

Although this may be true, an imitation strategy can still enhance firm performance because a successful new entry does not need to be valuable, rare, and inimitable in terms

imitation strategies
Copying the practices of other firms

of every aspect of the firm's operations. Rather, imitation of others' practices that are peripheral to the competitive advantage of the firm offers a number of advantages.

Entrepreneurs may simply find it easier to imitate the practices of a successful firm than to go through the process of a systematic and expensive search that still requires a decision based on imperfect information.[19] In essence, imitation represents a substitute for individual learning and is well illustrated by the following quote from the president of Rexhaul Industries (a firm that sells cheaper recreational vehicles than its competitors): "In this industry, we call it R&C: research and copy."[20]

Imitating some of the practices of established successful firms can help the entrepreneur develop the skills necessary to be successful in the industry, rather than attempting to work out which skills are required and develop these skills from scratch. This use of imitation allows the entrepreneur to quickly acquire the skills that will be rewarded by the industry without necessarily having to go through the process of first determining what those key success factors actually are. It is a mechanism that allows the entrepreneur to skip a step in the stages of solving a puzzle (or at least to delay the need, and the importance, of solving that particular step).

Imitation also provides organizational legitimacy. If the entrepreneur acts like a well-established firm, it is likely to be perceived by customers as well established. Imitation is a means of gaining status and prestige. Customers feel more comfortable doing business with firms that they perceive to be established and prestigious. This is particularly the case for service firms. For example, a new consulting firm will need to go out of its way to look like an established prestigious firm, even though some of its trappings (e.g., a prime location office, leather chairs and couches, and a well-tailored suit) put a strain on resources and are only incidental to the quality of the service.

Types of Imitation Strategies

Franchising is an example of a new entry that focuses on imitation to reduce the risk of downside loss for the franchisee. A franchisee acquires the use of a "proven formula" for new entry from a franchisor. For example, an entrepreneur might enter the fast food industry by franchising a McDonald's store in a new geographic location. This entrepreneur is imitating the business practices of other McDonald's stores (in fact, imitation is mandatory) and benefits from an established market demand; an intellectual property–protected name and products; and access to knowledge of financial, marketing, and managerial issues.

This new entry is unique because it is the only McDonald's store in a dedicated geographical area (although it must compete with Burger King, KFC, etc.). More broadly, this McDonald's store is differentiated from potential competitors in the same geographic space. Much of the risk of new entry for the entrepreneur has been reduced through this imitation strategy (Chapter 14 discusses franchising in more detail).

Franchising is not the only imitation strategy. Some entrepreneurs will attempt to copy successful businesses. For example, new entry can involve copying products that already exist and attempting to build an advantage through minor variations. This form of imitation is often referred to as a *"me-too" strategy*. In other words, the successful firm occupies a prime position in the minds of customers, and now the imitator is there too and hopes to be considered by the customers. Variation often takes the form of making minor changes to the launch product being offered, taking an existing product or service (which is unprotected by intellectual property rights) to a new market not currently served, or delivering the product to customers in a different way.

"me-too" strategy
Copying products that already exist and attempting to build an advantage through minor variations

Ice cream shops are an example of a "me-too" imitation strategy, where new entrants have imitated successful stores but have also been able to differentiate themselves from those already in the industry by offering some form of variation. We have seen competing ice cream shops imitate each other by offering similar shop layouts and locations (e.g., inside malls), the same choice of flavors and cones (e.g., waffle cones), and similar promotional strategies (such as, "Taste before you buy"). Often the point of variation is simply the location of the store.

In the ice cream retail industry we have noticed that new entrants are increasingly relying on even greater levels of imitation to provide the necessary competitive advantage—more and more new entrants are entering into a franchise agreement with Baskin-Robbins, Häagen-Dazs, or other international franchisors. These franchisors have introduced a national or global brand name and reputation (previously only regional), standardized operating procedures, interstore communication, and economies of scale in marketing.[21]

However, a "me-too" imitation strategy might be more difficult to successfully implement than first expected. The success of the firm being copied may depend on its underlying organizational knowledge and corporate culture. Peripheral activities may not produce the desired outcomes when used in a different organizational context. Furthermore, entrepreneurs are often legally prevented from other avenues of imitation, such as the use of registered trademarks and brand names.

Overall, an imitation strategy can potentially reduce the entrepreneur's costs associated with research and development, reduce customer uncertainty over the firm, and make the new entry look legitimate from day one. In pursuing an imitation strategy for new entry, the entrepreneur should focus on imitating those elements of the business that are not central to the firm's competitive advantage. These central aspects of advantage must be valuable, rare, and inimitable for the firm to achieve high performance over an extended period of time.

Managing Newness

New entry can occur through the creation of a new organization. The creation of a new organization offers some challenges not faced by entrepreneurs who manage established firms. These *liabilities of newness* arise from the following unique conditions.

liabilities of newness
Negative implications arising from an organization's newness

- New organizations face costs in learning new tasks. It may take some time and training to customize employees' skills to the new tasks they are asked to perform.

- As people are assigned to the roles of the new organization, there will be some overlap or gaps in responsibilities. This will often cause conflict until the boundaries around particular roles are more formally set (once management has gained sufficient knowledge to do so) and/or until they have been informally negotiated by the parties to the conflict.

- Communication within the organization occurs through both formal and informal channels. A new organization has not yet had the opportunity to develop informal structures, such as friendships and organizational culture. It takes time for a new firm to establish these informal structures.

Managing a new firm requires special attention to educating and training employees so that their knowledge and skills will develop quickly to meet the needs of their tasks, to facilitate conflicts over roles, and to foster social activities that will in turn quickly foster informal relationships and a functional corporate culture. If these liabilities of newness can be overcome, then the entrepreneur can benefit from some *assets of newness*. These assets acknowledge the advantages that a new organization has over a mature one, particularly in environments that are changing.

assets of newness
Positive implications arising from an organization's newness

Although mature organizations have established routines, systems, and processes that increase the efficiency of their operations, these routines, systems, and processes can be a liability when there is a need for those firms to adapt to changes in their environment.

Previous practices create a momentum along the same path, and redirection is difficult. Mature firms also find it difficult to attain new knowledge because their thoughts are narrowed by what has been done in the past and what they are good at rather than by the external environment and what is needed.

In contrast, new firms find that their lack of established routines, systems, and processes means that they have a clean slate, which gives them learning advantages over older firms.[22] They do not need to unlearn old knowledge and old habits to learn new knowledge and create the new routines, systems, and processes that are more attuned with the changed environment.

A heightened ability to learn new knowledge represents an important source of competitive advantage that needs to be fostered by the entrepreneur. It is particularly advantageous in a continuously changing environment because the firm needs to incrementally build its strategy as it learns information while acting. Previous strategic planning will not be successful in such environments because the development of such an environment is not knowable in advance (unless the entrepreneur is extremely lucky).

Therefore, although entrepreneurs must be aware of, and manage, liabilities of newness, it is not all doom and gloom. Rather, new ventures have an important strategic advantage over their mature competitors, particularly in dynamic, changing environments. Entrepreneurs need to capitalize on these assets of newness by creating a learning organization that is flexible and able to accommodate this new knowledge in its future actions. This shifts the emphasis in understanding firm performance from a heavy reliance on strategic plans to greater emphasis on the strategic learning and flexibility of the entrepreneur and his or her management team.

IN REVIEW

SUMMARY

One of the essential acts of entrepreneurship is new entry—entry based on a new product, a new market, and/or a new organization. Entrepreneurial strategies represent the set of decisions, actions, and reactions that first generate, and then exploit over time, a new entry in a way that maximizes the benefits of newness and minimizes its costs. The creation of resource bundles is the basis for new entry opportunities. A resource bundle is created from the entrepreneur's market knowledge, technological knowledge, and other resources. The new entry has the potential of being a source of sustained superior firm performance if the resource bundle underlying the new entry is valuable, rare, and difficult for others to imitate. Therefore, those wishing to generate an innovation need to look to the unique experiences and knowledge within themselves and their team.

Having created a new resource combination, the entrepreneur needs to determine whether it is in fact valuable, rare, and inimitable by assessing whether this new product and/or new market is sufficiently attractive to be worth exploiting and then acting on that decision. The decision to exploit or not to exploit the new entry opportunity depends on whether the entrepreneur has what she or he believes to be sufficient information to make a decision and on whether the window is still open for this new entry opportunity. The entrepreneur's determination of sufficient information depends on the stock of information and the entrepreneur's level of comfort in making such a decision without perfect information.

Successful new entry requires that the entrepreneur's firm have an advantage over competitors. Entrepreneurs often claim that their competitive advantage arises from being first to market. Being first can result in a number of advantages that can enhance performance, such as cost advantages, reduced competition, securing important sources of supply and distribution, obtaining a prime position in the market, and gaining expertise through early participation. But first movers do not always prosper, and in fact there are conditions that can push a first mover toward performance disadvantages, such as high instability of the environment surrounding the entry, a lack of ability among the management team to educate customers, and a lack of ability among the management team to erect barriers to entry and imitation to extend the firm's lead time.

A new entry involves considerable risk for the entrepreneur and his or her firm. This risk of downside loss is partly derived from the entrepreneur's uncertainties over market demand, technological development, and the actions of competitors. Strategies can be used to reduce some or all of these uncertainties and thereby reduce the risk of downside loss. Two such strategies are market scope and imitation. Scope is a choice by the entrepreneur about which customer groups to serve and how to serve them—for example, the choice between a narrow and a broad scope. Imitation involves copying the practices of other firms, whether those other firms are in the industry being entered or in related industries; for instance, "me too" and franchising are both imitation strategies.

Entrepreneurship also can involve the creation of a new organization. The creation of a new organization offers some challenges for entrepreneurs that are not faced by those who manage established firms. These challenges, referred to as liabilities of newness, reflect a new organization's higher costs of learning new tasks, increased conflict over newly created roles and responsibilities, and the lack of a well-developed informal communication network. However, new organizations also may have some assets of newness, the most important of which is an increased ability to learn new knowledge, which can provide an important strategic advantage over mature competitors, particularly in dynamic, changing environments.

RESEARCH TASKS

1. Choose three major inventions that have led to successful products. Who were the inventors? How did they invent the technology? Why do you believe they were the first to invent this technology?

2. Find three examples of firms that pioneered a new product in a new market and were able to achieve long-run success based on that entry. Find three examples of firms that were not the pioneers but entered later to eventually overtake the pioneer as market leader. In your opinion, why were the successful pioneers successful, and why were the unsuccessful ones unsuccessful?

3. What is the failure rate of all new businesses? What is the failure rate of all new franchises? What inferences can you make from these numbers?

CLASS DISCUSSION

1. Come up with five examples of firms that have used imitation as a way of reducing the risk of entry. What aspects of risk was imitation meant to reduce? Was it successful? What aspects of the firm were not generated by imitation, made the firm unique, and were a potential source of advantage over competitors?

2. Provide two examples of firms with a broad scope, two with a narrow scope, and two that started narrow and became broader over time.

3. Is it a waste of time to detail the firm's strategy in the business plan when the audience for that plan (e.g., venture capitalists) knows that things are not going to turn out as expected and, as a result, places considerable importance on the quality of the management team? Why not submit only the resumes of those in the management team? If you were a venture capitalist, would you want to see the business plan? How would you assess the quality of one management team relative to another?

SELECTED READINGS

Ardichvili, Alexander; Richard Cardozo; and Sourav Ray. (2003). A Theory of Entrepreneurial Opportunity Identification and Development. *Journal of Business Venturing*, vol. 18, no. 1, pp. 105–24.

This paper proposes a theory of the opportunity identification process. It identifies the entrepreneur's personality traits, social networks, and prior knowledge as antecedents of entrepreneurial alertness to business opportunities. Entrepreneurial alertness, in its turn, is a necessary condition for the success of the opportunity identification triad: recognition, development, and evaluation. A theoretical model, laws of interaction, a set of propositions, and suggestions for further research are provided.

Baker, Ted; and Nelson E. Reed. (2005). Creating Something from Nothing: Resource Construction through Entrepreneurial Bricolage. *Administrative Science Quarterly*, vol. 50, no. 3, pp. 329–66.

In this article the authors studied 29 firms and demonstrated that entrepreneurs differ in their responses to severe resource constraints. Some entrepreneurs were able to render unique services by recombining elements at hand for new purposes that challenged institutional definitions and limits. This article introduces the concept of bricolage to explain many of these behaviors of creating something from nothing by exploiting physical, social, or institutional inputs that other firms rejected or ignored. Central to the study's contribution is the notion that companies engaging in bricolage refuse to enact the limitations imposed by dominant definitions of resource environments; rather they create their opportunities. (from journal's abstract)

Barney, Jay B. (2001). Resource-Based "Theories" of Competitive Advantage: A Ten-Year Retrospective on the Resource-Based View. *Journal of Management*, vol. 27, no. 6, pp. 643–751.

The resource-based view is discussed in terms of its positioning relative to three theoretical traditions: SCP-based theories of industry determinants of firm performance, neoclassical microeconomics, and evolutionary economics. It also discusses some of the empirical implications of each of these different resource-based theories.

Boulding, William; and Christen Markus. (2008). Disentangling Pioneering Cost Advantages and Disadvantages. *Marketing Science*, vol. 27, pp. 699–716.

In this paper, the authors empirically test three different sources of long-term pioneering cost advantage—experience curve effects, preemption of input factors, and preemption of ideal market space—and three different sources of pioneering cost disadvantage—imitation, vintage effects, and demand orientation. The complexity of their findings suggests that managers need to think carefully about their particular conditions before making assumptions about the cost and, therefore, profit implications of a pioneering strategy.

Bruton, Gary D.; and Yuri Rubanik. (2002). Resources of the Firm, Russian High Technology Startups, and Firm Growth. *Journal of Business Venturing*, vol. 17, no. 6, pp. 553–77.

This study investigates the extent to which founding factors in Russia help high-technology firms to prosper. It was found that the team establishing the business mitigated the liability of newness. However, in contrast to the culture of the United States, the culture of Russia does not produce negative results if the founding team grows very large. Additionally, it was shown that firms that pursued more technological products and entered the market later performed best.

Erikson, Truls. (2002). Entrepreneurial Capital: The Emerging Venture's Most Important Asset and Competitive Advantage. *Journal of Business Venturing*, vol. 17, no. 3, pp. 275–91.

This study presents a parsimonious model of entrepreneurial capital, defined as a multiplicative function of entrepreneurial competence and entrepreneurial commitment. The presence of both entrepreneurial competence and commitment lays the foundation for enterprise generation and performance. Inherent in this view on competence is the capacity to identify opportunities.

Fiol, C. Marlene; and Edward J. O'Connor. (2003). Waking Up! Mindfulness in the Face of Bandwagons. *Academy of Management Review*, vol. 28, no. 1, pp. 54–71.

This article models the interactions between mindfulness as a decision-maker characteristic and the decision-making context, and shows the impact of those interactions on managers' ability to discriminate in the face of bandwagons. The authors illustrate the framework by applying it to recent integration and disintegration bandwagon behaviors in the U.S. health care market.

Haynie, J. Michael; Dean A. Shepherd; and Jeffery S. McMullen. (2009). An Opportunity for Me? The Role of Resources in Opportunity Evaluation Decisions. *Journal of Management Studies*, vol. 46, no. 3, pp. 337–61.

The authors apply the prescriptions of the resource-based perspective to develop a model of entrepreneurial opportunity evaluation. They propose that opportunity evaluation decision policies are constructed as future-oriented, cognitive representations of "what will be," assuming one were to exploit the opportunity under evaluation. Their findings suggest that entrepreneurs are attracted to opportunities that are complementary to their existing knowledge resources; however, we also identify a set of opportunity-specific and firm-specific conditions that encourage entrepreneurs to pursue the acquisition and control of resources that are inconsistent with the existing, knowledge-based resources of the venture.

Keh, Hean T.; Maw Der Foo; and Boon C. Lim. (2002). Opportunity Evaluation under Risky Conditions: The Cognitive Processes of Entrepreneurs. *Entrepreneurship: Theory & Practice*, vol. 27, no. 2, pp. 125–49.

This study uses a cognitive approach to examine opportunity evaluation. It finds that illusion of control and belief in the law of small numbers are related to how entrepreneurs evaluate opportunities. The results also indicate that risk perception mediates opportunity evaluation.

Lieberman, Marvin B.; and David B. Montgomery. (1998). First-Mover (Dis)advantages: Retrospective and Link with the Resource-Based View. *Strategic Management Journal*, vol. 19, no. 12, pp. 1111–26.

This article suggests that the resource-based view and first-mover advantage are related conceptual strategic planning frameworks that can benefit from closer linkage. It presents an evolution of the literature based on these concepts.

McEvily, Susan K.; and Bala Chakravarthy. (2002). The Persistence of Knowledge-Based Advantage: An Empirical Test for Product Performance and Technological Knowledge. *Strategic Management Journal*, vol. 23, no. 4, pp. 285–306.

The authors find that the complexity and tacitness of technological knowledge are useful for defending a firm's major product improvements from imitation, but not for protecting its minor improvements. The design specificity of technological knowledge delayed imitation of minor improvements in this study.

Mitchell, Robert J.; and Dean A. Shepherd. (2010). To Thine Own Self Be True: Images of Self, Images of Opportunity, and Entrepreneurial Action. *Journal of Business Venturing,* vol. 25, issue 1, pp. 138–54.

In this study, the authors seek to complement recent research that relates "the self" to the opportunity-recognition process by deepening understanding of the self vis-à-vis this process. They do this by drawing on the self-representation literature and the decision-making literature to introduce two distinct types of images of self: images of vulnerability and images of capability. They found that both images of self—vulnerability and capability—impact one's image of opportunity. (from journal's abstract)

Robinson, William T.; and Sungwook Min. (2002). Is the First to Market the First to Fail? Empirical Evidence for Industrial Goods Businesses. *Journal of Marketing Research,* vol. 39, no. 1, pp. 120–29.

The main conclusion of this study is that the pioneer's temporary monopoly over the early followers plus its first-mover advantages typically offset the survival risks associated with market and technological uncertainties. These results are consistent with previous research in the sense that first-mover advantages that increase a pioneer's market share also help protect the pioneer from outright failure.

Teplensky, Jill D.; John R. Kimberly; Alan L. Hillman; and J. Stanford Schwartz. (1993). Scope, Timing and Strategic Adjustment in Emerging Markets: Manufacturer Strategies and the Case of MRI. *Strategic Management Journal,* vol. 14, pp. 505–27.

This study examines the realized strategies of domestic manufacturers in a growing, high-technological industrial market in the United States. It offers a typology of entry strategies focusing on issues of timing and scope and on the impact that these entry strategies have on a firm's performance.

Ucbasaran, Deniz; Mike Wright; Paul Westhead; and Lowell W. Busenitz. (2003). The Impact of Entrepreneurial Experience on Opportunity Identification and Exploitation: Habitual and Novice Entrepreneurs. In J. Katz and D. A. Shepherd (eds.), *Advances in Entrepreneurship: Firm Emergence and Growth,* vol. 6. (Greenwich, CT: JAI Press).

This paper synthesizes human capital and cognitive perspectives to highlight behavioral differences between habitual and novice entrepreneurs. Issues related to opportunity identification and information search as well as opportunity exploitation and learning are discussed.

Watson, Warren; Wayne Stewart, Jr.; and Anat BarNir. (2003). The Effects of Human Capital, Organizational Demography, and Interpersonal Processes on Venture Partner Perceptions of Firm Profit and Growth. *Journal of Business Venturing,* vol. 18, no. 2, pp. 145–65.

This study examines the effects of human capital, organizational demography, and interpersonal processes on partner evaluations of venture performance, defined as the presence of profit and growth. The results support this approach in analyzing venture teams, and it is proposed that this perspective be included in future venture viability assessment and used for intervention to enhance venture success.

Zahra, Shaker A.; Donald O. Neubaum; and Galal M. El–Hagrassey. (2002). Competitive Analysis and New Venture Performance: Understanding the Impact of Strategic Uncertainty and Venture Origin. *Entrepreneurship: Theory & Practice,* vol. 27, no. 1, pp. 1–29.

Using survey data from 228 new ventures, this study concludes that the formality, comprehensiveness, and user orientation of competitor analysis activities are positively associated with new venture performance. Strategic uncertainty and venture origin also significantly moderate the relationship between competitive analysis and new venture performance.

END NOTES

1. G. Lumpkin and G. G. Dess, "Clarifying the Entrepreneurial Orientation Construct and Linking It to Performance," *Academy of Management Review* 21, no. 1 (1996), pp. 135–72.
2. F. H. Knight, *Risk, Uncertainty and Profit* (New York: Houghton Mifflin, 1921); E. M. Olson, O. C. Walker, Jr., and R. W. Ruekert, "Organizing for Effective New Product Development: The Moderating Role of Product Innovativeness," *Journal of Marketing* 59 (January 1995), pp. 48–62; H. J. Sapienza and A. K. Gupta, "Impact of Agency Risks and Task Uncertainty on Venture Capitalist-Entrepreneur Relations," *Academy of Management Journal* 37 (1994), pp. 1618–32.
3. J. B. Barney, "Firm Resources and Sustained Competitive Advantage," *Journal of Management* 17 (1991), pp. 99–120.
4. This list is adapted from M. A. Hitt, R. D. Ireland, and R. E. Hoskisson, *Strategic Management: Competitiveness and Globalization,* 3rd ed. (London: South-Western Publishing Co., 1999).
5. S. P. Schnaars, *Managing Imitation Strategies: How Later Entrants Seize Markets from Pioneers* (New York: Free Press, 1994).
6. Nathan Rosenberg, "Trying to Predict the Impact of Tomorrow's Inventions," *USA Today* 123 (May 1995), pp. 88ff.
7. Ibid.
8. J. McMullen and D. A. Shepherd, "A Theory of Entrepreneurial Action," in J. Katz and D. A. Shepherd (eds.), *Advances in Entrepreneurship: Firm Emergence and Growth* (vol. 6) (Greenwich, CT: JAI Press, 2003), pp. 203–48.
9. D. A. Shepherd and M. Shanley, *New Venture Strategy: Timing, Environmental Uncertainty and Performance* (Newburg Park, CA: The Sage Series in Entrepreneurship and the Management of Enterprises, 1998).
10. M. B. Lieberman and D. B. Montgomery, "First Mover Advantages," *Strategic Management Journal* 9 (1988), pp. 127–40.
11. D. F. Abell, "Strategic Windows," *Journal of Marketing* 42, no. 3 (1978), pp. 21–26.
12. D. A. Aaker and G. S. Day, "The Perils of High Growth Markets," *Strategic Management Journal* 7 (1986), pp. 409–21; Shepherd and Shanley, *New Venture Strategy.*
13. Shepherd and Shanley, *New Venture Strategy.*
14. S. F. Slater, "Competing in High Velocity Markets," *Industrial Marketing Management* 24, no. 4 (1993), pp. 255–68.
15. Shepherd and Shanley, *New Venture Strategy.*
16. T. W. Ruefli, J. M. Collins, and J. R. LaCugna, "Risk Measures in Strategic Management Research: Auld Lang Syne?" *Strategic Management Journal* 20 (1999), pp. 167–94.
17. J. D. Teplensky, J. R. Kimberly, A. L. Hillman, and J. S. Schwartz, "Scope, Timing and Strategic Adjustment in Emerging Markets: Manufacturer Strategies and the Case of MRI," *Strategic Management Journal* 14 (1993), pp. 505–27.
18. Shepherd and Shanley, *New Venture Strategy.*
19. Ibid.
20. Schnaars, *Managing Imitation Strategies.*
21. Shepherd and Shanley, *New Venture Strategy.*
22. B. B. Lichtenstein, G. T. Lumpkin, and R. Shrader, "A Theory of Entrepreneurial Action," in J. Katz and D. A. Shepherd (eds.), *Advances in Entrepreneurship: Firm Emergence and Growth* (vol. 6) (Greenwich, CT: JAI Press, 2003).

2

FROM IDEA TO THE OPPORTUNITY

4

CREATIVITY AND THE BUSINESS IDEA

1
To identify various sources of ideas for new ventures.

2
To discuss methods available for generating new venture ideas.

3
To discuss creativity and the techniques for creative problem solving.

4
To discuss the importance of innovation.

5
To understand an opportunity assessment plan.

6
To discuss the aspects of the product planning and development process.

7
To discuss aspects of e-commerce and starting an e-commerce business.

OPENING PROFILE

PIERRE OMIDYAR

Anyone who has ever watched *Antiques Roadshow* or *The Collectors* knows that not only is one man's trash another man's treasure, but that treasure can be worth a fortune. Consider that ugly vase inherited from Great Aunt Mildred 20 years ago that has not seen the light of day since. It could be worth $5,000. The interesting thing about "worth" is that something is only as valuable as someone is willing to pay for it. If no one in the world felt that Aunt Mildred's vase was worth any money, then it would be insignificant. However, that small pocket of people, perhaps zealot collectors, assign value to the object and so it becomes "valuable."

www.ebay.com

It is this interesting sociological phenomenon that grabbed Pierre Omidyar's attention and led to the eventual establishment of eBay. The famous story of eBay's conception starts with a dinner conversation between Omidyar and his girlfriend as she lamented her troubles with her Pez dispenser collection. She complained that there were not enough fellow Pez collectors in their region of the world for her to trade with, which sparked Omidyar's idea to reach beyond geography and connect sellers and buyers around the world via the Internet. Although a nice, catchy story, it is not entirely true. During an interview in 2000 with the Academy of Achievement, Omidyar described the story as being "media-enhanced," and later spokespersons from eBay called it a "publicist's fabrication."[1] The girlfriend in the story is Pamela Wesley, who is now his wife and was his fiancée at the time of the story. Apparently the Pez story irks her, as she would rather be known for her success as a management consultant and her master's degree in molecular biology than for being a candy connoisseur.

The real story is that Omidyar had always been fascinated with the high-tech world and its ability to connect people. Born in Paris in 1967, his parents were both educated and successful in their own right, his father a surgeon and his mother a linguist. He was not a particularly good student, but made his way through Tufts University with a degree in computer science.[2] Always fascinated by software technology, he learned how to program computers early on and wrote simple software programs as early as high school. Omidyar states of his formative years before the advent of the World Wide Web, "I grew up in the software world. I grew up in a technology environment but it was all about building software packages that can solve people's problems and change the world."[3]

After college, he worked for a company that developed software for Macintosh computers, as well as Claris, a subsidiary of Apple. His first entrepreneurial venture was co-founded in 1991, with three of his friends, a software company called Ink Development. Due to a component of the business being dedicated to e-commerce, they later changed the name to eShop Inc.; the company was eventually sold to Microsoft.[4] Fascinated by the human challenges of e-commerce, Omidyar continued to experiment with developing prototypes to augment trade via the Internet during his time off from a full-time job at General Magic. To his amazement, his first sale on the Web was not a Pez dispenser, but a laser pointer that no longer worked. This odd transaction would become the start of an immense marketplace transition from brick and mortar to drag and click.

Although Omidyar did not invent the idea of online commerce, he did revolutionize it. While building eBay, he recognized the importance of the human transaction that was taking place behind the screens and keyboards. He thought of it in terms of how trade was carried out by even the earliest civilizations in order to get to the root of how business is conducted successfully. The fundamental principle that he understood, and that made eBay a success, is that people have to *trust* one another in order for trade to occur. It was this reasoning that led him to produce the check and balance system on eBay that is still in place today; this system has been re-created thousands of times over on other retail Web sites. Traders, buyers, and sellers on eBay can rate each other, file complaints, and give feedback in regard to their experience with others on the site. In this way, trust can be built and broken, and one's online reputation can make or break a trader's business. His unending belief in the intrinsic good in people helped him create a winning formula that others thought impossible. In this way, Omidyar was able to build what is impressively known today as "The World's Online Marketplace."

When it comes to entrepreneurship, Omidyar believes that success lies in having the courage to fail. People with good or even great ideas never find success because they are too afraid to move forward, stuck in the mentality that their dream cannot become reality. Citing internal uncertainty as the biggest hurdle to overcome, Omidyar says he is lucky that he was never convinced not to try something new. Whenever he had a new idea he thought, ". . . well, gee, you know, why not. I'll just go ahead and do it."[5]

Beyond courage and trying new things, it appears that having a passion for what you are doing is Omidyar's next biggest theme for success. His natural interest in computers and software as well as his instinctive curiosity regarding the human condition make eBay a perfect fit for his entrepreneurial endeavors. His passion is what helped drive him through the hard times, long hours, and grueling criticism. eBay was hard hit by critics in its early years for enabling trade of controversial items such as firearms and pornography. Rather than panicking, Omidyar looked at the issues analytically, weighing the pros and cons of censorship and decency. In the end, the firearms were banned and pornography was isolated from the rest of the site. Omidyar ensures access only to users of legal age. As a self-proclaimed "cheerleader" for eBay, his passion and belief in the trade system he created motivated him through the hard times, and helped him to persevere.

Known as one of the "nice guys" in the business world, the entrepreneur holds personal values as the key to operating a successful business. At the core of eBay, there is a fundamental belief that people are basically good, with the untrustworthy being the exception not the rule. His marketplace is distinctly different from other retail environments because of the lack of control by the company itself. While they control the design of the Web site, all of the products are self-imposed by the customers using the space. There are no sales clerks to train, layouts to design, or any of the traditional means with which retailers impact the customer experience. It may seem scary to some, but on eBay, the users control their own experiences by interacting with one another with limited intervention by the company. The consequence is that an eBay user may never use the service again due to one bad experience with another customer. Rather than trying to control the transaction, Omidyar's flexibility in handling his business seems to have helped it evolve and thrive on its own. Giving every customer the benefit of the doubt is paramount to the progress of such a business model. Omidyar takes a decided stance on his unwavering faith in people by espousing that same principle internally throughout the organization. He believes that because one cannot control the actions of others, ". . . the only thing you can do is have a certain set of values that you encourage people to adopt, and the only way your customers are going to adopt those values is if they see that you're living those values as well."[6] As with all good managers throughout the ages, Omidyar walks what he talks, which not only has afforded him a lucrative career, but has secured his high reputation as well.

At an estimated net worth of US$6.2 billion, securing him a high spot on the Forbes 400 Richest People in America list, Omidyar has continued to inspire confidence in others with immense philanthropy projects through the Omidyar Network. Established in 2004 by Pierre and his wife Pamela, the focus of the organization is to provide investment capital in areas of need. Based on the same principle as eBay that people are basically good, they use the tagline "every person has the power to make a difference" to get their point across. Through capital investments in microfinance, entrepreneurship, and property rights as well as an initiative dealing with media, markets, and transparency, their goal is to help larger-scale enterprises thrive in order to promote cataclysmic change from the bottom up. Inspired by the precedent he had set at eBay, the idea is to even the playing field in the global economy as he did with the retail sector. As stated on the foundation's Web site, "Because we are inspired by people's resourcefulness, ideas and ability to address even the world's most challenging problems, we believe that no matter what their economic, social or political starting point, people everywhere can be empowered to improve their own lives and the lives of those around them."[7]

An entrepreneurial inspiration, Pierre Omidyar continues to leave a positive mark on the global marketplace. He has proven himself as an innovator, entrepreneur, and businessman, but above all a humanitarian in the most fundamental sense. His belief in human good has propelled him far in life, and he continues to be a source of inspiration through his kindness, altruism, and above all unwavering faith in people.

At the heart of Pierre Omidyar's success story is the creativity and uniqueness of the initial business concept. This part of the new venture creation process is perhaps the most difficult to actualize. What specific features does the new product or service need? A wide variety of techniques can be used to obtain the new product idea. For some—such as Bob Reis of Final Technology, Inc., and Frank Perdue of Perdue Chickens—the idea came from work experience. No matter how it occurs, a sound, unique idea for a new product (or service), properly evaluated, is essential to successfully launching a new venture. Throughout this evaluation, or opportunity assessment, the entrepreneur must remember that most ideas do *not* provide the basis for a new venture; rather, it is important to sift through and identify those ideas that *can* provide such a basis so that they can be the entrepreneur's focus. A good method for doing this is to look at trends that will occur in the next decade.

TRENDS

A trend often provides one of the greatest opportunities for starting a new venture, particularly when the entrepreneur can be at the start of a trend that lasts for a considerable period of time. Seven trends that provide opportunities, indicated in Table 4.1, include: green trend, clean-energy trend, organic-orientation trend, economic trend, social trend, health trend, and Web trend.

Green Trend

The green sector is brimming with opportunities for entrepreneurs around the world. While today's consumers are very conscious about their spending habits, an increasing number are willing to pay more for green products. Water is one aspect of this green trend that provides opportunities, particularly in the area of irrigation, such as reclamation programs for golf courses and parks, smart irrigation systems, and consulting firms that increase water-use efficiency. Other business areas worth looking at include eco-friendly printing, recycling, and green janitorial services. For example, one entrepreneur is testing using worms to recycle food waste into fertilizer and another uses the same process as a source of fuel.

TABLE 4.1   Trends of the Next Decade
• Green • Clean energy • Organic orientation • Economic • Social • Health • Web

Clean-Energy Trend

One of the most pressing environmental concerns of consumers is clean energy. Many feel that the power of the 21st century will come from solar, wind, and geothermal sources. A significant factor that will accelerate this movement from coal being the power in the 19th century and oil in the 20th century is when solar costs are equal to the costs of electricity either from cost reductions and efficiency in solar conversion capacity and/or tax breaks for solar production and use. Smaller businesses and homeowners are a significant untapped market in this area. Several entrepreneurs install solar devices on single family homes at a low cost or with their revenue coming from the cost savings in electricity bills.

Organic-Orientation Trend

The organic trend is increasing significantly, particularly in the food sector, which has been accelerated by the shrinking price gap between organic and nonorganic foods. The sales growth in all organic foods including meat, dairy, fruits, vegetables, breads, and snack foods averages about 25 percent per year. Total organic nonfood sales are also growing, particularly in apparel. Oscar and Belle, started in 2007 by Anna Gustafson, provides organic apparel for babies. The baby clothing, size newborn to 2T, is distributed through retail outlets and online (oscarandbelle.com).

Economic Trend

The impact of the credit crunch, bank failures, and the housing slide and foreclosures has forced consumers to be much more careful in their spending. This increase in more frugal spending provides significant opportunities in such areas as garden products, business coaching, discount retailing, credit and debt management, virtual meetings, outsourcing, and the entire do-it-yourself movement. Still, many luxury products have not been significantly adversely affected.

Social Trend

The social trend is evident throughout the world with more networking events and opportunities occurring each week. These include the popular Facebook, MySpace, LinkedIn, and many other social networks as well as social networking for businesses. There are also opportunities in related areas of financial planning and travel as individuals want to have the ability to be financially solvent and viable in their longer life spans and enjoy the benefits of seeing new places with their children and grandchildren. Longevity Alliance, for example, is a one-stop advisory service offering counseling in long-term care and financial planning.

Health Trend

Health maintenance and concerns about health care provisions together are one of the biggest trends today that will continue in the next decade as the world population ages. This provides many opportunities for entrepreneurs, including cosmetic procedures, mind expansion such as the "brain gym" of Vibrant Brains, personal health portals, point-of-care testing facilities, fitness centers, fitness toys such as the latest Fit Flops and Wii Fit peripherals, fit food, convenient care clinics, and wellness coaches. Green Mountain Digital is developing a social network platform for nature lovers and was the leading selling app in birds.

Web Trend

The Web trend is creating many new forms of communication and purchasing, which is opening up massive opportunities for entrepreneurs. This has been driven by Web 2.0. The opportunities, with low-cost barriers to entry, are in numerous areas such as Web 2.0 consulting, blogging, online video, mobile applications (apps), and Wi-Fi apps. Platforms such as Apple and Android allow entrepreneurs to create and market their applications maintaining 70 percent of the revenues generated. Gaming has become a high growth industry with new and more interactive games emerging daily.

An entrepreneur should carefully monitor these trends to see if any produce ideas and opportunities that make sense. He or she should also look at the many sources of ideas as well.

SOURCES OF NEW IDEAS

Some of the more fruitful sources of ideas for entrepreneurs include consumers, existing products and services, distribution channels, the federal government, and research and development.

Consumers

Potential entrepreneurs should always pay close attention to potential customers. This attention can take the form of informally monitoring potential ideas and needs or formally arranging for consumers to have an opportunity to express their opinions. Care needs to be taken to ensure that the idea or need represents a large enough market to support a new venture.

Existing Products and Services

Potential entrepreneurs should also establish a formal method for monitoring and evaluating competitive products and services on the market. Frequently, this analysis uncovers ways to improve on these offerings that may result in a new product or service that has more market appeal and better sales and profit potential. Even existing companies need to do this. Sam Walton, founder of Walmart, would frequently visit competitive stores focusing not on what the competitive store did badly, but rather on what it was doing very well, so he could implement the idea at Walmart. Jameson Inns established a policy whereby the manager of each of its inns (hotels) weekly reports on competitive hotels and their prices in their market areas.

Distribution Channels

Members of the distribution channels are also excellent sources for new ideas because of their familiarity with the needs of the market. Not only do channel members frequently have suggestions for completely new products, but they can also help in marketing the entrepreneur's newly developed products. One entrepreneur found out from a salesclerk in a large department store that the reason his hosiery was not selling well was its color. By heeding the suggestion and making the appropriate color changes, his company became one of the leading suppliers of nonbrand hosiery in that region of the United States.

Federal Government

The federal government can be a source of new product ideas in two ways. First, the files of the Patent Office contain numerous new product possibilities. Although the patents themselves may not be feasible, they can frequently suggest other more marketable product

AS SEEN IN *BUSINESS NEWS*

THE SPEED OF INNOVATION: WHAT BIG PLAYERS CAN LEARN FROM THE NEW GUYS

In what seems to be only a handful of years, Google, Facebook, and Groupon have revolutionized the way companies have long thought about customer needs and the product innovation cycle. In today's rapidly changing business landscape, disruptive innovation has overruled the slower, more traditional research and development approach to product and service development and there is no turning back. A company's success is no longer based on the size of its portfolio but on its ability to effectively juggle commitment and consistency, uncertainty and opportunities, risks and returns, customer needs and wants, and most importantly its speed to adapt, innovate, and maintain its attractiveness.

How have Google, Facebook, and Groupon accomplished this and how can other companies follow suit? Below are a few key strategies that these disruptive innovators have mastered and that other enterprises of all sizes can learn from. How successfully one integrates these strategies into their corporation will determine if they can achieve a true competitive advantage.

1. **Spot the Trend and Create the Market.** Disruptive innovation is about responding to an unmet need and filling the void. Moving away from a product-centric mentality propels creativity to another level and allows firms to reach across their multiple resources (or lack of) to create in the true sense of the term.

2. **Fuse Company and Customer.** The new players in innovation have considerably narrowed the distance between their customers and themselves. Customers have become an integral part of what drives inspiration for products and services. Customer interaction is constant whether through beta testing or casual conversation. Today's innovators do not purely deliver new products. They are themselves users of their products, which motivates them to continue taking the product to the next level.

3. **Build an "A" Team.** Successful ventures will undeniably admit that their most valued investment and asset remain the people whom they employ and work with, and the company culture they collectively create. With the fast changing pace it is important to have harmonious internal organization and thought processes. Diversity of thoughts and experiences are very important but what will make or break a company and its products is how coordinated and united the team is.

4. **Focus and Deliver.** A company can no longer afford to be everything to everyone. A focused yet agile strategy to product development allows a company to solidify their product leadership in a specific area and be prepared to evolve and expand as time commands.

5. **Fail Successfully.** We have heard many times that it is not about the fall but more about the lessons learned along the way down. In few areas does this ring more true than in product innovation. Here, lessons learned are crucial, for within the lessons learned lie new opportunities.

6. **First to Market Wins.** Innovators must keep in mind that their competition is also fiercely working on spotting the trends and capitalizing on the opportunities. To succeed, the innovator must be the first to market with a new product or service and then rapidly continue to enhance the product to stay out in front of the competition.

Source: For more information on this topic see J. Engel, "Accelerating Corporate Innovation: Lessons from the Venture Capital Model," *Research Technology Management* (serial online) 54, no. 3 (May 2011), pp. 36–43.

ideas. Several government agencies and publications are helpful in monitoring patent applications. The *Official Gazette,* published weekly by the U.S. Patent Office, summarizes each patent granted and lists all patents available for license or sale. Also, the Government Patents Board publishes lists of abstracts of thousands of government-owned patents; a good resource for such information is the *Government-Owned Inventories Available for License.* Other government agencies, such as the Office of Technical Services, assist entrepreneurs in obtaining specific product information.

Second, new product ideas can evolve in response to government regulations. The Occupational Safety and Health Act (OSHA) mandated that first-aid kits be available in business establishments employing more than three people. The kits had to contain specific items that varied according to the company and the industry. For example, the weather-proofed first-aid kit needed for a construction company had to be different from the one needed by a company manufacturing facial cream or a company in retail trade. In response to OSHA, both established and newly formed ventures marketed a wide variety of first-aid kits. One new company, R&H Safety Sales Company, was successful in developing and selling first-aid kits that allowed companies to comply with the standards of the act with minimum time and effort.

Research and Development

The largest source of new ideas is the entrepreneur's own "research and development" efforts, which may be a formal endeavor connected with one's current employment or an informal lab in a basement or garage. One research scientist in a Fortune 500 company developed a new plastic resin that became the basis of a new product, a plastic molded modular cup pallet, as well as a new venture—the Arnolite Pallet Company, Inc.—when the Fortune 500 company was not interested in developing the idea and released it to the entrepreneur.

METHODS OF GENERATING IDEAS

Even with such a wide variety of sources available, coming up with an idea to serve as the basis for a new venture can still pose a problem, particularly since the idea is the basis for the business. The entrepreneur can use several methods to help generate and test new ideas, such as focus groups, brainstorming, brainwriting, and problem inventory analysis.

Focus Groups

focus groups   Groups of individuals providing information in a structured format

Focus groups have been used for a variety of purposes since the 1950s. In a focus group, a moderator leads a group of people through an open, in-depth discussion rather than simply asking questions to solicit participant response. For a new product area, the moderator focuses the discussion of the group in either a directive or a nondirective manner. The group of frequently 8 to 14 participants is stimulated by comments from each other in creatively conceptualizing and developing a new product idea to fill a market need. One company interested in the women's slipper market received its new product concept for a "warm and comfortable slipper that fits like an old shoe" from a focus group of 12 women from various socioeconomic backgrounds. The concept was developed into a new women's slipper that was a market success. Even the theme of the advertising message came from comments of the focus group members.

In addition to generating new ideas, the focus group is an excellent method for initially screening ideas and concepts. With the use of one of several procedures available, the results can be analyzed more quantitatively, making the focus group a useful method for generating new product ideas.[8]

Brainstorming

brainstorming   A group method for obtaining new ideas and solutions

The *brainstorming* method stimulates people to be creative by meeting with others and participating in organized group experience. Although most of the ideas generated by the group have no basis for further development, sometimes a good idea emerges. This has a greater frequency of occurrence when the brainstorming effort focuses on a specific product or market area. When using brainstorming, four rules need to be followed:

1. No criticism is allowed by anyone in the group—no negative comments.
2. Freewheeling is encouraged—the wilder the idea, the better.
3. Quantity of ideas is desired—the greater the number of ideas, the greater the likelihood of the emergence of useful ideas.
4. Combinations and improvements of ideas are encouraged; ideas of others can be used to produce still another new idea.

The brainstorming session should be fun, with no one dominating or inhibiting the discussion.

A large commercial bank successfully used brainstorming to develop a journal that would provide quality information to its industrial clients. The brainstorming among financial executives focused on the characteristics of the market, the information content, the frequency of issue, and the promotional value of the journal for the bank. Once a general format and issue frequency were determined, focus groups of vice presidents of finance of Fortune 1000 companies were held in three cities—Boston, Chicago, and Dallas—to discuss the new journal format and its relevancy and value to them. The results of these focus groups served as the basis for a new financial journal that was well received by the market.

Brainwriting

Brainwriting is a form of written brainstorming. It was created by Bernd Rohrbach at the end of the 1960s under the name Method 635 and differs from classical brainstorming by giving participants more time to think than in brainstorming sessions, where the ideas are expressed spontaneously. Brainwriting is a silent, written generation of ideas by a group of people. The participants write their ideas on special forms or cards that circulate within the group, which usually consists of six members. Each group member generates and writes down three ideas during a five-minute period. The form is passed on to the adjacent person, who writes down three new ideas, and so on, until each form has passed all participants. A leader monitors the time intervals and can reduce or lengthen the time given to participants according to the needs of the group. Participants can also be spread geographically with the sheets rotated electronically.

Problem Inventory Analysis

problem inventory analysis A method for obtaining new ideas and solutions by focusing on problems

Problem inventory analysis uses individuals in a manner analogous to focus groups to generate new product ideas. However, instead of generating new ideas themselves, consumers are provided with a list of problems in a general product category. They are then asked to identify and discuss products in this category that have the particular problem. This method is often effective since it is easier to relate known products to suggested problems and arrive at a new product idea than to generate an entirely new product idea by itself. Problem inventory analysis can also be used to test a new product idea.

An example of this approach in the food industry is illustrated in Table 4.2. One of the most difficult problems in this example was in developing an exhaustive list of problems, such as weight, taste, appearance, and cost. Once a complete list of problems is developed, individuals can usually associate products with the problem.

Results from product inventory analysis must be carefully evaluated as they may not actually reflect a new business opportunity. For example, General Foods's introduction of a compact cereal box in response to the problem that the available boxes did not fit well

TABLE 4.2   Problem Inventory Analysis

Psychological	Sensory	Activities	Buying Usage	Psychological/Social
A. Weight • Fattening • Empty calories B. Hunger • Filling • Still hungry after eating C. Thirst • Does not quench • Makes one thirsty D. Health • Indigestion • Bad for teeth • Keeps one awake • Acidity	A. Taste • Bitter • Bland • Salty B. Appearance • Color • Unappetizing • Shape C. Consistency/ texture • Tough • Dry • Greasy	A. Meal planning • Forget • Get tired of it B. Storage • Run out • Package would not fit C. Preparation • Too much trouble • Too many pots and pans • Never turns out D. Cooking • Burns • Sticks E. Cleaning • Makes a mess in oven • Smells in refrigerator	A. Portability • Eat away from home • Take lunch B. Portions • Not enough in package • Creates leftovers C. Availability • Out of season • Not in supermarket D. Spoilage • Gets moldy • Goes sour E. Cost • Expensive • Takes expensive ingredients	A. Serve to company • Would not serve to guests • Too much last-minute preparation B. Eating alone • Too much effort to cook for oneself • Depressing when prepared for just one C. Self-image • Made by a lazy cook • Not served by a good mother

Source: From *Journal of Marketing* by Edward M. Tauber. Copyright © 1975 by American Marketing Association (AMA-Chicago). Reproduced with permission of American Marketing Association via Copyright Clearance Center.

on the shelf was not successful, as the problem of package size had little effect on actual purchasing behavior. To ensure the best results, problem inventory analysis should be used primarily to identify product ideas for further evaluation.

CREATIVE PROBLEM SOLVING

creative problem solving
A method for obtaining new ideas focusing on the parameters

Creativity is an important attribute of a successful entrepreneur. Unfortunately, creativity tends to decline with age, education, lack of use, and bureaucracy. Creativity generally declines in stages, beginning when a person starts school. It continues to deteriorate through the teens and continues to progressively decrease through ages 30, 40, and 50. Also, the latent creative potential of an individual can be stifled by perceptual, cultural, emotional, and organizational factors. Creativity can be unlocked and creative ideas and innovations generated by using any of the *creative problem-solving* techniques indicated in Table 4.3.[9]

Brainstorming

The first technique, brainstorming, is probably the most well known and widely used for both creative problem solving and idea generation, previously discussed. In creative problem solving, brainstorming can generate ideas about a problem within a limited time frame

TABLE 4.3 Creative Problem-Solving Techniques	
• Brainstorming	• Forced relationships
• Reverse brainstorming	• Collective notebook method
• Brainwriting	• Attribute listing method
• Gordon method	• Big-dream approach
• Checklist method	• Parameter analysis
• Free association	

through the spontaneous contributions of participants. A good brainstorming session starts with a problem statement that is neither too broad (which would diversify ideas too greatly so that nothing specific would emerge) nor too narrow (which would tend to confine responses). Once the problem statement is prepared, usually 8 to 12 individuals are selected to participate. To avoid inhibiting responses, no group member should be a recognized expert in the field of the problem. All ideas, no matter how illogical, must be recorded, with participants prohibited from criticizing or evaluating during the brainstorming session.

Reverse Brainstorming

reverse brainstorming
A group method for obtaining new ideas focusing on the negative

Reverse brainstorming is similar to brainstorming, except that criticism is allowed. In fact, the technique is based on finding fault by asking the question, "In how many ways can this idea fail?" Since the focus is on the negative aspects of a product, service, or idea, care must be taken to maintain the group's morale. Reverse brainstorming can be effectively used better than other creative techniques to stimulate innovative thinking.[10] The process usually involves the identification of everything wrong with an idea, followed by a discussion of ways to overcome these problems. Reverse brainstorming almost always produces some worthwhile results as it is easier for an individual to be critical about an idea than to come up with a new idea.

Gordon Method

Gordon method   Method for developing new ideas when the individuals are unaware of the problem

The *Gordon method,* unlike many other creative problem-solving techniques, begins with group members not knowing the exact nature of the problem. This ensures that the solution is not clouded by preconceived ideas and behavioral patterns.[11] The entrepreneur starts by mentioning a general concept associated with the problem. The group responds by expressing a number of ideas. Then a concept is developed, followed by related concepts, through guidance by the entrepreneur. The actual problem is then revealed, enabling the group to make suggestions for implementation or refinement of the final solution.

Checklist Method

checklist method
Developing a new idea through a list of related issues

In the *checklist method,* a new idea is developed through a list of related issues or suggestions. The entrepreneur can use the list of questions or statements to guide the direction of developing entirely new ideas or concentrating on specific "idea" areas. The checklist may take any form and be of any length. One general checklist is as follows:[12]

- Put to other uses? New ways to use as-is? Other uses if modified?
- Adapt? What else is like this? What other ideas does this suggest? Does past offer parallel? What could I copy? Whom could I emulate?

GANDHIAN INNOVATION

Due to the worldwide economic downturn and the boom of a new economic class that is more value and environmentally conscious, consumer choice today is undeniably driven by two main factors—affordability and sustainability. Furthermore, the addition of two to three billion middle class consumers, most notably in China and India, has set the tone for a new kind of innovation, that of creating more with less for a broader consumer base. As Prahalad and Mashelkar have noted, this new trend bears strong ties to Mahatma Gandhi's teachings of inclusion such as "I would prize every invention of science made for the benefit of all." Referred to as "Gandhian Innovation" by Prahalad and Mashelkar, nowhere has this new model, whereby innovation is focused on the value to the consumer and not just the bottom line, become more prevalent than in India.

India in recent years has indeed mastered the art of developing products and services to solve seemingly unsolvable problems at incredibly low prices and they continue to push the envelope with innovations that evoke the notion of "Gandhian Innovation." Western companies have much to learn about this new type of innovation, and the pressure to do so is intensifying as the consumer landscape is rapidly changing with the rich, poor, and young in both developed and developing worlds demanding more reliable, practical, economic, and socially and environmentally friendly products and services. From healthcare to telecommunications to auto manufacturing, the pressure to radically innovate crosses all industries and markets. To achieve "Gandhian Innovation," focus must be on the customers' needs and requirements and there are two variables to be considered:

1. **Creating or acquiring new capabilities to solve problems.** Successful and innovative Indian companies have more often than not addressed problems with a less systemic, less traditional approach than their Western counterparts. An example of this was the "reverse pharmacology" approach used by Lupin, an Indian pharmaceutical company, to develop a herbal-based psoriasis treatment. Instead of following the traditional research and development process of development, lab testing, and then consumer testing, Lupin began by collaborating with a practitioner of traditional Indian medicine to develop the product in the field, then gathered clinical data, and lastly gained approval from the Drug Controller General of India to run lab tests. This method of development cost a fraction of what it would have to develop using the traditional approaches. Lupin has passed these savings on to the customers, charging patients only $100 per treatment as opposed to $15,000 for a comparable drug development using the traditional methods in the United States.

2. **Leveraging current technologies and business models to meet a need at a lower cost.** Successful and innovative companies in India have also mastered the process of stripping products down to their bare bones in order to give customers only the services they want at a far lower cost than a similar product with lots of rarely used bells and whistles. The most striking example of this is the creation of the US$2,000 Nano car by Tata Motors. In creating the Nano, Tata Motors worked within its contextual constraints, most notably price sensitivity, to provide the Indian market with a safe, functional, cost effective automobile. To accomplish this feat, they integrated the expertise of numerous foreign and Indian companies to build components that met the Nano specifications for safety and performance while keeping within the price points required. The Nano may only have two doors and a trunk that does not open but Indian consumers are happy to forgo these features for the ability to purchase a car at such a low price point.

As companies continue to move forward, the question innovators must continually ask themselves is how they can do more with less and sell to customers at a lower cost. When a company innovates with these objectives in mind, they will tap into the hearts and wallets of people worldwide who want affordable and sustainable products and services.

Source: For more information, see C. Prahalad and R. Mashelkar, "Innovation's Holy Grail," *Harvard Business Review* (serial online) 88, no. 7/8 (July 2010), pp.132–41.

- Modify? New twist? Change meaning, color, motion, odor, form, shape? Other changes?
- Magnify? What to add? More time? Greater frequency? Stronger? Larger? Thicker? Extra value? Plus ingredient? Duplicate? Multiply? Exaggerate?
- Minify? What substitute? Smaller? Condensed? Miniature? Lower? Shorter? Lighter? Omit? Streamline? Split up? Understated?
- Substitute? Who else instead? What else instead? Other ingredient? Other material? Other process? Other power? Other place? Other approach? Other tone of voice?
- Rearrange? Interchange components? Other pattern? Other layout? Other sequence? Transpose cause and effect? Change track? Change schedule?
- Reverse? Transpose positive and negative? How about opposites? Turn it backward? Turn it upside down? Reverse roles? Change shoes? Turn tables? Turn other cheek?
- Combine? How about a blend, an alloy, an assortment, an ensemble? Combine units? Combine purposes? Combine appeals? Combine ideas?

Free Association

free association
Developing a new idea through a chain of word associations

One of the simplest yet most effective methods that entrepreneurs can use to generate new ideas is *free association*. This technique is helpful in developing an entirely new slant to a problem. First, a word or phrase related to the problem is written down, then another and another, with each new word attempting to add something new to the ongoing thought processes, thereby creating a chain of ideas ending with a new product idea emerging.

Forced Relationships

forced relationships
Developing a new idea by looking at product combinations

Forced relationships, as the name implies, is the process of forcing relationships among some product combinations. It is a technique that asks questions about objects or ideas in an effort to develop a new idea. The new combination and eventual concept is developed through a five-step process:[13]

1. Isolate the elements of the problem.
2. Find the relationships between these elements.
3. Record the relationships in an orderly form.
4. Analyze the resulting relationships to find ideas or patterns.
5. Develop new ideas from these patterns.

Table 4.4 illustrates the use of this technique with paper and soap.

Collective Notebook Method

collective notebook method Developing a new idea by group members regularly recording ideas

In the *collective notebook method,* a small notebook that easily fits in a pocket—containing a statement of the problem, blank pages, and any pertinent background data—is distributed. Participants consider the problem and its possible solutions, recording ideas at least once, but preferably three times, a day. At the end of a week, a list of the best ideas is developed, along with any suggestions.[14] This technique can also be used with a group of individuals who record their ideas, giving their notebooks to a central coordinator who summarizes all the material and lists the ideas in order of frequency of mention. The summary becomes the topic of a final creative focus group discussion by the group participants.

TABLE 4.4   Illustration of Forced Relationship Technique

Elements: Paper and Soap		
Forms	Relationship/Combination	Idea/Pattern
Adjective	Papery soap	Flakes
	Soapy paper	Wash and dry travel aid
Noun	Paper soaps	Tough paper impregnated with soap and usable for washing surfaces
Verb-correlates	Soaped papers	Booklets of soap leaves
	Soap "wets" paper	In coating and impregnation processes
	Soap "cleans" paper	Suggests wallpaper cleaner

Source: Reprinted from William E. Souder and Robert W. Ziegler, "A Review of Creativity and Problem Solving Techniques," *Research Management* (July 1975), p. 37, with permission from Industrial Research Institute.

Attribute Listing

attribute listing
Developing a new idea by looking at the positives and negatives

Attribute listing is an idea-finding technique that requires the entrepreneur to list the attributes of an item or problem and then look at each from a variety of viewpoints. Through this process, originally unrelated objects can be brought together to form a new combination and possible new uses that better satisfy a need.[15]

Big-Dream Approach

big-dream approach
Developing a new idea by thinking without constraints

The *big-dream approach* to coming up with a new idea requires that the entrepreneur dream about the problem and its solution—in other words, think big. Every possibility should be recorded and investigated without regard to all the negatives involved or the resources required. Ideas should be conceptualized without any constraints until an idea is developed into a workable form.[16]

parameter analysis
Developing a new idea by focusing on parameter identification and creative synthesis

Parameter Analysis

A final method for developing a new idea—*parameter analysis*—involves two aspects: parameter identification and creative synthesis.[17] As indicated in Figure 4.1, step one

FIGURE 4.1   Illustration of Parameter Analysis

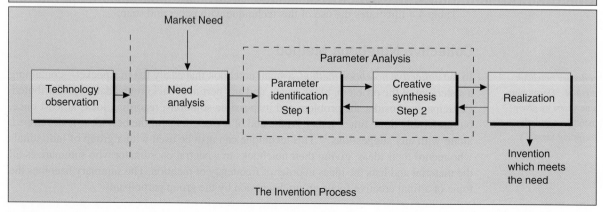

(parameter identification) involves analyzing variables in the situation to determine their relative importance. These variables become the focus of the investigation, with other variables being set aside. After the primary issues have been identified, the relationships between parameters that describe the underlying issues are examined. Through an evaluation of the parameters and relationships, one or more solutions are developed; this solution development is called creative synthesis.

INNOVATION

Innovation is the key to the economic development of any company, region of a country, or country itself. As technologies change, old products decrease in sales and old industries dwindle. Inventions and innovations are the building blocks of the future of any economic unit. Thomas Edison reportedly said that innovative genius is 1 percent inspiration and 99 percent perspiration.

Types of Innovation

There are various levels of innovation based on the uniqueness of the idea. Figure 4.2 shows three major types of innovation, in decreasing order of uniqueness: breakthrough innovation, technological innovation, and ordinary innovation. As you would expect, the fewest innovations are of the breakthrough type. These extremely unique innovations often establish the platform on which future innovations in an area are developed. Given that they are often the basis for further innovation in an area, these innovations, when possible, are protected by strong patents, trade secrets, and/or copyrights (see Chapter 6). Breakthrough innovations include such ideas as: penicillin, the steam engine, the computer, the airplane, the automobile, the Internet, and nanotechnology. One person in the field of nanotechnology who invents solutions to engineering problems is Chung-Chiun Liu, a professor and director of the Center for Micro and Nano Processing at Case Western Reserve University. Dr. Liu is a world expert on sensor technology and invents and builds nano

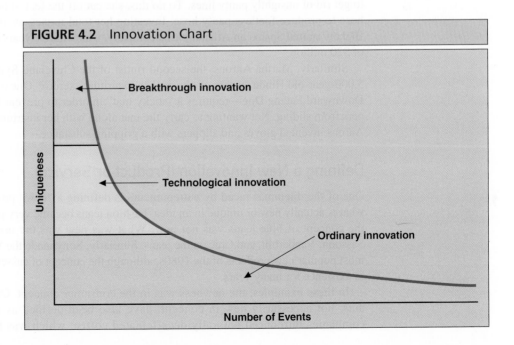

FIGURE 4.2 Innovation Chart

sensor systems for automotive, biomedical, commercial, and industrial applications. Despite publishing a majority of his inventions, Dr. Liu holds numerous patents in electrochemical and sensor technology, many of which have been licensed. One of his inventions is the technology for an electrochemical sensor system that can transmit findings to a nearby receiver. One of these nano devices can analyze the condition of motor oil from inside an engine. Another can measure blood glucose levels. Yet another can detect black mold in homes, hidden bombs, illegal drugs, and termites.

The next type of innovation—technological innovation—occurs more frequently than breakthrough innovation and in general is not at the same level of scientific discovery and advancement. Nonetheless, these are very meaningful innovations, as they do offer advancements in the product/market area. As such, they usually need to be protected. Such innovations as the personal computer, the flip watch for containing pictures, voice and text messaging, and the jet airplane are examples of technological innovations.

The company Hour Power Watch was based on a patented process where the watch can flip up revealing a cavity that can be used for pictures, pills, notes, and even nano dispensing and listening devices. Analiza, Inc., a bioscience company, invented, developed, and sells a system that allows drug manufacturers to quickly screen chemical compounds for the ones most suitable for new drugs. This automated discovery workstation simultaneously tests many different drug compounds, identifying the compounds most suitable for a new drug based on how the human body is likely to react to the compound. The company continues to explore other technological innovations such as an advanced blood test product for diagnosing cancer, a product for extending the shelf life of blood platelets, and a pregnancy test for cows.

The final type of innovation—ordinary innovation—is the one that occurs most frequently. These more numerous innovations usually extend an existing innovation into a better product or service or one that has a different—usually better—market appeal. These innovations usually come from market analysis and pull, not technology push. In other words, the market has a stronger effect on the innovation (market pull) than the technology (technology push). One ordinary innovation was developed by Sara Blakely, who wanted to get rid of unsightly panty lines. To do this, she cut off the feet of her control-top panty hose to produce footless panty hose. Investing her total money available ($5,000), Sara Blakely started Spanx, an Atlanta-based company, which in five years had annual earnings of $20 million.

Similarly, Martha Aarons, the second flutist of the Cleveland Symphony, practices a 5,000-year-old Hindu system of physical and spiritual exercise. One of the exercises—the Downward Facing Dog—requires a "sticky mat" in order to prevent the gloves and slippers from sliding. Not wanting to carry the mat along with her instrument on trips, Martha Aarons invented gloves and slippers with a gripping substance.

Defining a New Innovation (Product or Service)

One of the dilemmas faced by entrepreneurs is defining a "new" product or identifying what is actually new or unique in an idea. Fashion jeans became very popular even though the concept of blue jeans was not new. What was new was the use of names such as Sassoon, Vanderbilt, and Chic on the jeans. Similarly, Sony made the Walkman one of the most popular new products of the 1980s, although the concept of cassette players had been in existence for many years.

In these examples, the newness was in the consumer concept. Other types of products, not necessarily new in concept, have also been defined as new. When coffee companies introduced naturally decaffeinated coffee, which was the only change in the product, the initial promotional campaigns made definite use of the word *new* in the copy.

Other old products have simply been marketed in new packages or containers but have been identified as new products. When soft drink manufacturers introduced the can, some consumers viewed the product as new, even though the only difference from past products was the container. The invention of the aerosol can is another example of a change in the package or container that added an element of newness to old, established products, such as whipped cream, deodorant, and hair spray. Flip-top cans, plastic bottles, aseptic packaging, and the pump have also contributed to a perceived image of newness in old products. Some firms, such as detergent manufacturers, have merely changed the colors of their packages and then added the word *new* to the package and their promotional copy.

Panty hose are another product that has undergone significant marketing strategy changes. L'eggs (a division of Hanes Corporation) was the first to take advantage of supermarket merchandising, packaging, lower prices, and a new display.

In the industrial market, firms may call their products "new" when only slight changes or modifications have been made in the appearance of the product. For example, improvements in metallurgical techniques have modified the precision and strength of many raw materials that are used in industrial products, such as machinery. These improved characteristics have led firms to market products containing the new and improved metals as "new." Similarly, each new version of Microsoft Word usually has mostly minor improvements.

In the process of expanding their sales volume, many companies add products to their product line that are already marketed by other companies. For example, a drug company that added a cold tablet to its product line and a long-time manufacturer of soap pads that entered the dishwasher detergent market both advertised their products as new. In both cases the product was new to the manufacturer but not new to the consumer. With the increased emphasis on diversification in the world economy, this type of situation is quite common. Firms are constantly looking for new markets to enter to increase profits and make more effective use of their resources. Other firms are simply changing one or more of the marketing mix elements to give old products a new image.

Classification of New Products

New products may be classified from the viewpoint of either the consumer or the firm. Both points of view should be used by the entrepreneur to facilitate the success or failure of any new product.

From a Consumer's Viewpoint

There is a broad interpretation of what is a new product from the consumer's viewpoint. One attempt to identify new products classifies the degree of newness according to how much behavioral change or new learning is required by the consumer to use the product. This technique looks at newness in terms of its effect on the consumer rather than whether the product is new to a company, is packaged differently, has changed physical form, or is an improved version of an old or existing product.

The continuum shown in Figure 4.3 contains three categories based on the disrupting influence that use of the product has on established consumption patterns. Most new products tend to fall at the "continuous innovations" end of the continuum. Examples are annual automobile style changes, fashion style changes, package changes, or product size or color changes. Products such as compact discs, the Sony Walkman, and the iPod tend toward the "dynamically continuous" portion of the continuum. The truly new products, called "discontinuous innovations," are rare and require a great deal of new learning by the consumer because these products perform either a previously unfulfilled function or an

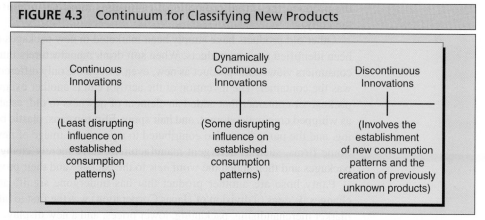

FIGURE 4.3 Continuum for Classifying New Products

Continuous Innovations	Dynamically Continuous Innovations	Discontinuous Innovations
(Least disrupting influence on established consumption patterns)	(Some disrupting influence on established consumption patterns)	(Involves the establishment of new consumption patterns and the creation of previously unknown products)

Source: Adapted from Thomas Robertson, "The Process of Innovation and the Diffusion of Innovation," *Journal of Marketing* (January 1967), pp. 14–19 with permission from American Marketing Association.

existing function in a new way. The Internet is one example of a discontinuous innovation that has radically altered our society's lifestyle. Another is digitalization and digital media. The basis for identifying new products according to their effect on consumer consumption patterns is consistent with the marketing philosophy that "satisfaction of consumer needs" is fundamental to a venture's existence.

From a Firm's Viewpoint   The innovative entrepreneurial firm, in addition to recognizing the consumer's perception of newness, should also classify its new products on some dimensions. One way of classifying the objectives of new products is shown in Figure 4.4. In this classification system, an important distinction is made between new products and new markets (i.e., market development). New products are defined in terms of the amount of improved technology, whereas market development is based on the degree of new segmentation.

FIGURE 4.4 New Product Classification System

Market Newness ↓   Technology Newness →

Product Objectives	No Technological Change	Improved Technology	New Technology
No market change		**Reformation** Change in formula or physical product to optimize costs and quality	**Replacement** Replace existing product with new one based on improved technology
Strengthened market	**Remerchandising** Increase sales to existing customers	**Improved product** Improve product's utility to customers	**Product life extension** Add new similar products to line; serve more customers based on new technology
New market	**New use** Add new segments that can use present products	**Market extension** Add new segments modifying present products	**Diversification** Add new markets with new products developed from new technology

The situation in which there is new technology *and* a new market is the most complicated and difficult and has the highest degree of risk. Since the new product involves new technology and customers that are not now being served, the firm will need a new and carefully planned marketing strategy. Replacements, extensions, product improvements, reformulations, and remerchandising involve product and market development strategies that range in difficulty depending on whether the firm has had prior experience with a similar product or with the same market.

OPPORTUNITY RECOGNITION

Some entrepreneurs need the ability to recognize a business opportunity; this is fundamental to the entrepreneurial process as well as growing a business. A business opportunity represents a possibility for the entrepreneur to successfully fill a large enough unsatisfied need that enough sales and profits result. There has been significant research done on the opportunity recognition process and several models developed.[18] One model that clearly identifies the aspects of this opportunity recognition process is indicated in Figure 4.5.

As is indicated, recognizing an opportunity often results from the knowledge and experience of the individual entrepreneur and, where appropriate, the entrepreneurial business. This prior knowledge is a result of a combination of education and experience, and the relevant experience could be work related or could result from a variety of personal experiences or events. The entrepreneur needs to be aware of this knowledge and experience and have the desire to understand and make use of it. The other important factors in this process are entrepreneurial alertness and entrepreneurial networks. There is an interaction effect between entrepreneurial alertness and the entrepreneur's prior knowledge of markets and customer problems. Those entrepreneurs who have the ability to recognize meaningful business opportunities are in a strategic position to successfully complete the product planning and development process and successfully launch new ventures.

Each and every innovative idea and opportunity should be carefully assessed by the global entrepreneur. One good way to do this is through developing an opportunity assessment plan, discussed in Chapter 5.

FIGURE 4.5   A Model of the Opportunity Recognition Process

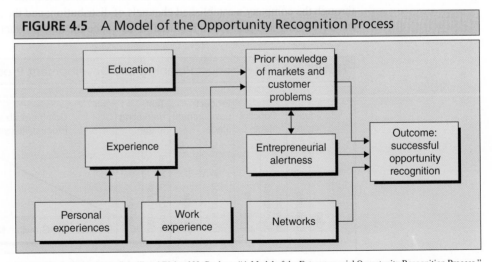

Source: From Alexander Ardichvili and Richard N. Cardozo, "A Model of the Entrepreneurial Opportunity Recognition Process," *Journal of Enterprising Culture* 8, no. 2 (June 2000). p. 103–119. Reprinted with permission of World Scientific Publishing Co, Inc.

PRODUCT PLANNING AND DEVELOPMENT PROCESS

Once ideas emerge from idea sources or creative problem solving, they need further development and refinement. This refining process—the product planning and development process—is divided into five major stages: idea stage, concept stage, product development stage, test marketing stage, and commercialization, which starts the *product life cycle* (see Figure 4.6).[19]

product life cycle The stages each product goes through from introduction to decline

product planning and development process The stages in developing a new product

Establishing Evaluation Criteria

At each stage of the *product planning and development process,* criteria for evaluation need to be established. These criteria should be all-inclusive and quantitative enough to screen the product carefully in the particular stage of development. Criteria should be established to evaluate the new idea in terms of market opportunity, competition, the marketing system, financial factors, and production factors.

A market opportunity in the form of a new or current need for the product idea must exist. The determination of market demand is by far the most important criterion of a proposed new product idea. Assessment of the market opportunity and size needs to consider the characteristics and attitudes of consumers or industries that may buy the product, the size of this potential market in dollars and units, the nature of the market with respect to its stage in the life cycle (growing or declining), and the share of the market the product could reasonably capture.

Current competing producers, prices, and marketing efforts should also be evaluated, particularly in terms of their impact on the market share of the proposed idea. The new idea should be able to compete successfully with products/services already on the market by having features that will meet or overcome current and anticipated competition. The new idea should have some unique differential advantage based on an evaluation of all competitive products/services filling the same consumer needs.

The new idea should have synergy with existing management capabilities and marketing strategies. The firm should be able to use its marketing experience and other expertise in this new product effort. For example, General Electric would have a far less difficult time adding a new lighting device to its line than Procter & Gamble. Several factors should be considered in evaluating the degree of fit: the degree to which the ability and time of the present sales force can be transferred to the new product; the ability to sell the new product through the company's established channels of distribution; and the ability to "piggyback" the advertising and promotion required to introduce the new product.

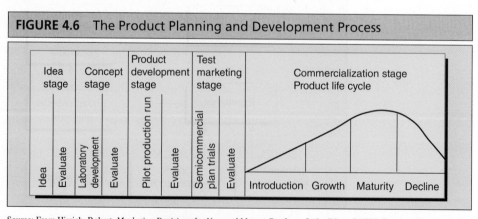

FIGURE 4.6 The Product Planning and Development Process

Source: From Hisrich, Robert, *Marketing Decisions for New and Mature Products,* 2nd edition, © 1991. Reprinted by permission of Pearson Education, Inc., Upper Saddle River, NJ.

ETHICS

CREATING AND MAINTAINING TRUST

Trust is a powerful tool of influence and management. People respond to authority not from a desire to follow orders, but because they trust the leader to steer them in the right direction and uphold his or her commitments. To be successful, the 21st century entrepreneur must abide by the rules of trust and lead by example. Cultivating trust is not only an ethical and moral necessity but also a practical business necessity as work environments built on trust are more productive. This is because people who establish trust and rapport with their employees are better able to motivate employees to be more efficient and work harder. As multiple studies have shown, employees are more willing to go the extra mile for entrepreneurs, managers, and companies they believe in. The essentials to cultivating trust in your company are:

1. **Be honest.** As much of a cliché as this may sound, honesty really is the best policy to align employee behavior with your company's mission and vision. If you are dishonest, you will set the tone for the organization, and employee dishonesty and disloyalty will exist throughout.

2. **Be consistent in what you say and do.** Uphold and respect your company's rules. If you break your own rules, you undermine yourself and will lose employees' trust.

3. **Do not cut corners under any circumstances.** Every entrepreneur will face enormous pressure at some point to take the easy road. However, behaving unethically even under times of high stress undermines trust and sets the precedent for repeated infringements going forward.

As powerful a tool as trust may be, it is also extremely fragile, can be easily destroyed, and is difficult, if not impossible, to rebuild. Trust can also be used in the wrong way, for example, to manipulate or take advantage of a person or situation, which can have devastating consequences on an organization. An example of how trust can be misused was the 1961 Milgram Experiment, conducted by Yale University psychologist Stanley Milgram. In this experiment, Milgram observed the degree to which participants would inflict electric shocks to fellow participants if they were instructed to do so by a "trusted" scientist. The results were staggering, showing that 62.5 percent of the participants followed the instructions of the "trusted" scientist and in this simulated environment would deliver a lethal shock of 450 volts to other participants. This study clearly showed the extent to which people will follow a leader or source of authority. From a managerial perspective, this has important implications. Entrepreneurs, managers, and companies must ensure they are leading the company and employees in the right direction. To avoid potential abuses, the best advice is to build, cultivate, and maintain an environment of trust throughout your company from the very beginning. Ensure that you and your management team are honest, consistent in your words and actions, and do not cut corners regardless of the situation. By incorporating these values into the company culture early on, you will establish yourself as a trusted employer and business partner for many years to come.

Source: For more information on this topic, see J. Hamm, "Trust Me," *Leadership Excellence* (serial online) 28, no. 6 (June 2011), pp. 9–10.

The proposed product/service idea should be able to be supported by and contribute to the company's financial well-being. The manufacturing cost per unit, the marketing expense, and the amount of capital need to be determined along with the break-even point and the long-term profit outlook for the product.

The compatibility of the new product's production requirements with existing plant, machinery, and personnel should also be evaluated. If the new product idea cannot be integrated into existing manufacturing processes, more costs such as plant and equipment are involved which need to be taken into account. All required materials for the production of the product need to be available and accessible in sufficient quantity.

When dealing with competition and competitive situations, concerns regarding ethics and ethical behavior frequently arise, as indicated in the Ethics box.

Entrepreneurs need to be concerned with formally evaluating an idea throughout its evolution. Care must be taken to be sure the product can be the basis for a new venture. This can be done through careful evaluation that results in a go or no-go decision at each of the stages of the product planning and development process: the idea stage, the concept stage, the product development stage, and the test marketing stage.

Idea Stage

idea stage First stage in product development process

Promising new product/service ideas should be identified and impractical ones eliminated in the *idea stage,* allowing maximum use of the company's resources. One evaluation method successfully used in this stage is the systematic market evaluation checklist, where each new idea is expressed in terms of its chief values, merits, and benefits. Consumers are presented with clusters of new product/service values to determine which, if any, new product/service alternatives should be pursued and which should be discarded. Many potential new idea alternatives can be evaluated with this method, with only the promising ideas further developed; resources are then not wasted on ideas that are incompatible with the market's values.

It is also important to determine the need for the new idea as well as its value to the entrepreneur/company. If there is no need for the suggested product, its development should not be continued. Similarly, the new product/service idea should not be developed if it does not have any benefit or value to the entrepreneur or firm. To accurately determine the need for a new idea, it is helpful to define the potential needs of the market in terms of timing, satisfaction, alternatives, benefits and risks, future expectations, price-versus-product performance features, market structure and size, and economic conditions. A form for helping in this need determination process is shown in Table 4.5. The factors in this table should be evaluated not only in terms of the characteristics of the potential new product/service but also in terms of the new product/service's competitive strength relative to each factor. This comparison with competitive products/services will indicate the proposed idea's strengths and weaknesses.

The need determination should focus on the type of need, its timing, the users involved with trying the product/service, the importance of controllable marketing variables, the overall market structure, and the characteristics of the market. Each of these factors should be evaluated in terms of the characteristics of the new idea being considered and the aspects and capabilities of present methods for satisfying the particular need. This analysis will indicate the extent of the opportunity available.

In the determination of the value of the new product/service to the firm, financial scheduling—such as cash outflow, cash inflow, contribution to profit, and return on investment—needs to be evaluated in terms of other product/service ideas as well as investment alternatives. Through the use of the form shown in Table 4.6, the dollar amount of each of the considerations important to the new idea should be determined as accurately as possible. The resulting figures can then be revised as better information becomes available and the product/service continues to be developed.

Concept Stage

concept stage Second stage in product development process

After a new product/service idea has passed the evaluation criteria in the idea stage, it should be further developed and refined through interaction with consumers. In the *concept stage,* the refined idea is tested to determine consumer acceptance. Initial reactions to the concept are obtained from potential customers or members of the distribution channel when appropriate. One method of measuring consumer acceptance is the

TABLE 4.5   Determining the Need for a New Product/Service Idea

Factor	Aspects	Competitive Capabilities	New Product Idea Capability
Type of Need			
Continuing need			
Declining need			
Emerging need			
Future need			
Timing of Need			
Duration of need			
Frequency of need			
Demand cycle			
Position in life cycle			
Competing Ways to Satisfy Need			
Doing without			
Using present way			
Modifying present way			
Perceived Benefits/Risks			
Utility to customer			
Appeal characteristics			
Customer tastes and preferences			
Buying motives			
Consumption habits			
Price versus Performance Features			
Price-quantity relationship			
Demand elasticity			
Stability of price			
Stability of market			
Market Size and Potential			
Market growth			
Market trends			
Market development requirements			
Threats to market			
Availability of Customer Funds			
General economic conditions			
Economic trends			
Customer income			
Financing opportunities			

Source: From Hisrich, Robert, *Marketing Decisions for New and Mature Products,* 2nd edition, © 1991. Reprinted by permission of Pearson Education, Inc., Upper Saddle River, NJ.

TABLE 4.6 Determining the Value of a New Product/Service Idea

Value Consideration	Cost (in $)
Cash Outflow	
R&D costs	
Marketing costs	
Capital equipment costs	
Other costs	
Cash Inflow	
Sales of new product	
Effect on additional sales of existing products	
Salvageable value	
Net Cash Flow	
Maximum exposure	
Time to maximum exposure	
Duration of exposure	
Total investment	
Maximum net cash in a single year	
Profit	
Profit from new product	
Profit affecting additional sales of existing products	
Fraction of total company profit	
Relative Return	
Return on shareholders' equity (ROE)	
Return on investment (ROI)	
Cost of capital	
Present value (PV)	
Discounted cash flow (DCF)	
Return on assets employed (ROA)	
Return on sales	
Compared to Other Investments	
Compared to other product opportunities	
Compared to other investment opportunities	

Source: From Hisrich, Robert, *Marketing Decisions for New and Mature Products,* 2nd edition, © 1991. Reprinted by permission of Pearson Education, Inc., Upper Saddle River, NJ.

conversational interview in which selected respondents are exposed to statements that reflect the physical characteristics and attributes of the product/service idea. Where competing products (or services) exist, these statements can also compare their primary features. Favorable as well as unfavorable product features can be discovered by analyzing consumers' responses, with the favorable features then being incorporated into the new product/service.

Features, price, and promotion should be evaluated for both the concept being studied and any major competing products by asking the following questions:

How does the new concept compare with competitive products/services in terms of quality and reliability?

Is the concept superior or deficient compared with products/services currently available in the market?

Is this a good market opportunity for the firm?

Similar evaluations should be done for all the aspects of the marketing strategy.

Product Development Stage

product development stage Third stage in product development process

In the *product development stage,* consumer reaction to the physical product/service is determined. One tool frequently used in this stage is the consumer panel, in which a group of potential consumers is given product samples. Participants keep a record of their use of the product and comment on its virtues and deficiencies. This technique is more applicable for product ideas and works for only some service ideas.

The panel of potential customers can also be given a sample of the product and one or more competitive products simultaneously. Then one of several methods—such as multiple brand comparisons, risk analysis, level of repeat purchases, or intensity of preference analysis—can be used to determine consumer preference.

Test Marketing Stage

test marketing stage Final stage before commercialization in product development process

Although the results of the product development stage provide the basis of the final marketing plan, a market test can be done to increase the certainty of successful commercialization. This last step in the evaluation process, the *test marketing stage,* provides actual sales results, which indicate the acceptance level of consumers. Positive test results indicate the degree of probability of a successful product launch and company formation.

E-COMMERCE AND BUSINESS START-UP

Throughout the evaluation process of a potential new idea as well as in the development of marketing strategy, the role of e-commerce needs to be continually assessed. E-commerce offers the entrepreneur the opportunity to be very creative and innovative. Its increasing importance is indicated in the continually increasing amount of both business-to-business and business-to-consumer e-commerce sales. E-commerce (Internet spending) continues to increase on an annual basis. According to comScore, in spite of continued economic uncertainty 2011 was a strong year for retail e-commerce. Total U.S. e-commerce spending reached $256 billion in 2011, an increase of 12 percent from 2010. Out of this $256 billion, travel e-commerce spending grew by 11 percent to $94.5 billion, while retail (nontravel) e-commerce spending jumped 13 percent to $161.5 billion for the year.

The fastest growing retail e-commerce category in 2011 was digital content and subscriptions, composed mainly of digital content downloads such as music, movies, TV shows, and e-books, at a growth rate of 26 percent. Consumer electronics ranked as the second fastest-growing category in 2011 at 18 percent, driven by low-priced flat panel TVs, tablets, and e-readers; jewelry and watches, which grew by 17 percent, also had a strong year as the economy recovered from the recession.

Factors that facilitated the high growth of commerce on a business-to-consumer or business-to-business basis include widespread use of personal computers, the adoption of intranets in companies, the acceptance of the Internet as a business communications platform, and faster and more secure systems. Numerous benefits—such as access to a broader customer base, lower information dissemination costs, lower transaction costs, and the interactive nature of the Internet—will continue to expand the volume of e-commerce.

Using E-Commerce Creatively

Electronic commerce is increasingly used by existing corporations to extend their marketing and sales channels, as well as being the basis for some new ventures. The Internet is especially important for small and medium-sized companies, as it enables them to minimize marketing costs while reaching broader markets. An entrepreneur starting an Internet commerce venture needs to address the same strategic and tactical questions as any other entrepreneur. Additionally, some specific issues of doing business online need to be addressed due to the new and perpetually evolving technology used in Internet commerce. An entrepreneur has to decide whether he or she will run the Internet operations within the company or outsource these operations to Internet specialists. In the case of in-house operations, computer servers, routers, and other hardware and software as well as support services such as Web site information have to be maintained. Alternatively, there are numerous possibilities for outsourcing the Internet business. The entrepreneur can hire Web developers to design the company's Web pages and then upload them on the server maintained by the Internet service provider. In this case, the entrepreneur's main task is to regularly update the information on the Web pages. Another option is to use the packages for e-commerce available from different software companies. The correct decision between in-house operations or outsourcing depends on the size of the Internet-related business, particularly where Internet operations are the company's primary business, and the relative costs of each alternative.

The two major components of Internet commerce are front-end and back-end operations. Front-end operations are encompassed in the Web site's functionality. Search capabilities, shopping cart, and secure payment are only a few examples. The biggest mistake made by many companies on the Internet is believing that an attractive, interactive Web site will secure success; this leads to underestimating the importance of back-end operations. Seamless integration of customer orders should be developed, with distribution channels and manufacturing capabilities that are flexible enough to handle any specific customer's desire. The integration of front-end and back-end operations represents the greatest challenge for doing Internet business and at the same time provides the opportunity for developing a sustained competitive advantage.

Web Sites

The use of Web sites by entrepreneurial firms has been increasing at a significant rate. About 90 percent of small businesses today have operating Web sites. However, the majority of small businesses and entrepreneurs feel that they do not have the technical capability to build and operate quality Web sites.

One of the keys to a good Web site is ease of use. In a 2008 ranking by Forrester of 114 Web sites according to usefulness, ease of use, and enjoyability, Barnes & Noble was ranked number one, followed by USAA, Borders, Amazon, Costco, and Hampton Inn/Suites.

In developing a Web site, an entrepreneur needs to remember that a Web site is a communication vehicle and should address the following questions: Who is the audience?

What are the objectives for the site? What do you want the consumers to do upon visiting the site? Is the Web site an integral part of the venture's total communications program? In addressing these questions, the entrepreneur needs to structure the Web site and organize the information to effectively engage the target market. This requires that the material be fresh, with new material added on a regular basis. The material should be interactive to engage the individual. And, of course the Web site needs to be known and as visible as possible.

One of the most important features of every Web site is search capability. It should be easy to find information about the products and services that a company offers over the Internet. This function can be accomplished through an advanced search tool, site map, or subject browsing. Other functions that should be available on every e-commerce Web site are shopping cart, secure server connection, credit card payment, and a customer feedback feature. Shopping cart is software that accepts product orders and automatically calculates and totals customers' orders based on the product availability information. Orders and other sensitive customer information should be transferred only through secure servers. Another important feature of the Web site is an e-mail response system that allows customers to send their feedback to the company.

There are three characteristics of successful Web sites: speed, speed, and speed. Additionally, a Web site should be easy to use, customized for specific market target groups, and compatible with different browsers. Ease of use goes hand in hand with speed; if visitors find Web pages easy to navigate, then they will be able to quickly find products, services, or information. One of the greatest advantages of the Internet is the simplicity of customization of the Web site content for different market segments. It should also take into consideration the international nature of the Internet and any nontargeted segments. For example, if a company is not planning to sell products beyond the U.S. border, then it should clearly indicate on its Web site that it is shipping its products only within the United States. If, on the other hand, the company is targeting international markets as well, then issues of translation and cultural adaptation need to be considered. As for the technical aspects, the designer should ensure that the Web site works properly in different browsers and platforms that are used by Internet visitors. Once the Web site is operational, it is important that it appears in all marketing materials, including business cards, company letterhead, and of course company advertising.

A good example of Web site development and operation is LinkedIn (http://www.linkedin.com/). The Santa Monica, California–based company is a business-related social networking site mainly used for professional networking. The goals of the Web site are to foster member growth, be the essential source of professional insights, increase monetization while creating value for their members, and expand internationally. To achieve these goals, the Web site allows its members to efficiently connect with an enormous reservoir of professionals from about every industry with its very easy-to-use search and filtering features. To achieve viral growth the site is enhanced with search engine optimization and integrated with many applications. The site invests heavily in targeting capabilities and analytics to efficiently and effectively identify candidates for a particular opportunity resulting in benefits for both members and customers. The platform is also being made available in more languages to further develop their brand across various international geographies.

There are some free Web site hosting solutions available to the entrepreneur. These include:

- Microsoft: http://www.microsoft.com/office/olsb/OLSB%20Home%20US.htm
  Six months free Web hosting and e-mails; a very good option.

- 000Webhost: http://www.000webhost.com/features
  Another fully free hosting company.
- Zymic: http://www.zymic.com/free-web-hosting/
  A free Web hosting site.
- Webs: http://www.webs.com/
  A free professional-looking Web site builder.

Tracking Customer Information

Electronic databases support the strategy of personalized one-to-one marketing. The database can not only track activity of the industry, segment, and company but also support personal marketing targeted at individual clients. The motivation for tracking customer information is to capture customer attention with customized one-to-one marketing. Care must be taken in doing this to follow the laws protecting the privacy of individuals.

Doing E-Commerce as an Entrepreneurial Company

The decision to develop a website and an e-commerce site for your business is essential today. Several product/service characteristics are necessary to make this work and to make it easy to facilitate transactions. First, the products should be able to be delivered economically and conveniently. Second, the product has to be interesting for a large number of people and be able to be distributed outside its own geographical location. Third, online operations have to be cost effective, easy to use, and secure. One student wanted to fulfill her passion of helping women in a poor village in Peru distribute their product. Her company started by selling on a newly created Web site.

Conflict between traditional and online marketing channels (channel conflict) arises because of disagreements between manufacturers and retailers, which eventually lead into a hostile, competing position of once-partnering companies. Partners in supply chains have to focus on their core competencies and outsource the noncore activities. When introducing the competing distribution channels, companies have to weigh the costs and benefits of that decision while taking into account the loss of existing business.

IN REVIEW

SUMMARY

The starting point for any successful new venture is the basic product or service to be offered. This idea can be generated internally or externally through various techniques.

The possible sources of new ideas range from the comments of consumers to changes in government regulations. Monitoring the comments of acquaintances, evaluating the new products offered by competitors, becoming familiar with the ideas contained in previously granted patents, and becoming actively involved in research and development are techniques for coming up with a good product idea. In addition, there are specific techniques entrepreneurs can use to generate ideas. For example, a better understanding of the consumer's true opinions can be gained from using a focus group. Another consumer-oriented approach is problem inventory analysis, through which consumers associate particular problems with specific products and then develop a new product that does not contain the identified faults.

Brainstorming, a technique useful in both idea generation and problem solving, stimulates creativity by allowing a small group of people to work together in an open, nonstructured environment. Other techniques useful in enhancing the creative process are checklists of related questions, free association, idea notebooks, and the "big-dream" approach. Some techniques are very structured, while others are designed to be more free form. Each entrepreneur should know the techniques available.

Once the idea or group of ideas is generated, the planning and development process begins. Each idea must be screened and evaluated to determine its appropriateness for further development. Ideas showing the most potential are then moved through the concept stage, the product development stage, the test marketing stage, and finally into commercialization. The product or idea can then be the basis of a successful venture.

RESEARCH TASKS

1. Choose a product or technology. Interview five consumers who buy that product and ask them what major problems they have with the product (or what major things they dislike about it). Then ask them to describe the attributes of the "perfect product" that would satisfy all their needs and replace the existing product. Next, interview the representatives of five companies that offer the product and ask them what they believe are the major problems customers experience with their product. Come up with some futuristic solutions.

2. Obtain a patent of a technology (e.g., go to the patent office Web site) and come up with 10 creative uses of the technology.

3. Choose three different products that you might be interested in purchasing and that are sold on the Internet. For each product, visit three Web sites and go through the process as if you were going to actually purchase the product. Which Web site was the best? Why? Which was the worst? Why? If you could create the perfect Web site, what features would it have?

CLASS DISCUSSION

1. Take the following problem statement and brainstorm solutions. Be prepared to present your three most "creative" solutions. Problem statement: "Customers too frequently use an airline and fly to a destination only to find out that their luggage has not arrived."

2. Choose a product and use the checklist method to develop new ideas. Be prepared to discuss your product and the three most creative ideas generated.

3. Do you think that the Internet can be a source of advantage for one firm over other firms or do you think that it is a necessity just to be able to compete? Be prepared to justify your answer.

SELECTED READINGS

Fillis, Ian; and Ruth Rentschler. (March 2010). The Role of Creativity in Entrepreneurship. *Journal of Enterprising Culture,* vol. 18, no. 1, pp. 49–81.

Ian Fillis and Ruth Rentschler first explore the classical definition of entrepreneurship which includes three major dimensions: innovation, risk-taking, and being proactive. The authors investigate the link between creativity and existing entrepreneurs. The authors argue that entrepreneurs are best poised to act on the opportunity created by globalization and technological advances because of their predisposition for creativity. As a result, they are able to create competitive advantages for their organizations.

Harryson, Sigvald J. (November 2008). Entrepreneurship through Relationships— Navigating from Creativity to Commercialization. *R&D Management*, vol. 38, no. 3, pp. 290–310.

Sigvald Harryson's paper investigates the importance of relationships in value creation for the entrepreneurial enterprises. Harryson argues that there are three unique network types: creativity networks, transformation networks, and process networks. The author suggests that a different leadership style is necessary during each unique phase, and relationships between stakeholders must be managed differently at each stage of the development process to create maximum value for the organization.

Korn, Melissa; and Amir Efrati. (September 1, 2011). Biz Stone Goes Back to College, This Time as Adviser to M.B.A.s. *Wall Street Journal*, p. B.6.

The Wall Street Journal interviewed Christopher Stone, Twitter, Inc.'s co-founder, who is serving as an Executive Fellow at the Haas School of Business for one year. Stone, a serial entrepreneur, discusses his own experience as an entrepreneur as well as teaching entrepreneurship to MBA students.

Lisa Girard. (June 3, 2011). 5 Creativity Exercises to Find your Passion. *Entrepreneur.com.* http://www.entrepreneur.com/article/219709.

In this article, the author suggests five techniques for entrepreneurs in using creativity to find their passions. The author argues that finding one's passion is the fastest route to launching a successful business. The steps for exploring creativity are: revisiting childhood passions, making a "creativity board" of images, making a list of people you want to emulate, doing what you love even before the business plan, and taking a break from "business thinking."

Fadel, Stephen. (January/February 2010). Resources to Encourage Entrepreneurial Creativity and Innovation. *Online*, vol. 34, pp. 22–24, 26–30.

The author of this article is a business reference librarian at the University of Maine, Orono. The article is a helpful resource for entrepreneurs seeking information and resources from a variety of lesser-known publications and other outlets, including sample business plans as well as industry-specific information.

END NOTES

1. P. Omidyar, "The World's Online Marketplace," Academy of Achievement, Interview, October 27, 2000.
2. J. Viegas, *Pierre Omidyar: The Founder of eBay* (Rosen Publishing Group, 2006).
3. Academy of Achievement, "Biography: Pierre Omidyar," 2000, Achievement.org: http://www.achievement.org/autodoc/page/omi0bio-1, retrieved September 23, 2011.
4. A&E Television Networks, "Pierre Omidyar Biography," 2011, Biography.com: http://www.biography.com/articles/Pierre-Omidyar-9542205, retrieved September 23, 2011.
5. Omidyar, "The World's Online Marketplace."
6. Ibid.
7. Omidyar Network, "About Us: Evolution," 2011, Omidyar.com: http://www.omidyar.com/about_us, retrieved October 2, 2011.
8. For an in-depth presentation on focus group interviews in general and quantitative applications, see "Conference Focuses on Focus Groups: Guidelines, Reports, and 'the Magic Plaque,'" *Marketing News,* May 21, 1976, p. 8; Keith K. Cox,

James B. Higginbotham, and John Burton, "Application of Focus Group Interviews in Marketing," *Journal of Marketing* 40, no. 1 (January 1976), pp. 77–80; and Robert D. Hisrich and Michael P. Peters, "Focus Groups: An Innovative Marketing Research Technique," *Hospital and Health Service Administration* 27, no. 4 (July–August 1982), pp. 8–21.

9. A discussion of each of these techniques can be found in Robert D. Hisrich and Michael P. Peters, *Marketing Decisions for New and Mature Products* (Columbus, OH: Charles E. Merrill, 1984), pp. 131–46; and Robert D. Hisrich, "Entrepreneurship and Intrapreneurship: Methods for Creating New Companies That Have an Impact on the Economic Renaissance of an Area," in *Entrepreneurship, Intrapreneurship, and Venture Capital* (Lexington, MA: Lexington Books, 1986), pp. 77–104.

10. For a discussion of this technique, see J. Geoffrey Rawlinson, *Creative Thinking and Brainstorming* (New York: John Wiley & Sons, 1981), pp. 124, 126; and W. E. Souder and R. W. Ziegler, "A Review of Creativity and Problem-Solving Techniques," *Research Management* 20 (July 1977), p. 35.

11. This method is discussed in J. W. Haefele, *Creativity and Innovation* (New York: Van Nostrand Reinhold, 1962), pp. 145–47; Sidney J. Parnes and Harold F. Harding (eds.), *A Source Book for Creative Thinking* (New York: Charles Scribner's Sons, 1962), pp. 307–23; and Souder and Ziegler, "A Review of Creativity and Problem-Solving Techniques," pp. 34–42.

12. Alex F. Osborn, *Applied Imagination* (New York: Scribner Book Companies, 1957), p. 318.

13. Rawlinson, *Creative Thinking,* pp. 52–59.

14. For a thorough discussion of the collective notebook method, see Haefele, *Creativity and Innovation,* p. 152.

15. Parnes and Harding, *A Source Book for Creative Thinking,* p. 308.

16. For a discussion of this approach, see M. O. Edwards, "Solving Problems Creatively," *Journal of Systems Management* 17, no. 1 (January–February 1966), pp. 16–24.

17. The procedure for parameter analysis is thoroughly discussed in Yao Tzu Li, David G. Jansson, and Ernest G. Cravalho, *Technological Innovation in Education and Industry* (New York: Reinhold, 1980), pp. 26–49, 277–86.

18. For some examples of this research and models, see Lenny Herron and Harry J. Sapienza, "The Entrepreneur and the Initiation of New Venture Launch Activities," *Entrepreneurship: Theory and Practice* (Fall 1992), pp. 49–55; C. M. Gaglio and R. P. Taub, "Entrepreneurs and Opportunity Recognition," Babson Research Conference (May 1992), pp. 136–47; L. Busenitz, "Research on Entrepreneurial Alertness," *Journal of Small Business Management* 34, no. 4 (1996), pp. 35–44; S. Shane, "Prior Knowledge and Discovery of Entrepreneurial Opportunities," *Organizational Science* 11, no. 4 (2000), pp. 448–69; Hean Tat Keh, Maw Der Foo, and Boon Chong Lim, "Opportunity Evaluation under Risky Conditions: The Cognitive Process of Entrepreneurs," *Entrepreneurship: Theory and Practice* (Winter 2002), pp. 125–48; and Noel J. Lindsay and Justin Craig, "A Framework for Understanding Opportunity Recognition," *Journal of Private Equity* (Winter 2002), pp. 13–25.

19. For a detailed description of this process, see Robert D. Hisrich and Michael P. Peters, *Marketing Decisions for New and Mature Products* (Columbus, OH: Charles E. Merrill, 1991), pp. 157–78.

5

IDENTIFYING AND ANALYZING DOMESTIC AND INTERNATIONAL OPPORTUNITIES

1

To understand the aspects and importance of identifying good domestic or international opportunities.

2

To be able to identify these opportunities.

3

To be able to create an opportunity assessment plan.

4

To present the problems and barriers of entering global markets.

5

To be able to select a global market.

6

To understand the options for entering a foreign market.

OPENING PROFILE

SALONI MALHOTRA

As the saying goes, necessity is the mother of invention, and nowhere in the world is there more need than in underdeveloped and emerging markets. Social entrepreneurs worldwide are aggressively working to find ways to increase quality of life in these regions. One such entrepreneur is Saloni Malhotra, a young Indian woman with a dream to create sustainable advancement for the people of her beloved country.

www.desicrew.in

India has made waves in the global economy with its recent insurgence as a competitor on a global scale. Now ranked as the ninth largest economy in the world and the fourth based on purchase power parity, India has played a crucial role in globalization and the rise of emerging markets since economic liberalization in 1991.[1,2] With a population of nearly 1.2 billion, it is not surprising that the people of India have become the country's greatest asset. As outsourcing started to become popular with corporations in the Western world, India stepped up and made sure they were the front-runner in providing an educated workforce for lucrative industries such as computer software and technology, telecommunications, and engineering. However, the demographic disparity that had existed for centuries among the people in the region became more apparent with the emergence of prosperity in the urban areas. The growing job market within the large cities such as New Delhi, Mumbai, Bangalore, Kolkata, and Chennai caused an urban migration from the countryside. However, the already overcrowded cities could not support the entire population, much less give them a better quality of life, and so the chasm continued to widen.

This rural-urban gap is not unique to India, but with such an immense population, it is more pronounced than in other areas of the world. With the cities supporting only 30 percent of the total population, an astounding 360 million people live in the rural areas of India that offer few options for generating income besides simple agriculture, even for citizens who have an education. That is to say, there are nearly 50 million more people living close to poverty in rural India than the number of people that populate the entire United States.

It was this phenomenon combined with an ambition to start her own company that convinced Saloni Malhotra to take a risk with what was considered at the time to be a difficult business model. With the help of her mentor, Professor Ashok Jhunjhunwala from IIT Madras, Malhotra proposed a for-profit venture that would address current social issues.[3] Rather than viewing the people living in rural villages as ignorant farmers, she believed that they are an untapped resource looking anxiously for any opportunity to live up to their potential. In order to utilize this workforce, she proposed taking one of the business models that had created so much prosperity in the cities and bringing it to the countryside. Thus, in 2007, after a couple of years of research, overcoming obstacles, and breaking down barriers, DesiCrew was born as the first socially motivated rural BPO (business process outsourcing).

Malhotra was only 26 years old when she founded her company. With the support of the Rural Technology and Business Incubator at IIT Madras, she was able to grow her small business into a viable and profitable entity, but not without jumping over numerous hurdles.[4] By definition, BPO is a method by which certain business operations or processes are outsourced or subcontracted to a third party. This method was previously used by manufacturing companies that found it was cheaper to set up factories in low-wage regions of the world and then transport goods to markets for sale. Later, the most popular BPO businesses were offshore call-centers, made especially famous by Indian companies. By the time Malhotra generated her idea, BPOs were synonymous with high-tech operations such as software development and business analytics.[5]

As BPOs moved up the value chain, her dream of creating rural centers seemed less and less possible. How can people program software if there is no electricity or Internet? Why would a client hire a company for business analysis if the employees can't speak English well? In order to answer these questions, Malhotra had to start from the bottom up. First, she had to establish some sort of infrastructure to enable vehicle transportation to and from the business centers, set up telecommunications systems, and ensure reliable power sources would be able to reach the centers. Although it was a slow process, she was able to create a distribution operations model with the main office in Chennai acting as the conduit between the client and the rural centers. In this manner, the BPO is accessible to the large corporations in the cities while conducting operations in the low-cost regions. The lower overhead cost of human capital is then passed on to the client. It is a win-win situation with the client enjoying lower costs of service and the people of the rural villages enjoying the opportunity to earn more money and generate income through knowledge work instead of agriculture.

The first rural centers Malhotra set up were focused on simpler tasks such as data entry and data conversion. However, as the centers became more structurally sound, their work became more significant. Through extensive employee training programs in basic office management, HR practices, computer usage, and data entry, DesiCrew was able to reach the crucial point at which their work was the same quality standard as their competitors in the city. Malhotra states that one of their biggest challenges in starting up the company was changing the mindset of the people in urban India that "work could be done out of the hinterland and with the same quality."[6] Once she proved the competency of the people, the validity of her business model began to take hold. With five established annuity clients and 21 clients overall, DesiCrew continues to expand into other rural areas of India.[7]

One resulting social impact of DesiCrew is reverse migration. By creating local knowledge work jobs, giving people proper training in transferable skills, and helping employees to make and save more money, the business model removes the need for people in villages to move to the cities. In the past, people born in the country who did not want to be farmers and/or who wanted the chance for a better life outside of their little village would have had to move to the nearest city to find a knowledge-based job. Although the city jobs paid well, the cost of living in the cities is significantly more than in the country, providing much less money to send home to their families. Although DesiCrew pays less than traditional BPOs, it allows the workers to remain at home where the cost of living is low. Continuing the economic growth cycle, the saved money is then spent in the village, rather than the city, helping to stimulate economic growth throughout the community. The change of keeping the rupees in circulation in the village provides an opportunity to increase quality of life for those who live and work there.

Nearly 70 percent of DesiCrew employees are female. Why the gender disparity? Culturally, women tend to live with their parents until they marry, at which time they move into their husband's home. In recent years, women began to leave home for school or to work in the cities to generate extra money for their families. However, once they get married, it is conventional for them to move into the home of their husband which is usually in a village. The education, training, or work experience the women gained before marriage is squandered due to a lack of jobs outside of the cities. When a company like DesiCrew sets up shop in one of these rural areas, they find plenty of women who are capable and eager to work. This not only boosts financial security for the family, but also gives the women an increased social standing. In turn, the women experience increased self-confidence that motivates them to work hard, learn more, and continue to develop.

Malhotra intends to continue building her company and hopes that it will increase to 1,000 employees within the next couple of years. In addition to physical expansion, she also envisions the company moving up the value chain in terms of services offered. She believes that if qualified people are given the right resources, such as education and training, they can do anything regardless of whether they are from a city or a village.[8] Teaching the villagers proper English is high on the priority list, as Malhotra believes that the company cannot move into more value-added work without being able to communicate directly with the hiring companies. In addition, considering India is a country with 15 official languages, the rural centers span multiple regional dialects. It is important for them to speak English not only because it is "the most important language for national, political, and commercial communication," as described by the CIA in the World Factbook, but also so the company can communicate internally as well.[9]

Saloni Malhotra's ambition to change the world for the better is not unique, but it is important in the sense that she acted on her ambition. In opposition to her parents' will for her to become an engineer (or a doctor), she decided to take a risk. Some still say her business model is crazy, even though the company is turning a profit, however meager.[10] In her view, adversity is well met if one has the support and mentorship of a good team and good friends. With such a young face at the forefront, DesiCrew continues to bring hope and prosperity to those who need it most.

INTRODUCTION

Unlike Saloni Malhotra, many entrepreneurs find it difficult to identify a market opportunity and expand the venture into new markets. To start and expand a venture, an entrepreneur needs to identify opportunities for domestic and international expansion. As a new venture grows and matures, a need can develop for different management skills as well as for a new infusion of the entrepreneurial spirit (corporate entrepreneurship), discussed in Chapter 2. Some entrepreneurs forget that in business the only constant is change. Entrepreneurs like Saloni Malhotra or Mal Mixon, CEO of Invacare, who understand this axiom, effectively manage change by continually adapting organizational culture, structure, procedures, strategic direction, and products in both a domestic and an international orientation. Entrepreneurs in such developed countries as the United States, Japan, the United Kingdom, and the European Union must sell their products in a variety of new and different domestic market areas early on in the development of their firms or, as in the case of Mal Mixon's Invacare, manufacture, market, and prosper in international markets.

Never before in the history of the world have there been such interesting and exciting international business opportunities. The opening of the once-controlled economies of Eastern and Central Europe, the former U.S.S.R., the People's Republic of China, and Vietnam to market-oriented enterprise and the advancement of the Pacific Rim are just a few of the myriad of possibilities for entrepreneurs wanting to start or grow in a foreign market.

As more and more countries become market oriented and developed, the distinction between foreign and domestic markets is becoming less pronounced. What was once only produced domestically is now produced internationally. This blurring of national identities will continue to accelerate as more and more products are introduced outside domestic boundaries earlier in the life of entrepreneurial firms.

In the past decade, organizations have been attempting to redefine themselves as truly global organizations. The pressure to internationalize is being felt in virtually every organization: nonprofit and for-profit, public and private, large and small. This need to internationalize is accelerating due to the self-interest of the organization as well as the impact of a variety of external events and forces. Who would have believed a decade ago that today seven-eighths of the markets of the world would have some degree of market economics? Who would have ever imagined some of the trading agreements occurring today? Or who would have imagined the rise of economic power in China to become one of the largest economies in the world?

These changes are well recognized by organizations, which are investing trillions of dollars in a world economy that features emerging markets as the vehicles of future growth and one in need of major investment in infrastructure. Just ask the potato farmers in the Chuvash Republic of Russia, who saw some of their crop rot because of inadequate distribution and warehousing, whether there is a need for such investment in infrastructure. Or, ask the economics professor in a developing country, who has to leave the university to find other employment due to the low university wages, whether massive investment is needed. Clearly, developing countries need training and education as well as infrastructure to support their development and growth in the next century.

There are new market opportunities in Latin and South America, Africa, the Pacific Rim, Vietnam, Iraq, and countries throughout the world that are in transition. These areas are becoming major attractions to companies that want to grow and establish a market position as these economies change and go through privatization and deregulation.

The internationalization of entrepreneurship and business creates wealth and employment that benefits individuals and nations throughout the world. International entrepreneurship is exciting as it combines the many aspects of domestic entrepreneurship with such other disciplines as anthropology, economics, geography, history, jurisprudence, and language.

In today's hypercompetitive world with rapidly changing technology, it is essential for an entrepreneur to at least consider entering a market outside the company's national borders.

OPPORTUNITY RECOGNITION AND THE OPPORTUNITY ASSESSMENT PLAN

The key to successful domestic and international entrepreneurship is to develop an idea that has a market with a need for the product or service idea conceived. The ideation process explained in Chapter 4 needs to be thought of in terms of satisfying a specific market need or as one entrepreneur stated, "making the customer whether a business, a consumer, or a government more profitable."

What is deemed to be "profitable" varies by the product/service idea and particularly whether the idea is an industrial product (business-to-business market) or a consumer product (business-to-consumer market). This is best accomplished through the development of an opportunity assessment plan.

An opportunity assessment plan is *not* a business plan. Compared to a business plan, it:

- Is shorter.
- Focuses on the opportunity, not the venture.
- Has no computer-based spreadsheet.
- Is the basis for making the decision to either act on an opportunity or wait until another, better opportunity comes along.

An opportunity assessment plan has four sections—two major sections and two minor sections. The first major section develops the product/service idea, analyzes the competitive products and companies, and identifies the uniqueness of the idea in terms of its unique selling propositions. This section includes:

- A description of the product or service.
- The market need for the product or service.
- The specific aspects of the product or service.
- The competitive products available filling this need and their features.
- The companies in this product market space.
- The unique selling propositions of this product or service.

Some data sources for determining competition and industry size are discussed in the next section later in this chapter.

The second major section of the opportunity assessment plan focuses on the market—its size, trends, characteristics, and growth rate. It includes:

- The market need filled.
- The social condition underlining this market need.
- Any market research data available to describe this market need.
- The size, trends, and characteristics of the domestic and/or international market.
- The growth rate of the market.

The third section (a minor one) focuses on the entrepreneur and the management team in terms of their background, education, skills, and experience. It should include answers to the following questions:

- Why does this opportunity excite you?
- How does the product/service idea fit into your background and experience?

- What business skills do you have?
- What business skills are needed?
- Do you know someone who has these skills?

The final section of the opportunity assessment plan develops a time line indicating what steps need to be taken to successfully launch the venture and translate the idea into a viable business entity. This minor section should focus on:

- Identifying each step.
- Determining the sequence of activities and putting these critical steps into some sequential order.
- Identifying what will be accomplished in each step.
- Determining the time and money required at each step.
- Determining the total amount of time and money needed.
- Identifying the source of this needed money.

INFORMATION SOURCES

There are many sources of information both on competitive companies and products/ services and the market size and characteristics available to the entrepreneur in identifying an appropriate opportunity. These will be discussed in terms of assistance, general information sources, industry and market information sources, competitive company and product information, government sources, search engines, trade associations, and trade publications.

Assistance

Information and assistance is readily available for entrepreneurs, particularly those starting a new venture. SCORE (www.score.org) is a nonprofit organization that provides free online and in-person assistance in about 400 chapter locations throughout the United States. The assistance takes the form of training, consulting, and mentoring provided mainly by retired executives and entrepreneurs.

Small Business Development Centers (sba.gov/aboutsba/sbaprograms/sbdc/sbdclocator/index.html) has small business development centers in over 1,100 locations throughout the United States. It provides counseling, training, and technical assistance on all aspects of starting and managing a new venture. Each location also has an on-site resource library. These centers are a part of the overall SBA (Small Business Administration) (sba.gov), which also provides a wide variety of resources and tools for the entrepreneur. One of the helpful items in the SBA's resource library is the Small Business Planner, a step-by-step guide for starting your new venture. The SBA also has a Women's Business Center and a Minority Business Center.

General Information

The U.S. Chamber Small Business Center (uschamber.com/sb) provides start-up assistance mainly through Web-based tools and resources. Its start-up toolkit is very helpful in starting a business as it focuses on everything from evaluating an idea to developing a business plan, accessing capital, and launching the venture. Other useful tools for various business documents, such as spreadsheet templates and other government forms, are also provided under the "Tools" section.

Other valuable Web sites providing useful information include:

1. *National Association of Small Business Investment Companies (nasbic.org).* Provides an online database of small venture capital firm members and a guide to obtaining SBIC financing.
2. *National Venture Capital Association (nvca.org).* Provides information on the venture capital industry as well as access to state and regional venture capital firms.
3. *National Business Incubation Association (nbia.org).* Provides information on the role of incubators, how to select the right incubator, and a listing of national and international incubators.
4. *FastTrac (www.fasttrac.org).* Funded by the Kauffman Foundation, provides educational programs for entrepreneurs throughout the United States.
5. *Active Capital (ACE-Net, activecapital.org).* Provides an opportunity for entrepreneurs to connect with accredited investors throughout the United States. Counseling, mentoring, and training are also provided.
6. *Collegiate Entrepreneurs' Organization (CEO, c-e-o.org).* Provides information on entrepreneurship programs at the undergraduate level at numerous colleges and universities.
7. *Consortium for Entrepreneurship Education (entre-ed.org).* Provides information on entrepreneurship programs and education throughout the United States.
8. *Ewing Marion Kauffman Foundation (kauffman.org).* Provides resources for entrepreneurship education and research and lists the angel (private investor) groups throughout the United States.

Industry and Market Information

There are a wide variety of databases available that provide significant information about the industry and market. These include:

1. *Plunkett.* Provides industry data, market research, trends and statistics on markets, and forecasts.
2. *Frost and Sullivan.* Provides very industry-specific information on industries such as aerospace and defense, chemicals/materials, telecom/IT, consumer products, electronics, energy, health care, industrial automation, and transportation.
3. *Euromonitor.* Provides consumer market sizes and marketing parameters as well as information on companies and brands.
4. *Gartner.* Provides information on technology markets.
5. *Gale Directory Library.* Provides industry statistics and a directory of nonprofit organizations and associations.

Competitive Company and Product Information

Besides personally investigating what is available by looking at the various options presently available for satisfying the market need, several sources supply significant information on competing products/services and their companies:

1. *Business Source Complete.* Provides company and industry information by scanning the Datamonitor reports.
2. *Hoovers.* Provides information on both large and small companies with links to competitors in the same NAICS (North American Industrial Classification System) category.
3. *Mergent.* Provides detailed company and product information on U.S. and international companies.

WHEN RECESSION KNOCKS, EXPAND GLOBALLY

Since the economic downturn of 2008, many companies have watched as their local markets contracted and company revenues decreased. In response to this drastic decline in sales, companies began looking for expansion opportunities in international markets where the desire for Western products and services has continued to grow steadily despite the recession in the United States and Europe. The countries primarily responsible for driving this increase in demand include the BRIC countries of Brazil, Russia, India, and China as well as the Middle Eastern countries of Saudi Arabia, Kuwait, Bahrain, and the U.A.E. These countries have two key characteristics making them attractive for foreign direct investment—their GDP is growing by more than 4 percent annually and they have an expanding middle class with increasing purchasing power. Expanding internationally strategically benefits entrepreneurial ventures by providing new sources of revenue, diversifying the portfolio investments to be less dependent on the home market, and increasing the brand value for all stakeholders. The decision to expand internationally should not be taken lightly though. As many companies discover, expanding internationally adds new complexities into the operations of the company, requires a substantial amount of financing, and requires customization of products and services to align with local cultures and tastes. Even with the best-laid plans, it is possible that one bad international experience could negatively impact domestic operations as well. Therefore, selecting the right country to enter is of utmost importance and requires careful research and analysis.

As a result of the 2008 financial crisis, one company that took the international leap was Wing Zone, an Atlanta-based restaurant chain. Finding domestic growth opportunities limited due to the

Government Sources

There are numerous information sources available from the U.S. government. These include the following:

- Census reports
  - factfinder.census.gov
  - www.census.gov/ipc/www/idb
  - www.census.gov/econ/census/ (ratios)
- Export/import authority
  - UN Comtrade
  - www.business.gov/expand/import-export
- North American Industrial Classification System (NAICS) and Standard Industrial Classification (SIC) codes
  - www.naics.com/info.htm
  - www.osha.gov/pls/imis/sic_manual.html
  - Similar information is provided by governments of other countries as well

Search Engines

There are many key terms for searching for the needed industry, market, and competitive information. Some of the better ones are:

- Search: _____ and statistics
- Search: _____ and market share
- Search: _____ and industry
- Search: _____ and association

significant decrease in customer demand as well as the inability of financial institutions to extend credit, the CEO and co-founder, Matt Friedman, decided to explore opportunities to expand internationally. Through their market research, Wing Zone discovered that chicken wing restaurants were not well known internationally despite the fact that chicken and spicy foods were established dietary staples worldwide. Wing Zone viewed this gap as a competitive advantage whereby they could enter the international market and quickly establish themselves as a global brand and industry leader. After significant research on consumer markets and cultural preferences, Wing Zone decided to open its first international franchise in Panama City, Panama. Opening the Panama location took 18 months in which time Mr. Friedman admits they encountered many unexpected issues requiring changes from their typical operating procedures. Some of these issues included expanding their floor plans to accommodate the Panamanian dining style and overcoming logistical issues related to the timely importing of their signature wing sauce. However, despite these growing pains, the Panama location was a quick success when it opened in November 2010 with their first week of operations being the busiest week for any Wing Zone location, domestic or international. With the Panama operations now in full swing, Wing Zone has turned their attentions elsewhere and is on track to continue their international expansion with contracts signed in the Bahamas, El Salvador, England, Ireland, Japan, Saudi Arabia, and Scotland.

Although expanding globally was not on the radar screen for Wing Zone before 2008, the financial downturn spurred Matt Friedman to explore other markets and, as a result, Wing Zone now finds itself with new sources of revenue, a more diversified portfolio of investments, and a global brand that will help them to survive future economic downturns.

Source: For more information on this topic, see J. Daley, "No Boundaries," *Entrepreneur* (serial online) 39, no. 5 (May 2011), pp. 98–103.

Trade Associations

Trade associations in the United States and throughout the world are also a good source for industry data about a particular country. Some trade associations do market surveys of their members' domestic and international activities and are strategically involved in international standards issues for their particular industry.

Trade Publications

There are numerous domestic and international publications specific to a particular industry that are also good sources of information. The editorial content of these journals can provide interesting information and insights on trends, companies, and trade shows by giving a more local perspective on the particular market and market conditions. Sometimes trade journals are the best, and often the only, source of information on competition and growth rates in a particular industry.

THE NATURE OF INTERNATIONAL ENTREPRENEURSHIP

international entrepreneurship
An entrepreneur doing business across his or her national boundary

International entrepreneurship is the process of an entrepreneur conducting business activities across national boundaries. It may consist of exporting, licensing, opening a sales office in another country, or something as simple as placing a classified advertisement in the Paris edition of the *International Herald Tribune*. The activities necessary for ascertaining and satisfying the needs and wants of target consumers take place in more than one country. When an entrepreneur executes his or her business model in more than one country, international entrepreneurship is occurring.

With a commercial history of only 300 years, the United States is relatively new to the international business arena. As soon as settlements were established American businesses began an active international trade with Europe. Foreign investors helped fund much of the early industrial trade as well as much of the early industrial base of the United States. The future commercial strength of the United States will depend on the ability of U.S. entrepreneurs and established U.S. companies to successfully do business in markets outside the country.

THE IMPORTANCE OF INTERNATIONAL BUSINESS TO THE FIRM

International business has become increasingly important to firms of all sizes—particularly today, when every firm is competing in a hypercompetitive global economy. There can be little doubt that today's entrepreneur must be able to move in the world of international business. The successful entrepreneur will be someone who fully understands how international business differs from purely domestic business and is able to respond accordingly, thereby successfully "going global."

INTERNATIONAL VERSUS DOMESTIC ENTREPRENEURSHIP

Although both international and domestic entrepreneurs are concerned with sales, costs, and profits, what differentiates domestic from international entrepreneurship is the variation in the relative importance of the factors affecting each decision. International entrepreneurial decisions are more complex due to such uncontrollable factors as economics, politics, technology, and culture (see Table 5.1).

Economics

In a domestic business strategy, a single country at a specified level of economic development is the focus of the firm's entrepreneurial efforts. The entire country is organized under a single economic system and has the same currency. Creating a business strategy for a multicountry area means dealing with differences in levels of economic development; currency valuations; government regulations; and banking, venture capital, marketing, and distribution systems. These differences impact each aspect of the entrepreneur's international business plan and method of doing business.

Stage of Economic Development

The United States is an industrially developed nation with regional variances. While needing to adjust the business plan according to regional differences, an entrepreneur

---

TABLE 5.1   International versus Domestic Business

- Economics
- Stage of economic development
- Current account
- Type of economic system
- Political–legal environment
- Language

doing business only in the United States does not have to worry about significant lacking of such fundamental infrastructures as roads, electricity, communication systems, banking facilities and systems, adequate educational systems, a well-developed legal system, and established business ethics and norms. These factors vary greatly in other countries, which impacts a firm's ability to successfully engage in international business.

Current Account

current account The trade status of imports/exports between countries

With the present system of flexible exchange rates, a country's *current account* (the difference between the value of a country's imports and exports over time) affects the valuation of its currency. The valuation of one country's currency affects business transactions between countries. Exchange rate divergences have occurred for Japanese automobile manufacturers and many products produced by Chinese firms, including steel and steel alloys.

Type of Economic System

Pepsi-Cola began considering the possibility of marketing in the former U.S.S.R. as early as 1959, following the visit of U.S. Vice President Richard Nixon. When Premier Nikita Khrushchev expressed his approval of Pepsi's taste, the slow wheels of East–West trade began moving, with Pepsi entering the former U.S.S.R. 13 years later. Instead of using its traditional type of franchise bottler in this entry, Pepsi used a barter-type arrangement that satisfied both the socialized system of the former U.S.S.R. and the U.S. capitalist system. In return for receiving technology and syrup from Pepsi, the former U.S.S.R. provided the company with Soviet vodka and the distribution rights in the United States. Many such *barter* or *third-party arrangements* have been used to do business in countries in various stages of development and transition.

barter A method of payment using nonmoney items

third-party arrangements Paying for goods indirectly through another source

Political–Legal Environment

The variety of different political and legal environments in the international market creates vastly different business problems, opening some market opportunities for entrepreneurs and eliminating others. One significant event in the political–legal environment involves the price fluctuations and significant increases and decreases in oil and other energy products.

A country's legal environment can influence each element of the business strategy of an entrepreneur. Pricing decisions in a country that has a value-added tax (VAT) will differ from pricing decisions made by the same entrepreneur in a country with no value-added tax. The value-added tax addition may increase the price above a price threshold and/or distort the advantage of ending a price in .79, .89, or .99. Advertising strategies are affected by variations in what can be said in the copy or in the support needed for advertising claims in different countries. Product decisions are affected by legal requirements with respect to labeling, ingredients, and packaging. Types of ownership and organizational forms vary widely throughout the world. The laws governing business arrangements also vary greatly, with more than 150 different legal systems and national laws.

While most entrepreneurs prefer to do business in stable and freely governed countries, good business opportunities often occur in different conditions. It is important to

political risk analysis
Prior to entering into
business in another
country, an assessment of
that country's political
policies and its stability

assess each country's policies and stability. This assessment is referred to as *political risk analysis*. While there is some political risk in every country, the range from country to country varies significantly, and even in a country with a history of stability and consistency, these conditions could change. There are three major types of political risks that might be present: operating risk (risk of interference with the operations of the venture), transfer risk (risk in attempting to shift assets or other funds out of the country), and—the biggest risk of all—ownership risk (risk where the country takes over the venture's property and employees). Conflict and changes in the solvency of the country are major risks to an entrepreneur in a particular country. This can take such forms as guerilla warfare, civil disturbances, and even terrorism where the entrepreneur's company and employees are targets.

A country's legal system, composed of the rules and laws that are used to regulate behavior as well as the processes by which the laws are enforced, also impacts the entrepreneur. The laws of a country regulate the business practices in that country, the manner in which business transactions are executed, and the rights and obligations involved in any business transaction between parties.

The entrepreneur should have an overall sense of the legal system of a country but usually needs legal counsel when it comes to specifics. Ideally this legal counsel would have its headquarters in the United States, with an office in the target country. Several areas are important to some extent for every entrepreneur: (1) property rights, (2) contract law, (3) product safety, and (4) product liability.

Countries vary significantly in the degree their legal system protects the property rights of the individual and the business. The property rights of a business are the resources owned, the use of these resources, and the income earned from this use. Besides buildings, equipment, and land, the protection of intellectual property is a very great concern, particularly for technology entrepreneurs. Intellectual property—such as a book, computer software, a score of music, a video, a formula for a new chemical or drug, or some other protected idea—is very important to a firm and needs to be protected when going outside the United States. Legal issues and property protection are discussed in Chapter 6. Few countries have laws and court procedures protecting intellectual property like those in the United States. You probably have heard how videos can be purchased in China at 10 percent of the cost in the United States—sometimes even before being officially released. Even this book—which has legal editions in several languages, including Arabic, Chinese, Hungarian, Indonesian, Portuguese, Russian, Slovenian, and Spanish—has an illegal edition in the Iranian language, as Iran does not recognize world copyright laws. Before entering a country, the entrepreneur needs to assess that country's protection of the intellectual property of the venture and the costs if these are copied illegally.

Another area of legal concern is the contract law of the country *and* how it is enforced. A contract specifies the conditions for an exchange and the rights and duties of the parties involved in this exchange. Contract law varies significantly from country to country, in part reflecting the two types of legal tradition—common law and civil law. Countries operating under common law include the United Kingdom, the United States, and most countries of the former British colonies. Countries operating under civil law include France, Germany, Japan, and Russia. Common law tends to be relatively nonspecific, so contracts under this law are longer and more detailed, with all the contingencies spelled out. Since civil law is much more detailed, contracts under it are much shorter.

In addition to the law itself, the entrepreneur needs to understand how the law might be enforced and the judicial system securing this enforcement. If the legal system of the country does not have a good track record of enforcement, the contract should contain an agreement that any contract disputes will be heard in the courts of another country. Since each

TABLE 5.2 Lost in Translation		
Even the best-laid business plans can be botched by a careless translator. Here's how some of America's biggest companies have managed to mess things up:		
Kentucky Fried Chicken	English: "Finger lickin' good."	Chinese: "Eat your fingers off."
Adolph Coors Co.	English: "Turn it loose."	Spanish: "Drink Coors and get diarrhea."
Otis Engineering Corp.	English: "Complete equipment."	Russian: "Equipment for orgasms."
Parker Pen Co.	English: "Avoid embarrassment."	Spanish: "Avoid pregnancy."
Perdue Farms Inc.	English: "It takes a tough man to make a tender chicken."	Spanish: "It takes a sexually excited man to make a chick affectionate."

From Anton Piech, "Speaking in Tongues," *Inc.* magazine, June 2003. Reprinted with permission of Mansueto Ventures LLC.

company might have some advantage in its home country, usually another country is selected. This aspect is very important for entrepreneurs operating in developing economies with little or even a bad history of enforcement. One company exporting Hungarian wine into Russia made sure any disputes in its Russian contracts would be heard in the Finnish court system rather than the Russian court system.

The final overall area of legal concern pertains to the laws of the country regarding product safety and liability. Again, these laws vary significantly among countries, from very high liability and damage awards in the United States to very low levels in Russia and China. These laws also raise an ethical issue for the entrepreneur, particularly one from the United States. When doing business in a country where the liability and product safety laws are much lower than in your home country, should you follow the more relaxed local standards or adhere to the stricter standards of your home country and risk not being competitive and losing the business?

Language

Sometimes one of the biggest problems for the entrepreneur is finding a translator and having an appropriate translation of the message. As indicated in Table 5.2, significant problems can occur with careless translation. To avoid such errors, care should be taken to hire a translator whose native tongue is the target language and whose expertise matches that of the original authors.

TECHNOLOGICAL ENVIRONMENT

Technology, like culture, varies significantly across countries. The variation and availability of technology are often surprising, particularly to an entrepreneur from a developed country. While U.S. firms produce mostly standardized, relatively uniform products that can be sorted to meet industry standards, this is not the case in many countries, making it more difficult to achieve a consistent level of quality.

New products in a country are created based on the conditions and infrastructure operating in that country. For example, U.S. car designers can assume wider roads and less expensive gasoline than European designers. When these same designers work on transportation vehicles for other parts of the world, their assumptions need to reflect the conditions in the country.

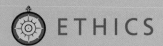

MARKETING CORPORATE SOCIAL RESPONSIBILITY

In recent years, the trend in companies, large and small, domestic and global, has been to position themselves as socially responsible. The concept of corporate social responsibility (CSR) has existed since the 1960s and describes a company's ability to operate in a sustainable, ecologically friendly manner that benefits shareholders as well as employees, and the community at large. In recent years, corporate social responsibility has become expected, due in part to legislative actions such as Great Britain's 2006 Companies Act that requires companies to report their environmental policies. The introduction of ISO 26000 in 2010 added further credibility to the movement by providing guidance on operating in a socially responsible manner to companies of all sizes, types, and economic states. In addition, new studies show that customers are responding to green initiatives, and increasingly expect companies to behave in a responsible manner. Employees are also increasingly reporting that personal alignment with a company's corporate social responsibility programs is an important criterion in their career search. With the expectations of politicians, customers, and employees all increasing relative to CSR, it is more important than ever before that companies openly communicate and market their CSR initiatives.

The first step to developing a social responsibility marketing campaign is to ensure the company has socially responsible corporate policies firmly established and operating throughout all locations. These policies should accurately reflect current operating procedures, be long term in scope, be valued by customers and employees, and be profitable for the company to execute. Many companies have successfully implemented CSR policies and developed very successful marketing campaigns, which in their own right have become strategic advantages that differentiated their companies from the competition. Some of the most successful companies are those whose founders had strong sustainable values and developed mission statements and organizational cultures that espoused these values into everyday operations, guiding the long-term decisions and direction of the company. Some examples of these companies include StonyField Farm, an organic dairy products producer, Tom's of Maine, a personal care company, and Patagonia, an outdoor clothing manufacturer.

CULTURE

Probably the single most important problem confronting the entrepreneur occurs when crossing cultures. While culture has been defined in many different ways, the term generally refers to common ways of thinking and behaving that are passed on from parents to children or transmitted by social organizations, developed, and then reinforced through social pressure. Culture is learned behavior and the identity of an individual and society.

Culture encompasses a wide variety of elements, including language, social structure, religion, political philosophy, economic philosophy, education, and manners and customs (see Figure 5.1). Language, sometimes thought of as the mirror of culture, is composed of verbal and nonverbal components. Messages and ideas are transmitted by the spoken words used, the voice tone, and nonverbal actions such as body position, eye contact, and gestures. An entrepreneur or someone on her team must have command of the language in the country in which business is being done. Not only is it important for information gathering and evaluation, but it is also essential for communication among those involved as well as eventually in developing the advertising campaign. Even though English has generally become the general language of business, dealing with languages other than English almost always requires local assistance, whether in the form of a local translator, a local market research firm, or a local advertising agency.

One U.S. entrepreneur was having a difficult time negotiating an agreement on importing a new high-tech microscope from a small entrepreneurial firm in St. Petersburg, Russia.

However, as corporations develop their CSR marketing strategy, it has become quickly apparent that the operating procedures of the company must align with the socially responsible image presented to consumers in their marketing campaigns. As evidenced by recent scandals including the 2008 financial services market crash, the 2009 Toyota safety recalls, and most recently the 2010 BP Deepwater Horizon catastrophe, when a company's day-to-day operating procedures do not align with the socially responsible image portrayed in their marketing, it can quickly give way to customer mistrust, anger, and a corporate image disaster. The BP Deepwater Horizon catastrophe may be a model case scenario of when brand image and reality do not align. BP started their corporate social responsibility program in the early 2000s and strategically marketed itself as a green company, utilizing the green and yellow sunburst logo while positioning its initials BP as "Beyond Petroleum" in advertisements. As early as 2002 though, critics surfaced to say that BPs green initiatives were not quite as proactive as the marketing campaign would lead customers to believe. This trend continued through 2010 when in the midst of the largest oil spill in history, BP's socially responsible image was called into question on multiple fronts in a global media frenzy that resulted in significant detriment to the BP brand and reputation. Had BP been more proactive in implementing the socially responsible policies they heavily marketed, perhaps the media fallout from the oil spill would not have been as severe and the BP brand and company reputation would not have been so badly impacted.

As the importance of implementing socially responsible programs continues to increase worldwide, it is important that companies develop social responsibility policies and programs and work in a sustainable, environmentally friendly manner beneficial to shareholders, employees, and the general community. For these companies, marketing their sustainable behaviors will endear them to politicians, customers, and employees alike, giving them a leg up on the competition and driving their business forward.

Source: For more information on this topic, see J. Balmer, S. Powell, and S. Greyser, "Explicating Ethical Corporate Marketing; Insights from the BP Deepwater Horizon Catastrophe: The Ethical Brand That Exploded and Then Imploded," *Journal of Business Ethics* (serial online) 102, no. 1 (August 2011), pp. 1–14; and J. Balmer, "The BP Deepwater Horizon Débâcle and Corporate Brand Exuberance," *Journal of Brand Management* (serial online) 18, no. 2 (October 2010), pp. 97–104.

The problems were resolved when the entrepreneur realized that the translations were not being done correctly and hired a new translator.

Equally important to the verbal language is the nonverbal or hidden language of the culture. This can be thought of in terms of several components—time, space, and business relationships. In most parts of the world, time is much more flexible than it is in the United States. For example, due to the variability in traffic and the possibility of significant congestion, it is difficult to set exact appointment times in Beijing or Hong Kong. "Irish time" means that a meeting usually starts anywhere from 15 to 30 minutes after the established posted time—which one U.S. professor at an Irish university found out when he was in the meeting room at the appointed starting time and no one showed up until 10 minutes later. The meeting actually started 15 minutes after that.

The second aspect of nonverbal language is space—in particular, how much room should exist between individuals when they talk. While Germans prefer more space than Americans, Arabic and Latin Americans like to stand closer when talking. Also, some cultures, like Hungarian, Russian, and Slavic, hug and even kiss when greeting a known business partner regardless of gender.

The final aspect of nonverbal language, business relationships, is also critical for the entrepreneur to understand. In most countries, it is far more important to interact with a potential business partner on a personal level before any transactions occur or even before business is discussed. One entrepreneur in Australia met the president, the management team, and the family on different social occasions before any business was discussed.

FIGURE 5.1   Various Aspects of Culture

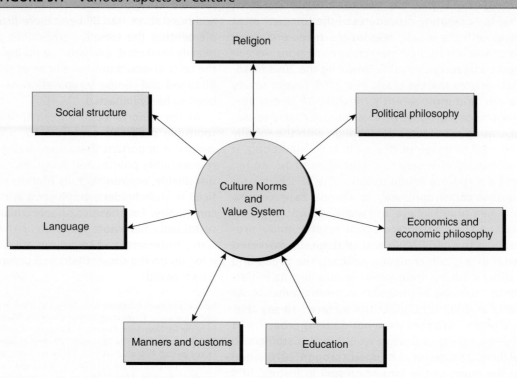

Social Structure

Social structure and institutions are also aspects of the culture. While the family unit in the United States usually consists of parent(s) and children, in many cultures it is extended to include grandparents and other relatives. This, of course, radically affects lifestyles, living standards, and consumption patterns.

Social stratification can be very strong in some cultures, significantly affecting the way people in one social strata behave and purchase. India, for example, is known for its hierarchical and relatively rigid social class system.

Reference groups in any culture provide values and attitudes that influence behavior. Besides providing overall socialization, reference groups develop a person's concept of self and provide a baseline for compliance with group norms. As such, they significantly impact an individual's behavior and buying habits.

The entrepreneur also needs to recognize that the social structure and institutions of a culture will impact the roles of manager and subordinate and how the two relate. In some cultures, cooperation between managers and subordinates is elicited through equality, while in other cultures, the two groups are separated.

Religion

Religion in a culture defines the ideas for life that are reflected in the values and attitudes of individuals and the overall society. The impact of religion on entrepreneurship, consumption, and business in general will vary depending on the strength and impact of the dominant religious tenets on the values and attitudes of the culture. Religion also provides the basis for some degree of transcultural similarity under shared beliefs and attitudes, as seen in some of the dominant religions of the world.

Political Philosophy

The political philosophy of an area also impacts its culture. The rules and regulations of a country significantly impact the entrepreneur and the way business is conducted. For example, embargoes or trade sanctions, export controls, and other business regulations may preclude an entrepreneur from doing business in a particular culture or at the very least will impact the attitudes and behaviors of people in that culture when business is transacted.

Economics and Economic Philosophy

The economics and economic philosophy of a country impact its culture and the entrepreneur. Whether the country overall is in favor of trade or trade restrictions, its attitudes toward balance of payments and balance of trade, its convertible or nonconvertible currency, and its overall trading policy all affect not only the decision about whether it is advantageous to do business in a certain market, but also the types and efficiency of any transactions occurring. Some countries use import duties, tariffs, subsidization of exports, and other restrictions to protect the country's own industry by having more exports than imports. Think how difficult it would be to do business in a country that restricted the exportation of profits.

Education

Both formal and informal education affect the culture and the way the culture is passed on. An entrepreneur needs to be aware not only of the education level and the literacy rate of a culture, but also the degree of emphasis on particular skills or career paths. China, Japan, and India, for example, emphasize the sciences and engineering more than many cultures.

   The technology level of the firm's products may be too sophisticated depending on the educational level of the culture. This level also influences whether customers are able to use the goods or services properly and whether they are able to understand the firm's advertising or other promotional messages.

Manners and Customs

Understanding manners and customs, the final aspect of culture, is particularly important for the entrepreneur in negotiations and gift giving. In negotiations entrepreneurs can come to an incorrect conclusion because their interpretations are based on their own frame of reference—not the frame of reference of the culture. For example: the silence of the Chinese and Japanese has been used effectively in negotiating with American entrepreneurs who interpret this (incorrectly) as a negative sign. Agreements in these countries, as well as other countries in Asia and the Middle East, take much longer because of the desire to discuss unrelated issues. Aggressively demanding last-minute changes is a mannerism used by Russian negotiators.

   Probably the area that requires the most sensitivity is gift giving. Gifts can be an important part of developing relationships in a culture, but great care must be taken to ascertain whether it is appropriate to give a gift, what type of gift to give, how to wrap the gift, and the manner in which the gift should be given. For example, in China a gift is given with two hands and is usually not opened at the time of giving but rather in the privacy of the recipient.

AVAILABLE DISTRIBUTION SYSTEMS

While the entrepreneur needs to be less concerned about worldwide logistics today, due to state-of-the-art transportation methods and the ensuing cost reductions, one of the entrepreneur's biggest challenges is related to the distribution channels in the target country. Distribution channels vary significantly from one country to another, and the channel of distribution in any country is a very powerful and strategic position, critical to the success of the global company.

In determining the best channel of distribution system for a country, the entrepreneur needs to consider several factors: (1) the overall sales potential, (2) the amount and type of competition, (3) the cost of the product, (4) the geographical size and density of the country, (5) the investment policies of the country, (6) exchange rates and any controls, (7) the level of political risk, and (8) the overall marketing plan. Each of these factors affects the choice of the distribution system that will yield the greatest sales and profit results in the country.

MOTIVATIONS TO GO GLOBAL

Unless they are born with a global mind-set, many entrepreneurs, particularly from the United States, will pursue international activities reluctantly. As indicated in Table 5.3, a variety of motivations can cause an entrepreneur to become involved in international business. Profits, of course, are one of the most significant reasons for going global. Usually, the expected profitability of going global is not reflected in the actual profits obtained. The profitability is adversely affected by the costs of getting ready to go global, an underestimation of the costs involved, and losses resulting from mistakes. The difference between the planned and actual results may be significant in the entrepreneur's first attempt to go global. Anything that the entrepreneur thinks won't happen most likely will, such as having significant shifts in foreign exchange rates.

The opportunity for profits is a strong motivation to sell to other markets. For a U.S.-based entrepreneurial firm, the 95 percent of the world's population living outside the United States offers a very large market opportunity. These sales may even be necessary to cover any significant research and development and start-up manufacturing costs that have been incurred in the domestic market. Without sales to international markets, these costs have to be spread over domestic sales alone, resulting in less profit, which can be a problem, particularly in price-sensitive markets.

Sales to other markets also may reflect another reason for going global—the home domestic market may be leveling or even declining. This is occurring in several markets in the United States due in part to the changing demographics in the country.

Sometimes an entrepreneur moves into international markets to avoid increased industry regulations or governmental or societal concerns about the firm's products or services.

TABLE 5.3   Motivations for Going Global
• Profits
• Competitive pressures
• Unique product(s) or service(s)
• Excess production capacity
• Declining home country sales
• Unique market opportunity
• Economies of scale
• Technological advantage
• Tax benefits

Cigarette companies such as Philip Morris, confronted with increased government regulations and antismoking attitudes, have aggressively pursued sales outside the United States, particularly in developing economies. Sometimes this has taken the form of purchasing existing companies in these foreign markets, which is what occurred in Russia.

When the entrepreneur's technology becomes obsolete in the domestic market and/or the product or service is near the end of its life cycle, there may be sales opportunities in foreign markets. One entrepreneur found new sales in the European Union for the company's gas-permeable hard contact lenses and solutions when the domestic market in the United States was negatively affected by highly competitive soft lenses. Volkswagen continued to sell its original VW Beetles in both Latin and South America for years after stopping its sales in the United States; after several years VW reentered the U.S. market.

Entrepreneurs often go global to take advantage of lower costs in foreign countries in such things as labor, manufacturing overhead, and raw materials. The HourPower Flip Watch could never be marketed at its price point in Things Remembered and JCPenney stores had it not been produced in China. Waterford is producing some products in Prague to help offset the higher labor costs in Ireland. There are often some cost advantages of having at least a distribution and sales office in a foreign market. Graphisoft, a Hungarian software company, found that its sales significantly increased in the United States when it opened a sales office in Los Angeles, California.

Several more esoteric motivations, beyond the traditional ones of sales and profits, also can motivate an entrepreneur to go global. One of the more predominant motivations is the desire to establish and exploit a global presence. When an entrepreneur goes global, many company operations can be internationalized and leveraged. For example, when going global, an entrepreneur will establish a global distribution system and an integrated manufacturing capability. Apple Computer has done this well, establishing solid profit margins throughout the established supply chain. Establishing these gives the entrepreneurial company a competitive advantage as they not only facilitate the firm's successful production and distribution of present products, but also help keep out competitive products. By going global, an entrepreneur can offer a variety of different products at better price points.

STRATEGIC EFFECTS OF GOING GLOBAL

While going global presents a wide variety of new environments and new ways of doing business, it is also accompanied by an entirely new set of wide-ranging problems. Carrying out business internationally involves a variety of new documents, such as commercial invoices, bills of lading, inspection certificates, and shippers' export declarations, as well as the need to comply with an entirely new set of domestic and international regulations.

One major effect of going global centers around the concept of proximity to the firm's customers and ports. Physical and psychological closeness to the international market affects the way business occurs. Geographic closeness to the foreign market may not necessarily provide a perceived closeness to the foreign customer. Sometimes cultural variables, language, and legal factors can make a foreign market that is geographically close seem psychologically distant. For example, some U.S. entrepreneurs perceive Canada, Ireland, and the U.K. as being much closer psychologically, due to similarities in culture and language, than Mexico, which may be closer in distance.

Three issues are involved in this psychological distance. First, the distance envisioned by the entrepreneur may be based more on perception than reality. Some Canadian and even Australian entrepreneurs focus too much on the similarities they share with the U.S. market, losing sight of the vast differences. These differences, which exist in every international market to varying extents, need to be taken into account to avoid costly mistakes. Second, closer psychological proximity does make it easier for an entrepreneurial firm to enter a

TAKING THE FAMILY BUSINESS GLOBAL

The decision to take a company global is difficult for large corporations and family businesses alike. Many factors must be considered including country economics, local markets, political and legal environments, as well as differences in language and culture. The decision to expand globally can be even more challenging for family-run companies, as they have an additional interest in maintaining family control of the company while expanding, limiting their use of more traditional entry methods such as joint ventures and acquisition. However, many family-owned companies have proven that a global expansion is still possible. These multinational family businesses originate in various countries and industry sectors and include companies such as Cargill (USA), Heineken (Holland), Michelin (France), Samsung (South Korea), and SC Johnson (USA). Based on their research, Casillas, Moreno, and Acedo suggest there are three key factors that determine if a family business will expand internationally—the international perspectives of the people actively engaged in the company, the international knowledge and exposure obtained by the company, and environmental factors such as the company's resources and capabilities.

The international perspectives of the people actively engaged in a company are crucial to determining if a family-owned company will become a multinational company. This group of influential people includes the founder, family members, employees, board, and outside consultants and advisors. The international perspectives of these individuals are based on their exposure to international cultures through studying abroad, working in large multinational companies, and personal travel experiences. The more positive international experiences that people have, the more likely they are to have a positive perspective toward internationalization, which will influence the company's vision and determine how the company responds to international opportunities. For some companies, the founder's original vision was of a global company and thus their global expansion was a natural progression as the business grew. An example of such a company is Heineken, whose founder envisioned a global presence from the very beginning and built the company into a global enterprise over three generations. Many companies start with a local vision but gain a more global perspective as younger generations enter the business with

market. It may be advantageous for the entrepreneur to start going global by selecting a market that is closer psychologically to gain some experience before entering markets that are more psychologically distant. Finally, the entrepreneur should also keep in mind that there are more similarities than differences between individual entrepreneurs regardless of the country. Each entrepreneur has gone through the entrepreneurial process, taken the risks, worked hard for success, and passionately loves the business idea.

FOREIGN MARKET SELECTION

With so many prospective countries available, two critical issues for the entrepreneur are foreign market selection and market entry strategies. Should you enter the top market prospect or should you employ a more regional focus? Should you choose the largest market possible or one that is easier to understand and navigate? Is a foreign market that is more developed preferable to one that is developing?

These are just some of the questions confronting the entrepreneur in deciding which market to enter. The market selection decision should be based on both past sales and competitive positioning as well as an assessment of each foreign market alternative. Data need to be collected on a systematic basis on both a regional and country basis. A region can be a collection of countries, such as the European Union, or an area within a country, such as the southeastern part of China.

A systematic process is needed so that a ranking of the foreign markets being considered can be established. Why is ranking markets so important? Ranking helps avoid the mistake of so many entrepreneurs—doing a poor job of establishing a rigorous market selection process

fresh ideas and perspectives. In either situation, having a team that is open to the idea of operating globally is the first factor to becoming a global company.

Obtaining international knowledge and experience within the company is another crucial factor in developing an international strategy. International knowledge and experience can be obtained from a number of sources including the founder, employees, consultants, industry leaders, and fellow entrepreneurs. As the international knowledge and experience grows within a company, the leadership will become more comfortable with the risks of expanding globally and will develop strategies to mitigate those risks appropriately. As a company begins entering foreign markets, the company will expand its understanding of their operating model and obtain invaluable experience in operating within a global arena, adjusting their business model to align with local cultures and business environments.

In addition to having an international perspective, knowledge, and experience, financial resources and organizational capabilities must be sufficient to maintain the domestic market while expanding globally. Resources currently allocated to the domestic market will need to be redeployed to support the global expansion strategy. By doing this, the company risks spreading resources too thin and being unable to adequately

support domestic customers and their business needs. Additionally, it is imperative the company has the capabilities to maintain a long-term commitment to global expansion. A company cannot expand globally for a short period and then return to operating only domestically. The global expansion must be sustained to be successful in the long term. This long-term vision must be included within the succession process as well, to ensure that as the baton is passed to the next generation, the vision of the overall company remains consistent.

In conclusion, it is possible for a family-owned company to become a multinational company while maintaining control of the company. In order to do this, the company needs a leadership team with an international perspective and receptive to exploring international opportunities, sufficient international knowledge and experience to develop and execute an international strategy, and adequate financial resources and organizational capabilities to focus on the global market in addition to the domestic environment. With all of these elements present, the local family business could quickly grow into a large, multinational family business.

Source: For more information on this topic, see J. Casillas, A. Moreno, and F. Acedo, "Internationalization of Family Businesses: A Theoretical Model Based on International Entrepreneurship Perspective," *Global Management Journal* (serial online) 2, no. 2 (December 2010), pp. 16–33.

and relying too much on assumptions and gut feel. The significant differences between global and domestic markets and the entire global decision process require that the market selection process be based on as much information as possible. These data should cover at least three years so that trends appear. The data collected and analyzed for market selection also will be used in developing the appropriate entry strategy and marketing plan.

While there are several market selection models available, one good method employs a five-step approach: (1) develop appropriate indicators, (2) collect data and convert into comparable indicators, (3) establish an appropriate weight for each indicator, (4) analyze the data, and (5) select the appropriate market from the market rankings.

In step 1, appropriate indicators need to be developed based on past sales, competitive research, experience, and discussions with other entrepreneurs doing global business. Specific indicators for the company need to be developed in three general areas: overall market size indicators, market growth indicators, and product indicators. Market size indicators generally center around: (1) population, (2) per capita income, (3) the market for the specific product (for consumer products), and (4) the types of companies and their sales and profits of particular products (for industrial products). In terms of market growth, the overall country growth (GDP) should be determined as well as the growth rate for the particular market of the venture. Finally, appropriate product indicators such as the size of the export of the specific product category to the market, the number of sales leads, and the level of interest should be established.

Step 2 involves collecting data for each of these indicators and making the data comparable. Both primary data (original information collected for the particular requirement) and secondary data (published data already existing) need to be collected. Typically, secondary data are collected first to establish what information (if any) still needs to be collected through primary research. When collecting international secondary data, there are several problems that can occur based on the stage of economic development of the country. These problems include: (1) comparability (the data for one country will not be the same as the data of another), (2) availability (some countries have much more country data than others, depending upon the stage of economic development), (3) accuracy (the data can be collected using rigorous standards or not as rigorous and even biased due to the interests of the government of the country), and (4) cost (only the United States has the Freedom of Information Act, which makes all government-collected data—with the exception of data related to security and defense—available to all). One entrepreneur was interested in setting up the first Western health club in Moscow. He was going to charge two rates: a higher hard currency rate to foreigners and a lower ruble rate to Russians and other citizens of countries in the former Soviet Union. In determining the best location, he was interested in identifying areas of the city where most foreigners lived. After significant searching to no avail and a high degree of frustration, he finally was able to buy the data needed from the former KGB (Soviet Union Security branch).

When researching foreign markets, the entrepreneur will usually want economic and demographic data such as population, GDP, per capita income, inflation rate, literacy rate, unemployment, and education levels. There are many sources for this and other foreign information in government agencies, Web sites, and embassies. One important source of data is the National Trade Data Bank (NTDB), which is managed by the U.S. Department of Commerce. The database has good information due in part to the large number of government agencies contributing information. Each country has its own database covering the data that comprises its Gross Domestic Product (GDP). This results in a large number of international reports such as Country Reports, Country Analysis Briefs (CABs), Country Commercial Guides (CCG), Food Market Reports, International Reports and Reviews, Department of State Background Notes, and Import/Export Reports.

Another good source of data is trade associations and U.S. and foreign embassies. While trade associations are a good source of domestic and international data, sometimes more specific information can be obtained by contacting the U.S. Department of Commerce industry desk officer or the economic attaché in the appropriate U.S. or foreign embassy.

The collected data for each selected indicator need to be converted to a point score so that each indicator of each country can be numerically ranked against the other countries. Various methods can be used to achieve this, each of which involves some judgment on the part of the entrepreneur. Another method is to compare country data for each indicator against global standards.

The third step is to establish appropriate weights for the indicators to reflect the importance of a particular indicator in predicting foreign market potential. For one company manufacturing hospital beds, the number and types of hospitals, the age of the hospitals and their beds, and the government's expenditure on health care and its socialized system were the best country indicators in selecting a foreign market. This procedure results in each indicator receiving a weight that reflects the relative importance of the indicator. The assignment of points and weights as well as the selection of indicators vary greatly from one entrepreneur to another and indeed are somewhat arbitrary. Regardless, this requires intensive thinking and internal discussion and results in far better market selection decisions being made.

Step 4 involves analyzing the results. When looking at the data, the entrepreneur should carefully scrutinize and question the results. He or she should also look for errors, as mistakes can be easily made. Also, a what-if analysis should be conducted by changing some of the weights and seeing how the results vary.

The final step—step 5—involves selecting a market to enter as well as follow-up markets so that an appropriate entry strategy can be selected and a market plan developed.

ENTREPRENEURIAL ENTRY STRATEGIES

There are various ways an entrepreneur can market products internationally. The method of entry into a market and the mode of operating overseas are dependent on the goals of the entrepreneur and the company's strengths and weaknesses. The modes of entering or engaging in international business can be divided into three general categories: exporting, nonequity arrangements, and direct foreign investment. The advantages and disadvantages of some of the modes are indicated in Table 5.4.

Exporting

exporting The sale and shipping of products manufactured in one country to a customer located in another country

Frequently, an entrepreneur starts doing international business through exporting. *Exporting* normally involves the sale and shipping of products manufactured in one country to a customer located in another country. There are two general classifications of exporting: direct and indirect.

TABLE 5.4   Various Entry Modes

Entry Mode	Advantage	Disadvantage
Exporting	Ability to capitalize on experiences in location selection	• High transport costs • Trade barriers • Problems with local marketing agents
Turn-key contracts	Ability to earn returns from process technology skills in countries where FDI is restricted	• Creation of efficient competitors • Lack of long-term market presence
Licensing	Low development costs and risks	• Lack of control over technology • Inability to realize location and experience curve economies • Inability to engage in global strategic coordination
Franchising	Low development costs and risks	• Lack of control over quality • Inability to engage in global strategic coordination
Joint ventures	• Access to local partner's knowledge • Shared development costs and risks • Politically acceptable	• Lack of control over technology • Inability to engage in global strategic coordination • Inability to realize location and experience curve economies
Wholly owned subsidiaries	• Protection of technology • Ability to engage in global strategic coordination • Ability to realize location and experience curve economies	• High costs and risks

indirect exporting In international business, involves having a foreign purchaser in the local market or using an export management firm

Indirect Exporting

Indirect exporting involves having a foreign purchaser in the local market or using an export management firm. For certain commodities and manufactured goods, foreign buyers actively seek out sources of supply and have purchasing offices in markets throughout the world. An entrepreneur wanting to sell in one of these overseas markets can deal with one of these buyers. In this case, the entire transaction is handled as though it were a domestic transaction, even though the goods will be shipped out of the country. This method of exporting involves the least amount of knowledge and risk for the entrepreneur.

Export management firms, another avenue of indirect exporting, are located in most commercial centers. For a fee, these firms will provide representation in foreign markets. Typically, they represent a group of noncompeting manufacturers from the same country who have no interest in becoming directly involved in exporting. The export management firm handles all the selling, marketing, and delivery, in addition to any technical problems involved in the export process.

direct exporting Involves the use of independent distributors or the company's own overseas sales office in conducting international business

Direct Exporting

If the entrepreneur wants more involvement without any financial commitment, *direct exporting* through independent distributors or the company's own overseas sales office is a way to get involved in international business. Independent foreign distributors usually handle products for firms seeking relatively rapid entry into a large number of foreign markets. This independent distributor directly contacts foreign customers and potential customers and takes care of all the technicalities of arranging for export documentation, financing, and delivery for an established rate of commission.

Entrepreneurs also can open their own overseas sales offices and hire their own salespeople to provide market representation. In starting out, the entrepreneur may send a U.S. or domestic salesperson to be a representative in the foreign market. As more business is done in the overseas sales office, warehouses are usually opened, followed by a local assembly process when sales reach a level high enough to warrant the investment. The assembly operation can eventually evolve into the establishment of manufacturing operations in the foreign market. Entrepreneurs can then export the output from these manufacturing operations to other international markets.

Nonequity Arrangements

nonequity arrangement A method by which an entrepreneur can enter a market and obtain sales and profits without direct equity investment in the foreign market

When market and financial conditions warrant the change, an entrepreneur can enter into international business by one of three types of *nonequity arrangements:* licensing, turn-key projects, and management contracts. Each of these allows the entrepreneur to enter a market and obtain sales and profits without direct equity investment in the foreign market.

licensing Involves giving a foreign manufacturer the right to use a patent, technology, production process, or product in return for the payment of a royalty

Licensing

Licensing involves an entrepreneur who is a manufacturer (licensee) giving a foreign manufacturer (licensor) the right to use a patent, trademark, technology, production process, or product in return for the payment of a royalty. The licensing arrangement is most appropriate when the entrepreneur has no intention of entering a particular market through exporting or direct investment. Since the process is low risk, yet provides a way to generate incremental income, a licensing agreement can be a good method for the entrepreneur to engage in international business. Unfortunately, some entrepreneurs have entered into these arrangements without careful analysis and have later found that they have licensed their largest competitor into business or that they are investing large sums of time and money in helping the licensor adopt the technology or know-how being licensed.

turn-key projects
A method of doing international business whereby a foreign entrepreneur supplies the manufacturing technology or infrastructure for a business and then turns it over to local owners

Turn-Key Projects Another method by which the entrepreneur can do international business without much risk is through *turn-key projects*. The underdeveloped or lesser-developed countries of the world have recognized their need for manufacturing technology and infrastructure and yet do not want to turn over substantial portions of their economy to foreign ownership. One solution to this dilemma has been to have a foreign entrepreneur build a factory or other facility, train the workers, train the management, and then turn it over to local owners once the operation is going—hence the name turn-key operation.

Entrepreneurs have found turn-key projects to be an attractive alternative. Initial profits can be made from this method, and follow-up export sales can also result. Financing is provided by the local company or the government, with periodic payments being made over the life of the project.

management contract
A nonequity method of international business in which an entrepreneur contracts his or her management techniques and skills to a (foreign) purchasing company

Management Contracts A final nonequity method the entrepreneur can use in international business is the *management contract*. Several entrepreneurs have successfully entered international business by contracting their management techniques and skills. The management contract allows the purchasing country to gain foreign expertise without giving ownership of its resources to a foreigner. For the entrepreneur, the management contract is another way of entering a foreign market without a large equity investment.

Direct Foreign Investment

The wholly owned foreign subsidiary has been a preferred mode of ownership for entrepreneurs using direct foreign investment for doing business in international markets. Joint ventures and minority and majority equity positions are also methods for making direct foreign investments. The percentage of ownership obtained in the foreign venture by the entrepreneur is related to the amount of money invested, the nature of the industry, and the rules of the host government.

minority interest A form of direct foreign investment in which the investing entrepreneur holds a minority ownership position in the foreign venture

Minority Interests Japanese companies have been frequent users of the minority equity position in direct foreign investment. A *minority interest* can provide a firm with a source of raw materials or a relatively captive market for its products. Entrepreneurs have used minority positions to gain a foothold or acquire experience in a market before making a major commitment. When the minority shareholder has something of strong value, the ability to influence the decision-making process is often far in excess of the amount of ownership.

joint venture The joining of two firms in order to form a third company in which the equity is shared

Joint Ventures Another direct foreign investment method used by entrepreneurs to enter foreign markets is the *joint venture*. Although a joint venture can take on many forms, in its most traditional form, two firms (for example, one U.S. firm and one German firm) get together and form a third company in which they share the equity.

Entrepreneurs use joint ventures most often in two situations: (1) when the entrepreneur wants to purchase local knowledge as well as an already established manufacturing facility, and (2) when rapid entry into a market is needed. Sometimes joint ventures are dissolved with one party assuming 100 percent ownership.

Even though using a joint venture to enter a foreign market is a key strategic decision, the keys to its success are not well understood, and the reasons for forming a joint venture today are different from those of the past. Previously, joint ventures were viewed as partnerships and often involved firms whose stock was owned by several other firms.

Joint ventures in the United States were first used by mining concerns and railroads as early as 1850. The use of joint ventures, mostly vertical joint ventures, started increasing significantly during the 1950s. Through the vertical joint venture, two firms could absorb the large volume of output when neither could afford the diseconomies associated with a smaller plant.

What has caused this significant increase in the use of joint ventures, particularly when many have not worked? Studies examining the success and failure of joint ventures have found many different reasons for their formation. One of the most frequent reasons an entrepreneur forms a joint venture is to share the costs and risks of a project. Projects where costly technology is involved frequently need resource sharing. This can be particularly important when an entrepreneur does not have the financial resources necessary to engage in capital-intensive activities.

Synergy between firms is another reason that an entrepreneur may form a joint venture. Synergy is the qualitative impact on the acquiring firm brought about by complementary factors inherent in the firm being acquired. Synergy in the form of people, customers, inventory, plant, or equipment provides leverage for the joint venture. The degree of the synergy determines how beneficial the joint venture will be for the companies involved.

Another reason for forming a joint venture is to obtain a competitive advantage. A joint venture can preempt competitors, allowing an entrepreneur to access new customers and expand the market base.

Entrepreneurs frequently use joint ventures to enter markets and economies that pose entrance difficulties or to compensate for a company's lack of foreign experience. This has been the case for the transition economies of Eastern and Central Europe and the former U.S.S.R. It is not surprising that it is easier to establish a joint venture in Hungary because that country has fewer registration requirements for establishing a joint venture than it does for registering a new business start-up.

Majority Interest   Another equity method by which the entrepreneur can enter international markets is through the purchase of a majority interest in a foreign business. In a technical sense, anything over 50 percent of the equity in a firm is *majority interest*. The majority interest allows the entrepreneur to obtain managerial control while maintaining the acquired firm's local identity. When entering a volatile international market, some entrepreneurs take a smaller position, which they increase up to 100 percent as sales and profits occur.

majority interest   The purchase of over 50 percent of the equity in a foreign business

Mergers   An entrepreneur can obtain 100 percent ownership to ensure complete control. Many U.S. entrepreneurs desire complete ownership and control in cases of foreign investments. If the entrepreneur has the capital, technology, and marketing skills required for successful entry into a market, there may be no reason to share ownership.

Mergers and acquisitions have been used significantly in international business as well as within the United States. During periods of intense merger activity, entrepreneurs may spend significant time searching for a firm to acquire and then finalizing the transaction. While any merger should reflect the basic principles of any capital investment decision and make a net contribution to shareholders' wealth, the merits of a particular merger are often difficult to assess. Not only do the benefits and costs of a merger need to be determined, but also special accounting, legal, and tax issues must be addressed. The entrepreneur, therefore, must have a general understanding of the benefits and problems of mergers as a strategic option as well as an understanding of the complexity of integrating an entire company into present operations.

There are five basic types of mergers: horizontal, vertical, product extension, market extension, and diversified activity. A *horizontal merger* is the combination of two firms that produce one or more of the same or closely related products in the same geographic area. The merger is motivated by economies of scale in marketing, production, or sales. An

horizontal merger   A type of merger combining two firms that produce one or more of the same or closely related products in the same geographic area *vertical merger* A type of merger combining two or more firms in successive stages of production

product extension merger A type of merger in which acquiring and acquired companies have related production and/or distribution activities but do not have products that compete directly with each other

market extension merger A type of merger combining two firms that produce the same products but sell them in different geographic markets

diversified activity merger A conglomerate merger involving the consolidation of two essentially unrelated firms

example of a horizontal merger is the acquisition of convenience food store chain South-land Stores by 7-Eleven Convenience Stores.

A *vertical merger* is the combination of two or more firms in successive stages of production that often involve a buyer–seller relationship. This form of merger stabilizes supply and production and offers more control of these critical areas. Examples are McDonald's acquiring its store franchises and Phillips Petroleum acquiring its gas station franchises. In each case, these outlets become company-owned stores.

A *product extension merger* occurs when acquiring and acquired companies have related production and/or distribution activities but do not have products that compete directly with each other. Examples are the acquisitions of Miller Brewing (beer) by Philip Morris (cigarettes), and Western Publishing (children's books) by Mattel (toys).

A *market extension merger* is a combination of two firms producing the same products but selling them in different geographic markets. The motivation is that the acquiring firm can economically combine its management skills, production, and marketing with those of the acquired firm. An example of this type of merger is the acquisition of Diamond Chain (a West Coast retailer) by Dayton Hudson (a Minneapolis retailer).

The final type of merger is a *diversified activity merger*. This is a conglomerate merger involving the consolidation of two essentially unrelated firms. Usually, the acquiring firm is not interested in either using its cash resources to expand shareholder wealth or actively running and managing the acquired company. An example of a diversified activity merger is Hillenbrand Industries (a caskets and hospital furniture manufacturer) acquiring American Tourister (a luggage manufacturer).

Mergers are a sound strategic option for an entrepreneur when synergy is present. Several factors cause synergy to occur and make two firms worth more together than apart. The first factor, economies of scale, is probably the most prevalent reason for mergers. Economies of scale can occur in production, coordination, and administration, and in the sharing of central services such as office management and accounting, financial control, and upper-level management. Economies of scale increase operating, financial, and management efficiency, thereby resulting in better earnings.

The second factor is taxation or, more specifically, unused tax credits. Sometimes a firm has had a loss in previous years but not enough profits to take advantage of the tax-loss carryover. Corporate income tax regulations allow the net operating losses of one company to reduce the taxable income of another when they are combined. By combining a firm that has a loss with a firm that has a profit, the tax-loss carryover can be used.

The final important factor for mergers refers to the benefits received in combining complementary resources. Many entrepreneurs will merge with other firms to ensure a source of supply for key ingredients, to obtain a new technology, or to keep the other firm's product from being a competitive threat. It is often quicker and easier for a firm to merge with another that already has a new technology developed—combining the innovation with the acquiring firm's engineering and sales talent—than it is to develop the technology from scratch.

Regardless of the entry mode, a successful entry strategy and growth in a global market often require the development of a global business plan. The global business plan varies somewhat from the domestic business plan discussed in Chapter 7. An outline of a typical global business plan is presented in Appendix 5A, at the end of this chapter.

ENTREPRENEURIAL PARTNERING

One of the best methods for an entrepreneur to enter an international market is to partner with an entrepreneur in that country. These foreign entrepreneurs know the country and culture and therefore can facilitate business transactions while keeping the entrepreneur current on business, economic, and political conditions. This partnering is facilitated by understanding the nature of entrepreneurship in the country.

There are several characteristics of a good partner. A good partner can help the entrepreneur achieve his or her goals such as market access, cost sharing, or core competency obtainment. Good partners also share the entrepreneur's vision and are unlikely to try to opportunistically exploit the partnership for their own benefit.

How does the entrepreneur go about selecting a good partner? First, he or she needs to collect as much information as possible on the industry and potential partners in the country. This information can be obtained from embassy officials, members of the country's chamber of commerce, firms doing business in that country, and customers of the potential partner. The entrepreneur also will need to attend any appropriate trade shows. References for each potential partner should be checked, and each reference should be asked for other references. Finally, it is most important that the entrepreneur meet several times with a potential partner to get to know the individual and the company as well as possible before any commitment is made.

BARRIERS TO INTERNATIONAL TRADE

There are varying attitudes throughout the world concerning trade. Starting around 1947 with the development of general trade agreements and the reduction of tariffs and other trade barriers, there has been an overall positive atmosphere concerning trade between countries.

General Agreement on Tariffs and Trade (GATT)

One of the longest-lasting agreements on trade is the General Agreement on Tariffs and Trade (GATT), which was established in 1947 under U.S. leadership. GATT is a multilateral agreement with the objective of liberalizing trade by eliminating or reducing tariffs, subsidies, and import quotas. GATT membership includes over 100 nations and has had eight rounds of tariff reductions, one of which is the Uruguay Round, which lasted from 1986 to 1993, and another is the Doha Development Round, which has been in progress since 2001. Another round should start in the 2010 time frame. In each round, mutual tariff reductions are negotiated between member nations and monitored by a mutually agreed-upon system. If a member country feels that a violation has occurred, it can ask for an investigation by the Geneva-based administrators of GATT. If the investigation uncovers a violation, member countries can be asked to pressure the violating country to change its policy and conform to the agreed-upon tariffs and agreements. Sometimes this pressure has not been sufficient to get an offending country to change. While GATT has assisted in developing more unrestricted trade, its voluntary membership gives it little authority to ensure that this type of trade will occur.

Trade Blocs and Free Trade Areas

Around the world, groups of nations are banding together to increase trade and investment between nations in the group and exclude those nations outside the group. One little-known agreement between the United States and Israel, signed in 1985, establishes a Free Trade Area (FTA) between the two nations. All tariffs and quotas except on certain agricultural products were phased out over a 10-year period. In 1989, an FTA went into effect between Canada and the United States that phased out tariffs and quotas between the two countries, which are each other's largest trading partners.

Many trading alliances have evolved in the Americas. In 1991, the United States signed a framework trade agreement with Argentina, Brazil, Paraguay, and Uruguay to support the development of more liberal trade relations. The United States has also signed bilateral trade agreements with Bolivia, Chile, Colombia, Costa Rica, Ecuador, El Salvador, Honduras, Peru, and Venezuela. The North American Free Trade Agreement (NAFTA) among the United States, Canada, and Mexico is a much publicized agreement to reduce trade barriers and quotas and encourage investment among the three countries. Similarly, the Americas, Argentina, Brazil, Paraguay, and Uruguay operate under the Treaty of Asunción, which created the Mercosur trade zone, a free trade zone among the countries.

Another important trading bloc is the European Community (EC). Unlike GATT or NAFTA, the EC is founded on the principle of supranationality, with member nations not being able to enter into trade agreements on their own that are inconsistent with EC regulations and having a common currency—the euro. As nations are added, the EC trading bloc becomes an increasingly important factor for entrepreneurs doing international business.

Entrepreneur's Strategy and Trade Barriers

trade barriers
Hindrances to doing international business

Clearly, *trade barriers* pose problems for the entrepreneur who wants to become involved in international business. First, trade barriers increase an entrepreneur's costs of exporting products or semifinished products to a country. If the increased cost puts the entrepreneur at a competitive disadvantage with respect to indigenous competitive products, it may be more economical to establish production facilities in the country. Second, voluntary export restraints may limit an entrepreneur's ability to sell products in a country from production facilities outside the country, which may also warrant establishing production facilities in the country in order to compete. Finally, an entrepreneur may have to locate assembly or production facilities in a country to conform to the local content regulations of the country.

IMPLICATIONS FOR THE GLOBAL ENTREPRENEUR

The cultural, political, economic, and distribution systems of a country clearly influence its attractiveness as a potential market and potential investment opportunity. Generally, the costs and political risks are lower in those market-oriented countries that are more advanced economically and politically. However, the long-run benefits to an entrepreneur are the country's future growth and expansion. This opportunity may indeed occur in less developed and less stable countries. The entrepreneur must carefully analyze the countries to determine the best one(s) (if any) to enter and then develop an appropriate entry strategy.

IN REVIEW _____

SUMMARY

Identifying both domestic and international market opportunities is becoming increasingly important to more and more entrepreneurs and to their countries' economies. International entrepreneurship—the conducting of business activities by an entrepreneur across national boundaries—is occurring much earlier in the growth of new ventures as opportunities open up in the hypercompetitive global arena. Several factors (economics, stage of economic development, balance of payments, type of system, political–legal environment, technological environment, and cultural environment) make decisions regarding international entrepreneurship more complex than those regarding domestic entrepreneurship.

Once an entrepreneur decides to be involved in international business, three general modes of market entry need to be considered: exporting, nonequity arrangements, and equity arrangements. Each mode includes several alternatives that provide varying degrees of risk, control, and ownership.

Entrepreneurs in the United States can find their counterparts in a wide variety of economies. Entrepreneurship is thriving from Dublin to Hong Kong, providing new products and services, new jobs, and new opportunities for partnering.

RESEARCH TASKS

1. Interview three managers of multinational businesses to ascertain the benefits generated from engaging in international business as well as some of the challenges (problems).
2. Choose a country. Research and be prepared to report on that country's (a) stage of economic development, (b) political–legal environment, (c) cultural environment, and (d) technological environment. If you were advising an entrepreneur who was considering entering this country to sell his or her products, what would you say were the major strategic issues? (Be specific to the country chosen.)
3. Choose a transition economy. Research that country and its recent economic progress. Do you believe its economy will flourish or stagnate? Why? What can that country's government do (if anything) to "help" the economy flourish?
4. Choose a specific industry in a specific country. Which mode of entry has been used the most by foreign firms entering this industry in this country? Explain why, using examples of successful entry and examples of unsuccessful entry.

CLASS DISCUSSION

1. Make sure, if possible, there is one foreign student in each small group. The group needs to discuss, and then report back to class on, the nature of business and entrepreneurship in the foreign student's home country. Such a discussion should include the country's (a) stage of economic development, (b) political–legal environment, (c) technological environment, and (d) cultural environment. Also explore how entrepreneurship and business failure are perceived in this country.
2. We typically focus on firms from well-developed economies entering markets of less developed economies. Do firms from less developed economies have a chance of success if they enter developed markets, such as the United States? What competitive advantage could a firm from a less developed economy rely on in entering developed markets? What would likely be the best entry mode?
3. Is going international something that only large and established firms should pursue after they have achieved success in their domestic markets "right off the bat"? Which sorts of products are more amenable to "going international" by small and new firms?

SELECTED READINGS

Baron, Robert A. (February 2006). Opportunity Recognition as Pattern Recognition: How Entrepreneurs "Connect the Dots" to Identify New Business Opportunities. *Academy of Management Perspectives,* vol. 20, no. 1, pp. 104–19.

The author discusses entrepreneurship using a human cognition pattern recognition framework. He discusses the value of pattern recognition to entrepreneurs who can recognize patterns to identify new or emerging trends in the marketplace. The paper ends by suggesting that entrepreneurs can utilize this framework to be better trained in opportunity recognition.

Ellis, Paul. (January 2011). Social Ties and International Entrepreneurship: Opportunities and Constraints Affecting Firm Internationalization. *Journal of International Business Studies,* vol. 42, no. 1, pp. 99–127.

The author argues that opportunity recognition is a subjective process influenced by the entrepreneur's relation with other individuals. The study, which focused on international ventures in China, determined that opportunities were sought rather than discovered, based on an individual's ties with others. The article also suggests that these ties can have a negative influence on international discovery because of the limits of the entrepreneur's network.

Puhakka, Vesa. (January 2010). Versatile and Flexible Use of Intellectual Capital in Entrepreneurial Opportunity Discovery. *Journal of Management Research,* vol. 2, no. 1, pp. 1–26.

The author explores the relationship between entrepreneurial intellectual capital and opportunity business strategy alignment among entrepreneurs. The study concludes that entrepreneurs utilize a combination of formal knowledge, management experience, intrinsic motivation, and creativity to identify and capitalize on unique opportunities. Flexibility in managing intellectual capital is important in the opportunity recognition process.

Ramos-Rodríguez, Antonio-Rafael; José-Aurelio Medina-Garrido; José-Daniel Lorenzo-Gómez; and José Ruiz-Navarro. (December 2010). What You Know or Who You Know? The Role of Intellectual and Social Capital in Opportunity Recognition. *International Small Business Journal,* vol. 28, pp. 566–82.

In this article, the authors study the influence of individual knowledge and access to information in the opportunity recognition process. They argue that social networks are critical in allowing the entrepreneur to develop the ability to recognize new opportunities in the marketplace.

Tang, Jintong. (June 2009). How Entrepreneurs Discover Opportunities in China: An Institutional View. *Asia Pacific Journal of Management,* vol. 27, no. 3, pp. 461–79.

This paper explores entrepreneurial opportunity recognition in China. The author argues that entrepreneurship is derived from a combination of individual and environmental characteristics which include human capital, social capital, social skills, environment, and personal experience. The study concludes that entrepreneurs must be able to leverage both personal and external resources to facilitate effective opportunity recognition.

END NOTES

1. Central Intelligence Agency, *The World Factbook: India* (Langley: CIA, 2011).
2. "India's Surprising Economic Miracle," *The Economist,* September 30, 2010.
3. S. Malhotra, "About DesiCrew," July 28, 2009 (H. Narayanan, Interviewer).
4. J. Ribeiro, "In India, Rural Workers Run Call Centers" (n.d.), *ABC News,* http://abcnews.go.com/Technology/PCWorld/storyid=5000185, retrieved October 5, 2011.

5. K. Murugesh, "Current BPO Industry Trends 2010," *SiliconIndia* (February 2010).
6. Malhotra, "About DesiCrew."
7. "About Us: Who We Are!" DesiCrew Solutions Pvt. Ltd., 2009, *DesiCrew,* http://desicrew.in/about-us.html, retrieved October 6, 2011.
8. Malhotra, "About DesiCrew."
9. Central Intelligence Agency, *The World Factbook: India.*
10. "About Us: Who We Are!" DesiCrew Solutions.

APPENDIX 5A EXAMPLE OUTLINE OF AN INTERNATIONAL BUSINESS PLAN

I. EXECUTIVE SUMMARY
One-page description of the project.

II. INTRODUCTION
The type of business proposed, followed by a brief description of the major product and/or service involved. A brief description of the country proposed for trade, the rationale for selecting the country, identification of existing trade barriers, and identification of sources of information (research resources and interviews).

III. ANALYSIS OF THE INTERNATIONAL BUSINESS SITUATION
A. Economic, Political, and Legal Analysis of the Trading Country
1. Describe the trading country's economic system, economic information important to your proposed product and/or service, and the level of foreign investment in that country.
2. Describe the trading country's governmental structure and stability, and how the government controls trade and private business.
3. Describe laws and/or governmental agencies that affect your product and/or service (i.e., labor laws, trade laws, etc.).

B. Trade Area and Cultural Analysis
1. Geographic and demographic information, important customs and traditions, other pertinent cultural information, and competitive advantages and disadvantages of the proposed business opportunity.

IV. PLANNED OPERATION OF THE PROPOSED BUSINESS
A. Proposed Organization
Type of ownership and rationale; start-up steps to form the business; planned personnel (or functional) needs; proposed staffing to handle managerial, financial, marketing, legal, and production functions; proposed organization chart; and brief job descriptions, if necessary.

B. Proposed Product/Service
1. Product and/or service details include potential suppliers, manufacturing plans, and inventory policies, if applicable. Include necessary supplies if a service is provided.
2. Transportation information includes costs, benefits, risks of the transportation method, and documents needed to transport the product.

C. Proposed Strategies
1. Pricing policies include what currency will be used, costs, markups, markdowns, relation to competition, and factors that could affect the price of the product (e.g., competition, political conditions, taxes, tariffs, and transportation costs).

2. Promotional program details include promotional activities, media availability, costs, one-year promotional plan outline, and local customs related to business readiness.

V. PLANNED FINANCING
   A. Projected Income and Expenses
   1. Projected income statements for first year's operation.
   2. Balance sheet for the end of the first year.
   3. A brief narrative description of the planned growth of the business, including financial resources, needs, and a brief three-year plan projection.

VI. BIBLIOGRAPHY

VII. APPENDIX

6

PROTECTING THE IDEA AND OTHER LEGAL ISSUES FOR THE ENTREPRENEUR

1
To identify and distinguish intellectual property assets of a new venture including software and Web sites.

2
To understand the nature of patents, the rights they provide, and the filing process.

3
To understand the purpose of a trademark and the procedure for filing.

4
To learn the purpose of a copyright and how to file for one.

5
To identify procedures that can protect a venture's trade secrets.

6
To understand the value of licensing to either expand a business or start a new venture.

7
To recognize the implications of new legislation that affects the board of directors and internal auditing processes for public companies.

8
To illustrate important issues related to contracts, insurance, and product safety and liability.

SALAR KAMANGAR

In 2006 Google acquired YouTube for $1.65 billion. This was less than two years after YouTube had registered its domain youtube.com. Salar Kamangar, at the time, was Google's youngest vice president and had been responsible for Google's Apps, one of which was Google's Video, a model similar to that of YouTube. However, Salar felt that Google's Video was not going to catch up to or dominate YouTube, so the company made the decision, with Salar's leadership, to purchase the young company. Salar was adamant that despite its copyright issues and less than clear business model YouTube was the future with incredible potential. All of this came at what many felt was an exorbitant cost but Salar stood his ground and became the most passionate voice for Google to make this purchase.

www.youtube.com

Salar Kamangar was born in Tehran but left at the age of two prior to the Iranian revolution. He received his bachelor's degree from Stanford University in 1998 in biological sciences. During his college years he was president of PARSA Community Foundation, a Persian nonprofit organization that had a great deal to do with the evolution of his strong entrepreneurial spirit. At a Stanford job fair he met Sergey Brin, one of the cofounders of Google, and was hired as its ninth employee. He did not have much of a job description in those early days so he basically did anything that the cofounders did not want to do. However, he eventually became a rising star and was immortalized at Google for co-developing AdWords, which is the foundation for Google's syndication on partner sites that also provides the company's major source of revenue.

After running Google's Apps for four years he yearned for something new and different. As he says, "I enjoy problem solving." He likes taking an idea, operationally zinging it, and seeing it evolve into a successful and profitable idea. As a result of his yearnings he engaged Google management in the effort to purchase YouTube that was finalized in 2006. At that time there were a number of questions regarding YouTube that Salar attacked with the same intensity with which he had earlier developed AdWords. The first problem that he addressed was how this site could make money. He saw opportunity here that was not being pursued by the former founders. Kamangar spent many hours meeting with Chad Hurley and Steve Chen, the founders of YouTube, hammering out details on how to evolve their relationship and make the company profitable. Eventually Hurley and Chen stepped down and Kamangar became CEO of YouTube. Kamangar's strategy was to adapt to the change in the video market. When Google purchased YouTube there were just two types of videos: television videos and computer videos. Now videos can be seen everywhere, such as on phones, tablets, computers, and televisions. Because of this Kamangar began adding professionally produced content for YouTube such as music videos, live concerts, and sporting events.

In 2011 YouTube expanded its movie rental service with the addition of 3,000 titles from major Hollywood studios such as Sony Pictures Entertainment, Warner Brothers, Universal Pictures, and independents such as Lionsgate Films. These movies were available to viewers the same day as on-demand services at a price of $3.99. In addition to Hollywood studios, Kamangar began to encourage more amateurs to develop content, many of whom had already amassed huge audiences on the site. Some studios, however, declined to participate, citing their concern about copyright infringement. Controlling what amateurs uploaded on YouTube was seen by these studios as a legal nightmare and thus they were reluctant to participate.

Copyright infringement was the second most pressing problem that Kamangar faced when Google purchased YouTube and he assumed responsibility for its future. In order to minimize copyright infringement Kamangar implemented a content tracking system called ContentID. This system allows any uploaded material to be compared with more than 100 million videos in the system and if there is any unauthorized content the owners of the material are alerted. They may then choose to have the material removed or they can allow it to continue. In one instance the owners of copyrighted music were alerted that a portion of a copyrighted song was included in a YouTube video. Instead of removing it YouTube recommended that the company place an ad for the purchase of the entire music. The ad resulted in a significant profit to the music studio without removal of the uploaded material and avoided any copyright infringement issues.

In addition to the content matching Kamangar has introduced YouTube Copyright School that establishes criteria for what can or cannot be uploaded. According to Kamangar, education is critical to minimizing copyright infringement. Although some Hollywood people still feel that YouTube has not done enough to crack down on illicit content, the company continues to attract more and more production firms. With all of these new services YouTube viewership doubled its revenue in 2011 with 160 million mobile views a day tripling the number from 2010. Google does not report YouTube's earnings but analysts say that it will bring in about $450 million in revenue for 2011 and also earn a profit.

Kamangar feels the future is bright for YouTube but the window of opportunity is limited. His aggressive entrepreneurial style continues to move YouTube in a positive direction making it one of the leaders in the video market.[1]

WHAT IS INTELLECTUAL PROPERTY?

intellectual property
Any patents, trademarks, copyrights, or trade secrets held by the entrepreneur

Intellectual property—which includes patents, trademarks, copyrights, and trade secrets—represents important assets to the entrepreneur and should be understood even before engaging the services of an attorney. Too often entrepreneurs, because of their lack of understanding of intellectual property, ignore important steps that they should have taken to protect these assets. This chapter will describe all the important types of intellectual property, including software and Web sites, which have become unique problems to the Patent and Trademark Office.[2]

NEED FOR A LAWYER

Since all business is regulated by law, the entrepreneur needs to be aware of any regulations that may affect his or her new venture. At different stages of the start-up, the entrepreneur will need legal advice. It is also likely that the legal expertise required will vary based on such factors as whether the new venture is a franchise, an independent start-up, or a buyout; whether it produces a consumer versus an industrial product; whether it is nonprofit; and whether it involves some aspect of computer software, exporting, or importing.

We begin with a discussion of how to select a lawyer. Since most lawyers have developed special expertise, the entrepreneur should carefully evaluate his or her needs before hiring one. By being aware of when and what legal advice is required, the entrepreneur can save much time and money. Many of the areas in which the entrepreneur will need legal assistance are discussed in this chapter.

HOW TO SELECT A LAWYER

Lawyers, like many other professionals, are specialists not just in the law but in specific areas of the law. The entrepreneur does not usually have the expertise or know-how to handle possible risks associated with the many difficult laws and regulations. A competent attorney is in a better position to understand all possible circumstances and outcomes related to any legal action.

In today's environment, lawyers are much more up-front about their fees. In fact, in some cases these fees, if for standard services, may even be advertised. In general, the lawyer may work on a retainer basis (stated amount per month or year) by which he or she provides office and consulting time. This does not include court time or other legal fees related to the action. This gives the entrepreneur the opportunity to call an attorney as the need arises without incurring high hourly visit fees.

In some instances the lawyer may be hired for a one-time fee. For example, a patent attorney may be hired as a specialist to help the entrepreneur obtain a patent. Once the patent is obtained, this lawyer would not be needed, except perhaps if there was any litigation regarding the patent. Other specialists for setting up the organization or for purchase of real estate may also be paid on a service-performed basis. Whatever the fee basis, the entrepreneur should confront the cost issue initially so that no questions arise in the future.

Choosing a lawyer is like hiring an employee. The lawyer with whom you work should be someone you can relate to personally. In a large law firm, it is possible that an associate or junior partner would be assigned to the new venture. The entrepreneur should ask to meet with this person to ensure that there is compatibility.

ADVICE TO AN ENTREPRENEUR REGARDING THE ROLE OF INTELLECTUAL PROPERTY IN SOFTWARE START-UPS

An empirical study in 2008 that was conducted by four Berkeley faculty has some revealing statistics regarding the role of patents for software start-ups. Some 700 software entrepreneurs were surveyed to ascertain their use of intellectual property to attain a competitive advantage in their markets. Interestingly, about 33 percent of the participants indicated that a patent was the least important mechanism among seven options for achieving a competitive advantage. The sample largely included CEOs and CTOs drawn from a population of high-tech firms registered with Dun & Bradstreet and from the VentureXpert (VX) database (all venture-backed firms).

The researchers were interested in determining whether high-tech start-ups were taking advantage of the patent system to protect their intellectual property. It was believed that early stage high-tech firms would be more sensitive to Intellectual Property Rights since they would likely lack some of the advantages, such as well-defined marketing channels and access to cheap credit, held by more mature firms.

The most important reasons for seeking patents, as reported by survey respondents, were to prevent competitors from copying the innovation, to enhance the firms' reputation, and to secure investment and improve the likelihood of an IPO. However, there were distinct differences in the importance of patents depending on whether the respondent was from the D & B database or the VentureXpert database. About 75 percent of the D & B sample had not received a patent nor were they seeking one. Over two-thirds of the venture-backed firms, however, had or were seeking patents. Reasons for this discrepancy were not addressed in survey questions but the researchers feel that this difference was due to the influence of the venture capitalists.

The major reasons for not seeking a patent were the costs of patenting and the costs associated with enforcing a patent. Respondents indicated that the average cost of obtaining a software patent was just below $30,000. Just behind the cost factors was the possibility that the software could not be patented.

Since patents were not considered important in achieving a competitive advantage, "what was the most important factor in gaining a competitive advantage?" Among software start-ups, first mover advantage was the single most important strategy in achieving a competitive advantage. This sharply contrasts with biotech firms where patents are ranked the most important factor in attaining a competitive advantage. In addition, complementary assets such as the licensing of software or being able to offer a proprietary complement to an open source program were considered next most important.

The study provides much more comprehensive data that will require extensive data analysis for future publications. Comparisons between the patent rates of different sectors of the software industry, as well as differences between patent holders and non-patent holders, are research issues that need to be addressed.

ADVICE TO AN ENTREPRENEUR

Consider the following:

1. What advice would you give to a business colleague who is about to start a new high-tech firm that has developed a new accessory for computer tablets? Would you recommend that she seek a patent immediately?

2. What factors should she consider in the process of debating whether a patent would be appropriate?

3. Why do you think it is so expensive to develop a software patent?

Source: Stuart J. H. Graham, Robert P. Merges, Pam Samuelson, and Ted Sichelman, "High Technology Entrepreneurs and the Patent System: Results of the 2008 Berkeley Patent Survey," 24 Berkeley Technology L.J. 1255 (2010).

A good working relationship with a lawyer will ease some of the risk in starting a new business and will give the entrepreneur necessary confidence. When resources are very limited, the entrepreneur may consider offering the lawyer stock in exchange for his or her services. The lawyer then will have a vested interest in the business and will likely provide more personalized services. However, in making such a major decision, the entrepreneur must consider any possible loss of control of the business.

LEGAL ISSUES IN SETTING UP THE ORGANIZATION

The form of organization as well as franchise agreements are discussed in Chapters 9 and 14 and will not be addressed in detail here. Since there are many options that an entrepreneur can choose in setting up an organization (see Chapter 9), it will be necessary to understand all the advantages and disadvantages of each regarding such issues as liability, taxes, continuity, transferability of interest, costs of setting up, and attractiveness for raising capital. Legal advice for these agreements is necessary to ensure that the most appropriate decisions have been made.

PATENTS

patent   Grants holder protection from others making, using, or selling a similar idea

A *patent* is a contract between the government and an inventor. In exchange for disclosure of the invention, the government grants the inventor exclusivity regarding the invention for a specified amount of time. At the end of this time, the government publishes the invention and it becomes part of the public domain. As part of the public domain, however, there is the assumption that the disclosure will stimulate ideas and perhaps even the development of an even better product that could replace the original.

Basically, the patent gives the owners a negative right because it prevents anyone else from making, using, or selling the defined invention. Moreover, even if an inventor has been granted a patent, in the process of producing or marketing the invention he or she may find that it infringes on the patent rights of others. The inventor should recognize the distinction between utility and design patents and some of the differences in international patents that are discussed later in this chapter.

- *Utility patents.* When speaking about patents, most people are referring to utility patents. A utility patent has a term of 20 years, beginning on the date of filing with the Patent and Trademark Office (PTO). Any invention requiring FDA approval has also been amended to extend the term of the patent by the amount of time it takes the FDA to review the invention. Initial filing fees for a utility patent for a small entity can vary from $82 online to $165 by mail. Additional fees exist depending on the number of claims made in the patent application.

  A utility patent basically grants the owner protection from anyone else making, using, and/or selling the identified invention and generally reflects protection of new, useful, and unobvious processes such as film developing, machines such as photocopiers, compositions of matter such as chemical compounds or mixtures of ingredients, and articles of manufacture such as the toothpaste pump.

- *Design patents.* Covering new, original, ornamental, and unobvious designs for articles of manufacture, a design patent reflects the appearance of an object. These patents are granted for a 14-year term and, like the utility patent, provide the inventor with a negative right excluding others from making, using, or selling an article having the ornamental appearance given in the drawings included in the patent. The initial filing fee for each design application for a small entity is $110.

There are also issuance fees, depending on the size of the item. These fees are much lower than for a utility patent.

Traditionally, design patents were thought to be useless because it was so easy to design around the patent. However, there is renewed interest in these patents. Examples are shoe companies such as Reebok and Nike that have become more interested in obtaining design patents as a means of protecting their ornamental designs. These types of patents are also valuable for businesses that need to protect molded plastic parts, extrusions, and product and container configurations.

- *Plant patents.* These are issued under the same provisions as utility patents and are for new varieties of plants. These patents represent a limited area of interest, and thus very few of these types of patents are issued.

Patents are issued by the PTO. In addition to patents, this office administers other programs and many online services for the entrepreneur, such as software for filing patents and forms for trademarks and copyrights, discussed later in this chapter. Although the Disclosure Document Program ended in 2007, it has been replaced by the Provisional Patent Application Program.

In March 2011 the U.S. Senate passed The America Invents Act that is designed to streamline the USPTO system. The tremendous backlog of requests for patents has increased the average time to receive a patent to 34 months. The new legislation changes the system to a first-to-file that now rewards firms that can file quickly rather that those who may be the first to think of the idea. Whether this rewards bigger companies that have larger resources more than small start-ups is still being debated.[3]

International Patents

As international marketing increases in our age of rapid technological development, it has become even more important for U.S. companies to seek some protection in global markets. As a result of the concern over imitations and knock-offs International Patenting has become a significant IP strategy for many start-ups.[4]

In response, the Patent Cooperation Treaty (PCT)—with over 142 participants—was established to facilitate patent filings in multiple countries in one office rather than filing in each separate country. Administered by the World Intellectual Property Organization (WIPO) in Geneva, Switzerland, it provides a preliminary search that assesses whether the filing firm will face any possible infringements in any country. The company can then decide whether to proceed with the required filing of the patent in each country. It has a 30-month time frame to file for these in-country patents. Although there have been some problems in getting reports on time there has been renewed cooperation between international patent offices such as the USPTO, European Patent office (EPO), and the Japan Patent Office (JPO). As a result, patent applications have been getting fast track examination, enhancing the process. Other countries (Republic of Korea, for instance) may be joining this process in the near future.[5]

The Provisional Application

provisional patent application The initial application to the U.S. Patent and Trademark Office providing evidence of first to market

It is recommended that the entrepreneur first file a *provisional patent application* to establish a date of conception of the invention. This provisional application replaces the disclosure document that was previously accepted by the PTO. The disclosure document was more loosely defined in its requirements and often led to issues when more than one person claimed the patent rights. In addition, the new provisional application is consistent with European procedures and can be critical when there is a foreign company involved in the patent application. Basically, this application gives the entrepreneur who files the rights to the patent based on the simple concept of first to file. As stated previously the requirements of the provisional application are somewhat more complete than the prior disclosure document since the entrepreneur must prepare a clear and concise description of the invention. In addition to the written material, drawings may be included, if deemed necessary to understand the invention. Upon receipt of the information, the PTO will file the application on behalf of the inventor. The actual filing of the patent in its final form must occur no later than 12 months after the provisional disclosure document is filed.

Before actually applying for the patent it is advisable to retain a patent attorney to conduct a patent search. After the attorney completes the search, a decision can be made as to the patentability of the invention.

The Patent Application

The patent application must contain a complete history and description of the invention as well as claims for its usefulness. The actual form can be downloaded from the Patent and Trademark Office Web site. In general, the application will be divided into the following sections:

- *Introduction.* This section should contain the background and advantages of the invention and the nature of problems that it overcomes. It should clearly state how the invention differs from existing offerings.

- *Description of invention.* Next the application should contain a brief description of the drawings that accompany it. These drawings must comply with PTO requirements. Following this would be a detailed description of the invention, which may include engineering specifications, materials, components, and so on, that are vital to the actual making of the invention.

- *Claims.* This is probably the most difficult section of the application to prepare since claims are the criteria by which any infringements will be determined. They serve to specify what the entrepreneur is trying to patent. Essential parts of the invention should be described in broad terms so as to prevent others from getting around the patent. At the same time, the claims must not be so general that they hide the invention's uniqueness and advantages. This balance is difficult and should be discussed and debated with the patent attorney.

In addition to the preceding sections, the application should contain a declaration or oath that is signed by the inventor or inventors. Your attorney will supply this form. The completed application is then ready to be sent to the PTO, at which time the status of the invention becomes patent pending. This status is important to the entrepreneur because it now provides complete confidential protection until the application is approved. At that time, the patent is published and thus becomes accessible to the public for review.

A carefully written patent should provide protection and prevent competitors from working around it. However, once granted, it is also an invitation to sue or be sued if there is any infringement.

The fees for filing an application will vary, depending on the patent search and on claims made in the application. Attorney fees are also a factor in completing the patent application. Applicants may also file online using the EFS Web service provided by the PTO. This online service enables applicants to file their application without the need for special software, resulting in faster application processing.

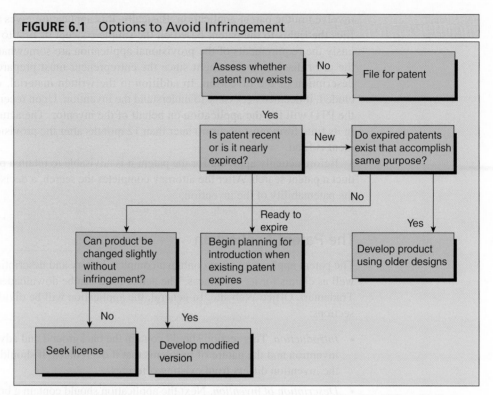

FIGURE 6.1 Options to Avoid Infringement

Source: Adapted from H. D. Coleman and J. D. Vandenberg, "How to Follow the Leader," *Inc.* (July 1988), pp. 81–82.

Patent Infringement

To this point, we have discussed the importance of and the procedures for filing a patent. It is also important for the entrepreneur to be sensitive about whether he or she is infringing on someone else's patent. The fact that someone else already has a patent does not mean the end of any illusions of starting a business. Many businesses, inventions, or innovations are the result of improvements on, or modifications of, existing products. Copying and improving on a product may be perfectly legal (no patent infringement) and actually good business strategy. If it is impossible to copy and improve the product to avoid patent infringement, the entrepreneur may try to license the product from the patent holder. Figure 6.1 illustrates the steps that an entrepreneur should follow as he or she considers marketing a product that may infringe on an existing patent. The entrepreneur can now make use of the Internet to identify Web sites and services that can assist in the search process. If there is an existing patent that might involve infringement by the entrepreneur, licensing may be considered. If there is any doubt as to this issue, the entrepreneur should hire a patent attorney to ensure that there will not be any possibility of patent infringement. Table 6.1 provides a simple checklist that should be followed by an entrepreneur to minimize any patent risks.

BUSINESS METHOD PATENTS

With the growth of Internet use and software development has emerged the use of business method patents. For example, Amazon.com owns a business method patent for the single-clicking feature used by a buyer on its Web site to order products. A number of years ago eBay was sued by Tom Woolston and his company MercExchange claiming a violation of a patent he owned that covered many fundamental aspects of eBay's operations, such as the buying and

TABLE 6.1 Checklist for Minimizing Patent Risks
• Seek a patent attorney who has expertise in your product line.
• The entrepreneur should consider a design patent to protect the product design or product look.
• Before making an external disclosure of an invention at a conference or to the media, or before setting up a beta site, the entrepreneur should seek legal counsel since this external disclosure may negate a subsequent patent application.
• Evaluate competitor patents to gain insight into what they may be developing.
• If you think your product infringes on the patent of another firm, seek legal counsel.
• Verify that all employment contracts with individuals who may contribute new products have clauses assigning those inventions or new products to the venture.
• Be sure to properly mark all products granted a patent. Not having products marked could result in loss or damages in a patent suit.
• Consider licensing your patents. This can enhance the investment in a patent by creating new market opportunities and can increase long-term revenue.

selling of products through a reverse auction process. Priceline.com claims that it holds a patent related to its service where a buyer can submit a price bid for a particular service. Expedia was forced to pay royalties to Priceline.com after being sued for patent infringement by Priceline.com. Many firms that hold these types of patents have used them to assault competitors and subsequently provide a steady stream of income from royalties or licensing fees.[6]

Given the increase in the assaults and because of the growth of digital technologies such as the Internet, computer software, and telecommunications, concerns have evolved regarding these business method patents. Examples of the focus of these concerns are tax strategies, the determination of insurance rates, or how commodities are purchased through a third party. These business practice patents are now being threatened by a recent Supreme Court ruling that denied a patent for a process of hedging risks against weather-driven changes in energy prices. The Federal Circuit Court had denied the patent because it did not meet the machine or transformation test. This simply means that any business method or practice must be tied to a machine such as a computer. Thus, a mental process of calculations for hedging risks in energy prices did not include a machine or computer and therefore was not granted a patent. However, the Supreme Court's decision did not provide any new specific means to determine if a business method was patentable, leaving the future uncertain for these types of patents.[7]

START-UP WITHOUT A PATENT

Not all start-ups will have a product or concept that is patentable. In this case the entrepreneur should understand the competitive environment (see Chapters 7 and 8) to ascertain any advantages that may exist or to identify a unique positioning strategy (see Chapter 8). With a unique marketing plan, the entrepreneur may find that striking early in the market provides a significant advantage over any competitors. Maintaining this differential advantage will be a challenge but represents an important means of achieving long-term success.

TRADEMARKS

trademark A distinguishing word, name, or symbol used to identify a product

A *trademark* may be a word, symbol, design, or some combination of such, or it could be a slogan or even a particular sound that identifies the source or sponsorship of certain goods or services. Unlike the patent, a trademark can last indefinitely, as long as the mark

AS SEEN IN *BUSINESS NEWS*

PROVIDE ADVICE TO AN ENTREPRENEUR INVENTOR ABOUT HOW TO MAKE PATENTS PAY

The niche patent-licensing business of Acacia Research (ACTG) is bearing fruit—and it has proved to be quite lucrative. Titans like Apple (AAPL), Verizon (VZ), Siemens (SI), Dell Inc. (DELL) and more recently Microsoft (MSFT) have opted to license certain patents held by Acacia. For Acacia, that makes the business all the more rewarding.

What's tiny Acacia's business strategy? It teams up with small, little-known tech companies and takes licenses on their patented technologies. Acacia then goes after companies it believes have infringed those patents. Fortunately for Acacia, it has settled quite a number of such patent violations out of court. And those companies that settle infringement claims usually end up paying fees.

The latest company to come to terms with Acacia is Microsoft, which entered into a settlement that included a licensing agreement for technology that allows them to provide geographical information for Internet maps.

In 2008, Apple signed two tech licenses with Acacia, and Verizon Wireless took a license on a process that synchronizes IP addresses between wireless network devices, says Acacia Chairman and CEO Paul Ryan. In its 18 years of existence Acacia has filed at least 337 patent-related lawsuits. Acacia says it reaches out of court settlements with about 95 percent of the lawsuits it files.

So far, Acacia has been on a rapid growth path, according to both CEO Ryan and analysts. In 2010 Acacia expected its sales to increase to $68.8 million, almost double the revenue of $34.8 million it achieved in 2006.

Acacia's "growth prospects remain strong," says analyst Sean O'Neill of Singular Research, who rates Acacia a buy. Analysts, however, are still concerned that these litigations are costing the industry billions of dollars each year. Ryan has indicated that it costs each side about $10 to $15 million over the time it takes for a settlement to be achieved.

In 2010 Acacia reported earnings of about $34 million and continues to grow. In August of 2011 Acacia settled with Force 10 Networks Inc. and Siemens Product Lifecycle Management Software Inc., resulting in significant unknown revenue.

If, as CEO Ryan predicts, more prominent companies sign agreements to settle patent infringements, Acacia's top and bottom lines would leap, along with its stock price.

Even though CEO Ryan is confident that Acacia will have more agreements forthcoming, some firms such as Cognex (CGNX) have begun to stand up to them, winning their lawsuit after a long struggle in the courts.

ADVICE TO AN ENTREPRENEUR

A friend of yours has read the above article and wants to know if he could benefit from some of the patents he owns, just as Acacia was able to do. How would you advise him to proceed to learn if any of his patents are being used by other companies? He also wants to know if Acacia may be interested in any of his patents and what he could do to find out.

Source: Adapted from "Acacia Research Finds Ways to Make Patents Pay," by Gene Marcial, www.businessweek.com; "Acacia: The Company Tech Loves to Hate," by Rachel King, www.businessweek.com; and www.yahoo.com (ACRI stock quotes).

continues to perform its indicated function. For all registrations filed after November 16, 1989, the trademark is given an initial 10-year registration with 10-year renewable terms. In the fifth to sixth year, the registrant is required to file an affidavit with the PTO indicating that the mark is currently in commercial use. If no affidavit is filed, the registration is canceled. Between the ninth and tenth year after registration, and every 10 years thereafter, the owner must file an application for renewal of the trademark. Otherwise, the registration is canceled. (There is a six-month grace period.)

Trademark law allows the filing of a trademark solely on the intent to use the trademark in interstate or foreign commerce. The filing date then becomes the first date use of the mark. This does not imply that the entrepreneur cannot file after the mark has already been in use. If this is the case, the entrepreneur may file a sworn statement that the mark is in commercial use, listing the date of first use. A properly worded declaration is included in the PTO application form.

It is also possible to file for a trademark if you intend to use this mark in the future. You are allowed to file in good faith along with a sworn statement in the application that there is intent to use the trademark. Actual use of the trademark must occur before the PTO will register the mark.[8]

Trademarks vary widely in their application and use. There are many famous trademarks that we sometimes take for granted but represent an important asset to the company. For example, the red tab attached to the left rear pocket identifies Levi Strauss jeans, the Dutch Boy is well recognized in paints, the McDonald's arch is internationally recognized in the fast food industry, the roar of a lion identifies the motion pictures of Metro-Goldwyn-Mayer, and the apple with a bite missing is well recognized as Apple Computer. These are only a few examples of significant trademarks.[9]

Registering a trademark can offer significant advantages or benefits to the entrepreneur. Table 6.2 summarizes some of these benefits.

Registering the Trademark

As indicated earlier, the PTO is responsible for the federal registration of trademarks. To file an application, the entrepreneur must complete a simple form that can be downloaded and either submitted by mail or filed electronically using the Trademark Electronic Application System (TEAS) available on the PTO Web site.

Filing of the trademark registration must meet four requirements: (1) completion of the written form, (2) a drawing of the mark, (3) five specimens showing actual use of the mark, and (4) the fee. Each trademark must be applied for separately. Upon receipt of this information, the PTO assigns a serial number to the application and sends a filing receipt to the applicant.

The next step in the registering process is a determination by the examining attorney at the PTO as to whether the mark is suitable for registration. Within about three months, an initial determination is made as to its suitability. Any objections by the entrepreneur must be raised within six months, or the application is considered abandoned. If the trademark is refused, the entrepreneur still has the right to appeal to the PTO.

Once accepted, the trademark is published in the *Trademark Official Gazette* to allow any party 30 days to oppose or request an extension to oppose. If no opposition is filed, the registration is issued. This entire procedure usually takes about 13 months from the initial filing.

TABLE 6.2 Benefits of a Registered Trademark

- It provides notice to everyone that you have exclusive rights to the use of the mark throughout the territorial limits of the United States.
- It entitles you to sue in federal court for trademark infringement, which can result in recovery of profits, damages, and costs.
- It establishes incontestable rights regarding the commercial use of the mark.
- It establishes the right to deposit registration with customs to prevent importation of goods with a similar mark.
- It entitles you to use the notice of registration (®).
- It provides a basis for filing trademark application in foreign countries.

COPYRIGHTS

copyright Right given to prevent others from printing, copying, or publishing any original works of authorship

A *copyright* protects original works of authorship. The protection in a copyright does not protect the idea itself, and thus it allows someone else to use the idea or concept in a different manner.

The copyright law has become especially relevant because of the tremendous growth of the use of the Internet, especially to download music, literary work, pictures, and videos, to name a few. Although software was added to copyright law in 1980, the issues surrounding access to material on the Internet have led to major legal battles for the entertainment industry.

When Napster made its entrance in 1999, Internet users were able to exchange music files at will. The music industry scrambled and fought against this use since its sales of CDs were significantly impacted. After three years, the music industry was able to win its battle with Napster. In addition, the Supreme Court ruled that StreamCast and Grokster, which both have extensive peer-to-peer file sharing software, must implement content filters in their software to reduce any copyright-infringing capabilities.[10]

As discussed in the opening profile, YouTube has had issues with uploaded material that has been copyrighted. However, they have found ways to avoid litigation through education and unique content identification software that alerts holders of copyrighted material. Many of the Hollywood production companies, however, still are skeptical about whether YouTube can maintain copyright controls over such a significant amount of uploading to the site.

Copyright protection related to the Internet will continue to be a concern and a gray area until precedents and regulations are made clear. Although these issues seem complicated, the registering procedure for copyright protection is fairly simple.

Copyrights are registered with the Library of Congress and will not usually require an attorney. To register a work, the applicant can send a completed application (available online at www.copyright.gov), two copies of the work, and the required filing fees (the initial filing fee is $35 if filed online or $45 if filed by mail, but other fees may apply based on the number of works included). As a general rule for works created after January 1, 1978, the term of the copyright is the life of the author plus 70 years.

Besides computer software, copyrights are desirable for such things as books, scripts, articles, poems, songs, sculptures, models, maps, blueprints, collages, printed material on board games, data, and music. In some instances, several forms of protection may be available. For example, the name of a board game may be protected by trademark, the game itself protected by a utility patent, the printed matter or the board protected by a copyright, and the playing pieces covered by a design patent.

TRADE SECRETS AND NONCOMPETITION AGREEMENTS

trade secret Protection against others revealing or disclosing information that could be damaging to business

In certain instances, the entrepreneur may prefer to maintain an idea or process as confidential and to sell or license it as a *trade secret*. The trade secret will have a life as long as the idea or process remains a secret. Noncompete agreements are documents that are prepared by an employer and signed by an employee in order for the company to protect valuable assets ranging from product information to clients, marketing ideas, and unique strategies.

A trade secret is not covered by any federal law but is recognized under a governing body of common laws in each state. Employees involved in working with an idea or process may be asked to first sign a confidential information agreement that will protect against their giving out the trade secret either while an employee or after leaving the

ETHICS

NONCOMPETE AGREEMENTS: DO EMPLOYEES HAVE AN ETHICAL RESPONSIBILITY TO RESTRAIN FROM REVEALING TRADE SECRETS TO A NEW EMPLOYER?

State courts differ in the way they interpret or even if they allow the enforceability of noncompetition agreements. However, the debate continues as to whether an employee should reveal trade secrets when a competitor offers that person a new position. How much responsibility should the employee have in revealing to the new employer that he or she is under some type of noncompete agreement with their former employee? The issue becomes even more significant if the individual is being hired away just so that the employee can be questioned about a trade secret. Three cases are mentioned below with somewhat different results and interpretations.

First, an Ohio State Court in the case of Acordia of Ohio, LLC v. Fishel, et al. ruled that noncompete agreements were not enforceable and that the four employees who left positions to work for a competitor did not misappropriate any trade secrets and were not in violation of loyalty, nor in violation of interfering with business relationships. In this case the court determined that the four employees did not pursue former clients until they were employed by the new firm and therefore there was no breach of duty.

In a second case, a New York District Court ruled that Aternity, Inc., a software company, had the right to prevent a former sales manager, who had signed a noncompete agreement, from working for its principal competitor, soliciting existing customers, or revealing trade secrets for a period of one year. In this case the employee had been terminated from Aternity, Inc., and prior to leaving had sent himself a number of e-mails containing confidential information. To the court this was a clear case of intent by the employee and therefore the court decision was quite clear.

In a third case former brothers-in-law together developed the idea of a medical device to help individuals whose larynxes had been surgically removed to produce clearer speech. One of the individuals, Joel Just, then formed JustMed, Inc., to continue development of the product. The brother-in-law Michael Bryce was offered 130,000 shares in return for a $25,000 investment. No written agreement was signed, and when Bryce did not receive his due stock certificates and discovered a discrepancy in the number of shares he owned compared to Just, he decided to delete all copies of the source code from JustMed computers. In this case the court ruled that Bryce was an employee of JustMed that owned the copyright to the software and found Bryce liable for violating the company's trade secret. However, this decision was later reversed and the court held that Bryce made no specific use of the code other than to make a point about the stock discrepancy. He had also returned the source code after the initial court case. Thus, according to the court there was no misappropriation of a trade secret.

As we can see from the variability of court decisions the issue of whether a noncompete agreement has legal substance is still debatable. The significance of these agreements also depends on the industry, such as services where employees have made personal contacts with clients that may be asked to follow them to the new company where they will be employed. One important issue here is whether an employee who willfully seeks new employment using a trade secret as a negotiating tool is ethically irresponsible. It seems apparent that it is better to have a noncompetition agreement with employees if there is any possibility of trade secrets being passed on to competitors.

Source: See *Business Torts Reporter,* April 2009, pp. 142–43; *Business Torts Reporter,* September 2010; and S. Robertson, "How Safe Are Non-compete Agreements?" *American Agent and Broker,* May 2010, pp. 50–55.

organization. This also applies to client names or lists that may be contacted when employed by a competitor. A simple example of a trade secret nondisclosure agreement is illustrated in Table 6.3. The entrepreneur should hire an attorney to help draw up any such agreement. The holder of the trade secret has the right to sue any signee who breaches such an agreement.

TABLE 6.3 A Simple Trade Secret Nondisclosure Agreement

WHEREAS, New Venture Corporation (NVC), Anywhere Street, Anyplace, U.S.A., is the Owner of information relating to; and

WHEREAS, NVC is desirous of disclosing said information to the undersigned (hereinafter referred to as "Recipient") for the purposes of using, evaluating, or entering into further agreements using such trade secrets as an employee, consultant, or agent of NVC; and

WHEREAS, NVC wishes to maintain in confidence said information as trade secret; and

WHEREAS, the undersigned Recipient recognizes the necessity of maintaining the strictest confidence with respect to any trade secrets of NVC.

Recipient hereby agrees as follows:

1. Recipient shall observe the strictest secrecy with respect to all information presented by NVC and Recipient's evaluation thereof and shall disclose such information only to persons authorized to receive same by NVC. Recipient shall be responsible for any damage resulting from any breach of this Agreement by Recipient.

2. Recipient shall neither make use of nor disclose to any third party during the period of this Agreement and thereafter any such trade secrets or evaluation thereof unless prior consent in writing is given by NVC.

3. Restriction on disclosure does not apply to information previously known to Recipient or otherwise in the public domain. Any prior knowledge of trade secrets by the Recipient shall be disclosed in writing within (30) days.

4. At the completion of the services performed by the Recipient, Recipient shall within (30) days return all original materials provided by NVC and any copies, notes, or other documents that are in the Recipient's possession pertaining thereto.

5. Any trade secrets made public through publication or product announcements are excluded from this agreement.

6. This agreement is executed and delivered within the State of _____ and it shall be construed, interpreted, and applied in accordance with the laws of that State.

7. This agreement, including the provision hereof, shall not be modified or changed in any manner except only in writing signed by all parties hereto.

Effective this _____ day of _____ 20 _____

RECIPIENT: _____

NEW VENTURE CORPORATION:

By: _____

Title: _____

Date: _____

What or how much information to give to employees is difficult to judge and is often determined by the entrepreneur's judgment. Historically, entrepreneurs tended to protect sensitive or confidential company information from anyone else by simply not making them privy to this information. Today, there is a tendency to take the opposite view, that the more information entrusted to employees, the more effective and creative employees can be. The argument is that employees cannot be creative unless they have a complete understanding of what is going on in the business.

Most entrepreneurs have limited resources, so they choose not to find means to protect their ideas, products, client lists, or services. This could become a serious problem in the future, since gathering competitive information legally is so easy to accomplish, unless the entrepreneur takes the proper precautions. For example, it is often easy to learn competitive information through such means as trade shows, transient employees, media interviews or announcements, and even Web sites. In all instances, overzealous employees are the problem. To try to control this problem, entrepreneurs should consider some of the ideas listed below.

- Train employees to refer sensitive questions to one person.
- Provide escorts for all office visitors.
- Avoid discussing business in public places.
- Keep important travel plans secret.
- Control information that might be presented by employees at conferences or published in journals.
- Use simple security such as locked file cabinets, passwords on computers, and shredders where necessary.
- Have employees and consultants sign nondisclosure agreements.
- Debrief departing employees on any confidential information.
- Avoid faxing and e-mailing any sensitive information.
- Mark documents confidential when needed.

Unfortunately, protection against the leaking of trade secrets is difficult to enforce. Historically, noncompete agreements have not been very successful in courts. However, the effectiveness of a noncompete agreement depends more on the agreement and the scenario in which it is being used. The reason that many noncompetes are thrown out of court is that they are poorly structured and written. For example, trying to keep an ex-employee from competing anywhere in the industry or over a large market area is not very likely to be enforced by the courts. Well-written agreements will hold up in court if they are fair to all parties and have a reasonable duration and geographic coverage. A few good points are worth considering when preparing a noncompetition agreement: (a) Determine if the employee can harm the company if he or she left, (b) hire a competent labor law attorney to make sure the agreement is fair and likely to be enforced, (c) provide incentives for the employee at hiring by offering a bonus for signing a noncompete agreement, (d) specify what is included in the noncompete such as client lists, confidential software code, or product information, and (e) consider other options besides a noncompete such as a nonpiracy or nondisclosure of confidential information covenant.[11] More important, legal action can be taken only after the secret has been revealed. It is not necessary for the entrepreneur to worry extensively about every document or piece of information. As long as minimal precautions are taken, most problems can be avoided, primarily because leaks usually occur inadvertently.

LICENSING

licensing Contractual agreement giving rights to others to use intellectual property in return for a royalty or fee

Licensing may be defined as an arrangement between two parties, where one party has proprietary rights over some information, process, or technology protected by a patent, trademark, or copyright. This arrangement, specified in a contract (discussed later in this chapter), requires the licensee to pay a royalty or some other specified sum to the holder of the proprietary rights (licensor) in return for permission to copy the patent, trademark, or copyright.

Thus, licensing has significant value as a marketing strategy to holders of patents, trademarks, or copyrights to grow their business in new markets when they lack resources or experience in those markets. It is also an important marketing strategy for entrepreneurs who wish to start a new venture but need permission to copy or incorporate the patent, trademark, or copyright with their ideas.

A patent license agreement specifies how the licensee would have access to the patent. For example, the licensor may still manufacture the product but give the licensee the rights to market it under their label in a noncompetitive market (i.e., foreign market). In other instances, the licensee may actually manufacture and market the patented product under its own label. This agreement must be carefully worded and should involve a lawyer, to ensure the protection of all parties.

Licensing a trademark generally involves a franchising agreement. The entrepreneur operates a business using the trademark and agrees to pay a fixed sum for use of the trademark, pay a royalty based on sales volume, buy supplies from the franchisor (examples would be Shell, Dunkin' Donuts, Pepsi Cola or Coca Cola bottlers, or Midas muffler shops), or some combination of these. Franchising is discussed later in the text as an option for the entrepreneur as a way to start a new business or as a means of financing growth.

Copyrights are another popular licensed property. They involve rights to use or copy books, software, music, photographs, and plays, to name a few. In the late 1970s, computer games were designed using licenses from arcade games and movies. Television shows have also licensed their names for board games or computer games. Celebrities will often license the right to use their name, likeness, or image in a product (i.e., Tiger Woods golf clothing, Jessica Simpson perfume, Elvis Presley memorabilia, or Mickey Mouse lunch boxes). This is actually analogous to a trademark license.

Licensing has become a revenue boom for many Fortune 500 companies. These firms spend billions of dollars each year on the research and development of new technologies that they will never bring to market. As a result, they will often license patents, trademarks, and other intellectual property to small companies that can profit from them. Microsoft Corporation, with its IP Ventures Division, is a great example of a firm that has offered technologies for biometric identity authentication, counterfeit-resistant labels, face detection and tracking, and other intellectual property that it does not know how to market or has no intent to market.[12] Recently Microsoft licensed with Hewlitt Packard, Dell, and Fujitsu to allow them to utilize Azure cloud-based applications for their customers.[13] These agreements have generated millions of dollars in revenue for Microsoft. IBM continues to generate significant revenues from its licensing strategies. Recently IBM licensed with EMC Corporation to allow customers to utilize both products in mainframe environments.[14] Recently also, in another unique licensing agreement, Flat World Knowledge Inc. licensed the use of its electronic business textbooks in seven core introductory business courses at Virginia State University.[15]

Although technology is one of the largest generators of licensing revenue, there are other significant players in this market. The entertainment industry, particularly motion picture studios such as Disney, DreamWorks, Fox, Sony, and Warner Brothers, generates millions of dollars for its bottom line with licensing agreements for clothing, toys, games, and other related items. Disney is by far the world leader in licensing. In 2009 it amassed $27 billion in licensing revenue. With the recent release of *Cars2* and the acquisition of Marvel comics the company expects to continue to grow its licensing revenue. Action heroes seem to be the most recent popular trend for licensing. For example, Sony and Paramount have benefited from the release of the *Green Lantern* and *Green Hornet* movies.[16]

Fox recently achieved a huge success with its hit television program "Glee." As a result of this success Fox has signed licensing agreements for numerous products such as musical greeting cards, games, toys, and clothing.[17] McDonald's, on the other hand, after losing its long-standing licensing agreement with Disney, has moved on and signed licensing agreements with other motion picture studios such as DreamWorks Animation SKG and Pixar Animation Studios.[18]

Licensing is also popular around special sporting events, such as the Olympics, marathons, bowl games, and tournaments. Licenses to sell T-shirts, clothing, and other accessories require written permission in the form of a license agreement before sales are allowed.

Licensing represents opportunities for many firms to expand into new markets, expand product lines, or simply reach more customers within its existing target markets. This strategy has become necessary in markets where revenue has become stagnant. Firms like Fox and others mentioned above look to take advantage of any specific success they have had with a product by leveraging this success through licensing agreements. Restaurants such as Cheesecake Factory, Panera Bread, and Burger King are putting their name on numerous products such as frozen and ready to eat foods. The National Basketball Association has even stepped up its efforts to increase revenues in licensing agreements using team logos on take-out pizzas, toasters, and sandwich presses.[19]

Before entering into a licensing agreement, the entrepreneur should ask the following questions:

- Will the customer recognize the licensed property?
- How well does the licensed property complement my products or services?
- How much experience do I have with the licensed property?
- What is the long-term outlook for the licensed property? (For example, the loss of popularity of a celebrity can also result in an end to a business involving that celebrity's name.)
- What kind of protection does the licensing agreement provide?
- What commitment do I have in terms of payment of royalties, sales quotas, and so on?
- Are renewal options possible and under what terms?

Licensing is an excellent option for the entrepreneur to increase revenue, without the risk and costly start-up investment. To be able to license requires the entrepreneur to have something to license, which is why it is so important to seek protection for any product, information, name, and so on, with a patent, trademark, or copyright. On the other hand, licensing can also be a way to start a new venture when the idea may infringe on someone else's patent, trademark, or copyright. In this instance, the entrepreneur has nothing to lose by trying to seek a license agreement from the holder of the property.

Licensing continues to be a powerful marketing tool. With the advice of a lawyer, entrepreneurs may find that licensing opportunities are a way to minimize risk, expand a business, or complement an existing product line.

PRODUCT SAFETY AND LIABILITY

product safety and liability Responsibility of a company to meet any legal specifications regarding a new product covered by the Consumer Product Safety Act

It is very important for the entrepreneur to assess whether any product that is to be marketed in the new venture is subject to any regulations under the Consumer Product Safety Act. The original act, which was passed in 1972 and then amended in 1990, created a five-member commission that has the power to prescribe safety standards for more than 15,000 types of consumer products. In August of 2008 there were significant changes that were made into law, now requiring stricter standards for potentially hazardous and unsafe products.

Large fines as well as recalls of any products that are deemed unsafe are the typical outcomes of any action enforced by the commission. For example, in 2007 U.S. companies were forced to make more than 100 recalls involving about 9 million toys. Polly Pocket play sets and Batman action figures highlighted these recalls, given that these products were found to have high lead content or that they contained small accessories that could be potentially hazardous if swallowed by a child. The public outcry from these recalls was a major factor in getting Congress to act quickly on the new legislation. In the past two decades, the Consumer Product Safety Commission had been operating on tighter budgets and smaller staff and was not able to oversee the large number of new products being launched or imported each year. With a new budget, significantly larger staff, and support from the administration it is expected that the commission will now be able to take a more active role in making sure that firms meet the new legal requirements for product safety. Stricter enforcement as well as the threat of significant increases in fines for violations should improve the situation.[20] In the last two years product recalls of toys have declined with the stricter regulations but recalls of automobiles, over-the-counter drugs, and food products have continued to make the news. Toyota, Honda, and Suzuki had major recalls due to defects in various functions. Johnson and Johnson lost over $2 billion attributed to recalls of Tylenol, Motrin, Mylanta, and Benadryl. In the food industry outbreaks of salmonella and E-coli have led to recalls of eggs, ground turkey, and peanut butter, to name a few.

Entrepreneurs should be aware of the threats of these recalls, especially if they are part of the channels of any of these high risk products. Food and toys especially should be evaluated prior to any business development.[21]

INSURANCE

Some of the problems relating to product liability were discussed in the previous section. Besides being cautious, it is also in the best interests of the entrepreneur to purchase insurance in the event that problems do occur. Service-related businesses such as day-care centers, amusement parks, and shopping centers have had significant increases in the number of lawsuits.

In general, most firms should consider coverage for those situations as described in Table 6.4. Each of these types of insurance provides a means of managing risk in the new business. The main problem is that the entrepreneur usually has limited resources in the beginning. Thus, it is important to first determine whether any of these types of insurance are needed. Note that some insurance, such as disability and vehicle coverage, is required by law and cannot be avoided. Other insurance, such as life insurance of key employees, is not required but may be necessary to protect the financial net worth of the venture. Once the entrepreneur determines what types of insurance are needed, then a decision can be made as to how much insurance and from what company. It is wise to get quotes from more than one insurance firm since rates and options can also vary. The total insurance cost represents an important financial planning factor, and the entrepreneur needs to consider increasing premiums in cost projections.

Skyrocketing medical costs have probably had the most significant impact on insurance premiums. This is especially true for workers' compensation premiums, which for some entrepreneurs have doubled or tripled in the last few years.

Entrepreneurs also have to consider health care coverage which in some cases such as in Massachusetts is mandatory for any full-time employees. This is an important benefit to employees and will require the venture to incur a significant expense if it is

TABLE 6.4 Types of Insurance and Possible Coverage

Types of Insurance	Coverage Possible
Property	• Fire insurance to cover losses to goods and premises resulting from fire and lightning. Can extend coverage to include risks associated with explosion, riot, vehicle damage, windstorm hail, and smoke. • Burglary and robbery to cover small losses for stolen property in cases of forced entry (burglary) or if force or threat of violence was involved (robbery). • Business interruption will pay net profits and expenses when a business is shut down because of fire or other insured cause.
Casualty	• General liability covers the costs of defense and judgments obtained against the company resulting from bodily injury or property damage. This coverage can also be extended to cover product liability. • Automobile liability is needed when employees use their own cars for company business.
Life	• Life insurance protects the continuity of the business (especially a partnership). It can also provide financial protection for survivors of a sole proprietorship or for loss of a key corporate executive.
Workers' compensation	• May be mandatory in some states. Provides benefits to employees in case of work-related injury.
Bonding	• This shifts responsibility to the employee for performance of a job. It protects company in case of employee theft of funds or protects contractor if subcontractor fails to complete a job within an agreed-upon time frame.

required by state law. Rates to the company will vary significantly depending on the plan and its various options. Health insurance premiums are less expensive if there is a large group of insured participants. This is, of course, difficult for a start-up venture but can be resolved by joining a group such as a professional association that offers such coverage.

However, if you are a self-employed entrepreneur, the options are limited. If you are leaving a corporate position, consider extending your health care benefits with COBRA. This usually allows you to continue on the same health care policy you were on for about three years. However, you now will have to pay the entire premium on the policy. If your COBRA has expired or one is not available, you can consider contacting your state insurance department, which can supply a list of insurance companies that provide individual health care insurance. Policies that have higher deductibles can also be considered because of their lower premiums. For additional assistance in these matters it is recommended that the entrepreneur contact the Association of Health Insurance Agents, the Health Insurance Association of America, or the U.S. Labor Department, all located in Washington, D.C.

Seeking advice from an insurance agent is often difficult because the agent is trying to sell insurance. However, there are specialists at universities or the Small Business Administration who can provide this advice at little or no cost.

SARBANES-OXLEY ACT

After a lengthy period of reported corporate misconduct involving companies such as Enron and Arthur Andersen, Congress passed the Sarbanes-Oxley Act in 2002. Although this act has provided a mechanism for greater control over the financial activities of public companies, it also has created some difficulties for start-ups and smaller companies. Recently Congress provided some relief for small businesses by making them exempt from section 404 of the Sarbanes-Oxley Act. This section requires businesses to attest to the soundness of the firm's internal controls and financial statements. This section had been blamed for burdening small businesses with the cost of these controls and in some cases was believed to discourage these firms from going public.[22]

The act contains a number of provisions, and no attempt will be made here to cover them all. Instead an overview of the law's requirements will be discussed. The complete law or relevant sections can be downloaded from the Internet.

The Sarbanes-Oxley Act covers a wide range of corporate governance activities. Under this law, CEOs are required to vouch for financial statements through a series of internal control mechanisms and reports. Directors must meet background, length of service, and responsibilities requirements regarding internal auditing and control. Any attempt to influence the auditor or impede the internal auditing process is considered a criminal act. In addition, the law covers bank fraud; securities fraud; and fraud by wire, radio, or TV.[23]

With the passage of this law there has been some concern as to the interpretation of this law and subsequent directors' liability. For example, will this law discourage qualified individuals from being members of important boards because of their concern for negative publicity that could be initiated by a disgruntled employee or stockholder?

Foreign companies that trade on U.S. stock exchanges are often delisted since there are major conflicts with the provisions of the new law and the laws of that foreign country. For example, independent audit committees, required by the new law, conflict with some foreign countries' rules and customs. This is only one example of the many conflicts that presently exist with foreign laws and customs.[24]

At present, private companies are not included in this act. However, there could be some future controls established to prevent any of these governance issues in private companies. Private companies are also subject to control if they consult with a public company and in any way influence that public company in any wrongdoing established by the Sarbanes-Oxley Act.

The other option, of course, is for the entrepreneur to set up a board of advisors instead of an extended board of directors. Advisors would not be subject to liability since they do not formulate final policy for the venture but only provide recommendations to the actual board of directors, which in this case could consist of the management of the start-up venture. If a venture capitalist or even an angel investor were involved, they would require a board seat, in which case the use of a board of advisors would not likely be acceptable and liability protection would be necessary.

CONTRACTS

contract A legally binding agreement between two parties

The entrepreneur, in starting a new venture, will be involved in a number of negotiations and *contracts* with vendors, landlords, and clients. A contract is a legally enforceable agreement between two or more parties as long as certain conditions are met. Table 6.5 identifies these conditions and the outcomes (breaches of contract) should one party not live up to the terms of the contract. It is very important for the entrepreneur to understand the

TABLE 6.5   Contract Conditions and Results of a Breach of Contract

Contract Conditions

- An offer is made. It can be oral or written but is not binding until voluntary acceptance of offer is given.
- Voluntary acceptance of offer.
- Consideration (something of value) is given by both parties.
- Both parties are competent and/or have the right to negotiate for their firms.
- Contract must be legal. Any illegal activities under a contract are not binding. An example might be gambling.
- Any sales of $500 or more must be in writing.

Results of a Contract Breach

- The party in violation of a contract may be required to live up to the agreement or pay damages.
- If one party fails to live up to its end of a contract, the second party may also agree to drop the matter and thus not live up to the agreement as well. This is referred to as contract restitution.

fundamental issues related to contracts while also recognizing the need for a lawyer in many of these negotiations.

Often business deals are concluded with a handshake. Ordering supplies, lining up financing, reaching an agreement with a partner, and so on, are common situations in which a handshake consummates the deal. Usually, when things are operating smoothly, this procedure is sufficient. However, if there are disagreements, the entrepreneur may find that there is no deal and that he or she may be liable for something never intended. The courts generally provide some guidelines based on precedence of cases. One rule is to never rely on a handshake if the deal cannot be completed within one year.

In addition to the one-year rule of thumb, the courts insist that a written contract exist for all transactions over $500. Even a quote on a specified number of parts from a manufacturer may not be considered a legal contract. For example, if an entrepreneur asked for and received a quote for 10 items and then ordered only 1 item, the seller would not have to sell that item at the original quoted price unless a written contract existed. If the items totaled over $500, even the quoted price could be changed without a written contract.

Most sellers would not want to try to avoid their obligations in the preceding example. However, unusual circumstances may arise that force the seller to change his or her mind. Thus, the safest way to conduct business deals is with a written contract, especially if the amount of the deal is over $500 and is likely to extend beyond one year.

Any deal involving real estate must be in writing to be valid. Leases, rentals, and purchases all necessitate some type of written agreement.

Although a lawyer might be necessary in very complicated or large transactions, the entrepreneur cannot always afford one. Therefore, it is helpful for the entrepreneur to understand that before signing a contract he or she should do the following:

1. Understand the terms and conditions in the contract.
2. Cross out anything that you do not agree to.
3. Do not sign if there are blank spaces (these can be crossed out).
4. Make a copy for your files after signing.

IN REVIEW

SUMMARY

This chapter explores some of the major concerns regarding intellectual property of the entrepreneur, as well as other important legal issues such as product safety, insurance, contracts, and the Sarbanes-Oxley Act. The problems with intellectual property have become more complicated with the growth of the Internet. It is important for the entrepreneur to seek legal advice in making any intellectual property legal decisions such as patents, trademarks, copyrights, and trade secrets. Lawyers have specialties that can provide the entrepreneur with the most appropriate advice under the circumstances. There are also resources identified in the chapter that should be considered before hiring an attorney. Some of this information can save time and money for the entrepreneur.

A patent requires a patent attorney, who assists the entrepreneur in completing an application to the Patent and Trademark Office with the history and description of the invention, as well as claims for its usefulness. An assessment of the existing patent(s) will help to ascertain whether infringement is likely and to evaluate the possibilities of modifying the patented product or licensing the rights from the holder of the patent. A provisional patent can be filed that will give the entrepreneur 12 months to finalize the patent. Being the first to file with a provisional patent can be very useful to provide immediate notification of ownership of the patent rights as well as provide time to develop business strategies.

A trademark may be a word, symbol, design, or some combination, or a slogan or sound that identifies the source of certain goods or services. Trademarks give the entrepreneur certain benefits as long as the following four requirements are met: (1) completion of the written application form, (2) submission of a drawing of the mark, (3) submission of five specimens showing actual use of the mark, and (4) payment of the required fees.

Copyrights protect original works of authorship. Copyrights are registered with the Library of Congress and do not usually require an attorney. Copyrights have become relevant to the use of the Internet, especially to download music, literary works, pictures, or videos.

Noncompete agreements are still not always enforced depending on the state and how well the agreement is stated. It is most important to be specific as to what is covered as well as to avoid exaggeration of geographic coverage and time allowed for the existence of the noncompete provisions. Licensing is a viable means of starting a business using someone else's product, name, information, and so on. It is also an important strategy that the entrepreneur can use to expand the business without extensive risk or large investments.

The entrepreneur should also be sensitive to possible product safety and liability requirements. Careful scrutiny of possible product problems, as well as insurance, can reduce the risk. Other risks relating to property insurance, life insurance, health insurance, workers' compensation, and bonding should be evaluated to ascertain the most cost-effective program for the entrepreneur.

Contracts are an important part of the transactions that the entrepreneur will make. As a rule of thumb, oral agreements are invalid for deals over one year and over $500. In addition, all real estate transactions must be in writing to be valid.

The Sarbanes-Oxley Act was passed in 2002 and places a great burden on public companies to streamline their financial reporting, modify the role and responsibility of boards of directors, and basically provide more checks and balances to avoid repeating the scandals of WorldCom, Enron, and others. There are a number of provisions of the law, and entrepreneurs should be aware of any relevant requirements, particularly if there is intent to take the company public. At this point the law applies only to public companies, but there are possible interactions with private firms as well as likely changes to these laws that will require continued scrutiny by entrepreneurs.

RESEARCH TASKS

1. Using the Internet, obtain copies of three patents that are at least three years old. What are the elements that are common across these patents? What are the differences? Which do you believe will be the greatest success? Can you find any evidence of products that are now on the market that incorporate any of these patented technologies?

2. Search press reports for patent infringement cases. Describe the process and the outcome. Of particular value are examples that list the legal costs of defending patent infringements and the amount awarded for a successful defense.

3. What are some of the world's most famous trademarks? Use data to back up your answer.

4. Provide a real-life example for each of the following different types of product liability: (a) negligence, (b) warranty, (c) strict liability, and (d) misrepresentation. When possible, report both the details and the payouts.

5. How much does it cost to apply for and obtain a patent?

CLASS DISCUSSION

1. Provide three examples of situations where a noncompete agreement would be necessary. In each of these three examples what should be included in the noncompete agreement to protect the venture?

2. Should copyrighted music be available on the Internet free of charge, even if it is against the wishes of the artist and the recording company? Consider both sides of the argument to make a more convincing argument.

3. To what extent should the government be involved in creating and enforcing safety laws and to what extent should companies (and industries) be responsible for creating their own standards and self-policing those standards?

SELECTED READINGS

Blum, Jonathan. (August 2011). Protect Yourself. *Entrepreneur,* vol. 39, issue 8, pp. 64–68.

> *The America Invents Act was recently passed by the U.S. Senate and it changes the U.S. Patent law. Now an entrepreneur must be the first to file in order to be granted the legal rights to a patent. In the past the first to invent was used as a basis by the courts in a patent challenge.*

Caixing, Liu; and David Yang. (June 2011). An Analysis of the Impact of the Sarbanes-Oxley Act on Earnings Management. *Advances in Management,* vol. 4, issue 6, pp. 25–31.

This is a study that examines whether the Sarbanes-Oxley Act (SOA) mitigates earnings management and thus improves financial reporting quality. The results reported here also indicate that not only does SOA mitigate earnings management but it affects high discretionary accrual firms more than low discretionary accrual firms.

Donahey, Scott M. (February/April 2010). Unique Considerations for the International Arbitration of Intellectual Property Disputes. *Dispute Resolution Journal,* vol. 65, issue 1, pp. 38–47.

This article explores how to structure international arbitration of international patent disputes. It identifies several factors that influence lawyers to include arbitration clauses. It also presents rules for suggested arbitration agreements in international patent disputes.

Fernandez-Ribas, Andrea. (July 2010). International Patent Strategies of Small and Large Firms: An Empirical Study of Nanotechnology. *Review of Policy Research,* vol. 27, issue 4, pp. 457–73.

The focus of this article is to investigate the extent small firm foreign patents differ from their larger counterparts. The sample was taken from U.S.-owned small and large businesses that applied for international patents through the World International Patent Organization. Results indicate an important contribution of small firms to the globalization of patents. Small firms also need to consider more opportunities in foreign markets with patent protection.

Gardner, Timothy M.; Jason Stansbury; and David Hart. (July 2010). The Ethics of Lateral Hiring. *Business Ethics Quarterly,* vol. 20, issue 2, pp. 341–69.

The method of critical genealogy is used to demonstrate that the norms that discourage lateral hiring or "poaching" are strategies used by powerful employers to control the turnover of their employees, making them subjects of the employer's power. Ethical responsibility should be with the employee as well as with any alternate employer looking to make lateral hiring decisions.

Leland, Thomas. (Winter 2009). Thinking Ahead in Today's Job Market: Do Not Forget about Post-Employment Restrictions When Hiring. *Employee Relations Law Journal,* vol. 35, issue 3, pp. 9–19.

This article points out that businesses that are hiring or laying off people need to understand employees' information, knowledge, and skill and the enforceability of any agreements that the employee has made not to compete with his or her former employer. The enforceability of these agreements is discussed in detail.

Orcutt, John L. (2009). The Case Against Exempting Smaller Reporting Companies from Sarbanes-Oxley Section 404: Why Market-Based Solutions Are Likely to Harm Ordinary Investors. *Fordham Journal of Corporate and Financial Law,* vol. 14, issue 2, pp. 325–414.

This article presents an overview of a case against exempting smaller reporting firms from Sarbanes-Oxley Section 404 and its intended benefits. It explores the evidence regarding substantial compliance costs of section 404 and its probable net effect. The special attributes of smaller firms are expected to warrant special attention by policy makers.

Pikas, Bohdan; Anastasia Pikas; and Candice Lymburner. (2011). The Future of the Music Industry. *Journal of Marketing Development and Competitiveness,* vol. 5, issue 3, pp. 139–49.

With the significant advances in technology that allow people to obtain music for free the music industry cannot rely on the sales of CDs as a primary source of revenue. Either the industry needs to decide to spend millions defending against illegal downloading of music or it should succumb to the release of free music. This study of a sample of 1,158 firms compares compliance costs for various categories of firms and provides cross sectional analysis of board independence, growth expectations, and R&D expenditures.

Robertson, Scott. (May 2010). How Safe Are Non-Compete Agreements? *American Agent and Broker,* vol. 82, issue 5, pp. 50–55.

This article focuses on the safety of noncompetition agreements in insurance agencies such as anti-piracy clauses and infringement of trade secrets in the U.S. The article reports that courts do not enforce noncompete agreements and will sanction agency owners for pursuing legal action against producers who take business with them.

Strand, John L. (January 2011). Facebook: Trademarks, Fan Pages, and Community Pages. *Intellectual Property and Technology Law Journal,* vol. 23, issue 1, pp. 10–13.

The article discusses the new challenges faced by trademark holders because of the creation of Facebook community pages in the U.S. Companies are having problems controlling their profiles on the Web and this paper discusses suggestions for the protection of a company's mark on these community pages.

END NOTES

1. See D. Sack, "Blown Away," *Fast Company* (February 2011), pp. 58–65, 104; J. Ashton, "Goodbye Amateurs as YouTube Takes On Television," *The London Times,* August 14, 2011, p. 6; "YouTube Violators to Copyright School," *Variety,* April 11, 2011, p. 4; D. C. Chmielewski, "Company Town; YouTube Movie Rental Service Gains 3,000 Titles," *Los Angeles Times,* May 10, 2011, p. 3.
2. Patent and Trademark Office, U.S. Department of Commerce Web site (www.uspto.gov).
3. J. Blum, "Protect Yourself," *Entrepreneur* (August 2011), pp. 64–68.
4. See www.uspto.gov/patents/int_index.jsp.
5. J. Pooley, "WIPO's Plans for Improving the PCT," *Managing Intellectual Property* (July/August 2010), pp. 84–85.
6. R. C. Scheinfeld and J. D. Sullivan, "Internet-Related Patents: Are They Paying Off?" *New York Law Journal,* December 10, 2002, p. 5.
7. B. W. Hattenbach and K. J. Weatherwax, "Bilski v. Kappos: A Divided Court Narrowly Reaffirms Patentability of Business Methods," *Intellectual Property and Technology Law Journal* (September 2010), pp. 15–18.
8. See www.uspto.gov/main/trademarks.htm.
9. See http://inventors.about.com.
10. "Face the Music," *Economist,* April 2, 2005, pp. 57–58.
11. C. Burand, "Protect Your Assets with Non-Compete Agreements," *Agent and Broker* (October 2009), pp. 14–15.
12. "Patents: Cuffing Innovation," *Electronics Design,* April 28, 2005, pp. 49–55.
13. I. Grant, *Computer Weekly,* July, 20, 2010, p. 10.
14. M. Anzani, "EMC/IBM Extend Interoperability Licensing for Storage," *Mainframe Computing* (April 2011), p. 8.
15. "FWK Forges Licensing Agreement: Interest in Licensing Spreads," *Educational Marketer,* August 16, 2010, pp. 1–3.
16. B. White-Sax, "Ever-Green Brands to Add Color to Licensing Segment," *Drug Store News,* August 23, 2010, p. 101.
17. T. L. Stanley, "In Tough Times Licensing Biz Sticks to Sure Things," *Brandweek,* June 7, 2010, p. 4.
18. M. Marr and S. Grey, "McDonald's Woos New Partners as Disney Pact Nears End," *The Wall Street Journal*, Eastern Edition, June 6, 2005, pp. B1–B2.

19. Stanley, "In Tough Times Licensing Biz Sticks to Sure Things."

20. A. Nicholas, "Dangerous Goods," *Inside Counsel* (November 2008), pp. 16–18.

21. See, J. Neff, "Can J & J Brand Family Stage Recall Recovery?" *Advertising Age,* May 23, 2011, pp. 1–21; and T. Perazzo, "The Industry Pitfall," *Food and Drug* (Summer 2011), pp. 76–77.

22. "Two Cheers for Sarbanes-Oxley," *Economist,* July 3, 2010, p. 64.

23. D. Chambers, "Did Sarbanes-Oxley Lead to Better Financial Reporting?" *Accounting and Auditing* (September 2010), pp. 24–27.

24. P. S. Foote and J. Chen, "Accounting Standards, Disclosure Requirements, and Foreign Company Listings on Stock Exchanges," *Chinese Business Review* (September 2008), p. 35.

3

FROM THE OPPORTUNITY TO THE BUSINESS PLAN

7

THE BUSINESS PLAN: CREATING AND STARTING THE VENTURE

LEARNING OBJECTIVES

1
To define what the business plan is, who prepares it, who reads it, and how it is evaluated.

2
To understand the scope and value of the business plan to investors, lenders, employees, suppliers, and customers.

3
To identify information needs and sources for each critical section of the business plan.

4
To enhance awareness of the value of the Internet as an information resource and marketing tool.

5
To present examples and a step-by-step explanation of the business plan.

6
To present helpful questions for the entrepreneur at each stage of the planning process.

7
To understand how to monitor the business plan.

OPENING PROFILE

BELINDA GUADARRAMA

The business plan, although it is often criticized as being "dreams of glory," is probably the single most important document to the entrepreneur at the start-up stage. Potential investors are not likely to consider investing in a new venture until the business plan has been completed. In addition, the business plan helps the entrepreneur maintain perspective as to what needs to be accomplished.

www.gcmicro.com

The development and preparation of a business plan can entail many obstacles and takes a strong commitment by an entrepreneur before it can actually be completed and then implemented. No one knows this better than Belinda Guadarrama, the president and CEO of GC Micro Corporation. Her company supplies computer hardware and software to Fortune 1000 companies as well as the defense and aerospace industry.

As the entrepreneur of this now multi-million-dollar company, Belinda was recognized by two Hispanic organizations—the U.S. Hispanic Chamber of Commerce and the Latin Business Association—as Hispanic Businesswoman of the Year 2002. Her firm has been consistently ranked among the 500 largest Hispanic-owned companies, and in each of the last three years has received the Boeing Performance Excellence Award and the U.S. Department of Agriculture Woman-Owned Business Contractor of the Year award.

Although today she is a successful entrepreneur, the journey was a long and arduous process with a number of highs and lows. After graduating from Trinity University and taking a number of graduate courses at the University of Texas at Austin, she began working for the Texas attorney general as the director of personnel and training. She later moved to California during the 1980s technology boom to work for a mail-order software company. Like many others, she arrived at work one day to find a note on the door indicating that the business was closed.

At that point Belinda made the decision to start her own business. She felt it was a great time to take some risks since she had no job and limited prospects. In 1986, with a few former co-workers, she launched GC Micro Corporation. To raise initial capital and money for other expenses while a business plan was being developed, she sold her house and cashed in her retirement money. She made a conscious decision at this point to put everything on the line. Eventually, with business plan in hand, she began knocking on doors to try to raise money for the start-up. It was then that she began to face some of the lows in the entrepreneurial process as she incurred one rejection after another. She could not even get a bank to lend her $5,000 to keep going. Fortunately, she persisted until she came upon the Small Business Administration (SBA) loan program that guarantees a large percentage of a loan through a local participating bank. After submitting her plan through this program, she received her first loan from a local bank.

Raising the start-up capital was only one of the early obstacles that she overcame. Being a woman and a Latina, she had to overcome many negative stereotypes. In one meeting with a potential client she was told that as a minority woman she did not have sufficient management qualifications to represent its product line and was hence turned down. However, her hard work and persistence paid off, and at the end of the first year of business the company attained revenue of $209,000. With this success, the client that had turned her down changed its mind and she became an authorized dealer for its products.

Other success followed, and soon she was pursuing contracts with the U.S. Department of Defense. In researching this market, she discovered that many government contractors are required to include a percentage of minority-owned businesses as subcontractors. She also discovered that there were not enough minority-owned businesses, presenting great opportunities for her venture. However, as she continued to investigate her opportunities she found she was blocked from records to which she had previously had access. She decided to pursue this in court, knowing that this could put her entire business on the line. Subsequently, the case *GC Micro Corporation v. the Defense Logistics Agency* reached the courts and then dragged on for several years. During this time her business was in jeopardy since many companies stated they would no longer work with her. Eventually she won her case. Her reputation as someone not afraid to take a stand and with strong leadership skills spread throughout the industry.

The company has become one of the few just-in-time (JIT) system contract suppliers, earning the company a number of best supplier awards in California. Guadarrama's entrepreneurial skills have also spilled over to civic-minded activities, supporting such programs as the California Latino-Chicano High School Drop-Out Prevention Program, the Canal Community Alliance, the Ochoa Migrant Farm Workers Camp, and the Gilroy YMCA. Belinda's success is a tribute to her strong entrepreneurial character. She was not afraid of the hard work required to plan her business—and she was not afraid to stand up for what she felt was right. Her commitment to the community has made her an inspiration to many other Hispanic businessmen and women.

GC Micro Corporation now has 14 warehouses across the United States and is an authorized dealer for about 200 manufacturers such as Sun Microsystems, IBM, Hewlett-Packard, Storage Tek, Cisco, Dell, Apple, and Sony. Now with 30 employees, sales revenue has reached $35 million.[1]

PLANNING AS PART OF THE BUSINESS OPERATION

Before we begin a discussion of the business plan, it is important for the reader to understand the different types of plans that may be part of any business operation. Planning is a process that never ends for a business. It is extremely important in the early stages of any new venture when the entrepreneur will need to prepare a preliminary business plan. The plan will become finalized as the entrepreneur has a better sense of the market, the product or services to be marketed, the management team, and the financial needs of the venture. As the venture evolves from an early start-up to a mature business, planning will continue as management seeks to meet its short-term or long-term business goals.

For any given organization, it is possible to find financial plans, marketing plans, human resource plans, production plans, and sales plans, to name a few. Plans may be short-term or long-term, or they may be strategic or operational. Plans will also differ in scope depending on the type of business or the anticipated size of the start-up operation. Even though they may serve different functions, all these plans have one important purpose: to provide guidance and structure to management in a rapidly changing market environment.

Some experts feel that the business plan does not ensure that an entrepreneur will be successful. These researchers indicate that there are many entrepreneurs such as Steve Jobs, Bill Gates, and Michael Dell that succeeded without a business plan. However, there is also strong evidence from many in this field that believe that an inexperienced entrepreneur can gain significant learning experience by engaging in the preparation of a business plan, especially when many variables and uncertainties are involved in the venture launch. Even without a completed business plan the entrepreneur would have been forced to think through many important scenarios that may be involved in the market. Even the above entrepreneurs would have thought through many of these scenarios. The process involved in preparing a business plan is ultimately what is important since planning in future stages of growth of the venture will be necessary. Thus, we continue to stress the importance of a good business plan not only for initial start-up but also for subsequent changes in strategy and for growing the new venture.[2]

WHAT IS THE BUSINESS PLAN?

business plan Written document describing all relevant internal and external elements and strategies for starting a new venture

The *business plan* is a written document prepared by the entrepreneur that describes all the relevant external and internal elements involved in starting a new venture. It is often an integration of functional plans such as marketing, finance, manufacturing, and human resources. As in the case of Belinda Guadarrama, it addresses the integration and coordination of effective business objectives and strategies when the venture contains a variety of products and services. It also addresses both short-term and long-term decision making for the first three years of operation. Thus, the business plan—or, as it is sometimes referred to, the game plan or road map—answers the questions, Where am I now? Where am I going? and How will I get there? Potential investors, suppliers, and even customers will request or require a business plan.

If we think of the business plan as a road map, we might better understand its significance. Let's suppose you were trying to decide whether to drive from Boston to Los Angeles (mission or goal) in a motor home. There are a number of possible routes, each requiring different time frames and costs. Like the entrepreneur, the traveler must make some important decisions and gather information before preparing the plan.

The travel plan would consider external factors such as emergency car repair, weather conditions, road conditions, sights to see, and available campgrounds. These factors are basically uncontrollable by the traveler but must be considered in the plan, just as the entrepreneur would consider external factors such as new regulations, the economy, competition, social changes, changes in consumer needs, or new technology.

On the other hand, the traveler does have some idea of how much money is available; how much time he or she has; and the choices of highways, roads, campgrounds, sights, and so forth. Similarly, the entrepreneur has some control over manufacturing, marketing, and personnel in the new venture.

The traveler should consider all these factors in determining what roads to take, what campgrounds to stay in, how much time to spend in selected locations, how much time and money to allow for vehicle maintenance, who will drive, and so on. Thus, the travel plan responds to three questions: Where am I now? Where am I going? and How do I get there? Then the traveler in our example—or the entrepreneur, the subject of our book—will be able to determine how much money will be needed from existing sources or new sources to achieve the plan.

We saw in the opening example of this chapter how Belinda Guadarrama used the business plan to address these questions. The functional elements of the business plan are discussed here but are also presented in more detail in the chapters that follow.

WHO SHOULD WRITE THE PLAN?

The business plan should be prepared by the entrepreneur; however, he or she may consult with many other sources in its preparation. Lawyers, accountants, marketing consultants, and engineers are useful in the preparation of the plan. Some of these needed sources can be found through services offered by the Small Business Administration (SBA), the Senior Corps of Retired Executives (SCORE), small-business development centers (SBDCs), universities, and friends or relatives. The Internet also provides a wealth of information as well as actual sample templates or outlines for business planning. Most of these sources are free of charge or have minimal fees for workshop attendance or to purchase or download any information. In many instances entrepreneurs will actually hire or offer equity (partnership) to another person who might provide the appropriate expertise in preparing the business plan as well as become an important member of the management team.

To help determine whether to hire a consultant or to make use of other resources, the entrepreneur can make an objective assessment of his or her own skills. Table 7.1 is an illustration of a rating to determine what skills are lacking and by how much. For example, a sales engineer designed a new machine that allows a user to send a 10-second personalized message in a greeting card. The greeting card had particular appeal in foreign countries. A primary concern was how best to market the machine: as a promotional tool a firm could use for its distributors, suppliers, shareholders, or employees; or as a retail product for end

TABLE 7.1   Skills Assessment

Skills	Excellent	Good	Fair	Poor
Accounting/taxes				
Planning				
Forecasting				
Marketing research				
Sales				
People management				
Product design				
Legal issues				
Technology				

users. Also it was necessary to assess these skills as they may apply to any international market opportunities. This entrepreneur, in assessing his skills, rated himself as excellent in product design and sales, good in organizing, and only fair or poor in the remaining skills. To supplement the defined weaknesses, the entrepreneur found a partner who could contribute those skills that were lacking or weak. Through such an assessment, the entrepreneur can identify what skills are needed and where to obtain them.

SCOPE AND VALUE OF THE BUSINESS PLAN—WHO READS THE PLAN?

The business plan may be read by employees, investors, bankers, venture capitalists, suppliers, customers, advisors, and consultants. Who is expected to read the plan can often affect its actual content and focus. Since each of these groups reads the plan for different purposes, the entrepreneur must be prepared to address all their issues and concerns. In some ways, the business plan must try to satisfy the needs of everyone, whereas in the actual marketplace the entrepreneur's product will be trying to meet the needs of selected groups of customers.

However, there are probably three perspectives that should be considered in preparing the plan. First is the perspective of the entrepreneur, who understands better than anyone else the creativity and technology involved in the new venture. The entrepreneur must be able to clearly articulate what the venture is all about. Second is the marketing perspective. Too often, an entrepreneur will consider only the product or technology and not whether someone would buy it. Entrepreneurs must try to view their business through the eyes of their customer. This customer orientation is discussed further in Chapter 8. Third, the entrepreneur should try to view his or her business through the eyes of the investor. Sound financial projections are required; if the entrepreneur does not have the skills to prepare this information, then outside sources can be of assistance.[3]

The depth and detail in the business plan depend on the size and scope of the proposed new venture. An entrepreneur planning to market a new high-tech machine will need a comprehensive business plan, largely because of the nature of the product and market. An entrepreneur who plans to open a retail clothing store will not need the comprehensive coverage required by a new high-tech machine manufacturer. A new e-commerce business, however, may require a very different focus, particularly on how to market the Web site that will offer the goods and services. Thus, differences in the scope of the business plan may depend on whether the new venture is a service, involves manufacturing, or is a consumer good or industrial product. The size of the market, competition, and potential growth may also affect the scope of the business plan.

The business plan is valuable to the entrepreneur, potential investors, or even new personnel, who are trying to familiarize themselves with the venture, its goals, and objectives. The business plan is important to these people because:

- It helps determine the viability of the venture in a designated market.
- It provides guidance to the entrepreneur in organizing his or her planning activities.
- It serves as an important tool in helping to obtain financing.

Potential investors are very particular about what should be included in the business plan. As stated above, even if some of the information is based on assumptions, the thinking process required to complete the plan is a valuable experience for the entrepreneur since it forces him or her to assess such things as cash flow and cash requirements. In addition, the thinking process takes the entrepreneur into the future, leading him or her to consider important issues that could impede the road to success.

DON'T EXPECT A FEE FOR MAKING AN INTRODUCTION

Q: *I'm an independent record producer. About 30 years ago, I introduced a close friend to a recording artist, and we all became friends and produced a song together. We lost touch with the artist, who is now a millionaire, but recently my friend contacted him, and they plan to form a partnership. Since I introduced them initially, do I deserve any monetary compensation from their joint venture?* —R.B., Manasquan, N.J.

A: The compensation you're asking about might be termed a "finder's fee," in which an individual gets a flat fee or a percentage of a business deal that he or she helped arrange, typically by making an introduction. "A finder's fee is associated with the performance of some type of service. The finder acts as an agent and thus is entitled to a fee for performance," says Robert Chell, a longtime business consultant in Indian Wells, Calif.

However, in your case, that introduction took place 30 years ago, and then the parties lost touch. After many years passed, your friend took it upon himself to reestablish contact with the (apparently now-successful) recording artist and form a new partnership.

Since you didn't make the introduction this time—the parties already knew each other, and you weren't asked to be a conduit—it is pretty tough to make the case that you deserve compensation from their joint venture, Chell says: "If you'd done something specific this time—maybe. But in this case, maybe not."

Other experts agreed. "If the business relationship began and ended with the production of the song way back in 1979, then an expectation of some reward, monetary or otherwise, is not in order," says Sheldon Kopin, president of JBS Associates, a management consulting firm in Cincinnati.

Source: Reprinted with permission from Karen E. Klein, "Don't Expect a Fee for Making an Introduction." September 15, 2009, www.businessweek.com/smallbiz.

The process also provides a self-assessment by the entrepreneur. Usually, he or she feels that the new venture is assured of success. However, the planning process forces the entrepreneur to bring objectivity to the idea and to reflect on such questions as: "Does the idea make sense? Will it work? Who is my customer? Does it satisfy customer needs? What kind of protection can I get against imitation by competitors? Can I manage such a business? Whom will I compete with?" This self-evaluation is similar to role playing, requiring the entrepreneur to think through various scenarios and consider obstacles that might prevent the venture from succeeding. The process allows the entrepreneur to plan ways to avoid such obstacles. It may even be possible that, after preparing the business plan, the entrepreneur will realize the obstacles cannot be avoided or overcome. Hence, the venture may be terminated while still on paper. Although this certainly is not the most desirable conclusion, it would be much better to terminate the business endeavor before investing further time and money.

HOW DO POTENTIAL LENDERS AND INVESTORS EVALUATE THE PLAN?

As stated earlier, there are a number of cookie-cutter or computer-generated software packages or samples on the Internet that are available to assist the entrepreneur in preparing a business plan. These sources, however, should be used only to assist in its preparation, since the business plan should address the needs of all the potential readers or evaluators and should reflect the strengths of management and personnel, the product or service, and available resources. There are many different ways to present a quality business plan and thus any attempt to imitate or fit your strategy and objectives into a cookie-cutter approach could have very negative results. The plan needs to focus on the above-mentioned factors and should ultimately consider its purpose.

It is conceivable that the entrepreneur will prepare a first draft of the business plan from his or her own personal viewpoint without consideration of the constituencies that will ultimately read and evaluate the plan's feasibility. As the entrepreneur becomes aware of who will read the plan, appropriate changes will be necessary. For example, one constituency may be suppliers, who may want to see a business plan before signing a contract to produce either components or finished products or even to supply large quantities of materials on consignment. Customers may also want to review the plan before buying a product that may require significant long-term commitment, such as a high-tech telecommunications system. In both cases the business plan should consider the needs of these constituencies, who may pay more attention to the experience of the entrepreneur(s) and his or her projection of the marketplace.

Another group that may evaluate the plan are the potential suppliers of capital. These lenders or investors will likely vary in terms of their needs and requirements in the business plan. For example, lenders are primarily interested in the ability of the new venture to pay back the debt including interest within a designated period of time. Banks want facts with an objective analysis of the business opportunity and all the potential risks inherent in the new venture. It is also important that, along with a solid business plan, the entrepreneur develop a strong personal relationship with the loan officer of the bank. Even the government lending programs can be supportive of business planning.

Bill Kronmiller and Paul Neutgens, partners at American Steel, a steel fabricating business in Montana, looked at the recent economic decline as an opportunity to expand their business. With lower construction costs and the opportunity to participate in the SBAs Emerging Leaders program, their plan was to build a new facility that would give them a better cash flow position, happier employees, and the ability to take on bigger projects. The SBA Emerging Leaders program, now in 27 cities, includes about 100 hours of classroom training, mentoring, and interaction with business leaders. An SBA loan resulting from this program for about $1.4 million allowed these entrepreneurs to take their business plan to a new level, to hire new employees, and to do their part in the national economic recovery.[4]

Typically, lenders focus on the four Cs of credit: character, cash flow, collateral, and equity contribution. Basically, what this means is that lenders want the business plan to reflect the entrepreneur's credit history, the ability of the entrepreneur to meet debt and interest payments (cash flow), the collateral or tangible assets being secured for the loan, and the amount of personal equity that the entrepreneur has invested.

Investors, particularly venture capitalists, have different needs since they are providing large sums of capital for ownership (equity) with the expectation of cashing out within five to seven years. Investors often place more emphasis on the entrepreneur's character than lenders do, and often spend much time conducting background checks. This is important not only from a financial perspective but also because the venture capitalist will play an important role in the actual management of the business. Hence, investors want to make sure that the entrepreneur is compliant and willing to accept this involvement. These investors will also demand high rates of return and will thus focus on the market and financial projections during this critical five- to seven-year period.

In preparing the business plan, it is important for entrepreneurs to consider the needs of external sources and not merely provide their own perspective. This will keep the plan from being an internalized document that emphasizes only the technical advantages of a product or market advantages of a service, without consideration of the feasibility of meeting market goals and long-term financial projections.

ETHICS

PROTECTING YOUR BUSINESS IDEA

One of the serious concerns that entrepreneurs voice relates to how to protect their business ideas, when they are also advised to share their business plans with many friends and associates. Since these plans provide comprehensive discussion of the new venture, the concern is understandable. Most individuals who are asked to comment and review a business plan would act in an ethical and professional manner in providing any advice to entrepreneurs. However, there are also many examples of situations in which a family member, friend, or business associate has been accused of "stealing" an idea.

The best strategy for an entrepreneur, outside of seeking the advice of an attorney, is to ask all readers who are not representing a professional firm (such as a venture capitalist) to sign a noncompete or nondisclosure agreement. An example of such an agreement can be found in Chapter 6. Those representing a professional organization (such as a bank or venture capitalist) need not be asked to complete a nondisclosure form since they would be insulted and would be inclined to reject the venture before they had even read the plan.

Entrepreneurs, in sharing their business plan with others, often become paranoid, fearing that their idea will be stolen by one of the external readers. Most external advisors and potential investors are bound by a professional code of ethics, and the entrepreneur should not be deterred from seeking external advice (see Ethics box).

PRESENTING THE PLAN

Often, colleges and universities or locally sponsored business meetings offer an opportunity for selected entrepreneurs to present their business plans in a competitive and structured setting. Typically, each selected entrepreneur is asked to present the highlights of his or her business plan in a defined time frame. The entrepreneur is expected to "sell" his or her business concept in this designated period of time. This implies that the entrepreneur must decide what to say and how to present the information. Typically the entrepreneur will focus on why this is a good opportunity, providing an overview of the marketing program (how the opportunity will convert to reality) and the results of this effort (sales and profits). Concluding remarks might reflect the recognized risks and how the entrepreneur plans to address them.

Audiences at these presentations usually include potential investors who are given an opportunity to ask pointed questions regarding any of the strategies conveyed in the business plan presentation. After the completion of all the scheduled business plan presentations, a winner is usually declared, with a financial reward that can range from $10,000 to $500,000. The benefit of these competitions is not necessarily the financial award since there can be only one winner. However, since the audience is made up of professional investors, there is always the opportunity for any one of the business plans presented to attract the attention of a venture capitalist or private investor. This interest may result in further negotiations and perhaps a future investment in the new venture. For a list of these competitions with requirements and prizes go to http://www.bizplancompetitions.com/competitions/.

INFORMATION NEEDS

Before committing time and energy to preparing a business plan, the entrepreneur should do a quick feasibility study of the business concept to see whether there are any possible barriers to success. The information, obtainable from many sources, should focus on marketing, finance, and production. The Internet, discussed later in the chapter, can be a valuable resource for the entrepreneur. It should also be noted here that if an entrepreneur is seeking an international market that the process would be the same. Differences in documentation in the business plan of course would exist, just as if the entrepreneur were focused on different industries in the US. Before beginning the feasibility study, the entrepreneur should clearly define the goals and objectives of the venture. These goals help define what needs to be done and how it will be accomplished. These goals and objectives also provide a framework for the business plan, marketing plan, and financial plan.

Goals and objectives that are too general or that are not feasible make the business plan difficult to control and implement. For example, an entrepreneur starting a sporting goods store that specialized in offbeat sports (e.g., rollerblading, skateboarding, and snowboarding) developed a business plan that called for six stores to be opened by year two of the start-up. A friend and business confidant read the plan and immediately asked the entrepreneur to explain how and where these stores would be located. Not having a clear understanding of the answers to these questions suggested to the entrepreneur that his business objectives needed to be much more reasonable and that they needed to be clarified in the marketing and strategy segments of the plan. The business associate explained to the entrepreneur that a business plan is similar to building a house, in that it is necessary that each step in the process be related to the goals and objectives or outcome of the construction. From this experience the entrepreneur rewrote the business plan to reflect more reasonable goals and objectives.

Marlo Scott, in the middle of a recession, is proving that with the right market niche start-up opportunities still exist. In New York City she has utilized an untapped niche—a cupcake, beer, and wine bar—all part of an upscale bistro called Sweet Revenge. Marlo has found a way to market cupcakes by searching successful concepts in the restaurant industry. She also sought information by taking pictures, talking to bartenders, studying lighting and furniture, and noticing color combinations and so on to identify what an upscale bistro should look like. Her information led to a fast financial success with revenue in year one of half a million dollars including sales of about 143,000 cupcakes. She has appeared on the Martha Stewart television show, been the critic's choice on Time Out New York website, and been featured in *Bon Appetit* magazine. Future planning includes apparel, lotions, perfumes, soaps, and wedding cakes.[5]

From the first example, we can see the importance of feasible, well-defined goals and objectives in the business plan. In the second example, we note that a well-defined business strategy based on market information can provide a more effective focus of the business model. Once this solid foundation is in place, strategy decisions can then be established that will allow the company to achieve those goals and objectives.

Market Information

One of the initial pieces of information needed by the entrepreneur is the market potential for the product or service. To ascertain the size of the market, it is first necessary for the entrepreneur to define the market. For example, is the product most likely to be purchased by men or women? People of high income or low income? Rural or urban dwellers? Highly educated or less educated people? A well-defined target market will make it easier to project market size and subsequent market goals for the new venture. For example, let's assume that an entrepreneur in the Boston area notes the success of businesses such as Au Bon Pain and Panera Bread Company and thus is considering launching a food business that offers the convenience of "fast food" but with the taste of a sit-down restaurant. With a huge tourism trade the entrepreneur decides on a mobile (food cart) crepe business that will include a number of carts situated in high-traffic areas.

To build a strong marketing plan with reasonable and measurable market goals and objectives the entrepreneur will need to gather information on the industry and market. Most entrepreneurs have difficulty with this stage and do not often know where to begin. The best way to start is to first visualize this process as an inverted pyramid (see Figure 7.1). This means that we start with very broad-based data and information and work down until we can develop a positioning strategy and quantifiable goals and objectives. All this information can then be used in the industry analysis and marketing planning sections of the business plan that are discussed later in this chapter. (Also see Chapter 8.)

As noted in Figure 7.1, we begin the process by evaluating general environmental trends. This would include household income trends, population shifts, food consumption habits and trends, travel, and employment trends. This information can be found in sources such as the U.S. Census Bureau, Bureau of Labor Statistics, Forrester, Reuter Business Insights, and Statistical Abstracts, to name a few. These sources are available in the local college or university library. Some sources such as the U.S. Census Bureau can be found online or in the local community library. Table 7.2 provides a partial list of sources that

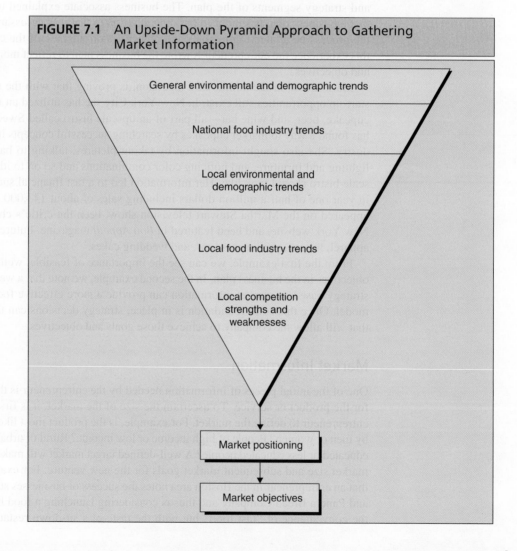

FIGURE 7.1 An Upside-Down Pyramid Approach to Gathering Market Information

- General environmental and demographic trends
- National food industry trends
- Local environmental and demographic trends
- Local food industry trends
- Local competition strengths and weaknesses

Market positioning

Market objectives

can be considered for typical census-related data. Forrester and Business Insights are private services and can be obtained from libraries or by purchasing specific reports on your industry or market. For international markets, population, economic, and demographic information can be accessed at such Web sites as www.euromonitor.com, www.census.gov/international, www.internetworldstats.com, and www.imf.org (the international monetary fund). Most of this international data is organized by country and by continent.

TABLE 7.2   Sources of Data on Environmental Trends, Industry Trends, Financial Ratios, and Other Benchmarks

Source	Description
1. U.S. Census (www.census.gov)	
A. U.S. Population Statistics for 2010	Data includes population by area.
B. *Service Annual Survey*	Includes dollar volume of receipts in selected service industries. Also includes year-to-year ratios.
C. *County Business Patterns, Metro Business Patterns, and Zip Code Business Patterns*	Economic data of small areas by industry for analyzing market potential, budgeting, and forecasting.
D. *Statistical Abstracts*	Statistics on social and economic variables at national, state, and metropolitan levels.
E. *Annual Survey of Manufacturers*	Statistics such as industry outputs, inputs, and operating data on manufacturing activity, by industry groups.
F. *Current Industrial Reports*	Regular reports measuring production and shipments of wide range of products.
2. Industry and Market Data	
A. *Encyclopedia of American Industries*	Industry trends and market data compiled on all SIC-coded firms.
B. Standard & Poor's (NetAdvantage and Market Insight)	Wide array of industry and market survey data on private and public firms.
C. U.S. Government	Find data and statistics on banking, earnings (www.usa.gov/business), economic analysis, trade data, and more.
D. *Market Share Reporter*	Compilation of market share statistics across array of products and services.
E. *RDS TableBase*	Provides market share, rankings, industry/product forecasts.
F. Other sources on industry or market trends are *MarketLine, Forrester, Investext, Dun & Bradstreet,* and *Mintel Reports.*	These reports may be purchased or accessed through a university library.
3. Financial and Industry Operating Ratios	
A. *RMA eStatement Studies* (Robert Morris Associates)	Compilation of 150,000 financial statements of banking customers with ratios and benchmarks.
B. *Almanac of Business and Industrial Financial Ratios* (Leo Troy)	Historical compilation of financial data on 4.7 million companies.
C. *Industry Norms and Key Ratios* (Dun & Bradstreet)	Ratios and financial percentages of over 1 million financial statements.
D. *Financial Studies of the Small Business*	Ratios of over 30,000 firms with capitalization under $2 million.
E. Bizminer (www.bizminer.com)	Local and regional market research reports, financial ratios on 5,500 lines of business covering a wide range of industries. Most cost less than $100.

The next step is the assessment of trends in the national food service industry. We would look for data on total food sales and commercial restaurant sales by type of restaurant. This information can be found in such sources as Dun and Bradstreet's AllBusiness, *Encyclopedia of American Industries,* the www.usa.gov Web site, and S&P's NetAdvantage. Standard and Poor's also provides very specific data on the food industry such as in its *Industry Surveys: Restaurants and the National Restaurant Association.* Also see Table 7.2 for more in-depth information on some of the important sources of information that can be used in this analysis.

Notice that the first two stages in Figure 7.1 focus on the national market, and the next two stages consider trends in the local market where the business will be located. This consists of general local economic trends and an assessment of the local food service industry. The sources may include the same ones mentioned above except data related only to the local market would be considered. In addition, the state of Massachusetts publishes data on tourism (the *Massachusetts Travel Industry Report*) and economic trends (U.S. Census Bureau). Also implicit in this local food service industry analysis is the regulatory environment. Each state has distinct regulations regarding alcohol and food delivery license requirements. If an international location was being considered the entrepreneur would follow the same procedure by searching for local data. This may be more difficult to obtain in another country. If not available, then it would be necessary for the entrepreneur to spend time in this market and speak to local businesses, channel members, and consumers. These data can also be found online or in your local library.

The final step is an analysis of the local competitive environment. In this example the entrepreneur would need to identify any restaurants, food stands, or push-cart food services that could be competitors. This list can be found in the yellow pages, local town hall (food license bureau), or through observation. Each local competitor's strengths and weaknesses should be assessed. This can be judged by using marketing research (discussed in Chapter 8); evaluating the competitors' Web sites, advertising, menus, and locations; and reviewing any published articles that have appeared in the local media. A spreadsheet can then be prepared with the list of competitors in the first column, followed by columns devoted to their strengths and weaknesses.

Once all this analysis has been completed, the entrepreneur is ready to clarify the product or service offering, actual market positioning in the competitive environment, and market objectives. These are part of the marketing plan and are discussed in more detail in Chapter 8. These data, in addition to contributing to the preparation of the marketing plan, lay the groundwork for the financial projections and forecasts discussed in Chapter 10.

Operations Information Needs

The relevance of a feasibility study of the manufacturing operations depends on the nature of the business. Most of the information needed can be obtained through direct contact with the appropriate source. The entrepreneur may need information on the following:

- *Location.* The company's location and its accessibility to customers, suppliers, and distributors need to be determined.
- *Manufacturing operations.* Basic machine and assembly operations need to be identified, as well as whether any of these operations would be subcontracted and to whom.
- *Raw materials.* The raw materials needed and suppliers' names, addresses, and costs should be determined.
- *Equipment.* The equipment needed should be listed, with its cost and whether it will be purchased or leased.

- *Labor skills.* Each unique skill needed, the number of personnel required for each skill, pay rate, and an assessment of where and how these skills will be obtained should be determined.

- *Space.* The total amount of space needed should be determined, including whether the space will be owned or leased.

- *Overhead.* Each item needed to support manufacturing—such as tools, supplies, utilities, and salaries—should be determined.

Most of the preceding information should be incorporated directly into the business plan. Each item may require some research, but this information is necessary to those who will assess the business plan and consider funding the proposal.

FINANCIAL INFORMATION NEEDS

Before preparing the financial section of the business plan, the entrepreneur will need to prepare a budget that includes a list of all possible expenditures in the first year and a list of all revenue sources, including sales and any external available funds. Thus the budget includes capital expenditures, direct operating expenses, and cash expenditures for nonexpense items. The revenue from sales must be forecast from market data, as discussed earlier. Forecasting is discussed in more detail in Chapter 8. To prepare the actual budget (see Chapter 10) the entrepreneur will need to identify benchmarks in the industry that can be used in preparing the final pro forma statements in the financial plan. These benchmarks or norms establish reasonable assumptions regarding expenditures based on industry history and trends. This is a very acceptable method to arrive at the necessary projected costs for the new venture.

We return to our crepe business example. In projecting his costs for operating the business, our entrepreneur might choose to consider the many secondary sources that provide percentage norms for such costs. For example, these sources would provide percentage norms in the industry for such costs as food, beverages, equipment, personnel, and licenses. Expenditures such as rent, utilities, insurance, and personnel costs can also be ascertained from newspapers or advertisements, or from phone conversations with real estate agents, insurance agents, equipment suppliers, and the utility companies in the area.

The benchmarks or financial ratios needed to prepare financial statements can be found in such sources as *Financial Studies of the Small Business* (Financial Research Associates), *Industry Norms and Key Business Ratios* (Dun & Bradstreet), *Annual Statement Studies* (Robert Morris Associates), *RMA eStatement Studies,* and the *Almanac of Business and Financial Ratios* (Leo Troy). More detailed information on the services these sources provide can be found in Table 7.2. It is also possible to find benchmarks by reviewing 10K reports of similar public competitors. Trade associations and trade magazines also may publish valuable data that can supplement the preceding sources to prepare the financial statements in the business plan. These pro forma statements will need to be prepared monthly in the first year and then either quarterly or annually for the next two years. Some investors require five-year projections, so the entrepreneur may need to clarify exactly what is needed by those who review the business plan.

USING THE INTERNET AS A RESOURCE TOOL

The changing world of technology offers great opportunities for entrepreneurs to be able to access information for many business activities efficiently, expediently, and at very little cost. The Internet can serve as an important source of information in the preparation of the business plan for such segments as the industry analysis, competitor analysis, and measurement of market potential, to name a few. Entrepreneurs will also find the Internet a valuable resource in later-stage planning and decision making. Besides being a business intelligence resource, the Internet also provides opportunities for marketing strategy; through its Web site, a firm can provide information on the company, its products and services, and ordering instructions.

According to data published by the Department of Commerce, online sales have continued to increase in spite of the economic downturn. In 2011 online sales are expected to reach approximately $197 billion, an increase of about 12 percent over 2010. In Western Europe online sales have risen 13 percent in 2011 to about $125 billion. Increased gas prices and convenience are the major reasons for the increase in e-commerce sales.[6]

An entrepreneur in the process of writing a business plan can also access one of the popular search engines: Google, Yahoo!, BING, MSN, AOL, or Ask Jeeves. Simply conducting a search of a topic (for example, "online sporting goods") may reveal several Web sites, articles, or sources of information to assist the entrepreneur in writing the business plan. Use of these search engines has become a commonplace procedure now to answer questions or gather information either for personal use or business purposes.

An entrepreneur should access competitors' Web sites to gain more knowledge about their strategy in the marketplace. Internet service is not costly and is an important vehicle for the entrepreneur to gather information about the market, competition, and customers as well as to distribute, advertise, and sell company products and services.

In addition to accessing Web sites, the entrepreneur can also investigate social networks, blogs, and discussion groups. A discussion group is an online forum where one can discuss a topic specific to the Web site with others. Individuals post responses to questions on the Web site. Blogs refer more to talking to or about something rather than creating a dialogue. Social networks are the fastest growing new trend in technology. They are Web sites where those with similar interests can communicate using such sites as MySpace, Twitter, LinkedIn, Windows Live Spaces, or Facebook. These are the most popular networks in the U.S. and they serve many uses depending on the needs of the entrepreneur. Marketing strategies utilizing these social networks are discussed in Chapter 8. Using Usenet, which represents the newsgroups on the Internet, the entrepreneur can use keywords to identify the most appropriate newsgroups. These newsgroups represent potential customers who can be asked specific questions on their needs, competitive products, and potential interest in the new venture's products and services. Individuals who are members of the newsgroups will then respond to these questions, providing valuable information to the entrepreneur.

Compared with alternative sources the entrepreneur need only make a small investment in hardware and software to be ready to use these online services. With its continuous improvements and modifications, the Internet will continue to provide invaluable opportunities for the entrepreneur in planning the start-up or the growth of a venture.

WRITING THE BUSINESS PLAN

The business plan could take hundreds of hours to prepare, depending on the experience and knowledge of the entrepreneur as well as the purpose it is intended to serve. It should be comprehensive enough to give any potential investor a complete picture and understanding of the new venture, and it should help the entrepreneur clarify his or her thinking about the business.

Many entrepreneurs incorrectly estimate the length of time that an effective plan will take to prepare. Once the process has begun, however, the entrepreneur will realize that it is invaluable in sorting out the business functions of a new venture.

The outline for a business plan is illustrated in Table 7.3. This outline is only meant to be a guide. As we discussed earlier in this chapter the entrepreneur should be aware that each business plan may be different depending on the purpose of the plan and who will be reading it. However, most of the items in this outline are critical elements in a general plan and should be

TABLE 7.3   Outline of a Business Plan

I. Introductory Page
   A. Name and address of business
   B. Name(s) and address(es) of principal(s)
   C. Nature of business
   D. Statement of financing needed
   E. Statement of confidentiality of report

II. Executive Summary—Two to three pages summarizing the complete business plan

III. Industry Analysis
   A. Future outlook and trends
   B. Analysis of competitors
   C. Market segmentation
   D. Industry and market forecasts

IV. Description of Venture
   A. Product(s)
   B. Service(s)
   C. Size of business
   D. Office equipment and personnel
   E. Background of entrepreneur(s)

V. Production Plan
   A. Manufacturing process (amount subcontracted)
   B. Physical plant
   C. Machinery and equipment
   D. Names of suppliers of raw materials

VI. Operations Plan
   A. Description of company's operation
   B. Flow of orders for goods and/or services
   C. Technology utilization

VII. Marketing Plan
   A. Pricing
   B. Distribution
   C. Promotion
   D. Product forecasts
   E. Controls

VIII. Organizational Plan
   A. Form of ownership
   B. Identification of partners or principal shareholders
   C. Authority of principals
   D. Management team background
   E. Roles and responsibilities of members of organization

IX. Assessment of Risk
   A. Evaluate weakness(es) of business
   B. New technologies
   C. Contingency plans

X. Financial Plan
   A. Assumptions
   B. Pro forma income statement
   C. Cash flow projections
   D. Pro forma balance sheet
   E. Break-even analysis
   F. Sources and applications of funds

XI. Appendix (contains backup material)
   A. Letters
   B. Market research data
   C. Leases or contracts
   D. Price lists from suppliers

addressed by the entrepreneur. Each of the items in the outline is detailed in the following paragraphs of this chapter. Key questions in each section are also appropriately detailed.

Introductory Page

This is the title or cover page that provides a brief summary of the business plan's contents. The introductory page should contain the following:

The name and address of the company.

The name of the entrepreneur(s), telephone number, fax number, e-mail address, and Web site address if available.

A paragraph describing the company and the nature of the business.

The amount of financing needed. The entrepreneur may offer a package (e.g., stock or debt). However, many venture capitalists prefer to structure this package in their own way.

A statement of the confidentiality of the report. This is for security purposes and is important for the entrepreneur.

This title page sets out the basic concept that the entrepreneur is attempting to develop. Investors consider it important because they can determine the amount of investment needed without having to read through the entire plan. An illustration of this page can be found in Table 7.4.

Executive Summary

This section of the business plan is prepared after the total plan is written. About two to three pages in length, the executive summary should stimulate the interest of the potential investor. This is a very important section of the business plan and should not be taken lightly by the entrepreneur since the investor uses the summary to determine if the entire business plan is worth reading. Thus, it should highlight in a concise and convincing manner the key points in the business plan.

TABLE 7.4 Sample Introductory Page

KC CLEANING SERVICE
OAK KNOLL ROAD
BOSTON, MA 02167
(617) 969-0010
www.cleaning.com

Co-owners: Kimberly Peters, Christa Peters

Description of Business:

This business will provide cleaning service on a contract basis to small and medium-sized businesses. Services include cleaning of floors, carpets, draperies, and windows, and regular sweeping, dusting, and washing. Contracts will be for one year and will specify the specific services and scheduling for completion of services.

Financing:

Initial financing requested is a $100,000 loan to be paid off over six years. This debt will cover office space, office equipment and supplies, two leased vans, advertising, and selling costs.

This report is confidential and is the property of the co-owners listed above. It is intended for use only by the persons to whom it is transmitted, and any reproduction or divulgence of any of its contents without the prior written consent of the company is prohibited.

Generally the executive summary should address a number of issues or questions that anyone picking up the written plan for the first time would want to know. For example:

What is the business concept or model?

How is this business concept or model unique?

Who are the individuals starting this business?

How will they make money and how much?

If the new venture has a strong growth plan and in five years expects to be positioned for an initial public offering (IPO), then the executive summary should also include an exit strategy. If the venture is not initially expecting this kind of growth, the entrepreneurs should avoid any discussion of an exit strategy in the executive summary.

Any supportive evidence, such as data points from marketing research or legal documents or contracts that might strengthen the case on the preceding issues, also should be included. Under no circumstances should the entrepreneur try to summarize every section of the plan, especially since the emphasis placed on the preceding issues depends on who is reading the plan.

It should be remembered that this section is only meant to highlight key factors and motivate the person holding the plan to read it in its entirety. Key factors for some plans might be the people involved. For example, if one of the entrepreneurs has been very successful in other start-ups, then this person and his or her background needs to be emphasized. If the venture has a contract in hand with a large customer, then this would be highlighted in the executive summary. It is similar to the opening statement a lawyer might make in an important court trial or the introductory statements made by a salesperson in a sales call.

Environmental and Industry Analysis

It is important to put the new venture in a proper context by first conducting an *environmental analysis* to identify trends and changes occurring on a national and international level that may impact the new venture. This process was described earlier in this chapter. Examples of these environmental factors are:

environmental analysis
Assessment of external uncontrollable variables that may impact the business plan

Economy. The entrepreneur should consider trends in the GNP, unemployment by geographic area, disposable income, and so on.

Culture. An evaluation of cultural changes may consider shifts in the population by demographics, for example, the impact of the baby boomers or the growing elderly population. Shifts in attitudes, such as "Buy American," or trends in safety, health, and nutrition, as well as concern for the environment, may all have an impact on the entrepreneur's business plan.

Technology. Advances in technology are difficult to predict. However, the entrepreneur should consider potential technological developments determined from resources committed by major industries or the U.S. government. Being in a market that is rapidly changing due to technological development will require the entrepreneur to make careful short-term marketing decisions as well as to be prepared with contingency plans given any new technological developments that may affect his or her product or service.

Legal concerns. There are many important legal issues in starting a new venture; these were discussed in Chapter 6. The entrepreneur should be prepared for any future legislation that may affect the product or service, channel of distribution, price, or promotion strategy. The deregulation of prices, restrictions on media advertising (e.g., ban on cigarette ads or requirements for advertising to children), and safety regulations affecting the product or packaging are examples of legal restrictions that can affect any marketing program.

All the preceding external factors are generally uncontrollable. However, as indicated, an awareness and assessment of these factors using some of the sources identified can provide strong support for the opportunity and can be invaluable in developing the appropriate marketing strategy.

industry analysis
Reviews industry trends and competitive strategies

As stated earlier (see Figure 7.1), this process can be visualized as an upside-down pyramid leading to specific market strategy and objectives. Once an assessment of the environment is complete, the entrepreneur should conduct an *industry analysis* that will focus on specific industry trends. Some examples of these factors are:

Industry demand. Demand as it relates to the industry is often available from published sources. Knowledge of whether the market is growing or declining, the number of new competitors, and possible changes in consumer needs are all important issues in trying to ascertain the potential business that might be achieved by the new venture. The projected demand for the entrepreneur's product or service will require some additional marketing research, which will be discussed in Chapter 8.

Competition. Most entrepreneurs generally face potential threats from larger corporations. The entrepreneur must be prepared for these threats and should be aware of who the competitors are and what their strengths and weaknesses are so that an effective marketing plan can be implemented. Most competitors can be easily identified from experience, trade journal articles, advertisements, Web sites, or even the yellow pages.

There are numerous sources that the entrepreneur can consult to attain general industry and competitive data for inclusion in this part of the business plan. Some of these were mentioned earlier in this chapter (also review Table 7.2), in relation to our discussion of the gathering of market information. Many of these sources can be found in local or university libraries. They include: *Encyclopedia of American Industries, Encyclopedia of Emerging Industries, Standard and Poor's Industry Surveys, MarketLine Business Information Centre, Forrester, Investext Plus,* and *Mintel Reports.* Each of these sources focuses on different types of industries or markets and can be easily evaluated as to their benefit either by an online search (such as Google) or by a visit to a local library. Most of these sources also provide published reports that are available for purchase.

The last part of the business plan's industry analysis section should focus on the specific market, which would include such information as who the customer is and what the business environment is like in the specific market and geographic area where the venture will compete. Thus, any differences in any of the preceding variables that reflect the specific market area in which the new venture will operate must be considered. This information is particularly significant to the preparation of the marketing plan section of the business plan, which is discussed in Chapter 8.

In addition to the numerous industry sources given, there are also many market databases that can be researched for relevant data to incorporate into this section of the business plan. Market share and size of market often can be assessed from databases such as: *TableBase* and *Business & Industry, Market Share Reporter, Economic Census, County Business Patterns, Current Industrial Reports, Service Annual Survey,* and *Monthly Retail and Food Service Sales and Inventories.* More specific data on demographic trends and possible target market numbers can be found in: *Profiles of General Demographic Characteristics 2010 Census/Population, Mediamark Reporter,* and *Lifestyle Market*

TABLE 7.5   Critical Issues for Environmental and Industry Analysis
1. What are the major economic, technological, legal, and political trends on a national and an international level?
2. What are total industry sales over the past five years?
3. What is anticipated growth in this industry?
4. How many new firms have entered this industry in the past three years?
5. What new products have been recently introduced in this industry?
6. Who are the nearest competitors?
7. How will your business operation be better than this?
8. Are the sales of each of your major competitors growing, declining, or steady?
9. What are the strengths and weaknesses of each of your competitors?
10. What trends are occurring in your specific market area?
11. What is the profile of your customers?
12. How does your customer profile differ from that of your competition?

Analyst. Finally, state-by-state population, demographic, and housing data usually are available from each state's Web site.

A list of some key questions the entrepreneur should consider for this section of the business plan is provided in Table 7.5.

Description of Venture

description of the
venture Provides
complete overview of the
product(s), service(s), and
operations of a new
venture

The *description of the venture* should be detailed in this section of the business plan. This will enable the investor to ascertain the size and scope of the business. This section should begin with the mission statement or company mission of the new venture. This statement basically describes the nature of the business and what the entrepreneur hopes to accomplish with that business. This mission statement or business definition will guide the firm through long-term decision making. After the mission statement, a number of important factors that provide a clear description and understanding of the business venture should be discussed. Key elements are the product(s) or service(s), the location and size of the business, the personnel and office equipment that will be needed, the background of the entrepreneur(s), and the history of the venture. Table 7.6 summarizes some of the important questions the entrepreneur needs to answer when preparing this section of the business plan.

The location of any business may be vital to its success, particularly if the business is retail or involves a service. Thus, the emphasis on location in the business plan is a function of the type of business. In assessing the building or space the business will occupy, the entrepreneur may need to evaluate such factors as parking; access from roadways to facility; and access to customers, suppliers, distributors, delivery rates, and town regulations or zoning laws. An enlarged local map may help give the location some perspective with regard to roads, highways, access, and so forth.

Recently an entrepreneur considered opening a new doughnut shop at a location diagonally across from a small shopping mall on a heavily traveled road. Traffic counts indicated a large potential customer base if people would stop for coffee, and so on, on their way to work. After enlarging a local map, the entrepreneur noted that the morning flow of traffic

---

TABLE 7.6   Describing the Venture

1. What is the mission of the new venture?
2. What are your reasons for going into business?
3. Why will you be successful in this venture?
4. What development work has been completed to date?
5. What is your product(s) and/or service(s)?
6. Describe the product(s) and/or service(s), including patent, copyright, or trademark status.
7. Where will the business be located?
8. Is your building new? old? in need of renovations? (If renovation is needed, state costs.)
9. Is the building leased or owned? (State the terms.)
10. Why is this building and location right for your business?
11. What office equipment will be needed?
12. Will equipment be purchased or leased?
13. What experience do you have and/or will you need to successfully implement the business plan?

---

required drivers to make a left turn into the doughnut shop, crossing the outbound lane. Unfortunately, the roadway was divided by a concrete center strip with no break to allow for a left-hand turn. The only possibility for entry into the shop required the customer to drive down about 400 yards and make a U-turn. It would also be difficult for the customer to get back on the roadway traveling in the right direction. Since the town was unwilling to open the road, the entrepreneur eliminated this site from any further consideration.

This simple assessment of the location, market, and so on, saved the entrepreneur from a potential disaster. Maps that locate customers, competitors, and even alternative locations for a building or site can be helpful in this evaluation. Some of the important questions that might be asked by an entrepreneur are as follows:

How much space is needed?

Should I buy or lease the building?

What is the cost per square foot?

Is the site zoned for commercial use?

What town restrictions exist for signs, parking, and so forth?

Is renovation of the building necessary?

Is the facility accessible to traffic?

Is there adequate parking?

Will the existing facility have room for expansion?

What is the economic and demographic profile of the area?

Is there an adequate labor pool available?

What are local taxes?

Are sewage, electricity, and plumbing adequate?

If the building or site decision involves legal issues, such as a lease, or requires town variances, the entrepreneur should hire a lawyer. Problems relating to regulations and

TABLE 7.7 Production Plan

1. Will you be responsible for all or part of the manufacturing operation?
2. If some manufacturing is subcontracted, who will be the subcontractors? (Give names and addresses.)
3. Why were these subcontractors selected?
4. What are the costs of the subcontracted manufacturing? (Include copies of any written contracts.)
5. What will be the layout of the production process? (Illustrate steps if possible.)
6. What equipment will be needed immediately for manufacturing?
7. What raw materials will be needed for manufacturing?
8. Who are the suppliers of new materials and what are the appropriate costs?
9. What are the costs of manufacturing the product?
10. What are the future capital equipment needs of the venture?

If a Retail Operation or Service:

1. From whom will merchandise be purchased?
2. How will the inventory control system operate?
3. What are the storage needs of the venture and how will they be promoted?
4. How will the goods flow to the customer?
5. Chronologically, what are the steps involved in a business transaction?
6. What are the technology utilization requirements to service customers effectively?

leases can be avoided easily, but under no circumstances should the entrepreneur try to negotiate with the town or a landlord without good legal advice.

Production Plan

production plan Details how the product(s) will be manufactured

If the new venture is a manufacturing operation, a *production plan* is necessary. This plan should describe the complete manufacturing process. If some or all of the manufacturing process is to be subcontracted, the plan should describe the subcontractor(s), including location, reasons for selection, costs, and any contracts that have been completed. If the manufacturing is to be carried out in whole or in part by the entrepreneur, he or she will need to describe the physical plant layout; the machinery and equipment needed to perform the manufacturing operations; raw materials and suppliers' names, addresses, and terms; costs of manufacturing; and any future capital equipment needs. In a manufacturing operation, the discussion of these items will be important to any potential investor in assessing financial needs.

Table 7.7 summarizes some of the key questions in this section of the business plan. If the new venture does not include any manufacturing functions, this section should be eliminated from the plan.

Operations Plan

All businesses—manufacturing or nonmanufacturing—should include an operations plan as part of the business plan. This section goes beyond the manufacturing process (when the new venture involves manufacturing) and describes the flow of goods and services from production to the customer. It might include inventory or storage of manufactured products, shipping, inventory control procedures, and customer support services. A non-manufacturer such as a retailer or service provider would also need this section in the business plan to explain the chronological steps in completing a business transaction. For example, an Internet retail sports clothing operation would need to describe how and where the products offered would be purchased, how they would be stored, how the inventory would be managed, how products would be shipped, and, importantly, how a customer would log on and complete a transaction. In addition, this would be a convenient place for the entrepreneur to discuss the role of technology in the business transaction process. For any Internet retail operation, some explanation of the technology requirements needed to efficiently and profitably complete a successful business transaction should be included in this section.

It is important to note here that the major distinction between services and manufactured goods is services involve intangible performances. This implies that they cannot be touched, seen, tasted, heard, or felt in the same manner as manufactured products. Airlines, hotels, car rental agencies, theaters, and hospitals, to name a few, rely on business delivery or quality of service. For these firms, performance often depends on location, facility layout, and personnel, which can, in turn, affect service quality (including such factors as reliability, responsiveness, and assurance). The process of delivering this service quality is what distinguishes one new service venture from another and thus needs to be the focus of an operations plan. Some key questions or issues for both the manufacturing and nonmanufacturing new venture are summarized in Table 7.7.

Marketing Plan

marketing plan
Describes market conditions and strategy related to how the product(s) and service(s) will be distributed, priced, and promoted

The *marketing plan* (discussed in detail in Chapter 8) is an important part of the business plan since it describes how the product(s) or service(s) will be distributed, priced, and promoted. Marketing research evidence to support any of the critical marketing decision strategies as well as for forecasting sales should be described in this section. Specific forecasts for a product(s) or service(s) are indicated to project the profitability of the venture. The budget and appropriate controls needed for marketing strategy decisions are also discussed in detail in Chapter 8. Potential investors regard the marketing plan as critical to the success of the new venture. Thus, the entrepreneur should make every effort to prepare as comprehensive and detailed a plan as possible so that investors can be clear as to what the goals of the venture are and what strategies are to be implemented to effectively achieve these goals. Marketing planning will be an annual requirement (with careful monitoring and changes made on a weekly or monthly basis) for the entrepreneur and should be regarded as the road map for short-term decision making.

Organizational Plan

organizational plan
Describes form of ownership and lines of authority and responsibility of members of new venture

The *organizational plan* is the part of the business plan that describes the venture's form of ownership—that is, proprietorship, partnership, or corporation. If the venture is a partnership, the terms of the partnership should be included. If the venture is a corporation, it is important to detail the shares of stock authorized and share options, as well as the names, addresses, and resumes of the directors and officers of the corporation. It is also helpful to provide an organization chart indicating the line of authority and the responsibilities of the members of the organization. Table 7.8 summarizes some of the key questions the entrepreneur needs to answer in preparing this section of the business plan. This information provides the potential investor with a clear understanding of who controls the organization and how other members will interact in performing their management functions. Chapter 9 provides more detail on this part of the business plan.

TABLE 7.8   Organization Structure
1. What is the form of ownership of the organization?
2. If a partnership, who are the partners and what are the terms of agreement?
3. If incorporated, who are the principal shareholders and how much stock do they own?
4. How many shares of voting or nonvoting stock have been issued and what type?
5. Who are the members of the board of directors? (Give names, addresses, and resumes.)
6. Who has check-signing authority or control?
7. Who are the members of the management team and what are their backgrounds?
8. What are the roles and responsibilities of each member of the management team?
9. What are the salaries, bonuses, or other forms of payment for each member of the management team?

Assessment of Risk

assessment of risk
Identifies potential hazards and alternative strategies to meet business plan goals and objectives

Every new venture will be faced with some potential hazards, given its particular industry and competitive environment. It is important that the entrepreneur make an *assessment of risk* in the following manner. First, the entrepreneur should indicate the potential risks to the new venture. Next should be a discussion of what might happen if these risks become reality. Finally, the entrepreneur should discuss the strategy that will be employed to either prevent, minimize, or respond to the risks should they occur. Major risks for a new venture could result from a competitor's reaction; weaknesses in the marketing, production, or management team; and new advances in technology that might render the new product obsolete. Even if these factors present no risks to the new venture, the business plan should discuss why that is the case.

Financial Plan

financial plan
Projections of key financial data that determine economic feasibility and necessary financial investment commitment

Like the marketing, production, and organization plans, the *financial plan* is an important part of the business plan. It determines the potential investment commitment needed for the new venture and indicates whether the business plan is economically feasible. (The financial plan is discussed in more detail in Chapter 10.)

Generally, three financial areas are discussed in this section of the business plan. First, the entrepreneur should summarize the forecasted sales and the appropriate expenses for at least the first three years, with the first year's projections provided monthly. The form for displaying this information is illustrated in Chapter 10. It includes the forecasted sales, cost of goods sold, and the general and administrative expenses. Net profit after taxes can then be projected by estimating income taxes.

The second major area of financial information needed is cash flow figures for three years, with the first year's projections provided monthly. Since bills have to be paid at different times of the year, it is important to determine the demands on cash on a monthly basis, especially in the first year. Remember that sales may be irregular, and receipts from customers also may be spread out, thus necessitating the borrowing of short-term capital to meet fixed expenses such as salaries and utilities. A form for projecting the cash flow needs for a 12-month period can be found in Chapter 10.

The last financial item needed in this section of the business plan is the projected balance sheet. This shows the financial condition of the business at a specific time. It summarizes the assets of a business, its liabilities (what is owed), the investment of the entrepreneur and any partners, and retained earnings (or cumulative losses). A form for the balance sheet is included in Chapter 10, along with more detailed explanations of the items

AN UNUSUAL START-UP: ELEVATOR PITCH FOR COFFEE POUCHES

A softball teammate tells you about a new product he has heard about that substitutes for chewing tobacco. You have recently sold your business in California and you are looking for some opportunities to invest your money in an interesting start-up. As a longtime athlete in high school and college you have continued to play softball in local leagues and would love to entertain some way to invest in a product that would involve professional athletes. Would you consider investing in the new product?

We all watch baseball players that are often chewing tobacco and constantly spitting, much to the dismay of viewing audiences. Pat Pezet and Matt Canepa have a solution to the chewing tobacco problem as well as a great substitute for those who need a caffeine boost and do not have the ability to make a cup of coffee. Their innovation is chewable flavored coffee pouches that contain about as much caffeine as a quarter cup of coffee as well as a small amount of vitamins. They come in two flavors: mint chocolate and mocha. Matt and Pat were both amateur and minor league baseball players and were finishing their degrees at California Polytechnic State University when one night while working on an economic project, they decided to stuff wads of coffee grinds in their mouths instead of making a pot of coffee. The caffeine "kicked in" and they both decided that they might be on to something.

After this discovery the two friends won a couple of business plan competitions that netted them funds and interest from investors who heard their presentation. In 2009 with their business plan and initial funding they launched Grinds. As a rollout they targeted minor and major league baseball players with Grinds as a substitute for chewing tobacco. Word of mouth quickly elevated their success such that a number of players have become testimonials for the product.

Revenues in 2011 are expected to break the six figure mark by the end of the year. With limited funds they have utilized social networks such as Twitter and Facebook to get the word out about their product. They are considering FDA approval since the product is considered a supplement. Other options are to increase the flavors offered and to consider other channels of distribution such as retail stores.

Source: Adapted from www.getgrinds.com; www.twitter.com/getGRINDS; www.facebook.com/getGRINDS; and "Grinding It Out," by Matt Villano, *Entrepreneur* (September 2011), p. 21.

included. Any assumptions considered for the balance sheet or any other item in the financial plan should be listed for the benefit of the potential investor.

Appendix

The appendix of the business plan generally contains any backup material that is not necessary in the text of the document. Reference to any of the documents in the appendix should be made in the plan itself.

Letters from customers, distributors, or subcontractors are examples of information that should be included in the appendix. Any documentation of information—that is, secondary data or primary research data used to support plan decisions—should also be included. Leases, contracts, or any other types of agreements that have been initiated also may be included in the appendix. Finally, price lists from suppliers and competitors may be added.

USING AND IMPLEMENTING THE BUSINESS PLAN

The business plan is designed to guide the entrepreneur through the first year of operations. It is important that the implementation of the strategy contain control points to ascertain progress and to initiate contingency plans if necessary. Some of the controls necessary in manufacturing, marketing, financing, and the organization are discussed in subsequent chapters. Most important to the entrepreneur is that the business plan not end up in a drawer somewhere once the financing has been attained and the business launched.

There has been a tendency among many entrepreneurs to avoid planning. The reason often given is that planning is dull or boring and is something used only by large companies. This may be an excuse; perhaps the real truth is that some entrepreneurs are afraid to plan.[7] Planning is an important part of any business operation. Without good planning, the entrepreneur is likely to pay an enormous price. All one has to do is consider the planning done by suppliers, customers, competitors, and banks to realize that it is important for the entrepreneur. It is also important to realize that without good planning the employees will not understand the company's goals and how they are expected to perform in their jobs.

Bankers are the first to admit that few business failures result from a lack of cash but, instead, that businesses fail because of the entrepreneur's inability to plan effectively. Intelligent planning is not a difficult or impossible exercise for the inexperienced entrepreneur. With the proper commitment and support from many outside resources, such as those shown in Table 7.2, the entrepreneur can prepare an effective business plan.

In addition, the entrepreneur can enhance effective implementation of the business plan by developing a schedule to measure progress and to institute contingency plans. These frequent readings or control procedures will be discussed next.

Measuring Plan Progress

During the introductory phases of the start-up, the entrepreneur should determine the points at which decisions should be made as to whether the goals or objectives are on schedule. Typically, the business plan projections will be made on a 12-month schedule. However, the entrepreneur cannot wait 12 months to see whether the plan has been successfully achieved. Instead, on a frequent basis (i.e., the beginning of each month) the entrepreneur should check the profit and loss statement; cash flow projections; and information on inventory, production, quality, sales, collection of accounts receivable, and disbursements for the previous month. Company Web sites should also be assessed as part of this process. This feedback should be simple but should provide key members of the organization with current information in time to correct any major deviations from the goals and objectives outlined. A brief description of each of these control elements is given here:

- *Inventory control.* By controlling inventory, the firm can ensure maximum service to the customer. The faster the firm gets back its investment in raw materials and finished goods, the faster that capital can be reinvested to meet additional customer needs.

- *Production control.* Compare the cost figures estimated in the business plan with day-to-day operation costs. This will help to control machine time, worker hours, process time, delay time, and downtime cost.

- *Quality control.* This will depend on the type of production system but is designed to make sure that the product performs satisfactorily.

- *Sales control.* Information on units, dollars, specific products sold, price of sales, meeting of delivery dates, and credit terms is useful to get a good perspective of the sales of the new venture. In addition, an effective collections system for accounts receivable should be set up to avoid aging of accounts and bad debts.

- *Disbursements.* The new venture should also control the amount of money paid out. All bills should be reviewed to determine how much is being disbursed and for what purpose.

- *Web site control.* With more and more sales being supported or garnered from a company's Web site, it is very important to continually evaluate the Web site to ascertain its effectiveness in meeting the goals and objectives of the plan. There are many services and software packages available to assist the entrepreneur in this process. These service companies and software alternatives are too numerous to mention here but can easily be identified from an Internet search.[8]

Updating the Plan

The most effective business plan can become out-of-date if conditions change. Environmental factors such as the economy, customers, new technology, or competition—and internal factors such as the loss or addition of key employees—can all change the direction of the business plan. Thus, it is important to be sensitive to changes in the company, industry, and market. If these changes are likely to affect the business plan, the entrepreneur should determine what revisions are needed. In this manner, the entrepreneur can maintain reasonable targets and goals and keep the new venture on a course that will increase its probability of success.

WHY SOME BUSINESS PLANS FAIL

Generally, a poorly prepared business plan can be blamed on one or more of the following factors:

- Goals set by the entrepreneur are unreasonable.
- Objectives are not measurable.
- The entrepreneur has not made a total commitment to the business or to the family.
- The entrepreneur has no experience in the planned business.
- The entrepreneur has no sense of potential threats or weaknesses to the business.
- No customer need was established for the proposed product or service.

Setting objectives requires the entrepreneur to be well informed about the type of business and the competitive environment. Objectives should be specific and not so mundane as to lack any basis of control. For example, the entrepreneur may target a specific market share, units sold, or revenue. These objectives are measurable and can be monitored over time.

In addition, the entrepreneur and his or her family must make a total commitment to the business to be able to meet the demands of a new venture. For example, it is difficult to operate a new venture on a part-time basis while still holding onto a full-time position. And it is also difficult to operate a business without an understanding from family members as to the time and resources that will be needed. Lenders or investors will not be favorably inclined toward a venture that does not have full-time commitment.

Generally, a lack of experience will result in failure unless the entrepreneur can either attain the necessary knowledge or team up with someone who already has it. For example, an entrepreneur trying to start a new restaurant without any experience or knowledge of the restaurant business would be in a disastrous situation.

The entrepreneur should also document customer needs before preparing the plan. Customer needs can be identified from direct experience, letters from customers, or marketing research. A clear understanding of these needs and how the entrepreneur's business will effectively meet them is vital to the success of the new venture.

IN REVIEW

SUMMARY

This chapter has established the scope and value of the business plan and has outlined the steps in its preparation. The business plan may be read by employees, investors, lenders, suppliers, customers, and consultants. The scope of the plan will depend on who reads it, the size of the venture, and the specific industry for which the venture is intended.

The business plan is essential in launching a new venture. The result of many hours of preparation will be a comprehensive, well-written, and well-organized document that will serve as a guide to the entrepreneur and as an instrument to raise necessary capital and financing.

Before beginning the business plan, the entrepreneur will need information on the market, manufacturing operations, and financial estimations. This process can be viewed as an upside-down pyramid, beginning with a very broad-based analysis down to specific market positioning and the determination of specific goals and objectives. The Internet represents a low-cost service that can provide valuable information on the market, customers and their needs, and competitors. This information should be evaluated based on the goals and objectives of the new venture. These goals and objectives also provide a framework for setting up controls for the business plan.

The chapter presents a comprehensive discussion and outline of a typical business plan. Each key element in the plan is discussed, an information-gathering process is described, and examples are provided. Control decisions are presented to ensure the effective implementation of the business plan. In addition, some insights as to why business plans fail are discussed.

RESEARCH TASKS

1. There are many software packages that aim to help entrepreneurs write a business plan. Research the Internet and select three of these software packages. What is different about them? How are they similar? How can they assist an entrepreneur in the preparation of his final business plan?
2. Find five business plans in your library. What are the common topics covered across all five plans? What are the differences? Choose the one that you believe is the best written and then describe why you believe it is better than the others.
3. Speak to five entrepreneurs and find out why they have (or do not have) a business plan. For those who do have a business plan, find out when it was written, the purpose for which it was created, and whether it has been used and/or kept up-to-date.

CLASS DISCUSSION

1. Given the difficulties in accurately predicting the future, is a business plan useful? Provide three reasons for writing one and three reasons for not preparing a plan. What is your conclusion and why?
2. What makes an excellent business plan?
3. Would the entrepreneur be better off spending more time selling his or her product rather than investing so much time in writing a business plan?

4. If a business plan is to be used to raise capital, then why would the entrepreneur want to advertise the firm's major risks by detailing them in the business plan?

5. What is the purpose of the business plan if the audience is (a) the entrepreneur, (b) an investor, or (c) a key supplier? How might the plan be adapted for these different audiences? Or do you believe that it is better to simply have one business plan that serves all audiences?

SELECTED READINGS

Bartes, František. (2011). Action Plan—Basis of Competitive Intelligence Activities. *Economics and Management,* vol. 16, pp. 664–69.

Competitive intelligence has become an important business practice. The author argues that competitive intelligence is often improperly understood. His view is that it is a means of forecasting the future. It then becomes the basis of planning and important strategic decision making.

Bekiaris, Maria; and Dan Warne. (September 2010). Starter Kit. *Money,* pp. 36–38.

This article provides important questions and answers related to starting a new business. The plan is regarded as one of the most important steps to get a new venture on the right path. Responses to questions regarding registering a business, setting up a company bank account, determining insurance needs, where to get help, and how to set up an efficient office are all addressed.

Bewayo, Edward D. (2010). Pre-Start-Up Preparations: Why the Business Plan Isn't Always Written. *Entrepreneurial Executive,* vol. 15, pp. 9–23.

This paper summarizes the results of a survey of 355 small business owners in New Jersey. It found that 50 percent of these businesses prepared a business plan. The main reasons for not preparing a plan was either because the venture did not need financing or the entrepreneurs had prior experience that substituted for a business plan. However, about half of those entrepreneurs that had experience still felt compelled to prepare a business plan. There was also a high correlation between the preparation of a plan and the need for external financing.

Deeter-Schmelz, Dawn R.; Rosemary P. Ramsey; and Jule B. Gassenheimer. (Summer 2011). Bleu Ribbon Chocolates: How Can Small Businesses Adapt to Changing Environment? *Marketing Education Review,* vol. 21, issue 2, pp. 177–82.

A small regional manufacturer of chocolates that markets to trade accounts, corporate-owned stores, and online/mail is faced with declining sales in a poor economy and changes in consumer life styles. The paper focuses on serious strategic issues such as changing the product line, considering more in-source manufacturing, reducing the number of company-owned stores, increasing sales to retail outlets, or just waiting for the economy to turn around.

Finley, Daniel C. (January/February 2011). A Plan for Success. *Advisor Today,* vol. 106, issue 1, pp. 58–59.

Highlighted here are views on how to accomplish goals set in the planning process. The author addresses the importance of building a blueprint with details on goals and strategy to meet these goals.

Gjerde, Thomas J.; and Thomas J. Harlow. (2010 Supplement). Valuing a Turnaround Plan for a Company in the Restaurant Equipment Business. *Journal of the International Academy for Case Studies,* pp. 39–48.

A case study on TastySlush's plan to restore its reputation is discussed in this paper. It provides a case study of why this company failed to maintain quality and durability in its frozen dessert and beverage equipment. A consultant was hired to provide a turnaround plan to revive the company's reputation in the food equipment business.

Komoszewski, Jim. (March 2011). Creating a Business Plan. *Investment Advisor,* vol. 31, issue 3, pp. 60–64.

This article discusses the importance of financial advisors to prepare and implement a business plan. It outlines the elements of a note card plan in order to guide investors to define goals, build a strategy, and implement changes in their business.

Robinson, Sherry; and Hans Anton Stubberud. (2011). Gender Differences in Entrepreneurs' Perceived Problems, Profits, and Plans. *International Journal of Entrepreneurship,* vol. 15, pp. 25–44.

This is a study of European business owners that had started their business and were still in operation after three years. Thus they were considered successful. Impediments to selling products and services due to competition and lack of demand were most often mentioned. Gender differences were also reported, with women incurring lower levels of profitability.

Schnuer, Jenna. (September 2011). Rebuild Rebuild. *Entrepreneur,* vol. 39, issue 9, pp. 76–78.

This is a good example of how to control and track inventory using a mobile device application called Thrive. The owner of a home furnishing store utilized this application to improve his business strategy.

END NOTES

1. See Katherine A. Diaz, "A Champion for Small Business: GC Micro's Belinda Guadarrama Breaks Barriers," *HispanicTrends.com* (Spring 2003), pp. 1–6; "GC Micro's 'Huge Step': Petaluma Computer Contractor Selected to Provide Equipment for Federal Agencies," *The Press Democrat,* November 7, 2007; and www.gcmicro.com.
2. See Kate Lister, "Myth of the Business Plan," *Entrepreneur* (January 2011), pp. 64–65; "A Simple Plan," *Entrepreneur* (August 2010), p. 38; and Sarah Simoneaux and Chris Stroud, "A Business Plan: The GPS for Your Company," *Journal of Pension Benefits: Issues in Administration* 18, issue 2 (Winter 2011), pp. 92–95.
3. Jack Kwicien, "Put Your Plan into Action," *Employee Benefit Advisor* (April 2011), pp. 60–62.
4. See http://www.sba.gov/about-offices-content/2/3126/success-stories.
5. Jennifer Wang, "A Refined Taste," *Entrepreneur* (April 2011), pp. 28–34.
6. See www.Fortune3.com; and www.hometextilestoday.com.
7. See Jason Daley, "First Lesson: Trust Your Gut," *Entrepreneur* (March 2010), p. 106; and Carl Richards, "Planning without Fear," *Financial Planning* (April 2010), pp. 93–94.
8. Allan Kent, "Choosing the Right CMS for Your Website," *NZ Business* (May 2011), pp. 46–47.

8

THE MARKETING PLAN

1

To understand the relevance of industry and competitive analysis
to the market planning process.

2

To describe the role of marketing research in determining
marketing strategy for the marketing plan.

3

To illustrate an effective and feasible procedure for the entrepreneur
to follow in engaging in a market research study.

4

To define the steps in preparing the marketing plan.

5

To explain the marketing system and its key components.

6

To illustrate different creative strategies that may be used to differentiate
or position the new venture's products or services.

OPENING PROFILE

RUSSELL ROTHSTEIN

Marketing strategies for promoting a new venture or a small business are often limited because of financial constraints. However, with the advent of social networking, small businesses have found new opportunities for promoting their products and services. The use of social networking as a marketing tool will be discussed in more detail later in this chapter. The notion of providing this service to small companies has led to the inspiration of Russell Rothstein, the founder of SaleSpider.com. This is a free social networking site that is designed to assist small businesses expand their networks and opportunities by connecting with contractors and suppliers, hosting and viewing webinars and videos, placing free classified ads, and gaining free access to sales leads and business opportunities.

www.SaleSpider.com

Russell Rothstein, whom we may refer to as a serial entrepreneur, has successfully launched a number of new ventures. His first endeavor was Bizware, a software supply chain for retail petroleum and major convenience stores. He built this venture into the industry market leader before selling it in 1995. Prior to launching SaleSpider.com Rothstein founded NorthPath, which offered sales leads and field sales outsourcing to leading technology companies. While at NorthPath, Rothstein noted that the company was attracting a high percentage of small businesses. Most of these companies were looking for opportunities to increase their business and sales revenue at a reasonable cost. With this knowledge Rothstein in 2006 decided to launch SaleSpider. com which would be dedicated to entrepreneurs all over the world managing small and medium-sized businesses.

SaleSpider.com has over 870,000 users and is the largest online community specifically dedicated to entrepreneurs that are interested in new income-generating business leads and networking connections. Based in Toronto, Canada, Rothstein indicates that about 95 percent of the users are from the United States. Rothstein credits the venture's success to timing as he noted how social networking sites such as Facebook and MySpace were very successful but limited in providing assistance to small businesses. Rothstein says that it is not enough to just connect people to one another. To be successful, particularly for a business, it is important to add value to social networking. Thus came the launch of SaleSpider.com.

Any business can use SaleSpider for free and with a few clicks can easily create an account, identify connections and alliances in new markets, identify sales leads and contract opportunities, post a classified ad, or even participate in an online trade show. Rothstein also recently launched Hot Deals to the site. This link provides members discounts for hotel rooms, car rentals, Web hosting, and even business loans.

Although a free site, SaleSpider has three revenue sources. The largest source of revenue is from advertising by firms that are targeting the small business market. These ads can range from $20,000 to $50,000 per month depending on the geography and industry targeted. Online newsletters and mobile marketing are also revenue sources.

Competition for SaleSpider typically includes any of the social networking sites. Facebook, one of the most popular personal profile sites, has recognized the business market and recently added a link called the Like button that allows businesses to connect to consumers. It provides a vast web of personal recommendations and helps businesses to target ads to specific target markets using Facebook. Many companies use Facebook to stay in touch with their customers that have joined their network. LinkedIn is another social network site specifically designed for business people to update their resumes and stay in touch with business associates and contacts. Because of their large base of users both of these sites are capable of adding services for their users that could be a threat to Rothstein. Twitter, an online social networking and microblogging service, enables users to send posts to others. These posts (called tweets) could be business related and have been used by some firms to inform consumers of new products, changes in services, and so on. However, this network is primarily a personal networking site that reports personal events or experiences. Even with the existence of these competitors, Rothstein sees SaleSpider as being the first of its kind with multiple specific services for small firms that has allowed it to become the number one business networking site. He feels that continued efforts to attract new users and to continue to provide more beneficial services will help SaleSpider to remain successful.

Recently Rothstein and SaleSpider were singled out by *Entrepreneur* and *Forbes* magazines as a hot new small business. Growing at the rate of more than 30,000 new users per month, social networking is still in its infancy, Rothstein believes. The challenges facing Rothstein and SaleSpider will be to remain cash flow positive and to continue to provide new opportunities for members to generate income and new business leads.[1]

As we can see from the example of SaleSpider.com many opportunities exist in a competitive environment. Russell Rothstein's efforts in creating the venture began with an understanding and assessment of the needs of a particular segment of the market. Developing an appropriate strategy to meet those needs includes an understanding and assessment of the industry, which is where we will begin our discussion in this chapter.

INDUSTRY ANALYSIS

Prior to the preparation of the marketing plan the entrepreneur will need to complete the industry analysis section of the business plan. The primary focus of the industry analysis is to provide sufficient knowledge of the environment (national and local market) that can affect marketing strategy decision making. In Chapter 7 we described this information-seeking process as an upside-down pyramid (see Figure 7.1). It begins with the broadest-based assessment of environmental and industry trends. Then it proceeds to more local market environmental and industry trends, including competition. The entrepreneur should review this section of Chapter 7 to understand what information is included and how it can be obtained.

Secondary sources can provide much of the information needed on each of these issues. Sample sources along with an appropriate example are also identified in Chapter 7. In addition to the secondary sources, the entrepreneur may also decide that a market research initiative is needed to secure more specific information on such variables as customer needs, competitive strengths and weaknesses, price, promotion, distribution, and product or service benefits. This market research project may add important valuable insights that can assist the entrepreneur in determining the most effective market position, setting market goals and objectives, and determining what action programs are necessary to meet those goals and objectives. The steps in the market research process and the avenues available to the entrepreneur for obtaining assistance in this process are discussed later in this chapter.

One of the important benefits of the upside-down pyramid approach to industry analysis is that the entrepreneur can begin to understand competitors' strengths and weaknesses, which may provide valuable insight into how to position the products or services of the new venture. Techniques for recording and evaluating this information on the competitive environment are discussed in the following section.

Competitor Analysis

The entrepreneur should begin this step by first documenting the current strategy of each primary competitor. This can be organized by using the model in Table 8.1. The information on competitors can be gathered initially by using as much public information as possible and then complementing this with a marketing research project. Newspaper articles, Web sites, catalogs, promotions, interviews with distributors and customers, and any other marketing strategy or company information available should be reviewed. A simple Google, Yahoo!, or MSN search can link the entrepreneur to many good sources of information on competitors. A library search using such databases as Business Source Complete, LexisNexis, Factiva, or Hoover's can also provide access to any newsworthy articles on specific competitors. These articles should be scanned for information on competitor strategies and should identify the names of individuals who were interviewed, referenced, or even mentioned in the article. Any of these individuals as well as the author of the article can then be contacted to obtain further information. All the information can then be summarized in the model provided in Table 8.1. Once the strategy has been summarized, the entrepreneur should begin to identify the strengths and weaknesses of each competitor, as shown in the table.

All the information included in Table 8.1 can then be utilized to formulate the market positioning strategy of the new venture. Will the new venture imitate a particular competitor or will it try to satisfy needs in the market that are not being filled by any other company? This analysis will enlighten the entrepreneur and provide a solid basis for any

TABLE 8.1   An Assessment of Competitor Marketing Strategies and Strengths and Weaknesses

	Competitor A	Competitor B	Competitor C
Product or service strategies			
Pricing strategies			
Distribution strategies			
Promotion strategies			
Strengths and weaknesses			

marketing decision making discussed in the marketing plan. If a more formal data collection process is being considered, the following paragraphs will help explain the steps in gathering primary data as well as some of the secondary sources that can provide data to the entrepreneur.

MARKETING RESEARCH FOR THE NEW VENTURE

Information for developing the marketing plan may necessitate conducting some marketing research. Marketing research involves the gathering of data to determine such information as who will buy the product or service, what is the size of the potential market, what price should be charged, what is the most appropriate distribution channel, and what is the most effective promotion strategy to inform and reach potential customers. Since marketing research costs vary significantly, the entrepreneur will need to assess available resources and the information needed. There are also some research techniques that are not costly and can provide, at least initially, significant evidence to support the market potential for the new venture. One of these techniques is the focus group, which is discussed later in this section.

Marketing research may be conducted by the entrepreneur or by an external supplier or consultant. There are also opportunities for entrepreneurs to contact their local colleges or universities to identify faculty who teach marketing and are willing to have external clients for student research projects. Suggestions on how to conduct market research are discussed next.

Market research begins with a definition of objectives or purpose. This is often the most difficult step since many entrepreneurs lack knowledge or experience in marketing and often don't even know what they want to accomplish from a research study. This, however, is the very reason why marketing research can be so meaningful to the entrepreneur.[2]

Step One: Defining the Purpose or Objectives

The most effective way to begin is for the entrepreneur to sit down and make a list of the information that will be needed to prepare the marketing plan. For example, the entrepreneur may think there is a market for his or her product but not be sure who the customers will be or even whether the product is appropriate in its present form. Thus, one objective would be to ask people what they think of the product or service and whether they would buy it, and to collect some background demographics and attitudes of these individuals. This would satisfy the objective or problem that the entrepreneur defined earlier. Other objectives may be to determine the following:

- How much would potential customers be willing to pay for the product or service?
- Where would potential customers prefer to purchase the product or service?
- Where would the customer expect to hear about or learn about such a product or service?

Step Two: Gathering Data from Secondary Sources

Secondary sources, discussed earlier in this chapter and in Chapter 7, offer a means of gathering information for the industry analysis section of the business plan. There are many other market research secondary sources that may be used to address the specific objectives of the project identified in step one. As mentioned, trade magazines, newspaper articles, libraries, government agencies, and the Internet can provide much information on the industry market and competitors. The Internet can even be used to gather informal primary data through chat groups.

Commercial data may also be available, but the cost may be prohibitive to the entrepreneur. However, business libraries may subscribe to some of these commercial services such as Nielsen Indexes, Audits and Surveys' National Market Indexes, and Information Resources, Inc.

Before considering either primary sources or commercial sources of information, the entrepreneur should exhaust all free secondary sources. At the federal level, the U.S. Census Bureau publishes a wide range of census reports, as does the Department of Commerce. Other excellent sources at the state and local levels are the State Department of Commerce, chambers of commerce, local banks, state departments of labor and industry, and local media. A comprehensive list of Web sites (some are fee based and others are free) as well as a number of excellent databases can be found in Table 8.2. Some of the fee-based sources may actually be accessible through a local university or community library. In addition to all the sources of data described in Table 8.2, the entrepreneur should also review any possible sources of research data at the Small Business Administration Web site (www.sba.gov).

The most important purpose of reviewing secondary sources is to obtain information that will assist the entrepreneur in making the best decisions regarding the marketing of a product or service. Improvements in information technology today make this a very effective source in gathering information on customers, competitors, and market trends. Completion of this task will also determine if more data are needed, in which case a primary data gathering will then need to be planned.

Step Three: Gathering Information from Primary Sources

Information that is new is primary data. Gathering primary data involves a data collection procedure—such as observation, networking, interviewing, focus groups, or experimentation—and usually a data collection instrument, such as a questionnaire.

Observation is the simplest approach. The entrepreneur might observe potential customers and record some aspect of their buying behavior. Networking, which is more of an informal method to gather primary data from experts in the field, can also be a valuable low-cost method to learn about the marketplace. One study of new ventures found that the most successful ventures (based on growth rate) were focused on information about

TABLE 8.2 Sources of Secondary Market Research Data

Commercial Sources

Each of these sources provides a wide range of research support and data on industries, consumer behavior, products, and technology. Some of these firms publish reports that may be accessible at a university library or online. The fees range from free to very expensive, but many of these are worth a look.

The Nielsen Company (www.nielsen.com)	Audits and Surveys (www.gfkauditsandsurveys.com)
Hoover's (www.hoovers.com)	IBISWorld (www.ibisworld.com)
IRI (www.iriweb.org)	IDC (www.idc.com)
TableBase (www.gale.cengage.com)	Harris Poll (www.harrispollonline.com)
MarketDataEnterprises (www.marketdataenterprises.com)	CQG (www.cqg.com)

Web-Related Demographic/Consumer Research Information

These sites are typically free online or accessible at a local university library.

American Consumer Satisfaction (www.bus.mich.edu/research). Maintained and produced by the University of Michigan, it provides an index of satisfaction toward a wide range of products and services.

Bureau of Labor Statistics (www.stats.bls.gov). Provides information on consumer buying habits related to different consumer and household characteristics.

ClickZ (www.clickz.com/stats). Provides news-related statistical information on digital marketing issues such as advertising and consumer behavior.

Statistical Abstracts of the United States (www.census.gov/compendia/statab/). Guide to summary statistics on a wide range of social, political, and economic variables. Available on state and county levels.

U.S. Census Bureau (www.census.gov). Contains demographic data in tables from the U.S. Census Bureau.

Free Internet Marketing Resources

Marketing for Success (www.marketingforsuccess.com/free-stuff.html). This site provides articles, data on how much to spend on marketing, audio answers, profit calculators, networking guide, and advertising analysis, as well as a free newsletter.

Free Demographics (www.freedemographics.com). This site allows you to analyze and compare any demographic variable by geographic area using census data.

InfoTrends (www.infotrends.com/freedemo.html). Allows you to search one year of market data free. Provides data on sales, shipments, market share, and other important market statistics on the information technology industry.

MarketingSherpa (www.marketingsherpa.com). Publishes many free reports with tips, benchmark guides, and marketing ideas. Provides advice on how to improve any fee-related searches.

Other Library Databases

Bloomberg. Provides real-time integrated market data and news for all market sectors.

Business Source Complete. Contains more than 3,000 full-text articles covering a wide range of topics in economics, finance, accounting, marketing, and general management.

Forrester. In-depth marketing research reports in emerging technologies and their impact on business.

LexisNexis. Covers a wide range of industry news topics such as market trends, finance, technology, accounting, tax information, and law reviews.

Mediamark Research (MRI). Published survey of product usage and media exposure of all persons 18 years and older in a wide range of markets.

Mintel Reports. Provides market research reports on U.S. and European marketplace on such sectors as consumer goods, travel, tourism, finance, Internet, retail, and food and drink. The focus is on market size and trends in these sectors.

AS SEEN IN *BUSINESS NEWS*

PROVIDE ADVICE TO AN ENTREPRENEUR ON SOCIAL MEDIA STRATEGY

In the 1990s, the Internet was a bunch of banners and brochures. Now we have social networks, which allow for much richer two-way interactions. Instead of just signposts on the Web, we have the opportunity to build outposts where people can be seen and heard. Here's my advice on how to use both tools effectively.

YOUR MAIN SITE IS YOUR HOME BASE

There are two things your website should do well: execute a solid call to action and give people a way to connect with you further. If you squint at your website no one will know what you want the person to do next. If this is the case then the site needs to be fixed. It is the first opportunity to do business with a potential customer. No matter how complex your business, your site should give visitors a really clear and obvious action to take.

Second, how easy have you made it for a person to contact you? That is your second chance to get the individual's business. Rethink your contact options.

The purpose of a great home base is that people who talk with you on the various social networks will feel warm and comfortable about taking the next steps with you. Most people's websites are cluttered, making it unclear what users are supposed to do next. Yours will be different once you have the top two items in hand.

SOCIAL NETWORKS ARE OUTPOSTS

If you think of social networks as places where things other than your business happen, then you're starting to get how this all works. People

aren't there to find you. They're there for their own purposes. Your job is to have an outpost there and to listen, so that when someone expresses a need you can address, you'll have the ability to start a relationship. This is what I mean by talking signs. Your outpost shouldn't just contain a bunch of witty advertising. Your Facebook page should consist of more than well-crafted offers.

The real win is in making relationships that stick. At the outposts, the goal is not to talk about yourself and your offers. It's about engaging with others, making relationships, and being accessible, should the need arise. Some tips:

- Set up Google Alerts (google.com/alerts) to search on not just your company and product name, but also to pinpoint ways people might identify a problem that your product or service can solve.

- Use Twitter Search (search twitter.com) to do the same.

- Talk with others about their interests long before you talk about your company.

- When you take on new customers, ask if you can follow them on Twitter and suggest they "like" your Facebook page. Invite them to communicate with you through these outposts.

- Spend 30 minutes a day for two weeks working on these spaces. Eventually 30 minutes won't be enough time, but for now it's a good way to start.

Source: Reprinted with permission of Wright's Media, "Talking Signs," by Chris Brogan, June 2011, *Entrepreneur*, p. 76.

competitors, the customer, and the industry, using networking, trade associations, and recent publications. Less successful ventures were more focused on gathering information on general economic and demographic trends and hence had less of a sense of what was happening in their specific target market.[3]

Interviewing or surveying is the most common approach used to gather market information. It is more expensive than observation but is more likely to generate more meaningful information. Interviews may be conducted in person, by telephone, through the mail, or online, an approach growing in popularity, particularly for firms with an existing customer base. Each of these methods offers advantages and disadvantages to the entrepreneur and should be evaluated accordingly.[4] Table 8.3 provides comparisons of each of these three methods of data collection.

TABLE 8.3	A Comparison of Survey Methods				
Characteristics of Methods					
Method	**Costs**	**Flexibility**	**Response Rate**	**Speed**	**Depth**
Telephone	Can be inexpensive, depending on telephone distance and length of interview.	Some flexibility; possible to clarify or explain questions.	Good response rate possible (possible 80%) depending on not-at-homes or refusals.	Fastest method of obtaining information. Can contact many respondents in a short period.	Least detailed because of 8- to 10-minute time limitation.
Mail	Can be inexpensive, depending on number of units mailed and weight.	No flexibility since questionnaire is self-administered. Instrument needs to be self-explanatory.	Poorest response rate since respondent has choice of whether to complete questionnaire.	Slowest method because of time required to mail and wait for respondents to complete and return questionnaire.	Some depth possible since respondent completes questionnaire at his or her leisure.
Personal	Most expensive technique. Requires face-to-face contact.	Most flexible of all methods because of face-to-face contact.	The most effective response rate because of face-to-face contact.	Somewhat slow because of dead time needed for travel.	Most detailed because of open-ended questions.
Internet	Inexpensive.	No flexibility since self-administered.	Good response rate but some have limits on number of questions.	Very fast method since questionnaire is sent electronically.	Some depth possible since respondent completes questionnaire at his or her leisure.

The Internet is becoming an important resource for new ventures to gather information both formally and informally. The informal sources typically involve the use of Facebook, Twitter, or LinkedIn. Entrepreneurs can solicit feedback on many related company or product issues utilizing these social networks. More formal research methods such as the use of Web-based survey tools may involve some expense. SurveyMonkey and Zoomerang are the most popular of these Internet survey tools. The information box later in this chapter provides more information regarding the application and benefits of these Web survey tools.

The questionnaire, or data collection instrument, used by the entrepreneur should include questions specifically designed to fulfill one or more of the objectives the entrepreneur listed earlier. Questions should be designed so they are clear and concise, do not bias the respondent, and are easy to answer. Table 8.4 illustrates a sample questionnaire employed by an entrepreneur trying to assess the need for a personal errand service. The questions are designed to satisfy the objectives of the entrepreneur, which are to ascertain the need, location, and determination of the most important services to offer and price. Support in the design of questionnaires can often be attained through small-business development centers, members of the Service Corps of Retired Executives (SCORE), or students in marketing research classes at a local college or university. Since the instrument is important in the research process, it is recommended that entrepreneurs seek assistance if they have no experience in designing questionnaires.

TABLE 8.4 Sample Questionnaire for Personal Errand Service

1. Of the following, please check the three most frequent errands that you are likely to carry out during the workweek.
   _____ Dry cleaners   _____ Post office
   _____ Drugstore   _____ Bank
   _____ Shopping for clothing items   _____ Shopping for nonclothing and nongrocery items
   _____ Buying a gift   _____ Automotive service or repair
   _____ Other _____   _____ Other _____
          Please specify   Please specify

2. Of the following, please indicate which items you would be willing to pay for someone to carry out for you.
   _____ Dry cleaners   _____ Post office
   _____ Drugstore   _____ Bank
   _____ Shopping for clothing items   _____ Shopping for nonclothing and nongrocery items
   _____ Buying a gift   _____ Automotive service or repair
   _____ Other _____   _____ Other _____
          Please specify   Please specify

3. What do you consider the two most important reasons for having someone else complete an errand? (Check only two.)
   _____ Waiting in lines
   _____ Inconvenient location
   _____ Imposes on my relaxation time
   _____ Difficult work schedule
   _____ Traffic
   _____ Other _____
          Please specify
   _____ Other _____
          Please specify

4. If an errand service was conveniently available to you, how much would you be willing to pay for a standard errand such as delivering or picking up dry cleaning, going to the post office, or picking up a prescription?
   _____ $3.00   _____ $4.00   _____ $5.00
   _____ $6.00   _____ $7.00   _____ $8.00
   _____ $9.00   _____ $10.00   _____ More than $10.00

5. Please indicate by rank ordering (1 being highest rank, 2 being second highest rank, and so on) your preference for the most convenient location for a personal errand service.
   _____ In my building
   _____ Near my office
   _____ Near the train station
   _____ Prefer to have item(s) delivered to my office

6. The following information is needed for categorizing the results of the survey. Please check the appropriate box.
   Sex: _____ Male   _____ Female
   Marital/household status: _____ Bachelor
                            _____ Single parent
                            _____ Married, both spouses working
                            _____ Married, one spouse working
   Age: _____ Under 25
                 _____ 25–34
                 _____ 35–44
                 _____ 45–54
                 _____ 55 and over
   Household income:
                 _____ Under $40,000
                 _____ $40,000–$54,000
                 _____ $55,000–$69,000
                 _____ $70,000–$84,000
                 _____ $85,000–$99,000
                 _____ $100,000 and above

Focus groups are a more informal method for gathering in-depth information. A focus group is a sample of 10 to 12 potential customers who are invited to participate in a discussion relating to the entrepreneur's research objectives. The focus group discusses issues in an informal, open format, enabling the entrepreneur to ascertain certain information.

For example, two entrepreneurs were considering a chain of hair salons that would specialize in hair styling and hair care services for African Americans. To understand the hair care needs and most effective marketing strategy for this market, focus groups of a cross section of African American women were organized. The focus groups were designed to ascertain what services should be offered, the demand for these services, pricing strategy, and the most effective advertising/promotion strategy. The information gathered was then used in the preparation of the marketing plan.

Someone other than the entrepreneur should lead the focus groups. Often this is a good project for students at a college or university in a marketing research class.

Step Four: Analyzing and Interpreting the Results

Depending on the size of the sample, the entrepreneur can hand-tabulate the results or enter them on a computer. In either case, the results should be evaluated and interpreted in response to the research objectives that were specified in the first step of the research process. Often, summarizing the answers to questions will give some preliminary insights. Then data can be cross-tabulated to provide more focused results. For example, the entrepreneur may want to compare the results to questions by different age groups, sex, occupation, location, and so on. The Web-based survey tools mentioned above and discussed later in the Advice to an Entrepreneur box also can provide data analysis support. Continuing this fine-tuning can provide valuable insights, particularly regarding the segmentation of the market, which is discussed later in this chapter.

DIFFERENCE BETWEEN A BUSINESS PLAN AND A MARKETING PLAN

An entrepreneur should understand the differences between a marketing plan and a business plan. The marketing plan focuses on all marketing activities of a venture for one year or more. The marketing plan will vary significantly for a firm depending on the industry, target market, and the size and scope of the organization. It is an integral part of a business plan, yet, as discussed below, it also is a standalone document that needs to be managed on a short-term basis to ascertain whether the venture is meeting its goals and objectives. The business plan on the other hand is the road map for the entire organization over time. It focuses on not just marketing issues but also such decisions as research and development, operations, manufacturing, personnel, financial projections and analysis, and future growth strategies. It also should be updated on a regular basis to help management to stay focused and to meet organization goals.

UNDERSTANDING THE MARKETING PLAN

Once the entrepreneur has gathered all the necessary information, he or she can sit down to prepare the marketing plan. As stated above, the marketing plan represents a significant element in the business plan for a new venture. The marketing plan should be prepared annually, assessing the goals and objectives for the next year, and also should be integrated with the firm's more long-term strategic plan (three- to five-year plan). It serves a number of important functions or purposes. Primarily the marketing plan establishes how the entrepreneur will effectively compete and operate in the marketplace and thus meet the business goals and objectives of the new venture. Once the strategies of how the business will operate have been established, the entrepreneur can assign costs to these strategies, which then serves the important purpose of establishing budgets and making financial projections. The marketing plan, like any other type of plan, may be compared to a road map used to guide a traveler. It is designed to provide answers to three basic questions:[5]

1. Where have we been? When used as a stand-alone document (operational plan), this would imply some background on the company, its strengths and weaknesses, some background on the competition, and a discussion of the opportunities and threats in the marketplace. When the marketing plan is integrated as part of the business plan, this segment would focus on some history of the marketplace, marketing strengths and weaknesses of the firm, and market opportunities and threats.

2. Where do we want to go (in the short term)? This question primarily addresses the marketing objectives and goals of the new venture in the next 12 months. In the initial business plan, the objectives and goals often go beyond the first year because of the need to project profits and cash needs for the first three years.

3. How do we get there? This question discusses the specific marketing strategy that will be implemented, when it will occur, and who will be responsible for the monitoring of activities. The answers to these questions are generally determined from the marketing research carried out before the planning process is begun. Budgets will also be determined and used in the income and cash flow projections.

Management should understand that the marketing plan is a guide for implementing marketing decision making and not a generalized, superficial document. The mere organization of the thinking process involved in preparing a marketing plan can be helpful to the entrepreneur because to develop the plan, it is necessary to formally document and describe as many marketing details as possible that will be part of the decision process during the next year. This process will enable the entrepreneur not only to understand and recognize the critical issues but also to be prepared in the event that any change in the environment occurs.

As stated above, each year the entrepreneur should prepare an annual marketing plan before any decisions are made regarding production or manufacturing, personnel changes, or financial resources needed. This annual plan becomes the basis for planning other aspects of the business and for developing budgets for the year. Table 8.5 provides a suggested outline for the marketing plan. Variations of this outline will depend on the market and nature of the product or service, as well as the general company mission. The remainder of this chapter focuses on the short-term aspects of the marketing plan, while not ignoring the fact that the entrepreneur will also need to provide market projections for years 2 and 3 as part of the business plan.

TABLE 8.5 Outline for a Marketing Plan

Situation analysis
   Background of venture
   Strengths and weaknesses of venture
   Market opportunities and threats
   Competitor analysis
Marketing objectives and goals
Marketing strategy and action programs
Budgets
Controls

CHARACTERISTICS OF A MARKETING PLAN

The marketing plan should be designed to meet certain criteria. Some important characteristics that must be incorporated in an effective marketing plan are as follows:

- It should provide a strategy for accomplishing the company mission or goal.
- It should be based on facts and valid assumptions. Some of the facts needed are illustrated in Table 8.6. It must provide for the use of existing resources. Allocation of all equipment, financial resources, and human resources must be described.
- An appropriate organization must be described to implement the marketing plan.
- It should provide for continuity so that each annual marketing plan can build on it, successfully meeting longer-term goals and objectives.
- It should be simple and short. A voluminous plan will be placed in a desk drawer and likely never used. However, the plan should not be so short that details on how to accomplish a goal are excluded.
- The success of the plan may depend on its flexibility. Changes, if necessary, should be incorporated by including what-if scenarios and appropriate responding strategies.
- It should specify performance criteria that will be monitored and controlled. For example, the entrepreneur may establish an annual performance criterion of 10 percent of market share in a designated geographic area. To attain this goal, certain expectations should be made at given time periods (e.g., at the end of three months we should have a 5 percent share of market). If not attained, then new strategy or performance standards may be established.

marketing plan Written statement of marketing objectives, strategies, and activities to be followed in business plan

marketing system Interacting internal and external factors that affect venture's ability to provide goods and services to meet customer needs

It is clear from the preceding discussion that the market plan is not intended to be written and then put aside. It is intended to be a valuable document that is referred to often and a guideline for the entrepreneur during the next time period.

Since the term *marketing plan* denotes the significance of marketing, it is important to understand the *marketing system*. The marketing system identifies the major interacting components, both internal and external to the firm, that enable the firm to successfully

---

TABLE 8.6   Facts Needed for Market Planning

- Who are the users, where are they located, how much do they buy, from whom do they buy, and why?
- How have promotion and advertising been employed and which approach has been most effective?
- What are the pricing changes in the market, who has initiated these changes, and why?
- What are the market's attitudes concerning competitive products?
- What channels of distribution supply consumers, and how do they function?
- Who are the competitors, where are they located, and what advantages/disadvantages do they have?
- What marketing techniques are used by the most successful competitors? By the least successful?
- What are the overall objectives of the company for the next year and five years hence?
- What are the company's strengths? Weaknesses?
- What are one's production capabilities by product?

FIGURE 8.1   The Marketing System

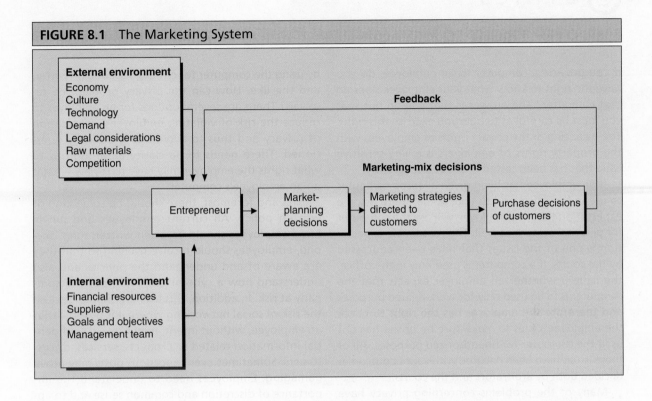

provide products and/or services to the marketplace. Figure 8.1 provides a summary of the components that constitute the marketing system.[6]

As can be seen from Figure 8.1, the environment (external and internal) plays a very important role in developing the market plan. These factors should be identified and discussed in the industry analysis section of the business plan discussed earlier in this chapter. It should also be noted that these factors are typically uncontrollable but need to be recognized as part of the marketing plan.

In addition to the external environmental factors, there are internal environmental factors which, although more controllable by the entrepreneur, can also affect the preparation of the marketing plan and implementation of an effective marketing strategy. Some of the major internal variables are as follows:

- *Financial resources.* The financial plan, discussed in Chapter 10, should outline the financial needs for the new venture. Any marketing plan or strategy should consider the availability of financial resources as well as the amount of funds needed to meet the goals and objectives stated in the plan.

- *Management team.* It is extremely important in any organization to make appropriate assignments of responsibility for the implementation of the marketing plan. In some cases the availability of a certain expertise may be uncontrollable (e.g., a shortage of certain types of technical managers). In any event, the entrepreneur must build an effective management team and assign the responsibilities to implement the marketing plan.

- *Suppliers.* The suppliers used are generally based on a number of factors such as price, delivery time, quality, and management assistance. In some cases, where raw materials are scarce or there are only a few suppliers of a particular raw material or part, the

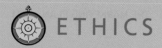

ETHICS

EMPLOYEE'S RIGHT TO PRIVACY

If you provide a computer to an employee, do you have the right to know what your employee does on that computer? The answer is that you do but that you must be careful as to how you exercise this right. The balancing of the privacy rights of employees with the property rights of employers is a very sensitive issue that has been tested in the courts recently.

If an employee has been given a laptop computer to use in the office and to take home, there is some expectation that the employee will use the computer for personal reasons as well. This reasonable expectation is one of the issues that have been addressed by the courts. If a computer is used only in the office, the issue is whether an employer expects that the computer is to be used only for work-related purposes and therefore the employer has the right to check the employee's files to make sure he or she has not used the computer for unauthorized purposes. All of these issues have been debated with various outcomes decided both by arbitrators and the courts.

Many of the problems concerning privacy have come to the fore because of the attention being given to the high risk of cyberattacks on company computers if and when an employee creates potential vulnerability by using the computer for e-mails, Facebook, Twitter, and the like. How can the privacy problem be resolved? There are several options for an employer to reduce the risk of violating employees' expectation of privacy and thus to avoid being ethically questioned. There needs to be clarity all around as to what rights the employer may have to review what is on an employee's computer.

First and foremost, there should be some kind of written policy. All current employees and newly hired employees should be given written rules. Second, employees should receive training so that they are aware of and understand the policies and also understand how a cyberattack could put the company at risk. In addition, this training should disclose the risk of social networking where it is possible that an employee, without intent, might reveal confidential information related to products, services, or customers. Sometimes even innocuous posts may prove damaging. Employees need to understand the importance of discretion and common sense and to apply these to their use of company computers in the same way that they would guard their own personal financial data.

---

entrepreneur has little control over the decision. Since the price of supplies, delivery time, and so on, are likely to impact many marketing decisions, it is important to incorporate these factors into the marketing plan.

- *Company mission.* As indicated in Chapter 7, every new venture should define the nature of its business. This statement helps to define the company's mission and basically describes the nature of the business and what the entrepreneur hopes to accomplish with that business. This mission statement or business definition will guide the firm through long-term decision making.

THE MARKETING MIX

marketing mix
Combination of product, price, promotion, and distribution and other marketing activities needed to meet marketing objectives

The preceding environmental variables will provide much important information in deciding what will be the most effective marketing strategy to be outlined in the marketing plan. The actual short-term marketing decisions in the marketing plan will consist of four important marketing variables: product or service, pricing, distribution, and promotion. These four factors are referred to as the *marketing mix*. Each variable will be described in detail in the strategy or action plan section of the marketing plan discussed later in this chapter. Although flexibility may be an important consideration, the entrepreneur needs a strong base to provide direction for the day-to-day marketing decisions. Some of the critical decisions in each area are described in Table 8.7.

TABLE 8.7   Critical Decisions for Marketing Mix

Marketing Mix Variable	Critical Decisions
Product	Quality of components or materials, style, features, options, brand name, packaging, sizes, service availability, and warranties
Price	Quality image, list price, quantity, discounts, allowances for quick payment, credit terms, and payment period
Channels of distribution	Use of wholesalers and/or retailers, type of wholesalers or retailers, how many, length of channel, geographic coverage, inventory, transportation, and use of electronic channels
Promotion	Media alternatives, message, media budget, role of personal selling, sales promotion (displays, coupons, etc.), use of social networking, website design, and media interest in publicity

STEPS IN PREPARING THE MARKETING PLAN

Figure 8.2 illustrates the various stages involved in preparing the marketing plan. Each of these stages, when completed, will provide the necessary information to formally prepare the marketing plan. Each of the steps is outlined and discussed, using examples to assist the reader in fully understanding the necessary information and procedure for preparing the marketing plan.[7]

Defining the Business Situation

situation analysis
Describes past and present business achievements of new venture

The *situation analysis* is a review of where we have been. It responds to the first of the three questions mentioned earlier in this chapter. It also considers many of the factors that were defined in both the environmental analysis section of the business plan (see Chapter 7) and the industry analysis section discussed earlier in this chapter.

To fully respond to this question, the entrepreneur should provide a review of past performance of the product and the company. If this is a new venture, the background will be more personal, describing how the product or service was developed and why it was developed (e.g., to satisfy consumer needs). If the plan is being written after the new venture has started up, it would contain information on present market conditions and performance of the company's goods and services. Any future opportunities or prospects should also be included in this section of the plan.

The industry and competitive environment has already been discussed in an earlier section of the business plan. Thus, at this point the entrepreneur should simply review some of the key elements of this section to help provide a context for the marketing segmentation and actions that will be stated in this section of the business plan.

Defining the Target Market: Opportunities and Threats

target market   Specific group of potential customers toward which venture aims its marketing plan

market segmentation
Process of dividing a market into definable and measurable groups for purposes of targeting marketing strategy

Either from the industry analysis or from the marketing research done earlier, the entrepreneur should have a good idea of who the customer or *target market* will be. Knowledge of the target market provides a basis for determining the appropriate marketing action strategy that will effectively meet its needs. The defined target market will usually represent one or more segments of the entire market. Thus, it is important even before beginning the research to understand what market segmentation is before determining the appropriate target market.

Market segmentation is the process of dividing the market into small homogeneous groups. Market segmentation allows the entrepreneur to more effectively respond to the

FIGURE 8.2 Sample Flowchart of a Marketing Plan

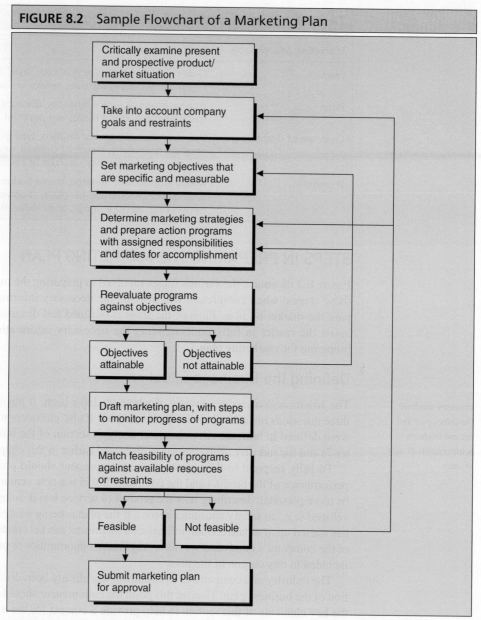

Source: Reproduced with permission from The Conference Board, Inc. Adapted from David S. Hopkins, *The Marketing Plan* (1981), p. 17 © 1981, The Conference Board, Inc.

needs of more homogeneous consumers. Otherwise the entrepreneur would have to identify a product or service that would meet the needs of everyone in the marketplace.

Henry Ford's vision was to manufacture a single product (one color, one style, one size, etc.) for the mass market. His Model T was produced in large numbers on assembly lines, enabling the firm to reduce costs through specialization of labor and materials. Although his strategy was unique, any successful mass-market strategy employed today would be unlikely.

In 1986, Paul Firestone of Reebok discovered that many consumers who bought running shoes were not athletes. They bought the shoes for comfort and style. Firestone then developed a marketing plan that was targeted directly to this segment.

The process of segmenting and targeting customers by the entrepreneur should proceed as follows:[8]

I. Decide what general market or industry you wish to pursue.
II. Divide the market into smaller groups based on characteristics of the customer or buying situations.
   A. Characteristics of the customer
      1. Geographic (e.g., state, country, city, region)
      2. Demographic (e.g., age, sex, occupation, education, income, and race)
      3. Psychographic (e.g., personality and lifestyle)
   B. Buying situation
      1. Desired benefits (e.g., product features)
      2. Usage (e.g., rate of use)
      3. Buying conditions (e.g., time available and product purpose)
      4. Awareness of buying intention (e.g., familiarity of product and willingness to buy)
III. Select segment or segments to target.
IV. Develop a marketing plan integrating product, price, distribution, and promotion.

Let's assume that an entrepreneur is considering offering an after-school student shuttle service in a local community in the suburbs of Boston. The service will be marketed to households that have high income, both spouses working (most likely professionals), and young children typically between 10 and 15 years old. The shuttle service is designed to taxi children (10 to 15 years old) using a minivan or similar vehicle to medical or other related appointments and after-school activities. These activities would be non-school-related activities since schools would most likely offer bus service for their students.

The first decision to be made, since we know the target market, is to identify candidate communities that would match the user profile. Town census research and any other available secondary sources are a logical starting place and will reveal demographic data on income, ages of children, and employment. Once this step is complete and a few towns have been identified, the entrepreneur can then conduct marketing research in the identified towns that seem to match the target market profile. This would help the entrepreneur understand the needs and buying intentions of any potential target market. The analysis from this research would then assist the entrepreneur in selecting the community in which to launch the service.

The buying situation is dependent on the venture's establishing credibility in the community. Even if specific households can be targeted, the marketing strategy (particularly sales strategy) will need to concentrate on first establishing credibility and community trust. This can be accomplished in a number of ways but will likely begin with an effort to gain the support of the key townspeople, such as school administrators, PTA members, or other local agencies. In addition, marketing actions will need to focus on getting the target market's attention and creating an awareness of the benefits that this service can provide. For example, the venture might choose to sponsor school events and activities, appoint local respected community members to its board, place advertisements in local newspapers, or send company information through direct mail.

The major issues initially involve careful targeting, using the approach mentioned earlier, as well as understanding the needs of this target market. With a clear understanding of who the customer is and a combined sales effort and marketing program, the entrepreneur can be more assured of sales growth and increased revenue. A continued presence in the community may also allow the entrepreneur to expand this shuttle service to include other segments of the market, such as senior citizens. Once credibility has been established in one community, it will be easier to expand to other communities.

Considering Strengths and Weaknesses

It is important for the entrepreneur to consider strengths and weaknesses in the target market. For example, to refer back to the student shuttle service venture, its primary strengths in its market are: there is no existing competition, the company has the support of local schools, and its usage base in the selected community is an excellent match for the projected target market. In addition, the experience gained from initiating this service in one community will be a major factor in soliciting new business in other communities.

Weaknesses could relate to the venture's inability to gain complete credibility in the town—given such widespread concern regarding the abduction and molestation of children. Credibility could be easily—and negatively—affected by any bad publicity. Also the success of the venture will depend heavily on the reliability of its drivers, who may not be sensitive to consumer needs. Thus, it will be important to carefully select and train all drivers.

An entrepreneur's evaluation of his or her venture's strengths and weaknesses would also vary if the market sought is international. A lack of understanding of the culture and differences in consumer buying habits could be critical in any attempt to reach these markets. For example, Mei Xu, whose start-up Maryland candle company Pacific Trade International now sells in her native China, has generated $85 million in sales. She understood that the market in China was extremely fragmented and that Chinese women prefer candles with floral scents whereas Americans prefer different scents. She believes that the reason many American small businesses do not have success in markets like China is because they do not understand the international markets and often try to go there simply with what they perceive is the strength of the strategy that they may have successfully used in the U.S.[9]

Establishing Goals and Objectives

marketing goals and objectives Statements of level of performance desired by new venture

Before any marketing strategy decisions can be outlined, the entrepreneur must establish realistic and specific goals and objectives. These *marketing goals and objectives* respond to the question: "Where do we want to go?" and should specify things such as market share, profits, sales (by territory and region), market penetration, number of distributors, awareness level, new product launching, pricing policy, sales promotion, and advertising support.

For example, the entrepreneur of a new frozen diet product may determine the following objectives for the first year: 10 percent market penetration, 60 percent of market sampled, distribution in 75 percent of the market. All these objectives must be considered reasonable and feasible given the business situation described earlier.

All the preceding goals and objectives are quantifiable and can be measured for control purposes. However, not all goals and objectives must be quantified. It is possible for a firm to establish such goals or objectives as: research customer attitudes toward a product, set up a sales training program, improve packaging, change name of product, or find new distributor. It is a good idea to limit the number of goals or objectives to between six and eight. Too many goals make control and monitoring difficult. Obviously, these goals should represent key areas to ensure marketing success.

Defining Marketing Strategy and Action Programs

marketing strategy and action plan Specific activities outlined to meet the venture's business plan goals and objectives

Once the marketing goals and objectives have been established, the entrepreneur can begin to develop the *marketing strategy and action plan* to achieve them. These strategy and action decisions respond to the question: "How do we get there?" As indicated earlier, these decisions reflect on the marketing mix variables. Some possible decisions that might be made for each variable are discussed next.

Product or Service   This element of the marketing mix indicates a description of the product or service to be marketed in the new venture. This product or service definition may consider more than the physical characteristics. For example, Dell Computer's product is computers, which is not distinctive from many other existing competitors. What makes the products distinctive is the fact that they are assembled from off-the-shelf components and are marketed with direct-marketing and Internet techniques promising quick delivery and low prices. Dell also provides extensive customer service with e-mail and telephone available to the customer to ask technical or nontechnical questions. Thus, the product is more than its physical components. It involves packaging, the brand name, price, warranty, image, service, delivery time, features, style, and even the Web site that will be seen by most customers. When considering market strategy, the entrepreneur will need to consider all or some of these issues, keeping in mind the goal of satisfying customer needs.

Pricing   Prior to setting the price, the entrepreneur, in the majority of situations, will need to consider three important elements: costs, margins or markups, and competition. There are some exceptions, which are discussed at the end of this section on pricing. Also explained is the interaction of these elements in the pricing process. Appropriate examples involving the use of each element are also discussed in the next few paragraphs.

Costs. One of the important initial considerations in any pricing decision is to ascertain the costs directly related to the product or service. For a manufacturer this would involve determining the material and labor costs inherent in the production of the product. For a nonmanufacturer, such as a clothing retailer, this would involve determining the cost of the goods from the suppliers. For a service venture, such as our student shuttle service, there are no manufacturing costs or costs of goods such as those that exist for a clothing retailer. Instead, the service venture's costs relate entirely to labor and overhead expenses.

Whether a manufacturer, retailer, or service venture, the entrepreneur would need to ascertain the approximate costs for overhead (some examples would be utilities, rent, promotion, insurance, and salaries). Let's assume a manufacturer of a special oxygen-based rug cleaner incurs a materials and labor cost of $2.20 per unit (24 ounces). Estimated sales are 500,000 units, with overhead at this level of sales at $1 million or $2.00 per unit. Total costs would add to $4.20, and a unit profit of 30 percent of cost or $1.26 would mean a final price of $5.46.

For a retail example of pricing let's consider a clothing store that sells T-shirts. Let's assume the company buys the T-shirts for $5.00 (cost of goods) from a supplier. Overhead costs are estimated to be $10,000, and the entrepreneur expects to sell 5,000 units for a unit overhead cost of $2.00 per shirt. An additional $2.00 is added for profit, resulting in a final price of $9.00.

For our shuttle service example, the entrepreneur estimates that the cost per mile is approximately $6.00. This includes the depreciation of the vehicle, insurance, driver salary, utilities, advertising, and all other operating costs. Each vehicle is expected to travel about 60 miles per day and service about 30 students. Thus total cost per day would be $360, or $12 per student. Adding a profit of $3.00 would set the final price for this service at $15.00 per student or ride.

In each of these examples the entrepreneur may find it necessary to consider the role of competition and markups (discussed later) as well as an overall positioning strategy before finalizing price.

Markups or margins. In many industries, such as jewelry, beauty supplies, furniture, and clothing, the retailers of the products use a standard markup to price goods in their stores. For example, a standard markup for beauty supplies is 100 percent on cost. Thus, if the retailer buys nail polish for $1.50 per unit, the markup would be $1.50 and the final price to the consumer would be $3.00. Given that the retailer maintains costs equivalent to the industry standards, this markup would be expected to cover overhead costs and some profit. Standard markups can be ascertained from trade publications or by asking suppliers. A retailer may look at the $3.00 price and decide that, since competition offers the same product for $2.99, he or she would like to offer the item at $2.89. The lower markup and hence lower profit accepted by the entrepreneur in this case is a strategy used to increase demand in the short term (market penetration strategy) but could influence the competition to also lower its price, thus eventually reducing the profit margins for everyone.

Competition. Often, when products cannot be easily differentiated (see the earlier T-shirt example), the entrepreneur is forced to charge the same price as the competition. For the oxygen-based rug cleaner, the entrepreneur may find it possible to justify a higher price (say $6.50) than the competition's price of $5.75 because the product has unique benefits (oxygen and other ingredients). The clothing retailer may be able to charge more than $9.00 for the T-shirt if it is unique enough. If competitors' T-shirts are $9.00 but the quality of our clothing retailer's shirts is graphically superior, then a higher than $9.00 price may be charged. Otherwise, if consumers are unable to discern any difference, the price will need to be equivalent to that of the competition. In our student shuttle example, it is more difficult to compare prices with competitors since the competition is more indirect. Here we might compare taxicab prices or bus prices. However, this service is more likely to be considered a convenience by the target market, and as such, price may not be a concern. The target market is also in the upper-income category, and therefore convenience may be more important than the cost of the service.

A higher price may also be supported by market research data. Innovations such as technology products (3D televisions or interactive games such as those for the Wii) or new drug products may warrant a higher price or skimming strategy for the new venture to recover some of its high development costs. In a nondifferentiated product market (such as clothing or a portable radio), marketing research may reveal that consumers are willing to pay more if you offer service benefits such as free home delivery, guarantees on the life of the item, or free long-term repair. Although these services would increase the costs to the entrepreneur, they would establish a distinctive image for the product in a nondifferentiated product category, allowing a higher price and, potentially, a higher quality image than that of the competition.

Generally, in a nondifferentiated product market there is little room for price variations from the competition. Any attempt to increase profits in this situation would have to come from reduced costs. For those situations where the product or service is unique in the marketplace, the entrepreneur has more flexibility and should have a clear understanding of the inherent costs. The important thing to remember is that there is a total cost and profit margin to get to the final price. Changing one of these items will impact the other two factors in some manner.

Distribution   This factor provides utility to the consumer; that is, it makes a product convenient to purchase when it is needed. This variable must also be consistent with other marketing mix variables. Thus, a high-quality product will not only carry a high price but should also be distributed in outlets that have a quality image.

Channel of distribution strategy considerations are summarized in Table 8.8. If the market for a new venture is highly concentrated, such as a major metropolitan area, the entrepreneur may consider direct sales to the customer or to a retailer rather than using a wholesaler. If the

TABLE 8.8   Major Considerations in Channel Selection

Degree of Directness of Channel

- Market conditions—Concerned whether end users are concentrated (direct) or dispersed (indirect) in market.
- Product attributes—Concerned with whether product is large (direct) or small (indirect), bulky (direct), perishable (direct), hazardous (direct), expensive (direct).
- Cost benefits—Considers the cost benefits in selection of channel members; many benefits (indirect) minimal or no benefit (direct).
- Venture attributes—Considers financial strength, size, channel experience, and marketing strategy of venture.

Number of Channel Members

- Intensive—Selection of as many retailers and/or wholesalers as possible.
- Selective—Choose only small number of channel members based on some set of criteria or requirements.
- Exclusive—Select only one wholesaler and/or retailer.

Criteria in Selection of Channel Members

- Reputation
- Services provided

Number of Channels

- One channel for one target market or multiple target markets.
- Multiple channels for one target market or multiple target markets.

market is dispersed across a wide geographic area, the cost of direct sales may be prohibitive and the use of a longer channel with wholesalers and retailers may be necessary.

Attributes of the product also affect the channel decision. If the product is very expensive, perishable, or bulky, a more direct channel would make sense because the costs of handling and shipping would drive the costs up to a prohibitive level.

Middlemen such as wholesalers and retailers can add important value to the product. Their costs for providing these benefits are much lower than the costs for a small, single-product start-up because they operate with economies of scale by representing many other businesses. They can provide functions such as storage, delivery, a sales staff, promotion or advertising, and maintenance that would not be feasible for a start-up venture. Middlemen also have important experience in the marketplace that can support and assist the entrepreneur in his or her marketing strategy.

Environmental issues may also be important in channel strategy. Special considerations and regulations regarding such products as chemicals or food and drug products, to name a few, are too costly for a small start-up to absorb. Competitor strategy is also important to consider since alternative choices may help to differentiate the product. For example, Dell Computer initially chose to use direct mail and the Internet to distribute its products, creating a major differentiation from its direct competitors. Once it became established in the market, it then sought other channels such as electronics retailers.

A new venture may also consider brokers' or manufacturers' representatives to reach retailers or end users. Manufacturers' representatives do not take title or physical possession of any products. Their role is to act on behalf of a number of noncompeting companies that will share the cost of their services. In our oxygen-based rug cleaner example, the entrepreneur may consider contracting with manufacturers' representatives that sell commercial products (such as cleaning supplies, furniture, or carpeting) that would add the rug cleaner as a complement to their other products. They would be paid a commission only when a product was sold (usually 6 to 8 percent depending on the product). Manufacturers' representatives could also be used to market to the consumer or household market. In this case the entrepreneur may look for those representatives that are presently marketing household cleaners or other similar products to retail outlets. Orders then would be sent directly to the new venture and would be shipped from there to the end user. This saves on the costs of a sales staff, storage, and multiple shipping points. Brokers are similar to manufacturers' representatives and are common in food or dry goods businesses. These types of representatives are also available in many international markets and represent an effective source of market data as well as a means to reach the target market with experienced sales people.

In selecting the channel, the entrepreneur should look at all the preceding factors. In some instances it may be necessary to use more than one channel to service customers more efficiently as well as increase sales potential. Clothing retailers such as Sports Authority, L. L. Bean, Macy's, Walmart, and Target, to name a few, all sell their products using multiple channels such as retail stores, Web sites, catalogs, and newspapers. Each of these may require a different communications channel to enable the customer to buy the desired products. These channels will also vary when engaged in international sales as the nature of these channels is sometimes culturally dependent. Channel decisions will also change over time. As the venture grows, the entrepreneur may find that hiring its own sales force is more efficient and is no longer cost prohibitive.

Promotion   It is usually necessary for the entrepreneur to inform potential consumers about the product's availability or to educate the consumer, using advertising media such as print, radio, television or electronic media. Usually television is too expensive unless the entrepreneur considers cable television a viable outlet. A local service or retail company such as a pet store may find that using community cable stations is the most cost-effective method to reach customers. Larger markets can be reached using the Internet, direct mail, trade magazines, or newspapers. The entrepreneur should carefully evaluate each alternative medium, considering not just costs but the effectiveness of the medium in meeting the market objectives mentioned earlier in the marketing plan. As stated earlier, a Web site and social networks may also be valuable to create awareness and to promote the products and services of the new venture. Web sites can now be easily designed with little experience using online services such as www.1and1.com or www.intuit.com. You can create your own Web site, establish a domain name, conduct Web hosting, and initiate an online store at very low costs.

With limited budgets many entrepreneurs that need to be creative in their promotions are turning to social media. For example, Quintin Middleton was convinced that there was a market for American-made carving knives. Out of his home this initial hobby of crafting high quality knives has turned into a successful business that targets chefs. Invites on Facebook to about 800 people in the food industry resulted in 400 fans, many of whom were willing to pay Middleton $300 to $400 for a custom knife. He now is selling these custom knives as fast as he can make them.[10]

Tom First is not new to being creative, as he learned as one of the founders of Nantucket Nectars. Tom recently launched a new venture Owater, a nutrient-enhanced water. Not able to compete with larger companies in this market, Tom has chosen to promote his product through an intensive sampling campaign. Owater may do as many as six or seven sampling events a day in key markets such as Boston, Chicago, Denver, Los Angeles, New York, and Philadelphia. The ability to focus on specific large markets has enhanced sales at a rate that would have been much more costly using more traditional mass media.[11]

AS SEEN IN *BUSINESS NEWS*

WEB-BASED MARKETING RESEARCH: ADVICE TO AN ENTREPRENEUR

Although marketing research is considered a must for most entrepreneurs it is often avoided because of its perceived cost. However, technology advances now provide many options for the entrepreneur to collect research data that are not costly and can be extremely beneficial in preparing a business plan, growth strategy, or just getting customer feedback.

For example, Vapur Inc., a new single product venture (a reusable and collapsible water bottle), needed input from its target market regarding the design of its product. In just six weeks it was able to quickly generate ideas from a number of crowdsourcing sites such as Eyeka, Hypios, and Jovoto at a low cost. It gave prizes to the best designs selected by the online participants. In another example, Bonobos, an online men's clothier, discovered through Twitter that a prototype dress shirt it gave away was too tight. The company also uses Facebook to ask research-related questions that assist them in the launch of new products.

To conduct more formal marketing research, web-based survey tools such as SurveyMonkey and Zoomerang may be used. SurveyMonkey and Zoomerang allow a limited number of questions (10 and 12, respectively) and up to 100 responses per survey for free. They charge a nominal monthly fee for larger surveys. There are other web-based survey tools such as SurveyGizmo, FluidSurveys, QuestionPro, and eSurveysPro that are also available at varied costs. They all offer some limited free service and have many benefits such as custom templates, multiple languages, and cross tabulation, to name a few.

The pros and cons of web-based surveys are in many ways similar to mail surveys and personal interviewing. An online survey may permit you to ask as many questions as you may need and also allows you to use branching (ability to ask a follow-up question to a yes response). It is also possible to include open-ended questions in addition to multiple choice or ranking questions. The negative to these web-based surveys is, like the mail survey, there is no face to face contact with the participant. This negative, however, is sometimes considered a positive because of bias that can be easily introduced by the interviewer in a face to face survey.

In the end, the value and benefits of web-based surveys outweigh the costs and negatives. Since entrepreneurs are often limited in time and resources, web-based surveys are an efficient and effective method to gather important market information.

Source: See Riva Richmond, "Entrepreneurs Seek Input from Outsiders," *The Wall Street Journal Online,* December 23, 2010; Jeff Dickey-Chasins, "Getting Inside the Mind of Your Target Candidate," *Journal of Corporate Recruiting Leadership* (June 2011), p. 39; and Robert Gordman, "Targeting Your Most Profitable Customers," *Retail Merchandiser* (July/August 2010), pp. 18–20.

Marketing Strategy: Consumer versus Business-to-Business Markets

Marketing strategy decisions for a consumer product may be very different from the decisions for a business-to-business product. In business-to-business markets the entrepreneur sells the product or service to another business that uses the product or service as part of its operations. Dell Computer markets its products to both consumers and businesses. In marketing to consumers, the company uses direct mail and the Internet, and to businesses it uses its own sales force. This sales force calls on businesses with the intent of selling a large volume of PCs or accessories in one transaction. The consumer marketing effort, however, does support the business marketing effort since the advertising and promotions will be seen or read by both markets. Consumer markets involve sales to households for personal consumption. Food, beverages, household products, furniture, and computers would be a few examples.

Usually business-to-business marketing strategy involves a more direct channel of distribution because of the volume of each transaction and the need to relate product knowledge to the business buyers. Advertising and promotion for the business-to-business market involve more trade magazine advertising, direct sales, and trade shows. For a start-up venture, attendance at a trade show can be one of the most effective means to reach many potential buyers in one location. At trade shows it is important to distribute material on the venture's products and services and to keep a log of all interested visitors to the trade show booth. Have visitors sign in or leave their business cards. From the log or business cards, a list can then be prepared and used as a prospect list for sales reps. It is also important that, right after the trade show, a follow-up letter be sent to all visitors thanking them for their interest and explaining how they might be contacted.

Overall, the marketing mix for the consumer or business markets is the same. However, the techniques and strategies within the mix of these factors will often vary significantly.

All these marketing mix variables will be described in detail in the marketing strategy or action plan section of the marketing plan. As indicated earlier, it is important that the marketing strategy and action programs be specific and detailed enough to guide the entrepreneur through the next year.

Budgeting the Marketing Strategy

Effective planning decisions must also consider the costs involved in the implementation of these decisions. If the entrepreneur has followed the procedure of detailing the strategy and action programs to meet the desired goals and objectives, costs should be reasonably clear. If assumptions are necessary, they should be clearly stated so that anyone else who reviews the written marketing plan (e.g., a venture-capital firm) will understand these implications.

This budgeting of marketing action and strategy decisions will also be useful in preparing the financial plan. Details of how to develop a financial plan are discussed in Chapter 10.

Implementation of the Market Plan

The marketing plan is meant to be a commitment by the entrepreneur to a specific strategy. It is not a formality that serves as a superficial document to outside financial supporters or suppliers. It is meant to be a formal vehicle for answering the three questions posed earlier in this chapter and a commitment to make adjustments as needed or dictated by market conditions. Someone in the venture should be assigned the responsibility of coordinating and implementing the plan.

Monitoring the Progress of Marketing Actions

Generally, monitoring of the plan involves tracking specific results of the marketing effort. Sales data by product, territory, sales rep, and outlet are a few of the specific results that should be monitored. What is monitored is dependent on the specific goals and objectives outlined earlier in the marketing plan. Any "weak" signals from the monitoring process will provide the entrepreneur with the opportunity to redirect or modify the existing marketing effort to allow the firm to achieve its initial goals and objectives.

In addition to monitoring the progress of the existing plan, the entrepreneur should also be prepared for contingencies. For example, reliance on a single supplier in a geographic area that is vulnerable to hurricanes could be disastrous if that supplier were to be shut down as a result of a hurricane. Adjustments in marketing actions are usually minor if the plan has been effectively developed and implemented. If the entrepreneur is constantly faced with significant changes in the marketing strategy, then it is likely that the plan was not prepared properly. Weaknesses in market planning are usually the result of poor analysis of the market and competitive strategy, unrealistic goals and objectives, or poor implementation of the outlined plan actions. There are also acts of God—such as weather or war—that can affect a marketing plan. These are usually difficult to predict but may be considered in a contingency plan.

IN REVIEW

SUMMARY

Before beginning the marketing plan section of the business plan, the entrepreneur should provide a comprehensive review and assessment of the industry and market trends at the national and local levels. In addition, a comprehensive assessment of competitor strategies and their strengths and weaknesses should be documented. From this analysis the entrepreneur can begin to formulate the marketing plan section of the business plan. The marketing plan designates the response to three questions: Where have we been? Where are we going? and How do we get there?

To be able to respond effectively to these questions, it is generally necessary for the entrepreneur to conduct some marketing research. This research may involve secondary sources or a primary data collection process. Information from the research will be very important in determining the marketing mix factors or the marketing strategy to be implemented in the marketing plan. With the advances in technology there are more opportunities for entrepreneurs to conduct research utilizing Web survey tools and social networking outlets.

The marketing plan entails a number of major steps. First, it is important to conduct a situation analysis to assess the question, "Where have we been?" Market segments must be defined and opportunities identified. This will help the entrepreneur determine a profile of the customer. Goals and objectives must be established. These goals and objectives must be realistic and detailed (quantified if possible). Next, the marketing strategy and action programs must be defined. Again, these should be detailed so that the entrepreneur clearly understands how the venture is going to get where it wants to go.

The marketing strategy section or action plan describes how to achieve the goals and objectives already defined. There may be alternative marketing approaches that could be used to achieve these defined goals. It is especially important to consider alternative marketing approaches when entering international markets. The use of creative strategies such as Internet marketing may give the entrepreneur a more effective entry into the market.

The action programs should also be assigned to someone to ensure their implementation. If the plan has been detailed, the entrepreneur should be able to assign some costs and budgets for implementing the marketing plan. During the year, the marketing plan will be monitored to discern the success of the action programs. Any "weak" signals will provide the entrepreneur with the opportunity to modify the plan and/or develop a contingency plan.

Careful scrutiny of the marketing plan can enhance its success. However, many plans fail, not because of poor management or a poor product but because the plan was not specific or had an inadequate situation analysis, unrealistic goals, or did not anticipate competitive moves, product deficiencies, and acts of God.

RESEARCH TASKS

1. Participate in an online focus group. Then conduct research on the advantages and disadvantages of conducting a focus group online versus a "face-to-face" focus group.
2. Choose an industry and then use the library or the Internet to find data from secondary sources that will be highly useful in developing a marketing plan.

3. Find an example of a small business that is using social media such as Facebook, Twitter, or LinkedIn to promote their products or services. How effective do you think this strategy is? Give some advantages and disadvantages of the use of social media by this company.

4. Find a marketing strategy that is being used now that you believe will be ineffective. Be prepared to justify your answer.

CLASS DISCUSSION

1. What are the three most effective advertisements on television? Why are they effective? What are the three least effective advertisements on television? Why are they ineffective? Are they really ineffective if you have been able to recall them?

2. Define a customer group and then invent a product and come up with a price, promotion, and distribution strategy. Have some fun in coming up with a particularly creative marketing mix.

3. Is market segmentation just a nice way of using "stereotypes" to sell your products? Can people really be classified so easily into groups that share common needs, wants, and demands?

SELECTED READINGS

Boyles, Trish. (2011). Small Business and Web 2.0 Hope or Hype? *Entrepreneurial Executive*, vol. 16, pp. 81–96.

Web 2.0 is defined by its increased interactivity in web applications in an open and collaborative platform. Web 2.0 advocates that the platform eliminates size advantages for businesses, allowing small companies to effectively compete with larger ones. This author argues that small businesses will need to weigh the risks of not participating in Web 2.0 applications since she feels that it will become an important basis of competition. The author provides reasons for participating and useful research avenues are identified.

Brooks, Neil; and Lyndon Simkin. (Spring 2011). Measuring Marketing Effectiveness: An Agenda for SMEs. *Marketing Review*, vol. 11, issue 1, pp. 3–24.

This article reviews many marketing effectiveness measures and concludes that none are the single best solution. Many of these measures are not applicable for small companies. As a result SMEs often manage their marketing without adequate planning and control. The authors argue that some measurement is better than none and recommends that SMEs focus on segmentation and positioning as a starting point.

Chawla, Sudhir; Dan Khanna; and Chen Jin. (April 2010). Are Small Business Critical Success Factors Same in Different Countries? *SIES Journal of Management*, vol. 7, issue 1, pp. 1–12.

This paper considers critical success factors exhibited by small businesses in China. Comparisons are made to similar earlier studies performed in the U.S. and Mexico. Critical success factors found in common with Mexican small businesses are marketing effort and competitive forces. Unique to China however are critical factors such as financial needs, location, and the fact there are few support services in China.

Colapinto, Robert. (October 2010). Way to Grow. *CA Magazine*, vol. 143, issue 8, pp. 28–33.

Detailed planning for products and services is the focus of this article. Expansion requires detailed planning for sales and marketing, which includes knowledge of customers and suppliers as well as the impact of promotions and advertising.

Deeter-Schmelz, Dawn R.; Rosemary P. Ramsey; and Jule B. Gassenheimer. (Summer 2011). Bleu Ribbon Chocolates: How Can Small Businesses Adapt to a Changing Environment? *Marketing Education Review*, vol. 21, issue 2, pp. 177–82.

In this article the authors highlight a small regional manufacturer of high quality chocolate that sells its products through trade accounts, corporate-owned stores, and online/mail. The company had not ever done any strategic planning but with the trend toward healthier foods and the weak economy as well as poor sales the question was raised here as to what the company should do. What should be its strategic direction? Alternative solutions such as changing the product line, increasing sales to retail outlets, laying off employees, or just waiting out the weak economy are discussed.

Duff, Amy. (June 2011). Candour Culture. *Director*, vol. 64, issue 10, pp. 50–53.

One of the important issues addressed here is how a business can enhance its brand through the use of social media. The use of Twitter and Facebook offers companies an opportunity to be more human and to be more interactive with consumers. Observers note that smaller companies have an advantage in social media because of less concern for control and more emphasis on flexibility and marketing their expertise.

Jin, Liiyin. (2011). Improving Response Rates in Web Surveys with Default Settings. *International Journal of Market Research*, vol. 53, issue 1, pp. 75–94.

Researchers are using Internet instruments more often such as e-mail and online surveys to collect data. However, web survey response rates are fairly low, which threatens their effectiveness. This article discusses ways to increase the response rate. From the study reported here it was found that default settings affect participation and survey length influences a respondent's willingness to participate. It was also found that default settings changed both consumer participation and e-mail invitation permission rates due to the "trade-off aversion" principle.

Kiedrowski, Claire. (September 2011). Growing Through Adversity. *Point of Beginning*, vol. 36, issue 12, pp. 32–33.

This is a good article that discusses different marketing strategies that an entrepreneur utilized in a poor economy. She identifies some important strategies such as cross training employees, upgrading hardware, utilizing social networks for promotion, and maximizing marketing opportunities and sales leads by participating in professional associations and societies.

Kobylanski, Andrzej; and Radoslaw Szulc. (2011). Development of Marketing Orientation in Small and Medium Sized Enterprises: Evidence from Eastern Europe. *International Journal of Management and Marketing Research*, vol. 4, issue 1, pp. 49–59.

One of the most important aspects that determine an organization's market position is the entrepreneur's approach to market orientation and marketing actions. The aim of this study was to investigate the process of marketing orientation development in SMEs in Eastern Europe where the economy has changed from central planning to a free market. The results from the study suggest that customer orientation is critical for SMEs yet most of these firms still may be characterized as sales oriented rather than marketing oriented.

Nazur, Muhammad Suhail; and Faiz M. Shaikh. (June 2011). Determinants of Export Performance of Small and Medium Enterprises. *Journal of Business Strategies*, vol. 5, issue 1, pp. 21–31.

These authors have developed a model that may provide a broader understanding of the export behavior of SMEs in order to enhance their export performance. This need exists because such a large number of these firms are unable to perform effectively in international markets. Determinants from this study are classified into firm characteristics, management characteristics, and export marketing capabilities.

END NOTES

1. "The Business Matchmaker," *Entrepreneur* (May 2011), p. 43; "How Social Media is Changing Business," *BusinessNewsDaily.com* (April 2011); and www.SaleSpider.com.
2. Joseph F. Hair, Jr., Mary Wolfinbarger, Robert P. Bush, and David J. Ortinau, *Essentials of Marketing Research,* 2nd ed. (New York: McGraw-Hill/Irwin, 2010), pp. 25–36.
3. M. P. Peters and C. Bush, "Market Information Scanning Activities and Growth in New Ventures: A Comparison of Service and Manufacturing Businesses," *Journal of Business Research* (May 1996), pp. 81–89.
4. Hair et al., *Essentials of Marketing Research,* pp. 80–89.
5. R. D. Hisrich and M. P. Peters, *Marketing Decisions for New and Mature Products*, 2nd ed. (Upper Saddle River, NJ: Prentice Hall, 1991), pp. 63–78.
6. R. Kerin, S. Hartley, and W. Rudelius, *Marketing*, 10th ed. (New York: McGraw-Hill/Irwin, 2011), pp. 39–45.
7. D. R. Lehman and R. S. Winer, *Analysis for Marketing Planning*, 7th ed. (New York: McGraw-Hill/Irwin, 2008), pp. 10–11.
8. Kerin et al., *Marketing*, pp. 221–40.
9. Devin Leonard, "Mei Xu," *Bloomberg Businessweek,* March 28, 2011, p. 60.
10. Margaret Littman, "A Sharp Idea," *Entrepreneur* (October 2011), p. 17.
11. Gwen Moran, "Try Sampling," *Entrepreneur* (October 2008), p. 84.

APPENDIX 8A: MARKETING PLAN OUTLINES

Exhibit 1. Marketing Plan for a Consumer Products Company.

Exhibit 2. Marketing Plan for a Business-to-Business Company.

Exhibit 3. Marketing Plan for a Service Company.

EXHIBIT 1	Marketing Plan for a Consumer Products Company

I. ANALYZE AND DEFINE THE BUSINESS SITUATION—past, present, and future
An analysis of where we are, perhaps how we got there. Data and trend lines should go back three to five years.
Suggested items to cover:
- A. The scope of the market (class of trade)
- B. Sales history by products, by class of trade, by regions
- C. Market potential, major trends anticipated
- D. Distribution channels
    1. Identification of principal channels (dealer or class of trade), sales history through each type
    2. Buying habits and attitudes of these channels
    3. Our selling policies and practices
- E. The customer or end user
    1. Identification of customers making the buying decision, classified by age, income level, occupation, geographical location, etc.
    2. Customer attitudes on product or services, quality, price, etc. Purchase or use habits that contribute to attitudes
    3. Advertising history: expenditures, media and copy strategy, measurements of effectiveness
    4. Publicity and other educational influences
- F. The product or services:
    1. Story of the product line, quality development, delivery and service
    2. Comparison with other approaches to serve the customers' needs
    3. Product research; product improvements planned

II. IDENTIFY PROBLEMS AND OPPORTUNITIES
- A. In view of the facts cited in (I) above, what are the major problems that are restricting or impeding our growth?
- B. What opportunities do we have for
    —Overcoming the above problems?
    —Modifying or improving the product line or adding new products?
    —Serving the needs of more customers in our market or developing new markets?
    —Improving the efficiency of our operation?

III. DEFINE SPECIFIC AND REALISTIC BUSINESS OBJECTIVES
- A. Assumptions regarding future conditions
    —Level of economic activity
    —Level of industry activity
    —Changes in customer needs
    —Changes in distribution channels
    —Changes beyond our control, increased costs, etc.
- B. Primary marketing objectives (the establishment of aim points and goals). Consider where you are going and how you will get there. Objectives are the necessary base of any plan since a plan must have precise direction.
- C. Overall strategy for achievement of primary objectives. The division's overall strategy to accomplish its primary objective—sample: shifting of sales emphasis, products, or classes of trade; changes for improvement of sales coverage, etc.
- D. Functional (departmental) objectives. (In this section "explode" your primary objectives into subobjectives, or goals, for each department. Show the interrelation vertically, by marketing project. Show time schedule on objectives below.)
    1. Advertising and promotion objectives
    2. Customer service objectives
    3. Product modification objectives
    4. New product objectives
    5. Expense control objectives
    6. Workforce objectives
    7. Personnel training objectives
    8. Market research objectives

IV. DEFINE MARKETING STRATEGY AND ACTION PROGRAMS—to accomplish the objectives
- A. Here, *detail the action steps*, priorities, and schedules relating to each of the functional objectives above. If, for example, one of your estimates was "an increase in sales of product X from 10,000 to 20,000 units," now is the time to pinpoint specific customers. In order to explain who must do what, and when, you can show the interaction of the departments listed above (III-D) and how their objectives serve to meet this increased demand.
- B. If one of your objectives was to introduce a new product by "x" date, now show the details and deadlines, production schedule, market introduction plans, advertising and merchandising support, sales and service training needed, etc. Define responsibility and dates for each step.
- C. Alternatives—In the event of a delay in a project or program, what alternative plans are available?

V. CONTROL AND REVIEW PROCEDURES
How will the execution of the plan be monitored?
- A. What kinds of "feedback" information will be needed?
- B. When and how will reviews be scheduled (departments, regions, etc.)?
- C. Date for full-scale review of progress vs. plan.

Source: David S. Hopkins, *The Marketing Plan* (New York: The Conference Board, 1981). Reprinted with permission of The Conference Board.

EXHIBIT 2   Marketing Plan for a Business-to-Business Company

Marketing Plan Outline

For each major product/product category: Time Period—One, Three, and Five-Plus Years

I. MANAGEMENT SUMMARY

What is our marketing plan for this product in brief?

This is a one-page summary of the basic factors involving the marketing of the product in the plan period, along with the results expected from implementing the plan. It is intended as a brief guide for management.

II. ECONOMIC OUTLOOK

What factors in the overall economy and industry will affect the marketing of the product in the plan period, and how?

This section will contain a summary of the specific economic and industry factors that will affect the marketing of this product during the plan period.

III. THE MARKET—qualitative

Who or what kinds of market segments constitute the major prospects for this product?

This section will define the qualitative nature of our market segments. It will include definitive descriptions and profiles of major distributors, specifiers, users, and/or consumers of the product.

IV. THE MARKET—quantitative

What is the potential market for this product?

This section will apply specific quantitative measures to this product. Here we want to include numbers of potential customers, dollar volume of business, our current share of the market—any specific measures that will outline our total target for the product and where we stand competitively now.

V. TREND ANALYSIS

Based on the history of this product, where do we appear to be headed?

This section is a review of the past history of this product. Ideally, we should include annual figures for the last five years showing dollar volume, accounts opened, accounts closed, share of market, and all other applicable historical data.

VI. COMPETITION

Who are our competitors for this product, and how do we stand competitively?

This section should define our current competition. It should be a thoughtful analysis outlining who our competitors are, how successful they are, and what actions they might be expected to take regarding this product during the coming year.

VII. PROBLEMS AND OPPORTUNITIES

Internally and externally, are there problems inhibiting the marketing of this product, or are there opportunities we have not taken advantage of?

This section will include a frank commentary on both inhibiting problems and unrealized opportunities. It should include a discussion of the internal and external problems we can control, for example, by changes in policies or operational programs. It should also point to areas of opportunity regarding this product that we are not now exploring.

VIII. OBJECTIVES AND GOALS

Where do we want to go with this product?

This section will outline the immediate short- and long-range objectives for this product. Short-range goals should be specific and will apply to next year. Intermediate to long-range goals will necessarily be less specific and should project for the next three to five years and beyond. Objectives should be stated in two forms.

(1) Qualitative—reasoning behind the offering of this product and what modifications or other changes we expect to make.

(2) Quantitative—number of accounts, dollar volume, share of market, and profit goals.

IX. ACTION PROGRAMS

Given past history, the economy, the market, competition, etc., what must we do to reach the goals we have set for this product or service?

This section will be a description of the specific actions we plan to take during the coming plan period to ensure reaching the objectives we have set for the product in VIII. These would include the full range of factors comprising our marketing mix. The discussion should cover what is to be done, schedules for completion, methods of evaluation, and assignment of accountability for executing the program and measuring results.

Source: David S. Hopkins, *The Marketing Plan* (New York: The Conference Board, 1981). Reprinted with permission of The Conference Board.

EXHIBIT 3   Marketing Plan for a Service Company

Marketing Plan Outline

For each major bank service:

I. MANAGEMENT SUMMARY
What is our marketing plan for this service in brief?

This is a one-page summary of the basic factors involving the marketing of the service next year along with the results expected from implementing the plan. It is intended as a brief guide for management.

II. ECONOMIC PROJECTIONS
What factors in the overall economy will affect the marketing of this service next year, and how?

This section will include a summary of the specific economic factors that will affect the marketing of this service during the coming year. These might include employment, personal income, business expectations, inflationary (or deflationary) pressures, etc.

III. THE MARKET—quantitative
Who or what kinds of organizations could conceivably be considered prospects for this service?

This section will define the qualitative nature of our market. It will include demographic information, industrial profiles, business profiles, and so on, for all people or organizations that could be customers for this service.

IV. THE MARKET—quantitative
What is the potential market for this service?

This section will apply specific quantitative measures to this bank service. Here we want to include numbers of potential customers, dollar volume of business, our current share of the market—any specific measures that will outline our total target for the service and where we stand competitively now.

V. TREND ANALYSIS
Based on the history of this service, where do we appear to be headed?

This section is a review of the past history of this service. Ideally, we should include quarterly figures for the last five years showing dollar volume, accounts opened, accounts closed, share of market, and all other applicable historical data.

VI. COMPETITION
Who are our competitors for this service, and how do we stand competitively?

This section should define our current competition, both bank and nonbank. It should be a thoughtful analysis outlining who our competitors are, how successful they are, why they have (or have not) been successful, and what actions they might be expected to take regarding this service during the coming year.

VII. PROBLEMS AND OPPORTUNITIES
Internally and externally, are there problems inhibiting the marketing of this service, or are there opportunities we have not taken advantage of?

This section will contain a frank commentary on both inhibiting problems and unrealized opportunities. It should include a discussion of the internal and external problems we can control, for example, changes in policies or operational procedures. It should also point to areas of opportunity regarding this service that we are not now exploiting.

VIII. OBJECTIVES AND GOALS
Where do we want to go with this service?

This section will outline the immediate short- and long-range objectives for this service. Short-range goals should be specific and will apply to next year. Long-range goals will necessarily be less specific and should project for the next five years. Objectives should be stated in two forms:
(1) Qualitative—reasoning behind the offering of this service and what modifications or other changes we expect to make.
(2) Quantitative—number of accounts, dollar volume, share of market, profit goals.

IX. ACTION PROGRAMS
Given past history, the economy, the market, competition, and so on, what must we do to reach the goals we have set for this service?

This section will be a description of the specific actions we plan to take during the coming year to ensure reaching the objectives we have set for the service in VIII. These would include advertising and promotion, direct mail, and brochure development. It would also include programs to be designed and implemented by line officers. The discussion should cover what is to be done, schedules for completion, methods of evaluation, and officers in charge of executing the program and measuring results.

9

THE ORGANIZATIONAL PLAN

1
To understand the importance of the management team in launching a new venture.

2
To understand the advantages and disadvantages of the alternative legal forms for organizing a new venture.

3
To explain and compare the S corporation and limited liability company as alternative forms of incorporation.

4
To learn the importance of both the formal and the informal organization.

5
To illustrate how the board of directors or board of advisors can be used to support the management of a new venture.

6
To understand what difficulties may arise when owners are reluctant to delegate or give up responsibility.

OPENING PROFILE

ERIC RYAN AND ADAM LOWRY

We have learned in this text that being a successful entrepreneur involves effective analysis, planning, and strategy. Growth of a new venture also requires a commitment of not only the founders but also the employees in order to sustain growth and profitability over an extended period of time. No one respects the importance of creating and nurturing a vibrant corporate culture more than Eric Ryan and Adam Lowry, co-founders of Method Products Inc., a San Francisco manufacturer of eco-friendly cleaning products.

Ryan, a former adman, and Lowry, a former climate scientist, recognized the relevance of corporate culture after embarking on their launch of their first cleaning products. According to Ryan, since their business involves cleaning products, which are not the most exciting products, it is important to maintain employee excitement.

Their beginning as entrepreneurs started in 2000 because both were unhappy in their jobs and both wanted to create something that was their own. After spending many hours dreaming about ideas in 2000 they came up with a plan to revolutionize the cleaning world with eco-friendly products that would be made from nontoxic ingredients, would be just as effective as existing products, and would also have very pleasant odors. They both believed that the green cleaning sector had huge potential but any innovations had to be just as effective as existing products.

Lowry began their quest by looking at alternatives for the common chemicals that were contained in laundry detergents. Most cleaning products required solvents to remove any stubborn stains that were made from petroleum and were likely to be harmful to the environment. With his background as a scientist Lowry discovered a natural solvent that was made from corn stover, a waste product of maize production. In addition he found other biodegradable alternatives to water softening agents that included phosphates and a way to extract detergents from coconut oil. After these discoveries they realized that they needed more than just natural ingredients since packaging also had to meet their green definition. This is where Ryan's experience as an adman came in as he designed packages made with PET plastic, which is one of the most recyclable and sustainable forms of plastic. Finally, they discovered that in the northern part of the Pacific Ocean, where currents create a large garbage area of plastic about the size of Texas, they could collect waste plastic and convert it into bottles for their products.

In 2001 they produced their first four cleaning items and convinced the managers of 20 independent grocers to try them. In September 2001 they received $1 million in venture capital financing. With this financing they then set their sights on national retailers and eventually landed Target, where one of the buyers was intrigued by the fact that such a small company was able to sustain a profit. The company then began to grow as more and more interest was created in their natural eco-friendly products. It was at this point that both Ryan and Lowry realized that they must be sure to create a friendly and positive culture among their employees that would keep them motivated and effective during this growth period.

Ryan and Lowry feel that employee morale is a key to enjoying continued growth and success. They feel that the more that you employ efforts to formalize employee rules and regulations the faster any positive culture slips away. The challenge was keeping the morale that came with early success alive as the company grew into a larger organization. As a small company Method was closely integrated; if any employee felt something was needed, all he or she needed to do was to walk over to the right person and ask them to take care of it. As the company grew, however, this became more difficult and as a result they needed to introduce more process, but without smothering their vibrant culture.

Given their concerns they thought about ways to maintain the positive and vibrant culture at Method by establishing what they called a "ministry of culture." Initially they defined this ministry of culture as a means to maintain qualities that you might envision in an ideal workplace where employees were not overwhelmed with rules and regulations.

In search of the right model they consulted with some exemplary companies such as Apple, Google, Pixar, Nike, Starbucks, and Innocent that they respected as having the kind of culture they sought. As a result Ryan and Lowry came up with three themes for their organization. First of all it was necessary to hire great people. Rather than focusing just on expertise it was imperative to make sure the person had the attitude that matched the company. Second, it was important to emphasize their culture to new hires from the very beginning and make it clear to new hires that they were being employed because they fit in. Third, employees deserved lots of feedback as to how they were doing their jobs in terms of the company's values and culture. Employees needed a sense of purpose at their jobs that was more a shared value than a rule.

In the end they recruited a handful of team members from various departments to work with the company's leadership to try to distil their culture into a few core values. The team was defined as the Values Pod. The values they arrived at came from the bottom up and were embraced by the entire organization. The final list was as follows:

- Keep Method weird.
- What would MacGyver do?
- Innovate, don't imitate.
- Collaborate like crazy.
- Care.

Now known as their Methodology, these values have become instilled in the organization and are the backbone of its culture. To integrate them into the day to day operations these values were printed on cards that illustrate how each value translates into decision making and behavior.

With its vibrant culture and core values established, the company has grown into one of the largest green cleaning firms. It is expected to surpass $110 million in sales in 2011. The company's list of products has grown to include laundry products, general cleaning items, and hand washes marketed in eight countries. Ryan and Lowry are very selective in their retail distribution given their focus on green products. Although their products are about 5 to 10 percent more expensive than environmentally unfriendly brands, Ryan and Lowry are confident that their sales will grow as consumers continue to be concerned about the environment and use more and more eco-friendly products.[1]

DEVELOPING THE MANAGEMENT TEAM

We can see from the Method Products Inc. example the importance of employees and their loyalty and commitment to the organization. Also significant to potential investors is the management team and its ability and commitment to the new venture.

Investors will usually demand that the management team not attempt to operate the business as a sideline or part-time venture while employed full time elsewhere. It is assumed that the management team is prepared to operate the business full time and at a modest salary. It is unacceptable for the entrepreneurs to try to draw a large salary out of the new venture, and investors may perceive any attempt to do so as a lack of psychological commitment to the business. Later in this chapter, the roles of various team members are discussed, particularly as the firm evolves into a legitimate ongoing concern. In addition, the entrepreneur should consider the role of the board of directors and/or a board of advisors in supporting the management of the new venture. At this point, however, the entrepreneur needs to consider the alternatives regarding the legal form of the organization. Each of these forms has important implications for taxes, liability, continuity, and financing the new venture.

LEGAL FORMS OF BUSINESS

C corporation Most common form of corporation, regulated by statute and treated as a separate legal entity for liability and tax purposes

There are three basic legal forms of business formation with some variations available depending on the entrepreneurs' needs. The three basic legal forms are (1) proprietorship, (2) partnership, and (3) corporation, with variations particularly in partnerships and corporations. The newest form of business formation is the limited liability company (LLC), which is now possible in all 50 states and the District of Columbia. The typical corporation form is known as a *C corporation*. Table 9.1 describes the legal factors involved in each of these forms with the differences in the limited liability partnership (LLP) and S corporation noted where appropriate. These three basic legal forms are compared with regard to ownership, liability, start-up costs, continuity, transferability of interest, capital requirements, management control, distribution of profits, and attractiveness for raising capital. Later in the chapter, the S corporation

ADVICE TO AN ENTREPRENEUR: ISSUES TO CONSIDER IN DELEGATING RESPONSIBILITY

Leadership in a start-up is extremely important in order to keep the organization on plan. Delegation of responsibility by an entrepreneur may be considered the soul of management in an organization yet entrepreneurs are often reluctant to give up responsibility and instead try to make most decisions on their own. This can destroy motivation among employees. Some of the reasons often given for why an entrepreneur is unwilling to delegate are:

1. My employees lack experience.
2. My employees are too busy.
3. By the time I explain the task I can do it myself.
4. I cannot trust an employee to make this decision.
5. Any mistakes would be too costly to my business.

In spite of all of these excuses delegation is the easiest and most efficient way to get things done. Any entrepreneur unwilling to delegate is shortchanging his or her employees in a manner that could lead to poor company performance.

Some of the key factors to consider in delegating are as follows:

1. Choose the right people to perform the task. It is important to recognize what you do best and what you are not capable of performing very well. Identify the best employee for the task by making a list of their strengths and weaknesses.
2. It is also best to start the process by delegating smaller tasks so that the level of expertise can be identified and then delegation can be increased over time.
3. Be flexible. People may perform the task differently than you would. As long as the same goal is achieved the process can be different depending on the individual.
4. Build in checkpoints and goals for the task at hand. Timetables and meetings to check on the

status of the task are important to both the entrepreneur and the employee.

5. Provide feedback to employees on tasks well done. As the leader of an organization you want to foster an effective collaborative environment where employees are motivated and willing to give suggestions.

History indicates that many entrepreneurs try to perform too many tasks in the new venture, often spreading themselves too thin and thus negatively affecting all their tasks. Assigning and delegating tasks is part of being a good leader and in the long run will enhance the confidence and motivation of all employees.

ADVICE TO AN ENTREPRENEUR

An entrepreneur who is getting ready to launch a new business has read the information above and comes to you with some questions.

1. How can I be sure that an employee will perform the task at hand the way I want him to without my spending a lot of time explaining how to complete the task? If I have to spend all this time explaining, I can probably better complete this task on my own.
2. I am particular about how to go about solving a problem. My employees may have a different idea on how to solve this problem. Should I give them my opinion of how to go about performing the task at hand?
3. How can I know for sure that delegating responsibility will make me a better leader in my organization?

Sources: Scott Eblin, "Delegating While Managing Risk," *Executive Leadership* (May 2010), p. 7; Michelle Thompson-Dolberry, "Drive Business by Delegating," *NAFE Magazine* (Winter 2011), p. 30; Tamara Holmes, "The Do's and Don'ts of Delegating," *Black Enterprise* (September 2010), p. 104.

and the LLC are compared and discussed as alternative forms of business, especially for the new venture.

It is very important that the entrepreneur carefully evaluate the pros and cons of the various legal forms of organizing the new venture. This decision must be made before the submission of a business plan and request for venture capital.

TABLE 9.1   Factors in Three Forms of Business Formation

Factors	Proprietorship	Partnership	Corporation
Ownership	Individual.	No limitation on number of partners.	No limitation on number of stockholders.
Liability of owners	Individual liable for business liabilities.	In general partnership, all individuals liable for business liabilities. Limited partners are liable for amount of capital contribution. In limited liability partnership (LLP), there is no liability except when negligence exists.	Amount of capital contribution is limit of shareholder liability.
Costs of starting business	None, other than filing fees for trade name.	Partnership agreement, legal costs, and minor filing fees for trade name.	Created only by statute. Articles of incorporation, filing fees, taxes, and fees for states in which corporation registers to do business.
Continuity of business	Death dissolves the business.	Death or withdrawal of one partner terminates partnership unless partnership agreement stipulates otherwise. Death or withdrawal of one of limited partners has no effect on continuity.	Greatest form of continuity. Death or withdrawal of owner(s) will not affect legal existence of business.
Transferability of interest	Complete freedom to sell or transfer any part of business.	General partner can transfer his/her interest only with consent of all other general partners. Limited partner can sell interest without consent of general partners. No transfer of interest in an LLP.	Most flexible. Stockholders can sell or buy stock at will. Some stock transfers may be restricted by agreement. In S corporation, stock may be transferred only to an individual.
Capital requirements	Capital raised only by loan or increased contribution by proprietor.	Loans or new contributions by partners require a change in partnership agreement. In LLP partnership, entity raises money.	New capital raised by sale of stock or bonds or by borrowing (debt) in name of corporation. In S corporation, only one class of stock and limited to 100 shareholders.
Management control	Proprietor makes all decisions and can act immediately.	All general partners have equal control, and majority rules. Limited partners have limited control. Can vary in an LLP.	Majority stockholder(s) have most control from legal point of view. Day-to-day control in hands of management, who may or may not be major stockholders.
Distribution of profits and losses	Proprietor responsible and receives all profits and losses.	Depends on partnership agreement and investment by partners.	Shareholders can share in profits by receipt of dividends.
Attractiveness for raising capital	Depends on capability of proprietor and success of business.	Depends on capability of partners and success of business.	With limited liability for owners, more attractive as an investment opportunity.

The evaluation process requires the entrepreneur to determine the priority of each of the factors mentioned in Table 9.1, as well as tax factors discussed later in this chapter. These factors will vary in importance, depending on the type of new business.

The variations of organizational structure as well as the advantages and disadvantages are numerous and can be quite confusing to the entrepreneur. In the next section of this chapter, some of these differences are clarified to assist the entrepreneur in making the best decision regarding organizational structure.

Ownership

proprietorship Form of business with single owner who has unlimited liability, controls all decisions, and receives all profits

partnership Two or more individuals having unlimited liability who have pooled resources to own a business

corporation Separate legal entity that is run by stockholders having limited liability

In the *proprietorship,* the owner is the individual who starts the business. He or she has full responsibility for the operations. In a *partnership,* there may be some general partnership owners and some limited partnership owners. There are also limited liability partnerships (LLPs) in which the partnership is treated as a legal entity. In the *corporation,* ownership is reflected by ownership of shares of stock. Unlike the S corporation, where the maximum number of shareholders is 100, there is no limit as to the number of shareholders who may own stock in a corporation.

Liability of Owners

Liability is one of the most critical reasons for establishing a corporation rather than any other form of business. The proprietor and general partners are liable for all aspects of the business. Since the corporation is an entity or legal "person," which is taxable and absorbs liability, the owners are liable only for the amount of their investment unless there is negligence or fraud involved. In the case of a proprietorship or regular partnership, no distinction is made between the business entity and the owner(s). Then, to satisfy any outstanding debts of the business, creditors may seize any assets the owners have outside the business.

In a partnership, the general partners usually share the amount of personal liability equally, regardless of their capital contributions, unless there is a specific agreement to the contrary. The only protection for the partners is insurance against liability suits and each partner putting his or her assets in someone else's name. The government may disallow the latter action if it feels this was done to defraud creditors.

In a general partnership there also may be limited partners. These limited partners are liable for only what they contribute to the partnership. This amount, by law, must be registered at a local courthouse, thus making this information public. The LLP has become very popular among larger law firms and accounting CPA firms. It is actually a form of limited liability company (LLC), where the firm elects this status when filing its entity classification with the IRS on Form 8832. Thus the advantages of the LLP are the same as the LLC, allowing the partners to protect their personal assets from liability risk. The LLP will be distinguished from the general partnership as appropriate in our comparison of the various forms of organization that follows.[2]

Costs of Starting a Business

The more complex the organization, the more expensive it is to start. The least expensive is the proprietorship, where the only costs incurred may be for filing for a business or trade name. In a partnership, in addition to filing a trade name, a partnership agreement is needed. This agreement requires legal advice and should explicitly convey all the responsibilities, rights, and duties of the parties involved. A limited partnership may be somewhat more complex than a general partnership because it must comply strictly with statutory requirements.

The corporation can be created only by statute. This generally means that before the corporation may be legally formed, the owners are required to (1) register the name and articles of incorporation and (2) meet the state statutory requirements (some states are more lenient than others). In complying with these requirements, the corporation will likely incur filing fees, an organization tax, and fees for doing business in each state. Legal advice is necessary to meet all the statutory requirements.

Continuity of Business

One of the main concerns of a new venture is what happens if one of the entrepreneurs (or the only entrepreneur) dies or withdraws from the business. Continuity differs significantly for each of the forms of business. In a sole proprietorship, the death of the owner results in the termination of the business. Sole proprietorships are thus not perpetual, and there is no time limit on how long they may exist.

The partnership varies, depending on whether it is a general partnership or a limited liability partnership (LLP). In a general partnership, the death or withdrawal of one of the partners results in termination of the partnership unless the partnership agreement stipulates otherwise. Thus, the partnership agreement may contain stipulations that allow for a buy-out of the deceased or withdrawn partner's share, based on some mechanism or predetermined value. It also may be possible to have a member of the deceased partner's family take over as a partner and share in the profits accordingly. Life insurance owned by the partnership can be valuable protection for the partnership, often providing the funds necessary to buy out the deceased partner's share.

If there are limited liability partners in a general partnership, their death or withdrawal has no effect on the continuity of the business. A limited partner also may be replaced depending on the partnership agreement.

In a limited liability partnership (LLP), the death or withdrawal of a partner has no effect on the partnership. The deceased or withdrawn partner may be replaced much like any employee of a corporation.

The corporation has the most continuity of all the forms of business. Death or withdrawal has no impact on the continuation of the business. Only in a closely held corporation, where a few people hold all the shares, may there be some problems trying to find a market for the shares. Usually, the corporate charter requires that the corporation or the remaining shareholders purchase the shares. In a public corporation this, of course, would not be an issue.

Transferability of Interest

There can be mixed feelings as to whether the transfer of interest in a business is desirable. In some cases the entrepreneur(s) may prefer to evaluate and assess any new owners before giving them a share of the business. On the other hand, it is also desirable to be able to sell one's interest whenever one wishes. This may be of particular significance when there is the need to consider a succession plan or strategy. This is discussed in more detail in Chapter 15. Each form of business offers different advantages as to the transferability of interest.

In the sole proprietorship, the entrepreneur has the right to sell or transfer any assets in the business. Limited partners, if existing in a general partnership organization, have more flexibility and may typically sell their interest at any time without consent of the general partners. The new limited partner's rights will remain the same as those of the prior partner. However, this may vary depending on the partnership agreement. General partners usually cannot sell their interest without first refusal from the remaining general partners, even if the partnership agreement allows for the transfer of interest.

In an LLP, the transfer of interest of one limited partner is typically not allowable. As stated previously, the LLP has become popular among law and CPA firms. Limited partners also may vary in distinction (e.g., there may be associate partners or junior partners), in which case they also may not share the same profit percentages as full partners. Full partners in law or CPA firms may elect to sell the business, but such a decision usually requires the approval of all or a majority.

The corporation has the most freedom in terms of selling one's interest in the business. Shareholders may transfer their shares at any time without consent from the other shareholders. The disadvantage of the right is that it can affect the ownership control of a corporation through election of a board of directors. Shareholders' agreements may provide some limitations on the ease of transferring interest, usually by giving the existing shareholders or corporation the option of purchasing the stock at a specific price or at the agreed-on price. Thus, they sometimes can have the right of first refusal. In the S corporation, the transfer of interest can occur only as long as the buyer is an individual.

Capital Requirements

The need for capital during the early months of the new venture can become one of the most critical factors in keeping a new venture alive. The opportunities and ability of the new venture to raise capital will vary, depending on the form of business.

For a proprietorship, any new capital can come only from loans by any number of sources or by additional personal contributions by the entrepreneur. In borrowing money from a bank, the entrepreneur in this form of business may need collateral to support the loan. Often, an entrepreneur will take a second mortgage on his or her home as a source of capital. Any borrowing from an outside investor may require giving up some of the equity in the proprietorship. Whatever the source, the responsibility for payment is in the hands of the entrepreneur, and failure to make payments can result in foreclosure and liquidation of the business. However, even with these risks the proprietorship is not likely to need large sums of money, as might be the case for a partnership or corporation.

In the partnership, loans may be obtained from banks but will likely require a change in the partnership agreement. Additional funds contributed by each of the partners will also require a new partnership agreement. As in the proprietorship, the entrepreneurs are liable for payment of any new bank loans.

In the corporation, new capital can be raised in a number of ways. The alternatives are greater than in any of the other legal forms of business. Stock may be sold as either voting or nonvoting. Nonvoting stock will of course protect the power of the existing major stockholders. Bonds also may be sold by the corporation. This alternative would be more difficult for the new venture since a high bond rating will likely occur only after the business has been successful over time. Money also may be borrowed in the name of the corporation. As stated earlier, this protects the personal liability of the entrepreneur(s).

Management Control

In any new venture, the entrepreneur(s) will want to retain as much control as possible over the business. Each of the forms of business offers different opportunities and problems as to control and responsibility for making business decisions.

In the proprietorship, the entrepreneur has the most control and flexibility in making business decisions. Since the entrepreneur is the single owner of the venture, he or she will be responsible for and have sole authority over all business decisions.

The partnership can present problems over control of business decisions if the partnership agreement is not concise regarding this issue. Usually, in a partnership the majority rules unless the partnership agreement states otherwise. It is quite important that the partners be friendly toward one another and that delicate or sensitive decision areas of the business be spelled out in the partnership agreement.

The existence of limited partners in a general partnership offers a compromise between the partnership and the corporation. In this type of organization, we can see some of the separation of ownership and control. The limited partners in the venture have no control over business decisions. As soon as the limited partner is given some control over business decisions, he or she then assumes personal liability and can no longer be considered a limited partner. In the LLP, the rights of all partners are clearly defined in the partnership agreement. As mentioned earlier, these types of organizations use titles such as junior partner, associate partner, and so on as a means of designating management responsibilities.

Control of day-to-day business in a corporation is in the hands of management, who may or may not be major stockholders. Control over major long-term decisions, however, may require a vote of the major stockholders. Thus, control is separated based on the types of business decisions. In a new venture, there is a strong likelihood that the entrepreneurs who are major stockholders will be managing the day-to-day activities of the business. As the corporation increases in size, the separation of management and control becomes more probable.

Stockholders in the corporation can indirectly affect the operation of the business by electing someone to the board of directors who reflects their personal business philosophies. These board members, through appointment of top management, then affect the operation and control of the day-to-day management of the business.

Distribution of Profits and Losses

Proprietors receive all distributions of profits from the business. As discussed earlier, they are also personally responsible for all losses. Some of the profits may be used to pay back the entrepreneur for any personal capital contributions that are made to keep the business operating.

In the partnership, the distribution of profits and losses depends on the partnership agreement. It is likely that the sharing of profits and losses will be a function of the partners' investments. However, this can vary depending on the agreement. As in the proprietorship, the partners may assume liability. Limited partners in a general partnership, or the formation of an LLP, are alternatives that protect those limited partners against personal liability but that may also reduce their share in any profits.

Corporations distribute profits through dividends to stockholders. These distributions are not likely to absorb all the profits that may be retained by the corporation for future investment or capital needs of the business. Losses by the corporation will often result in no dividends. These losses will then be covered by retained earnings or through other financial means discussed earlier.

Attractiveness for Raising Capital

In both the proprietorship and the partnership, the ability of the entrepreneurs to raise capital depends on the success of the business and the personal capability of the entrepreneur. These two forms are the least attractive for raising capital, primarily because of the problem of personal liability. Any large amounts of capital needed in these forms of business should be given serious consideration.

The corporation, because of its advantages regarding personal liability, is the most attractive form of business for raising capital. Shares of stock, bonds, and/or debt are all opportunities for raising capital with limited liability. The more attractive the corporation, the easier it will be to raise capital.

TAX ATTRIBUTES OF FORMS OF BUSINESS

The tax advantages and disadvantages of each of the forms of business differ significantly. Some of the major differences are discussed next. There are many minor differences that, in total, can be important to the entrepreneur. If the entrepreneur has any doubt about these advantages, he or she should get outside advice. Table 9.2 provides a summary of the major tax advantages of these forms of business.

TABLE 9.2   Tax Attributes of Various Legal Forms of Business

Attributes	Proprietorship	Partnership	Corporation
Taxable year	Usually a calendar year.	Usually calendar year, but other dates may be used.	Any year-end can be used at beginning. Any changes require changes in incorporation.
Distribution of profits to owners	All income appears on owner's return.	Partnership agreement may have special allocation of income. Partners pay tax on their pro rata shares of income on individual return even if income not immediately distributed.	No income is allocated to stockholders.
Organization costs	Not amortizable.	Amortizable over 60 months.	Amortizable over 60 months.
Dividends received	$100 dividend exclusion for single return and $200 on joint return.	Dividend exclusion of partnership passes to partner (conduit).	80% or more of dividend received may be deducted.
Capital gains	Taxed at individual level. A deduction is allowed for long-term capital gains.	Capital gain to partnership will be taxed as a capital gain to the partner (conduit).	Taxed at corporate level.
Capital losses	Carried forward indefinitely.	Capital losses can be used to offset other income. Carried forward indefinitely (conduit).	Carry back three years and carry over five years as short-term capital loss offsetting only capital gains.
Initial organization	Commencement of business results in no additional tax for individual.	Contributions of property to a partnership not taxed.	Acquisition of stock for cash entails no immediate taxes. Transfer of property in exchange for stock may be taxable if stock value greater than contributed property.
Limitations on losses deductible by owners	Amount at risk may be deducted except for real estate activities.	Partnership investment plus share of recourse liability if any. At-risk rules may apply except for real estate partnership.	No losses allowed except on sale of stock or liquidation of corporation. In S corporation, shareholder's investment in corporation is deductible.
Medical benefits	Itemized deductions for medical expenses in excess of percentage of adjusted gross income on individual's return. No deduction for insurance premium.	Cost of partner's benefits not deductible to business as an expense. Possible deduction at partner level.	Cost of employee-shareholder coverage deductible as business expense if designed for benefit of employee.
Retirement benefits	Limitations and restrictions basically same as regular corporation.	Same as for corporations.	Limitations on the benefits that can be derived and on the benefits that can be contributed to a defined contribution plan.

Tax Issues for Proprietorship

For the proprietorship, the IRS treats the business as the individual owner. All income appears on the owner's return as personal income. Thus, the proprietorship is not regarded by the IRS as a separate tax entity. As can be seen in Table 9.2, this treatment of taxes affects the taxable year, distribution of profits to owners, organization costs, capital gains, capital losses, and medical benefits. Each of these is treated as if it were incurred by the individual owner and not the business.

The proprietorship has some tax advantages when compared with the corporation. First, there is no double tax when profits are distributed to the owner. Another advantage is that there is no capital stock tax or penalty for retained earnings in the business. Again, these advantages exist because the proprietorship is not recognized as a separate tax entity; all profits and losses are part of the entrepreneur's tax return.

Tax Issues for Partnership

The partnership's tax advantages and disadvantages are similar to those of the proprietorship, especially regarding income distributions, dividends, and capital gains and losses. Limited partners in a traditional general partnership have the advantage of limited liability (they are liable only for the amount of their investment), but they can share in the profits at a percentage stipulated in the partnership agreement. The LLP is treated the same as the LLC for tax purposes, and all profits are distributed through the partners in some designated fashion as personal income.

Both the partnership and proprietorship are organizational forms that serve as nontaxable conduits of income and deductions. These forms of business do have a legal identity distinct from the partners or owners, but this identity is only for accounting reporting.

It is especially important for partnerships to report income since this serves as the basis for determining the share of each partner. The income is distributed based on the partnership agreement. The owners then report their share as personal income and pay taxes based on this amount.

Tax Issues for Corporation

Since the IRS recognizes the corporation as a separate tax entity, it has the advantage of being able to take many deductions and expenses that are not available to the proprietorship or partnership. The disadvantage is that the distribution of dividends is taxed twice, as income of the corporation and as income of the stockholder. This double taxation can be avoided if the income is distributed to the entrepreneur(s) in the form of salary. Bonuses, incentives, profit sharing, and so on, are thus allowable ways to distribute income of the corporation as long as the compensation is reasonable in amount and payment was for services rendered.

The corporate tax may be lower than the individual rate. The entrepreneur is best advised to consider the tax pros and cons and decide on that basis. Projected earnings may be used to calculate the actual taxes under each form of business to identify the one that provides the best tax advantage. Remember, tax advantages should be balanced by liability responsibility in the respective form of business.

THE LIMITED LIABILITY COMPANY VERSUS THE S CORPORATION

Although the perception among entrepreneurs is that the C corporation is the entity desired by investors, the actual entity desired by venture capitalists is the limited liability company (LLC), which is similar to the S corporation. The emergence of the LLC as a more popular alternative has resulted from a change in regulation. Regulations now allow an LLC to be automatically taxed as a partnership, unless the entrepreneur actively makes another choice (taxed as a corporation). This easing of election is one important factor that has enhanced the LLC's popularity.

The S corporation (the S refers to Subchapter S of the Internal Revenue Code) had been the most popular choice of organization structure by new ventures and small businesses.

However, the growth rate of the formation of S corporations has actually declined in the last few years primarily because of acceptance of the LLC in all states and amendments in several states making the LLC more attractive.[3]

S CORPORATION

S corporation Special type of corporation where profits are distributed to stockholders and taxed as personal income

The *S corporation* combines the tax advantages of the partnership and the corporation. It is designed so that venture income is declared as personal income on a pro rata basis by the shareholders. In fact, the shareholders benefit from all the income and the deductions of the business. Before the passing of the Small Business Job Protection Act of 1996, the rules governing the S corporation were considered too rigid. The passage of the 1996 law loosened some of the restrictions that existed in regard to number of shareholders, ownership of stock of another corporation, role of trusts as stockholders, classes of stock, and a number of other changes. In 2004, Congress again responded to some of the criticisms of the restrictions on S corporations as compared to LLCs. As a result a number of changes were made, such as an increase in the number of shareholders to 100, allowing family members to be treated as one stockholder, allowing IRAs to own shares in banks that are declared S corporations, as well as some modifications regarding the transfer of stock in a divorce. The intent was to make the S corporation as advantageous as the LLC since it is difficult to change status once a firm has declared itself an S corporation. There have been more recent decisions in 2010 and 2011 made by Congress (Small Business Job Acts) that have had some minor impact on the S corporation. It is important for the entrepreneur to be aware of such changes especially regarding tax implications.[4]

One of the issues with the S corporation is that its status must be carefully monitored and maintained. For example, its tax status as a pass-through entity (with its income taxed as personal income of shareholders) still requires an affirmative election of shareholders. If the S corporation status is ever lost, it usually cannot be reelected for five years and with some costs. As stated earlier, the differences between the S corporation and the LLC are generally minimal but should be evaluated on a case-by-case basis because of the existing company and shareholder circumstances.

Advantages of an S Corporation

The S corporation offers the entrepreneur some distinct advantages over the typical corporation, or C corporation. However, there are also disadvantages.[5] In those instances when the disadvantages are great, the entrepreneur should elect the C corporation form. Some of the advantages of the S corporation are as follows:

- Capital gains or losses from the corporation are treated as personal income or losses by the shareholders on a pro rata basis (determined by number of shares of stock held). The corporation is thus not taxed.
- Shareholders retain the same limited liability protection as the C corporation.
- The S corporation is not subject to a minimum tax, as is the C corporation.
- Stock may be transferred to low-income-bracket family members (children must be 14 years or older).
- Stock may be voting or nonvoting.
- This form of business may use the cash method of accounting.
- Corporate long-term capital gains and losses are deductible directly by the shareholders to offset other personal capital gains or losses.

ETHICS

LAWYERS EXPLAIN THE STEPS TO TAKE IF YOUR BUSINESS PARTNER VIOLATES HIS OR HER OBLIGATIONS TO THE BUSINESS

My business partner and I have owned a technology company for six years. It's an S-Corporation and we are 50-50 shareholders, each with a board position. Our bylaws are boilerplate and our stockholder agreement is pretty weak, focusing on when we can or can't sell the business. Recently I found out that for the first four years, my partner was getting paid by one of the corporation's customers through a local university to work in the same technology we do in the company. Is this a conflict of interest on his part? What should I do?

C. G. (Rome, NY)

Yes, this is a conflict of interest. In legal terms it's called "a diversion of corporate opportunity." This means your partner took work for himself that the corporation could have done. This is most likely a breach of your partner's fiduciary obligations and his duty of loyalty to the corporation, says Stuart Blake, co-founder and chief executive officer of the General Counsel, a law firm based in Newport Beach, Calif. It's also a serious breach of trust between the two of you as partners.

Relying on boilerplate documents and a weak shareholder agreement may make this dilemma more serious. "This is the pitfall of not having an attorney help draft your corporate documents when you set up your S-corp. With a more detailed agreement, including buy/sell provisions, noncompete clauses, and conflict-of-interest provisions, you could extricate yourself from this situation much more easily," Blake says.

PUT THE EVIDENCE IN BLACK AND WHITE

What you should do depends largely on what you want from your partner and from the corporation, says Rubin Ferziger, a business attorney based in New York. Do you want to continue with the corporation, but recover the lost profits and perhaps other damages? Are you considering dissolving the corporation and going off on your own? Does your business depend on your partner or could you carry on alone?

"Take your shareholder agreement to an attorney and explain what has happened," Ferziger suggests. "You should also discuss the situation with your family and with an accountant who is not affiliated with your partner."

Make sure you have documentary evidence about the competing work your partner did, says Ray Gallo, a Los Angeles attorney with Gallo & Associates. "Having it in black and white minimizes the possibilities for arguments and litigation. Present the evidence to a lawyer you engage to act as counsel to the corporation to make this determination," Gallo says.

If the lawyer concludes your partner has violated his duties, sit down with your partner promptly, Gallo says. If you want to continue working together, both of you should agree that he won't do this again and—ideally—that he'll put the money he made into the corporation. "Hopefully it'll go well," he says. "If not, you'll have to choose whether the money at issue is worth fighting over. Either way, you'll have to decide whether this is a guy you should continue in business with. If your gut reaction is that he cheated you, the answer is no."

Source: Reprinted with permission Karen E. Klein, "Resolving a Conflict of Interest," *BusinessWeek Online*, June 26, 2008, p. 16.

Disadvantages of an S Corporation

Although the advantages appear to be favorable for the entrepreneur, this form of business is not appropriate for everyone. The disadvantages of the S corporation are as follows:

- Even with the regulations passed in 1996 and 2004, there are still some restrictions regarding qualification for this form of business. More recent Small Business Job Acts passed in each of the past two years have also had some impact on the S corporation and should be consulted when considering this form of organization.

- Depending on the actual amount of the net income, there may be a tax advantage to the C corporation. This will depend on the company payout ratio, the corporate tax rate, the capital gains tax rate for the investor, and the personal income tax rate of the investor.

- The S corporation may not deduct most fringe benefits for shareholders.
- The S corporation must adopt a calendar year for tax purposes.
- Only one class of stock (common stock) is permitted for this form of business.
- The net loss of the S corporation is limited to the shareholder's stock plus loans to the business.
- S corporations cannot have more than 100 shareholders.

THE LIMITED LIABILITY COMPANY

As stated earlier, the new flexibility offered by LLC status has enhanced its choice by entrepreneurs. The tax rules for an LLC fall under Subchapter K, and this business form is considered a partnership-corporation hybrid with the following characteristics:

- Whereas the corporation has shareholders and partnerships have partners, the LLC has members.
- No shares of stock are issued, and each member owns an interest in the business as designated by the articles of organization, which is similar to the articles of incorporation or certificates of partnership.
- Liability does not extend beyond the member's capital contribution to the business. Thus, there is no unlimited liability, which can be detrimental in a proprietorship or general partnership.
- Members may transfer their interest only with the unanimous written consent of the remaining members.
- The Internal Revenue Service now automatically treats LLCs as partnerships for tax purposes, unless another option is elected. Thus, as mentioned earlier in this chapter, members may elect to designate the firm as a partnership or a corporation.
- The standard acceptable term of an LLC is 30 years. Dissolution is also likely when one of the members dies, the business goes bankrupt, or all members choose to dissolve the business. Some states allow continuity with majority or unanimous consent of the members. One of the important characteristics of the LLC is that the laws governing its formation differ from state to state. Thus, a firm that is operating in more than one state may be subject to different treatment. An analysis of these differences should be considered before choosing this form of organization.

Advantages of an LLC

A number of advantages of an LLC over an S corporation are described here.[6]

- In a highly leveraged enterprise, the LLC offers the partnership a distinct advantage over an S corporation in that the partners can add their proportionate shares of the LLC liabilities to their partnership interests.
- States vary on the requirements of taxation but the LLC may have tax advantages in most states.[7]
- One or more (without limit) individuals, corporations, partnerships, trusts, or other entities can join to organize or form an LLC. This is not feasible in an S corporation.
- Members are allowed to share income, profit, expense, deduction, loss and credit, and equity of the LLC among themselves. This is the only form of organization that offers all these features.

The one major concern with the LLC is in international business, where the context of unlimited liability is still unclear. Otherwise the LLC offers all the distinct advantages of a C corporation but with a pass-through tax to the members. Owners of an LLC can neither be paid as employees nor participate in certain employee benefits. Instead they are paid in the form of guaranteed payments with no federal or state withholding involved. Thus, members are responsible for filing estimated taxes on a regular basis. The LLC appears to be the favorite choice for venture capitalists since it offers more flexibility based on the advantages already discussed. However, entrepreneurs should compare all the alternative forms of organization before election. This should be done with the advice of a tax attorney, since once a decision is made, it may be difficult to change without some penalty.

DESIGNING THE ORGANIZATION

Generally, the design of the initial organization will be simple. In fact, the entrepreneur may find that he or she performs all the functions of the organization alone. This is a common problem and a significant reason for many failures. The entrepreneur sometimes thinks that he or she can do everything and is unwilling to give up responsibility to others or even include others in the management team. In most cases when this occurs, the entrepreneur will have difficulty making the transition from a start-up to a growing, well-managed business that maintains its success over a long period of time. Regardless of whether one or more individuals are involved in the start-up, as the workload increases, the organizational structure will need to expand to include additional employees with defined roles in the organization. Effective interviewing and hiring procedures will need to be implemented to ensure that new employees will effectively grow and mature with the new venture. All the design decisions involving personnel and their roles and responsibilities reflect the formal structure of the organization. In addition to this formal structure there is an informal structure or organization culture that evolves over time that also needs to be addressed by the entrepreneur. Although we are speaking of an organization culture rather than an organization design, the entrepreneur can have some control over how it evolves. Since issues related to this culture can be just as critical as the formal design of the organization for ensuring a successful and profitable enterprise, they will be discussed in more detail in the next section of this chapter.

For many new ventures, predominantly part-time employees may be hired, raising important issues of commitment and loyalty. However, regardless of the number of actual personnel involved in running the venture, the organization must identify the major activities required to operate it effectively.

The design of the organization will be the entrepreneur's formal and explicit indication to the members of the organization as to what is expected of them. Typically these expectations can be grouped into the following five areas:[8]

- *Organization structure.* This defines members' jobs and the communication and relationship these jobs have with each other. These relationships are depicted in an organization chart.

- *Planning, measurement, and evaluation schemes.* All organization activities should reflect the goals and objectives that underlie the venture's existence. The entrepreneur must spell out how these goals will be achieved (plans), how they will be measured, and how they will be evaluated.

- *Rewards.* Members of an organization will require rewards in the form of promotions, bonuses, praise, and so on. The entrepreneur or other key managers will need to be responsible for these rewards.

- *Selection criteria*. The entrepreneur will need to determine a set of guidelines for selecting individuals for each position.
- *Training*. Training, on or off the job, must be specified. This training may be in the form of formal education or learning skills.

The organization's design can be very simple—that is, one in which the entrepreneur performs all the tasks (usually indicative of a start-up)—or more complex, in which other employees are hired to perform specific tasks. As the organization becomes larger and more complex, the preceding areas of expectation become more relevant and necessary.

As the organization evolves, the manager or entrepreneur's decision roles also become critical for an effective organization. As an entrepreneur, the manager's primary concern is to adapt to changes in the environment and seek new ideas. When a new idea is found, the entrepreneur will need to initiate development either under his or her own supervision or by delegating the responsibility to someone else in the organization (see Advice to an Entrepreneur box that appears earlier in this chapter). In addition to the role of adaptor, the manager will also need to respond to pressures such as an unsatisfied customer, a supplier reneging on a contract, or a key employee threatening to quit. Much of the entrepreneur's time in the start-up will be spent "putting out fires."

Another role for the entrepreneur is that of allocator of resources. The manager must decide who gets what. This involves the delegation of budgets and responsibilities. The allocation of resources can be a very complex and difficult process for the entrepreneur since one decision can significantly affect other decisions. The final decision role is that of negotiator. Negotiations of contracts, salaries, prices of raw materials, and so on, are an integral part of the manager's job, and since he or she can be the only person with the appropriate authority, it is a necessary area of decision making.

BUILDING THE MANAGEMENT TEAM AND A SUCCESSFUL ORGANIZATION CULTURE

In conjunction with the design of the organization the entrepreneur will need to assemble the right mix of people to assume the responsibilities outlined in the organization structure. Some of the issues identified in the organization design will be revisited here since they are not only critical to the building of the team but are just as important in establishing a positive and successful organization culture. Recall in our opening profile how important culture in the organization was to Eric Ryan and Adam Lowry at Method Inc. They maintain that a vibrant culture is a critical factor in the successful growth of any new venture. This strategy must be maintained through the stages of start-up and growth of the enterprise. There are some important issues to address before assembling and building the management team. In essence the team must be able to accomplish three functions:

- Execute the business plan.
- Identify fundamental changes in the business as they occur.
- Make adjustments to the plan based on changes in the environment and market that will maintain profitability.

Although these functions may seem simple and easy to achieve, the people engaged and the culture promoted by the entrepreneur are critical in accomplishing these functions. As we discussed in the organization design section previously, the entrepreneur will first need to assume the responsibility of determining what skills and abilities are needed to meet the goals in the business plan. Not only are the skills and abilities important, but the entrepreneur also will need to consider the personality and character of each individual to create a viable organization culture. The organization culture will be a blend of attitudes, behaviors, dress, and communication styles that make one business different from another. There is no specific technique for accomplishing this since every organization will be different. One thing that is important is that the entrepreneur(s) need to be able to delegate responsibility in order to create a vibrant organizational culture. (See again the issues in delegating discussed in the Advice to an Entrepreneur box that appears earlier in this chapter.) We will explore some of the important considerations and strategies in recruiting and assembling an effective team and hence in creating an effective and positive organization culture.

First, the entrepreneur's desired culture must match the business strategy outlined in the business plan. For example, Fran Bigelow, founder of Fran's Chocolates in Seattle, has been able to get her team to consider themselves artisans, focus on detail, and strive for perfection. Fran feels that this strategy is effective for her venture because of her premium product line but might result in disaster for someone marketing a high-volume, low-cost manufactured product. Fran's success with this strategy has made her a celebrity among chefs such as Bobby Flay and has been featured in *Good Housekeeping* and *People* magazines.[9]

Second, the leader of the organization must create a workplace where employees are motivated and rewarded for good work. Paul English, the co-founder of Kayak, a travel search engine, is a strong believer in the team concept in his organization. As the head of a service organization he is committed to doing most of the hiring as well as firing of people. The company has an open environment with few private offices. English's office is in the open and he spends half his day walking around and interacting with his employees working on product and design strategy. Since everyone is in the open he encourages people to help each other when a customer issue becomes serious or complicated. He answers all e-mails and he personally answers the hot line on which customers can call to complain. He spends time socializing with employees, going out to lunch, playing basketball, jogging, playing volleyball and tennis. When making hiring decisions English tries to get people to accept the position before they know the salary or title. He promises to make people productive and that working for Kayak will be the most fun job they ever had. Since he spends a lot of his time recruiting, his priorities are team, then customer, and then profit. His leadership has created a very unique organization culture that has obviously worked for Kayak.[10]

Third, the entrepreneur should be flexible enough to try different things. This is not always possible in a very small organization but has been the successful strategy in the growth of Google. The leadership of this company has an abundance of talent, and the attitude of management is that this talent needs to be given enough flexibility to make decisions, as long as they do so within the model established by the company. Founders Larry Page and Sergey Brin encourage all their employees to use 20 percent of their time pursuing any interesting projects that are not part of their regular duties. They also are encouraged to post any ideas they have on an interactive in-house message board. In addition to free food, pool tables, and beanbag chairs and other perks, the company hosts an all-employee meeting on Fridays where anyone can challenge any decisions made by the organization.[11]

Fourth, it is necessary to spend extra time in the hiring process. There is sometimes a tendency to want to hurry the process of finding the appropriate skills to fill the organization's needs. As stated earlier, there is more to a person than his or her skills. Character is also an important factor in building an effective organization culture. Paul English whom we discussed above as one of the founders of a now large organization, still spends most of his time hiring new employees that will fit in the organization's culture. One thing that can be implemented is a hiring plan that establishes the procedure for screening, interviewing, and assessing all candidates. Job descriptions, along with specifications of the type of person who will match the desired culture, should be documented for this process.

Next, the entrepreneur needs to understand the significance of leadership in the organization. Leadership should help to establish core values and provide the appropriate tools so

ELEVATOR PITCH FOR UNIQUE TRAVEL START-UP

A friend of yours that likes to travel but dislikes typical tours saw a write-up on a new unique travel company that offers tours from local experts that are unusual and interesting. This friend inquired and discovered that this start-up is looking for capital to expand to other cities and has approached you to ask if you might be interested in investing in this company. Would you be willing to invest in this start-up? How can this new venture deal with the possibility that there may not be enough sellers of activities for tours in any of the expansion cities? What issues might they face with competition?

Vayable's mission is to promote cultural understanding and to provide customers with a new and unique way to explore the world. Launched by Jamie Wong and Shelly Roche, both travel lovers, they decided that in the $27 billion travel industry no one was offering activities for travelers that are unique. Instead of the standard city bus tour why not go on a street art tour led by a graffiti artist in San Francisco,

feast on ethnic foods in New York City's neighborhoods, or go on a wine tasting tour in Paris, all tours guided by local artists and experts. Top destinations at present are San Francisco (company base), New York, Los Angeles, Paris, London, and Berlin. Projected 2012 revenue is $1.5 million. The company received seed money but needs about $500,000 to expand their operations and marketing efforts to other cities. Revenue is received from sellers (15 percent of cost of tour) and from the buyers of the tours (3 percent of cost of tour).

Any local person that wants to offer a unique tour is interviewed by the co-founders either in person or on Skype. All the tours that are submitted by the local persons are reviewed before they are permitted to appear on the Web site or in any marketing material.

Sources: See www.vayable.com; Alexis Terrazas, "Company Offers Quirky Tours in San Francisco and Beyond," January 4, 2012, www.sfexaminer.com; and "After Dark, New Worlds," October 21, 2011, www.online.wsj.com.

that employees can effectively complete their jobs. An approach such as, "We're all in this together, no one is bigger than anyone else, and here are the rules we live by," can lead to greater challenges and job satisfaction. A reward system can play an important role in providing consistent and positive behavior patterns.

Finding the most effective team and creating a positive organization culture is a challenge for the entrepreneur but is just as critical as having an innovative, marketable product. It is an important ingredient in an organization's success.

THE ROLE OF A BOARD OF DIRECTORS

An entrepreneur may find it necessary in his or her organization plan to establish a board of directors or board of advisors. The board of advisors is discussed in the next section. The board of directors may serve a number of functions: (1) reviewing operating and capital budgets, (2) developing longer-term strategic plans for growth and expansion, (3) supporting day-to-day activities, (4) resolving conflicts among owners or shareholders, (5) ensuring the proper use of assets, or (6) developing a network of information sources for the entrepreneurs. These functions may be a formal part of the organization, with responsibilities assigned to the directors depending on the needs of the new venture.

Most important in establishing these responsibilities is the consideration of the impact of the Sarbanes-Oxley Act passed in 2002. Passage of this act resulted because of accounting irregularities, fraud, bankruptcy, insider trading, excessive management compensation, and other illegal or unethical actions that have become newsworthy in the years leading up to 2002 (see Chapter 6 for more discussion of the Sarbanes-Oxley Act). Although there is still some concern about the effectiveness of the new law, its intent is to establish a more independent functioning board. This is particularly relevant in public companies where the board members must represent all shareholders and are responsible for "blowing the whistle" on any discrepancies that may be suspected. In spite of its intent, this act has come under criticism in light of the economic crisis that led to the demise of a number of large financial services companies. However, many feel that it is not the law that is the problem but more the issues of having the right mix of board members. It is expected that because of the economic crisis there will be a greater demand on boards to master the reforms of Sarbanes-Oxley and to be more attentive to the expertise of appointed board members.[12]

Many start-up ventures do not plan to have a formal board of directors. However, if there are equity investors, they will usually insist on the formation of a board and at least one board seat. Julia Stamberger and Pam Jelaca, cofounders of GoPicnic, a company that sells snack boxes and packaged meals to airlines, corporations, hotels, and event planners, did not have a board in place and realized after their infusion of equity financing that they would need to establish one. They found that the experience of the board was very positive because it forced them into a discipline of financial reporting that they tended to avoid in the past. This financial focus has helped them to prioritize things that are essential to their fast-growing business. The success of the ready-to-eat boxed lunches and meals with on-board airline clients led the way for GoPicnic's growth into new markets. In addition to airlines, GoPicnic has created meal boxes for hotels, tourism, corporate events, and college and camp food service programs. In January 2011, GoPicnic introduced eight new ready-to-eat boxed lunches for the retail market, which are available at nationwide grocery, specialty, and mass merchandise stores, as well as online.[13]

Naomi Poe, the founder of Better Batter Gluten Free Flour, faced a similar scenario. Needing an infusion of cash, she asked a couple of business acquaintances whether they would become board members as well as invest in her company. They accepted her invitation to become board members and invested $30,000 that allowed her to grow her start-up venture.[14]

As we can see from the preceding examples, the purpose of the board of directors is to provide important leadership and direction for the new venture, and it should be carefully chosen to meet the requirements of the Sarbanes-Oxley Act and also the following criteria:[15]

- Select individuals who have specific skills needed for your business, have experience in your industry, and are committed to the venture's mission.
- Select candidates who are willing to spend enough time to be informed directors who can assist the company in making important decisions.
- Select candidates who are willing to exchange ideas, using their experience, in making board decisions.

Candidates should be identified using referrals of business associates or from any of the external advisors such as banks, investors, lawyers, accountants, or consultants. Ideally, the board should consist of 3, 5, 7, or some odd number of members to avoid deadlock and with limited terms to allow for continuous infusion of new ideas from different people.

Board of director performance needs to be regularly evaluated by the entrepreneurs. It is the chair's responsibility to provide an appraisal of each board member. To provide this appraisal, the chairperson (and/or founders) should have a written description of the responsibilities and expectations of each member.

Compensation for board members can be shares of stock, stock options, or dollar payment. Often the new venture will tie compensation to the performance of the new venture. Compensation is important since it reinforces the obligation of board members. If board members were only volunteers, they would tend to take the role lightly and not provide any value to the entrepreneur.

THE BOARD OF ADVISORS

Compared to a board of directors, a board of advisors would be more loosely tied to the organization and would serve the venture only in an advisory capacity for some of the functions or activities mentioned before. It has no legal status, unlike the board of directors, and hence is not subject to the regulations stipulated in the Sarbanes-Oxley Act. These boards are likely to meet less frequently or depending on the need to discuss important venture decisions. A board of advisors is very useful in a family business where the board of directors may consist entirely of family members.

The selection process for advisors can be similar to the process for selecting a board of directors, including determining desired skills and interviewing potential candidates. Advisors may be compensated on a per-meeting basis or with stock or stock options. Just as in the case of the board of directors, the members should be evaluated as to their contribution to meeting the mission of the new venture.

Boards of advisors can provide an important reality check for the entrepreneur or owner of any noncorporate type of business. Silicon Valley serial entrepreneur Cynthia Kocialski has started three companies and argues that every start-up can benefit from a board of advisors. She states that you need to select advisors that are proficient in different parts of the business and understand the industry well. She argues that having too many advisors can become confusing and complicated and recommends six members for the board. In addition, she feels that the advisory board members at an early stage may not be the same ones needed later in the growth of the company.[16]

Haroon Mokhtarzada gave up an opportunity to work with a prestigious law firm while a law student at Harvard Law School in order to start a business venture. He and his two brothers had been experimenting with a Web design business that would allow anyone including their nontechnical mother to build a Web site. As students he and his brothers launched the business and within a few short years had 50 million registered users. What gave him the impetus to grow this company was an advisor who recommended that Haroon try to raise capital and grow this business into something substantial. At this point he began building a strong board. Mokhtarzada's model for creating a board of advisors is based on three recommendations:[17]

1. Identify potential members that share your vision so that they will look out for your best interests.
2. Offer the members a quarter to a half point of equity so that they will not only offer their expertise but will provide valuable contacts to grow the business.
3. Timing is important when you add or bring in advisors. Use them at critical points in business decision making such as raising capital, entering new markets, or hiring high level managers.

Ecotech Institute, the first and only college that focuses its curriculum on training people for careers in renewable energy, recently assembled a who's who of diverse industry leaders to serve as its local board of advisors. Ecotech also utilizes a national advisory board that is instrumental in shaping curriculum that matches what employers want.[18]

As we can see from these diverse examples, the board of advisors represents an alternative or complementary option for the entrepreneur and to organizations of all sizes in providing expertise and direction in critical areas. Even large corporations will often assemble an advisory board to assist them in specific areas of the business. The flexibility in size, background requirements, number of meetings, and compensation makes these boards a very desirable alternative to the more formal boards of directors.

THE ORGANIZATION AND USE OF ADVISORS

The entrepreneur will usually use outside advisors such as accountants, bankers, lawyers, advertising agencies, and market researchers on an as-needed basis. These advisors, who are separate from the more formal board of advisors, can also become an important part of the organization and thus will need to be managed just like any other permanent part of the new venture.

The relationship of the entrepreneur and outside advisors can be enhanced by seeking out the best advisors and involving them thoroughly and at an early stage. Advisors should be assessed or interviewed just as if they were being hired for a permanent position. References should be checked and questions asked to ascertain the quality of service as well as compatibility with the management team.

Hiring and managing outside experts can be effectively accomplished by considering these advisors as advice suppliers. Just as no manager would buy raw materials or supplies without knowledge of their cost and quality, the same approval can apply for advisors. Entrepreneurs should ask these advisors about fees, credentials, references, and so on, before hiring them.

Even after the advisors have been hired, the entrepreneur should question their advice. Why is the advice being given? Make sure you understand the decision and its potential implications. There are many good sources of advisors, such as the Small Business Administration, other small businesses, chambers of commerce, universities, friends, and relatives. Careful evaluation of the entrepreneur's needs and the competency of the advisor can make advisors a valuable asset to the organization of a new venture.

IN REVIEW

SUMMARY

One of the most important decisions the entrepreneur(s) must make in the business plan is the legal form of business. The three major legal forms of business are the proprietorship, partnership, and corporation. Each differs significantly and should be evaluated carefully before a decision is made. This chapter provides considerable insight and comparisons regarding these forms of business to assist the entrepreneur in this decision.

The S corporation and the limited liability company are alternative forms of business that are gaining popularity. Each of these allows the entrepreneur to retain the protection from personal liability provided by a corporation as well as the tax advantages provided by a partnership. There are important advantages as well as disadvantages to these forms of business, and entrepreneurs should carefully weigh both before deciding.

The organization plan for the entrepreneur also requires some major decisions that could affect long-term effectiveness and profitability. It is important to begin the new venture with a strong management team that is committed to the goals of the new venture. The management team must be able to work together effectively toward these ends.

History indicates that many entrepreneurs try to perform too many tasks in the new venture, often spreading themselves too thin and thus negatively affecting all their tasks. Assigning and delegating tasks is part of being a good leader and in the long run will enhance the confidence and motivation of all employees and contribute to a strong management team.

The design of the organization requires the entrepreneur to specify the types of skills needed and the roles that must be filled. These would be considered part of the formal organization. In addition to the formal organization, the entrepreneur must consider the informal organization or culture that is desired to match the strategy stipulated in the business plan. This organization culture represents the attitudes, behaviors, dress, and communication styles that can differentiate one company from another. Both of these are important in establishing an effective and profitable organization.

A board of directors or board of advisors can provide important management support for an entrepreneur starting and managing a new venture. Boards of directors are now governed by the Sarbanes-Oxley Act, which was passed because of a rash of illegal and unethical behaviors that were newsworthy. The intent of this new law is to make the board of directors more independent and to make its members accountable to the shareholders. The law is particularly relevant to public companies and has less impact on privately held companies. The board of advisors is a good alternative to a board of directors when the stock is held privately or in a family business.

In spite of the new regulations, a board of directors or advisors can still provide excellent support for an organization. Either one can be formed in the initial business planning phase or after the business has been formed and financed. In either case the selection of board members should be made carefully, so that members will take their roles seriously and will be committed to their roles and responsibilities.

Advisors will also be necessary in the new venture. Outside advisors should be evaluated as if they were being hired as permanent members of the organization. Information on their fees and referrals can help determine the best choices.

RESEARCH TASKS

1. In this country, what proportion of all businesses are (a) proprietorships, (b) partnerships, (c) private companies, and (d) public companies? Provide an example of an industry that has a large share of proprietorships. Why is this the case? Provide an example of an industry that has a large share of partnerships. Why is this the case? Provide an example of an industry that has a large share of private companies. Why is this the case? Provide an example of an industry that has a large share of public companies. Why is this the case?

2. Review current business magazines and identify one large public corporation and one start-up that have a board of advisors. How will these boards be used differently or similarly? How would you expect a board of advisors to interact with a board of directors?

3. Study the local newspaper and choose three good examples and three poor examples of job advertisements. Be prepared to explain your choices.

4. Interview two entrepreneurs and ask them how they delegate responsibility in their organization. Ask them how they feel about delegating responsibility or involving an employee when a critical decision that could impact the financial stability of their company is necessary.

CLASS DISCUSSION

1. Why would entrepreneurs open themselves up to personal financial losses by choosing a proprietorship rather than a company form of organization?

2. Why do suppliers sometimes ask entrepreneurs of small companies to provide personal guarantees for a line of business credit? If an entrepreneur is asked (forced) to provide personal guarantees, then what personal protection does a company as a legal form really provide?

3. Does the old saying "You get what you pay for" apply to a board of directors or a board of advisors?

4. Identify three corporations that are different in their legal form of organization (for example an S corporation, an LLC, and a C corporation). How are these companies different? How are they similar? What advantages and disadvantages does each company achieve by maintaining their legal form or organization?

SELECTED READINGS

Blackman, Irv. (August 2011). To Be or Not to Be an S Corp Is the Question. *Contractor Magazine,* vol. 58, issue 8, pp. 34, 38.

This article provides a good overview on the differences between a C corporation and an S corporation. It focuses on the advantages and disadvantages of these two types of organizations when taxes are an issue. Tax deductions under the two types of organizations are also discussed.

Castellano, Joseph; Susan S. Lightle; and Bud Baker. (September 2011). The Role of Boards of Directors in the Financial Crisis. *CPA Journal,* vol. 81, issue 9, pp. 54–57.

Boards of Directors should engage in risk management and should be selected for membership based on their industry-specific experience and on their ability to make critical decisions during a financial crisis. All board members should understand the operation and financial compliance issues of the organization. In addition these authors suggest that board members should avoid a group think mindset and be able to make independent decisions.

Duden, Antje. (December 2011). Trust and Leadership: Learning Culture in Organizations. *International Journal of Management Cases,* vol. 13, issue 4, pp. 218–23.

The author refers to organization theorists such as Schein and Burns and Stalker that classify organizations regarding learning culture. These classifications are discussed and the author argues that creating organizational culture means creating the basis for learning organizations which in turn will affect success.

Hargis, Michael; and Don B. Bradley III. (June 2011). Strategic Human Resource Management in Small and Growing Firms: Aligning Valuable Resources. *Academy of Strategic Management Journal,* vol. 10, issue 2, pp.105–25.

Human capital is one of the primary factors a business can rely on to differentiate their products and services to build a competitive advantage. These authors argue however that few studies directly guide management of these types of firms through the people management decisions that will be faced during the various life cycles of the business. Two studies are discussed that examine selection, training, and compensation practices of small business managers. They also provide a framework to guide these managers through the important decisions points in the business life cycle.

Kwiatek, Harlan J.; Karen Nakamura; and Margarete Chalker. (June 2010). State Tax Considerations of Passthrough Entities: Potential Concerns and Pitfalls. *Tax Advisor,* vol. 41, issue 6, pp. 418–22.

> *This article discusses taxes and regulation issues that vary from state to state in passthrough organizations such as partnerships, LLCs, and S corporations. Tax consequences can vary widely in each state and need to be evaluated carefully before deciding on a legal form or organization.*

McKenzie, Meredyth. (January 2011). Efficient Guidance: How to Maintain an Effective Board of Directors. *Smart Business Columbus,* vol. 19, issue 4, p. 42.

> *An interview with an experienced director is discussed. The focus of the interview is to identify the qualities looked for when selecting a board member. It is felt that the board member must be assertive and prepared to be effective. The interview also focuses on the difference between a board of directors and a board of advisors.*

Prescott, Gregory L.; Ellen K. Madden; and Mark R. Foster. (November 2010). Forms of Business Ownership: A Primer for Commercial Lenders. *Commercial Lending Review,* vol. 25, issue 6, pp. 27–31, 54.

> *This is an excellent article that reviews the common forms of business ownership. In particular the article discusses the risk factors involved in these different types of structures. The authors discuss issues related to ownership, legal status, and taxation.*

Stamper, Connie. (June/July 2010). Hiring Tips for Small Business Leaders. *CMA Management,* vol. 84, issue 4, pp. 11–13.

> *The article stresses the importance of making great hiring decisions even though there is no in-house human resource department because of the size of the firm. It suggests that every hiring process should involve a well-written job description and a determination of the desired technical abilities and experience needed. Leaders of any business should follow up with all new hires.*

Ward, John L.; and Corey Hansen. (July 2008). How to Assemble a Board of Advisors. *INC,* vol. 30, issue 7, pp. 61–64.

> *This is an excellent article that provides some important guidelines to consider when assembling a board of advisors. It begins with a determination of the venture's key success factors. The board members should be considered only if they fulfill the need to build the business. Thus, the experience should be consistent with the long-term goals of the company.*

Westerlund, Elnar J. (March 2011). Four Simple Steps to Organizational Excellence. *Profit,* vol. 30, issue 1, p. 27.

> *The best practices needed to achieve organizational excellence are the focus of this article. It discusses a survey of the best small and medium employers in Canada that found that organizations with high employment engagement had the highest quality scores. The four best practices identified are teamwork, using one's influence as a leader, evaluating employees based on company goals, and being creative with staff development.*

END NOTES

1. See "The Madness Behind Method," *INC* (October 2011), pp. 26–27; Kate Walsh, "For Hands That Do Dishes with Non-Toxic Ingredients," *The Sunday Times,* November 20, 2011, p. 19; "The Method of Creating and Nurturing Amazing Corporate Culture," www.fastcompany.com, September 12, 2011; and Lindsay Riddell, "Method Stays in the Green," *San Francisco Business Times Online,* September 9, 2011.

2. Stephen L. Nelson, "What's the Difference Between an LLC and LLP?" www.llcexplained.com.

3. Agnes Gesiko, "Structure Counts! The Tax Implications Arising from the Formation, Operation, and Liquidation of C Corporations, S Corporations, Partnerships and Limited Liability Companies," *Corporate Business Taxation Monthly* (November 2008), pp. 39–49.

4. Hughlene Burton and Stewart S. Karlinsky, "Current Developments in S Corporations," *Tax Adviser* (November 2011), pp. 766–74.

5. Gregory L. Prescott, Ellen K. Madden, and R. Mark Foster, "Forms of Business Ownership: A Primer for Commercial Lenders," *Commercial Lending Review* (November–December 2010), pp. 27–32, 54–55.

6. BizFilings, "LLC vs. S Corp: Which Business Type Is Right for Me?" www.bizfilings.com/learn/llc-vs-s-corp.aspx.

7. Karen Nakamura and Margarete Chalker, "State Tax Considerations of Pass-through Entities: Potential Concerns and Pitfalls," *The Tax Advisor* (June 2010), pp. 418–22.

8. J. W. Lorsch, "Organization Design: A Situational Perspective," in J. R. Hackman, E. E. Lawler III, and W. Porter (eds.), *Perspectives on Behavior in Organizations,* 2nd ed. (New York: McGraw-Hill, 1983), pp. 439–47.

9. Fran's Chocolates. "News and Events," https://www.franschocolates.com/about/articles.php.

10. Liz Welch, "The Way I Work," *INC* (February 2010), pp. 99–101.

11. "Google's 5 Tools to Lure and Retain the Best," *The HR Specialist* (August 2010), pp. 1–2.

12. Xiaodong Qui and James A. Largay III, "Do Active Boards of Directors Add Value to Their Firms?" *Academy of Management Perspectives* 25, issue 1 (February 2011), pp. 98–99.

13. See www.gopicnic.com; and David Worrell, "Board Relations," *Entrepreneur* (November 2008), p. 56.

14. Gwen Moran, "Pocket Money," *Entrepreneur* (February 2011), p. 66.

15. See Robert C. Pozen, "Building Better Boards," *Accounting Today* (April 2011), pp. 16–17; and "Meet Members' Governance Expectations," *Credit Union Directors Newsletter* (December 2011), p. 4.

16. Christopher Hann, "Advice and Consent," *Entrepreneur* (August 2011), p. 20.

17. Joel Holland, "It Passes the Mom Test," *Entrepreneur* (January 2011), p. 63.

18. "Ecotech Institute Names Its Local Board of Advisors," *marketwire.com,* January 3, 2012.

10

THE FINANCIAL PLAN

LEARNING OBJECTIVES

1

To understand the role of budgets in preparing pro forma statements.

2

To understand why positive profits can still result in a negative cash flow.

3

To learn how to prepare monthly pro forma cash flow, income, balance sheet, and sources and applications of funds statements for the first year of operation.

4

To explain the application and calculation of the break-even point for the new venture.

5

To illustrate the alternative software packages that can be used for preparing financial statements.

OPENING PROFILE

TONY HSIEH

Not too many entrepreneurs have the goal of reaching a billion dollars in sales. At the age of 35, Tony Hsieh (pronounced "Shay") has reached this goal as the CEO and entrepreneurial brain behind Zappos.com. His serious entrepreneurial endeavors began after graduation from Harvard University at the age of 23. He and classmate Sanjay Madan saw opportunities for advertisers who wanted to consolidate large ad buys into a single package and subsequently launched LinkExchange in the early 1990s. LinkExchange offered small sites free advertising on a 2-to-1 basis. What this meant was that for every two ads a member displayed on their site, they would be granted one free ad on another member's site. The excess ad credits not used were then sold by LinkExchange to nonmembers, resulting in a substantial revenue stream. After getting investment capital in 1997, the company was seen as a serious player in the Internet advertising market and was subsequently purchased by Microsoft for $265 million in 1998. After this success Tony co-founded Venture Frogs, which invested in Internet start-ups such as Ask Jeeves, Tellme Networks, and Zappos.com. In 1999, as an investor he began to look more seriously at the long-term potential of Zappos.com. Initially, he was an advisor and consultant to Zappos.com, but eventually he joined the company full time in 2000 as co-CEO. He later took over the reins completely and moved the operation to Las Vegas because of the lower real estate rates and abundance of call-center workers. Under his leadership the company grew from $1.6 million in sales in 2000 to more than $1 billion in sales in 2008. In fact the company doubled its sales every year from 1999 to 2008.

Tony realized when he joined Zappos.com that the Internet had not become a major player as a shopping choice for consumers. He discovered that the footwear industry, at $40 billion per year, was mostly a result of retail store sales and that only 5 percent of the sales came from mail-order catalogs. He saw this as a huge opportunity for the company, particularly since he believed that the Web would surpass mail-order business as a percentage of total sales. Thus, he saw 5 percent of $40 billion as a reasonable goal for his business.

Tony's business model was unique and to some retailers costly, yet it has been extremely successful. Part of Hsieh's approach is to focus on customer service. Zappos offers free shipping, fast delivery, and a 365-day return policy. He even relocated his warehouse to Kentucky to be nearer the UPS hub and to ensure the fast delivery of the products offered,

www.zappos.com

which has recently expanded to clothing, handbags, and accessories. The company's focus on customer service is designed to make sure the customer has a quality experience from beginning to end. In addition, all employees once hired must complete a four-week customer loyalty training program to make sure they understand the culture that has made the company so successful. To ensure that the hires are serious, Tony makes a visit during the second week and offers anyone $2,000 if they would like to drop out and quit the program. Only 1 percent of the hires have taken him up on the offer. The unique culture of the company also includes such things as happy hours, a nap room, fully paid health insurance, and life-related issue support that Tony pays for out of his own pocket. His philosophy regarding these strategies is that only a happy employee can provide great service.

Once Zappos wins over a customer (75 percent of the customers are repeaters), the company tries to ensure their continued interest by keeping them engaged in various online and social media outlets. Customers are invited to submit reviews and to share their experience with others. This not only enhances each customer's loyalty but also attracts new customers.

In 2005 the Amazon.com founder visited Zappos headquarters looking to buy the company. At that time Hsieh turned them down thinking that the company would probably reach profitability and about $1 billion in sales. However by 2009 the company began to feel the cash flow crunch because of the poor economy. In addition the line of credit from the bank was asset-backed at about 50 percent of the value of the inventory, which gave the company little flexibility with cash flow. With the credit crunch and a board that wanted to see more profits Tony felt that he could be forced out as CEO unless he made some drastic decisions to improve profitability. At this point Amazon.com came calling again and offered to buy the company but let it operate as an independent entity with Tony still at the helm. With a $1.2 billion buyout the company now would have the resources to expand its marketing efforts and increase its sales and profits. A new board was formed and the company now had the cash resources to move on. In 2010 the company increased its net sales about 50 percent. Zappos continues to make strides as an independent company and Tony Hsieh continues to contribute his entrepreneurial strategies to a new age in the company's history.[1]

The financial plan provides the entrepreneur with a complete picture of how much and when funds are coming into the organization, where funds are going, how much cash is available, and the projected financial position of the firm. It provides the short-term basis for budgeting control and helps prevent one of the most common problems for new ventures—lack of cash. We can see from the preceding example how important it is to understand the role of the financial plan. Without careful financial planning, in its early stages, especially in light of the costly customer services, Zappos.com could have suffered serious cash flow problems. Eventually growth capital cash flow for Zappos did become an issue but now as an independent part of Amazon.com, Zappos can continue to meet its financial goals.

The financial plan must explain to any potential investor how the entrepreneur plans to meet all financial obligations and maintain the venture's liquidity in order to either pay off debt or provide a good return on investment. In general, the financial plan will need three years of projected financial data to satisfy any outside investors. The first year should reflect monthly data.

This chapter discusses each of the major financial items that should be included in the financial plan: pro forma income statements, pro forma cash flow, pro forma balance sheets, and break-even analysis. As we saw in the Zappos.com example, Internet start-ups have some unique financial characteristics, which are included in the discussion that follows.

OPERATING AND CAPITAL BUDGETS

Before developing the pro forma income statement, the entrepreneur should prepare operating and capital budgets. If the entrepreneur is a sole proprietor, then he or she is responsible for the budgeting decisions. In the case of a partnership, or where employees exist, the initial budgeting process may begin with one of these individuals, depending on his or her role in the venture. For example, a sales budget may be prepared by a sales manager, a manufacturing budget by the production manager, and so on. Final determination of these budgets will ultimately rest with the owners or entrepreneurs.

As can be seen in the following, in the preparation of the pro forma income statement, the entrepreneur must first develop a sales budget that is an estimate of the expected volume of sales by month. The key element in the budget is projected sales. There are a number of different approaches that can be used to forecast sales from very quantitative methods to more qualitative approaches. Techniques such as regression, time series analysis, and exponential smoothing are beyond the scope of this text. In many instances the entrepreneur can rely on more qualitative techniques to estimate sales. Some of these are discussed below. From the sales forecasts the entrepreneur will then determine the cost of these sales. In a manufacturing venture the entrepreneur could compare the costs of producing these internally or subcontracting them to another manufacturer. Also included will be the estimated ending inventory needed as a buffer against possible fluctuations in demand and the costs of direct labor and materials.

Table 10.1 illustrates a simple format for a production or manufacturing budget for the first three months of operation. This provides an important basis for projecting cash flows for the cost of goods produced, which includes units in inventory. The important information from this budget is the actual production required each month and the inventory that is necessary to allow for sudden changes in demand. As can be seen, the production required in the month of January is greater than the projected sales because of the need to retain 100 units in inventory. In February the actual production will take into consideration the inventory from January as well as the desired number of units needed in inventory for that month. This continues for each month, with inventory needs likely increasing as sales increase. Thus, this budget is a real determination of how much will be spent and for what purpose money will be used. The pro forma income statement discussed later in this chapter does not include the cost of inventory as an expense until it is actually sold (reflected on statement as cost of goods). Thus, in those ventures in which high levels of inventory are necessary or where demand fluctuates significantly because of seasonality, this budget can be a very valuable tool to assess cash needs.

TABLE 10.1 A Sample Manufacturing Budget for First Three Months			
	Jan.	Feb.	Mar.
Projected sales (units)	5,000	8,000	12,000
Desired ending inventory	100	200	300
Available for sale	5,100	8,200	12,300
Less: beginning inventory	0	100	200
Total production required	5,100	8,100	12,100

FORGIVENESS OR PERMISSION? SHOULD AN EMPLOYER ALLOW AN EMPLOYEE TO WORK ON A SIDE BUSINESS?

The question is fraught with ethical issues. The word *thorny* comes to mind, which is why we called on Gregory Fairchild. As an associate professor of business administration at the University of Virginia's Darden School of Business, Fairchild teaches strategy, entrepreneurship, and ethics. He says the outside-work question can often be distilled to a fairly simple equation: "To what degree is there an implicit versus an explicit agreement about working on a side business?"

Yet Fairchild concedes that even explicit agreements can contain "a reasonable amount of gray," and thus be subject to all manner of lawyerly interpretation. On occasion, Fairchild says he's granted a Darden employee permission to pursue outside work, only to be overruled by the university's human resources or legal staff.

Of course, the issue of outside work becomes especially important when an entrepreneur seeks to protect intellectual property. And while certain industries come most readily to mind—defense, biotech, IT—Fairchild says outside-work policies can pose a dilemma in any company of any size.

The key to employer and employee seeing eye to eye lies in their mutual transparency. Entrepreneurs should first seek legal counsel before enacting an outside-work policy, as laws on these matters differ from state to state, and then clearly explain to employees what is (and is not) allowed. Employees are often surprised when employers not only grant an outside-work request, Fairchild says, but also ask to invest in the venture. Still, he notes, "There are some people who believe it's easier to ask forgiveness than permission."

The ethical issues are more nuanced when a start-up is involved. Because a start-up is an inherently risky proposition, Fairchild says, employees might feel they have a right to hedge their career bets by pursuing outside work. Yet a violation of a start-up's outside-work policy is often felt more acutely than, say, at a Fortune 500 firm.

"The start-up firm's need in the bootstrapping stage is so critical," he says. "So to know resources were porous, so to speak, leaves people feeling more violated than in more established organizations."

Fairchild suggests that entrepreneur and employee alike apply what he calls the mirror test. When you look at yourself in the mirror, he says, "Do you have even a flinch of a moment where you wonder if what you're doing is kosher? If you do, it's worth a conversation."

Source: Reprinted with permission of Wright's Media, "Forgiveness or Permission?" Christopher Hann, January 2012, *Entrepreneur*, p.21.

After completing the sales budget, the entrepreneur can then focus on operating costs. First a list of fixed expenses (these are expenses that are incurred regardless of sales volume) such as rent, utilities, salaries, advertising, depreciation, and insurance should be completed. Estimated costs for many of these items can be ascertained from personal experience or industry benchmarks, or through direct contact with real estate brokers, insurance agents, and consultants. Industry benchmarks for preparing financial pro forma statements were discussed in the financial plan section of Chapter 7 (see Table 7.2 for a list of financial benchmark sources). Anticipation of the addition of space, new employees, and increased advertising can also be inserted in these projections as deemed appropriate. There are also expenses that vary from month to month based on sales activity or changes in marketing strategy. Examples might include labor, materials, transportation, or entertainment. These variable expenses must be linked to strategy in the business plan. Table 10.2 provides an example of an operating budget. In this example, we can see that salaries increase in month 3 because of the addition of a shipper, advertising increases because the primary season for this product is approaching, and payroll taxes increase because of the additional employee. This budget, along with the manufacturing budget illustrated in Table 10.1, provides the basis for the pro forma statements discussed in this chapter.

Capital budgets are intended to provide a basis for evaluating expenditures that will impact the business for more than one year. For example, a capital budget may project

TABLE 10.2   A Sample Operating Budget for First Three Months ($000s)

Expense	Jan.	Feb.	Mar.
Salaries	$23.2	$23.2	$26.2
Rent	2	2	2
Utilities	0.9	0.9	0.9
Advertising	13.5	13.5	17
Selling expenses	1	1	1
Insurance	2	2	2
Payroll taxes	2.1	2.1	2.5
Depreciation	1.2	1.2	1.2
Office expenses	1.5	1.5	1.5
Total expenses	$47.4	$47.4	$54.3

expenditures for new equipment, vehicles, computers, or even a new facility. It may also consider evaluating the costs of make or buy decisions in manufacturing or a comparison of leasing, buying used, or buying new equipment. Because of the complexity of these decisions, which can include the computation of the cost of capital and the anticipated return on the investment using present value methods, it is recommended that the entrepreneur enlist the assistance of an accountant.

FORECASTING SALES

As stated earlier there are many different methods for projecting sales, some very quantitative and some more qualitative. Most start-ups would not likely use any of the quantitative techniques but would rely on more qualitative methods. Our focus here will be to try to understand how to project sales simply and reasonably using more qualitative methods. To begin with, the entrepreneur should research everything he or she can find about other start-ups in the same industry. Reviewing their experience can often provide reasonable expectations for early sales. Local chambers of commerce, or any other business organization, may provide contacts and information on what might be expected in first year sales. No matter what approach entrepreneurs use, they must be aware that sales estimates may be wrong. As a result it is sometimes beneficial for the entrepreneur to provide sales estimates at different levels of activity. For example, sales estimates may be shown at one level and also at levels such as 5 percent less or 10 percent less. Each sales estimate may reflect different assumptions about the market and show costs and profits or losses with each sales forecast.

Since the pro forma income statement requires monthly projections, it is important not to just make a sales forecast and divide by 12. Sales may vary each month depending on the seasonality of the product and need to be reflected in the monthly projections. In addition, changes in strategy may also affect sales and would need to be included in the estimates. Using as much information as possible to project sales can make the pro forma statements more meaningful.

PRO FORMA INCOME STATEMENTS

The marketing plan discussed in Chapter 8 provides an estimate of sales for the next 12 months. Since sales are the major source of revenue and since other operational activities and expenses relate to sales volume, it is usually the first item that must be defined.

TABLE 10.3   MPP Plastics Inc., Pro Forma Income Statement, First Year by Month ($000s)

	Jan.	Feb.	Mar.	Apr.	May	June	July	Aug.	Sept.	Oct.	Nov.	Dec.	Totals
Sales	20.0	32.0	48.0	70.0	90.0	100.0	100.0	100.0	80.0	80.0	120.0	130.0	970.0
Less: Cost of goods sold	10.0	16.0	24.0	35.0	45.0	50.0	50.0	50.0	40.0	40.0	60.0	65.0	485.0
Gross profit	10.0	16.0	24.0	35.0	45.0	50.0	50.0	50.0	40.0	40.0	60.0	65.0	485.0
Operating expenses													
Salaries*	23.2	23.2	26.2	26.2	26.2	26.2	26.2	26.2	26.2	26.2	26.2	26.2	308.4
Rent	2.0	2.0	2.0	2.0	2.0	2.0	2.0	2.0	2.0	2.0	2.0	2.0	24.0
Utilities	0.9	0.9	0.9	0.8	0.8	0.8	0.9	0.9	0.9	0.8	0.8	0.9	10.3
Advertising	13.5	13.5	17.0	17.0	17.0	17.0	14.0	14.0	14.0	21.0[†]	17.0	17.0	192.0
Sales expenses	1.0	1.0	1.0	1.0	1.0	1.0	1.0	1.0	1.0	1.0	1.0	1.0	12.0
Insurance	2.0	2.0	2.0	2.0	2.0	2.0	2.0	2.0	2.0	2.0	2.0	2.0	24.0
Payroll taxes	2.1	2.1	2.5	2.5	2.5	2.5	2.5	2.5	2.5	2.5	2.5	2.5	29.2
Depreciation[‡]	1.2	1.2	1.2	1.2	1.2	1.2	1.2	1.2	1.2	1.2	1.2	1.2	14.4
Office expenses	1.5	1.5	1.5	1.7	1.8	2.0	2.0	2.0	1.8	1.8	2.2	2.2	22.0
Total operating expenses	47.4	47.4	54.3	54.4	54.5	54.7	51.8	51.8	51.6	58.5	54.9	55.0	636.3
Gross profit	(37.4)	(31.4)	(30.3)	(19.4)	(9.5)	(4.7)	(1.8)	(1.8)	(11.6)	(18.5)	5.1	10.0	(151.3)

*Added shipper in month 3.
[†]Trade show.
[‡]Plant and equipment of $72,000 depreciated straight line for five years.

pro forma income
Projected net profit
calculated from projected
revenue minus projected
costs and expenses

Table 10.3 summarizes all the profit data during the first year of operations for MPP Plastics. This company makes plastic moldings for such customers as hard goods manufacturers, toy manufacturers, and appliance manufacturers. As can be seen from the *pro forma income* statement in Table 10.3, the company begins to earn a profit in the eleventh month. Cost of goods sold remains consistent at 50 percent of sales revenue.

In preparation of the pro forma income statement, sales by month must be calculated first. As indicated above, sales may be projected using many different techniques. Again, it is important to try to estimate variations in sales that may result from changes in such factors as marketing strategy or seasonality. As would be expected, it will take a while for any new venture to build up sales. The costs for achieving these increases can be disproportionately higher in some months, depending on the given situation in any particular period.

Sales revenue for an Internet start-up is often more difficult to project since extensive advertising will be necessary to attract customers to the Web site. For example, a giftware Internet company can anticipate no sales in the first few months until awareness of the Web site has been created. Heavy advertising expenditures (discussed subsequently) also will be incurred to create this awareness. Given existing data on the number of "hits" by a similar type of Web site, a giftware Internet start-up could project the number of average hits expected per day or month. From the number of hits, it is possible to project the number of consumers who will actually buy products from the Web site and the average dollar amount per transaction. Using a reasonable percentage of these "hits" times the average transaction will provide an estimate of sales revenue for the Internet start-up.

The pro forma income statements also provide projections of all operating expenses for each of the months during the first year. As discussed earlier and illustrated in Table 10.2, each of the expenses should be listed and carefully assessed to make sure that any in-creases in expenses are added in the appropriate month.[2] For example, selling expenses such as travel, commissions, and entertainment should be expected to increase somewhat as territories are expanded and as new salespeople or representatives are hired by the firm. Selling expenses as a percentage of sales also may be expected to be higher initially since more sales calls will have to be made to generate each sale, particularly when the firm is an unknown. The cost of goods sold expense can be determined either by directly computing the variable cost of producing a unit times the number of units sold or by using an industry standard percentage of sales. For example, for a restaurant, the National Restaurant Asso-ciation or Food Marketing Institute publishes standard cost of goods as a percentage of sales. These percentages are determined from members and studies completed on the res-taurant industry. Other industries also publish standard cost ratios, which can be found in sources such as those listed in Table 7.2. Trade associations and trade magazines will also often quote these ratios in industry newsletters or trade articles.

Salaries and wages for the company should reflect the number of personnel employed as well as their role in the organization (see the organization plan in Chapter 9). As new personnel are hired to support the increased business, the costs will need to be included in the pro forma statement. In March, for example, a shipper is added to the staff. Other in-creases in salaries and wages may also reflect raises in salary.

The entrepreneur should also consider increasing selling expenses as sales increase, adjusting taxes because of the addition of new personnel or raises in salary, increasing of-fice expenses relative to the increase in sales, and modifying the advertising budget as a result of seasonality or simply because in the early months of start-up the budget may need to be higher to increase visibility. These adjustments actually occur in our MPP Plastics example (Table 10.3) and are reflected in the month-by-month pro forma income state-ment for year 1. Any noteworthy changes that are made in the pro forma income statement are also labeled, with explanations provided.

In addition to the monthly pro forma income statement for the first year, projections should be made for years 2 and 3. Generally, investors prefer to see three years of income projections. Year 1 totals have already been calculated in Table 10.3. Table 10.4 illustrates the yearly totals of income statement items for each of the three years. Calculation of the percent of sales of each of the expense items for year 1 can be used by the entrepreneur as a guide for determining projected sales and expenses for year 2; those percentages then can be considered in making the projections for year 3. In addition, the calculation of percent of sales for each year is useful as a means of financial control so that the entrepreneur can ascertain whether any costs are too high relative to sales revenue. In year 3, the firm expects to significantly increase its profits as compared with the first and second years. In some instances, the entrepreneur may find that the new venture does not begin to earn a profit until sometime in year 2 or 3. This often de-pends on the nature of the business and start-up costs. For example, a service-oriented busi-ness may take less time to reach a profitable stage than a high-tech company or one that requires a large investment in capital goods and equipment, which will take longer to recover.

In the pro forma statements for MPP Plastics (Tables 10.3 and 10.4), we can see that the venture begins to earn a profit in the eleventh month of year 1. In the second year, the company does not need to spend as much money on advertising and, with the sales increase, shows a modest profit of $16,300. However, in year 3 we see that the venture adds an additional employee and also incurs a 26 percent increase in sales, resulting in a net profit of $127,900.

In projecting the operating expenses for years 2 and 3, it is helpful to first look at those expenses that will likely remain stable over time. Items like depreciation, utilities, rent, insurance, and interest are likely to remain steady unless new equipment or additional space is purchased. Some utility expenses such as heat and power can be computed by using in-dustry standard costs per square foot of space that is utilized by the new venture. Selling

TABLE 10.4 MPP Plastics Inc., Pro Forma Income Statement, Three-Year Summary ($000s)

	Percent	Year 1	Percent	Year 2	Percent	Year 3
Sales	100.0	970.0	100.0	1,264.0	100.0	1,596.0
Less: Cost of goods sold	50.0	485.0	50.0	632.0	50.0	798.0
Gross profit	50.0	485.0	50.0	632.0	50.0	798.0
Operating expenses						
Salaries	31.8	308.4	24.4	308.4	21.8	348.4
Rent	2.5	24.0	1.9	24.0	1.5	24.0
Utilities	1.1	10.3	0.8	10.3	0.7	10.3
Advertising	19.8	192.0	13.5	170.0	11.3	180.0
Sales expenses	1.2	12.0	1.0	12.5	0.8	13.5
Insurance	2.4	24.0	1.9	24.0	1.5	24.0
Payroll & misc. taxes	3.0	29.2	2.3	29.2	2.0	32.0
Depreciation	1.5	14.4	1.1	14.4	0.9	14.4
Office expenses	2.3	22.0	1.8	22.5	1.5	23.5
Total operating expenses	65.6	636.3	48.7	615.3	42.0	670.1
Gross profit (loss)	(15.6)	(151.3)	1.3	16.3*	8.0	127.9*
Taxes	0.0	0.0	0.0	0.0	0.0	0.0
Net profit	(15.6)	(151.3)	1.3	16.3	8.0	127.9

*No taxes are incurred in profitable years 2 and 3 because of the carryover of losses in year 1.

expenses, advertising, salaries and wages, and taxes may be represented as a percentage of the projected net sales. When calculating the projected operating expenses, it is most important to be conservative for initial planning purposes. A reasonable profit that is earned with conservative estimates lends credibility to the potential success of the new venture.

For the Internet start-up, capital budgeting and operating expenses will tend to be consumed by equipment purchasing or leasing, inventory, and advertising expenses. For example, the giftware Internet company introduced earlier would need to purchase or lease an extensive amount of computer equipment to accommodate the potential buyers from the Web site. Inventory costs would be based on the projected sales revenue just as would be the case for any retail store. Advertising costs, however, would need to be extensive to create awareness for the giftware Web site. These expenses would typically involve a selection of search engines such as Yahoo!, Bing, and Google; links from the Web sites of magazines such as *Woman's Day, Family Circle,* and *Better Homes and Gardens;* and extensive media advertising in magazines, television, radio, and print—all selected because of their link to the target market.

PRO FORMA CASH FLOW

Cash flow is not the same as profit. Profit is the result of subtracting expenses from sales, whereas cash flow results from the difference between actual cash receipts and cash payments. Cash flows only when actual payments are received or made. For example, if someone owes you $100 for work you completed you have earned that amount as income. If you wanted to spend this $100 at the supermarket you would have to get them to let you buy on credit (you would owe them the amount of the groceries) or you would pay with a credit card. The fact is that at that point you have income of $100 (no cash yet) and expenses of $100 (not yet paid in cash). Similarly for a business sales may not be regarded as cash since it is common for buyers to have at least 30 days to make the payment. In addition, not all bills are paid immediately. Just as your buyer has at least 30 days to make payment, you would likely do the same for any of your purchases. These purchases on credit, however, would still be counted as expenses on your income statement.[3] On the other hand, cash payments to reduce the principal on a loan do not constitute a business expense but do constitute a reduction of cash. Only the interest on the loan would be considered an expense. Also, depreciation on capital assets is an expense, which reduces profits, not a cash outlay.

For an Internet start-up such as our giftware company discussed earlier, the sales transaction would involve the use of a credit card in which a percentage of the sale would be paid as a fee to the credit card company. This is usually between 1 and 3 percent depending on the credit card. Thus, for each sale only 97 to 99 percent of the revenue would be net revenue because of this fee.

As stated at the beginning of this chapter, one of the major problems that new ventures face is cash flow. On many occasions, profitable firms fail because of lack of cash. Thus, using profit as a measure of success for a new venture may be deceiving if there is a significant negative cash flow.

For strict accounting purposes there are two standard methods used to project cash flow, the indirect and the direct method. The most popular of these is the indirect method, which is illustrated in Table 10.5. In this method the objective is not to repeat what is in the income statement but to understand there are some adjustments that need to be made to the net income based on the fact that actual cash may or may not have actually been received

TABLE 10.5   Statement of Cash Flows: The Indirect Method

Cash Flow from Operating Activities (+ or − Reflects Addition or Subtraction from Net Income)	
Net income	XXX
Adjustments to net income:	
Noncash nonoperating items	
+ depreciation and amortization	XXX
Cash provided by changes in current assets or liabilities:	
Increase(+) or decrease(−) in accounts receivable	XXX
Increase(+) or decrease(−) in inventory	XXX
Increase(+) or decrease(−) in prepaid expenses	XXX
Increase(+) or decrease(−) in accounts payable	XXX
Net cash provided by operating activities	XX,XXX
Cash Flow from Other Activities	
Capital expenditures (−)	(XXX)
Payments of debt (−)	(XXX)
Dividends paid (−)	(XXX)
Sale of stock (+)	XXX
Net cash provided by other activities	(XXX)
Increase (Decrease) in Cash	XXX

PROVIDE ADVICE TO AN ENTREPRENEUR ABOUT SOLVING THEIR CASH-FLOW PROBLEM TO STAY IN BUSINESS

Hot & Cold Inc., a plumbing and heating supply company in the heart of Virginia's Shenandoah Valley, is headed for the slaughterhouse. As the housing boom grew, so did sales, from $7 million a year to $14 million over four years. But as the company expanded, its problems multiplied, and no amount of sales could cover the warts. As the economy faltered and poor management continued, revenue started dropping by more than $2 million a year.

Crunching the numbers over the past five years shows lost opportunity and bad financial management have cost the company about $5 million in profits. Overtime alone is about $250,000 a year. Today Hot & Cold is at $6 million in sales and is running at a loss in excess of $1 million. The bank is nervous, and ready to pull the plug on its line of credit. The steady supply of new business has dried up, and the three owners' lives are on the line. The old cash cow is chopped meat.

To keep the company alive, they've mortgaged their homes, maxed out their credit cards at usurious interest rates, and cashed in their 401(k)s. Worker morale is low, and employees are phoning it in because they are convinced they'll be out of a job tomorrow. As a result, the few remaining clients are unhappy, and threatening to take their business elsewhere.

SOLUTION: CONTROL, CONTROL, CONTROL

The owners of Hot & Cold have three choices: Walk away at great personal financial ruin; hope for a big client to fly to their rescue and help them pay off their huge debt; or take control of their own business. They're teetering on the verge of bankruptcy, but it's not too late.

The three guys who took over from the family who founded Hot & Cold have no training as managers. These are hard-working, talented contractors and engineers with great knowledge of how to carry plumbing and installation projects to completion. But, for most of their careers, they worked for somebody else.

First they need to sit down with each department head and develop an adopting plan for cash management. They need to be clear in their instructions, and forceful in their insistence that there will be dire consequences for failure to comply. Hold department meetings at 8 a.m. on Monday, issue marching orders, then meet again on Friday at 6 p.m. to see what did and did not get done. Every job needs to be monitored by microscope from start to finish.

It'll hurt. Hot & Cold requires drastic internal overhaul, including deep cuts in operating costs. They can't be "tepid" about this. At least 20 percent of their workforce of 50 will have to be fired. This business needs to get serious about collecting the cash that clients owe them, even if they have to take a hit by offering cash discounts or accepting partial payment just to bring the money in.

I also recommend that they meet face to face with their banker. If they've followed my advice so far, they will be able to point to the cost measures already in place and forestall foreclosure on their loan.

ADVICE TO AN ENTREPRENEUR

An entrepreneur friend saw the above article and has asked you for some advice:

1. My receivables are averaging about 75 days. Should I be concerned that this will affect my cash flow?

2. What can I do to get faster payments on my billing?

3. My business is profitable, but I seem to always run short of cash at the end of each month? Why is that?

Source: Reprinted with permission from George Cloutier with Samantha Marshall, "Solve Your Cash-Flow Problem to Stay in Business," *Businessweek.* July 24, 2009.

or disbursed. For example, a sales transaction of $1,000 may be included in net income, but if the amount has not yet been paid, no cash has been received. Thus, for cash flow purposes there is no cash available from the sales transaction. For simplification and internal monitoring of cash flow purposes, many entrepreneurs prefer a simple determination of cash in less cash out. This method provides a fast indication of the cash position of the new venture at a point in time and is sometimes easier to understand.

It is important for the entrepreneur to make monthly projections of cash like the monthly projections made for profits. The numbers in the cash flow projections are constituted from the pro forma income statement with modifications made to account for the expected timing of the changes in cash. If disbursements are greater than receipts in any time period, the entrepreneur must either borrow funds or have cash in a bank account to cover the higher disbursements. Large positive cash flows in any time period may need to be invested in short-term sources or deposited in a bank to cover future time periods when disbursements are greater than receipts. Usually the first few months of the start-up will require external cash (debt) to cover the cash outlays. As the business succeeds and cash receipts accumulate, the entrepreneur can support negative cash periods.

pro forma cash flow
Projected cash available calculated from projected cash accumulations minus projected cash disbursements

Table 10.6 illustrates the *pro forma cash flow* over the first 12 months for MPP Plastics. As can be seen, there is a negative cash flow based on receipts less disbursements for the first 11 months of operation. The likelihood of incurring negative cash flows is very high for any new venture, but the amount and length of time before cash flows become positive will vary, depending on the nature of the business. In Chapter 13 we discuss how the entrepreneur can manage cash flow in the early years of a new venture. For this chapter, we will focus on how to project cash flow before the venture is launched.

The most difficult problem with projecting cash flows is determining the exact monthly receipts and disbursements. Some assumptions are necessary and should be conservative so that enough funds can be maintained to cover the negative cash months. In this firm, it is anticipated that 60 percent of each month's sales will be received in cash with the remaining

TABLE 10.6 MPP Plastics Inc., Pro Forma Cash Flow, First Year by Month ($000s)

	Jan.	Feb.	Mar.	Apr.	May	June	July	Aug.	Sept.	Oct.	Nov.	Dec.
Receipts												
Sales	12.0	27.2	41.6	61.2	82.0	96.0	100.0	100.0	88.0	80.0	104.0	126.0
Disbursements												
Equipment purchase	72.0	—	—	—	—	—	—	—	—	—	—	—
Cost of goods	8.0	14.8	22.4	37.6	43.0	49.0	50.0	50.0	42.0	40.0	56.0	60.0
Salaries	23.2	23.2	26.2	26.2	26.2	26.2	26.2	26.2	26.2	26.2	26.2	26.2
Rent	2.0	2.0	2.0	2.0	2.0	2.0	2.0	2.0	2.0	2.0	2.0	2.0
Utilities	0.9	0.9	0.9	0.8	0.8	0.8	0.9	0.9	0.9	0.8	0.8	0.9
Advertising	13.5	13.5	17.0	17.0	17.0	17.0	14.0	14.0	14.0	21.0	17.0	17.0
Sales expense	1.0	1.0	1.0	1.0	1.0	1.0	1.0	1.0	1.0	1.0	1.0	1.0
Insurance	2.0	2.0	2.0	2.0	2.0	2.0	2.0	2.0	2.0	2.0	2.0	2.0
Payroll & misc. taxes	2.1	2.1	2.5	2.5	2.5	2.5	2.5	2.5	2.5	2.5	2.5	2.5
Office expenses	1.5	1.5	1.5	1.7	1.8	2.0	2.0	2.0	1.8	1.8	2.2	2.2
Inventory*	0.2	0.4	0.6	0.6	0.8	0.8	1.0	1.0	1.0	1.0	1.2	1.2
Total disbursements	126.4	61.4	76.1	91.4	97.1	103.3	101.6	101.6	93.4	98.3	110.9	115.0
Cash flow	(114.4)	(34.2)	(34.5)	(30.2)	(15.1)	(7.3)	(1.6)	(1.6)	(5.4)	(18.3)	(6.9)	11.0
Beginning balance†	300.0	185.6	151.4	116.9	86.7	71.6	64.3	62.7	61.1	55.7	37.4	30.5
Ending balance	185.6	151.4	116.9	86.7	71.6	64.3	62.7	61.1	55.7	37.4	30.5	41.5

*Inventory is valued at cost or average of $2.00/unit.
†Three founders put up $100,000 each for working capital through the first three years. After the third year the venture will need debt or equity financing for expansion.

40 percent paid in the subsequent month. Thus, in February we can see that the cash receipts from sales totaled $27,200. This resulted from cash sales in February of 60 percent of $32,000, or $19,200, plus the 40 percent of sales that occurred in January (.40 × $20,000 = $8,000) but was not paid until February, thus resulting in the total cash received in February of $27,200. This process continues throughout the remaining months in year 1.

Similar assumptions are made for the cost of goods disbursement. It is assumed in our example that 80 percent of the cost of goods is paid in the month that it is incurred, with the remainder paid in the following month. Thus, referring back to Table 10.3, we can note that in February the actual cost of goods was $16,000. However, we actually pay only 80 percent of this in the month incurred—but we also pay 20 percent of the cost of goods sold that is still due from January. Thus, the actual cost of goods cash outflow in February is .8 × $16,000 + .2 × $10,000, or a total of $14,800.

Using conservative estimates, cash flows can be determined for each month. These cash flow projections assist the entrepreneur in determining how much money he or she will need to raise to meet the cash demands of the venture. In our example, the venture starts with a total of $300,000, or $100,000 from each of the three founders. We can see that by the twelfth month, the venture begins to turn a positive cash flow from operations, still leaving enough cash available ($41,500) should the projections fall short of expectations. If the entrepreneurs in our example had to use debt for the start-up, then they would need to show the interest payments in the income statement as an operating expense and indicate the principal payments to the bank as a cash disbursement, not as an operating expense. This issue often creates cash flow problems for entrepreneurs when they do not realize that debt is a cash disbursement only and that interest is an operating expense.

It is most important for the entrepreneur to remember that the pro forma cash flow, like the income statement, is based on best estimates. A start-up venture in a weak economy may find it necessary to revise cash flow projections frequently to ensure that their accuracy will protect the firm from any impending disaster. The estimates or projections should include any assumptions so that potential investors will understand how and from where the numbers were generated.[4]

In the case of both the pro forma income statement and the pro forma cash flow, it is sometimes useful to provide several scenarios, each based on different levels of success of the business. These scenarios and projections not only serve the purpose of generating pro forma income and cash flow statements but, more importantly, familiarize the entrepreneur with the factors affecting the operations.

PRO FORMA BALANCE SHEET

The entrepreneur should also prepare a projected balance sheet depicting the condition of the business at the end of the first year. The balance sheet will require the use of the pro forma income and cash flow statements to help justify some of the figures.[5]

pro forma balance sheet
Summarizes the projected assets, liabilities, and net worth of the new venture

The *pro forma balance sheet* reflects the position of the business at the end of the first year. It summarizes the assets, liabilities, and net worth of the entrepreneurs. In other words it tells the entrepreneur a measure of the company's solvency. For example, a ratio analysis of current assets (those expected to be converted into cash within the year) to current liabilities (those that must be paid within the current year) indicates how well the firm can pay its bills. A ratio of less than 1 to 1 would indicate that the company needs an infusion of cash in order to meet its current obligations.

Every business transaction affects the balance sheet, but because of the time and expense, as well as need, it is common to prepare balance sheets at periodic intervals (i.e., quarterly or annually). Thus, the balance sheet is a picture of the business at a certain moment in time and does not cover a period of time.

TABLE 10.7   MPP Plastics Inc., Pro Forma Balance Sheet, End of First Year ($000s)

Assets		
Current assets		
Cash	$41.5	
Accounts receivable	52.0	
Inventory	1.2	
Total current assets		$ 94.7
Fixed assets		
Equipment	72.0	
Less depreciation	14.4	
Total fixed assets		57.6
Total assets		$152.3
Liabilities and Owners' Equity		
Current liabilities		
Accounts payable	$13.0	
Total liabilities		$ 13.0
Owners' equity		
K. Peters	100.0	
C. Peters	100.0	
J. Welch	100.0	
Retained earnings	(160.7)	
Total owners' equity		139.3
Total liabilities and owners' equity		$152.3

Table 10.7 depicts the balance sheet for MPP Plastics. As can be seen, the total assets equal the sum of the liabilities and owners' equity. Each of the categories is explained here:

assets Items that are owned or available to be used in the venture operations

- *Assets.* These represent everything of value that is owned by the business. Value is not necessarily meant to imply the cost of replacement or what its market value would be but is the actual cost or amount expended for the asset. The assets are categorized as current or fixed. Current assets include cash and anything else that is expected to be converted into cash or consumed in the operation of the business during a period of one year or less. Fixed assets are those that are tangible and will be used over a long period of time. These current assets are often dominated by receivables or money that is owed to the new venture from customers. Management of these receivables is important to the cash flow of the business since the longer it takes for customers to pay their bills, the more stress is placed on the cash needs of the venture. A more detailed discussion of the management of receivables is presented in Chapter 13.

liabilities Money that is owed to creditors

- *Liabilities.* These accounts represent everything owed to creditors. Some of these amounts may be due within a year (current liabilities), and others may be long-term debts. There are no long-term liabilities in our MPP Plastics example because the venture used funds from the founders to start the business. However, should the entrepreneurs need to borrow money from a bank for the future purchase of equipment or for additional growth capital, the balance sheet would show long-term liabilities in the form of a note payable equal to the principal amount borrowed. As stated earlier, any interest on this note would appear as an expense in the income statement, and the payment of any principal would be shown in the cash flow statement. Subsequent end-of-year balance sheets would show only the remaining amount of principal due on the note payable. Although prompt payment of what is owed (payables) establishes good credit ratings and a good relationship with suppliers, it is often necessary to delay payments of bills to more effectively manage cash flow. Ideally, any business owner wants bills to be paid on time by suppliers so that he or she can pay any bills owed on time. Unfortunately, during recessions, many firms hold back payment of their bills to better manage cash flow. The problem with this strategy is that while the entrepreneur may think that slower payment of bills will generate better cash flow, he or she may also find that customers are thinking the same thing, with the result that no one gains any cash advantage. More discussion of this issue is also included in Chapter 13.

owner equity The amount owners have invested and/or retained from the venture operations

- *Owner equity.* This amount represents the excess of all assets over all liabilities. It represents the net worth of the business. The $300,000 that was invested into the business by MPP Plastics' three entrepreneurs is included in the owners' equity or net worth section of the balance sheet. Any profit from the business will also be included in the net worth as retained earnings. In our MPP Plastics example, retained earnings is negative, based on the net loss incurred in year 1. Thus, revenue increases assets and owners' equity, and expenses decrease owners' equity and either increase liabilities or decrease assets.

BREAK-EVEN ANALYSIS

In the initial stages of the new venture, it is helpful for the entrepreneur to know when a profit may be achieved. This will provide further insight into the financial potential for the start-up business. Break-even analysis is a useful technique for determining how many units must be sold or how much sales volume must be achieved to break even.

We already know from the projections in Table 10.3 that MPP Plastics will begin to earn a profit in the eleventh month. However, this is not the break-even point since the firm has obligations for the remainder of the year that must be met, regardless of the number of units sold. These obligations, or fixed costs, must be covered by sales volume for a company to break even. Thus, *breakeven* is that volume of sales at which the business will neither make a profit nor incur a loss.

breakeven Volume of sales where the venture neither makes a profit nor incurs a loss

The break-even sales point indicates to the entrepreneur the volume of sales needed to cover total variable and fixed expenses. Sales in excess of the break-even point will result in a profit as long as the selling price remains above the costs necessary to produce each unit (variable cost).[6]

The break-even formula is derived in Table 10.8 and is given as:

$$B/E(Q) = \frac{TFC}{SP - VC/\text{Unit (marginal contribution)}}$$

where $B/E(Q)$ = break-even quantity
TFC = total fixed costs
SP = selling price
VC/Unit = variable costs per unit

As long as the selling price is greater than the variable costs per unit, some contribution can be made to cover fixed costs. Eventually, these contributions will be sufficient to pay all fixed costs, at which point the firm has reached breakeven.

TABLE 10.8   Determining the Break-Even Formula

By definition, breakeven is where Total Revenue (*TR*)	= Total Costs (*TC*)
Also by definition:	
(*TR*)	= Selling Price (*SP*) × Quantity (*Q*)
and (*TC*)	= Total Fixed Costs (*TFC*)* + Total Variable Costs (*TVC*)†
Thus: *SP* × *Q* = *TFC* + *TVC*	
Where *TVC*	= Variable Costs/Unit (*VC*/Unit)‡ × Quantity (*Q*)
Thus *SP* × *Q* = *TFC* + (*VC*/Unit × *Q*)	
(*SP* × *Q*) − (*VC*/Unit × *Q*)	= *TFC*
Q (*SP* − *VC*/Unit)	= *TFC*
Finally, Breakeven(*Q*)	$= \dfrac{TFC}{SP - VC/Unit}$

*Fixed costs are those costs that, without change in present productive capacity, are not affected by changes in volume of output.
†Variable costs are those that are affected in total by changes in volume of output.
‡The variable costs per unit is all those costs attributable to producing one unit. This cost is constant within defined ranges of production.

The major weakness in calculating the breakeven lies in determining whether a cost is fixed or variable. For new ventures these determinations will require some judgment. However, it is reasonable to regard costs such as depreciation, salaries and wages, rent, and insurance as fixed. Materials, selling expenses such as commissions, and direct labor are most likely to be variable costs. The variable costs per unit usually can be determined by allocating the direct labor, materials, and other expenses that are incurred with the production of a single unit.

Recall that in our MPP Plastics example the venture produces plastic molded parts for the toy industry and hard goods and appliance manufacturers. Since the company is likely to be selling a large volume of these parts at various prices, it is necessary to make an assumption regarding the average selling price based on production and sales revenue. The entrepreneurs determine that the average selling price of all these components is $4.00/unit. From the pro forma income statement (Table 10.4), we see that fixed costs in year 1 are $636,300. We also know from our example that cost of goods sold is 50 percent of sales revenue, so we can assume a variable cost per unit of $2.00. Using these calculations we can then determine the venture's break-even point (B/E) in units as follows:

$$B/E = \frac{TFC}{SP - VC/\text{Unit}}$$

$$= \frac{\$636,300}{\$4.00 - \$2.00}$$

$$= \frac{\$636,300}{\$2.00}$$

$$= 318,150 \text{ units}$$

Any units beyond the 318,150 that are sold by the venture will result in a profit of $2.00 per unit. Sales below this number will result in a loss for the company. In cases where the firm produces more than one product and it is feasible to allocate fixed costs to each product, then it is possible to calculate a break-even point for each product. Fixed costs are

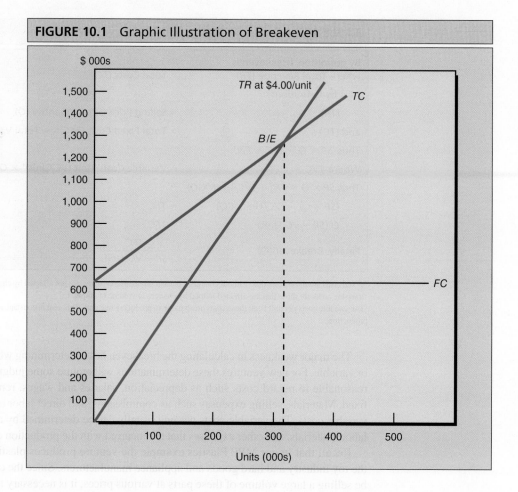

FIGURE 10.1 Graphic Illustration of Breakeven

determined by weighting the costs as a function of the sales projections for each product. For example, if it is assumed that 40 percent of the sales are for product X, then 40 percent of fixed costs should be allocated to that product.

In our MPP Plastics example, the large number of different products and the size lots of customer purchases prohibit any individual product break-even calculation. In this case we estimate the average selling price of all components for use in our calculations.

One of the unique aspects of breakeven is that it can be graphically displayed, as in Figure 10.1. In addition, the entrepreneur can try different states of nature (e.g., different selling prices, different fixed costs and/or variable costs) to ascertain the impact on breakeven and subsequent profits.

PRO FORMA SOURCES AND APPLICATIONS OF FUNDS

pro forma sources and applications of funds
Summarizes all the projected sources of funds available to the venture and how these funds will be disbursed

The *pro forma sources and applications of funds* statement illustrates the disposition of earnings from operations and from other financing. Its purpose is to show how net income and financing were used to increase assets or to pay off debt.

It is often difficult for the entrepreneur to understand how the net income for the year was disposed of and the effect of the movement of cash through the business. Questions often asked are, Where did the cash come from? How was the cash used? and What happened to asset items during the period?

AS SEEN IN *BUSINESS NEWS*

ELEVATOR PITCH FOR BROADCASTR.COM

As a potential investor you are always looking for start-ups that might be a good investment. You notice a number of articles relating to a new app for your iPhone and Android that sounds interesting. After reading the description below you consult with a good friend who is also a private investor to discuss this new business. What would you expect to be the major issues that would be discussed in this meeting? If you were in their shoes, what would you decide?

Broadcastr.com is a new app that allows you to create and share audio and video experiences or stories about places that are important or significant. Located in New York City there are four full-time employees and six freelancers and interns. Co-founders Andy Hunter and Scott Lindenbaum launched the beta site in March 2011 with the goal of relating interesting and compelling stories on location-based mobile technology. The way it works is that a person who wants to relate a significant event such as a visit to a historical site, a meal at a unique restaurant, or even a funny incident can record a story about this experience on their iPhone or Android. The Web site will also have this option in the near future. So far story submissions are increasing at the rate of 25 percent per month.

Recently the company partnered with Simon & Schuster to provide eight exclusive audio excerpts from Pulitzer Prize winner David McCullough's audio book *The Great Bridge.* Users can now access the free app that provides these excerpts that come together to provide a streaming half hour walking tour of the bridge.

A major issue is, how does the company generate revenue? Several means of generating revenue are being considered such as content sponsorships and partnerships. For example, the company has partnered with Fodor's so anyone can find all kinds of guidebook content relating to travel, food, and places to visit. Thus users can purchase some of this premium content information while traveling. The company is also planning to introduce more ads to its service, all limited to less than 30 seconds. Revenue will also be generated by organizations wishing to place premium content on the site. As of early 2012 there were 12,000 stories uploaded to the site. About 20 percent of these were placed by one of the many partners.

Sources: See Ericka Chickowski, "A Spoken-Word GPS," *Entrepreneur* (January 2012), p. 42; Katherine Boehret, "Find a Story to Hear Wherever It May Be," *The Wall Street Journal Online,* March 2, 2011; and www.broadcastr.com.

Table 10.9 shows the pro forma sources and applications of funds for MPP Plastics Inc. after the first year of operation. Many of the funds were obtained from personal funds or loans. Since at the end of the first year a profit was earned, it too would be added to the sources of funds. Depreciation is added back because it does not represent an out-of-pocket

TABLE 10.9	MPP Plastics Inc., Pro Forma Sources and Applications of Funds, End of First Year	
Source of funds		
Personal funds of founders	$ 300,000	
Net income (loss) from operations	(151,300)	
Add depreciation	14,400	
Total funds provided		$163,100
Application of funds		
Purchase of equipment	$ 72,000	
Inventory	1,200	
Total funds expended		73,200
Net increase in working capital		89,900
		$163,100

expense. Thus, typical sources of funds are from operations, new investments, long-term borrowing, and sale of assets. The major uses or applications of funds are to increase assets, retire long-term liabilities, reduce owner or stockholders' equity, and pay dividends. The sources and applications of funds statement emphasizes the interrelationship of these items to working capital. The statement helps the entrepreneur as well as investors to better understand the financial well-being of the company as well as the effectiveness of the financial management policies of the company.

SOFTWARE PACKAGES

There are a number of financial software packages available for the entrepreneur that can track financial data and generate any important financial statement. For purposes of completing the pro forma statements, at least in the business planning stage, it is probably easiest to use a spreadsheet program, since numbers may change often as the entrepreneur begins to develop budgets for the pro forma statements. Microsoft Excel is the most widely used spreadsheet software and is relatively simple to use.

The value of using a spreadsheet in the start-up phase for financial projections is simply being able to present different scenarios and assess their impact on the pro forma statements. It helps to answer such questions as, What would be the effect of a price decrease of 10 percent on my pro forma income statement? What would be the impact of an increase of 10 percent in operating expenses? and How would the lease versus purchase of equipment affect my cash flow? This type of analysis, using the computer spreadsheet software, will provide a quick assessment of the likely financial projections given different scenarios.

It is recommended in the start-up stage, where the venture is very small and limited in time and resources, that the software selected be very simple and easy to use. The entrepreneur will need software to maintain the books and to generate financial statements. Most of these software packages allow for check writing, payroll, invoicing, inventory management, bill paying, credit management, and taxes.

The software packages vary in price and complexity. Some are Web-based and can be accessed at little or no expense depending on the specific needs of the user. One of the simplest and probably the most widely used small business accounting software package is Intuit's Quickbooks. The premiere edition costs about $349 for the first year and $299 for each year thereafter. Or alternatively you can pay monthly ($79 for the first month and $39/month thereafter). Peachtree (Sage Software) and AccountEdge (Acclivity) are solid competitors to Quickbooks at a cost of about $349 and $299, respectively, depending on the needs of the user.[7]

IN REVIEW

SUMMARY

This chapter introduces several financial projection techniques. A single fictitious example of a new venture (MPP Plastics Inc.) is used to illustrate how to prepare each pro forma statement. Each of the planning tools is designed to provide the entrepreneur with a clear picture of where funds come from, how they are disbursed, the amount of cash available, and the general financial well-being of the new venture.

The pro forma income statement provides a sales estimate in the first year (monthly basis) and projects operating expenses each month. These estimates are determined from the appropriate budgets, which are based on marketing plan projections and objectives.

Cash flow is not the same as profit. It reflects the difference between cash actually received and cash disbursements. Some cash disbursements are not operating expenses (e.g., repayment of loan principal); likewise, some operating expenses are not a cash disbursement (e.g., depreciation expense). Many new ventures have failed because of a lack of cash, even when the venture is profitable.

The pro forma balance sheet reflects the condition of the business at the end of a particular period. It summarizes the assets, liabilities, and net worth of the firm.

The break-even point can be determined from projected income. This measures the point where total revenue equals total cost.

The pro forma sources and applications of funds statement helps the entrepreneur to understand how the net income for the year was disposed of and the effect of the movement of cash through the business. It emphasizes the interrelationship of assets, liabilities, and stockholders' equity to working capital.

Software packages to assist the entrepreneur in accounting, payroll, inventory, billing, and so on are readily available. There are now many options for the entrepreneur including Web-based accounting services that can range from no cost to a nominal monthly fee depending on the financial need of the company. Even the more sophisticated software packages vary on what is offered so the entrepreneur should evaluate them carefully and get assistance in selection if necessary.

RESEARCH TASKS

1. Go online and identify some of the new Web-based financial software packages. How are they different? What advantages do Quickbooks, Peachtree, or AccountEdge have over these Web-based services?

2. Companies planning to make an initial public offering (IPO) must submit a financial plan as part of their prospectus. From the Internet, collect a prospectus from two different companies and analyze their financial plans. What were the major assumptions made in constructing these financial plans? Compare and contrast these financial plans with what we would expect of a financial plan as part of a business plan.

3. A start-up has sales in the first three months of $20,000 yet there is not enough funds in the checking account to meet the payroll. How do you explain this? What can the owner do to assess this situation and improve upon it to meet financial obligations?

CLASS DISCUSSION

1. Is it more important for an entrepreneur to track cash or profits? Does it depend on the type of business and/or industry? What troubles will an entrepreneur face if she or he tracks only profits and ignores cash? What troubles will an entrepreneur face if she or he tracks only cash and ignores profits?

2. What volume of sales is required to reach breakeven for the following business: The variable cost of producing one unit of the product is $5, the fixed costs of plant and labor are $500,000, and the selling price of a single product is $50. It is not always easy to classify a cost as fixed or variable. What happens to the breakeven calculated above if some of the fixed costs are reclassified as variable

costs? What happens if the reverse is the case (i.e., some of the variable costs are reclassified as fixed costs)?

3. How useful is a financial plan when it is based on assumptions of the future and we are confident that these assumptions are not going to be 100 percent correct? Does it make more sense for the entrepreneur to evaluate and modify financial plans monthly or wait for results from quarterly reports? Why or why not?

SELECTED READINGS

Christie, Nancy L.; John Brozovsky; and Sam Hicks. (September 2010). International Financial Reporting Standards for Small and Medium Sized Entities: An Update for the Commercial Loan Officer. *Commercial Lending Review*, vol. 25, issue 5, pp. 28–34.

This article provides some explanation and research on the major differences between generally accepted accounting principles (GAAP) and international financial reporting standards (IFRS). In particular the study focuses on the differences of each with regard to income statements, balance sheets, and cash flow. One conclusion is that the IFRS for small and medium-sized firms are simpler accounting principles for private U.S. firms.

Cloutier, George. (May 3, 2010). Negotiate Payments to Stay in Business. *BusinessWeek.com.*

This author describes a client that found himself near bankruptcy when sales plummeted as a result of the recession. However, the owner was not aware of the discrepancy on the books between accounts receivables and accounts payables. The company was taking too long to collect payments but was quick to pay vendors and landlords. Instituting faster collection and increasing their days before paying bills even slightly enhanced cash flow and allowed the company to continue in business.

Estes, Jim; and Richard S. Savich. (March 2011). A Comparison of Financial Analysis Software for Use in Financial Planning for Small Businesses. *Journal of Financial Service Professionals*, vol. 65, issue 2, pp. 48–55.

According to these authors there are no specific methods or tools that help small businesses with their financial planning. A number of software packages that are designed to assist the small business owner with financial ratios and overall efficiency of the business operations are discussed. These also help with determining the valuation of the business for sale and succession planning.

Ittelson, Thomas R. (2009). *Financial Statements: A Step by Step Guide to Understanding and Creating Financial Reports.* Franklin Lakes, NJ: The Career Press.

This paperback book provides an excellent overview of all financial statements. It is clear and concise with lots of examples. It provides a very good overview of how to analyze financial statements with discussion on how to utilize information from the analysis. Ratio analysis is discussed as well as the time and value of money with explanations of the Internal Rate of Return (IRR) and Net Present Value (NPV).

Kearns, Suzanne. (November/December 2011). Nine Ways to Collect Bad Debt. *Home Business*, pp. 44–47.

In our weak economy business owners are struggling with stagnant accounts receivables. This author provides nine ways in which a business owner can improve collection of invoices to improve cash flow and reduce the threat of bad debt.

Lister, Kate. (May 2011). Go with the Flow. *Entrepreneur,* vol. 39, issue 5, p. 44.

Cash management is considered an important issue in the success opportunities for an entrepreneur. Basic principles of cash flow accounting are discussed. Techniques on how to project cash flow as well as a discussion of the importance of using marketing research to forecast sales and income are included in the article.

Philips, Michael; Steven Anderson; and John Volker. (July 2010). Understanding Small Private Retail Firm Growth Using the Sustainable Growth Model. *Journal of Finance and Accountancy,* vol. 3, pp. 1–11.

This paper is a research study of financial ratios among privately held retailers in different stages of their growth cycle. The study focuses on four financial categories: profitability, activity, leverage, and liquidity. Results indicated that small or early growth cycle stage firms performed differently than larger or later growth cycle firms in all categories and across all time periods.

Rogers, Steven. (2009). *Entrepreneurial Finance: Finance and Business Strategies for the Serious Entrepreneur,* 2nd ed. New York: McGraw-Hill/Irwin.

This book is written by a successful entrepreneur and targets prospective and existing entrepreneurs that are not financial managers. It is user friendly, providing the fundamentals needed for financial management as well as an integration of this analysis with marketing, sales, human resources, and strategic planning. The book has major sections dedicated to cash flow management, valuation, financial statement analysis, and raising capital.

Taylor, Audrey; and Tristan Saario. (Autumn 2011). Winning the Fight: Using Target Mapping to Leverage Fixed Costs and Meet Customer Needs. *Management Accounting Quarterly,* vol. 13, issue 1, pp. 31–39.

Many small businesses are struggling during the current economic downturn and need more effective ways to leverage their fixed costs. Using a martial arts business as an example these authors show how target mapping can be utilized to allow for more effective planning to reach the right target market. Target mapping starts with a goal, then a list of obstacles preventing the goal from being achieved, and finally strategies that can overcome any of the obstacles. These are then put into a plan. They show how this technique was incorporated in a new plan at little expense using the original facilities to provide a positive cash flow.

Taylor, Mandie. (June 2008). How to Identify Short- and Long-Term Liquidity Needs Accurately. *Journal of Corporate Treasury Management,* pp. 291–96.

This is a good article that describes the need to manage cash effectively to ensure that funding is secured at an early date. These strategies involve producing a reliable cash projection with appropriate cash budget. This forecast or projection of cash needs is a work in progress and should be monitored regularly to ensure reliability.

Tozzi, John. (March 28, 2011). A Cash Flow is the Recession's Legacy. *Bloomberg Businessweek,* issue 4222, pp. 59–60.

One of the dilemmas for small businesses that results from the weak economy is that vendors are demanding payments more quickly and customers are making payments more slowly. This creates cash flow problems and in turn makes it more difficult to obtain bank financing to cover the discrepancy. One solution is to try to find vendors that are more reasonable with payment plans and avoid those that demand upfront payments for supplies.

Youngwirth, Joni. (September/October 2011). Connecting Personal Passages with the Business Life Cycle. *Practice Management Solutions,* pp. 24–25.

As with personal aging so do small businesses mature. The small business owner should try to identify the stage of the business cycle that the business falls in. Each stage offers unique challenges to the firm and understanding these stages can help the firm anticipate changes and subsequently plan appropriately to maintain financial success.

END NOTES

1. See Sara Wilson, "Build a Billion-Dollar Business," *Entrepreneur* (March 2009), pp. 45–47; Jeffrey M. O'Brien, "Zappos Knows How to Kick It," *Fortune* (February 2009), pp. 54–60; David Moin, "Q & A: Tony Hsieh," *Women's Wear Daily,* June 4, 2010, p. 14; and Max Chafkin, "Why I Sold Zappos," *INC* (June 2010), pp. 100–4.
2. J. Chris Leach and Ronald W. Melicher, *Entrepreneurial Finance,* 4th ed. (Mason, OH: South-Western Cengage Learning, 2012), pp. 126–28.
3. Kate Lister, "Go with the Flow," *Entrepreneur* (May 2011), pp. 88–89.
4. Steven Rogers, *Entrepreneurial Finance,* 2nd ed. (New York: McGraw-Hill/Irwin, 2009), pp. 97–101.
5. Ibid., pp. 92–97.
6. Roger Kerin, Steven Hartley, and William Rudelius, *Marketing,* 10th ed. (New York: McGraw-Hill/Irwin, 2011), pp. 336–40.
7. See Jeffrey Wilson, "The Best Free Small Business Software," www.pcmag.com, March 24, 2011; Venessa Wong, "The Battle for Accounting Software," www.BusinessWeek.com, October 22, 2010; and Jonathan Blum, "Books Smart," *Entrepreneur* (August 2011), pp. 41–42.

4

FROM THE BUSINESS PLAN TO FUNDING THE VENTURE

11

SOURCES OF CAPITAL

1
To identify the types of financing available.

2
To understand the role of commercial banks in financing new ventures, the types of loans available, and bank lending decisions.

3
To discuss Small Business Administration (SBA) loans.

4
To understand the aspects of research and development limited partnerships.

5
To discuss government grants, particularly Small Business Innovation Research grants.

6
To understand the role of private placement as a source of funds.

OPENING PROFILE

SCOTT B. WALKER

Some entrepreneurs are born and others are created through focus, energy, and desire. Scott Walker is the latter type, developing his own lifelong learning curriculum in creating opportunities and taking risks.

Walker was born an Air Force brat; his family was posted at stations across the country throughout his childhood. This training, including six different grade schools and three high schools in three different states, gave him the ability to get along anywhere, to be comfortable with different types of people, and to be self-sufficient.

www.epic-aviation.com

After receiving a BA from Utah State University in 1977, Walker selected a graduate school that would initiate his career as an entrepreneur. Thunderbird School of Global Management provided an environment for learning how an interesting idea can become a business—as well as exposure to the broader world as represented by students and faculty from around the globe. Walker graduated in 1981 with an MBA.

The banking world and its activity in mergers and acquisitions was Walker's first professional stop. Based in Dallas, he centered much of his effort on the oil and gas industry, including working with T. Boone Pickens and his Mesa Petroleum Co.

After a number of years in banking with such firms as Lloyd's Bank and GE Capital, Walker noticed that many of the people he respected in this industry were leaving to work on riskier, more nontraditional and stimulating ventures. This appealed to him, so he searched for an established entrepreneur who could show him the basics. That person was William Conley, a friend and successful entrepreneur, who was starting an Internet backbone infrastructure company to provide Internet points of presence, or POPs. Walker was the second employee and CFO of the fledgling technology firm in 1995. After one year of hard work with few paychecks, the firm was sold to GTE. It remains a portion of the Internet backbone today.

Following that first taste of risk taking, Walker returned to the corporate world as CFO of Precept Business Services, a $200 million company. When Conley again touched base with Walker in 1998, he was ready for a new challenge, the establishment of a not-for-profit educational assistance company. This company, one2one Learning

Foundation, provided individualized curriculum programs for children not enrolled in traditional public or private institutions.

Early in 1999, Walker became CEO of TelePay, a firm that provided large recurring billers with a way to have their consumers pay their bills using an automated telephone service known as interactive voice response, or IVR (the "press 1 for . . ." technology), through credit cards, ATM debit cards, and ACH or electronic checks. The company had only four employees but had very loyal clients despite a number of nagging technical glitches. Walker's first step was to completely rebuild the system on a single software platform to be able to scale up from 1,000 transactions to 10 million transactions. His second step was to bring on a senior sales executive who could leverage the loyalty of the existing customers into references for new prospects.

After renaming the company BillMatrix Corporation, the team started to develop a stellar client list. Walker built out the senior executive staff, adding a COO, CFO, and both client and consumer support personnel. The company was cash flow positive since the first month of his tenure and revenue grew over 100 percent year after year, every year. Because of its cash flow, the company did not require venture capital for growth, thereby keeping the majority control of the company and all of the decision-making processes in the hands of the senior executives. The company continued to grow, adding new technologies, and by 2005 had over 300 employees.

In 2005, the electronic payments industry was a hot area and the time was ripe for maximizing the value of an acquisition. Walker led the company in a buyout process with a large number of interested parties. The resulting transaction was an acquisition of BillMatrix by Fiserv, Inc. (NASDAQ: FISV) of Brookfield, Wisconsin, for $350 million in August 2005. This was the second largest acquisition in dollar value for Fiserv, which built itself primarily by acquisition into a $3.4 billion company with over 16,000 clients worldwide and 22,000 employees.

In early 2006, in a meeting with an old friend, Jim Tehan, Jim was complaining about all of the problems with contract fillers. Jim owned a sun care line, Aloe Gator. Tehan decided to acquire an existing contract filler. They tried to purchase a company—Nature's Formula (about $16+ million revenues)—one of the largest operations in North Texas. The company's largest customer was Victoria's Secret ($12 million contract). When the deal did not go through, Walker and three other individuals decided to build a contract filler company from scratch. In November, a lease was signed on 90,000 square feet of empty warehouse space. Offices, mechanical and production rooms, and a warehouse were built. The company, ProCore Laboratories, was open for business in early March 2007, and the first official product batch was filled in early April. Positive cash flow was achieved by December that year. The major difference between ProCore and all the rest of the industry was that the company employed an internal operating system to manage and monitor by batch.

The focus of ProCore was on quality and partnership. The company has quality standards that will not be compromised. The company proved that if it provided consistent product quality in every batch, customer sales increased. First year (2007) revenues were around $1.26 million.

ProCore was hard hit by the 2008 recession. Several customers who had been paying their bills ceased to pay or went out of business and multiple customers were sued for payment. One customer tried to bilk ProCore for over $500,000. In addition, consumer buying habits changed. The ProCore business model moved from local contract fill to large corporate customers. Not being the primary filler, ProCore was used to experimenting. Multiple products were manufactured, which would have led to increased business but nearly all the test products failed to generate sufficient revenue. ProCore struggled to find its niche. After three business models, the company finally settled on a winning model to thrive in the current depressed economic environment. ProCore focused on NBEs (National Brand Equivalent). This is a product tested by an independent third party lab to conform in all respects to a brand product. Typically, the NBE is represented by a "compare to" label situated next to the brand product. In all regards, the NBE is the same product as the brand but with a value component. ProCore is now moving to gain certification of several products. Current certified products include Pedialyte and Pepto Bismol. Additional products in the pipeline are cough and cold liquids and antacids. After continued substantial investment to keep the company alive, ProCore is returning to health and will experience a profitable 2012. Jim Tehan's belief is that Procore forecasts $40 million in annual revenue in the next three years.

Walker also followed another track into a completely new industry. After his departure from BillMatrix in May 2008, he took several months off to spend time with his family. In October 2008, Bill Conley and he started pursuing an aviation fuel distribution company, EPIC Aviation located in Oregon, and negotiated the acquisition of 25 percent of equity for a reasonable price. The deal closed in mid-2008. BP owned 50 percent and the remaining 25 percent was in the hands of the current owner/operator. The company had been operated as a family business for 40 years. During late 2008, the Conley/Walker team had attempted to acquire the 50 percent equity position from BP, but due to the economy and the "bank implosion," EPIC's current bank would not approve the transaction. During 2009, EPIC replaced its current bank with a new bank able to provide sufficient working capital. In the initial attempt to acquire BP's interest, a "put" was negotiated by the owner/operator to Conley/Walker. The owner/operator decided in early 2010 to exercise this "put" as he was turning 65 and stated his intention to retire from the day to day management of EPIC by the end of the year. Walker took over operations following the owner's retirement and the Conley/Walker team now owned 50 percent of the company. In April 2010, BP's Gulf incident occurred. By midsummer, it was apparent that the spill was not a short-term issue and BP's interest in retaining its 50 percent ownership in EPIC was again available. In early August, a letter of intent (LOI) was negotiated by Walker to acquire the remaining 50 percent currently owned by BP for a reasonable price. Walker became CEO of the company in December 2010 and the BP share purchase was completed in February 2011.

As the new CEO Walker focused on many non–best of breed business practices and implemented immediate changes. One of the main issues was the company's balance sheet.

EPIC was fully maximized under its working capital line leaving no additional capacity to borrow. Walker identified multiple assets of a noncore nature and some of these such as aircraft, inventories, Fixed Based Operator (FBO) leases at market value were liquidated.

By summer 2011, the funded bank debt was being paid off rapidly with a target of complete debt repayment by October, and 2011 was one of the most profitable years for the company in the last 10 years.

Walker transitioned the day to day operations of EPIC to a new COO in December 2011 to work with Bill Conley who had successfully negotiated with the Chinese government–owned entity, China National Aviation Fuel Group (CNAF), to joint venture and begin the development of general aviation (business and personal air-craft) for China. CNAF is responsible for all jet fuel distribution in China. This oppor-tunity was officially awarded to EPIC in late November 2011. The Chinese general aviation (GA) market is exploding rapidly and there is no formal GA infrastructure or operations. EPIC is now responsible for implementing all operational aspects of an FBO network throughout China. Approximately 250 FBOs are planned to be built at existing airports, including new independent GA airports to be constructed.

Today, Walker is dedicated to being an "entrepreneurial philanthropist." While he is a generous monetary donor to his alma mater—Thunderbird School of Global Management—he also provides the more important gift of time with students who are looking for the same knowledge he needed early in his career. His goal is to help the next generation get a quicker start on their ventures by sharing his knowledge about how to build a strong business around a good idea. Among his many talents, Scott B. Walker understands how to successfully finance and capitalize a venture, the focus of this chapter.

AN OVERVIEW

One of the most difficult problems in the new venture creation process is obtaining financ-ing. For the entrepreneur, available financing needs to be considered from the perspective of debt versus equity and using internal versus external funds.

Debt or Equity Financing

debt financing
Obtaining borrowed funds for the company

There are two general types of financing available: debt financing and equity financing. *Debt financing* is a financing method involving an interest-bearing instrument, usually a loan, the payment of which is only indirectly related to the sales and profits of the venture. Typically, debt financing (also called asset-based financing) requires that some asset (such as a car, house, inventory, plant, machine, or land) be used as collateral.

Debt financing requires the entrepreneur to pay back the amount of funds borrowed as well as a fee expressed in terms of the interest rate. There can also be an additional fee, sometimes referred to as points, for using or being able to borrow the money. If the financing is short term (less than one year), the money is usually used to provide working capital to finance inventory, accounts receivable, or the operation of the business. The funds are typically repaid from the resulting sales and profits during the year. Long-term debt (lasting more than one year) is frequently used to purchase some asset such as a piece of machinery, land, or a building, with part of the value of the asset (usually from 50 to 80 percent of the total value) being used as collateral for the long-term loan. Particularly when interest rates are low, debt (as opposed to equity) financing allows the entrepreneur to retain a larger ownership portion in the venture and have a greater return on the equity. The entrepreneur needs to be careful that the debt is not so large that regular interest payments become difficult if not impossible to make, a situation that will inhibit growth and development and possibly end in bankruptcy. Using debt as the financing instrument is called leveraging the firm. The higher the amount of leverage (debt/total assets), the greater the risk in the venture.

equity financing
Obtaining funds for the company in exchange for ownership

Equity financing does not require collateral and offers the investor some form of ownership position in the venture. The investor shares in the profits of the venture, as well as any disposition of its assets on a pro rata basis based on the percentage of the business owned. Key factors favoring the use of one type of financing over another are the availability of funds, the assets of the venture, and the prevailing interest rates. Frequently, an entrepreneur meets financial needs by employing a combination of debt and equity financing.

All ventures will have some equity, as all ventures are owned by some person or institution. Although the owner may sometimes not be directly involved in the day-to-day management of the venture, there is always equity funding involved that is provided by the owner. The amount of equity involved will of course vary by the nature and size of the venture. In some cases, the equity may be entirely provided by the owner, such as in a small ice cream stand or pushcart in the mall or at a sporting event. Larger ventures may require multiple owners, including private investors and venture capitalists. This equity funding can provide the basis for debt funding, which together make up the capital structure of the venture.

Internal or External Funds

Financing is also available from both internal and external funds. The funds most frequently employed are internally generated funds. Internally generated funds can come from several sources within the company: profits, sale of assets, reduction in working capital, extended payment terms, and accounts receivable. In every new venture, the start-up years involve putting all the profits back into the venture; even outside equity investors do not expect any payback in these early years. The needed funds can sometimes be obtained by selling little-used assets. Assets, whenever possible, should be on a rental basis (preferably on a lease with an option to buy), not an ownership basis, as long as there is not a high level of inflation and the rental terms are favorable. Also, activities should be outsourced whenever possible. This helps the entrepreneur conserve cash, a practice that is particularly critical during the start-up phase of the company's operation.

A short-term, internal source of funds can be obtained by reducing short-term assets: inventory, cash, and other working-capital items. Sometimes an entrepreneur can generate the needed cash for a period of 30 to 60 days through extended payment terms from suppliers. Although care must be taken to ensure good supplier relations and continuous sources of supply, taking a few extra days to pay can generate needed short-term funds. A final method of internally generating funds is collecting bills (accounts receivable) more quickly. Key account holders should not be irritated by implementation of this practice, as certain customers have established payment practices. Mass merchandisers, for example, pay their bills to supplying companies in 60 to 90 days, regardless of a supplying company's accounts receivable policy, the size of the company, or the discount offered for prompt payment. If a company wants this mass merchandiser to carry its product, it will have to live with this payment schedule.

TABLE 11.1   Guide for Alternative Sources of Financing

Source of Financing	Length of Time		Cost			Control		
	Short Term	Long Term	Fixed Rate Debt	Floating Rate Debt	Percent of Profits	Equity	Covenants	Voting Rights
Self								
Family and friends								
Suppliers and trade credit								
Commercial banks								
Government loan programs								
R&D limited partnerships								
Private investors (angels)								
Venture capital								
Private equity placements								
Public equity offerings								
Other government programs								

One entrepreneur who is very successful at leveraging the discounts from vendors is home product distributor Jeff Schreiber. Schreiber always tries to take advantage of any discounts for prompt payments, and he obtained over $15,000 in early payment savings in one year alone.[1]

The other general source of funds is external to the venture. Alternative sources of external financing need to be evaluated on three bases: the length of time the funds are available, the costs involved, and the amount of company control lost. In selecting the best source of funds, each of the sources indicated in Table 11.1 needs to be evaluated along these three dimensions. The more frequently used sources of funds (self, family and friends, commercial banks, private investors (angels), R&D limited partnerships, government loan programs and grants, venture capital, and private placement) indicated in the table are discussed at length in the following pages.

Whenever an entrepreneur deals with items external to the firm, particularly with people and institutions that could become stakeholders, some ethical dilemmas can occur.

PERSONAL FUNDS

Few, if any, new ventures are started without the personal funds of the entrepreneur. Not only are these the least expensive funds in terms of cost and control, but they are absolutely essential in attracting outside funding, particularly from banks, private investors, and venture capitalists. Often referred to as blood equity, the typical sources of personal funds include savings, life insurance, or mortgage on a house or car. These outside providers of capital feel that the entrepreneur may not be sufficiently committed to the venture if he or she does not have money invested. As one venture capitalist succinctly said, "I want the entrepreneurs so financially committed that when the going gets tough, they will work through the problems and not throw the keys to the company on my desk."

This level of commitment is reflected in the percentage of total assets that the entrepreneur has available that are committed to the venture, not necessarily the amount of money committed. An outside investor wants an entrepreneur to have committed all available assets,

AS SEEN IN *BUSINESS NEWS*

START-UP CHILE

What better way to attract intelligent, creative entrepreneurs to your country than by offering equity-free capital? This is exactly what Chile is doing with Start-Up Chile, a USD $40 million program that gives early stage entrepreneurs up to USD $40,000 to launch their entrepreneurial idea or venture in Chile. During its first year of operation in 2010, Start-Up Chile supported 22 entrepreneurial teams from 14 different countries. The following year, in 2011, Start-Up Chile had 300 entrepreneurial teams in the program and the program plans to have over 1,000 teams by 2014.

Chile has three objectives for the Start-Up Chile program—to establish Chile as the innovation and entrepreneurial hub of Latin America, to improve the approach Chileans have toward entrepreneurship, and to develop more globally minded Chilean entrepreneurs. A crucial element to the success of these objectives is the collaborative nature of the program that emphasizes relationship building between Chileans and the international entrepreneurs in the program. To nurture these relationships, Start-Up Chile gives entrepreneurs access to financial, political, and social networks throughout the country. In return, Start-Up Chile participants share their knowledge and expertise with local Chilean entrepreneurs and businesses through presentations and workshops at local universities. Through this sharing of networks and information, the Chilean government is hopeful that these relationships will continue to be maintained after program participants leave Chile and over time develop a worldwide, creative network.

To participate in the Start-Up Chile program, entrepreneurs from around the world compete in one of three application rounds held each year. Applications have covered a wide variety of entrepreneurial ideas including travel Web sites, high-tech gadgets, software, and solar panels. A Chilean innovation board along with a group of Silicon Valley experts reviews the completed applications from each round and determines the best entrepreneurial ideas. The entrepreneurs behind these ideas are then invited to come to Chile and participate in the program. Participants are granted a one-year work visa and are reimbursed for 90 percent of their business expenses while in Chile up to a maximum of USD $40,000. This money is given without an equity requirement and the entrepreneurs are able to return to their home countries after a minimum of 24 weeks of work within the country. To help the entrepreneurs get the most from their time in Chile, Start-Up Chile also provides each team with an office, network introductions, and access to a group of over 160 highly qualified mentors who work closely with the participants to help them navigate the complex and sometimes overwhelming process of starting a new business, especially while operating in a foreign country. Through this elaborate support system, entrepreneurs are able to accomplish many things in a relatively short period of time and are positioned for continued success after leaving Chile.

Source: To learn more about Start-Up Chile and apply for the program, visit their Web site at www.startupchile.org. Also see R. Sheila, "Government-Backed Start-Up Chile Effort Eyes Silicon Valley," *Investors Business Daily* (serial online), March 7, 2011, p. A06.

an indication that he or she truly believes in the venture and will work all the hours necessary to ensure success. Whether this is $1,000, $100,000, or $250,000 depends on the assets of the entrepreneur available. *Entrepreneurs should always remember that it is not the amount but rather the fact that all monies available are committed that makes outside investors feel comfortable with their commitment level and therefore more willing to invest.*

FAMILY AND FRIENDS

After the entrepreneur, family and friends are a common source of capital for a new venture. They are most likely to invest due to their relationship with the entrepreneur. This helps overcome one portion of uncertainty felt by impersonal investors—knowledge of the entrepreneur. Family and friends provide a small amount of equity funding for new ventures, reflecting in part the small amount of capital needed for most new ventures. Although it is relatively easy to obtain money from family and friends, like all sources of capital, there are positive and negative aspects. Although the amount of money provided may be small, if it is in the form of equity financing, the family members or friends then have an ownership position in the venture and all rights and privileges of that position. This may make them feel they have a direct input into the operations of the venture, which may have a negative effect on employees, facilities, or sales and profits. Although this possibility must be guarded against as much as possible, frequently family and friends are not problem investors and in fact are more patient than other investors in their timetable for a return on their investment.

To avoid problems in the future, the entrepreneur must present the positive and negative aspects and the nature of the risks of the investment opportunity to try to minimize the negative impact on the relationships with family and friends should problems occur. One thing that helps to minimize possible difficulties is to keep the business arrangements strictly business. Any loans or investments from family or friends should be treated in the same businesslike manner as if the financing were from an impersonal investor. Any loan should specify the rate of interest and the proposed repayment schedule of interest and principal. The timing of any future dividends must be disclosed in terms of an equity investment. If the family or friend is treated the same as any investor, potential future conflicts can be avoided. It is also beneficial to the entrepreneur to settle everything up front and in writing. It is amazing how short memories become when money is involved. All the details of the financing must be agreed upon before the money is put into the venture. Such things as the amount of money involved, the terms of the money, the rights and responsibilities of the investor, and what happens if the business fails must all be agreed upon and written down. A formal agreement with all these items helps avoid future problems.

Finally, the entrepreneur should carefully consider the impact of the investment on the family member or friend before it is accepted. Particular concern should be paid to any hardships that might result should the business fail. Each family member or friend should be investing in the venture because they think it is a good investment, not because they feel obligated. They should receive income statements showing results on a regular basis—usually every quarter or at least every six months.

COMMERCIAL BANKS

Commercial banks are by far the source of short-term funds most frequently used by the entrepreneur when collateral is available. The funds provided are in the form of debt financing and, as such, require some tangible guaranty or collateral—some asset with value. This collateral can be in the form of business assets (land, equipment, or the building of the venture), personal assets (the entrepreneur's house, car, land, stock, or bonds), or the assets of the cosigner of the note.

Types of Bank Loans

asset base for loans
Tangible collateral valued at more than the amount of money borrowed

There are several types of bank loans available. To help ensure repayment, these loans are based on the assets or the cash flow of the venture. The *asset base for loans* is usually accounts receivable, inventory, equipment, or real estate.

Accounts Receivable Loans   Accounts receivable provide a good basis for a loan, especially if the customer base is well known and creditworthy. For those creditworthy customers, a bank may finance up to 80 percent of the value of their accounts receivable. When customers such as the government are involved, an entrepreneur can develop a factoring arrangement whereby the factor (the bank) actually "buys" the accounts receivable at a value below the face value of the sale and collects the money directly from the account. In this case, if any of the receivables is not collectible, the factor (the bank) sustains the loss, not the business. The cost of factoring the accounts receivable is of course higher than the cost of securing a loan against the accounts receivable without factoring being involved, since the bank has more risk when factoring. The costs of factoring involve the interest charge on the amount of money advanced until the time the accounts receivable are collected, the commission covering the actual collection, and protection against possible uncollectible accounts.

Inventory Loans

Inventory is another of the firm's assets that is often a basis for a loan, particularly when the inventory is more liquid and can be easily sold. Usually, the finished goods inventory can be financed for up to 50 percent of its value. Trust receipts are a unique type of inventory loan used to finance floor plans of retailers, such as automobile and appliance dealers. In trust receipts, the bank advances a large percentage of the invoice price of the goods and is paid on a pro rata basis as the inventory is sold.

Equipment Loans

Equipment can be used to secure longer-term financing, usually on a 3- to 10-year basis. Equipment financing can fall into any of several categories: financing the purchase of new equipment, financing used equipment already owned by the company, sale-leaseback financing, or lease financing. When new equipment is being purchased or presently owned equipment is used as collateral, usually 50 to 80 percent of the value of the equipment can be financed depending on its salability. Given the entrepreneur's tendency to rent rather than own, sale-leaseback or lease financing of equipment is widely used. In the sale-leaseback arrangement, the entrepreneur "sells" the equipment to a lender and then leases it back for the life of the equipment to ensure its continued use. In lease financing, the company acquires the use of the equipment through a small down payment and a guarantee to make a specified number of payments over a period of time. The total amount paid is the selling price plus the finance charges.

Real Estate Loans

Real estate is also frequently used in asset-based financing. This mortgage financing is usually easily obtained to finance a company's land, plant, or another building, often up to 75 percent of its value.

Cash Flow Financing

The other type of debt financing frequently provided by commercial banks and other financial institutions is cash flow financing. These *conventional bank loans* include lines of credit, installment loans, straight commercial loans, long-term loans, and character loans. Lines of credit financing is perhaps the form of cash flow financing most frequently used by entrepreneurs. In arranging for a line of credit to be used as needed, the company pays a "commitment fee" to ensure that the commercial bank will make the loan when requested and then pays interest on any outstanding funds borrowed from the bank. Frequently, the loan must be repaid or reduced to a certain agreed-upon level on a periodic basis. Character loans are particularly difficult to obtain without a third party co-signer.

conventional bank loan
Standard way banks lend
money to companies

Installment Loans

Installment loans can also be obtained by a venture with a track record of sales and profits. These short-term funds are frequently used to cover working capital needs for a period of time, such as when seasonal financing is needed. These loans are usually for 30 to 40 days.

Straight Commercial Loans

A hybrid of the installment loan is the straight commercial loan, by which funds are advanced to the company for 30 to 90 days. These self-liquidating loans are frequently used for seasonal financing and for building up inventories.

Long-Term Loans When a longer time period for use of the money is required, long-term loans are used. These loans (usually available only to strong, mature companies) can make funds available for up to 10 years. The debt incurred is usually repaid according to a fixed interest and principal schedule. The principal, however, can sometimes start being repaid in the second or third year of the loan, with only interest paid the first year.

Character Loans When the business itself does not have the assets to support a loan, the entrepreneur may need a character (personal) loan. These loans frequently must have the assets of the entrepreneur or other individual pledged as collateral or the loan cosigned by another individual. Assets that are frequently pledged include cars, homes, land, and securities. One entrepreneur's father pledged a $50,000 certificate of deposit as collateral for his son's $40,000 loan. In extremely rare instances, the entrepreneur can obtain money on an unsecured basis for a short time when a high credit standing has been established.

Bank Lending Decisions

One problem for the entrepreneur is determining how to successfully secure a loan from the bank. Banks are generally cautious in lending money, particularly to new ventures, since they do not want to incur bad loans. Regardless of geographic location, commercial loan decisions are made only after the loan officer and loan committee do a careful review of the borrower and the financial track record of the business. These decisions are based on both quantifiable information and subjective judgments.[2]

The bank lending decisions are made according to the five Cs of lending: character, capacity, capital, collateral, and conditions. Past financial statements (balance sheets and income statements) are reviewed in terms of key profitability and credit ratios, inventory turnover, aging of accounts receivable, the entrepreneur's capital invested, and commitment to the business. Future projections on market size, sales, and profitability are also evaluated to determine the ability to repay the loan. Several questions are usually raised regarding this ability. Does the entrepreneur expect to use the loan for an extended period of time? If problems occur, is the entrepreneur committed enough to spend the effort necessary to make the business a success? Does the business have a unique differential advantage in a growth market? What are the downside risks? Is there protection (such as life insurance on key personnel and insurance on the plant and equipment) against disasters?

Although the answers to these questions and the analysis of the company's records allow the loan officer to assess the quantitative aspects of the loan decision, the intuitive factors, particularly the first two Cs—character and capacity—are also taken into account. This part of the loan decision—the gut feeling—is the most difficult part to assess. The entrepreneur must present his or her capabilities and the prospects for the company in a way that elicits a positive response from the lender. This intuitive part of the loan decision becomes even more important when there is little or no track record, limited experience in financial management, a nonproprietary product or service (one not protected by a patent or license), or few assets available.

Some of the concerns of the loan officer and the loan committee can be reduced by providing a good loan application. While the specific loan application format of each bank differs to some extent, generally the application format is a "mini" business plan that consists of an executive summary, business description, owner/manager profiles, business projections, financial statements, amount and use of the loan, and repayment schedule. This information provides the loan officer and loan committee with insight into the creditworthiness of the individual and the venture as well as the ability of the venture to make enough sales and profit to repay the loan and the interest. The entrepreneur should evaluate several alternative banks, select the one that has had positive loan experience in the particular business area, call for an appointment, and then carefully present the case for the loan to the loan officer. Presenting a positive business image and following the established protocol are necessary to obtain a loan from a commercial bank.

Generally, the entrepreneur should borrow the maximum amount that can possibly be repaid as long as the prevailing interest rates and the terms, conditions, and restrictions of the loan are satisfactory. It is essential that the venture generate enough cash flow to repay the interest and principal on the loan in a timely manner. The entrepreneur should evaluate the track record and lending procedures of several banks to secure the money needed on the most favorable terms available. This "bank shopping procedure" will provide the needed funds at the most favorable rates.

ROLE OF THE SBA IN SMALL-BUSINESS FINANCING

Frequently, an entrepreneur is missing the necessary track record, assets, or some other ingredient to obtain a commercial bank loan. When the entrepreneur is unable to secure a regular commercial bank loan, an alternative is a guaranty from the Small Business Administration (SBA). The SBA offers numerous loan programs to assist small businesses. In each of these, the SBA is primarily a guarantor of loans made by private and other institutions. The Basic 7(a) Loan Guaranty is the SBA's primary business loan program. This program helps qualified small businesses obtain financing when they cannot obtain business loans through regular lending channels. The proceeds from such a loan can be used for a variety of business purposes, such as working capital; machinery and equipment; furniture and fixtures; land and building; leasehold improvements; and even, under some conditions, debt refinancing.

To get a 7(a) loan, the entrepreneur must be eligible. While repayment ability from the cash flow of the business is of course essential, other criteria include good character, management capability, collateral, and owner's equity contribution. Eligibility factors for all 7(a) loans include size, type of business, use of proceeds, and the availability of funds from other sources. All owners of 20 percent or more are required to personally guarantee SBA loans.

The SBA 7(a) loan program has a maximum loan amount of $5 million. In the case of a $5 million loan, the maximum guarantee to the lender by the SBA will be $3.75 million or 75 percent. Though the interest rates on the loan are negotiated between the borrower and the lender, they are subject to SBA maximums, which are pegged to the prime rate, the LIBOR rate, or an optional peg rate, and may be fixed or variable. For example, a fixed-rate loan of $50,000 or more must not exceed the base rate plus 2.25 percent if the maturity is less than seven years.

Most of the loans have the same guarantee features. The SBA can guarantee 85 percent of the loan for loans of $150,000 or less and 75 percent for loans between $150,000 and $5 million. Some differences occur in SBA Express loans (maximum guarantee of 50 percent) and export working capital loans (maximum guarantee of 90 percent). To help offset the costs of the SBA loan programs, lenders are charged a guaranty and servicing fee for each approved loan. These fees can be passed on to the borrower and vary depending on the amount of the loan.

In addition to the 7(a) loan program, the SBA has several other programs. The 504 loan program provides fixed-rate financing to enable small businesses to acquire machinery, equipment, or even real estate in order to expand or modernize. The maximum of the program is $5 million and $5.5 million for manufacturing and energy companies, and the loan can take a variety of forms, including a loan from a Community Development Company (CDC) backed by a 100 percent SBA-guaranteed debenture.

Another more recent SBA loan program that many entrepreneurs have used is the SBA Microloan, a 7(m) loan program. This program provides short-term loans of up to $50,000 to small businesses for working capital or the purchase of inventory, supplies, furniture, fixtures, machinery, or equipment. The loan cannot be used to pay existing debts. The small business receives the loan from a bank or other organization, with the loan being guaranteed in full by the SBA. Other specific SBA loans include: International Trade and Export Working Capital loans ($5 million maximum), Export Express loans ($500,000 maximum), and CDC/504 loans ($1.5 million maximum when meeting job creation criteria or $20 million maximum when meeting a public policy goal). The entrepreneur should check with the SBA to see whether a loan program is available, if a loan cannot be obtained without the SBA guarantee.

RESEARCH AND DEVELOPMENT LIMITED PARTNERSHIPS

research and development limited partnerships Money given to a firm for developing a technology that involves a tax shelter

Research and development limited partnerships are another possible source of funds for entrepreneurs in high-technology areas. This method of financing provides funds from investors looking for tax shelters. A typical R&D partnership arrangement involves a sponsoring company developing the technology with funds being provided by a limited partnership of individual investors. R&D limited partnerships are particularly good when the project involves a high degree of risk and significant expense in doing the basic research and development, since the risks, as well as the ensuing rewards, are shared.

Major Elements

The three major components of any R&D limited partnership are the contract, the sponsoring company, and the limited partnership. The contract specifies the agreement between the sponsoring company and the limited partnership, whereby the sponsoring company agrees to use the funds provided to conduct the proposed research and development that hopefully will result in a marketable technology for the partnership. The sponsoring company does not guarantee results but rather performs the work on a best-effort basis, being compensated by the partnership on either a fixed-fee or a cost-plus arrangement. The typical contract has several key features. The first is that the liability for any loss incurred is borne by the limited partners. Second, there are some tax advantages to both the limited partnership and the sponsoring company.

limited partner A party in a partnership agreement that usually supplies money and has a few responsibilities

The second component involved in this contract is the limited partners. Similar to the stockholders of a corporation, the *limited partners* have limited liability but are not a total taxable entity. Consequently, any tax benefits of the losses in the early stages of the R&D limited partnership are passed directly to the limited partners, offsetting other income and reducing the partners' total taxable incomes. When the technology is successfully developed in later years, the partners share in the profits. In some instances, these profits for tax purposes are at the lower capital gains tax rate as opposed to the ordinary income rate.

general partner The overall coordinating party in a partnership agreement

The final component, the sponsoring company, acts as the *general partner* developing the technology. The sponsoring company usually has the base technology but needs funds to further develop and modify it for commercial success. It is this base technology that the company is offering to the partnership in exchange for money. The sponsoring company usually retains the rights to use this base technology to develop other products and to use the developed technology in the future for a license fee. Sometimes, a cross-licensing agreement is established whereby the partnership allows the company to use the technology for developing other products.

Procedure

An R&D limited partnership generally progresses through three stages: the funding stage, the development stage, and the exit stage. In the funding stage, a contract is established between the sponsoring company and limited partners, and the money is invested for the proposed R&D effort. All the terms and conditions of ownership, as well as the scope of the research, are carefully documented.

In the development stage, the sponsoring company performs the actual research, using the funds from the limited partners. If the technology is subsequently successfully developed, the exit stage commences, in which the sponsoring company and the limited partners commercially reap the benefits of the effort. There are three basic types of arrangements for doing this: equity partnerships, royalty partnerships, and joint ventures.

In the typical equity partnership arrangement, the sponsoring company and the limited partners form a new, jointly owned corporation. On the basis of the formula established in the original agreement, the limited partners' interest can be transferred to equity in the new corporation on a tax-free basis. An alternative is to incorporate the R&D limited partnership itself and then either merge it into the sponsoring company or continue as a new entity.

A possible alternative to the equity partnership arrangement is a royalty partnership. In this situation, a royalty based on the sale of the products developed from the technology is paid by the sponsoring company to the R&D limited partnership. The royalty rates typically range from 6 to 10 percent of gross sales and often decrease at certain established sales levels. Frequently, an upper limit, or cap, is placed on the cumulative royalties paid.

A final exit arrangement is through a joint venture. Here the sponsoring company and the partners form a joint venture to manufacture and market the products developed from the technology. Usually, the agreement allows the company to buy out the partnership interest in the joint venture at a specified time or when a specified volume of sales and profit has been reached.

Benefits and Costs

As with any financing arrangement, the entrepreneur must carefully assess the appropriateness of establishing an R&D limited partnership in terms of the benefits and costs involved. Among the several benefits is that an R&D limited partnership provides the funds needed with a minimum amount of equity dilution while reducing the risks involved. In addition, the sponsoring company's financial statements are strengthened through the attraction of outside capital.

There are some costs involved in this financial arrangement. Typically, it is more expensive to establish than conventional financing. First, time and money are expended. An R&D limited partnership frequently takes a minimum of six months to establish and $50,000 in professional fees. These can increase to a year and $400,000 in costs for a major effort. And the track record is not as good, as most R&D limited partnerships are unsuccessful. Second, the restrictions placed on the technology can be substantial. To give up the technology developed as a by-product of the primary effort may be too high a price to pay for the funds. Third, the exit from the partnership may be too complex and involve too much fiduciary responsibility. These costs and benefits need to be evaluated in light of other financial alternatives available before an R&D limited partnership is chosen as the funding vehicle.

Examples

In spite of the many costs involved, there are numerous examples of successful R&D limited partnerships. Syntex Corporation raised $23.5 million in an R&D limited partnership to develop five medical diagnostic products. Genentech was so successful in developing human growth hormone and gamma interferon products from its first $55 million R&D limited partnership that it raised $32 million through a second partnership six months later to develop a tissue-type plasminogen activator. Trilogy Limited raised $55 million to develop a high-performance computer. And the list goes on. Indeed, R&D limited partnerships offer one financial alternative to fund the development of a venture's technology.

GOVERNMENT GRANTS

SBIR grants program
Grants from the U.S. government to small technology-based businesses

The entrepreneur can sometimes obtain federal grant money to develop and launch an innovative idea. The Small Business Innovation Research (SBIR) program, designed for the small business, was created as part of the Small Business Innovation Development Act. The act requires that all federal agencies with R&D budgets in excess of $100 million award a portion of their R&D funds to small businesses through the *SBIR grants program*. This act not only provides an opportunity for small businesses to obtain research and development money but also offers a uniform method by which each participating agency solicits, evaluates, and selects the research proposals for funding.

Eleven federal agencies are involved in the program (see Table 11.2). Each agency develops topics and publishes solicitations describing the R&D topic it will fund. Small businesses submit proposals directly to each agency using the required format, which is somewhat standardized, regardless of the agency. Each agency, using its established evaluation criteria, evaluates each proposal on a competitive basis and makes awards through a contract, grant, or cooperative agreement.

The SBIR grant program has three phases. Phase I awards are up to $100,000 for six months of feasibility-related experimental or theoretical research. The objective here is to determine the technical feasibility of the research effort and assess the quality of the company's performance through a relatively small monetary commitment. Successful projects are then considered for further federal funding support in Phase II.

Phase II is the principal R&D effort for those projects showing the most promise at the end of Phase I. Phase II awards are up to $750,000 for 24 months of further research and development. The money is to be used to develop prototype products or services. A small business receiving a Phase II award has demonstrated good research results in Phase I,

---

TABLE 11.2   Federal Agencies Participating in Small Business Innovation Research Program

- Department of Defense (DOD)
- National Aeronautics and Space Administration (NASA)
- Department of Energy (DOE)
- Department of Health and Human Services (DHHS)
- National Science Foundation (NSF)
- U.S. Department of Agriculture (USDA)
- Department of Transportation (DOT)
- Nuclear Regulatory Commission (NRC)
- Environmental Protection Agency (EPA)
- Department of Education (DOED)
- Department of Commerce (DOC)

DEVOTED EMPLOYEE BY DAY, ENTREPRENEUR BY NIGHT

To maintain a continuous source of income for living expenses as well as provide funding for a start-up company, many entrepreneurs choose to keep their day job during the early stages of their entrepreneurial venture. However, moonlighting, as this is commonly called, introduces complications that a successful entrepreneur must be cognizant of before starting a business after hours.

The first complication moonlighting entrepreneurs may encounter are noncompete agreements, employee policies, and contract clauses with their current employer that limit the entrepreneurial aspirations of the employee. Before starting any venture, an entrepreneur must read all policies and agreements with their employer to understand what limitations, if any, may apply to the entrepreneur's activities outside of normal work hours. Many employers have noncompete agreements that prevent the entrepreneur from marketing their products or services to their customers, possibly negating many of the valuable relationships and networks the entrepreneur built while working there. Another common limitation, especially in the technology industry, is employers who contractually retain the rights to all products and intellectual property developed by employees during and after normal work hours. In this situation, even if an employee develops a product or service that is unrelated to the business in which they are employed, their employer would retain all legal and intellectual property rights to that creation. To prevent issues in the future, it is advisable to review all employee policies and agreements closely before proceeding with your start-up activities.

The biggest and perhaps most stressful issue encountered by moonlighting entrepreneurs is time management, ensuring adequate time is allocated to both the day job and the start-up company. This can become especially tricky when the requirements of one's day job, start-up company, and social commitments conflict and the entrepreneur must determine where to spend the limited time available. Another potential source of conflict for the entrepreneur occurs when the day job requires additional time and focus, reducing the amount of time an entrepreneur can spend working on the start-up. Allocating more time to one's day job can occur for a short period of time with minimal impact; however, if extended over long periods of time, the resulting delay in start-up activities can be detrimental to the success of the venture. To properly maintain a balance between these competing interests, moonlighting entrepreneurs must have a great amount of focus, dedication, and perseverance.

Lastly, an entrepreneur must keep start-up activities completely separate from an employer's activities. A general rule of thumb for moonlighting entrepreneurs is to never discuss your start-up activities at the workplace. Although there will be individuals within the company who are supportive of your venture, word will quickly spread of your newfound passion and it may result in fellow employees and managers perceiving you as less committed to your job. In the worst-case scenario, this could result in termination. Also, while at work, entrepreneurs should work on entrepreneurial activities only during breaks or lunches and should never use the phones, computers, or printers of an employer for start-up activities as employers routinely track this usage and will know what was done using their equipment.

In the end, the ultimate goal of every moonlighting entrepreneur is to resign from the current employer and devote all available time and creative energy to the start-up company. Determining when is the right time to leave will depend on many factors and varies for every entrepreneur depending on financial situation and risk tolerance. Before submitting their resignation, entrepreneurs should have saved a minimum of six to nine months' wages as a buffer until the start-up company can begin paying a regular salary. Setting an exit goal, such as when sales reach $XXX, when total clients are XX, or by December 31, 20XX, and committing to leave one's job when that goal is obtained is an effective way for entrepreneurs to keep motivated and focused. Alas, when the day finally arrives for the entrepreneur to submit his or her resignation, it is still important to maintain good relations with the current employer and colleagues because one never knows when they may become your next big customer.

Source: For more information, see M. Goodman, "Boot-Strap Your Business," *Entrepreneur* (serial online) 39, no. 12 (December 2011), pp. 90–95.

developed a proposal of sound scientific and technical merit, and obtained a commitment for follow-on private-sector financing in Phase III for commercialization.

Phase III does not involve any direct funding from the SBIR program. Funds from the private sector or regular government procurement contracts are needed to commercialize the developed technologies in Phase III.

Procedure

Applying for an SBIR grant is a straightforward process. The government agencies participating (indicated in Table 11.2) publish solicitations describing the areas of research they will fund. Each of these annual solicitations contains documentation on the agency's R&D objectives, proposal format, due dates, deadlines, and selection and evaluation criteria. The second step involves the submission of the proposal by a company or individual. The proposal, which is 25 pages maximum, follows the standard proposal format. Each agency screens the proposals it receives. Knowledgeable scientists or engineers then evaluate those that pass the screening on a technological basis. Finally, awards are granted to those projects that have the best potential for commercialization. Any patent rights, research data, technical data, and software generated in the research are owned by the company or individual, not by the government.

The SBIR grant program is one viable method of obtaining funds for a technology-based entrepreneurial company that is independently owned and operated, employs 500 or fewer individuals, and has any organizational structure (corporation, partnership, sole proprietorship).

Another grant program available to the entrepreneur is the Small Business Technology Transfer (STTR) program, which was established by the Small Business Technology Transfer Act of 1992. Federal agencies with budgets over $1 billion are required to set aside 0.3 percent for small businesses. Five agencies participate in the STTR program—the Department of Defense (DOD), the Department of Energy (DOE), the Department of Health and Human Services (DHHS), the National Aeronautics and Space Administration (NASA), and the National Science Foundation (NSF). All these also participate in the SBIR program. While a comparison of the SBIR and STTR programs is found in Table 11.3, the two programs differ in two major ways: First, while in the SBIR program, the principal investigator must have his or her primary employment with the small business receiving the award. In contrast, for the duration of the project, there is no employment stipulation in the STTR program. Second, the STTR program requires research partners at universities or other nonprofit institutions, with at least 40 percent of the research conducted by the small business and at least 30 percent conducted by the partnering nonprofit institution. The SBIR program has a maximum of 33 percent [Phase I] and 50 percent [Phase II] in consulting costs. The procedure for obtaining an STTR award is the same as for the SBIR award.

Other Government Grants

There are other grants available to the entrepreneur at the federal, state, and local levels. These take many different forms and vary greatly depending on the objectives of the level of government involved and the geographic area. Sometimes the federal and some state governments provide training grants to companies locating in and/or hiring in what has been determined to be a labor surplus area. These training grants often take the form of paying 50 percent of the salary of the employee for up to the first year, at which time the employee should be fully productive. Companies locating in these areas often get some tax reductions at the state and federal levels for a period of time.

TABLE 11.3 Comparison of SBIR and STTR Programs

Requirements	SBIR	STTR
Applicant organization	Small-business concern (SBC)	Small-business concern (SBC)
Award period	Phase I—6 months, normally	Phase I—1 year, normally
	Phase II—2 years, normally	Phase II—2 years, normally
Award dollar guidelines	Phase I—$100,000, normally	Phase I—$100,000, normally
	Phase II—$750,000, normally	Phase II—$750,000, normally
Principal investigator (PI)	Employed by company more than 50% of her or his time *during award*.	Employment not stipulated.
	Minimum level of effort on the project not stipulated.	The PI must spend a minimum of 10% effort on the project and have a formal appointment with or commitment to the SBC.
Subcontract/consultant costs	Phase I—Total amount of contractual and consultant costs normally may not exceed 33% of total amount requested.	Phase I and Phase II—SBC must perform at least 40% of work, and the single, partnering U.S. nonprofit research institution (RI) must perform at least 30% of the work.
	Phase II—Total amount of contractual and consultant costs normally may not exceed 50% of total amount requested.	
Performance site	Must be entirely in United States.	Must be entirely in United States.
	Part of research must take place in company-controlled research space.	Part of research must take place in company-controlled research space and part in that of partnering U.S. research institution.

Many of the states and cities in the United States also have grant incentive programs for developing technology and technology companies located in the particular state and/or providing jobs in labor surplus areas. Often in terms of locating or building a facility in the state or city, these incentives take the form of a tax reduction for a period of time.

Grants are also available in many countries and cities throughout the world. The entrepreneur should investigate all possible grants available, particularly in deciding where to locate his or her company. For example, Vienna (Austria) has a grant program for entrepreneurs locating in the city.

PRIVATE PLACEMENT

Another source of funds for the entrepreneur is private investors, also called angels, who may be family and friends or wealthy individuals. Individuals who handle their own sizable investments frequently use advisors such as accountants, technical experts, financial planners, or lawyers in making their investment decisions. Business angels are discussed in more detail in Chapter 12.

Types of Investors

An investor usually takes an equity position in the company, can influence the nature and direction of the business to some extent, and may even be involved to some degree in the business operation. The degree of involvement in the day-to-day operations of the venture is an important point for the entrepreneur to consider in selecting an investor. Some investors want to be actively involved in the business; others desire at least an advisory role in the direction and operation of the venture. Still others are more passive in nature, desiring no active involvement in the venture at all. Each investor is primarily interested in recovering his or her investment plus a good rate of return.

Private Offerings

private offering A formalized method for obtaining funds from private investors

A formalized approach for obtaining funds from private investors is through a *private offering*. A private offering is different from a public offering or going public (as discussed in Chapter 12) in several ways. Public offerings involve a great deal of time and expense, in large part due to the numerous regulations and requirements involved. The process of registering the securities with the Securities and Exchange Commission (SEC) is an arduous task requiring a significant number of reporting procedures once the firm has gone public. Since this process was established primarily to protect unsophisticated investors, a private offering is faster and less costly when a limited number of sophisticated investors are involved who have the necessary business acumen and ability to absorb risk. These sophisticated investors still need access to material information about the company and its management. What constitutes material information? Who is a sophisticated investor? How many is a limited number? Answers to these questions are provided in Regulation D.

Regulation D

Regulation D Laws governing a private offering

Regulation D contains (1) broad provisions designed to simplify private offerings, (2) general definitions of what constitutes a private offering, and (3) specific operating rules—Rule 504, Rule 505, and Rule 506. Regulation D requires the issuer of a private offering to file five copies of Form D with the Securities and Exchange Commission (SEC) 15 days after the first sale, every 6 months thereafter, and 30 days after the final sale. It also provides rules governing the notices of sale and the payment of any commissions involved.

The entrepreneur issuing the private offering carries the burden of proving that the exemptions granted have been met. This involves completing the necessary documentation on the degree of sophistication of each potential investor. Each offering memorandum presented to an investor needs to be numbered and must contain instructions that the document should not be reproduced or disclosed to any other individual. The date that the investor (or the designated representative) reviews the company's information—that is, its books and records—as well as the date(s) of any discussion between the company and the investor need to be recorded. At the close of the offering, the offering company needs to verify and note that no persons other than those recorded were contacted regarding the offering. The book documenting all the specifics of the offering needs to be placed in the company's permanent file. The general procedures of Regulation D are further broadened by the three rules—504, 505, and 506. Rule 504 provides the first exemption to a company seeking to raise a small amount of capital from numerous investors. Under Rule 504, a company can sell up to $500,000 of securities to any number of investors, regardless of their sophistication, in any 12-month period. While there is no specific form of disclosure required, the issuing company cannot engage in any general solicitation or advertising. Some states do not allow investors to resell their shares unless the security is registered.

Rule 505 changes both the investors and the dollar amount of the offering. This rule permits the sale of $5 million of unregistered securities in the private offering in any 12-month period. These securities can be sold to any 35 investors and to an unlimited number of accredited investors. This eliminates the need for the sophistication test and disclosure requirements called for by Rule 504. What constitutes an "accredited investor"? Accredited investors include (1) institutional investors, like banks, insurance companies, investment companies, employee benefit plans containing over $5 million in assets, tax-exempt organizations with endowment funds of over $25 million, and private business development companies; (2) investors who purchase over $150,000 of the issuer's securities; (3) investors whose net worth is $1 million or more at the time of sale; (4) investors with incomes in excess of $200,000 in each of the last two years; and (5) directors, executive officers, and general partners of the issuing company.

Like Rule 504, Rule 505 permits no general advertising or solicitation through public media. When only accredited investors are involved, no disclosure is required under Rule 505 (similar to the issuance under Rule 504). However, if the issuance involves any unaccredited investors, additional information must be disclosed. Regardless of the amount of the offering, two-year financial statements for the two most recent years must be available unless such a disclosure requires "undue effort and expense." When this occurs for any issuing company other than a limited partnership, a balance sheet as of 120 days before the offering can be used instead. All companies selling private-placement securities to both accredited and unaccredited investors must furnish appropriate company information to both and allow any questions to be asked before the sale. Rule 506 goes one step further than Rule 505 by allowing an issuing company to sell an unlimited number of securities to 35 investors and an unlimited number of accredited investors and relatives of issuers. Still, no general advertising or solicitation through public media can be involved.

In securing any outside funding, the entrepreneur must take great care to disclose all information accurately. Investors generally have no problem with the company as long as its operations continue successfully and this success is reflected in an increase in valuation. But if the business turns sour, both investors and regulators scrutinize the company's disclosures in minute detail to determine if any technical or securities law violations occurred. When any violation of securities law is discovered, management and sometimes the company's principal equity holders can be held liable as a corporation and as individuals. When this occurs, the individual is no longer shielded by the corporation and is open to significant liability and potential lawsuits. Lawsuits under securities law by damaged investors have almost no statute of limitations, as the time does not begin until the person harmed discovers or should reasonably be expected to discover the improper disclosure. The suit may be brought in federal court in any jurisdiction in which the defendant is found or lives or transacts business. An individual can file suit as a single plaintiff or as a class action on behalf of all persons similarly affected. Courts have awarded large attorney's fees as well as settlements when any securities law violation occurs. Given the number of lawsuits and the litigious nature of U.S. society, the entrepreneur needs to be extremely careful to make sure that any and all disclosures are accurate. If this is not enough of an incentive, it should be kept in mind that the SEC can take administrative, civil, or criminal action as well, without any individual lawsuit involved. This action can result in fines, imprisonment, or the restoration of the monies involved.

BOOTSTRAP FINANCING

One alternative to acquiring outside capital that should be considered is bootstrap financing.[3] This approach is particularly important at start-up and in the early years of the venture when capital from debt financing (i.e., in terms of higher interest rates) or from equity financing (i.e., in terms of loss of ownership) is more expensive.

In addition to the monetary costs, outside capital has other costs as well. First, it usually takes between three and six months to raise outside capital or to find out that there is no outside capital available. During this time, the entrepreneur may not be paying enough attention to the important areas of marketing, sales, product development, and operating costs. A business usually needs capital when it can least afford the time to raise it. One company's CEO spent so much time raising capital that sales and marketing were neglected to such an extent that the forecasted sales and profit figures on the pro forma income statements were not met for the first three years after the capital infusion. This led to investor concern and irritation that, in turn, required more of the CEO's time.

Second, outside capital often decreases a firm's drive for sales and profits. One successful manager would never hire a person as one of his commission salespeople if he or she "looked too prosperous." He felt that if a person was not hungry, he or she would not push hard to sell. The same concept could apply to outside funded companies that may have the tendency to substitute outside capital for income.

Third, the availability of capital increases the impulse to spend. It can cause a company to hire more staff before they are needed and to move into more costly facilities. A company can easily forget the basic axiom of venture creation: staying lean and mean.

Fourth, outside capital can decrease the company's flexibility. This can hamper the direction, drive, and creativity of the entrepreneur. Unsophisticated investors are particularly a problem as they often object to a company's moving away from the focus and direction outlined in the business plan that attracted their investment. This attitude can encumber a company to such an extent that the needed change cannot be implemented or else is implemented very slowly after a great deal of time and effort has been spent in consensus building. This can substantially demoralize the entrepreneur who likes the freedom of not working for someone else.

Finally, outside capital may cause disruption and problems in the venture. Capital is not provided without the expectation of a return, sometimes before the business should be giving one. Also, particularly if certain equity investors are involved, the entrepreneur is under pressure to continuously grow the company so that an initial public offering can occur as soon as possible. This emphasis on short-term performance can be at the expense of the long-term success of the company.

Bootstrap financing involves using any possible method for conserving cash. While some entrepreneurs can take advantage of any supplier discounts available, entrepreneurs with restricted cash flow need to take as long as possible to pay without incurring interest or late payment fees or being cut off from any future items from the supplier. The entrepreneur should always ask about discounts for volume, frequent customer discounts, promotional discounts for featuring the vendor's product, and even "obsolescence money," which allows for upgrading to an enhanced product at no additional cost.

Savings can also be obtained by asking for bulk packaging instead of paying more for individually wrapped items as well as using co-op advertising with a channel member so that the cost of the advertisement is shared.

Consignment financing can also be used to help conserve cash. Some vendors allow entrepreneurs to place a standing order for the entire amount of goods to be used over a period of time but take shipment and make payment only as needed, therefore securing the lower price of a larger order without having to carry the cost of the inventory. These are just some examples. The only possible limitation in bootstrap financing is the imagination of the entrepreneur.

Most every entrepreneur at times needs some capital to finance growth, which would be too slow or nonexistent if internal sources of funds were used. Outside capital should be sought only after all possible internal sources of funds have been explored. And when outside funds are needed and obtained, the entrepreneur should not forget to stay intimately involved with the basics of the business.

IN REVIEW

SUMMARY

Every business venture requires capital. While capital is needed throughout the life of a business, an entrepreneur faces significant difficulties in acquiring capital at start-up. Before seeking outside financing, an entrepreneur should first explore all methods of internal financing, such as using profits, selling unused assets, reducing working capital, obtaining credit from suppliers, and collecting accounts receivable promptly. After all internal sources have been exhausted, the entrepreneur may find it necessary to seek funds through external financing. External financing can be in the form of debt or equity. When considering external financing, the entrepreneur needs to consider the length of time, cost, and amount of control of each alternative financial arrangement.

Commercial bank loans are the most frequently used source of short-term external debt financing. This source of funding requires collateral, which may be asset-based or may take the form of cash flow financing. In either case, banks tend to be cautious about lending and carefully weigh the five Cs: character, capacity, capital, collateral, and condition. Not every entrepreneur will qualify under the bank's careful scrutiny. When this occurs, an alternative for an entrepreneur is the Small Business Administration Guaranty Loan. The SBA guarantees a percentage of the loan, allowing banks to lend money to businesses that might otherwise be refused.

A special method of raising capital for high-technology firms is a research and development (R&D) limited partnership. A contract is formed between a sponsoring company and a limited partnership. The partnership bears the risk of the research, receiving some tax advantages and sharing in future profits, including a fee to use the research in developing any future products. The entrepreneur has the advantage of acquiring needed funds for a minimum amount of equity dilution while reducing his or her own risk in the venture.

Government grants are another alternative available to small businesses through the Small Business Innovation Research (SBIR) program. Businesses can apply for grants from 11 agencies. Other federal, state, and local (city) grants are often available.

Finally, the entrepreneur can seek private funding. Individual investors frequently require an equity position in the company and some degree of control. A less expensive and less complicated alternative to a public offering of stock is a private offering. By following the procedures of Regulation D and three of its specific rules—504, 505, and 506—an entrepreneur can sell private securities. When making a private offering, the entrepreneur must exercise care in accurately disclosing information and adhering precisely to the requirements of the SEC. Securities violations can lead to lawsuits against individuals as well as the corporation.

The entrepreneur needs to consider all possible sources of capital and select the one that will provide the needed funds with minimal cost and loss of control. Usually, different sources of funds are used at various stages in the growth and development of the venture, as occurred in the case of Scott Walker, a successful entrepreneur indeed.

RESEARCH TASKS

1. Interview a business loan officer at a bank to determine the bank's lending criteria for small businesses and new businesses. Does it use the five Cs? Which of the five Cs appears to be the most important?

2. Obtain a loan application from the local bank and categorize each question in terms of which of the five Cs it is attempting to assess.

3. Choose a type of business you would like to run. Then search the Internet for government grants that might be applicable for you and your business.

4. Interview three small-business owners about things they do (or have done) to bootstrap the financing of their business. How effective were these techniques? Be prepared to present this list to the class and describe how the techniques work.

CLASS DISCUSSION

1. What is the cheapest source of funds? When all other sources turn down your request for funding, what source is most likely to say yes? Why is this the case? Is the entrepreneur exploiting a personal relationship with this potential source of capital? What are the consequences of using this source of capital if the business goes bankrupt?

2. Should the government provide grants for entrepreneurs starting new businesses? Should the government guarantee loans for small businesses that are missing the necessary track record, assets, or other ingredients to obtain a commercial bank loan? What benefit do we, as a nation of taxpayers, receive from such grants and loan guarantees?

3. Why don't all firms use bootstrap financing? Are there any dangers with this approach? What are the benefits of having some financial slack (e.g., some extra cash in reserve)? What are the costs of that financial slack?

SELECTED READINGS

Anonymous. (April 2010). The New Face of Venture Capital: Family Offices. *Institutional Investor*, n/a.

This article discusses the absence of venture capital in the economy and the increase in investments in start-up organizations by family offices. The author highlights industries that are especially attractive to family offices; these include technology that contributes to society, investing in mature start-ups, and investing in established products (instead of concepts).

DeBaise, Colleen. (June 2, 2011). Seeking Venture Capital. *Wall Street Journal*.

The author discusses the pros and cons of funding a business with venture capital. She emphasizes the active participation of venture capital investors in the companies they invest in, which can include operations and active board participation. She also discusses the increasing challenge of obtaining venture capital–backed financing in the current economy.

Farrell, Christopher. (April 28, 2008). How Angel Investors Get Their Wings. *BusinessWeek*, no. 112.

Angel investors invest in promising start-ups too young and raw to attract the attention and money of professional venture capitalists. The credit crunch and economic downturn have some angels feeling skittish. But others see opportunity. Studies show that the best time to start a business is when the economy is down. That's because entrepreneurs with good ideas will find cheaper land, labor, supplier contracts, and other ingredients that go into starting a business. Angels who back such ventures can earn impressive long-term returns—one study cites a rate of return of about 27 percent, on average, or 2.6 times the investment in 3.5 years. The risks, of course, are steep. Still, 258,200 angels pumped $26 billion into 57,120 ventures last *year, according to the University of New Hampshire's Center for Venture Research. While many angels are current or former entrepreneurs, and that background can prove invaluable, they also need to develop investing skills.*

Gimmon, Eli. (2008). Entrepreneurial Team-starts and Teamwork: Taking the Investors' Perspective. *Team Performance Management*, vol. 14, no. 7/8, pp. 327–39.

This article includes the results of a research project, which evaluates the importance of entrepreneurial teamwork in venture capitalists' decisions to fund a venture. The entrepreneurial teams examined in this research are exclusively involved in high-technology pursuits, such as information technology and electronics. The author of this research is an Israeli business professor who bases his hypothesis on previous evidence that teamwork has a favorable effect on the success of entrepreneurial undertakings. The author's conclusions examine the habits of venture capitalists and angel investors from different geographical regions: U.S. investors, for example, do not value entrepreneurial teamwork as much as do British and Israeli investors.

Mehrotra, Devi. (Winter 2011). Financing New Businesses. *Yale Economic Review*, vol. 7, pp. 14–17.

The author discusses the Kauffman Firm Survey (KFS) which tracks start-up firm financing over several years beginning with year one. The survey authors, Alicia M. Robb and David T. Robinson, describe a financing pyramid that summarizes their results. Firm owners first secure outside debt, then owner equity, and lastly debt from outsiders. Their findings differ from earlier published research.

Westerman, James W.; Scott W. Geiger; and Linda A. Cyr. (December 2008). Employee Equity Incentives and Venture Capitalist Involvement: Examining the Effects on IPO Performance. *Journal of Developmental Entrepreneurship,* vol. 13, no. 4, pp. 409–23.

Many times entrepreneurs are hesitant to operate within the confines of other people's money. While the additional influx of cash is often welcome, seasoned entrepreneurs realize these handouts come at a price: independence. This article, for such naysayers, offers proof that accepting venture capital funding can ensure the success of a business, should it choose to go public. Also, the employees of these potential initial public offering firms are in better stead if their company has received venture capital funding.

Yallapragada, RamMohan R.; and Mohammad Bhuiyan. (November/December 2011). Small Business Entrepreneurships in the U.S. *Journal of Applied Business Research*, vol. 27, pp. 117–22.

The authors examine the importance of small business entrepreneurs to the U.S. economy and the factors that contribute to the success of these businesses. The article concludes with a discussion of financing options for small businesses, including SBA loans and micro-financing.

END NOTES

1. Crystal Detamore-Rodman, "Cash In, Cash Out," *Entrepreneur* (June 2003), pp. 53–54.
2. For a discussion of bank lending decisions, see A. D. Jankowicz and R. D. Hisrich, "Intuition in Small Business Lending Decisions," *Journal of Small Business Management* (July 1987), pp. 45–52; N. C. Churchill and V. L. Lewis, "Bank Lending to New and Growing Enterprises," *Journal of Business Venturing* (Spring 1986), pp. 193–206; R. T. Justis, "Starting a Small Business: An Investigation of the Borrowing Procedure," *Journal of Small Business Management* (October 1982), pp. 22–32; and L. Fertuck, "Survey of Small Business Lending Practices," *Journal of Small Business Management* (October 1982), pp. 42–48.
3. Bootstrap financing is discussed in Anne Murphy, "Capital Punishment," *Inc.* (November 1993), pp. 38–42; and Michael P. Cronin, "Paradise Lost," *Inc.* (November 1993), pp. 48–53.

12

INFORMAL RISK CAPITAL, VENTURE CAPITAL, AND GOING PUBLIC

LEARNING OBJECTIVES

1

To explain the basic stages of venture funding.

2

To discuss the informal risk-capital market.

3

To discuss the nature of the venture-capital industry
and the venture-capital decision process.

4

To explain all aspects of valuing a company.

5

To identify several valuation approaches.

6

To explain the process of going public.

OPENING PROFILE

RICHARD BRANSON

More emperor than CEO, Richard Branson with his Virgin Group empire has taken the world by storm as one of the most successful, enlightened, and outrageous entrepreneurs in the world today. Virgin Group has competed head to head with the biggest players in an impressive array of industries across the world for four decades. Led by

Sir Richard Branson (knighted for "services in entrepreneurship" on December 31, 1999), what started as a nearly failed magazine company has now evolved into over 200 businesses in over 30 countries.[1] According to the 2011 *Forbes* list of billionaires, Branson is worth about £2.58 billion (US$4.2 billion), making him the fifth richest person in the UK and 254th in the world.[2] What is his secret to success? Some would say his savvy business acumen, others his passion for life, still others his spectacular marketing ploys. What is certain is that Richard Branson's entrepreneurial spirit and enthusiastic optimism is virulent, affecting everyone with whom he comes in contact. Be it flying around the world in a hot air balloon or competing against the big three airline alliances as a start-up, Branson's spice for life and risk-taking behavior have made him a favorite corporate figure within the business community.

As all aspiring and failed entrepreneurs want to know from those who have succeeded, Branson's success story is true to his reputation as a nonconformist rebel. He was a poor student, not knowing until much later in life that part of his trouble in school was due to dyslexia. At the age of 16, he dropped out of his prep school to form a magazine called *Student*. It is reported that, informed of Branson's intentions to leave the school, the headmaster wrote him a note saying, "Congratulations, Branson. I predict you will either go to prison or become a millionaire."[3] How was he to know that *billionaire* would be more apropos?

Student magazine was not a profitable venture, although it did give its founder some credibility as a professional. Propelled by the anti-authoritarian sentiment that was pervasive among young adults in the late 60s, Branson convinced well-known celebrities such as Norman Mailer, Jean-Paul Sartre, and James Baldwin to contribute articles to his magazine about irreverent topics that mainstream magazines would not touch, a theme that would continue to characterize his career.[4] On the brink of financial failure, Branson came up with the idea to sell music records via mail order at a slightly discounted price, advertising the service in his already-circulating magazine. Thus, Virgin Records was born, allegedly named for the company staff's lack of commercial knowledge and experience as well as the compulsory shock value. The first retail store was opened on London's Oxford Street in 1971.

Virgin Records experienced early success as the first business of its kind with a direct focus on the 18–25-year-old sector. However, it was their expansion into record publishing that sealed the fate of Virgin as a thriving business. Branson signed Mike Oldfield to the label and together they released *Tubular Bells*, an instrumental piece that became an instant classic and put Virgin Records on the map. Following his intuition rather than popular opinion, Branson continued to sign artists to his record label that the more conventional companies would not consider due to irreverent content or behavior. Signing the Sex Pistols, who had previously been dropped from two major labels as a PR nightmare, skyrocketed Virgin Records to being the largest independent record label with a cadre of superstars including UB40, the Rolling Stones, and Paula Abdul.[5]

With Virgin Records earning revenues just shy of £50 million in 1983, Branson's entrepreneurial spirit got the best of him and he embarked on the greatest challenge of his career: Virgin Atlantic. Although lucrative, the airline industry is extremely risky and capital-intensive, not to mention it is monopolized by three powerful worldwide alliances. Undeterred by naysayers, Branson pursued the endeavor with the goal of creating an airline that focused on the customer rather than the bottom line, offering a multitude of amenities along with lower fares. Initial success faltered once the 90s hit with economic turmoil, spiking gas prices, and terrorism stifling the tourism industry. In order to keep the airline afloat, Branson was forced to sell Virgin Records for a highly inflated price (nearly $1 billion) to Thorn-EMI in 1992.[6] Selling his music company, the cherished cornerstone of his career, devastated Branson and he realized that being a prisoner to lenders would no longer be an option in his entrepreneurial pursuits.

Since Virgin's inception, the serial entrepreneur has expanded into a multitude of diverse industries including mobile phones, dot-coms, air and rail transportation, finance, retail, hotels and leisure, and radio. The strategy seems haphazard at best, absent at worst. What exactly is Virgin Group? Conglomerate? Incubator? A brand name licensed out to franchisees? The answer to all these questions is . . . yes. Branson has coined a new term to describe his empire as a "branded venture capital organization." He defines the hybrid business model as such: "We invest, along with a range of different institutional and trade partners, in a wide range of businesses that either share or have the prospect of sharing common brand values."[7] Balking at formal lending practices after the sale of his treasured music business, Branson decided to leverage the brand name he had built instead. In return for liquid capital from wealthy investors, Branson licenses the use of the Virgin name and maintains a controlling share of the company. In this manner, Branson has bought interest in more than 200 companies spanning the globe, with the goal of making Virgin one of the top 20 global brands in the world.

How did the Virgin name gain so much value as a brand? Branson cites two specific instances: the music business and Megastore concept that created a youthful image as it reached out to the Indy crowd in the late 70s, and Virgin Atlantic whose consumer focus created a reputation for quality, value, innovation, and fun. Taking Branson out of the equation is perhaps a compelling argument and one that could be duplicated by others. However, Branson is not exactly the run-of-the-mill CEO who like a puppeteer overlooks the empire he has built from behind a desk. Since *Student* magazine, Branson has been his own CMO, PR officer, and Director of Sales wrapped into one. A self-proclaimed "adventure capitalist," his many antics over the last few decades have turned heads and brought attention to himself and his business.

After making headlines for pushing the envelope with Virgin Records, he became obsessed with the goal of beating the record for crossing the Atlantic by boat. After his first attempt sank (literally) in 1985, he tried again the next year and won. Then Prime Minister Margaret Thatcher personally congratulated him on his feat. He then attempted the same sea crossing, but this time in a hot air balloon. Three attempts to circumnavigate the globe in that same balloon have failed, but won him headlines nonetheless. In addition to his aeronautical exploits, he writes his own blog, has hosted a reality TV show, appeared on an episode of *Baywatch*, and is a frequent columnist for *Entrepreneur* magazine among other media.[8] His most recent adventure challenge is commercial flight to the moon. Virgin Galactic is due to send its first passengers into outer space within the next couple of years. Tickets cost only $200,000 per person.[9]

Richard Branson's rock star image has ballooned him to celebrity status in recent years. Luxury goods companies are now hiring him to become the face of their products. As any celebrity, he gets paid well just by showing up to give a speech (about $300,000 per appearance according to one article in *Forbes*). However, unlike others whose fame and fortune morphed into lavish eccentricity, Branson's fortune has seemed to bring him more firmly down to earth. In 2005, the Virgin Group added a nonprofit foundation called Virgin Unite with the stated mission to help revolutionize the way that governments, businesses, and the social sector work together, driving business as a force for good.[10] Branson has indicated through both statement and action that entrepreneurship is a tool that can be used to better the world, especially in underdeveloped countries. He has also created the Branson Centre of Entrepreneurship, currently with two main regional focuses in South Africa and the Caribbean. Building on the idea of "business for good," the Centre helps local entrepreneurs to start, manage, and build their businesses with the goal of stimulating the local economies. On his role as business icon, Branson states, "Having become a global figure, you have responsibility to not waste it. It means I can set up organizations like the Ocean Elders or the Carbon War Room or the CDC in Africa using my entrepreneurial skills and financial resources to do so. If you put your celebrity status to good use, you can make a big difference."[11]

Although he does not have any formal credentials from educational institutions, Branson's seemingly limitless success makes budding entrepreneurs curious about his methods. In 2010, he wrote an article outlining his five secrets to success in *Entrepreneur* magazine, namely: (1) enjoy what you are doing, (2) create something that stands out, (3) create something that everybody who works for you is really proud of, (4) be a good leader, and (5) be visible.[12] Anyone would be hard-pressed to find examples where he has not taken his own advice. As exemplified in nearly every venture, Branson takes a decidedly people-centric approach to business. Making people happy, be they employees, customers, or beneficiaries of social initiatives, is the essence of his business strategy. A true entrepreneur, each day presents new ideas and challenges for Branson, and he enthusiastically accepts them with open arms. He has the world on the edge of their seats waiting to see what he will do next.

FINANCING THE BUSINESS

In evaluating the appropriateness of financing alternatives, particularly angel versus venture-capital financing, an entrepreneur must determine the amount and the timing of the funds required, as well as the projected company sales and growth. Conventional small businesses and privately held middle-market companies tend to have a difficult time obtaining external equity capital, especially from the venture-capital industry. Most venture capitalists like to invest in software, biotechnology, or high-potential ventures like the numerous ones of Richard Branson or Mark Zuckerberg's Facebook. The three types of funding as the business develops are indicated in Table 12.1. The funding problems, as well as the cost of the funds, differ for each type. *Early-stage financing* is usually the most difficult and costly to obtain. Two types of financing are available during this stage: seed capital and start-up capital. Seed capital, the most difficult financing to obtain through outside funds, is usually a relatively small amount of funds needed to prove concepts and

early-stage financing
One of the first financings obtained by a company

TABLE 12.1 Stages of Business Development Funding

Early-Stage Financing

• Seed capital	Relatively small amounts to prove concepts and finance feasibility studies
• Start-up	Product development and initial marketing, but with no commercial sales yet; funding to actually get company operations started

Expansion or Development Financing

• Second stage	Working capital for initial growth phase, but no clear profitability or cash flow yet
• Third stage	Major expansion for company with rapid sales growth; company is at breakeven or positive profit levels but is still private
• Fourth stage	Bridge financing to prepare company for public offering

Acquisition and Leveraged Buyout Financing

• Traditional acquisitions	Assuming ownership and control of another company
• Leveraged buyouts (LBOs)	Management of a company acquiring company control by buying out the present owners
• Going private	Some of the owners/managers of a company buying all the outstanding stock, making the company privately held again

finance feasibility studies. Since venture capitalists usually have a minimum funding level of above $500,000, they are rarely involved in this type of funding, except in the case of high-technology ventures of entrepreneurs who have a successful track record and need a significant amount of capital. The second type of funding is start-up financing. As the name implies, start-up financing is involved in developing and selling some initial products to determine if commercial sales are feasible. These funds are also difficult to obtain. Angel investors are active in these two types of financing.

development financing
Financing to rapidly expand the business

Expansion or *development financing* (the second basic financing type) is easier to obtain than early-stage financing. Venture capitalists play an active role in providing funds at this stage. As the firm develops in each stage, the funds for expansion are less costly. Generally, funds in the second stage are used as working capital to support initial growth. In the third stage, the company is at breakeven or a positive profit level and uses the funds for major sales expansion. Funds in the fourth stage are usually used as bridge financing in the interim period as the company prepares to go public.

acquisition financing
Financing to buy another company

Acquisition financing or leveraged buyout financing (the third type) is more specific in nature. It is issued for such activities as traditional acquisitions, leveraged buyouts (management buying out the present owners), and going private (a publicly held firm buying out existing stockholders, thereby becoming a private company).

risk-capital markets
Markets providing debt and equity to nonsecure financing situations

informal risk-capital market   Area of risk-capital markets consisting mainly of individuals

venture-capital market
One of the risk-capital markets consisting of formal firms

public-equity market
One of the risk-capital markets consisting of publicly owned stocks of companies

business angels   A name for individuals in the informal risk-capital market

There are three *risk-capital markets* that can be involved in financing a firm's growth: the *informal risk-capital market,* the *venture-capital market*, and the *public-equity market*. Although all three risk-capital markets can be a source of funds for stage-one financing, the public-equity market is available only for high-potential ventures, particularly when high technology is involved. Recently, some biotechnology companies raised their first-stage financing through the public-equity market; investors were excited about the potential prospects and returns in this high-interest area. This has also occurred in the areas of oceanography and fuel alternatives when there was a high level of interest. Although venture-capital firms also provide some first-stage funding, the venture must require the minimum level of capital. This can be anywhere from $500,000 to $3 million depending on the firm. A venture-capital company establishes this minimum level of investment due to the high costs in evaluating and monitoring a deal. By far the best source of funds for first-stage financing is the informal risk-capital market—the third type of risk-capital market.

INFORMAL RISK-CAPITAL MARKET

The informal risk-capital market is the most misunderstood type of risk capital. It consists of a virtually invisible group of wealthy investors, often called *business angels,* who are looking for equity-type investment opportunities in a wide variety of entrepreneurial ventures. Typically investing anywhere from $10,000 to $500,000, these angels provide the funds needed in all stages of financing, but particularly in start-up (first-stage) financing. Firms funded from the informal risk-capital market frequently raise second- and third-round financing from professional venture-capital firms or the public-equity market.

Despite being invisible to many entrepreneurs, the informal investment market contains the largest pool of risk capital in the United States. Although there is no verification of the size of this pool or the total amount of financing provided by these business angels, related statistics provide some indication. A 1980 survey of a sample of issuers of private placements by corporations, reported to the Securities and Exchange Commission under Rule 146, found that 87 percent of those buying these issues were individual investors or personal trusts, investing an average of $74,000.[13] Private placements filed under Rule 145 average over $1 billion per year. Another indication becomes apparent on examination of the filings

AS SEEN IN *BUSINESS NEWS*

ANGELLIST—THE FUTURE OF INVESTING?

AngelList is a free service used by start-up companies and investors to raise capital in a quick and efficient manner. With more than 7,600 introductions made before June 2011, this online tool has linked over 800 start-up companies directly to more than 1,200 potential angel investors. Historically, obtaining funding from angel investors was a long and tedious process for entrepreneurs that often required multiple introductions within their investment network before they found an investor who was truly interested in their start-up, and even then it was not guaranteed that funding would be obtained. From an angel investor's perspective, this informal network of connecting start-up companies with investors was equally frustrating and time consuming. Many investors voiced frustration at the process of attending meetings where the investor knew within minutes they were not interested in the start-up company, wasting the time and efforts of the investor as well as the entrepreneur. AngelList solves these issues for both entrepreneurs and investors by cutting out the middleman and allowing investors and entrepreneurs to interact directly.

AngelList functions like a marketplace (similar to Craig's List) to connect and introduce the two groups. To start the process, entrepreneurs submit their business plans and company information to AngelList. AngelList employees sort through these applications and select the top 5 percent based on their growth potential, the existence of a known angel investor or founder, or based on an endorsement from a known advisor or colleague. These applications are then forwarded to investors interested and experienced in the industry of the start-up company. Investors review the company profiles sent to them by AngelList and contact the entrepreneurs directly if they are interested in the company. Similar to entrepreneurs, investors are added to the site through a selection process. All AngelList investors are required to have at least one investment in the last year, prove they are a real person, and publicly list past investments. Investors who get in initially and are later determined not to be at par or do not make an investment in the subsequent 12 months are removed from the site. This process keeps investors active and prevents them from becoming silent observers, only involved with the website to monitor market trends and see what is up-and-coming in their industry.

The obvious and primary benefit of AngelList is the significant reduction in time for a start-up to find investors and secure funding, reducing what has historically taken many months to just a few weeks or, in some cases, only days. This significant reduction in time allows companies to move quicker, bringing their products to market faster than ever before. As a start-up company shows growth, they can raise additional angel funds through AngelList or move into the venture capital arena to continue expanding. As the popularity of AngelList grows, the capital investment process is changing with angel funding (typically $1 million or less) replacing the more traditional first round of funding from venture capital. The continually expanding network of entrepreneurs and investors from around the world is also creating new and exciting funding opportunities in places that have traditionally had less access to angel investors. With the streamlined, efficient, and worldwide access to capital that AngelList is creating, the future of angel investing will be changed forever.

Source: For more information, see T. Geron, "AngelList Takes Angel Investing to Warp Speed," *Forbes.com* (serial online), June 20, 2011, p. 3.

under Regulation D—the regulation exempting certain private and limited offerings from the registration requirements of the Securities Act of 1933, discussed in Chapter 11. In its first year, over 7,200 filings, worth $15.5 billion, were made under Regulation D. Corporations accounted for 43 percent of the value ($6.7 billion), or 32 percent of the total number of offerings (2,304). Corporations filing limited offerings (under $500,000) raised $220 million, an average of $200,000 per firm. The typical corporate issuers tended to be small, with fewer than 10 stockholders, revenues and assets less than $500,000, stockholders' equity of $50,000 or less, and five or fewer employees.[14]

Similar results were found in an examination of the funds raised by small technology-based firms prior to their initial public offerings. The study revealed that unaffiliated individuals (the informal investment market) accounted for 15 percent of these funds, while venture capitalists accounted for only 12 to 15 percent. During the start-up year, unaffiliated individuals provided 17 percent of the external capital.[15]

A study of angels in New England again yielded similar results. The 133 individual investors studied reported risk-capital investments totaling over $16 million in 320 ventures between 1976 and 1980. These investors averaged one deal every two years, with an average size of $50,000. Although 36 percent of these investments averaged less than $10,000, 24 percent averaged over $50,000. While 40 percent of these investments were start-ups, 80 percent involved ventures less than five years old.[16]

The size and number of these investors have increased dramatically, due in part to the rapid accumulation of wealth in various sectors of the economy. One study of consumer finances found that the net worth of 1.3 million U.S. families was over $1 million.[17] These families, representing about 2 percent of the population, accumulated most of their wealth from earnings, not inheritance, and invested over $151 billion in nonpublic businesses in which they have no management interest. Each year, over 100,000 individual investors finance between 30,000 and 50,000 firms, with a total dollar investment of between $7 billion and $10 billion. Given their investment capability, it is important to know the characteristics of these angels.

One article determined that the angel money available for investment each year was about $20 billion.[18] This amount was confirmed by another study indicating that there are about 250,000 angel investors who invest an amount of $10 billion to $20 billion annually in about 30,000 firms.[19] A recent study found that only about 20 percent of the angel investors surveyed tended to specialize in a particular industry, with the typical investment in the first round being between $29,000 to over $100,000.[20]

The characteristics of these informal investors, or angels, are indicated in Table 12.2. They tend to be well educated; many have graduate degrees. Although they will finance firms anywhere in the United States (and a few in other parts of the world), most of the firms that receive funding are within one day's travel. Business angels will make one to two deals each year, with individual firm investments ranging from $100,000 to $500,000 and the average being $340,000. If the opportunity is right, angels might invest from $500,000 to $1 million. In some cases, angels will join with other angels, usually from a common circle of friends, to finance larger deals.

Is there a preference for the type of ventures in which they invest? While angels invest in every type of investment opportunity, from small retail stores to large oil exploration operations, some prefer manufacturing of both industrial and consumer products, energy, service, and the retail/wholesale trade. The returns expected decrease as the number of years the firm has been in business increases, from a median five-year capital gain of 10 times for start-ups to 3 times for established firms over five years old. These investing angels are more patient in their investment horizons and do not have a problem waiting for a period of 7 to 10 years before cashing out. This is in contrast to the more predominant five-year time horizon in the formal venture-capital industry. Investment opportunities are rejected when there is an inadequate risk/return ratio, a subpar management team, a lack of interest in the business area, or insufficient commitment to the venture from the principals.

The angel investor market averages about $20 billion each year, which is about the same level of yearly investment of the venture-capital industry. The angel investment is in about eight times the number of companies. In normal economic conditions, the number of active investors is around 250,000 individuals in the United States, with five or six investors typically being involved in an investment.

referral sources Ways individual investors find out about potential deals

Where do these angel investors generally find their deals? Deals are found through referrals by business associates, friends, active personal research, investment bankers, and business brokers. However, even though these *referral sources* provide some deals, most angel investors are not satisfied with the number and type of investment referrals.

TABLE 12.2   Characteristics of Informal Investors

Demographic Patterns and Relationships

- Well educated, with many having graduate degrees.
- Will finance firms anywhere, particularly in the United States.
- Most firms financed within one day's travel.
- Majority expect to play an active role in ventures financed.
- Many belong to angel clubs.

Investment Record

- Range of investment: $100,000–$500,000
- Average investment: $340,000
- One to two deals each year

Venture Preference

- Most financings in start-ups or ventures less than 5 years old
- Most interest in financing:
  - Manufacturing—industrial/commercial products
  - Manufacturing—consumer products
  - Energy/natural resources
  - Services
  - Software

Risk/Reward Expectations

- Median 5-year capital gain of 10 times for start-ups
- Median 5-year capital gain of 6 times for firms under 1 year old
- Median 5-year capital gain of 5 times for firms 1–5 years old
- Median 5-year capital gain of 3 times for established firms over 5 years old

Reasons for Rejecting Proposals

- Risk/return ratio not adequate
- Inadequate management team
- Not interested in proposed business area
- Unable to agree on price
- Principals not sufficiently committed
- Unfamiliar with area of business

Fifty-one percent of the investors surveyed were either partially or totally dissatisfied with their referral systems and indicated that at least moderate improvement is needed.

A phenomenon that is spreading throughout the United States and the world, particularly Austria, Germany, Ireland, and the United Kingdom, is groups of angels—organized angel investor groups. Each angel group or club usually has a meeting for about two to three hours about 6 to 10 times each year. Some groups co-invest with other groups. The group as a whole does not have any money but serves as a convening and screening device for the presentations. The individual members of the group make the investment either individually or with others interested if any investment is made.

The typical club process is that you send the required form to the designated club member. Following initial screening, if the entrepreneur is chosen, then follow-up meetings with several club members occur. If the entrepreneur is selected to present at a future meeting, then the entrepreneur is provided guidance in terms of business plan refinement and the presentation. Usually 30 minutes is allocated for a presentation and questions, and then any interested club members meet with the entrepreneur to discuss further steps in the investment decision process. The approximately 300 organized angel investor groups are identified by the Kauffman Foundation (www.kauffman.org). Most, such as the Thunderbird Angel Network (TAN), can be accessed through a software program—GUST (gust.com).

In several cases, these organized clubs have spawned an angel fund, which is a pool of money dedicated to a specific region and several industries. The fund size is between $5 and $10 million. The few angel funds in existence operate very much like university-sponsored venture-capital funds, which will be discussed later in this chapter.

VENTURE CAPITAL

The important and little understood area of venture capital will be discussed in terms of its nature, the venture-capital industry in the United States, and the venture-capital process.

Nature of Venture Capital

equity pool   Money raised by venture capitalists to invest

Venture capital is another misunderstood area in entrepreneurship. Some think that venture capitalists do the early-stage financing of relatively small, rapidly growing technology companies. It is more accurate to view venture capital broadly as a professionally managed pool of equity capital. Frequently, the *equity pool* is formed from the resources of wealthy individuals or institutions who are limited partners. Other principal investors in venture-capital limited partnerships are pension funds, endowment funds, and other institutions, including foreign investors. The pool is managed by a general partner—that is, the venture-capital firm—in exchange for a percentage of the gain realized on the investment and a fee. The investments are in early-stage deals as well as second- and third-stage deals and leveraged buyouts. In fact, venture capital can best be characterized as a long-term investment discipline, usually occurring over a five-year period, that is found in the creation of early-stage companies, the expansion and revitalization of existing businesses, and the financing of leveraged buyouts of existing divisions of major corporations or privately owned businesses.

equity participation Taking an ownership position

In each investment, the venture capitalist takes an *equity participation* through stock, warrants, and/or convertible securities and has an active involvement in the monitoring of each portfolio company, bringing investment, financing planning, and business skills to the firm. The venture capitalist will often provide debt along with the equity portion of the financing.

Overview of the Venture-Capital Industry

Although the role of venture capital was instrumental throughout the industrialization of the United States, it did not become institutionalized until after World War II. Before World War II, venture-capital investment activity was a monopoly led by wealthy individuals, investment banking syndicates, and a few family organizations with a professional manager. The first step toward institutionalizing the venture-capital industry took place in 1946 with the formation of the American Research and Development Corporation (ARD) in Boston. The ARD was a small pool of capital from individuals and institutions put together by General Georges Doriot to make active investments in selected emerging businesses.

The next major development, the Small Business Investment Act of 1958, married private capital with government funds to be used by professionally managed small-business

AS SEEN IN *BUSINESS NEWS*

ENTREPRENEURS' PREFERENCES IN VENTURE CAPITAL

The quality and frequency of interaction between a venture capital firm and a start-up company are invaluable to the growth and long-term success of the company. Venture capital firms not only provide financial capital to the entity but also provide operational advice, financial experience, governance, and network connections. These nonfinancial contributions can be just as important to the growth and long-term success of an entity as the initial capital contribution. However, an entrepreneur must be cognizant of the fact that the quality of these nonfinancial contributions varies between venture capital firms. The most influential and beneficial venture capital firms to partner with are those who will be actively involved, helping to grow and expand the business. Entrepreneurs must be selective in choosing a venture capital firm with whom to partner, ensuring the venture capital firm selected will add the most value to the company.

To get the highest value out of their venture capital partners, most entrepreneurs prefer to work with independent private venture capital firms because their management teams are compensated based upon the profitability of the companies in which they invest (typically 20 percent of profits). This compensation structure aligns the venture capital team's interests with that of their investors as well as the entrepreneurs to grow and expand the company, motivating them to be involved with the operations of the business. By contrast the teams from corporate, financial, and government venture capital firms are often compensated with a yearly salary and performance-based bonuses. This compensation structure motivates their teams to be involved with their portfolio companies but to a far lesser extent than when compensation is solely tied to the profitability of the portfolio investments.

Venture capital firms with a proven track record of successful investments often have a reputation within the industry for making wise investment decisions and for adding significant value to the company post acquisition. On the surface, this appears to be an appealing credential that would cause entrepreneurs to prefer partnering with such organizations. However, counterintuitively, many entrepreneurs do not perceive a successful track record as being beneficial to them. This is because of the ongoing struggle between venture capital firms and entrepreneurs to capture the financial rewards of the company. Research and entrepreneurial feedback show that successful venture capital firms understand the value proposition they bring to a company and are often successful at negotiating a lower valuation price, obtaining a higher percent interest in the company, and then extracting all the additional value created by their interactions with the company. This leaves little monetary rewards for the entrepreneur and therefore makes entrepreneurs hesitant to partner with them. Serial entrepreneurs are well aware of this issue and due to their experience are typically better at mitigating this risk by effectively engaging the venture capital management teams to bring the most value to the company.

In addition to the two main considerations outlined above, some other important considerations an entrepreneur should take into account when selecting a venture capital firm include the speed of screening and due diligence, the fit between the company and the industry of the venture capital firm's other portfolio companies, the venture capital firm's understanding of the entrepreneurial process, the deal characteristics and the manner negotiations are conducted, the predictability and consistency of advice provided by the venture capital firm, and the degree of control that the venture capital firm requires from their portfolio companies. Before taking money from any venture capital firms, be sure to check with the management teams of some of the other portfolio companies. Those management teams may be the best source of information for what you can expect from the venture capital firm in question. Remember, the venture capital firm is going to spend a significant amount of time completing due diligence on every start-up company before investing. It is in the best interest of the start-up and the entrepreneur to do an equally detailed and thorough analysis before deciding with which venture capital firm they want to partner.

Source: For more information, see Ola Bengtsson and Wang Fredrick, "What Matters in Venture Capital? Evidence from Entrepreneurs' Stated Preferences," *Financial Management* (Blackwell Publishing Limited, serial online) 39, no. 4 (Winter 2010), pp. 1367–1401.

SBIC firms Small companies with some government money that invest in other companies

investment companies (*SBIC firms*) to infuse capital into start-ups and growing small businesses. With their tax advantages, government funds for leverage, and status as a private-capital company, SBICs were the start of the now formal venture-capital industry. The 1960s saw a significant expansion of SBICs with the approval of approximately 585 SBIC licenses that involved more than $205 million in private capital. Many of these early SBICs failed due to inexperienced portfolio managers, unreasonable expectations, a focus on short-term profitability, and an excess of government regulations. These early failures caused the SBIC program to be restructured, which in turn eliminated some of the unnecessary government regulations and increased the amount of capitalization needed. There are approximately 360 SBICs operating today, of which 130 are minority small-business investment companies (MESBICs) funding minority enterprises.

private venture-capital firms A type of venture-capital firm having general and limited partners

During the late 1960s, small *private venture-capital firms* emerged.[21] These were usually formed as limited partnerships, with the venture-capital company acting as the general partner that received a management fee and a percentage of the profits earned on a deal. The limited partners, who supplied the funding, were frequently institutional investors such as insurance companies, endowment funds, bank trust departments, pension funds, and wealthy individuals and families. There are over 900 of this type of venture-capital establishment in the United States.

Another type of venture-capital firm was also developed during this time: the venture-capital division of major corporations. These firms, of which there are approximately 100, are usually associated with banks and insurance companies, although companies such as 3M, Monsanto, Xerox, Intel, and Unilever house such firms as well. Corporate venture-capital firms are more prone to invest in windows on technology or new market acquisitions than are private venture-capital firms or SBICs. Some of these corporate venture-capital firms have not had strong results.

state-sponsored venture-capital fund A fund containing state government money that invests primarily in companies in the state

In response to the need for economic development, a fourth type of venture-capital firm has emerged in the form of the *state-sponsored venture-capital fund*. These state-sponsored funds have a variety of formats. While the size and investment focus and industry orientation vary from state to state, each fund typically is required to invest a certain percentage of its capital in the particular state. Generally, the funds that are professionally managed by the private sector, outside the state's bureaucracy and political processes, have performed better.

An overview of the types of venture-capital firms is indicated in Figure 12.1. Besides the four types previously discussed, there are now emerging university-sponsored venture-capital funds. These funds, usually managed as separate entities, invest in the technology of the

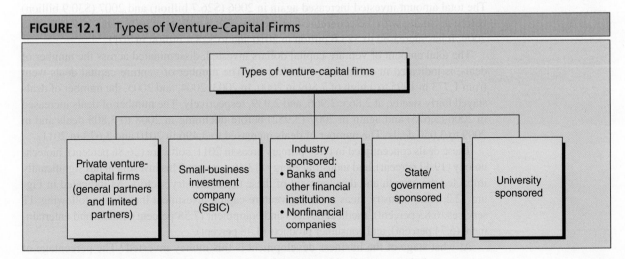

FIGURE 12.1 Types of Venture-Capital Firms

TABLE 12.3   Total Venture Dollars Invested and Number of Deals

Year	Total	# of Deals
1995	$ 7,879,331,900	1,773
1996	11,014,332,900	2,471
1997	14,612,026,900	3,084
1998	20,810,583,100	3,553
1999	53,475,711,500	5,396
2000	104,700,717,300	7,809
2001	40,703,455,300	4,456
2002	21,697,809,100	3,057
2003	19,585,475,700	2,865
2004	21,635,323,900	2,966
2005	23,173,465,300	3,155
2006	26,740,603,400	3,675
2007	30,885,861,100	3,952
2008	28,298,040,600	3,808
2009	19,667,943,200	3,056
2010	23,363,535,600	3,496
2011	29,119,041,600	3,752

Source: PricewaterhouseCoopers LLP/National Venture Capital Association MoneyTree™ Report, Data: Thomson Reuters.

particular university. At such schools as Stanford, Columbia, and MIT, students assist professors and other students in creating business plans for funding as well as assisting the fund manager in his or her due diligence, thereby learning more about the venture-funding process.

The venture-capital industry has not returned to the highest level of dollars invested in 1999, 2000, and 2001. While the total amount of venture-capital dollars invested increased steadily from $7.8 billion in 1995 to a high of $104.7 billion in 2000 (see Table 12.3),[22] the total dollars invested declined to $40.7 billion in 2001, $21.7 billion in 2002, and $19.6 billion in 2003. There was a slight increase to $21.6 billion in 2004 and $21.7 billion in 2005. The total amount invested increased again in 2006 ($26.7 billion) and 2007 ($30.9 billion) before declining with the economic downturn to $28.3 billion in 2008 and $19.7 billion in 2009. It has increased to $23.6 billion in 2010 and to $28.4 billion in 2011.

The total amount of venture-capital dollars invested, disseminated across the number of deals, is indicated in column 3 of Table 12.3. The number of venture-capital deals went from 1,773 in 1995 to a high of 7,809 in 2000. In 2003, 2004, and 2005, the number of deals stayed fairly steady, at 2,865, 2,966, and 2,939, respectively. The number of deals increased in 2006 (3,675) and again in 2007 (3,952) before declining in 2008 to 3,808 deals and in 2009 to 3,056 deals. The number of deals increased to 3,496 in 2010 and 3,673 in 2011.

These deals concentrated in three primary areas in 2011: software (26.86 percent), biotechnology (19.42 percent), and industrial energy (13.46 percent). This investment has significantly impacted the growth and development of these three industry sectors. As indicated in Figure 12.2, other industry areas receiving venture-capital investment include the following: IT services (6.83 percent), medical devices and equipment (7.58 percent), media and entertainment (5.74 percent), and consumer products (4.48 percent).

At what stage of the business development is this money invested? The percentage of venture-capital money raised by stage of the venture in 2011 is indicated in Figure 12.3.

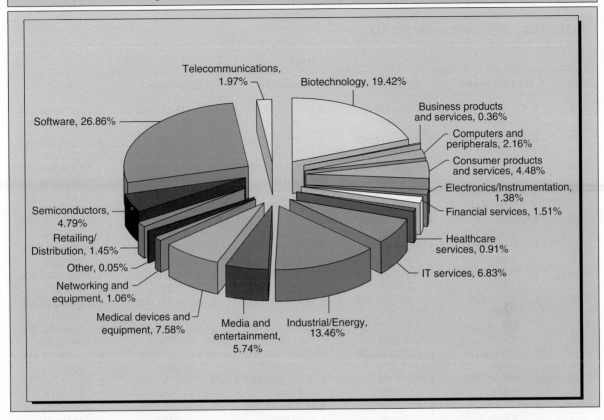

Numbers rounded to the nearest whole percent.

Source: PricewaterhouseCoopers LLP/National Venture Capital Association MoneyTree™ Report, Data: Thomson Reuters.

FIGURE 12.3 Percentage of Venture Dollars Raised by Stage in 2011

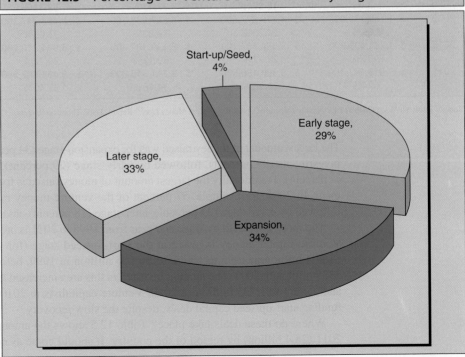

Source: PricewaterhouseCoopers LLP/National Venture Capital Association MoneyTree™ Report, Data: Thomson Reuters.

TABLE 12.4 Venture Investment Stages

Year	Start-Up/Seed	Early Stage	Stage Expansion	Later Stage	Total
1995	$ 1,704,471,700 21.32%	$ 2,541,970,600 31.79%	$ 1,712,698,300 21.42%	$ 2,036,641,700 25.47%	$ 7,995,782,300 100.00%
1996	$ 2,412,661,100 21.42%	$ 3,106,571,800 27.58%	$ 2,555,789,700 22.69%	$ 3,190,091,200 28.32%	$ 11,265,113,800 100.00%
1997	$ 3,047,368,500 20.49%	$ 3,674,240,600 24.71%	$ 3,669,504,700 24.68%	$ 4,479,777,100 30.12%	$ 14,870,890,900 100.00%
1998	$ 4,113,597,500 19.51%	$ 5,652,693,500 26.82%	$ 5,321,257,600 25.24%	$ 5,991,717,200 28.42%	$ 21,079,265,800 100.00%
1999	$ 6,605,334,400 12.22%	$ 10,993,285,200 20.34%	$ 13,130,681,200 24.29%	$ 23,318,742,800 43.14%	$ 54,048,043,600 100.00%
2000	$ 3,223,304,800 3.08%	$ 25,406,580,700 24.25%	$ 59,710,151,000 56.99%	$ 16,427,731,000 15.68%	$104,767,767,500 100.00%
2001	$ 778,015,300 1.92%	$ 8,602,168,900 21.20%	$ 23,008,875,900 56.70%	$ 8,188,266,600 20.18%	$ 40,577,326,700 100.00%
2002	$ 335,810,200 1.53%	$ 3,835,175,200 17.42%	$ 12,434,571,800 56.50%	$ 5,404,111,000 24.55%	$ 22,009,668,200 100.00%
2003	$ 347,769,000 1.76%	$ 3,559,772,100 18.00%	$ 10,100,836,400 51.07%	$ 5,768,505,400 29.17%	$ 19,776,882,900 100.00%
2004	$ 470,124,200 2.09%	$ 4,011,236,300 17.85%	$ 9,165,044,300 40.79%	$ 8,821,753,200 39.26%	$ 22,468,158,000 100.00%
2005	$ 897,707,300 3.87%	$ 3,819,745,600 16.48%	$ 8,663,870,300 37.39%	$ 9,792,142,100 42.26%	$ 23,173,465,300 100.00%
2006	$ 1,177,319,200 4.40%	$ 4,172,001,400 15.60%	$ 11,521,031,400 43.08%	$ 9,870,251,400 36.91%	$ 26,740,603,400 100.00%
2007	$ 1,267,968,200 4.11%	$ 5,486,760,800 17.76%	$ 11,677,215,200 37.81%	$ 12,453,916,900 40.32%	$ 30,885,861,100 100.00%
2008	$ 1,509,963,800 5.34%	$ 5,339,272,800 18.87%	$ 10,604,468,700 37.47%	$ 10,844,335,300 38.32%	$ 28,298,040,600 100.00%
2009	$ 1,749,330,000 8.89%	$ 4,776,877,600 24.28%	$ 6,647,988,500 33.80%	$ 6,493,747,100 33.03%	$ 19,667,943,200 100.00%
2010	$ 1,725,405,900 7.39%	$ 5,554,537,100 23.77%	$ 9,139,382,400 39.12%	$ 6,944,210,200 29.72%	$ 23,363,535,600 100.00%
2011	$ 919,111,100 3.24%	$ 8,300,156,500 29.20%	$ 9,711,345,000 34.16%	$ 9,494,462,800 33.40%	$ 28,425,075,400 100.00%

Source: PricewaterhouseCoopers LLP/National Venture Capital Association MoneyTree™ Report, Data: Thomson Reuters.

The largest amount of money raised was for expansion-stage (34 percent) and then later-stage investments (33 percent), followed by early-stage (29 percent), and start-up/seed stage (4 percent). Traditionally the largest amount of money raised is for expansion-stage investment. In 2002, for example, 57 percent of the venture money raised was for expansion, followed by early stage (23 percent), later stage (18 percent), and start-up (2 percent).

The money invested by stage and year from 1995 to 2011 is broken down in Table 12.4. Venture-capital money invested at the start-up/seed stage (for seed capital) went from $1,704 million in 1995 to a high of $6,605 million in 1999, before declining to a low of $335 million in 2002. The amount invested in this area increased to $1,749 million in 2009 and again to $1,725 million in 2010. Venture capitalists in 2010 still showed interest in funding start-up/seed capital deals, despite the slow recovery.

Where do these deals take place? Table 12.5 shows the amount of money invested in 2011 (28.4 billion) by region of the country. It should come as no surprise that the areas

TABLE 12.5   Venture-Capital Investments by Region (2011)

Region	# of Deals	%	$ Invested	%
Silicon Valley	1,158	31.53	11,629,888,100	40.91
New England	441	12.01	3,204,345,800	11.27
NY Metro	379	10.32	2,726,886,700	9.59
LA/Orange County	208	5.66	1,976,047,400	6.95
Texas	153	4.16	1,460,761,900	5.13
Midwest	269	7.32	1,431,536,600	5.04
Southeast	185	5.04	1,090,975,100	3.84
DC/Metroplex	163	4.44	941,395,100	3.31
San Diego	104	2.83	829,029,500	2.92
Northwest	156	4.25	787,638,100	2.77
Colorado	98	2.67	618,715,500	2.18
SouthWest	80	2.18	546,688,800	1.92
Philadelphia Metro	122	3.32	492,235,200	1.73
North Central	64	1.74	382,081,100	1.34
Upstate NY	21	0.57	119,334,700	0.42
South Central	62	1.69	115,715,900	0.41
Sacramento/N.Cal	7	0.19	71,199,900	0.25
AK/HI/PR	3	0.08	600,000	0.02
Grand Total	3,673	100.00	28,425,075,400	100.00

Source: PricewaterhouseCoopers LLP/National Venture Capital Association MoneyTree™ Report, Data: Thomson Reuters.

receiving the largest amount of venture capital were the Silicon Valley—$11.6 billion in 1,158 companies (31 percent); and New England—$3.2 billion in 441 companies (12 percent). Other areas receiving funding were metro New York—$2.7 billion in 379 companies (10 percent); Los Angeles/Orange County—$1.9 billion in 208 companies (5 percent); and Texas—$1.4 billion in 153 companies (4 percent).

Venture-Capital Process

venture-capital process
The decision procedure of a venture-capital firm

To be in a position to secure the funds needed, an entrepreneur must understand the philosophy and objectives of a venture-capital firm, as well as the *venture-capital process*. The objective of a venture-capital firm is to generate long-term capital appreciation through debt and equity investments. To achieve this objective, the venture capitalist is willing to make any changes or modifications necessary in the business investment. Since the objective of the entrepreneur is the survival of the business, the objectives of the two are frequently at odds, particularly when problems occur such as the numbers not being met.

A typical portfolio objective of venture-capital firms in terms of return criteria and risk involved is shown in Figure 12.4. Since there is more risk involved in financing a business earlier in its development, more return is expected from early-stage financing (50 percent ROI) than from acquisitions or leveraged buyouts (30 percent ROI), which are later stages of development. The significant risk involved and the pressure that venture-capital firms feel from their investors (limited partners) to make safer investments with higher rates of return have caused these firms to invest even greater amounts of their funds in later stages

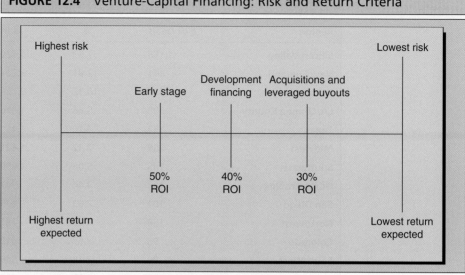

FIGURE 12.4 Venture-Capital Financing: Risk and Return Criteria

of financing. In these late-stage investments, there are lower risks, faster returns, less managerial assistance needed, and fewer deals to be evaluated.

The venture capitalist does not necessarily seek control of a company, but would rather have the firm and the entrepreneur at the most risk. The venture capitalist will want at least one seat on the board of directors. Once the decision to invest is made, the venture capitalist will do anything necessary to support the management team so that the business and the investment prosper. Whereas the venture capitalist expects to provide guidance as a member of the board of directors, the management team is expected to direct and run the daily operations of the company. A venture capitalist will support the management team with investment dollars, financial skills, planning, and expertise in any area needed.

Since the venture capitalist provides long-term investment (typically five to seven years or more), it is important that there be mutual trust and understanding between the entrepreneur and the venture capitalist. There should be no surprises in the firm's performance. Both good and bad news should be shared, with the objective of taking the necessary action to allow the company to grow and develop in the long run. The venture capitalist should be available to the entrepreneur to discuss problems and develop strategic plans.

The venture capitalist expects a company to satisfy three general criteria before he or she will commit to the venture. First, the company must have a strong management team that consists of individuals with solid experience and backgrounds, a strong commitment to the company, capabilities in their specific areas of expertise, the ability to meet challenges, and the flexibility to scramble wherever necessary. A venture capitalist would rather invest in a first-rate management team and a second-rate product than the reverse. The management team's commitment should be reflected in dollars invested in the company. Although the amount of the investment is important, more telling is the size of this investment relative to the management team's ability to invest. The commitment of the management team should be backed by the support of the family, particularly the spouse, of each key team player. A positive family environment and spousal support allow the entrepreneur and team members to spend the 60 to 70 hours per week necessary to start and grow the company. One successful venture capitalist makes it a point to have dinner with the entrepreneur and spouse, and even to visit the entrepreneur's home, before making an investment decision. According to the venture capitalist, "I find it difficult to believe an entrepreneur can successfully run and manage a business and put in the necessary time when the home environment is out of control."

The second criterion is that the product and/or market opportunity must be unique, having a differential advantage in a growing market. Securing a unique market niche is essential since the product or service must be able to compete and grow during the investment period. This uniqueness needs to be carefully spelled out in the marketing portion of the business plan and is even better when it is protected by a patent or a trade secret.

significant capital
appreciation Significant
capital appreciation is the
increase in value of the
organization during a
specific period of time

The final criterion for investment is that the business opportunity must have *significant capital appreciation*. The exact amount of capital appreciation varies, depending on such factors as the size of the deal, the stage of development of the company, the upside potential, the downside risks, and the available exits. The venture capitalist typically expects a 40 to 60 percent return on investment in most investment situations.

The venture-capital process that implements these criteria is both an art and a science.[23] The element of art is illustrated in the venture capitalist's intuition, gut feeling, and creative thinking that guide the process. The process is scientific due to the systematic approach and data-gathering techniques involved in the assessment.

The process starts with the venture-capital firm establishing its philosophy and investment objectives. The firm must decide on the following: the composition of its portfolio mix, including the number of start-ups, expansion companies, and management buyouts; the types of industries; the geographic region for investment; and any product or industry specializations.

preliminary screening
Initial evaluation of a deal

The venture-capital process can be broken down into four primary stages: preliminary screening, agreement on principal terms, due diligence, and final approval. The *preliminary screening* begins with the receipt of the business plan. A good business plan is essential in the venture-capital process. Most venture capitalists will not even talk to an entrepreneur who doesn't have one. As the starting point, the business plan must have a clear-cut mission and clearly stated objectives that are supported by an in-depth industry and market analysis and pro forma income statements. The executive summary is an important part of this business plan, as it is used for initial screening in this preliminary evaluation. Many business plans are never evaluated beyond the executive summary. When evaluating the business, the venture capitalist first determines if the deal or similar deals have been seen previously. The investor then determines if the proposal fits his or her long-term policy and short-term needs in developing a portfolio balance. In this preliminary screening, the venture capitalist investigates the economy of the industry and evaluates whether he or she has the appropriate knowledge and ability to invest in that industry. The investor reviews the numbers presented to determine whether the business can reasonably deliver the ROI required. In addition, the credentials and capability of the management team are evaluated to determine if they can carry out the plan presented.

The second stage is the agreement on principal terms between the entrepreneur and the venture capitalist. The venture capitalist wants a basic understanding of the principal terms of the deal at this stage of the process before making the major commitment of time and effort involved in the formal due diligence process.

due diligence The
process of deal evaluation

The third stage, detailed review and *due diligence,* is the longest stage, involving anywhere from one to three months. There is a detailed review of the company's history, the business plan, the resumes of the individuals, their financial history, and target market customers. The upside potential and downside risks are assessed, and there is a thorough evaluation of the markets, industry, finances, suppliers, customers, and management.

final approval A
document showing the
final terms of the deal

In the last stage, *final approval,* a comprehensive, internal investment memorandum is prepared. This document reviews the venture capitalist's findings and details the investment terms and conditions of the investment transaction. This information is used to prepare the formal legal documents that both the entrepreneur and venture capitalist will sign to finalize the deal.[24]

Locating Venture Capitalists

One of the most important decisions for the entrepreneur lies in selecting which venture-capital firm to approach. Since venture capitalists tend to specialize either geographically by industry (manufacturing industrial products or consumer products, high technology, or service) or by size and type of investment, the entrepreneur should approach only those that may have an interest in the investment opportunity. Where do you find this venture capitalist?

Although venture capitalists are located throughout the United States, the traditional areas of concentration are found in Los Angeles, New York, Chicago, Boston, and San Francisco. Most venture capital firms belong to the National Venture Capital Association and are listed on its Web site (www.nvca.org). An entrepreneur should carefully research the names and addresses of prospective venture-capital firms that might have an interest in the particular investment opportunity. There are also regional and national venture-capital associations. For a nominal fee or none at all, these associations will frequently e-mail the entrepreneur a directory that lists their members, the types of businesses their members invest in, and any investment restrictions. Whenever possible, the entrepreneur should be introduced to the venture capitalist. Bankers, accountants, lawyers, and professors are good sources for introductions.

Approaching a Venture Capitalist

The entrepreneur should approach a venture capitalist in a professional business manner. Since venture capitalists receive hundreds of inquiries and are frequently out of the office working with portfolio companies or investigating potential investment opportunities, it is important to begin the relationship positively. The entrepreneur should contact any potential venture capitalist to ensure that his/her business venture is in an area of investment interest. Then the business plan should be sent, accompanied by a short professional letter.

Since venture capitalists receive many more plans than they are capable of funding, many plans are screened out as soon as possible. Venture capitalists tend to focus and put more time and effort on those plans that are referred. In fact, one venture-capital group said that 80 percent of its investments over the last five years were in referred companies. Consequently, it is well worth the entrepreneur's time to seek out an introduction to the venture capitalist. Typically this can be obtained from an executive of a portfolio company, an accountant, a lawyer, a banker, or a business school professor.

The entrepreneur should be aware of some basic rules of thumb before implementing the actual approach and should follow the detailed guidelines presented in Table 12.6. First, great care should be taken in selecting the right venture capitalist to approach. Venture capitalists tend to specialize in certain industries and will rarely invest in a business outside those areas, regardless of the merits of the business proposal and plan. Second, recognize that venture capitalists know each other, particularly in a specific region of the country. When a large amount of money is involved, they will invest in the deal together, with one venture-capital firm taking the lead. Since this degree of familiarity is present, a venture-capital firm will probably find out if others have seen your business plan. Do not shop

---

TABLE 12.6   Guidelines for Dealing with Venture Capitalists

- Carefully determine the venture capitalist to approach for funding the particular type of deal. Screen and target the approach. Venture capitalists do not like deals that have been excessively "shopped."

- Once a discussion is started with a venture capitalist, do not discuss the deal with other venture capitalists. Working several deals in parallel can create problems unless the venture capitalists are working together. Time and resource limitations may require a cautious simultaneous approach to several funding sources.

- It is better to approach a venture capitalist through an intermediary who is respected and has a preexisting relationship with the venture capitalist. Limit and carefully define the role and compensation of the intermediary.

- The entrepreneur or manager, not an intermediary, should lead the discussions with the venture capitalist. Do not bring a lawyer, accountant, or other advisors to the first meeting. Since there are no negotiations during this first meeting, it is a chance for the venture capitalist to get to know the entrepreneur without interference from others.

- Be very careful about what is projected or promised. The entrepreneur will probably be held accountable for these projections in the pricing, deal structure, or compensation.

- Disclose any significant problems or negative situations in this initial meeting. Trust is a fundamental part of the long-term relationship with the venture capitalist; subsequent discovery by the venture capitalist of an undisclosed problem will cause a loss of confidence and probably prevent a deal.

- Reach a flexible, reasonable understanding with the venture capitalist regarding the timing of a response to the proposal and the accomplishment of the various steps in the financing transaction. Patience is needed, as the process is complex and time consuming. Too much pressure for a rapid decision can cause problems with the venture capitalist.

- Do not sell the project on the basis that other venture capitalists have committed themselves. Most venture capitalists are independent and take pride in their own decision making.

- Be careful about glib statements such as, "There is no competition for this product" or "There is nothing like this technology available today." These statements can reveal a failure to do one's homework or can indicate that a perfect product has been designed for a nonexistent market.

- Do not indicate an inordinate concern for salary, benefits, or other forms of current compensation. Dollars are precious in a new venture. The venture capitalist wants the entrepreneur committed to an equity appreciation similar to that of the venture capitalist.

- Eliminate to the extent possible any use of new dollars to take care of past problems, such as payment of past debts or deferred salaries of management. New dollars of the venture capitalist are for growth, to move the business forward.

---

among venture capitalists, as even a good business plan can quickly become "shopworn." Third, when meeting the venture capitalist, particularly for the first time, bring only one or two key members of the management team. A venture capitalist is investing in you and your management team and its track record, not in outside consultants and experts. Any consultants and/or experts can be called in when needed.

Finally, be sure to develop a succinct, well-thought-out oral presentation. This should cover the company's business, the uniqueness of the product or service, the prospects for growth, the major factors behind achieving the sales and profits indicated, the backgrounds and track records of the key managers, the amount of financing required, and the returns anticipated. This first presentation is critical, as is indicated in the comment of one venture capitalist: "I need to sense a competency, a capability, a chemistry within the first half hour of our initial meeting. The entrepreneur needs to look me in the eye and present his story clearly and logically. If a chemistry does not start to develop, I start looking for reasons not to do the deal."

Following a favorable initial meeting, the venture capitalist will do some preliminary investigation of the plan. If favorable, another meeting between the management team and the venture capitalist will be scheduled so that both parties can assess the other and determine if a good working relationship can be established and if a feeling of trust and confidence is evolving. During this mutual evaluation, the entrepreneur should be careful not to be too inflexible about the amount of company equity he or she is willing to share. If the entrepreneur is too inflexible, the venture capitalist might end negotiations. During this meeting, initial agreement of terms is established. If you are turned down by one venture capitalist, do not become discouraged. Instead, select several other nonrelated venture-capitalist candidates and repeat the procedure. A significant number of companies denied funding by one venture capitalist are able to obtain funds from other outside sources, including other venture capitalists.

VALUING YOUR COMPANY

A problem confronting the entrepreneur in obtaining outside equity funds, whether from the informal investor market (the angels) or from the formal venture-capital industry, is determining the value of the company. This valuation is at the core of determining how much ownership an investor is entitled to for a certain amount of funding for the venture. This is determined by considering the *factors in valuation*. This, as well as other aspects of securing funding, has a potential for ethical conflict that must be carefully handled.

factors in valuation
Nonmonetary aspects that affect the fund valuation of a company

Factors in Valuation

There are eight factors that vary by situation the entrepreneur should consider when valuing the venture. The first factor, and the starting point in any valuation, is the nature and history of the business. The characteristics of the venture and the industry in which it operates are fundamental aspects in every evaluation process. The history of the company from its inception provides information on the strength and diversity of the company's operations, the risks involved, and the company's ability to withstand any adverse conditions.

The valuation process must also consider the outlook of the economy in general as well as the outlook for the particular industry. This, the second factor, involves an examination of the financial data of the venture compared with those of other companies in the industry. Management's capability now and in the future is assessed, as well as the future market for the company's products. Will these markets grow, decline, or stabilize, and in what economic conditions?

The third factor is the book value (net value) of the stock of the company and the overall financial condition of the business. The book value (often called owner's equity) is the acquisition cost (less accumulated depreciation) minus liabilities. Frequently, the book value is not a good indication of fair market value, as balance sheet items are almost always carried at cost, not market value. The value of plant and equipment, for example, carried on the books at cost less depreciation may be low due to the use of an accelerated depreciation method or other market factors, making the assets more valuable than indicated in the book value figures. Land, particularly, is usually reflected lower than fair market value. For valuation, the balance sheet must be adjusted to reflect the higher values of the assets, particularly land, so that a more realistic company worth is determined. A good valuation should also value operating and nonoperating assets separately and then combine the two into the total fair market value. A thorough valuation involves comparing balance sheets and profit and loss statements for the past three years when available.

While book value develops the benchmark, the future earning capacity of the company, the fourth factor, is the most important factor in valuation. Previous years' earnings are generally not simply averaged but weighted, with the most recent earnings receiving the highest weighting. Income by product line should be analyzed to judge future profitability and value. Special attention should be paid to depreciation, nonrecurring expense, officers' salaries, rental expense, and historical trends.

The fifth valuation factor is the dividend-paying capacity of the venture. Since the entrepreneur in a new venture typically pays little if any in dividends, it is the future capacity to pay dividends rather than actual dividend payments made that is important. The dividend-paying capacity should be capitalized.

An assessment of goodwill and other intangibles of the venture is the sixth valuation factor. These intangible assets usually cannot be valued without reference to the tangible assets of the venture.

The seventh factor in valuation involves assessing any previous sale of equity. Previous equity transactions and their valuations accurately represent future sales particularly if recent. Motives regarding the new sale (if other than arriving at a fair price) and any change in economic or financial conditions during the intermittent period should be considered.

The final valuation factor is the market price of equity of companies engaged in the same or similar lines of business. This factor is used in the specific valuation method discussed later in this section. The critical issue is the degree of similarity between the publicly traded company and the company being valued.

Ratio Analysis

financial ratios Control mechanisms to test the financial strength of the new venture

Calculations of *financial ratios* can also be valuable as an analytical and control mechanism to test the financial well-being of a new venture. These ratios serve as a measure of the financial strengths and weaknesses of the venture, but should be used with caution since they are only one control measure for interpreting the financial success of the venture. There is no single set of ratios that should be used, nor are there standard definitions for all ratios. However, there are industry rules of thumb that the entrepreneur can use to interpret the financial data. Ratio analysis is typically used on actual financial results but can also provide the entrepreneur with some sense of where problems exist in the pro forma statements as well. Throughout this section we will use information taken from the financial statements of MPP Plastics (Chapter 10, Table 10.4 (year 2) and Table 10.7) to illustrate.

Liquidity Ratios

Current Ratio This ratio is commonly used to measure the short-term solvency of the venture or its ability to meet its short-term debts. The current liabilities must be covered from cash or its equivalent; otherwise the entrepreneur will need to borrow money to meet these obligations. The formula and calculation of this ratio when current assets are $94,500 and current liabilities are $13,600 is:

$$\frac{\text{Current assets}}{\text{Current liabilities}} = \frac{94,500}{13,600} = 6.96 \text{ times}$$

While a ratio of 2:1 is generally considered favorable, the entrepreneur should also compare this ratio with any industry standards. One interpretation of this result is that for every $1.00 of current debt, the company has $6.96 of current assets to cover it. This ratio indicates that MPP Plastics is liquid and can likely meet any of its obligations even if there were a sudden emergency that would drain existing cash.

Acid Test Ratio   This is a more rigorous test of the short-term liquidity of the venture because it eliminates inventory, which is the least liquid current asset. The formula given the same current assets and liabilities and inventory of $1,200 is:

$$\frac{\text{Current assets} - \text{Inventory}}{\text{Current liabilities}} = \frac{94,700 - 1,200}{13,600} = 6.9 \text{ times}$$

The result from this ratio suggests that the venture is very liquid since it has assets convertible to cash of $6.90 for every dollar of short-term obligations. Usually a 1:1 ratio would be considered favorable in most industries.

Activity Ratios

Average Collection Period   This ratio indicates the average number of days it takes to convert accounts receivable into cash. This ratio helps the entrepreneur to gauge the liquidity of accounts receivable or the ability of the venture to collect from its customers. Using the formula with accounts receivable of $52,000 and sales of $1,264,000 results in:

$$\frac{\text{Accounts receivable}}{\text{Average daily sales}} = \frac{52,000}{1,264,000/360} = 3.5 \text{ days}$$

This particular result needs to be compared with industry standards since collection will vary considerably. However, if the invoices indicate a 20-day payment required, then one could conclude that most customers pay on time.

Inventory Turnover   This ratio measures the efficiency of the venture in managing and selling its inventory. A high turnover is a favorable sign indicating that the venture is able to sell its inventory quickly. There could be a danger with a very high turnover that the venture is understocked, which could result in lost orders. Managing inventory is very important to the cash flow and profitability of a new venture. The calculation of this ratio when the cost of goods sold is $632,000 and the inventory is $4,200 is:

$$\frac{\text{Cost of goods sold}}{\text{Inventory}} = \frac{632,000}{4,200} = 150.5 \text{ times}$$

This would appear to be a good turnover as long as the entrepreneur feels that he or she is not losing sales because of understocking inventory.

Leverage Ratios

Debt Ratio   Many new ventures will incur debt to finance the venture. The debt ratio helps the entrepreneur to assess the firm's ability to meet all its obligations (short and long term). It is also a measure of risk because debt also consists of a fixed commitment in the form of interest and principal repayments. With total liabilities of $13,600 and total assets of $152,300, the debt ratio is calculated as:

$$\frac{\text{Total liabilities}}{\text{Total assets}} = \frac{13,600}{152,300} = 8.9\%$$

This result indicates that the venture has financed 8.9 percent of its assets with debt. On paper this looks very good, but it also needs to be compared with industry data.

Debt to Equity   This ratio assesses the firm's capital structure. It provides a measure of risk to creditors by considering the funds invested by creditors (debt) and investors (equity). The higher the percentage of debt, the greater the degree of risk to any of the creditors. The calculation of this ratio using the same total liabilities, with stockholder's equity being $148,700, is:

$$\frac{\text{Total liabilities}}{\text{Stockholder's equity}} = \frac{13,600}{139.3} = 97.6 \text{ times}$$

This figure is not meaningful due to the owner's negative equity reflecting the negative retained earnings of the company. The actual investment of the entrepreneurs or the equity base is about one-fourth of what is owed, giving a cushion to the creditors. MPP Plastics has a strong short-term cash position.

Profitability Ratios

Net Profit Margin   This ratio represents the venture's ability to translate sales into profits. You can also use gross profit instead of net profit to provide another measure of profitability. In either case it is important to know what is reasonable in your industry as well as to measure these ratios over time. The ratio and calculation when net profit is $16,300 and net sales are $1,264,000 is:

$$\frac{\text{Net profit}}{\text{Net sales}} = \frac{16,300}{1,264,000} = 1.2\%$$

The net profit margin for MPP Plastics, although low for an established firm, is also a great concern for a new venture. Many new ventures do not incur profits until the second or third year. In this case we have a favorable profit situation.

Return on Investment   The return on investment measures the ability of the venture to manage its total investment in assets. You can also calculate a return on equity, which substitutes stockholders' equity for total assets in the following formula and indicates the ability of the venture in generating a return to the stockholders. The formula and calculation of the return on investment when total assets are $152,300 and net profit is $16,300 is:

$$\frac{\text{Net profit}}{\text{Total assets}} = \frac{16,300}{152,300} = 10.7\%$$

The result of this calculation will also need to be compared with industry data. However, the positive conclusion is that the firm has earned a profit in its second year and has returned 10.7 percent on its asset investment.

There are many other ratios that could also be calculated. However, for a start-up these would probably suffice for an entrepreneur in assessing the venture's financial strengths and weaknesses. As the firm grows, it will be important to use these ratios in conjunction with all other financial statements to provide an understanding of how the firm is performing financially.

General Valuation Approaches

general valuation approaches Methods for determining the worth of a company

There are several *general valuation approaches* that can be used in valuing the venture. One of the most widely used approaches assesses comparable publicly held companies and the prices of these companies' securities. This search for a similar company is both an art and a science. First, the company must be classified in a certain industry, since companies in the same industry share similar markets, problems, economies, and potential of sales and earnings. The review of all publicly traded companies in this industry classification should evaluate size, amount of diversity, dividends, leverage, and growth potential until the most similar company is identified. This method is inaccurate when a truly comparable company is not found.

present value of future cash flow Valuing a company based on its future sales and profits

A second widely used valuation approach is the *present value of future cash flow*. This method adjusts the value of the cash flow of the business for the time value of money and the business and economic risks. Since only cash (or cash equivalents) can be used in reinvestment, this valuation approach generally gives more accurate results than profits. With this method, the sales and earnings are projected back to the time of the valuation decision when shares of the company are offered for sale. The period between the valuation and sale dates is determined, and the potential dividend payout and expected price-earnings ratio or liquidation value at the end of the period are calculated. Finally, a rate of return desired by investors is established, less a discount rate for failure to meet those expectations.

Another valuation method, used only for insurance purposes or in very unique circumstances, is known as *replacement value*. This method is used when, for example, there is a unique asset involved that the buyer really wants. The valuation of the venture is based on the amount of money it would take to replace (or reproduce) that asset or another important asset or system of the venture.

replacement value   The cost of replacing all assets of a company

The *book value* approach uses the adjusted book value, or net tangible asset value, to determine the firm's worth. Adjusted book value is obtained by making the necessary adjustments to the stated book value by taking into account any depreciation (or appreciation) of plant and equipment and real estate, as well as necessary inventory adjustments that result from the accounting methods employed. The following basic procedure can be used:

book value   The indicated worth of the assets of a company

Book value	$_____
Add (or subtract) any adjustments such as appreciation or depreciation to arrive at figure on next line—the fair market value	$_____
Fair market value (the sale value of the company's assets)	$_____
Subtract all intangibles that cannot be sold, such as goodwill	$_____
Adjusted book value	$_____

Since the book valuation approach involves simple calculations, its use is particularly good in relatively new businesses, in businesses where the sole owner has died or is disabled, and in businesses with speculative or highly unstable earnings.

The *earnings approach* is the most widely used method of valuing a company since it provides the potential investor with the best estimate of the probable return on investment. The potential earnings are calculated by weighting the most recent operating year's earnings after they have been adjusted for any extraordinary expenses that would not have normally occurred in the operations of a publicly traded company. An appropriate price-earnings multiple is then selected based on norms of the industry and the investment risk. A higher multiple will be used for a high-risk business and a lower multiple for a low-risk business. For example, a low-risk business in an industry with a seven-times-earnings multiple would be valued at $4.2 million if the weighted average earnings over the past three years were $0.6 million (7 × $0.6 million).

earnings approach   Determining the worth of a company by looking at its present and future earnings

An extension of this method is the *factor approach,* wherein the following three major factors are used to determine value: earnings, dividend-paying capacity, and book value. Appropriate weights for the particular company being valued are developed and multiplied by the capitalized value, resulting in an overall weighted valuation. An example is indicated here:

factor approach   Using the major aspects of a company to determine its worth

Approach (in 000s)	Capitalized Value	Weight	Weighted Value
Earnings: $40 × 10	$400	0.4	$160
Dividends: $15 × 20	$300	0.4	$120
Book value: $600 × 0.4	$240	0.2	$ 48
Average: $328			
10% discount: $33			
Per-share value: $295			

liquidation value Worth of a company if everything was sold today

A final valuation approach that gives the lowest value of the business is *liquidation value*. Liquidation value is often difficult to obtain, particularly when costs and losses must be estimated for selling the inventory, terminating employees, collecting accounts receivable, selling assets, and performing other closing-down activities. Nevertheless, it is also good for an investor to obtain a downside risk value in appraising a company.

General Valuation Method

One approach an entrepreneur can use to determine how much of the company a venture capitalist will want for a given amount of investment is indicated here:

$$\text{Venture-capitalist ownership (\%)} = \frac{\text{VC \$ investment} \times \text{VC investment multiple desired}}{\text{Company's projected profits in year 5} \times \text{Price-earnings multiple of comparable company}}$$

Consider the following example:

> A company needs $500,000 of venture-capital money.
>
> The company is anticipating profits of $650,000.
>
> The venture capitalist wants an investment multiple of 5 times.
>
> The price-earnings multiple of a similar company is 12.

According to the following calculations, the company would have to give up 32 percent ownership to obtain the needed funds:

$$\frac{\$500,000 \times 5}{\$650,000 \times 12} = 32\%$$

A more accurate method for determining this percentage is given in Table 12.7. The step-by-step approach takes into account the time value of money in determining the appropriate investor's share. The following hypothetical example uses this step-by-step procedure.

TABLE 12.7 Steps in Valuing Your Business and Determining Investors' Share

1. Estimate the earnings after taxes based on sales in the fifth year.

2. Determine an appropriate earnings multiple based on what similar companies are selling for in terms of their current earnings.

3. Determine the required rate of return.

4. Determine the funding needed.

5. Calculate, using the following formulas:

$$\text{Present value} = \frac{\text{Future valuation}}{(1 + i)^n}$$

where:

$$\text{Future valuation} = \text{Total estimated value of company in 5 years}$$

$$i = \text{Required rate of return}$$

$$n = \text{Number of years}$$

$$\text{Investors' share} = \frac{\text{Initial funding}}{\text{Present value}}$$

H&B Associates, a start-up manufacturing company, estimates it will earn $1 million after taxes on sales of $10 million. The company needs $800,000 now to reach that goal in five years. A similar company in the same industry is selling at 15 times earnings. A venture-capital firm, Davis Venture Partners, is interested in investing in the deal and requires a 50 percent compound rate of return on investment. What percentage of the company will have to be given up to obtain the needed capital?

$$\text{Present value} = \frac{\$1,000,000 \times 15 \text{ times earning multiple}}{(1 + 0.50)^5}$$

$$= \$1,975,000$$

$$\frac{\$800,000}{\$1,975,000} = 41\% \text{ will have to be given up}$$

Evaluation of an Internet Company

The valuation process for early-stage Internet companies is quite different from the traditional valuation process. Traditionally, private-equity companies would examine historical financials and operations as part of a very quantitative process using such things as discounted cash flow (DCF), comparables, and/or multiples of EBITDA (earnings before interest, taxes, depreciation, and amortization). Following this, the culture and management are examined in a more qualitative way. When institutional investors focus on earlier-stage companies—in particular Internet companies that have little or no history, no historical financials, and no comparables—a different approach has to be taken in the valuation process.

For these companies, the qualitative portion of due diligence carries much more weight than in other evaluations. The focus is more on the market itself. How big is it? How is it segmented? Who are the players? How will it evolve? Once these questions are resolved, the potential entrepreneurial company's financial projections are compared with the future market in terms of fit, realism, and opportunity. After getting comfortable with the market size and potential revenue of a company, the investor examines the management team. Is this a management team that will take the company "all the way"? Who will they need to bring in? How much should be set aside for an employee stock ownership plan (ESOP)? The more complete the management team is, the higher the valuation. If the management team is still thin, then a substantial portion of the company's assets needs to be set aside to attract and retain good employees. Different industries require different valuations. For example, an infrastructure business is viewed differently from a business-to-business firm.

After going through the process of deriving a value, the investor looks at all the opportunities available in the investor market. Generally, the value in early-stage technology companies is driven by a combination of market structure and management team maturity, modified by the supply and demand forces that exist in a market that is highly competitive for good, solid companies.

An entrepreneur seeking financing should keep in mind that markets are changing and traditional systems are being turned upside down. Investors and entrepreneurs who have a sense of how this is going to occur and can predict the impact new technologies will have on traditional and newly formed markets are the ones who will be more highly rewarded.

DEAL STRUCTURE

deal structure The form of the transaction when money is obtained by a company

In addition to valuing the company and determining the percentage of the company that may have to be given up to obtain funding, a critical concern for the entrepreneur is the *deal structure,* or the terms of the transaction between the entrepreneur and the funding source.

To make the venture look as attractive as possible to potential sources of funds, the entrepreneur must understand the needs of the investors as well as his or her own needs. The needs of the funding sources include the rate of return required, the timing and form of return, the amount of control desired, and the perception of the risks involved in the particular funding opportunity. While some investors are willing to bear a significant amount of risk to obtain a significant rate of return, others want less risk and less return. Other investors are more concerned about their amount of influence and control once the investment has been made.

The entrepreneur's needs revolve around similar concerns, such as the degree and mechanisms of control, the amount of financing needed, and the goals for the particular firm. Before negotiating the terms and the structure of the deal with the venture capitalist, the entrepreneur should assess the relative importance of these concerns to negotiate most strategically. Both the venture capitalist and the entrepreneur should feel comfortable with the final deal structure, and a good working relationship needs to be established to deal with any future problems that may arise.

GOING PUBLIC

going public Selling some part of the company by registering with the SEC

Going public occurs when the entrepreneur and other equity owners of the venture offer and sell some part of the company to the public through a registration statement filed with the securities commission of the country. In the United States, this is the Securities and Exchange Commission (SEC) pursuant to the Securities Act of 1933. The resulting capital infusion to the company from the increased number of stockholders and outstanding shares of stock provides the company with financial resources and generally with a relatively liquid investment vehicle. Consequently, the company will have greater access to capital markets in the future and a more objective picture of the public's perception of the value of the business. However, given the reporting requirements, the increased number of stockholders (owners), and the costs involved, the entrepreneur must carefully evaluate the advantages and disadvantages of going public before initiating the process. A list of these advantages and disadvantages is given in Table 12.8.

Advantages

The three primary advantages of going public are obtaining new equity capital, realizing an enhanced valuation due to the greater liquidity of an equity investment in the company, and enhancing the company's ability to obtain future funds. Whether it is first-stage, second-stage, or third-stage financing that is desired, a venture is in constant need of capital. The new

TABLE 12.8   Advantages and Disadvantages of Going Public

Advantages	Disadvantages
• Ability to obtain equity capital	• Increased risk of liability
• Enhanced ability to borrow	• Expense
• Enhanced ability to raise equity	• Regulation of corporate governance policies and procedures
• Liquidity and valuation	
• Prestige	• Disclosure of information
• Personal wealth	• Pressures to maintain growth pattern
	• Loss of control

capital provides the needed working capital, plant and equipment, or inventories and sup-plies necessary for the venture's growth and survival. Going public is often the best way to obtain capital on the best possible terms.

Going public generally results in a public trading market and provides a mechanism for valuing the company and allowing this value to be easily transferred among parties. Many family-owned or other privately held companies may need to go public so that the value of the company can be disseminated among the second and third generations. Venture capitalists view going public as one of the most beneficial ways to attain the liquidity necessary to exit a company with the best possible return on their investment. Other investors benefit as well due to easier liquidation of their investment when the company's stock takes on value and transferability. Because of this liquidity, the value of a publicly traded security is sometimes higher than shares of one that is not publicly traded. In addition, publicly traded companies often find it easier to acquire other companies by using their securities in the transactions.

As noted earlier, the third primary advantage is that publicly traded companies usually find it easier to raise additional capital, particularly debt. Money can often be borrowed more easily and on more favorable terms, the company's balance sheet is strengthened by the new equity capital, and the company has better prospects for raising future equity capital.

Disadvantages

initial public offering (IPO) The first public registration and sale of a company's stock

Although the advantages of going public are significant for a new venture, they must be carefully weighed against the numerous disadvantages. Some entrepreneurs want to keep their companies private, even in times of a hot stock market. Why do entrepreneurs avoid an *initial public offering (IPO)?*

Two major reasons are the increased reporting and the potential loss of control that can oc-cur in a publicly traded company. Yet, to stay on the cutting edge of technology, companies frequently need to sacrifice short-term profits for long-term innovation. This can require rein-vesting in technology that in itself may not produce any bottom-line results, particularly in the short run. Making long-term decisions can be difficult in publicly traded companies where sales and profit results indicate the capability of management via stock values.

Some of the most troublesome aspects of being public are the resulting loss of autonomy as well as increased duties to public stockholders and administrative burdens. The company must make decisions with respect to the fiduciary duties owed to the public shareholder, and it needs to disclose to the public all material information regarding the company, its opera-tions, and its management. One publicly traded company had to retain a more expensive in-vestment banker than would have been required by a privately held company to obtain an "appropriate" fairness opinion in a desired merger. The investment banker increased the ex-penses of the merger by $150,000, in addition to causing a three-month delay in the merger proceedings. Management of a publicly traded company also spends a significant amount of additional time and expense addressing queries from shareholders, press, and financial ana-lysts and ensuring compliance with the complicated accessing, reporting, and securities trad-ing regulations. CEOs of most publicly traded companies set aside one day per week for this.

Finally, when enough shares are sold to the public, the company can lose control of decision making, which can even result in the venture being acquired through an unfriendly tender offer.

With the enactment of the Sarbanes-Oxley Act in 2002, corporate governance and disclo-sure requirements of public companies and the practices and conduct of accountants and lawyers engaged by public companies became subject to significantly greater regulation en-forcement by the Securities and Exchange Commission and the stock exchanges. As a result, the expense and administrative responsibilities of being a public company, as well as the lia-bility risks of officers and directors, are greater than ever. Among the other consequences of the new regulation, the recruitment of qualified independent directors has become a much more difficult challenge for most public companies.

If all these disadvantages themselves have not caused the entrepreneur to look for alternative financing rather than an IPO, the expenses involved may. The major expenses of going public include accounting fees, legal fees, underwriter's fees, registration and blue-sky filing fees, and printing costs. The accounting fees involved in going public vary greatly, depending in part on the size of the company, the availability of previously audited financial statements, and the complexity of the company's operations. Generally, the costs of going public average $700,000, although they can be much greater when significant complexities are involved. Additional reporting, accounting, legal, and printing expenses can run anywhere from $50,000 to $250,000 per year, depending on the company's past practices in the areas of accounting and shareholder communications. In addition to the SEC reports that must be filed, a proxy statement and other materials must be submitted to the SEC for review before distribution to the stockholders. These materials contain certain disclosures concerning management, its compensation, and transactions with the company, as well as the items to be voted on at the meeting. Public companies must also submit an annual report to the shareholders containing the audited financial information for the prior fiscal year and a discussion of any business developments. The preparation and distribution of the proxy materials and annual report are some of the more significant items of additional expense incurred by a company after it is public.

Accounting fees for an initial public offering fluctuate widely but typically average $200,000. Fees are at the lower end of this range if the accounting firm has regularly audited the company over the past several years. They are at the higher end of the range if the company has no prior audits or if it engages a new accounting firm. The accounting fee covers the preparation of financial statements, the response to SEC queries, and the preparation of "cold comfort" letters for the underwriters described later in this chapter. The fees can be affected by the quality and reputation of the accounting firm used in the last three years before going public. Sometimes it becomes necessary to redo these last three years at additional cost if an appropriate firm had not been used.

Legal fees will vary significantly, typically ranging from $150,000 to $350,000. These fees generally cover preparation of corporate documents, preparation and clearing of the registration statement, negotiation of the final underwriting agreement, and closing of the sale of the securities to these underwriters. Additional legal fees may also be assessed and can be extensive, particularly if a major organization is involved. A public company also pays legal fees for the work involved with the Financial Industry Regulatory Authority (FINRA) and state blue-sky filings. The legal fees for FINRA and state blue-sky filings range from $8,000 to $30,000, depending on the size of the offering and the number of states in which the securities will be offered.

In most of the more significant public offerings, the company technically sells the shares to the underwriters, who then resell the shares to the public investors. The difference in the per-share price at which the underwriters purchase the shares from the company and the price at which they sell them to the public is the underwriters' discount, which usually ranges from 7 to 10 percent of the public offering price of the new issue. In some IPOs, the underwriters can also require additional compensation, such as warrants to purchase stock, reimbursement for expenses, and the right of first refusal on any future offerings. The FINRA regulates the maximum amount of the underwriters' compensation and reviews the actual amount for fairness before the offering can take place.

There are other expenses in the form of SEC, FINRA, and state blue-sky registration fees. Of these, the SEC registration fee is quite small: one-fiftieth of 1 percent of the maximum aggregate public offering price of the security. For example, the SEC fee would be $4,000 on a

$20 million offering. The minimum fee is $100. The SEC fee must be paid by certified or cashier's check. The FINRA filing fee is also small in relation to the size of the offering: $100 plus one-hundredth of 1 percent of the maximum public offering price. In the preceding example of a $20 million offering, this would be $2,100, with the FINRA fee being $5,100.

The final major expense, printing costs, typically ranges from $50,000 to $200,000. The registration statement and prospectus discussed later in this chapter account for the largest portion of these expenses. The exact amount of expenses varies, depending on the length of the prospectus, the use of color or black and white photographs, the number of proofs and corrections, and the number printed. It is important for the company to use a good printer because accuracy and speed are required in the printing of the prospectus and other offering documents.

Some help in stemming these rapidly increasing costs could come from more significant use of the Internet in the publication and distribution of prospectuses, as well as from other stockholder communications such as proxy statements and annual reports. However, use of this medium is still somewhat in its infancy state. The SEC is continually refining its rules in this regard in an effort to allow companies to take advantage of this technology while maintaining the disclosure principles originally developed in the 1930s.

Not only can going public be a costly event, but also the process leading up to it can be exasperating. Just ask Bing Yeh, who went through some trying circumstances starting when he decided to go public in July 1995 and ending when his company, Silicon Storage Technology (SST), issued its IPO on November 22 of that same year.[25] While the exact process varies with each company, the goal is the same as it was for SST—make sure the company is well received by Wall Street. For some companies, getting ready to go public can involve eliminating members of the management team and board, dropping marginal products, eliminating treasured perks such as the corporate jet, hiring a new accounting firm, subduing some personality traits, dressing up the senior management, or hiring new members of the management team. For Bing Yeh and SST, the makeover centered around four primary tasks: (1) hiring a chief financial officer, (2) reorganizing the financials, (3) writing a company biography, and (4) preparing for the road show (this is the time when management will present the company to potential investors).

Regardless of how much reading is done, like Bing Yeh, almost every entrepreneur is unprepared and wants to halt the preparation process at some point. Yet for a successful IPO, each entrepreneur must follow Yeh's example by listening to the advice being given and making any recommended changes.

TIMING OF GOING PUBLIC AND UNDERWRITER SELECTION

Two of the most critical issues in a successful public offering are the timing of the offering and the underwriting team. An entrepreneur should seek advice from several financial advisors as well as other entrepreneurs who are familiar with the process in making decisions in these two areas.

Timing

The critical question each entrepreneur must ask is, "Is the company ready to go public?" Some criteria to help answer this question are indicated in the following section.

First, is the company large enough? While it is not possible to establish rigid minimum-size standards that must be met before an entrepreneur can go public, New York investment banking firms prefer at least a 100,000 share offering at a minimum of $20 per share. This means that the company would have to have a post offering value of at least $50 million to support this $20 million offering, given that the company is willing to sell shares representing not more than 40 percent of the total number of shares outstanding after the offering is completed. This size of offering will occur only with past significant sales and earnings performance or a solid prospect for future growth and earnings.

Second, what is the amount of the company's earnings, and how strong is its financial performance? Not only is this performance the basis of the company valuation, but it also determines if a company can successfully go public and the type of firm willing to underwrite the offering. While the exact criteria vary from year to year, thereby reflecting market conditions, generally a company must have at least one year of good earnings and sales before its stock offering will be acceptable to the market. Larger underwriting firms have more stringent criteria, such as sales as high as $15 million to $20 million, a $1 million or more net income, and a 30 to 50 percent annual growth rate.

Third, are the market conditions favorable for an initial public offering? Underlying the sales and earnings, as well as the size of the offering, is the prevailing general market condition. Market conditions affect both the initial price that the entrepreneur will receive for the stock and the aftermarket, or the price performance of the stock after its initial sale. Some market conditions are more favorable for IPOs than others. Unless the need for money is so urgent that delay is impossible, the entrepreneur should attempt to take his or her company public in the most favorable market conditions.

Fourth, how urgently is the money needed? The entrepreneur must carefully appraise both the urgency of the need for new money and the availability of outside capital from other sources. Since the sale of common stock decreases the ownership position of the entrepreneur and other equity owners, the longer the time before going public, given that profits and sales growth occur, the less percentage of equity the entrepreneur will have to give up per dollar invested.

Finally, what are the needs and desires of the present owners? Sometimes the present owners lack confidence in the future viability and growth prospects of the business, or they have a need for liquidity. Going public is frequently the only method by which present stockholders may obtain the cash needed.

Underwriter Selection

managing underwriter
Lead financial firm in selling stock to the public

underwriting syndicate
Group of firms involved in selling stock to the public

Once the entrepreneur has determined that the timing for going public is favorable, he or she must carefully select a *managing underwriter* that will then take the lead in forming the *underwriting syndicate*. The underwriter is of critical importance in establishing the initial price for the stock of the company, supporting the stock in the aftermarket, and creating a strong following among security analysts.

Although most public offerings are conducted by a syndicate of underwriters, the entrepreneur needs to select the lead or managing underwriter(s). The managing underwriter will then develop the syndicate of underwriters for the initial public offering. An entrepreneur should ideally develop a relationship with several potential managing underwriters (investment bankers) at least one year before going public. Frequently, this occurs during the first- or second-round financing, when the advice of an investment banker helps structure the initial financial arrangements to position the company to go public later.

Since selecting the investment banker is a major factor in the success of the public offering, the entrepreneur should approach one through a mutual contact. Commercial banks, attorneys specializing in securities work, major accounting firms, providers of the initial financing, or prominent members of the company's board of directors can usually provide the needed suggestions and introductions. Also, because the relationship will be ongoing and will not end with the completion of the offering, the entrepreneur should employ several criteria in the selection process, such as reputation, distribution capability, advisory services, experience, and cost.

Since an initial public offering rarely involves a well-known company, the managing underwriter needs a good reputation to develop a strong syndicate team and provide confidence to potential investors. This reputation helps sell the public offering and supports the stock in the aftermarket. The ethics of the potential underwriter is an aspect that must be carefully evaluated.

The success of the offering also depends on the underwriter's distribution capability. An entrepreneur wants the stock of his or her company distributed to as wide and varied a base as possible. Since each investment banking firm has a different client base, the entrepreneur should compare client bases of possible managing underwriters. Is the client base strongly institutional or is it composed of individual investors? Or is it balanced between the two? Is the base more internationally or domestically oriented? Are the investors long term or speculators? What is the geographic distribution—local, regional, or nationwide? A strong managing underwriter and syndicate with a quality client base will help the stock sell and perform well in the aftermarket.

Some underwriters are better able than others to provide financial advisory services. Although this factor is not as important as the previous two in selecting an underwriter, financial counsel is frequently needed before and after the IPO. An entrepreneur should pose such questions as the following: Can the underwriter provide sound financial advice? Has the underwriter given good financial counsel to previous clients? Can the underwriter render assistance in obtaining future public or private financing? The answers to these questions will indicate the degree of ability among prospective underwriters.

As reflected in the previous questions, the experience of the investment banking firm is important. The firm should have experience in underwriting issues of companies in the same or at least similar industries. This experience will give the managing underwriter credibility, the capability to explain the company to the investing public, and the ability to price the IPO accurately.

The final factor to be considered in the choice of a managing underwriter is cost. Going public is a very costly proposition, and costs can vary significantly among underwriters. Costs associated with various possible managing underwriters must be carefully weighed against the other four factors. The key is to obtain the best possible underwriter and not try to cut corners, given the stakes involved in a successful initial public offering.

REGISTRATION STATEMENT AND TIMETABLE

Once the managing underwriter has been selected, a planning meeting should be held among those company officials responsible for preparing the registration statement, the company's independent accountants and lawyers, and the underwriters and their counsel. At this important meeting, frequently called the "all hands" meeting, a timetable is prepared that indicates dates for each step in the registration process. This timetable establishes the effective date of the registration, which determines the date of the final financial statements to be included. The timetable should indicate the individual(s) responsible for preparing the various parts of the registration and offering statement. Problems may arise in an initial public offering due to the timetable not being carefully developed and agreed to by all parties involved.

After the completion of the preliminary preparation, the first public offering normally requires six to eight weeks to prepare, print, and file the registration statement with the SEC. Once the registration statement has been filed, the SEC generally takes 6 to 12 weeks to declare the registration effective. Delays frequently occur in this process, especially (1) during heavy periods of market activity; (2) during peak seasons such as March, when the SEC is reviewing a large number of proxy statements; (3) when the company's attorney is not familiar with federal or state regulations regarding the registration process; (4) when issues arise over requirements of the SEC resulting from its review of the filing; or (5) when the managing underwriter is inexperienced.

full and fair disclosure
The nature of all material submitted to the SEC for approval

prospectus Document for distribution to prospective buyers of a public offering

registration statement Materials submitted to the SEC for approval to sell stock to the public

Form S-1 Form for registration for most initial public offerings of stock

In reviewing the registration statement, the SEC attempts to ensure that the document makes a *full and fair disclosure* of the material reported. The SEC has no authority to withhold approval of or require any changes in the terms of an offering that it deems unfair or inequitable, as long as all material information concerning the company and the offering is fully disclosed. However, the Financial Industry Regulatory Authority (FINRA) will review each offering, principally to determine the fairness of the underwriting compensation and its compliance with FINRA bylaw requirements.

The registration statement itself consists primarily of two parts: the *prospectus* (a legal offering document normally prepared as a brochure or booklet for distribution to prospective buyers) and the *registration statement* (supplemental information to the prospectus, which is available for public inspection at the office of the SEC and EDGAR). Both parts of the registration statement are governed principally by the Securities and Exchange Act of 1933 (the "1933 Act"), a federal statute requiring the registration of securities to be offered to the public. This act also requires that the prospectus be furnished to the purchaser at or before the making of any written offer or the actual confirmation of a sale. Specific SEC forms set forth the informational requirements for a registration. Most initial public offerings will use a *Form S-1* registration statement. Smaller offerings may be able to use the shorter forms SB-1 or SB-2.

The Prospectus

The prospectus portion of the registration statement is almost always written in a highly stylized narrative form, since it is the selling document of the company. While the exact format is decided by the company, the information must be presented in an organized, logical sequence and in an easy-to-read, understandable manner to obtain SEC approval. Some of the most common sections of a prospectus include the cover page; prospectus summary; description of the company; risk factors; use of proceeds; dividend policy; capitalization; dilution; selected financial data; the business, management, and owners; type of stock; underwriter information; and the actual financial statements.

The cover page includes information such as company name, type and number of shares to be sold, a distribution table, date of prospectus, managing underwriter(s), and syndicate of underwriters involved. There is a preliminary prospectus and then a final prospectus once it has been approved by the SEC. The preliminary prospectus is used by the underwriters to solicit investor interest in the offering while the registration is pending. The final prospectus contains all the changes and additions required by the SEC and the information concerning the price at which the securities will be sold. The final prospectus must be delivered with or prior to the written confirmation of purchase orders from investors participating in the offering.

The prospectus starts with a table of contents and summary. The prospectus summary highlights the important features of the offering, similar to the executive summary of a business plan that was discussed previously in Chapter 7.

A brief introduction of the company follows, which describes the nature of the business, the company's history, major products, and location.

Then a discussion of the risk factors involved is presented. Such issues as a history of operating losses, a short track record, the importance of certain key individuals, dependence on certain customers, significant level of competition, or market uncertainty are the typical risk factors revealed to ensure that the purchaser is aware of the speculative nature of the offering and the degree of risk involved in purchasing.

The next section, use of proceeds, needs to be carefully prepared since the actual use of the proceeds must be reported to the SEC after the offering. This section is of great interest to potential purchasers as it indicates the reason(s) the company is going public and its future direction.

The dividend policy section details the company's dividend history and any restrictions on future dividends. Most entrepreneurial companies have not paid any dividends but have retained their earnings to finance future growth.

The capitalization section indicates the overall capital structure of the company both before and after the public offering.

Whenever there is significant disparity between the offering price of the shares and the price paid for shares by officers, directors, or founding stockholders, a dilution section is necessary in the prospectus. This section describes the dilution, or difference between the share price paid by the public investors and the weighted average price at which all shares have been issued, including the pre-IPO shares sold to officers, directors, and founding stakeholders.

Form S-1 requires that the prospectus contain selected financial data for each of the last five years of company operation to highlight significant trends in the company's financial condition. There must also be a discussion of management's analysis of the company's financial condition and results of operations. This analysis should cover at least the last three years of operation.

The next section, the business, is the largest part of the prospectus. It provides information on the company, its industry, and its products, and includes the following: the historical development of the company; principal products, markets, and distribution methods; new products being developed; sources and availability of raw materials; backlog orders; export sales; number of employees; and nature of any patents, trademarks, licenses, franchises, and physical property owned; competition; and effects of governmental regulations.

Following the business section is a discussion of management and security holders. This section covers background information, ages, business experience, total remuneration, and stock holdings of directors, nominated directors, and executive officers. Also, any other stockholder (not in the preceding categories) who beneficially owns more than 5 percent of the company must be indicated.

The description of the capital stock section, as the name implies, indicates the par and stated value of the stock being offered, dividend rights, voting rights, liquidity, and transferability if more than one class of stock exists.

Following this, the underwriter information section explains the plans for distributing the securities, such as the amount of securities to be purchased by each underwriting participant involved.

The prospectus part of the registration statement concludes with the actual financial statements. Form S-1 normally requires audited balance sheets for the last two fiscal years, audited income statements and statements of retained earnings for the last three fiscal years, and unaudited interim financial statements as of 135 days prior to the date when the registration statement becomes effective. It is this requirement that makes it so important to pick a date for going public in light of year-end operations and to develop a good timetable. This will help avoid the time and costs of preparing additional interim statements.

The Registration Statement

This section of Form S-1 contains certain information regarding the offering, the past unregistered securities offering of the company, and any other undertakings by the company. The registration statement also includes exhibits such as the articles of incorporation, the underwriting agreement, company bylaws, stock option and pension plans, and initial contracts.

Procedure

red herring Preliminary prospectus of a potential public offering

Once the preliminary prospectus is filed as a part of the registration statement, it can be distributed to the underwriting group. This preliminary prospectus is called a *red herring,*

comment letter   A letter from the SEC to a company indicating corrections that need to be made in the submitted prospectus

pricing amendment   Additional information on price and distribution submitted to the SEC to develop the final prospectus

quiet period   90-day period in going public when no new company information should be released

blue-sky laws   Laws of each state regulating public sale of stock

aftermarket support   Actions of underwriters to help support the price of stock following the public offering

because a statement printed in red ink appears on the front cover. The registration statement is then reviewed by the SEC to determine the adequacy of the disclosure. Some deficiencies are almost always found and are communicated to the company via either telephone or a *comment letter.* This preliminary prospectus contains all the information that will appear in the final prospectus except that which is not known until shortly before the effective date: offering price, underwriters' commission, and amount of proceeds. These items are filed through a *pricing amendment* and appear in the final prospectus. The time between the initial filing of the registration statement and its effective date, usually around 2 to 10 months, is called the waiting period. During this time the underwriting syndicate is formed and briefed. Any company publicity regarding the proposed offering cannot be released during this period.

LEGAL ISSUES AND BLUE-SKY QUALIFICATIONS
Legal Issues

In addition to all the legal issues surrounding the actual preparation and filing of the prospectus, there are several other important legal concerns. Perhaps the one that is of the most concern to the entrepreneur is the *quiet period,* the period of time from when the decision to go public is made to 90 days following the date the prospectus becomes effective. Care must be taken during this period regarding any new information about the company or key personnel. Any publicity effort creating a favorable attitude about the securities to be offered is illegal. The guidelines established by the SEC regarding the information that can and cannot be released should be understood not only by the entrepreneur but by everyone else in the company as well. All press releases and other printed material should be cleared with the attorneys involved as well as the underwriter. The entrepreneur and key personnel must curtail speaking engagements and television appearances to avoid any possible problematic response to interviewer or audience questions. For example, one entrepreneur whose company was in the process of going public had to postpone a TV guest appearance on *The Today Show* with one of the authors of this textbook, where she was to discuss women entrepreneurs, not her company.

Blue-Sky Qualifications

The securities of certain smaller companies going public must also be qualified under the *blue-sky laws* of each state in which the securities will be offered. This is true unless the state has an exemption from the qualification requirements. These blue-sky laws may cause additional delays and costs to the company going public. Offerings of securities that will be traded on the more prominent stock exchanges or listed on the NASDAQ Global Market have been preempted from most state registration requirements by the National Securities Markets Improvement Act of 1996. Many states allow their state securities administrators to prevent an offering from being sold in their state on such substantive grounds as past stock issuances, too much dilution, or too much compensation to the underwriter, even though all required disclosures have been met and clearance has been granted by the SEC.

AFTER GOING PUBLIC

After the initial public offering has been sold, there are still some areas of concern to the entrepreneur. These include *aftermarket support,* relationship with the financial community, and reporting requirements.

Aftermarket Support

Once issued, the price of the stock is typically monitored, particularly in the initial weeks after its offering. Usually the managing underwriting firm will be the principal market maker in the company's stock and will be ready to purchase or sell stock in the interdealer market. To stabilize the market, and prevent the price from going below the initial public offering price, the underwriter will usually enter bids to buy the stock in the early stages after the offers, thereby giving aftermarket support. This support is important in allowing the stock not to be adversely affected by an initial drop in price.

Relationship with the Financial Community

Once a company has gone public, the financial community usually takes a greater interest. An entrepreneur will need an increasing portion of time to develop a good relationship with this community. The relationship established has a significant effect on the market interest and the price of the company's stock. Since many investors rely on analysts and brokers for investment advice, the entrepreneur should attempt to meet as many of these individuals as possible. Regular appearances before societies of security analysts should be a part of establishing this relationship, as well as public disclosures through formal press releases. Frequently, it is best to designate one person in the company to be the information officer, ensuring that the press, public, and security analysts are dealt with in a friendly, efficient manner. There is nothing worse than a company not responding in a timely manner to information requests.

Reporting Requirements

The company must file annual reports on Form 10-K, quarterly reports on Form 10-Q, and specific transaction or event reports on Form 8-K. The information in Form 10-K on the business, management, and company assets is similar to that in Form S-1 of the registration statement. Of course, audited financial statements are required.

The quarterly report on Form 10-Q primarily contains the unaudited financial information for the most recently completed fiscal quarter. No Form 10-Q is required for the fourth fiscal quarter.

A Form 8-K report must be filed within two to five days of such events as the acquisition or disposition of significant assets by the company outside the ordinary course of the business, the resignation or dismissal of the company's independent public accountants, or a change in control of the company.

Under the Sarbanes-Oxley Act, the due dates for reports have been accelerated. In addition, by adopting its Regulation FD, the Securities and Exchange Commission has tried to minimize selective disclosures of important corporate developments and information. Under this regulation, public companies are required to make immediate and broad public disclosures of important information at the same time they release the information to anyone outside the company.

The company must follow the proxy solicitation requirements in connection with holding a meeting or obtaining the written consent of security holders. The timing and type of materials involved are detailed in Regulation 14A under the Securities Exchange Act of 1934. These are but a few of the reporting requirements of public companies that must be carefully observed, since even inadvertent mistakes can have negative consequences for the company. The reports required must be filed on time.

IN REVIEW

SUMMARY

In financing a business, the entrepreneur determines the amount and timing of funds needed. Seed or start-up capital is the most difficult to obtain, with the most likely source being the informal risk-capital market (angels). These investors, who are wealthy individuals, average one or two deals per year, ranging from $100,000 to $500,000, and generally find their deals through referrals.

Although venture capital may be used in the first stage, it is primarily used in the second or third stage to provide working capital for growth or expansion. Venture capital is broadly defined as a professionally managed pool of equity capital. Since 1958, small-business investment companies (SBICs) have combined private capital and government funds to finance the growth and start-up of small businesses. Private venture-capital firms have developed since the 1960s, with limited partners supplying the funding. At the same time, venture-capital divisions operating within major corporations began appearing. States also sponsor venture-capital funds to foster economic development.

To achieve the venture capitalist's primary goal of generating long-term capital appreciation through investments in business, three criteria are used: The company must have strong management; the product/market opportunity must be unique; and the capital appreciation must be significant, offering a 40 to 60 percent return on investment. The process of obtaining venture capital includes a preliminary screening, agreement on principal terms, due diligence, and final approval. Entrepreneurs need to approach a potential venture capitalist with a professional business plan and a good oral presentation.

Valuing the company is of concern to the entrepreneur. Eight factors can be used as a basis for valuation: the nature and history of the business, the economic outlook, book value, future earnings, dividend-paying capacity, intangible assets, sales of stock, and the market price of stocks of similar companies. Numerous valuation approaches that can be used were discussed.

In the end, the entrepreneur and investor must agree on the terms of the transaction, known as the deal. When care is taken in structuring the deal, the entrepreneur and the investor will maintain a good relationship while achieving their goals through the growth and profitability of the business.

Going public—transforming a closely held corporation into one in which the general public has proprietary interest—is indeed arduous. An entrepreneur must carefully assess whether the company is ready to go public as well as whether the advantages outweigh the disadvantages of doing so.

Once the decision is made to proceed, a managing investment banking firm must be selected and the registration statement prepared. The expertise of the investment banker is a major factor in the success of the public offering. In selecting an investment banker, the entrepreneur should consider reputation, distribution capability, advisory services, experience, and cost. To prepare for the registration date, the entrepreneur must organize an "all hands" meeting of company officials, the company's independent accountants and lawyers, and the underwriters and their counsel. A timetable must be established for the effective date of registration and for the preparation of necessary financial documents, including the preliminary and final prospectuses.

Following the initial public offering, the entrepreneur should strive to maintain a good relationship with the financial community and adhere strictly to the reporting requirements of public companies.

RESEARCH TASKS

1. Go to a directory of venture capitalists and ascertain what percentage of funds for a typical venture-capital firm are invested in seed, start-up, expansion or development, and acquisitions or leveraged buyouts. What criteria do venture capitalists report using in their initial screening of business proposals?

2. Obtain an initial public offering prospectus for three companies. Use at least two different approaches for valuing each company.

3. Search the Internet for services that provide access to business angels or informal investors. How do these sites work? If you were an entrepreneur looking for funding, how much would it cost to use this service? How many business angels are registered on the typical database? How many entrepreneurs are registered on the typical database? How effective do you believe these services are? (Use data where possible to back up your answer.)

4. How many companies went public per year over the last 10-year period? How do you explain this variation in the "popularity" of going public?

5. Analyze the prospectuses of 10 companies that went public in 2005. In your opinion, which companies are likely to do well in the public offering, and which are less likely to do well? Conduct the following calculation to test your propositions: Stock price after 1 week − Offering price ÷ Offering price. Compare this price with the original IPO price.

6. Analyze the prospectuses of five companies going public. What are the reasons they state for going public? How are they going to use the proceeds? What are the major risk factors presented?

CLASS DISCUSSION

1. An investor provides an entrepreneurial firm with the capital that it needs to grow. Over and above providing the capital, in what other ways can the investor add value to the firm? What are the possible downsides of having a venture capitalist as an investor in the business?

2. Assume that you have been very lucky and have been given a considerable fortune. You want to become a business angel (straight after graduation). How would you go about setting up and running your "business angel" business? Be specific about generating deal flow, selection criteria, the desired level of control and involvement in the investee, etc.

3. What drives the market for IPOs? Why is it so volatile?

4. If you were an entrepreneur in a "hot" market, would you invest the substantial amount of time, energy, and other resources necessary to try and go public before the bubble bursts? Or would you prefer to utilize those resources to build your business and create value for customers?

SELECTED READINGS

Gupta, Udayan. (September 1, 2011). Using Venture Capital to Build Companies and Save the World. *Institutional Investor Magazine*, n/a.

This article discusses the current venture capital market and the role of venture capital firms in supporting innovation. The importance of a partnership between investors and entrepreneurs is examined.

Miller, Toyah L.; and Curtis L. Wesley II. (July 2010). Assessing Mission and Resources for Social Change: An Organizational Identity Perspective on Social Venture Capitalists' Decision Criteria. *Entrepreneurship Theory and Practice*, vol. 34, pp. 705–33.

This paper investigates the evaluation criteria used by social venture capital investors in identifying new investments. The authors determine that not all potential investors evaluate investments equally, but that generally entrepreneurial criteria is valued more than social criteria. Furthermore, the value of the social project to an investor is dependent on the investor's preference for social projects.

Zhang, Junfu. (February 2011). The Advantage of Experienced Start-up Founders in Venture Capital Acquisition: Evidence from Serial Entrepreneurs. *Small Business Economics*, vol. 36, pp. 187–208.

This article discusses the advantages of experienced entrepreneurs with venture-backed experience in the capital-raising process. The author suggests that entrepreneurs with funding experience that included venture capital were able to raise capital more quickly and easily in the first round of funding than either experienced entrepreneurs without capital-raising experience or inexperienced entrepreneurs. In the second round of financing, experienced entrepreneurs raised more funds than inexperienced entrepreneurs. The author emphasizes the importance of relationships with venture capital investors in the financing process.

Zheng, Yanfeng. (Spring 2011). In Their Eyes: How Entrepreneurs Evaluate Venture Capital Firms. *The Journal of Private Equity*, vol. 14, pp. 72–85.

The author investigates the criteria most valued by entrepreneurs in seeking venture capital investors. These criteria include late responses, ethics, geographic density, and the firm's success record.

END NOTES

1. "Profile: Richard Branson," *BBC News*, London, September 27, 2004.
2. "*Forbes* Billionaires 2011," *Forbes*, March 2011.
3. "Richard Branson: The P. T. Barnum of British Business," *Entrepreneur Media*, October 10, 2008, http://www.entrepreneur.com/article/197616.
4. Robert M. Grant, *Richard Branson and the Virgin Group of Companies in 2004*, Case 15 (Oxford: Blackwell Publishing, 2004).
5. "Richard Branson: The P. T. Barnum of British Business."
6. Grant, *Richard Branson and the Virgin Group of Companies in 2004*.
7. "Virgin," *Virgin—About Us*, September 20, 2011, http://www.virgin.com/about-us.
8. Zack O'Malley Greenburg, "Billionaire Richard Branson on Being a Rock Star Businessman," *Forbes*, September 19, 2011.
9. "Space Tickets," *Virgin Galactic*, September 20, 2011, http://www.virgingalactic.com/overview/space-tickets/.
10. "Virgin Unite," *About Virgin Unite*, September 21, 2011, http://www.virginunite.com/AboutVirginunite/Rest-of-World/.
11. Greenburg, "Billionaire Richard Branson on Being a Rock Star Businessman."

12. Richard Branson, "Richard Branson: Five Secrets to Business Success," *Entrepreneur,* September 9, 2010.

13. *Report of the Use of the Rule 146 Exemption in Capital Formation* (Washington, DC: Directorate of Economic Policy Analysis, Securities and Exchange Commission, 1983).

14. *An Analysis of Regulation D* (Washington, DC: Directorate of Economic Policy Analysis, Securities and Exchange Commission, 1984).

15. Charles River Associates, Inc., *An Analysis of Capital Market Imperfections* (Washington, DC: National Bureau of Standards, February 1976).

16. W. E. Wetzel, Jr., "Entrepreneurs, Angels, and Economic Renaissance," in R. D. Hisrich (ed.), *Entrepreneurship, Intrapreneurship, and Venture Capital* (Lexington, MA: Lexington Books, 1986), pp. 119–40. Other information on angels and their investments can be found in W. E. Wetzel, Jr., "Angels and Informal Risk Capital," *Sloan Management Review* 24 (Summer 1983), pp. 23–24; and W. E. Wetzel, Jr., "The Informal Venture Capital Market: Aspects of Scale and Market Efficiency," *Journal of Business Venturing* (Fall 1987), pp. 299–314.

17. R. B. Avery and G. E. Elliehausen, "Financial Characteristics of High-Income Families," *Federal Reserve Bulletin* (Washington, DC, March 1986).

18. M. Gannon, "Financing Purgatory: An Emerging Class of Investors Is Beginning to Fill the Nether Regions of Start-Up Financing—The Murky World between the Angels and the Venture Capitalists," *Venture Capital Journal* (May 1999), pp. 40–42.

19. S. Prowse, "Angel Investors and the Market for Angel Investments," *Journal of Banking and Finance* 23 (1998), pp. 785–92.

20. Joseph Bell, Kenneth Huggins, and Christine McClatchey, "Profiling the Angel Investor," *Proceedings, Small Business Institute Directors Association 2002 Conference,* February 7–9, 2002, San Diego, CA, pp. 1–3.

21. For the role of SBICs, see Farrell K. Slower, "Growth Looms for SBICs," *Venture* (October 1985), pp. 46–47; and M. H. Fleischer, "The SBIC 100—More Deals for the Bucks," *Venture* (October 1985), pp. 50–54.

22. Most of the information on the venture capital industry in this section as well as other information can be found in the PricewaterhouseCoopers/Thomson Venture Economics/National Venture Capital Association Money Tree™ Survey.

23. For a thorough discussion of the venture capital process, see B. Davis, "Role of Venture Capital in the Economic Renaissance of an Area," in R. D. Hisrich (ed.), *Entrepreneurship, Intrapreneurship, and Venture Capital* (Lexington, MA: Lexington Books, 1986), pp. 107–18; Robert D. Hisrich and A. D. Jankowicz, "Intuition in Venture Capital Decisions: An Exploratory Study Using a New Technique," *Journal of Business Venturing* 5 (January 1990), pp. 49–63; Robert D. Hisrich and Vance H. Fried, "The Role of the Venture Capitalist in the Management of Entrepreneurial Enterprises," *Journal of International Business and Entrepreneurship* 1, no. 1 (June 1992), pp. 75–106; Vance H. Fried, Robert D. Hisrich, and Amy Polonchek, "Research Note: Venture Capitalists' Investment Criteria: A Replication," *Journal of Small Business Finance* 3, no. 1 (Fall 1993), pp. 37–42; and Vance H. Fried and Robert D. Hisrich, "The Venture Capitalist: A Relationship Investor," *California Management Review* 37, no. 2 (Winter 1995), pp. 101–13.

24. A discussion of some of the important sectors in this decision process can be found in I. MacMillan, L. Zemann, and Subba Narasimba, "Criteria Distinguishing Successful from Unsuccessful Ventures in the Venture Screening Process," *Journal of Business Venturing* 2 (Spring 1987), pp. 123–38; Robert D. Hisrich and Vance H. Fried, "Towards a Model of Venture Capital Investment Decision-Making," *Financial Management* 23, no. 3 (Fall 1994), pp. 28–37; and Vance H. Fried, B. Elonso, and Robert D. Hisrich, "How Venture Capital Firms Differ," *Journal of Business Venturing* 10, no. 2 (March 1995), pp. 157–79.

25. For the full details of this story, see John Kerr, "The 100-Day Makeover," *Inc.* (May 1996), pp. 54–63.

5

FROM FUNDING THE VENTURE TO LAUNCHING, GROWING, AND ENDING THE NEW VENTURE

13

STRATEGIES FOR GROWTH AND MANAGING THE IMPLICATIONS OF GROWTH

1

To know where to look for (or how to create) possible growth opportunities.

2

To understand the human resource management challenges and to be prepared to effectively manage those challenges.

3

To understand the pressures of time and how to engage time management techniques.

4

To recognize that people differ and to understand how these differences impact their intentions and abilities to grow a business.

OPENING PROFILE

BRIAN AND JENNIFER MAXWELL

Brian Maxwell, an internationally ranked marathon runner and coach at the University of California, Berkeley, was leading a marathon race in England when at the 21-mile mark he began to experience dizziness and tunnel vision, which forced him to quit the race. His consumption of energy drinks on the day of the race had failed and motivated him to find a solution for a better energy source. He teamed up with Jennifer Biddulph, a student studying nutrition and food science (now a PhD chemist), and they began the quest for an energy bar that would taste good, be healthy and nutritious, and provide the appropriate ingredients to optimize performance. With $50,000 gathered from savings, they were determined to find a solution.[1]

During their three years of research, experts indicated to them that it would be impossible to produce a healthy product because of the large amounts of saturated fats necessary for lubricating machinery in the food bar manufacturing process. However, after many failures, they found the solution. They understood that their efforts required developing a food bar manufacturing process that would not require adding fats for lubrication of machinery and would produce a product that would meet the desired attributes. The product needed to provide a balance of simple carbohydrates for quick energy, complex carbohydrates for longer lasting energy, and low fat for easy digestion. Hundreds of recipes were tested with athletes until the most effective and best-tasting product was found. Continued requests among these athletes to have more of those "power bars" led to the final brand name, and in 1986 they officially formed the company, PowerBar Inc.

Initially the company was operated from Brian and Jennifer's basement. The first products, which went on sale in 1987, were the Malt-Nut and Chocolate flavors. After their marriage in 1988, they moved to a new facility and began hiring employees to meet the growing demand.

Their vision of finding a solution to a serious runner's energy source wasn't the only factor in forming this new venture. Both Brian and Jennifer were determined to create a work environment where employees would feel important and have a strong sense of pride in the company. They wanted a company that did not have all the things that they hated about jobs they had held previously. Thus, they created a work environment where employees are called team members, the dress is casual, and the focus is on sports. To Brian and Jennifer, it was important that their employees enjoyed the workplace and developed an important loyalty and commitment to the company's mission.

In the early part of the 1990s, sales for the new venture increased by 50 to 60 percent. In 1997 sales began to slow and increased by only 23 percent. In 1995 Brian and Jennifer turned down an opportunity to purchase Balance Bar, a producer of an energy bar that targeted the more casual athlete and those who were looking for a nutritious snack. They had believed that their company did not need to add any new products and could continue to grow with the one product. In retrospect, they realized this was a mistake in strategy and that the venture could not survive on the one product, especially when they saw sales begin to stall in 1995. At that time there were many new competitors who recognized the opportunities in a larger market by introducing energy bars for casual exercisers and snackers. So in 1997 Brian and Jennifer began efforts to find new products. In 1998 they launched PowerBar Harvest, a crunchy, textured energy bar available in a number of flavors that would target casual athletes and consumers looking for a nutritious snack. In 1999 a new creamy bar called Essentials and a new line of sports drinks were launched.

Today PowerBar is still the leader in the serious athlete market, and Harvest has just passed Clif bar to become the number three brand in this category. Sales in 1999 reached $135 million. The company also opened a state-of-the-art manufacturing facility in Idaho and two distribution centers in Idaho and North Carolina. It also established two subsidiaries in Canada and Germany as opportunities for sales growth in international markets occurred.

Brian still runs 40 to 50 miles per week. Jennifer was recently recognized in the first annual Working Women Entrepreneurial Excellence Awards competition by winning for Harvest in the Best Innovation category. In 2000, PowerBar was purchased by Nestlé USA, which intends to grow and expand it globally. Brian Maxwell will continue to play an integral role in the company.

In this chapter, important management decision areas are reviewed and discussed. Building a solid management team and a loyal employee base, recognized by entrepreneurs like Brian and Jennifer Maxwell as being very important during the early years, is discussed in detail, along with financial and marketing control decisions.

GROWTH STRATEGIES: WHERE TO LOOK FOR GROWTH OPPORTUNITIES

In Chapter 3 we discussed new entry as an essential act of entrepreneurship. A successful new entry provides the opportunity for the entrepreneur to grow his or her business. For example, introducing a new product into an existing market provides the opportunity to take market share from competitors; entry into a new market provides the opportunity to service a new group of customers; and a new organization has a chance to make, and build upon, its first sales. Although it is difficult to provide direct guidance to entrepreneurs on a step-by-step process for generating a highly attractive opportunity, in this chapter we provide a model that offers suggestions on where to look for growth opportunities in which the firm may already have a basis for a sustainable competitive advantage. We then investigate the implications of that growth for an economy, for the firm, and for the entrepreneur, as well as the possible need to negotiate for resources from external sources to sustain firm growth.

We know from Chapter 3 that opportunities for new entry are generated by the knowledge of the entrepreneur and from organizational knowledge. We use this as a basis for deciding on the best place to look for opportunities to grow the business. From a simple perspective, we can assume that the entrepreneur and the firm have knowledge about the product that they are currently producing and selling (the existing product) and have knowledge about the group of customers to which they are currently selling that product (the existing market).

Different combinations of different levels of these types of knowledge are represented in Figure 13.1 and provide a model of different growth strategies.[2] Most of these growth strategies can lead to a competitive advantage because they capitalize on some aspect of the entrepreneur's, and the firm's, knowledge base. These growth strategies are: (1) penetration strategies, (2) market development strategies, (3) product development strategies, and (4) diversification strategies.

Penetration Strategies

penetration strategy
A strategy to grow by encouraging existing customers to buy more of the firm's current products

A *penetration strategy* focuses on the firm's existing product in its existing market. The entrepreneur attempts to penetrate this product or market further by encouraging existing customers to buy more of the firm's current products. Marketing can be effective in encouraging more frequent repeat purchases. For example, a pizza company engages in an extensive marketing campaign to encourage its existing customer base of university students to eat its pizza three nights a week rather than only twice a week. This growth strategy does not involve anything new for the firm and relies on taking market share from competitors and/or expanding the size of the existing market. Therefore, this growth strategy attempts to better exploit its original entry.

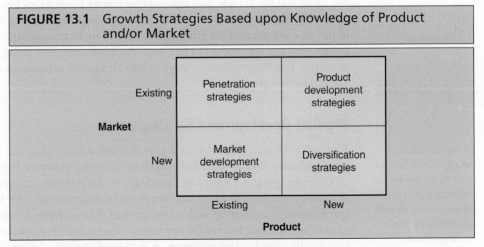

FIGURE 13.1   Growth Strategies Based upon Knowledge of Product and/or Market

Source: H. I. Ansoff, *Corporate Strategy: An Analytical Approach to Business Policy for Growth and Expansion* (New York: McGraw-Hill, 1965). With permission of the Ansoff Family Trust.

Market Development Strategies

market development strategy   Strategy to grow by selling the firm's existing products to new groups of customers

Growth also can occur through market development strategies. *Market development strategies* involve selling the firm's existing products to new groups of customers. New groups of customers can be categorized in terms of geographics or demographics and/or on the basis of new product use.

New Geographical Market   This simply refers to selling the existing product in new locations. For example, a firm selling its products in Singapore could start selling its products in Malaysia, Thailand, and Indonesia. This has the potential of increasing sales by offering products to customers who have not previously had the chance to purchase them. The entrepreneur must be aware of possible regional differences in customer preferences, language, and legal requirements that may necessitate a slight change in the product (or packaging).

New Demographic Market   Demographics are used to characterize (potential) customers based upon their income; where they live; their education, age, and sex; and so on. For an entrepreneur who is currently selling the firm's existing product to a specific demographic group, the business could grow by offering the same product to a different demographic group. For example, a studio currently produces and sells computer games (specializing in games on baseball and soccer) to males between the ages of 13 and 17. However, there is an opportunity for this company to expand its sales by also targeting males between the ages of 24 and 32 who are university educated, have high disposable incomes, and would likely enjoy the escapism of these computer game products.

New Product Use   An entrepreneurial firm might find out that people use its product in a way that was not intended or expected. This new knowledge of product use provides insight into how the product may be valuable to new groups of buyers. For example, when I moved from Australia to Chicago, I bought a baseball bat. I did not use the bat to play baseball; rather, I kept it beside my bed for security against anyone who might break into my apartment. Fortunately, I never had to use it, but I did sleep better knowing it was there. Recognition of this new product use could open up a whole new market for the manufacturers of baseball bats. Another example is four-wheel-drive vehicles. The original producers of this product thought that it would be used primarily for off-road recreational driving but found that the vehicle was also popular among housewives because it was big enough to take the children to school and carry all their bags and sporting equipment. Knowledge of this new use allowed the producers to modify their product slightly to better satisfy customers who use the product in this way. An advantage from using a market development strategy is that it capitalizes on existing knowledge and expertise in a particular technology and production process.

Product Development Strategies

product development strategy   A strategy to grow by developing and selling new products to people who are already purchasing the firm's existing products

Product development strategies for growth involve developing and selling new products to people who are already purchasing the firm's existing products. Experience with a particular customer group is a source of knowledge on the problems customers have with existing technology and ways in which customers can be better served. This knowledge is an important resource in coming up with a new product. For example, Disney Corporation built on its existing customer base of Disney movie viewers and developed merchandising products specifically aimed at this audience. A further advantage of using a product development strategy is the chance to capitalize on existing distribution systems and on the corporate reputation the firm has with these customers.

Diversification Strategies

diversification strategy
A strategy to grow by selling a new product to a new market

Diversification strategies involve selling a new product to a new market. Even though both knowledge bases appear to be new, some diversification strategies are related to the entrepreneur's (and the firm's) knowledge. In fact there are three types of related diversification that are best explained through a discussion of the value-added chain.

As illustrated in Figure 13.2, a value-added chain captures the steps it takes to develop raw materials into a product and get it into the hands of the customers. Value is added at every stage of the chain. For the value added, each firm makes some profit. If we focus on the manufacturer, opportunities for growth arise from backward integration, forward integration, and horizontal integration. *Backward integration* refers to taking a step back (up) on the value-added chain toward the raw materials, which in this case means that the manufacturer also becomes a raw materials wholesaler. In essence the firm becomes its own supplier. *Forward integration* is taking a step forward (down) on the value-added chain toward the customers, which in this case means that the firm also becomes a finished goods wholesaler. In essence the firm becomes its own buyer.

backward integration
A step back (up) in the value-added chain toward the raw materials

forward integration
A step forward (down) on the value-added chain toward the customers

Backward or forward integration provides an entrepreneur with a potentially attractive opportunity to grow his or her business. First, these growth opportunities are related to the firm's existing knowledge base, and the entrepreneur could therefore have some advantage over others with no such experience or knowledge. Second, being one's own supplier and/or buyer provides synergistic opportunities to conduct these transactions more efficiently than they are conducted with independent firms fulfilling these roles. Third, operating as a supplier and/or a buyer of the original business provides learning opportunities that could lead to new processes and/or new product improvements that would not have been available if this integration had not taken place.

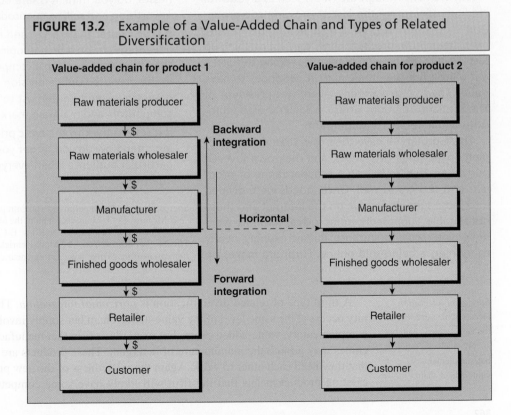

FIGURE 13.2 Example of a Value-Added Chain and Types of Related Diversification

AS SEEN IN *BUSINESS NEWS*

PROVIDE ADVICE TO AN ENTREPRENEUR ABOUT GROWING INTO NEW MARKETS USING THE INTERNET

Dot-com mania may have ended, but selling products and services online has scarcely begun. In fact, estimates from a variety of sources have total online retail sales increasing approximately 30 percent in 2002. And after years of similarly rapid growth, the absolute numbers aren't tiny either: Projections based on the U.S. Department of Commerce's conservative data reports indicate that online sales of goods and services topped $42 billion in 2002. And the Department of Commerce doesn't include online travel sales, which typically account for 40 percent or more of online revenue.

One thing driving online sales growth is the still-increasing number of people going online. Market trackers at Jupiter Media Metrix forecast the number of online Americans will double in five years to 132 million. Because about half of Internet users buy something online during any particular year, that translates to solid growth for online commerce.

The online market isn't just growing; it's also changing. To begin with, the shoppers themselves are transforming. Once mostly men, they're now mostly women. Though the Net is seen as a youthful medium, seniors are the fastest-growing age group. And though ethnic groups have lagged behind the mainstream in embracing online, they are catching up fast. "While the general market is tending to flatten out a little bit, the ethnic market continues to have rapid growth," says Derene Allen, vice president of The Santiago Solutions Group, a San Francisco multicultural marketing consulting firm.

These groups all have their own reasons for shopping online, their own styles, and their own favored purchases. They're buying a broader range of products and services as well. Once, goods were divided into those suitable for sale on the Internet and those not suitable. Supposedly, items such as furniture were not online-ready, for instance. But increasingly, nearly everything is being sold online. Furniture makes up most of the volume at PoshTots, a 16-person Glen Allen, Virginia, online seller of high-end children's products. "Our customers are buying cribs and beds," says Karen Booth Adams, 33-year-old co-founder, "and we sell a lot of playhouses."

Continuing growth of the online market calls for evolving business strategies as well. The frenzy to achieve the first-mover advantage that characterized the early years of online retail has subsided. Today, selling online is less about having the latest technology and more about having the best insight into customers. "It's back to tried-and-true principles of marketing," says Keith Tudor, professor of marketing at Kennesaw State University in Kennesaw, Georgia. "Look at your customers' wants, needs, and motivations."

ADVICE TO AN ENTREPRENEUR

An entrepreneur who runs a "bricks and mortar" retail business comes to you for advice:

1. With all the failures associated with dot-com businesses, do you think it is safe now for me to start advertising and selling my products online?

2. If I can't enter this market and rely on first-mover advantages or on a technological advantage, then how can I develop a competitive advantage in the proposed online division of my retail business? Do I need to enter just to keep up with my competitors and maintain market share?

3. If it reverts back to the basic principles of marketing, then how do you target your product at a particular audience when everyone is using the Internet?

Source: Reprinted with permission of Entrepreneur Media, Inc., "Net Meeting. Let Us Introduce You to the Most Important People on the Internet. If You Think You Know E-Commerce Consumers, This Might Surprise You," by Mark Henricks, February 2003, *Entrepreneur* magazine: www.entrepreneur.com.

horizontal integration
Occurs at the same level of the value-added chain but simply involves a different, but complementary, value-added chain

A third type of related diversification is *horizontal integration*. The growth opportunity occurs at the same level of the value-added chain but simply involves a different, but complementary, value-added chain. For example, a firm that manufactures washing machines may go into the manufacture of detergent. These products are complementary in that they need each other to work. Again the relatedness of the new product to the firm's existing product means that the firm will likely have some competencies in this new product and may provide learning opportunities. Further, horizontal integration provides the opportunity to increase sales of the existing product. For example, the existing product and the new product may be bundled and sold together, which may provide increased value to customers and increase sales. Examples of bundled products include computer hardware and software, televisions and video recorders, and telephones and answering machines.

What about introducing a new product into a new market that is not related to the existing business (i.e., not forward, backward, or horizontal integration)? The short answer is, "Don't do it." If it is not related to the current business, then what possible advantage can this firm have over competitors? Ego and the mistaken belief in the benefits of a firm's diversifying its risk lead some entrepreneurs to pursue unrelated diversification to their own peril.

Example of Growth Strategies

To illustrate the use of the preceding model to explore possibilities for firm growth, we consider the early days of the Head Ski Company, which, at that time, only produced and sold high-tech skis in the U.S. market. A *penetration strategy* for Head could be achieved through an increase in its marketing budget focused on encouraging existing customers to "upgrade" their skis more often. This could involve some sort of performance imperative that encourages customers to desire the most up-to-date skis with the newest technological features.

A *market development strategy* could involve Head's selling its skis in Europe, Argentina, and New Zealand. The advantage of moving into Argentina and New Zealand is that these markets are in the Southern Hemisphere and therefore sales are counterseasonal to those in the United States (and other Northern Hemisphere markets). Head could also start selling its skis to the mass market—those less affluent skiers who want a good-performance ski at a "reasonable" price.

To pursue a *product development strategy*, Head could develop and sell new products, such as hats, gloves, boots, and other ski accessories, to people who buy its skis. Head could also manufacture tennis racquets or mountain bikes—equipment that is used by its existing customer group when not skiing. These new products would build on its customer reputation for high-tech, high-quality products and could capitalize on existing distribution systems. For example, ski shops could sell Head tennis racquets and mountain bikes during the summer months, which would also smooth out seasonal variability in sales.

Diversification strategies also offer opportunities for growth. For example, backward integration could involve the design and manufacture of equipment used to make skis, forward integration could involve control of a chain of retail ski shops, and horizontal integration could involve ownership of ski mountains (lifts, lodges, etc.).

As this example demonstrates, the model offers a tool for entrepreneurs, to force them to think and look in different directions for growth opportunities where the firm may already have a basis for a sustainable competitive advantage. The pursuit and achievement of growth have an impact on the economy, the firm, and the entrepreneur.

IMPLICATIONS OF GROWTH FOR THE FIRM

Because growth makes a firm bigger, the firm begins to benefit from the advantages of size. For example, higher volume increases production efficiency, makes the firm more attractive to suppliers, and therefore increases its bargaining power. Size also enhances the legitimacy of the firm, because firms that are larger are often perceived by customers, financiers, and other stakeholders as being more stable and prestigious. Therefore, the growing of a business can provide the entrepreneur more power to influence firm performance. But as the firm grows, it changes. These changes introduce a number of managerial challenges. These challenges arise from the following pressures.

Pressures on Human Resources

Growth is also fueled by the work of employees. If employees are spread too thin by the pursuit of growth, then the firm will face problems of employee morale, employee burnout, and an increase in employee turnover. These employee issues could also have a negative impact on the firm's corporate culture. For example, an influx of a large number of new employees (necessitated by an increase in the number of tasks and to replace those that leave) will likely dilute the corporate culture, which is a concern, especially if the firm relies on its corporate culture as a source of competitive advantage.

Pressures on the Management of Employees

Many entrepreneurs find that as the venture grows, they need to change their management style, that is, change the way they deal with employees. Management decision making that is the exclusive domain of the entrepreneur can be dangerous to the success of a growing venture. This is sometimes difficult for the entrepreneur to realize since he or she has been so involved in all important decisions since the business was created. However, to survive, the entrepreneur will need to consider some managerial changes.

Pressures on the Entrepreneur's Time

One of the biggest problems in growing a firm is encapsulated in the phrase "If I only had more time." While this is a common problem for all managers, it is particularly applicable to entrepreneurs who are growing their businesses. Time is the entrepreneur's most precious yet limited resource. It is a unique quantity: The entrepreneur cannot store it, rent it, hire it, or buy it. It is also totally perishable and irreplaceable. No matter what an entrepreneur does, today's ration is 24 hours, and yesterday's time is already history. Growth is demanding of the entrepreneur's time, but as the entrepreneur allocates time to growth, it must be diverted from other activities, and this can cause problems.

There are actions the entrepreneur can take to better manage these issues and more effectively grow his or her business. We will now discuss some of these actions.

Pressures on Existing Financial Resources

Growth has a large appetite for cash. Investing in growth means that the firm's resources can become stretched quite thin. With financial resources highly stretched, the firm is more vulnerable to unexpected expenses that could push the firm over the edge and into bankruptcy. Resource slack (resources in reserve) is required to ensure against most environmental shocks and to foster further innovation.

ETHICS

LESSONS FROM ENRON

EVEN THE SMALLEST BUSINESS CAN LEARN WHAT *NOT* TO DO FROM THIS GIANT COMPANY

Q: What can a business owner learn from the mistakes of Enron?

A: So you wanted to own a multibillion-dollar corporation and fly around the world in the latest Lear jet. Then along comes Enron, the seventh largest company in the United States, a firm most folks probably never even heard of, and it ruins your dreams. And perhaps your 401(k), too. The excesses that caused this disintegration will be thoroughly examined by lawmakers and regulators. When their work is completed, even the innocent will find new government-mandated rules and regulations to make doing business more difficult. Well, don't despair—"mistakes were made," but lessons can be learned.

And don't think for a minute the Enron problem is something that only giant corporations face. Although the magnitude of its collapse won't be matched by the local print shop or pizza parlor, the collapse of even the smallest of businesses impacts many people. The failure of your business will greatly and negatively impact you, your partners, your employees, customers, and vendors as well as the families of each of those groups. As business owners, we have a duty to operate in a prudent, lawful, and ethical manner.

So what can we do? Every good business has a solid business plan and a realistic design for implementing that plan. While Enron is fresh in our minds, we think the first thing to do is to examine our business plan from the perspective of its fidelity to the prudence, legality, and ethics mentioned above, and then compare the business plan to the reality. Have business "necessities" caused us to step over the line? How will the deviations from the plan come back to bite us and those who depend on us? Try to recall your first day in business—it wasn't about bending the rules, it wasn't about living

high on the hog (or as they say today, living large), and it had nothing to do with cheating others—that first day was all about launching a dream and bringing others along. It's time to relight the flame.

As we said, on a local scale, the collapse of a small business will match the collapse of an Enron for those involved. If we get caught playing the business game dirty, we won't see ourselves on national TV, but our next-door neighbor will know that side of our character we've tried to hide. So will our families and close friends.

Let's think about the things we may be doing now, things that were never in our plan and were never a part of our dreams. And let's purge them from our business practices. A few of the common legal and ethical missteps some business owners take, which must be ended today, are:

- Paying personal expenses out of business funds and writing them off
- Not reporting all cash receipts
- Cheating customers on price, quality, delivery, or warranty
- Using misleading advertising
- Failing to pay our business bills on time
- Lying to employees, customers, and vendors

Some may think these lapses pale in comparison to the allegations against Enron. They don't. If you act illegally or unethically in your business, given the opportunity, you'd do so if your canvas were larger. Take a good look at the list above and ask yourself, "What is the penalty if I get caught?" Then ask yourself a more important question: "Is this who I really am?" Finally, fix it.

We may yet get to fly in that Lear jet, but we'll only deserve to if we're honest, hard-working business owners.

Source: Reprinted with permission of Entrepreneur Media, Inc., "Even the Smallest Business Can Learn What *Not* to Do from This Giant Company," by Rod Walsh and Dan Carrison, February 2002, *Entrepreneur* magazine: www.entrepreneur.com.

OVERCOMING PRESSURES ON EXISTING HUMAN RESOURCES

Generally, the new venture does not have the luxury of a human resource department that can interview, hire, and evaluate employees. Most of these decisions will be the responsibility of the entrepreneur and perhaps one or two other key employees. The process of human resource management should not be any different from what was previously discussed in Chapter 9, where we outline some of the important procedures for preparing job descriptions and specifications for new employees.

Some entrepreneurs are using professional employer organizations (PEOs). One such company is TriNet Employer Group Inc., which came to the rescue of Robert Teal, cofounder of a Silicon Valley start-up, Quinta Corporation. Robert had found it time consuming and costly to hire and retain employees. His banker suggested he consider TriNet. After an assessment of TriNet's services, he hired the firm to assume most of the human resource tasks of the new venture. This involved such things as recruiting, hiring, setting up benefit programs, payroll, and even firing decisions. This has given Robert more time to devote to other aspects of his growing venture.[3]

In growing the workforce, entrepreneurs face the decision of what proportion of the workforce should be permanent and what proportion should be part time, and this decision involves a number of trade-offs. On the one hand, a greater percentage of part-time workers represents a lower fixed cost, which provides the firm greater flexibility in dealing with changes in the external environment. On the other hand, personnel instability is more likely with part-time workers because turnover is typically higher[4] and part-time workers are less committed to the firm because they have less of a personal stake in its performance. Therefore, building a functional organizational culture is more difficult when the workforce has a greater proportion of part-time workers.

Regardless of the composition of the firm's workforce, mistakes will be made in the selection and hiring of some people. This leads to one of the most difficult decisions for an entrepreneur to make—the firing of incompetent employees. Having a fair employee evaluation process is essential in justifying the firing of an employee. Employees should be given feedback on a regular basis, and any problems should be identified with a proposed solution agreeable to the employee and the entrepreneur. In this manner, continued problems with the employee that necessitate a firing decision will be well documented.

An integral part of the firm's human resource strategy for effectively growing the business must take into consideration how to maintain the corporate culture despite the influx of new employees. New employees can be inculcated through early training sessions that perpetuate the stories and rituals that form the basis of the culture. But the majority of this responsibility falls on the shoulders of the entrepreneur. The entrepreneur must be the walking, talking embodiment of the culture, although in cases of rapid growth the work of the entrepreneur can be complemented by the work of a cultural ambassador. For example, as IKEA expanded internationally, Ingvar Kamprad took a number of steps to ensure that the corporate culture would still have an impact in foreign stores. For example, he documented the "IKEA way" and used cultural ambassadors and training sessions to inculcate new employees of new stores in foreign locations.

OVERCOMING PRESSURES ON THE MANAGEMENT OF EMPLOYEES

participative style of management The manager involves others in the decision-making process

As the venture grows, it changes. Managing change is often a complex task, one that is better undertaken with a participative style of management. A *participative style of management* is one in which the entrepreneur involves others in the decision-making process. There are a number of advantages to using a participative management style when a firm is growing. First, the complexity of growing a business and managing change increases the information-processing demands on the entrepreneur. Involving others in the decision-making process is a way of reducing these demands. Second, highly qualified managers and employees are an important resource for coming up with new ways to tackle current problems. Third, if employees are involved in the decision-making process, they

ELEVATOR PITCH FOR eVEST

A wealthy friend has asked you to keep your eye out for attractive businesses in which she can invest. Your wealthy friend is very busy, and you only want to introduce those businesses that are genuinely attractive. After hearing the following pitch, would you introduce Scott to your wealthy friend?

Entrepreneur: Scott Jordan, 38, founder and CEO of Scott eVest LLC.

Company: Clothing and licensing company featuring a line of vests/jackets with 16 to 22 pockets that discreetly hold tech gadgets.

Sales Projections for the Current Year: $5 million.

Weighed Down: "I was practicing law and commuting back and forth, carrying the things that most businesspeople carry with them nowadays—PDA, cell phone, an expandable keyboard. Working in a business casual environment, I would wear sports jackets just to have the extra pockets to put my stuff in. I started asking around and found the need for more pockets was common."

(Un) orderly Fashion: Now selling through www.scottevest.com, Jordan was initially wary of e-commerce when he started the company in 2001. "On the day [the site] went live, a Web site referred to it, and I got 50,000 hits and more than 100 orders. I didn't even have a manufacturer lined up. I had six samples. I had to juggle between sending them to retailers, catalog companies, and Asia for production pricing. Each one was like gold to me."

Apparel Appeal: On exhibit at Disneyland's Tomorrowland, the Scott eVest has appeared on *ER* and HBO's *The Wire*. "Every other day, I get a call from a branch of the military, CIA, Secret Service, INS. I'm told the president got one with the presidential seal on it."

Source: Reprinted with permission of Entrepreneur Media, Inc., "This Entrepreneur Will Never Find His Pockets Empty—No Matter How Many of Them He Has," by April Y. Pennington, February 2003, *Entrepreneur* magazine: www.entrepreneur.com.

are more prepared and more motivated to implement the decided course of action. Finally, in most cultures employees enjoy the added responsibility of making decisions and taking initiative. In such a case, a participative management style will enhance job satisfaction. The following captures some of the activities the entrepreneur can do to institute a more participative style of management and successfully grow the business.

Establish a Team Spirit A team spirit involves the belief by everyone in the organization that they are "in this thing together" and by working together great things can be achieved. Small but important actions by the entrepreneur can create this team spirit. For example, the entrepreneur should establish a "we" spirit—not a "me" spirit—in meetings and memoranda to employees as well as to other stakeholders.

Communicate with Employees Open and frequent communication with employees builds trust and diminishes fear. Often the fear of change associated with firm growth is worse than the reality of change, and communication will alleviate some of that anxiety. Open and frequent communication is a two-way street. The entrepreneur must listen to what is on the minds of his or her employees. The entrepreneur should solicit suggestions on how a department or the firm as a whole can more effectively manage growth and improve its performance.

Provide Feedback The entrepreneur should frequently provide feedback to employees. Feedback needs to be constructive such that it enables the employee to improve the quality of a particular task but does not attack the person and create a fear of failure. The entrepreneur should also seek feedback from others. For this feedback to be valuable it must be honest, which requires a culture that values open and honest communication. An entrepreneur confident in his or her own abilities, and with a desire to effectively grow the business, should be open to, and should encourage, this type of feedback.

Delegate Some Responsibility to Others   With an increasing number of tasks for the entrepreneur, he or she cannot be available to make every management decision. Key employees must be given the flexibility to take the initiative and make decisions without the fear of failure. This requires the entrepreneur to create a culture that values and rewards employees for taking initiative and sees failure as a positive attempt rather than a negative outcome.

Provide Continuous Training for Employees   By training employees, the entrepreneur increases employees' ability and capacity to improve their own performance at a particular task and, as a result, improves the chance of successfully growing the firm. Training should reflect the new management style by involving employees in deciding upon training session topics.

OVERCOMING PRESSURES ON ENTREPRENEURS' TIME

time management The process of improving an individual's productivity through more efficient use of time

Entrepreneurs can always make better use of their time, and the more they strive to do so, the more it will enrich their venture as well as their personal lives. How does one more effectively manage time? *Time management* is the process of improving an individual's productivity through more efficient use of time. The entrepreneur reaps numerous benefits from effectively managing his or her time, some of which follow.

Increased Productivity   Time management helps the entrepreneur determine the tasks of greatest importance and focuses his or her attention on successfully completing those tasks. This means that there will always be sufficient time to accomplish the most important things.

Increased Job Satisfaction   Increased productivity means that more of the important tasks are successfully completed, which in turn enhances the entrepreneur's job satisfaction. The entrepreneur is less likely to feel "swamped" and overwhelmed by the increasing number of tasks generated from firm growth. Getting more important things done and being more successful in growing and developing the venture will give the entrepreneur more job satisfaction.

Improved Interpersonal Relationships   Although the total time an entrepreneur spends with other individuals in the company may in fact decrease through better time management, the time spent will be of a higher quality (quality time), allowing him or her to improve relationships with others inside and outside the firm (including family). Furthermore, as others in the company experience less time pressure, better results, and greater job satisfaction, relationships within the firm become more harmonious and the firm can build an *esprit de corps*.

Reduced Time Anxiety and Tension   Worry, guilt, and other emotions tend to reduce the entrepreneur's information-processing capacity, which can lead to less effective assessments and decisions. Effective time management reduces concerns and anxieties, which "frees up" information processing and improves the quality of the entrepreneur's decisions.

Better Health   By reducing anxiety and tension and improving productivity, job satisfaction, and relationships with others, there is less psychological and physiological strain on the mind and body, resulting in improved health. Time management can also include scheduling time to eat well and exercise. Good health, and the energy that it brings, is vital for an entrepreneur growing his or her business.

Basic Principles of Time Management

Time management provides a process by which the entrepreneur can become a time saver, not a time server. This efficient use of time enables the entrepreneur to expand and grow the venture properly, increase personal and firm productivity, and lessen the encroachment of the business into his or her private life. An entrepreneur develops good time management by adhering to six basic principles, as follows.

Principle of Desire

principle of desire   A recognition of the need to change personal attitudes and habits regarding the allocation of time

The *principle of desire* requires that the entrepreneur recognize that he or she is a time waster, that time is an important resource, and that there is a need to change personal attitudes and habits regarding the allocation of time. Therefore, effective time management depends on the entrepreneur's willpower, self-discipline, and motivation to optimize his or her time.

Principle of Effectiveness

principle of effectiveness   A focus on the most important issues

The *principle of effectiveness* requires the entrepreneur to focus on the most important issues, even when under pressure. Whenever possible, an entrepreneur should try to complete each task in a single session, which requires that enough time be set aside to accomplish that task. This eliminates time wasted in catching up to where one left off. Although quality is of course important, perfectionism is not and often leads only to procrastination. The entrepreneur must not spend excessive time on trying to make a small improvement in one area when time would be better spent in another area.

Principle of Analysis

principle of analysis   Understanding how time is currently being allocated, and where it is being inefficiently invested

The *principle of analysis* provides information to the entrepreneur about how time is currently being allocated, which will also highlight inefficient or inappropriate investments of time. The entrepreneur should track his or her time over a two-week period, using a time sheet with 15-minute intervals, and then analyze how time has been spent, where time has been wasted, and how these "time traps" can be avoided in the future (using the other principles). For example, the entrepreneur should not "reinvent the wheel" in solving similar problems; rather, standardized forms and procedures should be developed for all recurring events and operations.

Principle of Teamwork

principle of teamwork   Acknowledgment that only a small amount of time is actually under one's control and that most of one's time is taken up by others

Analysis of time will likely reveal to the entrepreneur that only a small amount of time is actually under his or her control—most of his or her time is taken up by others. The *principle of teamwork* acknowledges the increasing importance of delegation for an entrepreneur of a growing firm; that is, the entrepreneur must require others to take responsibility for the completion of tasks previously undertaken by the entrepreneur. The entrepreneur must also help members of the management team become more sensitive to the time management concept when dealing with others in the company, especially in dealing with the entrepreneur. Note that managing one's time does not mean that the entrepreneur must make himself or herself inaccessible to others; rather, accessibility is increased because the time that is spent with others can now be fully focused on them.

principle of prioritized planning Categorization of tasks by their degree of importance and then the allocation of time to tasks based on this categorization

Principle of Prioritized Planning

The *principle of prioritized planning* requires the entrepreneur to categorize his or her tasks by their degree of importance and then to allocate time to tasks based on this categorization. For example, each day, an entrepreneur should list all tasks to be accomplished and indicate their degree of importance using a scale from 1 to 3, with 1 being most important, 2 somewhat important, and 3 moderately important. The entrepreneur can then focus on those tasks of most importance (those with a number 1). Furthermore, the entrepreneur can prioritize his or her time. For example, some entrepreneurs are most efficient in the morning, some during the afternoon, and some at night. The most efficient period of the day should be used to address the most important issues.

principle of reanalysis Periodic review of one's time management process

Principle of Reanalysis

The *principle of reanalysis* requires the entrepreneur to periodically review his or her time management process. In this reanalysis, entrepreneurs can often improve their time management by investigating more systemic (systemwide) issues and revisiting potential opportunities for delegation. For example, the clerical staff and close assistants should be well trained and encouraged to take the initiative, including sorting correspondence and returning phone calls based on importance, dealing with issues of low importance to the entrepreneur, and instituting routines such as standard letters for the entrepreneur to sign, a daily diary, reminder lists, operations board, and an efficient "pending" file. All meetings should be analyzed to ensure that they are being run effectively. If not, the person who runs the meeting should be trained to do so. The purpose of all committees should also be reanalyzed to ensure that they still provide value.

OVERCOMING PRESSURES ON EXISTING FINANCIAL RESOURCES

In Chapter 10 we detailed the role of the financial plan in effectively managing an entrepreneurial venture's financial resources. In this chapter we have acknowledged the pressures on a firm's financial resource brought on by growth. To overcome these pressures on existing financial resources, the entrepreneur could acquire new resources. The acquisition of new resources is expensive, whether in terms of the equity sold or the interest payments from debt. The need or the magnitude of the new resources required can be reduced through better management of existing resources. Such important management activities include applying effective financial control, managing inventory, and maintaining good records.

Financial Control

The financial plan, as an inherent part of the business plan, was discussed in Chapter 10. Just as we outlined how to prepare pro forma income and cash flow statements for the first three years, the entrepreneur will need some knowledge of how to provide appropriate controls to ensure that projections and goals are met. Some financial skills are thus necessary for the entrepreneur to manage the venture during these early years. Cash flows, the income statement, and the balance sheet are the key financial areas that will need careful management and control. Since Chapter 10 explains how to prepare these pro forma statements, the focus in this section will be controls and the management of these elements to alleviate financial "growing" pains.

TABLE 13.1 MPP Plastics Inc. (Statement of Cash Flow) July, Year 1 (000s)

	July	
	Budgeted	**Actual**
Receipts		
Sales	$ 24.0	$ 22.0
Disbursements		
Equipment	100.0	100.0
Cost of goods	20.8	22.5
Selling expenses	1.5	2.5
Salaries	6.5	6.5
Advertising	1.5	1.5
Office supplies	0.3	0.3
Rent	2.0	2.0
Utilities	0.3	0.5
Insurance	0.8	0.8
Taxes	0.8	0.8
Loan principal and interest	2.6	2.6
Total disbursements	$137.1	$140.0
Cash flow	(113.1)	(118.0)
Beginning balance	275.0	275.0
Ending balance	161.9	157.0

Managing Cash Flow   Since cash outflow may exceed cash inflow when growing a business, the entrepreneur should try to have an up-to-date assessment of his or her cash position. This can be accomplished by preparing monthly cash flow statements, such as that found in Table 13.1, and comparing the budgeted or pro forma statements with the actual results. The July budgeted amounts are taken from the pro forma cash flow statement of MPP Plastics. The entrepreneur can indicate the actual amounts next to the budgeted amounts. This will be useful for adjusting the pro forma for the remaining months, as well as for providing some indication as to where cash flow problems may exist.

Table 13.1 shows a few potential problem areas. First, sales receipts were less than anticipated. Management needs to assess whether this was due to nonpayment by some customers or to an increase in credit sales. If the lower amount is due to nonpayment by customers, the entrepreneur may need to try enforcing faster payment by sending reminder letters or making telephone calls to delinquent customers. Bounced checks from customers can also affect cash flow since the entrepreneur has likely credited the amount to the account and assumed that the cash is readily available. If the lower receipts are resulting from higher credit sales, the entrepreneur may need to either consider short-term financing from a bank or try to extend the terms of payment to his or her suppliers.[5]

Cash disbursements for some items were greater than budgeted and may indicate a need for tighter cost controls. For example, cost of goods was $22,500, which was $1,700 more than budgeted. The entrepreneur may find that suppliers increased their prices, which may require a search for alternative sources or even raising the prices of the products/services offered by the new venture. If the higher cost of goods resulted from the purchase of more supplies, then the entrepreneur should assess the inventory costs from the income statement. It is possible that the increased cost of goods resulted from the purchase of more supplies because sales were higher than expected. However, if these additional sales resulted in more credit sales, the entrepreneur may need to plan to borrow money to meet short-term cash needs. Conclusions can be made once the credit sales and inventory costs are evaluated.

The higher selling expenses also may need to be assessed. If the additional selling expenses were incurred to support increased sales (even if they were credit sales), then there is no immediate concern. However, if no additional sales were generated, the entrepreneur may need to review all these expenses and perhaps institute tighter controls.

Projecting cash flow in the early stages can also benefit by conducting sensitivity analysis. For each monthly expected cash flow, the entrepreneur can use 1 plus and minus 5 for an optimistic and pessimistic cash estimate, respectively. Thus, our MPP Plastics example (Table 13.1) might have projected in the prior month sales receipts of $24,000 and, using the 1 plus and minus 5 percent, would have a column indicating a pessimistic amount of $22,800 and an optimistic amount of $25,200. This sensitivity analysis would then be computed for all disbursements as well. In this manner the entrepreneur would be able to ascertain the maximum cash needs given a pessimistic outcome and could prepare for any cash needs.

For the very new venture it may be necessary to prepare a daily cash sheet. This might be particularly beneficial to a retail store, restaurant, or service business. Table 13.2 provides an illustration of the cash available at the beginning of the day with additions and deletions of cash recorded as indicated. This would provide an effective indication of any daily shortfall and give a clear sense of where problems exist or where errors have occurred.

TABLE 13.2 Daily Cash Activity (Date)

Beginning day's cash balance:		$XXX
Add:		
Day's cash sales (cash, charges, checks)	$XXX	
Collection of receivables	$XXX	
Total		$XXX
Less:		
Charge account sales (from day's cash sales)		$XXX
Total cash collected		$XXX
Cash disbursed:		
Cash refunds	$XXX	
Cash returns	$XXX	
Petty cash expenses (such as postage, travel, supplies, or repairs)	$XXX	
Total cash disbursed (subtract from total cash collected)		$XXX
Amount of cash that should be on hand		$XXX
Actual count of cash on hand		$XXX
Difference between what should be on hand and actual		$XXX

Note: If the final number is negative or positive, then an error has occurred in collections or payments.

Comparison of budgeted or expected cash flows with actual cash flows can provide the entrepreneur with an important assessment of potential immediate cash needs and indicate possible problems in the management of assets or control of costs. These items are discussed further in the next sections.

Managing Inventory   During the growth of a new venture, the management of inventory is an important task. Too much inventory can be a drain on cash flow since manufacturing, transportation, and storage costs must be borne by the venture. On the other hand, too little inventory to meet customer demands can also cost the venture in lost sales, or it can create unhappy customers who may choose another firm if their needs are not met in a timely manner.

Growing ventures typically tie up more cash in their inventory than in any other part of the business. Skolnik Industries, a $10 million manufacturer of steel containers for storage and disposal of hazardous materials, developed an inventory control system that allowed it to ship products to its customers within 24 to 48 hours. This was accomplished with a very lean inventory, thanks to the installation of a computerized inventory-control system that allows the firm to maintain records of inventory on a product-by-product basis. In addition to this capability, the system allows the company to monitor gross margin return on investment, inventory turnover, percentage of orders shipped on time, length of time to fill back orders, and percentage of customer complaints to shipped orders. Software to accomplish these goals is readily available and in many cases can even be modified to meet the exact needs of the business. The reports from this system are generated every two to four weeks in normal sales periods and weekly in heavy sales periods. This system not only provides Skolnik with an early warning system but also frees up cash normally invested in inventory and improves the overall profitability of the firm.[6] Perpetual inventory systems can be structured using computers or a manual system. As items are sold, inventory should be reduced. To check the inventory balance, it may be necessary to physically count inventory periodically.

Efficient electronic data interchanges (EDIs) among producers, wholesalers, and retailers can enable these firms to communicate with one another. Linking the needs of a retailer with the wholesaler and producer allows for a fast order entry and response. These systems also allow the firm to track shipments internationally.[7] The linking of firms in a computerized system has also been developed by the grocery and pharmaceutical industries using a software system called efficient consumer response (ECR). Supply chain members work together in this system to manage demand, distribution, and marketing such that minimum inventory levels are necessary to meet consumer demands. Computerized checkout machines are usually part of these systems so that linked members are able to anticipate inventory needs before stock-outs occur.[8]

Transport mode selection can also be important in inventory management. Some transportation modes, such as air transport, are very expensive. Rail and truck are the most often used methods of transportation when a next-day delivery for a customer is not necessary. Careful management of inventory through a computerized system and by working with customers and other channel members can minimize transportation costs. Anticipating customer needs can avoid stock-outs and the unexpected cost of having to meet a customer's immediate need by shipping a product by next-day air. These mistakes can be costly and are likely to significantly reduce the margins on any transaction.

TABLE 13.3   MPP Plastics Inc., Income Statement, First Quarter
Year 1 (000s)

		Actual (%)	Standard (%)
Net sales	$150.0	100.0%	100.0%
Less cost of goods sold	100.0	66.7	60.0
Gross margin	50.0	33.3	40.0
Operating expenses			
Selling expenses	11.7	7.8	8.0
Salaries	19.8	13.2	12.0
Advertising	5.2	3.5	4.0
Office supplies	1.9	1.3	1.0
Rent	6.0	4.0	3.0
Utilities	1.3	0.9	1.0
Insurance	0.6	0.4	0.5
Taxes	3.4	2.3	2.0
Interest	3.6	2.4	2.0
Depreciation	9.9	6.6	5.0
Miscellaneous	0.3	0.2	0.2
Total operating expenses	$ 66.3	42.5	38.7
Net profit (loss)	(13.7)	(9.1)	1.3

Managing Fixed Assets   Fixed assets generally involve long-term commitments and large investments for the new venture. These fixed assets, such as the equipment appearing in Table 13.3, will have certain costs related to them. Equipment will require servicing and insurance and will affect utility costs. The equipment also will be depreciated over time, which will be reflected in the value of the asset over time.

If the entrepreneur cannot afford to buy equipment or fixed assets, leasing could be considered as an alternative. Leasing may be a good alternative to buying, depending on the terms of the lease, the type of asset to be leased, and the usage demand on the asset. For example, leases for automobiles may contain a large down payment and possible usage or mileage fees that can make the lease much more expensive than a purchase. On the other hand, lease payments represent an expense to the venture and can be used as a tax deduction. Leases are also valuable for equipment that becomes obsolete quickly. The entrepreneur can take a lease for short periods, reducing the long-term obligation to any specific asset. As with any other make or buy decision, the entrepreneur should consider all costs associated with the decision as well as its impact on cash flows.

Managing Costs and Profits   Although the cash flow analysis discussed earlier in the chapter can assist the entrepreneur in assessing and controlling costs, it is also useful to compute the net income for interim periods during the year. The most effective use of the interim income statement is to establish cost standards and compare the actual with the budgeted amount for that time period. Costs are budgeted based on

TABLE 13.4   MPP Plastics Inc., Balance Sheet, First Quarter Year 1

Assets		
Current assets		
Cash	$ 13,350	
Accounts receivable (40% of $60,000 in sales the previous month)	24,000	
Merchandise inventory	12,850	
Supplies	2,100	
Current assets		$ 52,300
Fixed assets		
Equipment	$240,000	
Less depreciation	9,900	
Total fixed assets		$230,100
Total assets		282,400
Liabilities and Owners' Equity		
Current liabilities		
Accounts payable (20% of 40 CGS)	$ 8,000	
Current portion of L-T debt	13,600	
Total current liabilities		$ 21,600
Long-term liabilities		
Notes payable		223,200
Total liabilities		244,800
Owners' equity		
C. Peter's capital	$ 25,000	
K. Peter's capital	25,000	
Retained earnings	(13,400)	
Total owners' equity		$ 37,600
Total liabilities and owners' equity		$282,400

percentages of net sales. These percentages can then be compared with actual percentages and can be assessed over time to ascertain where tighter cost controls may be necessary.

Table 13.3 compares actual and expected (standard) percentages on MPP Plastic's income statement for its first quarter of operation. This analysis gives the entrepreneur the opportunity to manage and control costs before it is too late. Table 13.4 shows that cost of goods sold is higher than standard. Part of this may result from the initial small purchases of inventory, which did not provide any quantity discounts. If this is not the case, the entrepreneur should consider finding other sources or raising prices.

Most of the expenses appear to be reasonably close to standard or expected percentages. The entrepreneur should assess each item to determine whether these costs can be reduced or whether it will be necessary to raise prices to ensure future positive profits (although the effectiveness of raising prices is determined by the market and could substantially lower the number of items sold and reduce market share). As the venture begins to evolve into the second and third years of operation, the entrepreneur should also compare current actual costs with prior incurred costs. For example, in the second year of operation, the entrepreneur may find it useful to look back at the selling expenses incurred in the first year of operation. Such comparisons can be done on a month-to-month basis (i.e., January, year 1, to January, year 2) or even quarterly or yearly, depending on the volatility of the costs in the particular business.

Where expenses or costs have been much higher than budgeted, it may be necessary for the entrepreneur to carefully analyze the account to determine what is the exact cause of the overrun. For example, utilities represent a single expense account yet may include a number of specific payments for such things as heat, electricity, gas, and hot water. Thus, the entrepreneur should retain a running balance of all these payments to ascertain the cause of an unusually large utility expense. In Table 13.1 we see that the utility expense was $500, which was $200 over the budgeted amount, or a 67 percent increase. What caused the increase? Was any particular utility responsible for the overrun, or was it a result of higher oil costs, which affected all the utility expenses? These questions need to be resolved before the entrepreneur accepts the results and makes any needed adjustments for the next period.

Comparisons of the actual and budgeted expenses in the income statement can be misleading for those new ventures where there are multiple products or services. For financial reporting purposes to shareholders, bankers, or other investors, the income statement would summarize expenses across all products and services. This information, although helpful to provide an overview of the success of the venture, does not indicate the marketing cost for each product, the performance of particular managers in controlling costs, or the most profitable product(s). For example, selling expenses for MPP Plastics Inc. (Table 13.3) were $11,700. These selling expenses may apply to more than one product, in which case the entrepreneur would need to ascertain the amount of selling expense for each product. He or she may be tempted to prorate the expense across each product, which would not provide a realistic picture of the relative success of each product. Thus, if MPP Plastics Inc. produced three different products, the selling expense for each might be assumed to be $3,900 per product, when the actual selling expenses could be much more or less.

Some products may require more advertising, insurance, administrative time, transportation, storage, and so on, which could be misleading if the entrepreneur chooses to allocate these expenses equally across all products. In response to this problem, it is recommended that the entrepreneur allocate expenses as effectively as possible, by product. Not only is it important to evaluate these costs across each product, but also it is important to evaluate them by region, customer, distribution channel, department, and so on. Arbitrary allocation of costs should be avoided to get a real profit perspective of every product marketed by the new venture.

Taxes   Don't forget the tax agent! The entrepreneur will be required to withhold federal and state taxes for his or her employees. Each month or quarter (depending on the size of the payroll), deposits or payments will need to be made to the appropriate agency for funds withheld from wages. Generally, federal taxes, state taxes, Social Security, and Medicare are withheld from employees' salaries and are deposited later. The entrepreneur should be careful not to use these funds since, if payments are late, there will be high interest and penalties assessed. In addition to withholding taxes, the new venture may be required to pay a number of taxes, such as state and federal unemployment taxes, a matching FICA and Medicare tax, and other business taxes. These taxes will need to be part of any budget since they will affect cash flow and profits. To determine the exact amount, dates due, and procedures, the unemployment agency for the federal government and the appropriate state or the tax department can be contacted.

The federal and state governments will also require the entrepreneur to file end-of-year returns of the business. If the venture is incorporated, there may be state corporation taxes to be paid regardless of whether the venture earned a profit. The filing periods and tax responsibilities will vary for other types of organizations. Chapter 10 provides some insights into the tax responsibilities of proprietorships, partnerships, and corporations. As stated earlier, use of a tax accountant should also be considered to avoid any errors and provide advice in handling these expenses. The accountant can also assist the entrepreneur in planning or budgeting appropriate funds to meet any of these expenses.

Record Keeping   To support this effort toward financial control, it is helpful to consider using a software package to enhance the flow of this type of information. With a growing venture it may also be necessary to enlist the support and services of an accountant or a consultant to support record keeping and financial control. These external service firms can also help train employees using the latest and most appropriate technology to meet the needs of the venture.

A system for storing and using customer information becomes vitally important for a growing firm. Growth typically involves marketing to new customers, and a large influx of new customers can overwhelm more primitive systems. For example, previously customer information may have been stored in the memory of the different salespeople. However, as the sheer number of customers increases, the memory capacity of a salesperson may be exceeded and important information (and new and existing sales) could be lost.

Not only will a database increase the capacity to hold and process information, it begins to accumulate bits of knowledge contained within different individuals into an organizational knowledge that is accessible to everyone within the firm. By building organizational knowledge the entrepreneur is less dependent upon any one individual. For example, if the top salesperson were to die or otherwise leave the organization, then a considerable amount of important information could be lost to the firm. Specifically, customer information should be retained in a database that includes information on a contact person (including telephone number and address), as well as important data on the number of units and dollars of business transacted by each account. New accounts should also be designated for follow-up, such as welcoming customers and providing them with important information about the company and its products and services.

IMPLICATIONS OF FIRM GROWTH FOR THE ENTREPRENEUR

Firm growth introduces a number of managerial challenges for the entrepreneur; challenges with which they may be unfamiliar and ill equipped to deal. In the preceding, we have offered a number of tools that entrepreneurs can develop to more effectively cope with, and manage, the growth process. Some entrepreneurs lack the ability to make the transition to this more professional management approach. Another group of entrepreneurs may be able but unwilling to focus their attention on achieving those tasks necessary to successfully achieve firm growth.

For example, Pearce Jones, founder and president of Design Edge, controlled growth by putting a halt on all growth for one full year. The company realized that if it did not get control over growth, serious problems were likely. At this decision point, the company had quadrupled its number of employees and had invested in a new building. Even though each new employee was contributing an increase of $150,000 in sales, the margins were small. The additional debt from the new facility and the additional costs for employees led to this abrupt decision to cease hiring, deactivate marketing and sales, refuse any new business, and basically focus only on existing customers. Although Pearce admits this decision was emotionally painful, it led to dramatic changes as profits actually doubled and no employee turnover was experienced.[9]

Another example of a reluctance to grow is illustrated by this quote from the founder and CEO of Southwest Airlines (at the time), Herb Kelleher: "Southwest has had more opportunities for growth than it has airplanes. Yet, unlike other airlines, it has avoided the trap of growing beyond its means. . . . Employees just don't seem to be enamored of the idea that bigger is better."[10] Growth may not be pursued because there is a belief that in doing so firm profitability and/or the firm's chances of survival will be sacrificed.

Even if there is a belief that the pursuit of growth will improve firm performance and enhance personal wealth, some entrepreneurs will still avoid growing their business. These entrepreneurs are not necessarily motivated by financial gain. Consider an individual who chooses to start a business because she or he is tired of being controlled by others—this person wants the independence that comes from being one's own boss. Growth may not be an attractive option for this entrepreneur, because acquiring the necessary resources for growth will mean selling equity (for example, to a venture capitalist) or raising debt capital (for example, from a bank). Both sources of resources place limits on the entrepreneur's ability to make strategic decisions for the firm. In this case the entrepreneur may prefer to have full ownership, be debt free, and remain small.

Evan Douglas is a professor of entrepreneurship and dean of the University of the Sunshine Coast in Australia. His dream is to create and manage a business that rents a small number of yachts to tourists. The office (preferably a shack) would be on the beach somewhere on the Great Barrier Reef. When he achieves this dream, the last thing that he wants to do is to grow the business such that his task moves to one of professional manager and away from the task of "beach bum." His dream business is an example of a lifestyle business. Growth can be perceived by such lifestyle entrepreneurs as threatening the very reason for becoming an entrepreneur in the first place.

A Categorization of Entrepreneurs and Their Firms' Growth

Based on the preceding arguments, Figure 13.3 categorizes entrepreneurs in terms of two dimensions: The first dimension represents an entrepreneur's abilities to successfully make the transition to more professional management practices, and the second dimension represents an entrepreneur's growth aspirations. Depending on the entrepreneur's position along these two dimensions, four types of firm growth outcomes are identified.

Actual Growth of the Firm
Entrepreneurs in the upper-right quadrant possess both the necessary abilities to make the transition to a more professional management approach and the aspiration to grow their businesses. These are the entrepreneurs who are the most likely to achieve firm growth.

FIGURE 13.3   Four Types of Entrepreneurs* and Firm Growth

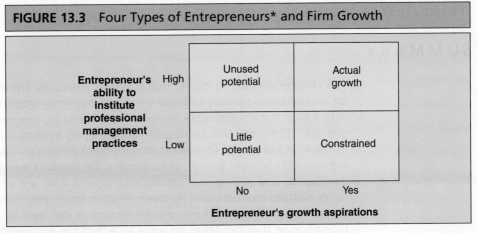

*Based on ability to make a transition to professional management and aspiration.

Source: Adapted from J. Wiklund and D. A. Shepherd, "Aspiring for and Achieving Growth: The Moderating Role of Resources and Opportunities," *Journal of Management Studies* (2003), vol. 40, no. 8, pp. 1919–42.

Unused Potential for Growth   Entrepreneurs in the upper-left quadrant possess the necessary abilities for transition *but* do not aspire to do so. These are the entrepreneurs of firms that have unused potential. A relatively large proportion of all lifestyle firms are represented by this classification.

Constrained Growth   Entrepreneurs in the lower-right quadrant aspire to grow their businesses *but* do not possess sufficient abilities to successfully satisfy this aspiration. These entrepreneurs are most likely to be frustrated by the firm's lack of growth and are in the most danger of failure because the firm may be pushed toward the pursuit of growth opportunities and beyond the entrepreneur's ability to cope. However, the entrepreneur might replace himself or herself as the CEO with a professional manager. This will allow the aspiration to be fulfilled (move to the upper-right quadrant). This does not necessarily mean that the entrepreneur will leave the business; rather, the entrepreneur might manage R&D, new products, and/or new markets where his or her strengths are highly valued and enhance rather than constrain the growth of the firm.

Little Potential for Firm Growth   Entrepreneurs in the lower-left quadrant possess neither the necessary abilities to make the transition to a more professional management approach *nor* the aspirations to grow their businesses. These businesses have little potential for growth, and due to the limited abilities of the entrepreneur to manage growth, these firms may actually perform better if they remain at a smaller scale.

Although the abilities of the entrepreneur and the existing resources of the firm can limit the effective pursuit of growth opportunities, the resources necessary for growth can be acquired externally—we refer to these sources as external growth mechanisms. These external mechanisms for growth, which include joint ventures, acquisitions, mergers, and so on, each offer a number of different advantages and disadvantages in providing the resources for effective growth, but all require the entrepreneur to negotiate a new relationship. For example, negotiation is a critical element to forming a joint venture.

Chapter 14 introduces the basic concepts and skills required for an entrepreneur to negotiate the best agreement with these potential growth partners—an agreement that maximizes the entrepreneur's interests. It then describes each external growth mechanism and its advantages and disadvantages.

IN REVIEW

SUMMARY

This chapter provides a model that suggests where an entrepreneur can look for (or create) opportunities to grow his or her business—opportunities that can provide a basis for a sustainable competitive advantage. The relevant growth strategies are: (1) penetration strategies—encouraging existing customers to buy more of the firm's products, (2) market development strategies—selling the firm's existing products to new groups of customers, (3) product development strategies—developing and selling new products to people who are already purchasing the firm's existing products, and (4) diversification strategies—selling a new product to a new market. Most of these growth strategies can lead to a competitive advantage because they capitalize on some aspect of the entrepreneur's, and the firm's, knowledge base.

Business growth has important implications for the firm and the entrepreneur. Because growth makes a firm bigger, the firm begins to benefit from the advantages of size but also introduces a number of managerial challenges. It puts pressure on existing financial resources, human resources, the management of employees, and the entrepreneur's time. There are actions the entrepreneur can take to better manage these pressures and more effectively grow his or her business.

To overcome pressures on existing human resources, the entrepreneur must address the question of what proportion of the workforce should be permanent and what proportion should be part time, should be prepared to fire incompetent employees, and, at the same time, should build and maintain a functional organizational culture. It is important that the entrepreneur interact with employees, so as to establish a team spirit; effect open and frequent communication to build trust and provide constructive feedback; provide key employees with the flexibility to take the initiative and make decisions without the fear of failure; and provide continuous training for employees.

Entrepreneurs can always make better use of their time, and the more they strive to do so, the more it will enrich their venture as well as their personal lives. Better use of time can lead to increased productivity, increased job satisfaction, improved interpersonal relationships with people inside and outside the business, reduced anxiety and tension, and possibly even better health. Efficient use of time enables the entrepreneur to expand and grow the venture properly, increase personal and firm productivity, and lessen the encroachment of the business into his or her private life. Effective time management requires adherence to six basic principles: desire, effectiveness, analysis, teamwork, prioritized planning, and reanalysis. To overcome pressures on existing financial resources, the entrepreneur should apply more effective financial control, record keeping, and inventory management techniques.

Some entrepreneurs lack the ability to make the transition to this more professional management approach, while others may be unwilling to do so. Entrepreneurs who possess both the necessary abilities and the aspiration are most likely to achieve firm growth. Entrepreneurs who possess the necessary abilities but do not aspire to do so will manage firms that have unused potential and/or lifestyle firms. Entrepreneurs who aspire to grow their business but do not possess sufficient abilities are most likely to be frustrated by the firm's lack of growth and are in the most danger of business failure unless the entrepreneur replaces himself or herself. Finally, entrepreneurs who possess neither the necessary abilities nor the aspirations to grow their businesses may run businesses that provide a sufficient income if the businesses remain at a smaller scale.

RESEARCH TASKS

1. Which are the three fastest-growing companies in the country? What opportunities have they pursued to achieve this level of growth? What growth mechanism have they used (internal, joint venture, acquisitions, franchising, etc.)?

2. Use research to come up with three examples of founding entrepreneurs who stepped aside once their firms had grown to a certain size and brought in "professional managers." In each case, what relationship did the entrepreneur continue to have with the firm after the transition? Provide an example of a founding entrepreneur being forced out of the position of CEO to be replaced by a professional manager.

3. Keep a record of how you use your time by documenting what you are doing every 15 minutes over a two-day period. Then analyze these records to determine where you waste time and what you could do to eliminate (or minimize) these time wasters.

4. What different software packages are available to help entrepreneurs with their different record-keeping and control activities? How effective do you believe software can be for each of these tasks?

CLASS DISCUSSION

1. The firm needs to make sales. What is the best way to motivate salespeople to make more sales and improve the performance of the firm? How would you effectively monitor their performance under the proposed motivation system? What are the pros and cons of your motivation and monitoring system?

2. Categorize those people in the class who you believe would be well-suited for starting a business and managing initial growth but would be less effective at conducting the professional management tasks when the firm became larger. What can they do to improve their ability to successfully make the transition with the firm? Categorize those people in your class who you believe would be well-suited to the role of professionally managing a larger (more established) firm but less effective at starting a firm and managing early growth. What can they do to improve their ability to manage a firm earlier in its development? Is there anybody in the class (except maybe yourself) who you believe would be equally effective at both tasks?

3. Think of a company that produces one product and sells it to one group of customers (or make one up). Advise the entrepreneur of the many opportunities there are for growth—opportunities for penetration strategies, market development strategies, product development strategies, and diversification strategies.

4. Are you a time waster or a time server? What time management techniques do you use? How can you better manage your time?

5. To what extent does the use of software help and hinder the entrepreneur's ability to perform the important tasks of record keeping and financial control?

SELECTED READINGS

Baum, J. Robert; Edwin A. Locke; and Ken G. Smith. (2001). A Multidimensional Model of Venture Growth. *Academy of Management Journal,* vol. 44, no. 2, pp. 292–304.

The authors formed an integrated model of venture growth. CEOs' specific competencies and motivations and firm competitive strategies were found to be direct predictors of venture growth. CEOs' traits and general competencies and the environment had significant indirect effects.

Chrisman, James; Ed McMullan; and Jeremy Hall. (2005). The Influence of Guided Preparation on the Long-Term Performance of New Ventures. *Journal of Business Venturing,* vol. 20, no. 6, pp. 769–91.

In this article the authors further develop a theory of guided preparation and new venture performance and test its fundamental relationships on a sample of 159 new ventures that had received outsider assistance 5 to 9 years earlier and had been in business for 3 to 8 years. The results suggest that the long-term growth of the ventures since start-up is significantly related to guided preparation. However, a curvilinear model, rather than a linear model, was found to best capture the relationships of interest.

Danneels, Erwin. (2002). The Dynamics of Product Innovation and Firm Competences. *Strategic Management Journal,* vol. 23, no. 12, pp. 1095–1122.

This study examines how product innovation contributes to the renewal of the firm through its dynamic and reciprocal relation with the firm's competencies.

Davidsson, Per; Bruce Kirchhoff; Abdulnasser Hatemi-J.; and Helena Gustavsson. (2002). Empirical Analysis of Business Growth Factors Using Swedish Data. *Journal of Small Business Management,* vol. 40, no. 4, pp. 332–50.

Although business growth differs among industrial sectors, youth, ownership independence, and small size are found to be major factors that underlie growth across all industries.

Delmar, Frédéric; Per Davidsson; and William B. Gartner. (2003). Arriving at the High-Growth Firm. *Journal of Business Venturing,* vol. 18, no. 2, pp. 189–217.

Using 19 different measures of firm growth (such as relative and absolute sales growth, relative and absolute employee growth, organic growth versus acquisition growth, and the regularity and volatility of growth rates over the 10-year period), the authors identified seven different types of firm growth patterns. These patterns were related to firm age and size as well as industry affiliation. Implications for research and practice are offered.

Eckhardt, Jonathan T.; and Scott A. Shane. (2011). Industry Changes in Technology and Complementary Assets and the Creation of High-Growth Firms. *Journal of Business Venturing,* vol. 26, Issue 4, pp. 412–30.

This study uses employment data to examine why some industries host more new high-growth firms than others. It finds that increases in the proportion of employment of scientists and engineers in industries are positively associated with counts of fast-growing new firms. The findings suggest that technological innovation is an important determinant of entrepreneurial opportunity. Further, they suggest that private new firms are an important means of organizing commercial innovation and that new firms may be less constrained by complementary assets than has been previously understood. (from journal's abstract)

Gielnik, Michael M.; Hannes Zacher; and Michael Frese. (In press). Focus on Opportunities as a Mediator of the Relationship Between Business Owners' Age and Venture Growth. *Journal of Business Venturing.*

Combining upper echelons and lifespan theories, this study investigated the mediating effect of focus on opportunities on the negative relationship between business owners' age and venture growth. They expected and found that mental health moderates the negative relationship between business owners' age and focus on opportunities—mental health helps maintain a high level of focus on opportunities with increasing age. (from journal's abstract)

Park, Choelsoon. (2003). Prior Performance Characteristics of Related and Unrelated Acquirers. *Strategic Management Journal,* vol. 24, no. 5, pp. 471–81.

This paper focuses on a single event of a large acquisition, which enables the authors to better identify the sequential relationships between prior firm profitability, prior industry profitability, and subsequent acquisition strategies. By doing so, this paper makes clearer the causal relationships between firm profitability, industry profitability, and acquisition strategies.

Pettus, Michael L. (2001). The Resource-Based View as a Developmental Growth Process: Evidence from the Deregulated Trucking Industry. *Academy of Management Journal,* vol. 44, no. 4, pp. 878–97.

This paper develops a resource-based perspective for predicting the sequencing of a firm's resources that best provides for firm growth. The sequencing that generated the highest firm growth combines a Penrosian (1959) perspective with the more recent resource-based literature.

Qian, Gongming. (2002). Multinationality, Product Diversification, and Profitability of Emerging U.S. Small- and Medium-Sized Enterprises. *Journal of Business Venturing,* vol. 17, no. 6, pp. 611–34.

This paper examines empirically individual and joint effects of multinationality and product diversification on profit performance for a sample of emerging small- and medium-sized enterprises (SMEs). The results suggest a curvilinear relationship between them: that is, they are positively related up to a point, after which a further increase in multinationality and product diversification was associated with declining performance.

Reuber, Rebecca A.; and Eileen Fischer. (2002). Foreign Sales and Small Firm Growth: The Moderating Role of the Management Team. *Entrepreneurship: Theory & Practice,* vol. 27, no. 1, pp. 29–46.

The premise of this article is that the management team of a small firm plays a key role in internationalization outcomes. Findings indicate that the behavioral integration of the management team moderates the relationship between foreign sales growth and overall firm growth.

Schulze, William S.; Michael H. Lubatkin; and Richard N. Dino. (2003). A Social Capital Model of High-Growth Ventures. *Academy of Management Journal,* vol. 46, no. 3, pp. 374–85.

In this article the authors use social capital theory to explain how human and social capital affect a venture's ability to accumulate financial capital during its growth stages and its performance during the two-year period after going public. They found indications that social capital leverages the productivity of a venture's resource base and provides the venture with a durable source of competitive advantage.

Shepherd, Dean A.; and Johan Wiklund. (2009). Are We Comparing Apples with Apples or Apples with Oranges? Appropriateness of Knowledge Accumulation across Growth Studies. *Entrepreneurship: Theory & Practice*, vol. 33, no. 1, pp. 105–23.

In this paper the authors conduct analyses on all Swedish firms incorporated during the 1994 to 1998 period (68,830 firms) and track their growth (or demise) over their first 6 years of existence. Although they typically find low shared variance between different growth measures, there is variability such that some measures demonstrate high and/or moderate concurrent validity. These findings have implications for how we delineate the boundaries of firm growth research and accumulate knowledge—when we are comparing apples with apples and when we are comparing apples with oranges. [Abstract from author.]

Wiklund, Johan; and Dean A. Shepherd. (2003). Aspiring for, and Achieving Growth: The Moderating Role of Resources and Opportunities. *Journal of Management Studies*, vol. 40, no. 8, pp. 1919–42.

In this article, the authors find that small-business managers' aspirations to expand their business activities are positively related to actual growth. However, the relationship between aspirations and growth appears more complex than stated. Education, experience, and environmental dynamism magnify the effect of growth aspirations on the realization of growth.

Wiklund, Johan; Per Davidsson; and Frédéric Delmar. (2003). What Do They Think and Feel about Growth? An Expectancy-Value Approach to Small Business Managers' Attitudes toward Growth. *Entrepreneurship: Theory & Practice*, vol. 27, no. 3, pp. 247–71.

This study focuses on small-business managers' motivation to expand their firms. The results suggest that concern for employee well-being comes out strongly in determining the overall attitude toward growth. The authors interpret this as reflecting a concern that the positive atmosphere of the small organization may be lost in growth, which might cause recurrent conflict for small-business managers when deciding about the future route for their firms.

Wiklund, Johan; Holger Patzelt; and Dean A. Shepherd. (2009). Building an Integrative Model of Small Business Growth. *Small Business Economics*, vol. 32, no. 4, pp. 351–74.

The purpose of this article is to develop an integrative model of small-business growth that is both broad in scope and parsimonious in nature. Based on an analysis of data from 413 small businesses, the authors derive a set of propositions that suggest how entrepreneurial orientation, environmental characteristics, firm resources, and managers' personal attitudes directly and/or indirectly influence the growth of small businesses. [Abstract from authors.]

Zimmerman, Monica A.; and Gerald J. Zeitz. (2002). Beyond Survival: Achieving New Venture Growth by Building Legitimacy. *Academy of Management Review*, vol. 27, no. 3, pp. 414–32.

In this article the authors argue that (1) legitimacy is an important resource for gaining other resources, (2) such resources are crucial for new venture growth, and (3) legitimacy can be enhanced by the strategic actions of new ventures. They review the impact of legitimacy on new ventures as well as sources of legitimacy for new ventures, present strategies for new ventures to acquire legitimacy, explore the process of building legitimacy in the new venture, and examine the concept of the legitimacy threshold.

END NOTES

1. See "PowerBar Reaps Bounty with New Harvest Bar; Crunched for Time, Americans Devour Energy Bars," *Business Wire*, August 4, 1998, p. 1; C. Adams, "A Lesson from PowerBar's Slow Start to Diversity," *The Wall Street Journal*,

June 14, 1999, p. 4; and "The PowerBar Story," Company Web site
www.powerbar.com.

2. H. I. Ansoff, *Corporate Strategy: An Analytical Approach to Business Policy for Growth and Expansion* (New York: McGraw-Hill, 1965).

3. "You Do the Work, They Do the Paperwork," *BusinessWeek,* November 17, 1997, p. 54.

4. K. Carley, "Organizational Learning and Personnel Turnover," *Organization Science* 3, no. 1 (1992), pp. 20–47.

5. E. Pofeldt, "Collect Calls," *Success* (March 1998), pp. 22–23.

6. J. Fraser, "Hidden Cash," *Inc.* (February 1991), pp. 81–82.

7. Ivan T. Hoffman, "Current Trends in Small Package Shipping," *International Business* (March 1994), p. 33.

8. "Unlocking the Secrets of ECR," *Progressive Grocer* (January 1994), p. 3.

9. I. Mochari, "Too Much, Too Soon," *Inc.* (November 1999), p. 119.

10. M. A. Hitt, R. D. Ireland, and R. E. Hoskisson, *Strategic Management: Competitiveness and Globalization*, 3rd ed. (London: South-Western College Publishing, 1999).

14

ACCESSING RESOURCES FOR GROWTH FROM EXTERNAL SOURCES

LEARNING OBJECTIVES

1
To understand how joint ventures can help an entrepreneur grow his or her business and acknowledge the challenges of finding, and maintaining, an effective joint venture relationship.

2
To be aware of the pros and cons of using acquisitions to grow a business and to know what to look for in an acquisition candidate.

3
To understand the possibilities of achieving growth through mergers and leveraged buyouts and the challenges associated with each.

4
To understand franchising from the perspective of both the entrepreneur looking to reduce the risk of new entry and the entrepreneur looking for a way to grow his or her business.

5
To understand the tasks of negotiation and develop the skills to more effectively conduct these tasks.

OPENING PROFILE

BILL GROSS

How does a start-up company take advantage of the seemingly endless opportunities of the Internet by using the creative talents of one person and then letting other selected entrepreneurs take over the responsibility of running these businesses? It sounds like a repeat of history when Thomas Edison made invention a business. But the new kid on the block is Bill Gross, whose vision is to grow his Idealab by nurturing and monitoring other Internet businesses that have resulted because of his ingenuity. He refers to Idealab as Internet start-ups in a box. Basically the concept is simple. Bill comes up with an idea for an Internet start-up. He locates someone, either a former executive or even an engineering student, who he thinks is right for the job. That person is then given the reins to start this venture all under the roof of an incubator-like operation, where Bill provides the structure and services necessary to make these start-ups rapidly grow into successful enterprises.

www.idealab.com

Bill describes Idealab as a combination of incubator, venture capitalist, and creative think tank. Like an incubator, it provides shared space and administrative services, it offers seed financing for a minority equity position (up to 49 percent), and it uses everyone to brainstorm on the most opportune technology applications. Started in 1996 in Pasadena, California, to date the company has created 30 Internet ventures, all at various stages of development. Each idea came from Gross or one of his Idealab staff managers. For each firm a CEO was found and hired using Bill's networking skills in the Internet industry and at Caltech, his alma mater. Then the core expert staff becomes involved to get these ventures up and running as quickly as possible. This involves developing the technology, conducting marketing research, preparing a business plan, hiring management, launching the venture, and finally either going public or selling the business. The seed financing that Idealab provides to these start-ups does not exceed $250,000. Bill believes that Internet start-ups do not need large amounts of capital to get started but, more importantly, do need knowledge, intelligence, and speed. Knowledge and intelligence are provided by Bill and the Idealab's staff experts, and speed focuses on the ability to quickly grow a start-up, but with few mistakes. According to Bill, these two elements are much

387

more important in the successful launch and growth of an Internet company than money.

Bill Gross personifies the real meaning of an entrepreneur. He probably holds the unique distinction in the field of entrepreneurship of not only starting many businesses but also turning all of them into successful enterprises. As an enterprising 12-year-old he noticed that the corner drugstore was selling candy at 9 cents, and at the Sav-On nearby it was selling for 7 cents. He quickly figured out that with no overhead he could make an easy profit on the price spread. Bill then moved on to his next successful enterprise by placing ads in *Popular Mechanics,* where he sold $25,000 worth of solar devices and plans. The proceeds from this effort were used to finance his freshman year's tuition at Caltech. While at Caltech he proceeded to launch GNP Inc., a stereo equipment maker. This enterprise not only was very successful but was recognized as one of *Inc.* magazine's top 500 growth ventures in 1982 and 1985. His next enterprise was created when Bill and his brother found a way to make Lotus 1-2-3 obey simple commands. Mitch Kapor, the founder of Lotus, was impressed with their software and purchased their business for $10 million.

The success streak continued with the launch of Knowledge Adventure in 1991. This venture developed and marketed educational software and was considered to be his most successful venture to date. He sold the business in 1997 for $100 million. Idealab actually was created in 1996 when Bill was stepping down from Knowledge Adventure and negotiating the sale.

A sample of some of the companies launched by Idealab includes CitySearch, which competes with Microsoft and provides online services for urban communities; EntertainNet, an Internet broadcaster that provides news and related information; and Answer.com, a Web site that will answer any question you might have and which has already been acquired by another company. Last year Bill expanded his operations into Silicon Valley. He wanted to be close to the action and take advantage of Idealab's ability to quickly transform some of these Internet opportunities into successful ventures.

Growing these start-ups is a challenge to Bill Gross, and although there is high risk in the Internet industry, Bill feels that Idealab will continue to stay focused on its mission.[1]

USING EXTERNAL PARTIES TO HELP GROW A BUSINESS

In Chapter 13, we detailed the financial pressures faced by entrepreneurs of growing firms. Over and above the effective management of one's own resources entrepreneurs can use the resources (financial, knowledge, and so on) of others to help grow the business. This can be achieved through joint ventures, acquisitions, and mergers. The first section of the chapter explores these modes of growth. Franchising is also an alternative means by which an entrepreneur may expand his or her business by having others pay for the use of the name, process, product, service, and so on. Using franchising as a growth mechanism is the primary focus of this chapter. Given the importance of franchising for both new entry and growth, this chapter explores franchising from the perspective of the entrepreneur looking to use franchising to reduce the risks of new entry and from the perspective of the entrepreneur looking to use franchising as a way to grow his or her business. Finally, regardless of the mode used, entrepreneurs need to be good negotiators. They need to negotiate with external parties to obtain the human and financial resources necessary to fuel business growth. We provide some useful advice in how to become a better negotiator.

JOINT VENTURES

With the increase in business risks, hypercompetition, and failures, joint ventures have occurred with increased regularity and often involve a wide variety of players.[2] Joint ventures are not a new concept, but rather have been used as a means of expansion by entrepreneurial firms for a long time.

joint venture Two or more companies forming a new company

What is a joint venture? A *joint venture* is a separate entity that involves a partnership between two or more active participants. Sometimes called strategic alliances, joint ventures can involve a wide variety of partners that include universities, not-for-profit organizations, businesses, and the public sector.[3] Joint ventures have occurred between such rivals as General Motors and Toyota as well as General Electric and Westinghouse. They have occurred between the United States and foreign concerns to penetrate an international market, and they have been a good conduit by which an entrepreneur can enter an international market.

Whenever close relationships between two companies are being developed, concerns about the ethics and ethical behavior of the potential partner may arise.

Types of Joint Ventures

Although there are many different types of joint venture arrangements, the most common is still between two or more private-sector companies. For example, Boeing, Mitsubishi, Fuji, and Kawasaki entered into a joint venture for the production of small aircraft to share technology and cut costs. Microsoft and NBC Universal formed a partnership to create a cable news channel (MSNBC). There is an elaborate cost-sharing arrangement between the different entities of the partnership.

Other private-sector joint ventures have had different objectives, such as entering new markets (Corning and Ciba-Geigy as well as Kodak and Cetus), entering foreign markets (AT&T and Olivetti), and raising capital and expanding markets (U.S. Steel and Phong Iron and Steel).

Some joint ventures are formed to do cooperative research. Probably the best known of these is the Microelectronics and Computer Technology Corporation (MCC). Supported by 13 major U.S. companies, this for-profit venture does long-range research with scientists who are loaned to MCC for up to four years before returning to their competing companies to apply the results of their research activities. MCC retains title to all the resulting knowledge and patents, making them available for license to the companies participating in the program. Another type of joint venture for research development is the Semiconductor Research Corporation, located in Triangle Park, North Carolina. A not-for-profit research organization, it began with the participation of 11 U.S. chip manufacturers and computer companies. The goal of the corporation is to sponsor basic research and train professional scientists and engineers to be future industry leaders. Members of SRC programs have invested $1.1 billion in cutting-edge semiconductor research supporting over 7,000 students and 1,598 faculty members at 237 universities worldwide.[4]

Industry–university agreements created for the purpose of doing research are another type of joint venture that has seen increasing usage. However, two major problems have kept these types of joint ventures from proliferating even faster. A profit corporation has the objective of obtaining tangible results, such as a patent, from its research investment and wants all proprietary rights. Universities want to share in the possible financial returns from the patent, but the university researchers want to make the knowledge available through research papers. In spite of these problems, numerous industry–university teams have been established. In one joint venture agreement in robotics, for example, Westinghouse retains patent rights while Carnegie-Mellon receives a percentage of any license royalties. The university also has the right to publish the research results as long as it withholds from publication any critical information that might adversely affect the patent.

The joint venture agreement between Celanese Corporation and Yale University, created for researching the composition and synthesis of enzymes, took a somewhat different form—cost sharing. Although Celanese assumes the expense of any needed supplies and equipment for the research, as well as the salaries of the postdoctoral researchers, Yale pays the salaries of the professors involved. The research results can be published only after a 45-day waiting period.

International joint ventures, discussed in Chapter 5, are rapidly increasing in number due to their relative advantages. Not only can both companies share in the earnings and growth, but the joint venture can have a low cash requirement if the knowledge or patents are capitalized as a contribution to the venture. Also, the joint venture provides ready access to new international markets that otherwise may not be easily attained. Finally, since talent and financing come from all parties involved, an international joint venture causes less drain on a company's managerial and financial resources than a wholly owned subsidiary.

There are several drawbacks to establishing an international joint venture. First, the business objectives of the joint venture partners can be quite different, which can result in problems in the direction and growth of the new entity. In addition, cultural differences in each company can create managerial difficulties in the new joint venture. Finally, government policies can sometimes have a negative impact on the direction and operation of the international joint venture.

In spite of these problems, the benefits usually outweigh the drawbacks, as evidenced by the frequency rate of establishing international joint ventures. For example, an international joint venture was established between Dow Chemical (United States) and Asaki Chemicals (Japan) to develop and market chemicals on an international basis. While Asaki provided the raw materials and was a sole distributor, Dow provided the technology and obtained distribution in the Japanese market. The arrangement eventually dissolved because of the concerns of the Japanese government and the fundamental difference in motives between the two partners: Dow was primarily concerned with the profits of the joint venture, whereas Asaki was primarily concerned with having a purchaser for its basic petrochemicals.

Factors in Joint Venture Success

Clearly, not all joint ventures succeed. An entrepreneur needs to assess this method of growth carefully and understand the factors that help ensure success as well as the problems involved before using it. The most critical factors for success are:

1. The accurate assessment of the parties involved to best manage the new entity in light of the ensuing relationships. The joint venture will be more effective if the managers can work well together. Without this chemistry, the joint venture has a low likelihood of success and may even fail.

2. The degree of symmetry between the partners. This symmetry goes beyond chemistry to objectives and resource capabilities. When one partner feels that he or she is bringing more to the table, or when one partner wants profits and the other desires product outlet (as in the case of the Asaki-Dow international joint venture), problems arise. For a joint venture to be successful, the managers in each parent company, as well as those in the new entity, must concur on the objectives of the joint venture and the level of resources that will be provided. Good relationships must be nurtured between the managers in the joint venture and those in each parent company.

3. The expectations of the results of the joint venture must be reasonable. Far too often, at least one of the partners feels that a joint venture will be the cure-all for other corporate problems. Expectations of a joint venture must be realistic.

4. The timing must be right. With environments constantly changing, industrial conditions being modified, and markets evolving, a particular joint venture could be a success one year and a failure the next. Intense competition leads to a hostile environment and increases the risks of establishing a joint venture. Some environments are just not conducive to success. An entrepreneur must determine whether the joint venture will offer opportunities for growth or will penalize the company, for example, by preventing it from entering certain markets.

A joint venture is not a panacea for expanding the entrepreneurial venture. Rather, it should be considered one of many options for supplementing the resources of the firm and responding more quickly to competitive challenges and market opportunities. The effective use of joint ventures as a strategy for expansion requires the entrepreneur to carefully appraise the situation and the potential partner(s). Other strategic alternatives to the joint venture—such as acquisitions, mergers, and leveraged buyouts—should also be considered.

ACQUISITIONS

acquisition Purchasing all or part of a company

Another way the entrepreneur can expand the venture is by acquiring an existing business. Acquisitions provide an excellent means of expanding a business by entering new markets or new product areas. One entrepreneur acquired a chemical manufacturing company after becoming familiar with its problems and operations as a supplier of the entrepreneur's company. An *acquisition* is the purchase of an entire company, or part of a company; by definition, the company is completely absorbed and no longer exists independently. An acquisition can take many forms, depending on the goals and position of the parties involved in the transaction, the amount of money involved, and the type of company.

Although one of the key issues in buying a business is agreeing on a price, successful acquisition of a business actually involves much, much more. In fact, often the structure of the deal can be more important to the resultant success of the transaction than the actual price. One radio station was successful after being acquired by a company primarily because the previous owner loaned the money and took no principal payment (only interest) on the loan until the third year of operation.

From a strategic viewpoint, a prime concern of the entrepreneurial firm is maintaining the focus of the new venture as a whole. Whether the acquisition will become the core of the new business or rather represents a needed capability—such as a distribution outlet, sales force, or production facility—the entrepreneur must ensure that it fits into the overall direction and structure of the strategic plan of the present venture.

Advantages of an Acquisition

For an entrepreneur, there are many advantages to acquiring an existing business:

1. *Established business.* The most significant advantage is that the acquired firm has an established image and track record. If the firm has been profitable, the entrepreneur need only continue its current strategy to be successful with the existing customer base.

2. *Location.* New customers are already familiar with the location.

3. *Established marketing structure.* An acquired firm has its existing channel and sales structure. Known suppliers, wholesalers, retailers, and manufacturers' reps are important assets to an entrepreneur. With this structure already in place, the entrepreneur can concentrate on improving or expanding the acquired business.

4. *Cost.* The actual cost of acquiring a business can be lower than other methods of expansion.

5. *Existing employees.* The employees of an existing business can be an important asset to the acquisition process. They know how to run the business and can help ensure that the business will continue in its successful mode. They already have established relationships with customers, suppliers, and channel members and can reassure these groups when a new owner takes over the business.

6. *More opportunity to be creative.* Since the entrepreneur does not have to be concerned with finding suppliers, channel members, hiring new employees, or creating customer awareness, more time can be spent assessing opportunities to expand or strengthen the existing business and tapping into potential synergies between the businesses.

Disadvantages of an Acquisition

Although we can see that there are many advantages to acquiring an existing business, there are also disadvantages. The importance of each of the advantages and disadvantages should be weighed carefully with other expansion options.

1. *Marginal success record.* Most ventures that are for sale have an erratic, marginally successful, or even unprofitable track record. It is important to review the records and meet with important constituents to assess that record in terms of the business's future potential. For example, if the store layout is poor, this factor can be rectified; but if the location is poor, the entrepreneur might do better using some other expansion method.

2. *Overconfidence in ability.* Sometimes an entrepreneur may assume that he or she can succeed where others have failed. This is why a self-evaluation is so important

before entering into any purchase agreement. Even though the entrepreneur brings new ideas and management qualities, the venture may never be successful for reasons that are not possible to correct. Often managers are overconfident in their ability to overcome cultural differences between their current business and the one being acquired.

3. *Key employee loss.* Often, when a business changes hands, key employees also leave. Key employee loss can be devastating to an entrepreneur who is acquiring a business since the value of the business is often a reflection of the efforts of the employees. This is particularly evident in a service business, where it is difficult to separate the actual service from the person who performs it. In the acquisition negotiations, it is helpful for the entrepreneur to speak to all employees individually to obtain some assurance of their intentions as well as to inform them of how important they will be to the future of the business. Incentives can sometimes be used to ensure that key employees will remain with the business.

4. *Overvaluation.* It is possible that the actual purchase price is inflated due to the established image, customer base, channel members, or suppliers. If the entrepreneur has to pay too much for a business, it is possible that the return on investment will be unacceptable. It is important to look at the investment required in purchasing a business and at the potential profit and establish a reasonable payback to justify the investment.

After balancing the pros and cons of the acquisition, the entrepreneur needs to determine a fair price for the business.

Synergy

The concept that "the whole is greater than the sum of its parts" applies to the integration of an acquisition into the entrepreneur's venture. The synergy should occur in both the business concept, with the acquisition functioning as a vehicle to move toward overall goals, and the financial performance. The acquisition should positively impact the bottom line, affecting both long-term gains and future growth. Lack of synergy is one of the most frequent causes of an acquisition's failure to meet its objectives.

Structuring the Deal

Once the entrepreneur has identified a good candidate for acquisition, an appropriate deal must be structured. Many techniques are available for acquiring a firm, each having a distinct set of advantages to both the buyer and seller. The deal structure involves the parties, the assets, the payment form, and the timing of the payment. For example, all or part of the assets of one firm can be acquired by another for some combination of cash, notes, stock, and/or employment contract. This payment can be made at the time of acquisition, throughout the first year, or extended over several years.

The two most common means of acquisition are the entrepreneur's direct purchase of the firm's entire stock or assets or the bootstrap purchase of these assets. In the direct purchase of the firm, the entrepreneur often obtains funds from an outside lender or the seller of the company being purchased. The money is repaid over time from the cash flow generated from the operations. Although this is a relatively simple and clear transaction, it usually results in a long-term capital gain to the seller and double taxation on the funds used to repay the money borrowed to acquire the company.

AS SEEN IN *BUSINESS NEWS*

PROVIDE ADVICE TO AN ENTREPRENEUR ABOUT ENTERING INTO AGREEMENTS

Entrepreneurs: James Tiscione, 49, and Anthony Tiscione, 79, founders of ACM Enterprises in Tucson, Arizona.

Product Description: The Auto Card Manager (ACM), a thin metal case that holds a driver's license and up to five credit cards. When users push one of the six buttons on the case, the selected credit card is dispensed.

Start-Up: $50,000 in 2000 and 2001, to pay for the first production run of 25,000 units.

Sales: $1.8 million in 2002.

The Challenge: Bringing a new product to market with a limited marketing budget.

James Tiscione didn't have a lot of money when he launched his business, but that didn't stop him from finding a way to bring his unusual product to market. Here are the steps he followed:

1. *Obtain a patent.* Tiscione started by visiting www.uspto.gov, the official Web site of the U.S. Patent and Trademark Office, to look for similar patents. "I looked at over 1,000 patents and found only two that were even remotely similar to mine," he says. "Only after completing the search did I go to a patent attorney." Doing some research on his own did more than just save Tiscione money: "I was trying to hedge my bets before investing dollars in attorney fees, engineering design, and prototypes. I also wanted to see what other ideas were out there. I was surprised no one else ever had the idea." Before long, Tiscione applied for a provisional patent,

which doesn't give inventors patent protection, but does allow them to show their ideas to people. "It is an inexpensive way of protection that allows inventors one year for research and development," Tiscione says. In 2001, he applied for his utility patent.

2. *Decide what help you need.* Because Tiscione had never developed a product before, he felt he lacked the experience he needed to launch the idea. He asked his father, Anthony, an inventor, for help in finalizing his product design. Tiscione also approached Steve Pagac, a marketing whiz who owned a real estate and investment firm. Says Tiscione, "Steve invested sweat equity in our venture, and he is responsible for lining up all our customers."

3. *Make a prototype.* Tiscione knew people wouldn't understand the ACM without trying it, so he made a prototype. Tiscione ended up choosing a prototype supplier in California. Once he began using the prototype, people started asking where they could buy one. The positive feedback played a major role in moving the business ahead.

4. *Locate a production source.* Tiscione's first stop was the Hong Kong Chamber of Commerce, which has an office in San Francisco. "They sent me a list of companies I e-mailed," he says. He narrowed it down to one—but only signed the final agreement after visiting the company several times and viewing a few trial production pieces.

To avoid these problems, the entrepreneur can make a bootstrap purchase, acquiring a small amount of the firm, such as 20 to 30 percent, for cash. He or she then purchases the remainder of the company with a long-term note that is paid off over time out of the acquired company's earnings. This type of deal often results in more favorable tax advantages to both the buyer and the seller.

Locating Acquisition Candidates

If an entrepreneur is seriously planning to buy a business, there are some sources of assistance. There are professional business *brokers* who operate in a fashion similar to a real estate broker. They represent the seller and will sometimes aggressively find buyers

brokers People who sell companies

5. *Explore all possibilities to find distribution outlets.* Tiscione and Pagac weren't sure which retailers would want to buy their product, so they started by approaching catalogs and stores such as Brookstone, The Sharper Image, and Things Remembered. "While the stores didn't bite, one promotional company did—AMG of Plymouth, Wisconsin," Tiscione says. "AMG signed an exclusive agreement with us for the promotional products market in 2001." Tiscione and Pagac also approached SkyMall, a specialty retailer that produces a cost-sharing catalog targeting in-flight airline passengers. "After two quarters ending in September," says Tiscione, "SkyMall reported that the ACM was the No. 1–selling product in [the catalog], and they agreed to carry the product through March." Tiscione and Pagac also contacted MJ Media, a TV marketer in Phoenix that signed a nonexclusive agreement to sell the ACM through TV ads. "We revamped our original agreement with MJ Media to include a broader base of distribution," Tiscione says. "Originally, the contract was for TV advertising only. Since then, MJ Media has expanded into Internet sales and master distribution to small distributors." Now, Tiscione has a broad range of customers selling his products. As a bonus, Taylor Gifts, a major consumer catalog, picked up the ACM for the 2002 Christmas season.

6. *Sign deals that maximize marketing exposure but limit financial risk.* Advertising and marketing expenses can kill a product—but Tiscione avoided these expenses by signing contracts with limited risk. Both AMG and MJ Media signed agreements to purchase the product from ACM and promote it themselves. Also, Tiscione's deal with SkyMall was cooperative. Tiscione paid nothing to be listed in SkyMall, but all the sales went to SkyMall up to a certain sales level. Once that level was reached, sales were split equally between SkyMall and ACM. At press time, ACM switched to a standard contract, which requires them to pay for the ad but allows them to retain all sales.

ADVICE TO AN ENTREPRENEUR

An inventor has read the preceding article and comes to you for advice. "This is exactly what I want to do," he says, "I don't have the expertise or the money to manufacture the product myself or to market and sell it. What I need is for someone else to do that for me. Here are my questions:

1. Is it really that simple to find and then establish a relationship with someone to produce my product? Should the producer have a manufacturing license or should I enter into a joint venture?

2. Same sorts of issues on the marketing end, but I also want to know how much control I can maintain over how the product is marketed and sold. Or should I not worry about that and let the experts do their thing?

3. One dilemma for me is how much money I should invest in the prototypes. The more money I invest, the better the prototype looks, but I don't want to waste money either."

Source: Reprinted with permission of Entrepreneur Media, Inc., "Play Your Cards Right. Presenting a Case Study in Striking the Best Deals to Launch Your Own Great Product on a Limited Budget," by Don Debelak, March 2003, *Entrepreneur* magazine: www.entrepreneur.com.

through either referrals, advertising, or direct sales. Since these brokers are paid a commission on the sale, they often expend more effort on their best deals.

Accountants, attorneys, bankers, business associates, and consultants may also know of good acquisition candidates. Many of these professionals have a good working knowledge of the business, which can be helpful in the negotiations.

It is also possible to find business opportunities in the classified sections of the newspaper or in a trade magazine. Since these listings are usually completely unknown, they may involve more risk but can be purchased at a lower price.

Determining the best option for an entrepreneur involves significant time and effort. The entrepreneur should gather as much information as possible, read it carefully, consult with advisors and experts, consider his or her own situation, and then make a constructive decision.

MERGERS

merger Joining two or more companies

A *merger*—or a transaction involving two, or possibly more, companies in which only one company survives—is another method of expanding a venture. Acquisitions are so similar to mergers that at times the two terms are used interchangeably. A key concern in any merger (or acquisition) is the legality of the purchase. The Department of Justice frequently issues guidelines for horizontal, vertical, and conglomerate mergers which further define the interpretation that will be made in enforcing the Sherman Act and Clayton Act. Since the guidelines are extensive and technical, the entrepreneur should secure adequate legal advice when any issues arise.

Why should an entrepreneur merge? There are both defensive and offensive strategies for a merger, as indicated in Figure 14.1. Merger motivations range from survival to protection to diversification to growth. When some technical obsolescence, market or raw material loss, or deterioration of the capital structure has occurred in the entrepreneur's venture, a merger may be the only means for survival. The merger can also protect against market encroachment, product innovation, or an unwarranted takeover. A merger can provide a great deal of diversification as well as growth in market, technology, and financial and managerial strength.

How does a merger take place? It requires sound planning by the entrepreneur. The merger objectives, particularly those dealing with earnings, must be spelled out with the resulting gains for the owners of both companies delineated. Also, the entrepreneur must carefully evaluate the other company's management to ensure that, if retained, it would be competent in developing the growth and future of the combined entity. The value and appropriateness of the existing resources should also be determined. In essence, this involves a careful analysis of both companies to ensure that the weaknesses of one do not compound those of the other. Finally, the entrepreneur should work toward establishing a climate of mutual trust to help minimize any possible management threat or turbulence.

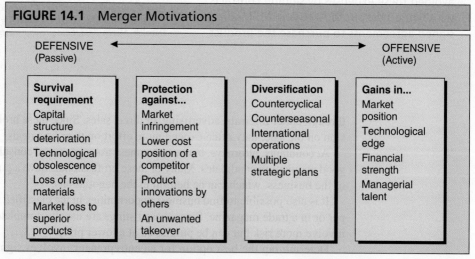

FIGURE 14.1   Merger Motivations

DEFENSIVE ←————————————————————→ OFFENSIVE
(Passive)   (Active)

Survival requirement	**Protection against...**	**Diversification**	**Gains in...**
Capital structure deterioration	Market infringement	Countercyclical	Market position
Technological obsolescence	Lower cost position of a competitor	Counterseasonal	Technological edge
Loss of raw materials	Product innovations by others	International operations	Financial strength
Market loss to superior products	An unwanted takeover	Multiple strategic plans	Managerial talent

Source: F. T. Haner, *Business Policy, Planning, and Strategy* (Cambridge, MA: Winthrop, 1976), p. 399.

The same methods for valuing an acquisition candidate can be used to determine the value of a merger candidate. The process involves the entrepreneur looking at the synergistic product/market position, the new domestic or international market position, any undervalued financial strength, whether or not the company is skilled in a related industry, and any underexploited company asset. A common procedure for determining value is to estimate the present value of discounted cash flows and the expected after-tax earnings attributable to the merger. This should be done on optimistic, pessimistic, and probable scenarios of cash flows and earnings using various acceptable rates of return.

LEVERAGED BUYOUTS

leveraged buyout (LBO)
Purchasing an existing venture by any employee group

A *leveraged buyout (LBO)* occurs when an entrepreneur (or any employee group) uses borrowed funds to purchase an existing venture for cash. Most LBOs occur because the entrepreneur purchasing the venture believes that he or she could run the company more efficiently than the current owners. The current owner is frequently an entrepreneur or other owner who wants to retire. The owner may also be a large corporation desiring to divest itself of a subsidiary that is too small or that does not fit its long-term strategic plans.

The purchaser needs a great amount of external funding since the personal financial resources needed to acquire the firm directly are frequently limited. Since the issuance of additional equity as a means of funding is usually not possible, capital is acquired in the form of long-term debt financing (five years or more), and the assets of the firm being acquired serve as collateral. Who usually provides this long-term debt financing? Banks, venture capitalists, and insurance companies have been the most active providers of the debt needed in LBOs.

The actual financial package used in an LBO reflects the lender's risk-reward profile. Whereas banks tend to use senior-debt issues, venture capitalists usually use subordinated debt issues with warrants or options. Regardless of the instrument used, the repayment plan established must be in line with the pro forma cash flows that the company expects to be generated. The interest rates are usually variable and are consistent with the current yields of comparable risk investment.

In most LBOs, the debt capital usually exceeds the equity by a ratio of 5 to 1, with some ratios as high as 10 to 1. This is significantly more debt relative to equity than in a typical firm's capital structure. Although this makes the financial risk great, the key to a successful LBO is not the relative debt-equity ratio but rather the ability of the entrepreneur taking over to cover the principal and interest payments through increased sales and profits. The ability depends on the skills of the entrepreneur and the strength and stability of the firm.

How does the entrepreneur determine whether a specific company is a good candidate for an LBO? This determination can be made through the following evaluation procedure:

1. The entrepreneur must determine whether the present owner's asking price is reasonable. Many subjective and quantitative techniques can be used in this determination. Subjective evaluations need to be made of the following: the competitiveness of the industry and the competitive position of the firm in that industry, the uniqueness of the offering of the firm and its stage in the product life cycle, and the abilities of management and other key personnel remaining with the firm. Quantitative techniques are used to evaluate the fairness of the asking price. The price-earnings ratio of the LBO prospect should be calculated and compared with those of comparable companies, as well as the present value of future earnings of the prospect and its book value.

2. The entrepreneur must assess the firm's debt capacity. This is particularly critical since the entrepreneur wants to raise as much of the capital needed as possible in the form of long-term debt. The amount of long-term debt a prospective LBO can carry depends on the prospect's business risk and the stability of its future cash flows. The cash flow must cover the long-term debt required to finance the LBO. Any financial amount that cannot be secured by long-term debt, due to the inadequacy of the cash flow, will need to be in the form of equity from the entrepreneur or other investors.

3. The entrepreneur must develop the appropriate financial package. The financial package must meet the needs and objectives of the providers of the funds as well as the company's and the entrepreneur's situation. Although each LBO financial package is tailored to the specific situation, there are usually some restrictions, such as no payment of dividends. Frequently, an LBO agreement with venture capitalists has warrants that are convertible into common stock at a later date. A sinking fund repayment of the long-term debt is frequently required.

There are many instances of both successful and unsuccessful LBOs. One of the most publicized involved R. H. Macy and Co., a well-known department store chain. Macy's was not in bad condition in terms of the traditional measures of sales per square foot, profitability, and return on assets. However, it had experienced a significant drop in profits and was losing talented middle executives. The LBO was accomplished by some 345 executives participating and sharing a 20 percent ownership in the $4.7 billion retailer. Ultimately, the LBO provided the following benefits: a new entrepreneurial spirit in management that fostered more loyalty in the employees; increased motivation among employees, with middle managers actually selling and earning sales floor bonuses during slack time; and a long-term planning direction for the board of directors that meets five times a year instead of once a month.

FRANCHISING

franchising An arrangement whereby a franchisor gives exclusive rights of local distribution to a franchisee in return for payment of royalties and conformance to standardized operating procedures

franchisor The person offering the franchise

franchisee The person who purchases the franchise

Franchising is "an arrangement whereby the manufacturer or sole distributor of a trademarked product or service gives exclusive rights of local distribution to independent retailers in return for their payment of royalties and conformance to standardized operating procedures."[5] The person offering the franchise is known as the *franchisor.* The *franchisee* is the person who purchases the franchise and is given the opportunity to enter a new business with a better chance to succeed than if he or she were to start a new business from scratch.

Advantages of Franchising—to the Franchisee

One of the most important advantages of buying a franchise is that the entrepreneur does not have to incur all the risks associated with creating a new business. Table 14.1 summarizes the important advantages of a franchise. Typically, the areas that entrepreneurs have problems with in starting a new venture are product acceptance, management expertise, meeting capital requirements, knowledge of the market, and operating and structural controls. In franchising, the risks associated with each are minimized through the franchise relationship, as discussed in the following.

Product Acceptance   The franchisee usually enters into a business that has an accepted name, product, or service. In the case of Subway, any person buying a franchise will be using the Subway name, which is well known and established throughout the United States.

TABLE 14.1   What You May Buy in a Franchise
1. A product or service with an established market and favorable image.
2. A patented formula or design.
3. Trade names or trademarks.
4. A financial management system for controlling the financial revenue.
5. Managerial advice from experts in the field.
6. Economies of scale for advertising and purchasing.
7. Head office services.
8. A tested business concept.

The franchisee does not have to spend resources trying to establish the credibility of the business. That credibility already exists based on the years the franchise has existed. Subway has also spent millions of dollars in advertising, thus building a favorable image of the products and services offered. An entrepreneur who tries to start a sandwich shop would be unknown to the potential customers and would require significant effort and resources to build credibility and a reputation in the market.

Management Expertise   Another important advantage to the franchisee is the managerial assistance provided by the franchisor. Each new franchisee is often required to take a training program on all aspects of operating the franchise. This training could include classes in accounting, personnel management, marketing, and production. McDonald's, for example, requires all its franchisees to spend time at its school, where everyone takes classes in these areas. In addition, some franchisors require their new franchisees to actually work with an existing franchise owner or at a company-owned store or facility to get on-the-job training. Once the franchise has been started, most franchisors will offer managerial assistance on the basis of need. Toll-free numbers are also available so that the franchisee can ask questions anytime. Local offices for the larger franchises continually visit the local franchisees to offer advice and keep owners informed of new developments.

The training and education offered is actually an important criterion that the entrepreneur should consider in evaluating any franchise opportunity. If the assistance in start-up is not good, the entrepreneur should probably look elsewhere for opportunities unless he or she already has extensive experience in the field.

Capital Requirements   As we've seen in previous chapters, starting a new venture can be costly in terms of both time and money. The franchise offers an opportunity to start a new venture with up-front support that could save the entrepreneur significant time and possibly capital. Some franchisors conduct location analysis and market research of the area that might include an assessment of traffic, demographics, business conditions, and competition. In some cases, the franchisor will also finance the initial investment to start the franchise operation. The initial capital required to purchase a franchise generally reflects a fee for the franchise, construction costs, and the purchase of equipment.

The layout of the facility, control of stock and inventory, and the potential buying power of the entire franchise operation can save the entrepreneur significant funds. The size of the parent company can be advantageous in the purchase of health care and business insurance, since the entrepreneur would be considered a participant in the entire franchise organization. Savings in start-up are also reflected in the pooling of monies by individual franchisees for advertising and sales promotion. The contribution by each franchisee is usually a function of the volume and the number of franchises owned. This allows advertising on both a local and a national scale to enhance the image and credibility of the business, something that would be impossible for a single operation.

Knowledge of the Market Any established franchise business offers the entrepreneur years of experience in the business and knowledge of the market. This knowledge is usually reflected in a plan offered to the franchisee that details the profile of the target customer and the strategies that should be implemented once the operation has begun. This is particularly important because of regional and local differences in markets. Competition, media effectiveness, and tastes can vary widely from one market to another. Given their experience, franchisors can provide advice and assistance in accommodating any of these differences.

Most franchisors will be constantly evaluating market conditions and determining the most effective strategies to be communicated to the franchisees. Newsletters and other publications that reflect new ideas and developments in the overall market are continually sent to franchisees.

Operating and Structural Controls Two problems that many entrepreneurs have in starting a new venture are maintaining quality control of products and services and establishing effective managerial controls. The franchisor, particularly in the food business, will identify suppliers that meet the quality standards established. In some instances, the supplies are actually provided by the franchisor. Standardization in the supplies, products, and services provided helps ensure that the entrepreneur will maintain quality standards that are so important. Standardization also supports a consistent image on which the franchise business depends for expansion.

Administrative controls usually involve financial decisions relating to costs, inventory, and cash flow, and personnel issues such as criteria for hiring and firing, scheduling, and training to ensure consistent service to the customer. These controls will usually be outlined in a manual supplied to the franchisee upon completion of the franchise deal.

Although all the preceding are advantages to the franchisee, they also represent important strategic considerations for an entrepreneur who is considering growing the business by selling franchises. Since there are so many franchise options for an entrepreneur, the franchisor will need to offer all the preceding services to succeed in the sale of franchises. One of the reasons for the success of such franchises as McDonald's, Burger King, KFC, Boston Market, Subway, Midas, Jiffy Lube, Holiday Inn, Mail Boxes Etc., and Merry Maids is that all these firms have established an excellent franchise system that effectively provides the necessary services to the franchisee.

Advantages of Franchising—to the Franchisor

The advantages a franchisor gains through franchising are related to expansion risk, capital requirements, and cost advantages that result from extensive buying power. Consider the success of the Subway chain. Clearly, Fred DeLuca would not have been able to achieve the size and scope of his business without franchising it. To use franchising as an expansion method, the franchisor must have established value and credibility that someone else is willing to buy.

AS SEEN IN *BUSINESS NEWS*

VENTURE CAPITAL'S FAVORITE STARTUPS

Over the past four quarters—even as the depths of the nation's economic problems became evident—venture capitalists invested more than $7 billion in seed and early-stage companies in more than 1,400 deals, according to the MoneyTree Report from the National Venture Capital Assn. That's more money raised by young companies than in any calendar year since the dot-com bubble burst in 2001.

In the largest deals of the past year, venture capital firms poured money into companies tackling the global problems of climate change and disease. The challenges are great—and investors bet that the payoffs will be, too—for the startups that successfully commercialize ideas like solar power, low-emission cars, and new medications.

Who are these hot startups? To find out, we followed the money, looking at deals that took place in the four most recent quarters available, from October 2007 to September 2008, based on the MoneyTree report, which uses data from Thomson Reuters. We then reached out to a selection of the seed and early-stage companies that raised the most money and profiled them in a slide show.

At the top of the list are some veteran entrepreneurs who have already proven themselves to investors by founding companies that led to acquisitions. The team behind Relypsa, a Santa Clara (Calif.) drug development company working on a treatment for life-threatening hyperkalemia in heart and kidney patients, sold their last company to Amgen (AMGN) for $420 million in 2007. Relypsa, founded months after the acquisition, raised $33 million in late 2007.

But even for well-capitalized startups with proven track records, the uncertain funding outlook means they have to make every dollar count. Gerrit Klaerner, Relypsa's chief operating officer, says startups that are only now thinking of ways to trim may be in trouble. "Operating a small company, I think you have to be lean and mean. If you start thinking about capital efficiency today, it's too late," he says.

For other businesses, the downturn carries the scent of opportunity. Ron Gonen, co-founder and chief executive officer of RecycleBank, says the sudden need for cities and households to conserve cash puts his company in a position to grow. The 85-employee New York firm runs recycling systems for cities that let residents earn points, based on the amount they recycle, that they can redeem at retailers. "Now that cities really need to save money and people are really looking for a way to get disposable income, we're at a unique time in our growth curve," Gonen says. He says families can earn up to $400 a year in RecycleBank points. RecycleBank, which raised $30 million last year on top of $15 million in an earlier round, takes a cut of the savings that the cities get from reducing how much trash they send to landfills.

Venture capitalists see other companies that focus on conservation, renewable power, and reducing the emissions that cause global warming as strong bets even in bad times.

"No matter how much worse the economy could get over the next six to 12 months, there are many who believe that clean tech kind of rides above the economic uncertainty," says Mark Heesen, president of the National Venture Capital Assn. Demand for clean power from governments around the globe, along with renewed attention to cutting emissions from the incoming Obama Administration, has convinced investors to bet on solar and wind power, as well as hybrid cars.

Likewise, Heesen says, biotechnology and medical device companies will continue to draw investors because the promise of their products to extend lives is so important. "We all are living longer, and we want to live longer, more productive lives, and biotech is at the cusp of that," he says. The startups Heesen predicts will suffer most from the downturn are IT firms that ultimately sell their products to consumers or businesses, because both are cutting spending.

Still, developing drugs or clean technology takes a lot of money, with long time frames for exits potentially made longer by an IPO drought and a tough market for acquisitions. One drug development company, IRX Therapeutics in New York, has raised more than $60 million since its founding more than a decade ago, mostly from high-net-worth individuals and some VCs, to develop treatments to restore immune function in head and neck cancer patients. "We're obviously a company without revenue in a business that eats capital," says Chief Financial Officer Jeffrey Hwang. He says the firm has had to cut staff by a third and delay clinical trials it planned for 2009, because he's not sure whether the funding will be there to complete them. "We're not going to start anything we can't finish," he says.

Heesen says many startups may face the same problem next year. He expects fewer companies to get funded. Those entrepreneurs that do will have to prove the value of their ideas and their ability to execute them even in a downturn.*

ADVICE TO AN ENTREPRENEUR

An individual who is looking to start and grow a business approaches you and asks you the following questions:

1. If I don't have the track record of starting and running a successful business, then what else can I do to enhance my likelihood of raising funds to start up and grow a new business?

2. Why are "green opportunities" so attractive during an economic downturn? Will they "disappear" when the economy "heats up"?

3. Biotech requires scientific knowledge and considerable money. Given the trends that make biotech attractive, what other businesses are also likely to be high growth?

*Source: Reprinted from December 19, 2008 issue of *BusinessWeek* by special permission, copyright © 2008 by The McGraw-Hill Companies, Inc., "Venture Capital's Favorite Startups," by John Tozzi, http://www.businessweek.com/smallbiz/content/dec2008/sb20081218_856857.htm.

Expansion Risk The most obvious advantage of franchising for an entrepreneur is that it allows the venture to expand quickly using little capital. This advantage is significant when we reflect on the problems and issues that an entrepreneur faces in trying to manage and grow a new venture (see Chapter 13). A franchisor can expand a business nationally and even internationally by authorizing and selling franchises in selected locations. The capital necessary for this expansion is much less than it would be without franchising. Just think of the capital that DeLuca would require to build 8,300 Subway sandwich shops.

The value of the franchise depends on the to-date track record of the franchisor and on the services offered to the entrepreneur or franchisee. Subway's low franchise fee has enhanced expansion opportunities, as more people can afford it.

Operating a franchised business requires fewer employees than a nonfranchised business. Headquarters and regional offices can be lightly staffed, primarily to support the needs of the franchisees. This allows the franchisor to maintain low payrolls and minimizes personnel issues and problems.

Cost Advantages The mere size of a franchised company offers many advantages to the franchisees. The franchisor can purchase supplies in large quantities, thus achieving economies of scale that would not have been possible otherwise. Many franchise businesses produce parts, accessories, packaging, and raw materials in large quantities, and then in turn sell these to the franchisees. Franchisees are usually required to purchase these items as part of the franchise agreement, and they usually benefit from lower prices.

One of the biggest cost advantages of franchising a business is the ability to commit larger sums of money to advertising. Each franchisee contributes a percentage of sales (1 to 2 percent) to an advertising pool. This pooling of resources allows the franchisor to conduct advertising in major media across a wide geographic area. If the business were not franchised, the company would have to provide funds for the entire advertising budget.

Disadvantages of Franchising

Franchising is not always the best option for an entrepreneur. Anyone investing in a franchise should investigate the opportunity thoroughly. Problems between the franchisor and the franchisee are common and have recently begun to receive more attention from the government and trade associations.

The disadvantages to the franchisee usually center on the inability of the franchisor to provide services, advertising, and location. When promises made in the franchise agreement are not kept, the franchisee may be left without any support in important areas. For example, Curtis Bean bought a dozen franchises in Checkers of America Inc., a firm that provides auto inspection services. After losing $200,000, Bean and other franchisees filed a lawsuit claiming that the franchisor had misrepresented advertising costs and had made false claims—including that no experience was necessary to own a franchise.[6]

The franchisee may also face the problem of a franchisor's failing or being bought out by another company. No one knows this better than Vincent Niagra, an owner of three Window Works franchises. Niagra had invested about $1 million in these franchises when the franchise was sold to Apogee Enterprises and then resold four years later to a group of investors. This caused many franchises to fail. The failure of these franchises has made it difficult for Niagra to continue because customers are apprehensive about doing business with him for fear that he will also go out of business. None of the support services that had been promised were available.[7]

The franchisor also incurs certain risks and disadvantages in choosing this expansion alternative. In some cases, the franchisor may find it very difficult to find quality franchisees. Poor management, in spite of all the training and controls, can still cause individual franchise failures and, therefore, can reflect negatively on the entire franchise system. As the number of franchises increases, the ability to maintain tight controls becomes more difficult.

Types of Franchises

There are three available types of franchises.[8] The first type is the dealership, a form commonly found in the automobile industry. Here, manufacturers use franchises to distribute their product lines. These dealerships act as the retail stores for the manufacturer. In some instances, they are required to meet quotas established by the manufacturers, but as is the case for any franchise, they benefit from the advertising and management support provided by the franchisor.

The most common type of franchise is the type that offers a name, image, and method of doing business, such as McDonald's, Subway, KFC, Midas, Dunkin' Donuts, and Holiday Inn. There are many of these types of franchises, and their listings, with pertinent information, can be found in various sources.[9]

A third type of franchise offers services. These include personnel agencies, income tax preparation companies, and real estate agencies. These franchises have established names and reputations and methods of doing business. In some instances, such as real estate, the franchisee has actually been operating a business and then applies to become a member of the franchise.

Franchising opportunities have often evolved from changes in the environment as well as important social trends. Several of these are discussed in the following.[10]

- *Good health.* Today people are eating healthier food and spending more time keeping fit. Many franchises have developed in response to this trend. For example, Bassett's Original Turkey was created in response to consumer interest in eating foods lower in cholesterol, and Booster Juice was created to provide fresh juice and smoothies as a healthy alternative to other snacks and drinks. Peter Taunton founded Snap Fitness Inc. in 2003 to offer patrons a convenient and affordable place to work out, and Gary Heavin created Curves for Women—a women-only fitness center.

- *Time saving or convenience.* More and more consumers prefer to have things delivered to them as opposed to going out of their way to buy them. In fact, many food stores now offer home delivery services. In 1990, Auto Critic of America Inc. was started as a mobile car inspection service. About the same time, Ronald Tosh started Tubs To Go, a company that delivers Jacuzzis to almost any location for an average of $100 to $200 per night.

- *Health care.* There is an increasing number of opportunities in health care for aging people. For example, Senior Helpers was founded in 2001 and started franchising in 2005 to offer care for seniors so that they can live independently in the comfort of their own home. HealthSource Chiropractic and Progressive Rehab started franchising in 2006 and offers chiropractic care with "Progressive Rehabilitation" where chiropractors work side by side with therapists, massage therapists, and athletic trainers.

- *The second baby boom.* Today's baby boomers have had babies themselves, which has resulted in the need for a number of child-related service franchises. Child care franchises such as KinderCare and Living and Learning are thriving. In 1989, two attorneys, David Pickus and Lee Sandoloski, opened Jungle Jim's Playland. This is an indoor amusement park with small-scale rides in a 20,000- to 27,000-square-foot facility. One franchise, Computertots, teaches classes on computers to preschoolers. This franchise has spread to 25 locations in 15 states.

INVESTING IN A FRANCHISE

Franchising involves many risks to an entrepreneur. Although we read about the success of McDonald's or Burger King, for every one of these successes there are many failures. Franchising, like any other venture, is not for the passive person. It requires effort and long hours, as any business does, since duties such as hiring, scheduling, buying, and accounting are still the franchisee's responsibility.

Not every franchise is right for every entrepreneur. He or she must evaluate the franchise alternatives to decide which one is most appropriate. A number of factors should be assessed before making the final decision.

1. *Unproven versus proven franchise.* There are some trade-offs in investing in a proven or unproven franchise business. Whereas an unproven franchise will be a less expensive investment, the lower investment is offset by more risk. In an unproven franchise, the franchisor is likely to make mistakes as the business grows. These mistakes could inevitably lead to failure. Constant reorganization of a new franchise can result in confusion and mismanagement. Yet, a new and unproven franchise can offer more excitement and challenge and can lead to significant opportunities for large profits should the business grow rapidly. A proven franchise offers lower risk but requires more financial investment.

2. *Financial stability of franchise.* The purchase of a franchise should entail an assessment of the financial stability of the franchisor. A potential franchisee should seek answers to the following questions:
   - How many franchises are in the organization?
   - How successful is each of the members of the franchise organization?
   - Are most of the profits of the franchise a function of fees from the sale of franchises or from royalties based on profits of franchisees?
   - Does the franchisor have management expertise in production, finance, and marketing?

   Some of the preceding information can be obtained from the profit-and-loss statements of the franchise organization. Face-to-face contact with the franchisor can also indicate the success of the organization. It is also worthwhile to contact some of the franchisees directly to determine their success and to identify any problems that have occurred. If financial information about the franchisor is unavailable, the entrepreneur may purchase a financial rating from a source such as Dun & Bradstreet. Generally, the following are good external sources of information:
   - Franchise association
   - Other franchisees
   - Government
   - Accountants and lawyers
   - Libraries
   - Franchise directories and journals
   - Business exhibitions

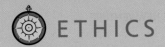

ETHICS

FAIR ENOUGH

To Be a Better Negotiator, Learn to Tell the Difference between a Lie and a *Lie*

No one really likes to think about how much lying goes on at the bargaining table. Of course not—it's troubling. On the one hand, we aspire to principled negotiation, win-win solutions, and civility with our opponents. On the other, our whole notion of negotiation is built on ethical quicksand: To succeed, you must deceive.

I'm not talking about the obvious cases, such as the bald lie. Those we all condemn, and in fact, our courts provide remedies for them—albeit slow, aggravating, inconsistent, and expensive ones. To me, it's the little lies, the omissions and evasions, that are more curious.

In negotiation, exaggerating benefits, ignoring flaws, or saying "I don't know" when in reality you do is not considered lying. Rather, it's sales ability. Declaring your bottom line to be non-negotiable (even when you're posturing) is not lying. It's a show of strength. Pretending to bend over backward to make meaningless concessions is not lying. It's applied psychology. Savvy businesspeople accept these rituals without undue introspection. Of course, the pathologically honest among us find them disturbing. But we have a place for those people . . . in the back room, far away from any bargaining table.

Still, some evasiveness and deception we consider out of bounds. Following are some tips for staying in bounds without getting clobbered.

On defense, vigilant skepticism is a tremendous asset. Reflect on everything you hear. Reflect on everything you don't. If you're suspicious, ask questions, especially ones that require more than just a simple yes or no answer. Keep probing until you're satisfied. J. P. Morgan used to say, "A man always has two reasons for the things he does—a good one and the real one." So after you get the good ones, ask for the real ones by saying, "And why else?" Also, get important promises in writing, and scrutinize their wording with and without your lawyer. To discourage dishonesty, tell your opponent you will independently verify the important stuff. If you can, do it. By the way, experts say it's easier to detect lying on the phone than in person. The voice all by itself (without distracting visual cues) is more of a giveaway.

To the terminally honest, I say: Negotiation is not group therapy. Generally, if you bare your soul, you will be fleeced. Respect the rules—or have someone else do your bargaining for you. If you're a liar (and you know who you are), I hope you get nailed big time. And if you're morally sturdy and find yourself unsure of what to say or omit, just keep Richard Nixon's comments about Watergate in mind: "I was not lying. I said things that later on seemed to be untrue."

Source: Reprinted with permission of Entrepreneur Media, Inc., "To Be a Better Negotiator, Learn to Tell the Difference between a Lie and a *Lie*," by Marc Diener, January 2002, *Entrepreneur* magazine: www.entrepreneur.com.

3. *Potential market for the new franchise.* It is important for the entrepreneur to evaluate the market that the franchise will attract. A starting point is evaluating the traffic flow and demographics of the residents from a map of the area. Traffic flow information may be observed by visiting the area. Direction of traffic flow, ease of entry to the business, and the amount of traffic (pedestrian and automobile) can be estimated by observation. The demographics of the area can be determined from census data, which can be obtained from local libraries or the town hall. It can also be advantageous to locate competitors on the map to determine their potential effect on the franchise business. Marketing research in the market area is helpful. Attitudes about and interest in the new business can be assessed in the market research. In some instances, the franchisor will conduct a market study as a selling point to the franchisee.

4. *Profit potential for a new franchise.* As in any start-up business, it is important to develop pro forma income and cash flow statements. The franchisor should provide projections to calculate the needed information.

TABLE 14.2 Information Required in Disclosure Statement

1. Identification of the franchisor and its affiliates and their business experience.

2. The business experience of each of the franchisor's officers, directors, and management personnel responsible for franchise services, training, and other aspects of the franchise programs.

3. The lawsuits in which the franchisor and its officers, directors, and management personnel have been involved.

4. Any previous bankruptcies in which the franchisor and its officers, directors, and management personnel have been involved.

5. The initial franchise fee and other initial payments that are required to obtain the franchise.

6. The continuing payments that franchisees are required to make after the franchise opens.

7. Any restrictions on the quality of goods and services used in the franchise and where they may be purchased, including restrictions requiring purchases from the franchisor or its affiliates.

8. Any assistance available from the franchisor or its affiliates in financing the purchase of the franchise.

9. Restrictions on the goods or services franchises are permitted to sell.

10. Any restrictions on the customers with whom franchises may deal.

11. Any territorial protection that will be granted to the franchisee.

12. The conditions under which the franchise may be repurchased or refused renewal by the franchisor, transferred to a third party by the franchisee, and terminated or modified by either party.

13. The training programs provided to franchisees.

14. The involvement of any celebrities or public figures in the franchise.

15. Any assistance in selecting a site for the franchise that will be provided by the franchisor.

16. Statistical information about the present number of franchises; the number of franchises projected for the future; and the number of franchises terminated, the number the franchisor has decided not to renew, and the number repurchased in the past.

17. The financial statements of the franchisor.

18. The extent to which the franchisees must personally participate in the operation of the franchise.

19. A complete statement of the basis of any earnings claims made to the franchisee, including the percentage of existing franchises that have actually achieved the results that are claimed.

20. A list of the names and addresses of other franchises.

In general, most of the preceding information should be provided in the disclosure statement or the prospectus. The Federal Trade Commission's Franchise Rule requires franchisors to make full presale disclosure in a document that provides information about 20 separate aspects of a franchise offering.[11] The information required in this disclosure is summarized in Table 14.2. Some of the information will be comprehensive and some will be sketchy. There are always weaknesses that must be evaluated before making a commitment. The disclosure statement represents a good resource, but it is also important to evaluate the other services mentioned earlier in this chapter.

Front-end procedure fees, royalty payments, expenses, and other information should be compared with those of franchises in the same field, as well as in different business areas. If a franchise looks good as an investment, the entrepreneur may request a franchise package from the franchisor, which usually contains a draft franchise agreement or contract. Generally, this package will require a deposit of $400 to $600, which should be fully refundable.

The contract or franchise agreement is the final step in establishing a franchise arrangement. Here a lawyer experienced in franchising should be used. The franchise agreement contains all the specific requirements and obligations of the franchisee. Things such as the exclusivity of territory coverage will protect against the franchisor's granting another franchise within a certain radius of the business. The renewable terms will indicate the length of the contract and the requirements. Financial requirements will stipulate the initial price for the franchise, the schedule of payments, and the royalties to be paid. Termination of franchise requirements should indicate what will happen if the franchisee becomes disabled or dies and what provisions are made for the family. Terminating a franchise generally results in more lawsuits than any other issue in franchising. These terms should also allow the franchisee to obtain fair market value should the franchise be sold. Even though the agreement may be standard, the franchisee should try to negotiate important items to reduce the investment risk.

OVERCOMING CONSTRAINTS BY NEGOTIATING FOR MORE RESOURCES

distribution task
Negotiating how the benefits of the relationship will be allocated between the parties

There are two primary tasks for an entrepreneur negotiating with another party for access to an external growth mechanism. The *distribution task* is the first—how the benefits of the relationship are distributed between the parties. That is, given a certain sized pie, the parties work out who gets what proportion of that pie. Second is the *integration task,* in which mutual benefits from the relationship are explored. This requires a collaborative mind-set so that the "size of the pie" can be increased.

integration task
Exploring possible mutual benefits from the relationship so that the "size of the pie" can be increased

Often people focus on the first task and ignore the second. However, making the pie bigger before distribution provides the opportunity to generate greater benefits for both parties and increases the likelihood of an agreement being reached. Besides, the collaborative and creative aspects of working together to find ways to increase the size of the pie are more enjoyable and more beneficial than a conflict resolution approach, which involves simply allocating outcomes under a purely distributive approach.

To negotiate in a way that maximizes benefits requires the entrepreneur to use information about one's own preferences and those of the other party to create an outcome that is mutually beneficial. This requires an initial assessment of oneself and the other party and the use of strategies to elicit more information during the negotiation interactions to better inform those initial assessments. Based on the work of Max Bazerman and Margaret Neale, two leading experts on negotiation, there are a number of assessments that an entrepreneur should make when negotiating with a growth partner.[12]

reservation price The price (the bundle of resources from the agreement) at which the entrepreneur is indifferent about whether to accept the agreement or choose the alternative

Assessment 1: What Will You Do If an Agreement Is Not Reached?   The answer to such a question provides an important basis for any negotiation strategy. The answer represents the entrepreneur's "best alternative to a negotiated agreement." This best alternative helps to determine a reservation price for the negotiation. The *reservation price* is the price (the bundle of resources from the agreement) at which the entrepreneur is indifferent about whether to accept the agreement or choose the alternative. For example, the best alternative to a negotiated agreement with a joint venture partner would be the benefits from pursuing growth at a slower rate using existing resources (knowledge, money, network, etc.). Recognizing that there is an alternative to this joint venture relationship, albeit a slower route, provides a minimum acceptable level of benefits that the negotiated outcome must reach.

bargaining zone The range of outcomes between the entrepreneur's reservation price and the reservation price of the other party

Assessment 2: What Will the Other Party to the Negotiation Do If an Agreement Is Not Reached?

It can be difficult for the entrepreneur to assess his or her own reservation prices, and it is even more difficult to assess those of the negotiation partner. If these prices can be determined, the entrepreneur has a good idea of the *bargaining zone,* or the range of outcomes between the entrepreneur's reservation price and the reservation price of the other party. Consideration of the bargaining zone encourages the entrepreneur not to focus prematurely on a settlement price but rather to consider the range of possible outcomes within the bargaining zone. If the bargaining zone can be determined by the entrepreneur while keeping his or her reservation price hidden from the other party, then the entrepreneur is in a position to negotiate an outcome that is largely beneficial to the entrepreneur and only marginally beneficial to the other party (i.e., just above the other party's reservation price). Of course, such an approach focuses on the distribution stage and not the integrative stage.

Assessment 3: What Are the Underlying Issues of This Negotiation? How Important Is Each Issue to You?

Answers to these questions focus the negotiation toward achieving aspects of the relationship that are most desirable for the entrepreneur by trading off aspects of less importance for those of greater importance. For example, an entrepreneur might be more concerned about having control over a joint venture than about his or her share of the profits generated by the joint venture. Recognizing the relative importance of these aspects of the relationship allows the entrepreneur to "sacrifice" equity (maybe through nonvoting shares) but obtain control (e.g., to have 51 percent of the stock and/or one more seat on the board of directors and the position of chairman of the board).

Assessment 4: What Are the Underlying Issues of This Negotiation? How Important Is Each Issue to the Other Party?

By understanding more about the other party, the entrepreneur has a greater opportunity to achieve integration (i.e., make the size of the pie bigger). This information provides the opportunity for the entrepreneur to sacrifice aspects that are of less importance to him or her but of high importance to the other party. Similarly, the entrepreneur can obtain from the other party aspects of high importance to him or her but of low importance to the other party. If this information is known to both parties, then it is likely that the outcome will be mutually beneficial (because the size of the pie has been increased).

Being aware of the assessments that need to be made is an important step toward a successful negotiation but requires strategies for eliciting information from the other party that can benefit the distributive and/or integrative elements of a negotiation. Again based on the work of Bazerman and Neale (1992),[13] we offer a number of these strategies. These strategies should be thought of as tools. No one tool is perfect for every job. Some jobs require that a number of different tools be used simultaneously, while other jobs require that the tools be used sequentially. The entrepreneur needs to make his or her own decision as to which strategies should be used and when. This may not be known in advance, and the entrepreneur might experiment with different strategies to get an idea of which ones will work best for the current negotiation.

Strategy 1: Build Trust and Share Information
As has been discussed, the best negotiated outcome likely arises from integration, where the parties find mutually beneficial trade-offs. To find them requires both parties to have information about each other's underlying issues and the relative importance of those issues. Although providing information is beneficial to integration, it can be detrimental to the entrepreneur in distributing benefits if the other party has kept hidden his or her own preferences (e.g., the other party is aware of the entrepreneur's reservation price but the entrepreneur is unaware of the other party's reservation price). Therefore, releasing information requires trust—a belief that the other party will not act opportunistically to the detriment of the entrepreneur.

Building trust is an important aspect of negotiation and is important for the ongoing relationship if an agreement is reached. One way to start this process is to share some information with the other party, such as the relative importance of a particular issue (not one's reservation price). The other party may reciprocate by also sharing information, as part of an incremental process of building trust. If possible, the entrepreneur should assess the other party's trustworthiness (maybe by investigating the other party's previous relationships). If the other party appears to be untrustworthy, then the worst outcome for the entrepreneur would be that an agreement is reached, because a relationship with an untrustworthy partner can be detrimental to the long-run performance of the firm.

Strategy 2: Ask Lots of Questions
Asking questions provides an opportunity to learn more about the preferences of the other party, because this information is the foundation for finding the trade-offs necessary for integrative agreements. Even if the other party does not answer certain questions, the nonanswer itself might provide some information. For example, an entrepreneur negotiating an exclusive license agreement could ask the potential licensee, "How much would it cost you to get out of your current contract with firm YY to free yourself up to license our technology?"

Strategy 3: Make Multiple Offers Simultaneously
Relationships are rarely defined by one dimension, and therefore there can be numerous possible offers based on combinations of different levels on different dimensions. Recognizing this, the entrepreneur can simultaneously make multiple offers. By determining which offer is the closest to being acceptable, the entrepreneur can infer which issues are of greatest importance to the other party. This information is valuable in reaching an integrative agreement. It also sends a signal to the other party that the entrepreneur is flexible.

Strategy 4: Use Differences to Create Trade-Offs That Are a Source of Mutually Beneficial Outcomes
Differences between the entrepreneur and the other party in expectations, risk preferences, and time preferences all provide opportunities to reach an integrative agreement. We can investigate these differences in the context of an entrepreneur negotiating a license agreement. One difference could be in expectation—the entrepreneur expects the introduction of the licensed technology into the other party's product to increase sales more substantially than the other party expects. This difference in expectation could be the basis for an integrative agreement. For example, both parties would prefer

to have a lower "up-front" fee for the technology and a greater royalty percentage. Both parties perceive that they do better based on their expectations of sales.

A similar license agreement would be mutually beneficial when the entrepreneur has less risk aversion than the other party—that is, when the entrepreneur is more willing to give up a certain gain from the up-front fee for a greater, but uncertain, stream of revenue from an increased royalty payment. Alternatively, differences in time preference could lead to the preceding negotiated license agreement. The entrepreneur prefers to accept less now for more later, whereas the licensee is prepared to pay more later, when the income from the license is generated.

IN REVIEW

SUMMARY

In this chapter we explored alternate means by which an entrepreneur can grow his or her business. Entrepreneurs can also achieve growth through joint ventures. The effective use of joint ventures as a strategy for expansion requires the entrepreneur to carefully appraise the situation and the potential partner(s). First, the entrepreneur needs an accurate assessment of the other party to best manage the new entity in light of the ensuing relationship. Second, there needs to be symmetry between the two (or more) firms in terms of "chemistry" and the combination of their resources. Third, expectations of the results of the joint venture must be reasonable. Far too often, at least one of the partners feels that a joint venture will be the cure-all for other corporate problems. Expectations of a joint venture must be realistic. Finally, the timing must be right.

Another way the entrepreneur can expand the venture is by acquiring an existing business. For an entrepreneur, there are many advantages to acquiring an existing business, such as gaining access to an established image and track record, familiar location, established distribution and resource channels, and knowledgeable and skilled employees. Besides, the cost of an acquisition can be cheaper than other mechanisms for growth. However, history suggests that acquisitions have only a marginal success record. Entrepreneurs seem to be overly confident about their ability to achieve envisioned synergies, integrate organizational cultures, and retain key employees. After balancing the pros and cons of the acquisition, the entrepreneur needs to determine a fair price for the business. Mergers and leveraged buyouts are other ways that entrepreneurs can grow their businesses.

Franchising was discussed as a means of new entry that can reduce the risk of downside loss for the franchisee and also as a way that an entrepreneur can expand his or her business by having others pay for the use of the business formula. For the franchisee, the advantages of franchising are that he or she enters into a business with an accepted name, product, or service; has access to managerial assistance provided by the franchisor; receives up-front support that could save the entrepreneur significant time and possibly capital; has access to extensive information about the market; and has other operating and structural controls to assist in the effective management of the business. However, there are a number of potential disadvantages, which usually center on the inability of the franchisor to provide the services, advertising, and location that were promised.

For the franchisor, the primary advantage of franchising is that he or she can expand the business quickly, using little personal capital. But the franchisor also incurs certain risks in choosing this expansion alternative. In some cases, the franchisor may find it very difficult to locate quality franchisees. Poor management, in spite of all the training and controls, can still cause individual franchise failures, and these can reflect negatively on the entire franchise system. As the number of franchises increases, the ability to maintain tight controls becomes more difficult.

An essential skill for all these alternatives is the ability of the entrepreneur to negotiate. Good negotiation involves two tasks. The first task involves determining how the benefits of the relationship are going to be distributed between the parties. The second task is exploring the mutual benefits that can be gained from the relationship. To negotiate in a way that maximizes benefits requires the entrepreneur to use information about one's own preferences and those of the other party to create an outcome that is mutually beneficial. This requires an initial assessment of oneself and the other party and the use of strategies to elicit more information during the negotiation interactions to better inform those initial assessments. To these ends, this chapter offered four important assessments an entrepreneur should make and four strategies that can be used to achieve a successful negotiation.

RESEARCH TASKS

1. Find information about three joint ventures that were failures, and be prepared to discuss the underlying reasons for the failure in each case.

2. Search on the Internet for franchises for sale. Choose three. What commonalities are there across the businesses and the information provided? What differences are there? For one of these businesses, obtain all franchise information. For this business, what are the benefits of being a franchisee rather than setting up an independent business? What are all the associated costs of being a franchisee for this business?

3. Interview three franchisees to better understand their relationship with the franchisor.

4. Find three types of business license agreements (only one of these should be a software license agreement). In what ways are these license agreements the same and in what ways are they different? Why have these companies decided to license their product or technology rather than simply sell it?

5. Find three reports of acquisitions that were unsuccessful. Why were these acquisitions deemed unsuccessful?

CLASS DISCUSSION

1. Being a franchisor seems to be a mechanism for growth, but what are the growth prospects for entrepreneurs who are franchisees? Isn't the entrepreneur limited in his or her ability to pursue all the different types of growth strategies? Is being a franchisee simply substituting one type of employment for another type of employment? How can a franchisee grow his or her business(es)?

2. Recently the Chinese government has been encouraging foreign firms to enter into joint venture relationships with local (Chinese) firms. What are the benefits to the

Chinese economy from these joint venture relationships? What are the benefits to the local Chinese firm? What are the benefits to the foreign firm? What is the impact of the joint venture on the foreign firm's domestic economy?

3. Identify a local franchise in your area, and determine where the competitors are located and where other franchises from the same organization are located. Evaluate the existing potential for the franchise.

4. Why are there so many different techniques for determining the worth of a firm? In any given situation, is there one "right answer" for a company's value? What effects do your answers to these questions have on the entrepreneur making an acquisition?

SELECTED READINGS

Bazerman, Max H.; and Jared R. Curhan. (2000). Negotiation. *Annual Review of Psychology,* vol. 51, no. 1, pp. 279–315.

This article focuses on the psychological study of negotiation, including the history of the negotiation game; the development of mental models on negotiation; the definition of negotiation rules based on concerns of ethics, fairness, and values; the impact of the selection of communication medium on the negotiation game; and the impact of cross-cultural issues on perception and of behavior on negotiation.

Chang, Sea Jin. (2004). Venture Capital Financing, Strategic Alliances, and the Initial Public Offerings of Internet Startups. *Journal of Business Venturing,* vol. 19, no. 5, pp. 721–41.

In this study the author examines how Internet start-ups' venture-capital financing and strategic alliances affect these start-ups' ability to acquire the resources necessary for growth. Using the initial public offering (IPO) event as an early-stage measure for an Internet start-ups' performance and controlling for the IPO market environment, this study found that three factors positively influence a start-up's time to IPO: (1) the reputations of participating venture-capital firms and strategic alliance partners, (2) the amount of money the start-up raised, and (3) the size of the start-up's network of strategic alliances.

Davies, Mark A. P.; Walfried Lassar; Chris Manolis; Melvin Prince; and Robert Winsor. (2011). A Model of Trust and Compliance in Franchise Relationships. *Journal of Business Venturing,* vol. 26, issue 3, pp. 321–40.

Using a foundation of relational exchange theory, the authors construct and test a model that demonstrates how two distinct forms of trust, based upon perceptions of franchisor integrity and franchisor competence, are critical to explaining the roles that relational conflict and satisfaction play in influencing franchisee compliance. Implications of these findings are then demonstrated to have compelling relevance to the effective management of franchise systems. (from journal's abstract)

Dietmeyer, Brian J.; and Max H. Bazerman. (2001). Value Negotiation. *Executive Excellence,* vol. 18, no. 4, p. 7.

This article advises executives on value negotiation, including developing wise trades in value creation, building trust and sharing information in an open and truthful manner, asking questions, making multiple offers simultaneously, and searching for postsettlement settlements.

George, Gerard; Shaker A. Zahra; and D. Robley Wood, Jr. (2002). The Effects of Business–University Alliances on Innovative Output and Financial Performance: A Study of Publicly Traded Biotechnology Companies. *Journal of Business Venturing,* vol. 17, no. 6, pp. 557–90.

Analysis of 2,457 alliances undertaken by 147 biotechnology firms shows that companies with university linkages have lower R&D expenses and higher levels of innovative output. However, the results do not support the proposition that companies with university linkages achieve higher financial performance than similar firms without such linkages.

Gonzalez-Diaz, Manuel; and Vanesa Solis-Rodriguez. (In press). Why Do Entrepreneurs Use Franchising as a Financial Tool? An Agency Explanation. *Journal of Business Venturing.*

When and why one type of entrepreneur (franchisor) attracts to its ventures another type of entrepreneur (franchisees) instead of passive investors is a central concern in entrepreneurship literature. Based on the informativeness principle of the principal-agent model, the authors claim that franchisees are not such an expensive financial tool as has been argued in the literature because their compensation (return) is more efficiently designed: it directly depends on variables which are under franchisee's control. They therefore link agency and financial explanations for franchising. Most of their findings show that, once the agency argument is controlled for, the higher the cost of alternative funds for the franchisor (estimated through different variables), the more the franchisor will rely on expansion through franchising as opposed to company ownership. (from journal's abstract)

Gulati, Ranjay; and Monica C. Higgins. (2003). Which Ties Matter When? The Contingent Effects of Interorganizational Partnerships on IPO Success. *Strategic Management Journal,* vol. 24, no. 2, pp. 127–45.

This paper investigates the contingent value of interorganizational relationships at the time of a young firm's initial public offering (IPO). Results show that ties to prominent venture-capital firms are particularly beneficial to IPO success during cold markets, while ties to prominent investment banks are particularly beneficial to IPO success during hot markets; a firm's strategic alliances with major pharmaceutical and health-care firms did not have such contingent effects.

Holmberg, Stevan R.; and Kathryn Boe Morgan. (2003). Franchise Turnover and Failure: New Research and Perspectives. *Journal of Business Venturing,* vol. 18, no. 3, pp. 403–19.

This paper's new franchise failure concept reconciles many prior, seemingly inconsistent study results based largely on franchisors' surveys. Overall franchisee turnover rates are significant and appear to have increased over time.

Katila, Riitta; Jeff Rosenberger; and Kathleen Eisenhardt. (2008). Swimming with Sharks: Technology Ventures, Defense Mechanisms and Corporate Relationships. *Administrative Science Quarterly,* vol. 53, no. 2, pp. 295–332.

This paper focuses on the tension that firms face between the need for resources from partners and the potentially damaging misappropriation of their own resources by corporate "sharks." The findings show that entrepreneurs take a risk when they need resources that established firms uniquely provide (i.e., financial and manufacturing) and when they have effective defense mechanisms to protect their own resources (i.e., secrecy and timing). [Abstract from authors.]

Kenis, Patrick; and David Knoke. (2002). How Organizational Field Networks Shape Interorganizational Tie-Formation Rates. *Academy of Management Review,* vol. 27, no. 2, pp. 275–94.

The authors investigate the impact of communication in field-level networks on rates of formation of interorganizational collaborative ties, such as strategic alliances and joint ventures.

Marino, Louis; Karen Strandholm; Kevin H. Steensma; and Mark K. Weaver. (2002). The Moderating Effect of National Culture on the Relationship between Entrepreneurial Orientation and Strategic Alliance Portfolio Extensiveness. *Entrepreneurship: Theory & Practice,* vol. 26, no. 4, pp. 145–61.

This article examines the moderating effect of national culture on the relationship between entrepreneurial orientation and strategic alliance portfolio extensiveness.

Michael, Steven C. (2000). Investment to Create Bargaining Power: The Case of Franchising. *Strategic Management Journal*, vol. 21, no. 4, pp. 497–517.

In this article the author argues that the franchisor can make investments in activities to increase its bargaining power and decrease conflict and litigation in a franchise system. Includes tapered integration, ownership of some units with franchisement of others, selection of inexperienced franchisees, and employment of a long training program.

Park, Seung H.; Roger R. Chen; and Scott Gallagher. (2002). Firm Resources as Moderators of the Relationship between Market Growth and Strategic Alliances in Semiconductor Start-Ups. *Academy of Management Journal*, vol. 45, no. 3, pp. 527–46.

The results of this study indicate that, in volatile markets, resource-rich firms access external resources through alliances whereas resource-poor firms are less likely to do so. However, in relatively stable markets, this relationship reverses, and resource-poor firms become more active in alliance formation.

Pearce II, John A.; and Louise Hatfield. (2002). Performance Effects of Alternative Joint Venture Resource Responsibility Structures. *Journal of Business Venturing*, vol. 17, no. 4, pp. 343–65.

The authors examine the relationship between the acquirers of a joint venture's (JV's) resources and the JV's performance in achieving its partners' goals in the United States. Topics covered include the impact of alternative resource responsibility structures on JV performance, variation in resources received by JVs, and implications for business theory development and practicing managers.

Sarkar, M. B.; R. A. J. Echambadi; and Jeffrey S. Harrison. (2001). Alliance Entrepreneurship and Firm Market Performance. *Strategic Management Journal*, vol. 22, no. 6/7, pp. 701–12.

This article extends entrepreneurship into the domain of alliances and examines the effect of alliance proactiveness on market-based firm performance, including the higher performance of firms that are proactive in forming alliances, and the moderating influences of firm size and environmental uncertainty on the relationship between alliance proactiveness and performance.

Wiklund, Johan; and Dean A. Shepherd. (2009). The Effectiveness of Alliances and Acquisitions: The Role of Resource Combination Activities. *Entrepreneurship: Theory & Practice*, vol. 33, no. 1, pp. 193–212.

Resource complementarity increases the potential value of alliances and acquisitions, but the extent to which the value potential of an alliance or an acquisition becomes realized depends on the ability of the firm to discover and conduct productive resource combinations. Using a sample of 319 small firms, the authors separate domestic from international alliances and acquisitions and show that alliances and acquisitions bring limited benefits to firms unless a deliberate effort is devoted to resource combination.

END NOTES

1. See J. Useem, "The Start-up Factory," *Inc.*, February 9, 1997, pp. 40–52; E. Matson, "He Turns Ideas into Companies—at Net Speed," *Fast Company* (December 1996), p. 34; and Idealab Web site, www.idealab.com.
2. For some different perspectives on joint ventures, see R. D. Hisrich, "Joint Ventures: Research Base and Use in International Methods," in Donald L. Sexton and John D. Kasarda (eds.), *The State of the Art of Entrepreneurship* (Boston: PWS-Kent, 1992), pp. 520–79; and J. McConnell and T. J. Nantell, "Corporate Combinations and Common Stock Returns: The Case of Joint Ventures," *Journal of Finance* 40 (June 1985), pp. 519–36.

3. For a discussion of some different types of joint ventures, see R. M. Cyert, "Establishing University–Industry Joint Ventures," *Research Management* 28 (January–February 1985), pp. 27–28; F. K. Berlew, "The Joint Venturer—A Way into Foreign Markets," *Harvard Business Review* (July–August 1984), pp. 48–49 and 54; and Kathryn Rudie Harrigan, *Strategies for Joint Ventures* (Lexington, MA: Lexington Books, 1985).

4. Semiconductor Research Corporation, www.src.org/member/about/src.asp.

5. D. D. Seltz, *The Complete Handbook of Franchising* (Reading, MA: Addison-Wesley, 1982), p. 1.

6. L. Bongiorno, "Franchise Fracas," *BusinessWeek,* March 22, 1993, pp. 68–71.

7. F. Huffman, "Under New Ownership," *Entrepreneur* (January 1993), pp. 101–5.

8. W. Siegel, *Franchising* (New York: John Wiley & Sons, 1983), p. 9.

9. *Directory of Franchising Organizations* (Babylon, NY: Pilot Industries, 1985).

10. K. Rosenburg, "Franchising, American Style," *Entrepreneur* (January 1991), pp. 86–93.

11. D. J. Kaufmann and D. E. Robbins, "Now Read This," *Entrepreneur* (January 1991), p. 100.

12. Max H. Bazerman and Margaret A. Neale, *Negotiating Rationally* (New York: Free Press, 1992).

13. Ibid.

15

SUCCESSION PLANNING AND STRATEGIES FOR HARVESTING AND ENDING THE VENTURE

LEARNING OBJECTIVES

1
To understand the planning that is necessary to allow for the effective succession of ownership or leadership in a business.

2
To examine the options in providing for an exit strategy, such as the sale of the business to employees (ESOP) or to an external source.

3
To illustrate differences in alternative types of bankruptcy under the Bankruptcy Act of 1978 (amended in 1984 and again in 2005).

4
To illustrate the rights of creditors and entrepreneurs in different cases of bankruptcy.

5
To provide the entrepreneur with an understanding of the typical warning signs of bankruptcy.

6
To illustrate how some entrepreneurs can turn bankruptcy into a successful business.

OPENING PROFILE

DAVID HARTSTEIN

It is not often that an entrepreneur achieves significant success with a new venture, sells it, sees it decline, and then returns to again move the venture into a new successful era. David Hartstein along with his partner Thomas G. Stemberg opened their first Kabloom flower shop in December 1998. Hartstein was the CEO and co-founder of Super Office, the first office superstore chain in Israel. Stemberg was former Chairman and CEO of Staples, Inc., where he orchestrated the growth of this successful chain to 1,300 stores worldwide.

www.kabloom.com

Kabloom's business model was to offer benefits not found in traditional florist shops, such as convenience to customers (locations would be easily accessible to both pedestrian and vehicular traffic), early and late hours, flowers shipped direct from growers to ensure freshness and quality, and ability to purchase flowers using the Internet (www.kabloom.com), telephone, or directly from retail shops. The plan was to offer a more European-style market, inviting customers to sample from the wide array of plants and fresh cut flowers each week. The company's goal was to operate 150 stores within three to four years. The strategy to achieve this growth was based on the same inventory controls and distribution methods that each of the co-founders had brought to the office supply business.

The idea for Kabloom can be traced to a dinner Hartstein had with Stemberg in 1997. Hartstein was looking for an idea for a new retail chain. At first he considered a Boston Chicken–type restaurant with a health foods menu. However, at dinner the two were discussing a flower chain that Stemberg had seen in Germany that might fit the U.S. market. Research on the idea indicated that Americans were not very high on flower consumption compared to their European counterparts. Hartstein found that part of this discrepancy was because of the several layers of middlemen that caused flower prices to be significantly higher in the U.S. Hartstein felt that they could eliminate many of these layers and save the consumer a significant amount of money on each purchase. For example, a dozen long-stem roses can be priced with a more direct distribution at about half the cost as through a traditional flower channel. With this strategy and its unique benefits Kabloom became an instant success, changing the industry culture in flower marketing. Hartstein was a finalist for the New England Entrepreneur of the Year Award in 2001.

In 2003 Hartstein decided to sell franchises so that he could reach more geographic markets quickly and with less internal resources. Hartstein's vision was to be the Starbucks of the flower industry. By the end of 2004 a total of 55 franchised stores had opened in 13 states. His goal at this point was to open an additional 100 franchised stores and increase revenue to about $50 million from the $12.7 million achieved in 2002. In 2004 Hartstein introduced MobileLime's™ unique cell phone technology so that shoppers could receive notifications of special promotions, earn rewards toward future purchases, and easily shop via a cell phone so their orders would be ready immediately for pickup.

In 2006 Hartstein decided to sell the company. At this point he had reached more than 120 stores in 29 states and had achieved e-commerce revenue of about $40 million. Under new ownership the company experienced weak sales as a result of a weak economy and the failure of many franchisees. After seeing that the company was reduced to 24 stores Hartstein decided to reacquire the company with the intent of not only achieving a business turnaround but also bringing to the business his new innovation he called the Moses Miracle.

The Moses Miracle is basically a water balloon that is tightly cinched around a bouquet's stems. It ensures that flowers will always remain fresh even when shipped across country. Competitors typically shipped their flowers dry, which can result in wilting. His patented innovation is a leakproof balloon that can be quickly and cheaply slipped over a bouquet's stems.

One of the major competitive advantages that Hartstein sees with his innovation is to be able to sell flowers in low overhead kiosks that don't need extensive plumbing or a large water supply. In addition, by locating these kiosks in high pedestrian traffic areas consumers can purchase flowers on their way to work since the flowers will stay fresh all day with the new patented Moses Miracle. Hartstein also plans to staff kiosks with veterans, giving them an opportunity to become an entrepreneur and receive a 17 percent cut of sales. The future success of Kabloom will not only depend on this new business strategy but also on the company's ability to compete with such online heavyweights as 1-800-Flowers.com, Teleflora, and FTD.[1]

This book has taken an in-depth view of the entire entrepreneurial process, from the idea to a business plan and then successful funding and growth strategies. However, the entrepreneur should also be prepared for a number of important issues that he or she may face in later years of the operations of the venture. We saw above that David Hartstein achieved great success initially with his business, but then after selling the firm found that it was moving in the wrong direction. Typically entrepreneurs are faced with the issues of whether or not to sell their business, have a family member or trusted employee succeed

AS SEEN IN *BUSINESS NEWS*

ADVICE TO AN ENTREPRENEUR: CREDIT CARD DEBT AND KEEPING YOUR CREDIT CLEAN

The ease of obtaining a credit card can often be troublesome to an entrepreneur. Often with the difficulty of getting loans and credit lines to finance receivables or to grow a new venture, an entrepreneur will turn to a credit card to provide much needed cash. However, as debt is accumulated the interest rate on these credit cards can reach the point where the monthly fees and interest are more than what the entrepreneur can afford to pay. If credit card debt becomes too high, future investors or partners may perceive your company as living off credit which could affect your future opportunities to get additional resources. A few pointers can help alleviate this problem.

First of all, if you need to use a credit card for a trade show, to travel, or to advertise, it is a good idea to make sure that you can realistically pay this off. Understand that the interest and monthly payments will become a cash flow issue if the amounts are too high. So consider this in any of your cash budgets. If receivables are slow it may make more sense to put a plan in place to call on your delinquent accounts and offer discounts for early payment. Follow-ups to these accounts on a regular basis can also sometimes speed up payments.

Second, do not apply for too many credit cards at any one time. Credit bureaus take this into consideration when calculating your credit score. It is better to stick with one credit card with a reasonable interest rate so that you can make payments on time and make any future lenders comfortable with you as a potential borrower.

Third, do not constantly shift money from one credit card to another just because there is a lower interest rate. This again is a red flag to credit bureaus and can negatively affect your credit rating.

Fourth, avoid any of the debt consolidation advertisements from companies that claim you can shed all or much of your debt. These typically make a bad situation worse and could push you into bankruptcy or certainly ruin your personal or company's credit rating.

Fifth, you should consistently review your credit scores. Credit reports can easily be obtained for free. Review them carefully to make sure there are no errors. Research indicates that about 79 percent of credit reports contain errors with 25 percent of these serious enough to affect your ability to obtain credit.

Lastly, do not declare personal bankruptcy in order to avoid paying off debt on credit cards that may be in your name. The ability to start over may seem like a good idea to you since you believe that this can save your venture. However, consumer finance companies are not so forgiving and a personal bankruptcy can stay on your credit report for as long as 10 years.

The bottom line is that credit cards can be useful short-term cash generators but they must be used with caution. Try to use them in a way that your budget will allow for timely payments. Try to keep small balances on any credit cards. It is sometimes more prudent to find other short-term cash sources such as loans from family or even finding a second job. Being financially responsible can go a long way in avoiding financial disaster in a start-up venture. Maintain good budgeting practices and continually review your revenue goals to ensure that you can really afford the debt you incur.

ADVICE TO AN ENTREPRENEUR

After reading the above, an entrepreneur friend comes to you for advice:

1. I recently noted that there is a trade show in Europe that offers a good opportunity for me to make contacts with potential customers and to expand my business globally. I do not have the funds on hand to pay for this trip. Does it make sense to use a credit card I just obtained in the mail to make this trip and potentially enhance my company's sales?

2. I have a second credit card in my name that has about a $5,000 balance. Should I use this card or consider the second card I just obtained in the mail that has a lower interest rate? Or should I transfer the debt to the lower interest card and then use this card for my business trip to Europe?

3. Why should I be concerned with personal debt as long as it is not in my company's name?

Source: Adapted from Rosalind Resnick, "Keep Your Credit Clean," *Entrepreneur* (July 2010), p. 74; J. D. Roth, "Give Yourself Some Credit," *Entrepreneur* (August 2011), p. 82; and Rosalind Resnick, "A Debt-Free Philosophy," *Entrepreneur* (October 2010), p. 118.

them, try to change the strategy and harvest any opportunities, or declare bankruptcy. These exit strategies are the topics of discussion in this chapter.

EXIT STRATEGY

Every entrepreneur who starts a new venture should think about an exit strategy. A number of possible exit strategies will be discussed in the following paragraphs. Exit strategies include an initial public offering (IPO), private sale of stock, succession by a family member or a nonfamily member, merger with another company, or liquidation of the company. The sale of the company could be to employees (an ESOP) or to an external source (a person or persons, or a company). The IPO, private sale of stock, and merger options are discussed elsewhere in this book (see Chapters 12 and 14).

Each of these exit strategies has its advantages and disadvantages, which are discussed in the following and in Chapters 12 and 14. The most important issue is that the entrepreneurs have an exit strategy or plan in place at the start-up stage, instead of waiting until it may be too late to effectively implement a desirable option.

SUCCESSION OF BUSINESS

By 2015 millions of baby boomers will be retired, causing a significant gap in the workforce. This will be a critical issue for small businesses that are looking to find successors. Only about 60 percent of businesses have a succession plan in place. For very small businesses this percentage is likely to be a lot lower.[2] In the next sections we will focus on important issues that can help the entrepreneur plan for the succession of the business to either a family member, an employee, or an external party. Table 15.1 provides a summary of important tips that should be considered in any succession plan.

If there is no one in the family interested in the business, it is important for the entrepreneur to either sell the business or train someone within the organization to take over. Each of these transfer possibilities is discussed in the following sections.

Transfer to Family Members

Successfully passing a business down to a family member faces tough odds. Research by the Family Business Institute indicates that only 30 percent of family businesses survive into the second generation and only 12 percent survive into the third generation. This data clearly supports the need for a succession plan.[3]

TABLE 15.1   Succession Planning Tips

- Allow sufficient time for the process by starting early.
- Estimate the firm's value or hire a consultant to do it for you.
- Evaluate potential successors on their merit—not on whether they remind you of yourself.
- If family members are being considered, make sure they have the skills and motivation necessary to carry on the business.
- Provide a transition period so that the successor can learn the business.
- Consider options such as employee stock option plans (ESOPs) for a management succession.
- Set a date for completion of the transition and stick to it.

An effective succession plan should also be communicated clearly to all employees. This is particularly relevant to key personnel who may be affected by the succession transition. The solution to minimize the emotional and financial turmoil that can often be created during a transfer to family members is a good succession plan.

An effective succession plan needs to consider the following critical factors:

- The role of the owner in the transition stage: Will he or she continue to work full time? Part time? Or will the owner retire?
- Family dynamics: Are some family members unable to work together?
- Income for working family members and shareholders.
- The current business environment during the transition.
- Treatment of loyal employees.
- Tax consequences.

The transfer of a business to a family member can also create internal problems with employees. This often results when a son or daughter is handed the responsibility of running the business without sufficient training. A young family member's chances of success in taking over the business are improved if he or she assumes various operational responsibilities early on. It is beneficial for the family member to rotate to different areas of the business to get a good perspective on the total operation. Other employees in these departments or areas will be able to assist in the training and get to know their future leader.

It is also helpful if the entrepreneur stays around for a while to act as an advisor to the successor. As stated in Table 15.1, however, there should be a set date for when this transition will end. Although having the entrepreneur act as an advisor during the transition stage can be helpful to the successor in making business decisions, it is also possible that this can result in major conflicts if the personalities involved are not compatible. In addition, employees who have been with the firm since start-up may resent the younger family member's assuming control of the venture. However, if the successor works in the organization during this transition period, he or she can justify assumption of the future role by proving his or her abilities.

Transfer to Nonfamily Members

Often, family members are not interested in assuming responsibility for the business. When this occurs, the entrepreneur has three choices: train a key employee and retain some equity, retain control and hire a manager, or sell the business outright.

Passing the business on to an employee ensures that the successor (or principal) is familiar with the business and the market. The employee's experience minimizes transitional problems. In addition, the entrepreneur can take some time to make the transition smoother.

The key issue in passing the business on to an employee is ownership. If the entrepreneur plans to retain some ownership, the question of how much becomes an important area of negotiation. The new principal may prefer to have control, with the original entrepreneur remaining as a minority owner, stockholder, or consultant. The financial capacity and managerial ability of the employee will be important factors in deciding how much ownership is transferred. In many cases the transfer or succession of a venture can take many years to meet all the requirements of the parties involved. Since evidence indicates that most entrepreneurs wait until it is too late, it is important to begin the process long before there is a need to sell or transfer the ownership of the business. The U.S. Department of Commerce indicates that about 70 percent of successful ventures never make it to the second generation of ownership.

Jim Holland, one of the founders and the CEO of retailer Backcountry.com, to this point believes that he is one of the exceptions, although only time will tell. Jim handed over control of his company in 2011 to a long-time employee, Jill Layfield. Jim is still engaged in the company but he encourages Jill to think for herself. He feels that during this transition his experience is important, but when she asks for his opinion on a major issue he always passes the final decision back to her.[4]

If the business has been in the family for some time and the succession to a family member may become more likely in the future, the entrepreneur may hire a manager to run the business. However, finding someone to manage the business in the same manner and with the same expertise as the entrepreneur may be difficult. If someone is found to manage the business, the likely problems are compatibility with the owners and willingness of this person to manage for any length of time without a promise of equity in the business. Executive search firms can help in the search process. It will be necessary to have a well-defined job description to assist in identifying the right person.

In nonfamily business situations, succession planning may take on a slightly different approach. In these businesses a key senior manager or group of managers may be stepping down or leaving the company. Since there are no family members involved, there may be a need to consider replacements from either external or internal sources. For a partnership the process may be clearly outlined in the partnership agreement and could simply involve a predetermined choice. However, there could also be a need to go outside the partnership and find a successor for the partnership. In this instance, as well as in an S corporation or an LLC, where there may be only a small number of shareholders, the succession plan should consider the following important issues:[5]

- Senior management of the company must be committed to any succession plan. The strategy must be one that everyone shares.
- It is important to have well-defined job descriptions and a clear designation of skills necessary to fulfill any and all positions.
- The process needs to be an open one. All employees should be invited to participate so that they will feel comfortable with the transition and thus minimize the possibility of their leaving the company.

The last option is to sell the business outright to either an employee or an outsider. The major considerations in this option are financial, which will likely necessitate the help of an accountant and/or lawyer. This alternative also requires that the value of the business be determined (see Chapter 12).

OPTIONS FOR SELLING THE BUSINESS

There are a number of alternatives available to the entrepreneur in selling the venture. Some of these are straightforward, and others involve more complex financial strategy. Each of these methods should be carefully considered and one selected, depending on the goals of the entrepreneur.

Direct Sale

This is probably the most common method for selling the venture. The entrepreneur may decide to sell the business because he or she wants to move on to some new endeavor or simply decides that it is time to retire. A sale to a larger company that can infuse much-needed capital may also provide opportunities for the company to grow and reach larger markets. If the entrepreneur has decided to sell the business but does not need to sell immediately, there are a number of strategies that should be considered early in the process.[6]

- A business can be more valuable if it is focused on a narrow, well-defined segment. In other words, a larger share in a small market niche can be more valuable than a smaller share in a large market.
- The entrepreneur should concentrate on keeping costs under control and focus on higher margins and profits.
- Get all financial statements in order, including budgets and cash flow projections.
- Prepare a management documentation of the business explaining how the business is organized and how it operates.
- Assess the condition of capital equipment. Up-to-date or state-of-the-art equipment can enhance the value of a company.
- Get tax advice, since the sale of a corporation will involve different tax considerations than those for a partnership, LLC, or S corporation.
- Get nondisclosures from key employees.
- Try to maintain a good management team, allowing them to have day-to-day contact with key customers to lessen the firm's dependence on owner–customer relations.
- There is no substitute for advance preparation and planning.

One of the important considerations of any business sale is the type of payment the buyer will use. Often, buyers will purchase a business using notes based on future profits. If the new owners fail in the business, the seller may receive no cash payment and possibly may have to take back the company, which is struggling to survive.

Business brokers in some instances may be helpful, since trying to actually sell a business will take time away from running it. Brokers can be discreet about a sale and may have an established network to get the word around. Brokers earn a commission from the sale of a business. Generally, these commissions are based on a sliding scale starting at about 10 percent for the first $200,000. The best way to communicate the business to potential buyers is through the business plan. A five-year comprehensive plan can provide buyers of the business with a future perspective and accountability of the value of the company (see Chapters 7 and 8).

As indicated earlier, an entrepreneur may find that selling out to a larger company can provide much-needed resources to achieve important market goals. It has also become a more common exit strategy given that IPOs, the more traditional growth funding option, have become more rare given the current economic environment.

Gurbaksh Chahal, a very successful serial entrepreneur, has started and sold two businesses to larger companies. Each time, he was able to use resources from the sale to start a new venture. His first endeavor at the age of 16 was ClickAgents, an advertising network that focused on performance-based advertising. At the age of 18 he sold this business to ValueClick for $40 million, an all stock merger. Chahal had a three year noncompete agreement with ValueClick. After the three years he started BlueLithium that specialized in behavioral targeting of banner advertising. It tracked Web users' online response habits. In 2007 he sold this company to Yahoo for $300 million in cash and remained as CEO during the transition period. In 2009 Chahal started his third venture, gWallet, an advertising company that focused on bringing brands into social media. After raising $12.5 million in venture financing and after his noncompete agreement expired, he rebranded the company as RadiumOne and launched an ad network that focused on overlaying social and intent data together. In 2011 his company raised another $21 million after investors valued this company at $200 million.[7]

Unlike our example earlier of Jim Holland, who remains CEO of Backcountry.com, the role of an entrepreneur who sells to an employee or passes the business on to a family member may vary depending on the sale agreement or contract with the new owner(s). Many buyers will want the seller to stay on for a short time to provide a smooth transition. Under these circumstances, the seller (entrepreneur) should negotiate an employment contract that specifies time, salary, and responsibility. If the entrepreneur is not needed in the business, it is likely that the new owner(s) will request that the entrepreneur sign an agreement not to engage in the same business for a specified number of years. These agreements vary in scope and may require a lawyer to clarify details.

An entrepreneur may also plan to retain a business for only a specified period of time, with the intent to sell it to the employees. This may be achieved using an employee stock option plan (ESOP) or through a management buyout, which allows the sale to occur to only certain managers of the venture.

Employee Stock Option Plan

employee stock option plan (ESOP) A two- to three-year plan to sell the business to employees

Under an *employee stock option plan (ESOP),* the business is sold to employees over a period of time. The ESOP establishes a new legal entity, called an employee stock ownership trust, that borrows the money against future profits. The borrowed money then buys the owner's shares and allocates them to individual employees' retirement accounts as the loan is paid off. The ESOP has the obligation to repay the loan plus interest out of the cash flow of the business. Typically, these ESOPs are a way to reward employees and clarify the succession process. In addition, ESOPs result in significant stock values for employees, provided that the company continues to succeed.

Presently there are about 11,500 ESOP companies in the United States, of which approximately 3,000 are wholly owned by the ESOP. ESOPs account for about 50 percent of the nation's 10 million employees (about 10 percent of the private sector workforce). In addition, about 330 (or 3 percent) are publicly traded companies.[8]

The ESOP has a number of advantages. First, it offers a unique incentive to employees that can enhance their motivation to put in extra time or effort. Employees recognize that they are working for themselves and hence will focus their efforts on innovations that contribute to the long-term success of the venture. Second, it provides a mechanism to pay back those employees who have been loyal to the venture, particularly during more difficult times. Third, it allows the transfer of the business under a carefully planned written agreement. Finally, the company can reap the advantage of deducting the contributions to the ESOP or any dividends paid on the stock.

ESOPs, due to a new law passed in 1996, are now possible for S corporations. However, there are some important differences in the tax treatment between the C corporation and the S corporation because of the pass-through feature of the S corporation (see Chapter 9). Because of the new tax law, the S corporation pays no income tax on the portion of the stock owned by the ESOP.

However, in spite of its favorable attributes, the ESOP has some disadvantages. This type of stock option plan is usually quite complex to establish. It requires a complete valuation of the venture to establish the amount of the ESOP package. In addition, it raises issues such as taxes, payout ratios, amount of equity to be transferred per year, and the amount actually invested by the employees. The agreement also must specify if the employees can buy or sell additional shares of stock once the plan has been completed. Clearly, because of the complexity of this type of plan, the entrepreneur will need the advice of experts if this type of plan is selected. A simpler method may be a more direct buyout by key employees of the venture.

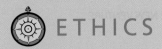

ETHICS

INVOLVING EMPLOYEES, BANKERS, AND BUSINESS ASSOCIATES IN THE PROBLEM

Who should be made aware when a venture is in trouble? How much responsibility does the entrepreneur have to his or her employees? How much should you tell your banker? Should clients be made aware of your problems? These are all legitimate yet difficult questions that an entrepreneur may struggle with when the business is on the verge of bankruptcy.

Some may feel that their only responsibility is to their family and themselves. Trying to get out of the dilemma with the least effect on your personal reputation and financial well-being could in fact make matters worse. Ethically and morally the entrepreneur is the leader of the organization, and trying to avoid responsibility will not rectify the situation.

In fact, there is evidence to indicate that involving your employees, banker, or other business associates can actually improve matters. Employees may take pay cuts or stock options to stay on with the company and try to turn the business around. Bankers can be your financial best friend and can recommend ways to save money and generate more cash flow. Your clients and suppliers can also support turnaround efforts by helping to provide needed cash during the crisis. One example was an entrepreneur who ran out of cash to produce a product being sold by a large supermarket chain. A meeting with the important client that revealed the situation (brought on by a competitor's lawsuit that was settled) led to a simple solution. The supermarket appreciated the honesty of the entrepreneur and agreed to prepay for all orders so that there would be sufficient cash to produce the product.

The entrepreneur needs to consider the past efforts of employees who made him or her successful in the first place. Thus, the best solution is participation. Get help rather than taking the selfish and perhaps immoral alternative. Honesty is the best strategy.

Management Buyout

It is conceivable that the entrepreneur only wants to sell or transfer the venture to loyal, key employees. Since the ESOP described earlier can be rather complicated and expensive, the entrepreneur may find that a direct sale would be simpler to accomplish.

Management buyouts usually involve a direct sale of the venture for some predetermined price. This would be similar to selling one's house. To establish a price, the entrepreneur would have an appraisal of all the assets and then determine the goodwill value established from past revenue.

Sale of a venture to key employees can be for cash, or it can be financed in any number of ways. A cash sale is unlikely if the value of the business is substantial. Financing the sale of the venture can be accomplished through a bank, or the entrepreneur could also agree to carry the note. This may be desirable to the entrepreneur in that the stream of income from the sale would be spread out over a determined period of time, enhancing cash flow and lessening the tax impact. Another method of selling the venture would be to use stock as the method of transfer. The managers buying the business may sell nonvoting or voting stock to other investors. These funds would then be used as a full or partial payment for the venture. The reason that other investors would be interested in buying stock or that a bank would lend the managers money is that the business is continuing with the same management team and with its established track record.

Other methods of transferring or selling a business are through a public offering or even a merger with another business. These topics are discussed in Chapter 14. Before determining the appropriate selling strategy, the entrepreneur should seek the advice of outsiders. Every circumstance is different, and the actual decision will depend on the entrepreneur's goals. Case histories of each of the preceding methods can also be reviewed to be able to effectively determine which option is best for the given circumstances.

BANKRUPTCY—AN OVERVIEW

Failure is not uncommon in many new ventures, especially in light of the poor global economic environment, the wars in Iraq and Afghanistan, and the continued battle against terrorism. According to the Small Business Administration, about half of all new start-ups fail in their first years. The failures are personally painful for the entrepreneur and too often could have been prevented if the entrepreneur had paid more attention to certain critical factors in the business operation. It is important to understand the issues involved in bankruptcy since it does occur and there may even be an opportunity to use the bankruptcy options to get the company back on solid financial ground.

Prior to the tightening of the bankruptcy laws by Congress in 2005, bankruptcies were running at about 1.6 million per year. In 2006 total filings dropped to about 618,000, a definite reflection of the new laws. However, since 2006 these filings have increased significantly, a result of the poor global economy. In 2010 the total filings again reached nearly 1.6 million with more than 56,000 of these business filings. This compared to 1.47 million filings in 2009 and 1.12 million in 2008. In 2011 business filings were running about 12 percent less than 2010. However, it should be noted that many of the nonbusiness filings could be failed proprietorships, partnerships, or home businesses. It is also important to understand that both business and nonbusiness bankruptcy filings are divided by chapter filings, which will be explained in more detail later.

The most common type of business bankruptcy is Chapter 7, or liquidation, which accounted for about 70 percent of the total in 2011. Chapter 11 bankruptcy provides an opportunity for a business to reorganize, prepare a new business plan (acceptable to the courts), and then, with time and achievement of new goals, to return to normal business operation. These bankruptcies represented about 21 percent of all business filings in 2011. The remaining business bankruptcies (about 9 percent) are Chapter 13 filings, which allow creditors to be repaid in an agreed-upon installment plan.[9]

Bankruptcy is a term that has been on the minds of many entrepreneurs in the past couple of years, as businesses face a weak domestic and global economy, increased competition, and rising costs of doing business. As stated before, bankruptcy may not always mean the end of a business since it can offer the entrepreneur an opportunity to reorganize under Chapter 11 or merge with another company. The results of each bankruptcy filing can be quite distinct because of the nature of the business or the uniqueness of an industry. Some of the following examples describe the possible mix of results or experiences that can occur from a bankruptcy filing.

Although a Chapter 11 filing is designed to allow a company to reorganize and then emerge with its operations again, there have been some serious concerns given the new restrictions signed into law in 2005. The Sharper Image filed for Chapter 11 bankruptcy in February 2008. Its intent was to close 90 of its 184 stores to save significant operating costs. However, because the new law has lessened the time that Chapter 11 firms can remain under court control, the management of The Sharper Image felt that there was not enough time to finance the restocking of the remaining stores, so the company instead chose liquidation to retain some value in the assets. Other retailers such as Wickes Furniture, Whitehall Jewelers, Levitz, and Bombay Company have had similar experiences. It is apparent that the new time restrictions have been particularly harsh to retailers.

In 2011 Think Global AS, a leading manufacturer of pure electric cars, was purchased by Boris Zingarevich, a successful international technology entrepreneur. The Norwegian carmaker had declared Chapter 11 bankruptcy after failing to raise much needed capital. However, unable to resolve its financial issues, the company was offered for sale and engaged potential bidders for the company. Zingarevich, whose investment operations are based in Russia, was the winning bidder. After winning the bid Zingarevich signed a partnership agreement with a leading U.S. automotive battery maker. He believed that with this partnership and with Europe's top automobile engineering, the new company would be very competitive in the global market.[10]

In February 2004 disaster struck for 72 franchise stores when Ground Round Grill & Bar announced that it was filing for bankruptcy. The franchise stores were owned by local proprietors under a license from the chain. The company also owned 59 restaurants. Founded in 1969, the restaurant had been a pioneer in the casual dining industry but now was faced with debt to unsecured creditors of between $10 million and $50 million. Sell-offs of a number of the restaurants had provided some funds, but any ability to survive the bankruptcy hit a snag when financing was delayed and the company defaulted on its loan payments. The franchisees, however, made some quick and innovative decisions and decided to organize themselves into a cooperative. With this new organization, the Independent Owners Cooperative, LLC, they were able to raise some internal and external funds to buy the brand from the bankruptcy court. In early 2011 the cooperative announced that it had become debt free after making its final bank payment. The cooperative now operates 30 restaurants located in 13 states. The new business model of a cooperative seems to be working as a number of the original franchise owners have now opened new restaurants.[11]

Bankrate is one of a few Internet stocks that were able to survive the dot-com bubble burst. After an IPO at $13 per share in May 1999, the stock reached a low of $1 per share in August 2002. Since that low point, the company has made a complete turnaround, primarily due to the leadership of Elizabeth DeMarse. The company Web site lists comparative rate tables and fee information on 100 financial products such as mortgages, credit cards, auto loans, and money markets. Most of its revenue, however, is accumulated from advertising on the site. Now under new leadership, the company has enhanced its product line with a network of companies such as Interest.com, Mortgage-calc.com, Nationwide Card Services, and Savingforcollege.com. Revenues have reached new highs of over $300 million but with inconsistent yet small negative profits.[12]

Some lessons that can be learned from those who have experienced bankruptcy are as follows:

- Many entrepreneurs spend too much time and effort trying to diversify in markets where they lack knowledge. They should focus only on known markets.
- Bankruptcy protects entrepreneurs only from creditors, not from competitors.
- It's difficult to separate the entrepreneur from the business. Entrepreneurs put everything into the company, including worrying about the future of their employees.
- Many entrepreneurs do not think their businesses are going to fail until it's too late. They should file early.
- Bankruptcy is emotionally painful. Going into hiding after bankruptcy is a big mistake. Bankruptcy needs to be shared with employees and everybody else involved.

Chapter 11 bankruptcy
Provides the opportunity to reorganize and make the venture more solvent

Chapter 13 bankruptcy
Voluntarily allows individuals with regular income the opportunity to make extended time payments

Chapter 7 bankruptcy
Requires the venture to liquidate, either voluntarily or involuntarily

As the preceding examples indicate, bankruptcy is serious business and requires some important understanding of its applications. The Bankruptcy Act of 1978 (with amendments added in 1984 and 2005) was designed to ensure a fair distribution of assets to creditors, to protect debtors from unfair depletion of assets, and to protect debtors from unfair demands by creditors. The Bankruptcy Act provides three alternative provisions for a firm near or at a position of insolvency. The three alternative positions are (1) reorganization, or *Chapter 11 bankruptcy;* (2) extended time payment, or *Chapter 13 bankruptcy;* and (3) liquidation, or *Chapter 7 bankruptcy.* All attempt to protect the troubled entrepreneur as well as provide a reasonable way to organize payments to debtors or to end the venture.

CHAPTER 11—REORGANIZATION

This is the least severe alternative to bankruptcy. In this situation the courts try to give the venture "breathing room" to pay its debts. Usually, this situation results when a venture has cash flow problems, and creditors begin to pressure the firm with lawsuits. The entrepreneur feels that, with some time, the business can become more solvent and liquid to meet its debt requirements. However, as we have seen in examples discussed earlier in this chapter, the new time restrictions regarding how long a Chapter 11 firm may continue under court control have made it particularly difficult for firms in retailing to reorganize effectively. However, it is still in the best interests of a company that has a chance to become solvent to seek protection under this option.

A major creditor, any party who has an interest, or a group of creditors will usually present the case to the court. Then a plan for reorganization will be prepared to indicate how the business will be turned around. The plan will divide the debt and ownership interests into two groups: those who will be affected by the plan and those who will not. It will then specify whose interests will be affected and how payments will be made.

Once the plan is completed, it must be approved by the court. All bankruptcies are now handled by the U.S. Bankruptcy Court, whose powers were restructured under the Bankruptcy Amendments and Federal Judgeship Act of 1984. Approval of the plan also requires that all creditors and owners agree to comply with the reorganization plan as presented to the courts. The decisions made in the reorganization plan generally reflect one or a combination of the following:[13]

1. *Extension.* This occurs when two or more of the largest creditors agree to postpone any claims. This acts as a stimulus for smaller creditors to also agree to the plan.
2. *Substitution.* If the future potential of the venture looks promising enough, it may be possible to exchange stock or something else for the existing debt.
3. *Composition settlement.* The debt is prorated to the creditors as a settlement for any debt.

Even though only 20 to 25 percent of those firms that file for Chapter 11 bankruptcy will make it through the process, it does present an opportunity to find a cure for any business problems. Some of these problems are resolvable, and without the Chapter 11 protection even these 20 to 25 percent that file would never have the opportunity to succeed. It should also be noted that some firms that make it through the process often find that they cannot succeed and thus either must liquidate or find a buyer.

There are a number of different reasons why companies do not successfully come out of Chapter 11 bankruptcy. Some firms wait too long before filing and others are faced with poor markets, intense competition, or as is the present case, a poor global economy. Even industries can be affected by poor economic conditions and intense competition. For example, the alternative or clean energy market in the U.S. has experienced many recent bankruptcies because of a poor economy and also from intense competition from China. Solyndra LLC was a heavily subsidized California solar company that may have difficulty avoiding liquidation from Chapter 11 bankruptcy because it depended so heavily on government subsidies that have just about dried up. It laid off 1,100 workers and is now under an investigation regarding the use of this subsidy money. In Massachusetts several firms in this industry have experienced bankruptcy issues. Evergreen Solar Inc. was once a start-up that was valued at over $1 billion that had to complete a bankruptcy auction of its assets that netted only $34 million. Others will have difficulty rising from Chapter 11 bankruptcy because the subsidies have dried up and because China has intensified its international marketing, offering products at much lower prices. However, in spite of these failures venture capitalists still regard this industry as a primary sector for investment with the right product line and unique technology.[14]

ELEVATOR PITCH FOR nPOWER PERSONAL ENERGY GENERATOR

Your former partner, who has been a very successful investor in start-ups, has called you to ask if you are aware of any good investments. He just cashed out of a very profitable sale of one of his companies and has funds to reinvest. You know he likes to hike and thought that after learning about the following startup, this may be a good option to propose to his former partner. What do you think?

Aaron LeMieux loves to hike but he has always complained about the extra batteries he needs to carry with him for a cell phone, iPod, and other electronic gadgets. Then one day he thought about trying to harvest all of the energy a person emits from hiking. LeMieux at the time was a mechanical engineer employed by a management consulting firm. He considered the idea very viable so he convinced his wife it would work, quit his job as a management consultant, emptied out his savings, and with these funds proceeded to develop a prototype. His original prototype weighed 11 ounces and was twice as long as a smart phone. The unit took energy from the human stride and turned it into 2.5 watts of electricity, which is enough energy to power any electronic gadget for a short time.

In 2007 he formed Tremont Electric and began raising funds from friends, family, and a local bank in order to set up manufacturing and marketing. It took him about two years to get everything in place and in mid-2011 the company began taking orders for the unit, priced at $159. The company is targeting backpackers or people on the move who do not have consistent access to charging. According to the company 26 minutes of walking is enough to top off a 3G smartphone for one minute of talking through a USB port. There is also speculation that portable battery and fuel cell manufacturers may in the future be interested in this unique technology.

Sources: Rachel Z. Arndt, "America's Most Promising Startups: Tremont Electric," www.businessweek.com/smallbiz; http://www.wired.com/gadgetlab/tag/npower-peg/; and Jefferson Graham, "Talking Tech at CES: Recharge Devices Naturally with nPower PEG," January 5, 2011, www.usatoday.com.

In general, entrepreneurs have a tendency to ignore the warning signs of bankruptcy. These signs may be avoided or ignored until there is an emergency, such as running out of cash. In the present volatile global economy this issue becomes even more evident, as we saw in the examples just given. Being aware of any warning signs is critical to giving an entrepreneur the opportunity to develop a new plan and alternative strategies.

Surviving Bankruptcy

The most obvious way to survive bankruptcy is to avoid it altogether. However, since bankruptcy is becoming such a common occurrence, it may be helpful for the entrepreneur to have a plan should he or she find it necessary to declare bankruptcy. Some suggestions for survival are listed here:

- Bankruptcy can be used as a bargaining chip to allow the entrepreneur to voluntarily restructure and reorganize the venture.
- File before the venture runs out of cash or has no incoming revenue so that expenses not protected by bankruptcy can be paid.
- Don't file for Chapter 11 protection unless the venture has a legitimate chance of recovery.
- Be prepared to have creditors examine all financial transactions for the last 12 months, seeking possible debtor fraud.
- Maintain good records.

- Understand completely how the protection against creditors works and what is necessary to keep it in place.
- If there is any litigation in existence, transfer it to the bankruptcy court, which may be a more favorable forum for the entrepreneur.
- Focus efforts on preparing a realistic financial reorganization plan.

Following some of these suggestions and being prepared should bankruptcy be necessary is the best advice that anyone could give to an entrepreneur. Preparation will prevent unfavorable conditions and could increase the likelihood of successfully coming out of bankruptcy.

CHAPTER 13—EXTENDED TIME PAYMENT PLANS

As of October 17, 2005, the ability of an entrepreneur to file for a Chapter 7 bankruptcy is now more difficult. The reforms in the Bankruptcy Code that were signed into law in April 2005 are based on the argument that a person should be obligated to repay some of his or her debt (Chapter 13 bankruptcy); therefore, these reforms make it more difficult to walk away from all debt by filing for Chapter 7 bankruptcy. Under this new law, individuals are required to obtain credit counseling within six months of filing and to take a means test to ascertain if they are eligible for either Chapter 7 or Chapter 13 bankruptcy. The means test states that individuals may not file for Chapter 7 bankruptcy if their income is at or above the state income median.

Under Chapter 13 bankruptcy, the individual creates a five-year repayment plan under court supervision. In each case, a court-appointed trustee receives money from the debtor and then is responsible for making scheduled payments to all creditors. This reform is more favorable to creditors than the old law. The only problem is that, according to the Bankruptcy Institute, about two of every three Chapter 13 filers ultimately fail to meet their planned obligations, thus resulting in a Chapter 7 filing.

Research now indicates mixed results regarding these reforms. The American Enterprise Institute recently published research that indicates that entrepreneurs that declared personal or business bankruptcy were able to start new businesses without much difficulty or many restrictions. The profitability of these restructured firms was just as successful as those that never declared bankruptcy. However, the research also reports that entrepreneurs that had declared bankruptcy had more difficulty getting loans or had to pay higher interest rates. They were able to recover and generate a good profit rate by finding other ways to finance their new companies. The issue remains, however, whether the reforms are making it easier or more difficult for entrepreneurs to recover from bankruptcy.[15]

CHAPTER 7—LIQUIDATION

The most extreme case of bankruptcy requires the entrepreneur to liquidate, either voluntarily or involuntarily, all nonexempt assets of the business.

voluntary bankruptcy
Entrepreneur's decision to file for bankruptcy

If the entrepreneur files a *voluntary bankruptcy* petition under Chapter 7, it constitutes a determination that his or her venture is bankrupt. Usually, the courts will also require a current income and expense statement.

involuntary bankruptcy
Petition of bankruptcy filed by creditors without consent of entrepreneur

Table 15.2 summarizes some of the key issues and requirements under the *involuntary bankruptcy* petition. As the table indicates, an involuntary bankruptcy can be very complicated and can take a long time to resolve. However, liquidation is in the best interests of the entrepreneur if there is no hope of recovering from the situation.

| | Number and Claims | Rights and Duties | |
Requirements	of Creditors	of Entrepreneur	Trustee
Debts are not being paid as they become due.	If 12 or more creditors, at least 3 with unsecured claims totaling $5,000 must sign petition.	Damages may be recovered if creditor files in bad faith.	Elected by creditors. Interim trustee appointed by court.
Custodian appointed within 120 days of filing petition.	If fewer than 12 creditors, 1 creditor whose unsecured claim is at least $5,000 must sign the petition.	If involuntary petition is dismissed by court, costs, fees, or damages may be awarded.	Becomes by law owner of all property considered nonexempt for liquidation.
Considered insolvent when fair value of all assets is less than debts. Called a balance sheet test.	A proof of claim must be filed within 90 days of first meeting of creditors.	Must file a list of creditors with courts. Must file a current income and expense statement.	Can set aside petitions; transfer of property to a creditor under certain conditions.

TABLE 15.2   Liquidation under Chapter 7 Involuntary Bankruptcy

STRATEGY DURING REORGANIZATION

Normally, reorganization under Chapter 11 or an extended payment plan under Chapter 13 takes a significant amount of time. During this period, the entrepreneur can speed up the process by taking the initiative in preparing a plan, selling the plan to secured creditors, communicating with groups of creditors, and not writing checks that cannot be covered.

The key to enhancing the bankruptcy process is keeping creditors abreast of how the business is doing and stressing the significance of their support during the process. Improving the entrepreneur's credibility with creditors will help the venture emerge from financial difficulties without the stigma of failure. But trying to meet face to face with groups of creditors usually results in turmoil and ill will, so these meetings should be avoided.

Bankruptcy should be a last resort for the entrepreneur. Every effort should be made to avoid it and keep the business operating.

KEEPING THE VENTURE GOING

Not all bankruptcies have unfavorable endings. Ground Round Grill & Bar and Think Global AS survived bankruptcies but did emerge under new ownership and a change in the business strategy.

Any entrepreneur who starts a business should pay attention to, as well as learn from, the mistakes of others. There are certain requirements that can help keep a new venture going and reduce the risk of failure. We can never guarantee success, but we can learn how to avoid failure.

Table 15.3 summarizes some of the key factors that can reduce the risk of business failure. The entrepreneur should be sensitive to each of these issues regardless of the size or type of business.

TABLE 15.3   Requirements for Keeping a New Venture Afloat

- Avoid excess optimism when the business appears to be successful.
- Always prepare good marketing plans with clear objectives.
- Make good cash projections and avoid capitalization.
- Keep abreast of the marketplace.
- Identify stress points that can put the business in jeopardy.

Many entrepreneurs have confidence in their abilities, which is necessary for them to be successful in their field. This confidence allows them to meet changing market conditions by implementing new strategies and directions for their firms to achieve future success where others may have failed. Two examples of this approach are Eli and Sheri Gurock and Hendrik and Lorette Vosloo. Eli and Sheri Gurock saw two big-name toy stores close their doors in their Massachusetts community. They believed that they could be successful with a community toy store by including a baby section that offered a wide variety of baby clothes and necessities. Their strategy was that expectant parents who shopped the store (named Magic Beans) would leave with the idea that this was also a great place to buy toys. In addition, even though toy sales tended to be very seasonal, sales of the baby necessities would create a good business environment all year long. Emphasizing themselves as a community business that had excellent follow-through service during and after the sale has led to an expansion to four stores, 34 employees, an effective Web site, and net sales estimated at about $3 million.[16]

Hendrik and Lorette Vosloo, looking for a new business, became very interested in a gourmet wine and olive oil store they had visited called the Cork and Olive Store. As a result they decided to purchase a franchise. About a year later the franchisor experienced financial problems such that Hendrik and Lorette could not get shipments of their best selling wines nor could they get any new items. When the franchisor declared Chapter 11, Hendrik and Lorette decided to continue on their own. They kept the name but retooled and stocked better wine and held more tastings. A year into their efforts the original franchisor sold the franchise to another group that hoped to bring it out of Chapter 11. However the retooling did not last and the franchisor declared Chapter 7. Although Hendrik and Lorette lost the major volume pricing advantage of being part of a franchise, they decided to add a second revenue stream and started a wine tasting bar and brought in gourmet foods. The new company is surviving in a difficult economy and is pleased to be independent and able to try new strategies to make the business more successful.[17]

The entrepreneurs in these examples recognized the need to develop different strategies or face failure. In the first case the need was to develop a unique mix of products that would help build a strong store image. In the second case the entrepreneurs realized that they needed to continue on their own even when the franchisor declared Chapter 11 bankruptcy. With a new strategy and retooling they survived even after the franchisor eventually had to liquidate in a Chapter 7 bankruptcy. We saw in Chapter 8 of this textbook the importance of market planning to help prepare for situations such as those described.

Good cash projections are also a serious consideration for the entrepreneur. Cash flow is one of the major causes for an entrepreneur to have to declare bankruptcy. Thus, in preparing cash projections, entrepreneurs should seek assistance from accountants, lawyers, or a federal agency such as the Small Business Administration. This may prevent the situation from reaching the point where it is too late for any hope of recovery.

Many entrepreneurs avoid gathering sufficient information about the market (see Chapter 7 of this textbook). Information is an important asset to any entrepreneur, especially regarding future market potential and forecasting the size of the immediate attainable market. Entrepreneurs will often try to guess what is happening in the market and ignore the changing marketplace. This could spell disaster, especially if competitors are reacting more positively to the market changes.

In the early stages of a new venture, it is helpful for the entrepreneur to be aware of stress points, that is, those points when the venture is changing in size, requiring new survival strategies. Early rapid rises in sales can be interpreted incorrectly so that the venture finds itself adding plant capacity, signing new contracts with suppliers, or increasing inventories, resulting in shrinking margins and being overleveraged. To offset this situation, prices are

TABLE 15.4 Warning Signs of Bankruptcy
• Management of finances becomes lax, so no one can explain how money is being spent.
• Directors cannot document or explain major transactions.
• Customers are given large discounts to enhance payments because of poor cash flow.
• Contracts are accepted below standard amounts to generate cash.
• Bank requests subordination of its loans.
• Key personnel leave the company.
• Materials to meet orders are lacking.
• Payroll taxes are not paid.
• Suppliers demand payment in cash.
• Customers' complaints regarding service and product quality increase.

increased or quality weakened, leading to lower sales. This becomes a vicious circle that can lead to bankruptcy.

Stress points can be identified based on the amount of sales. For example, it may be possible to recognize that sales of $1 million, $5 million, and $25 million may represent key decision marks in terms of major capital investment and operational expenses such as hiring new key personnel. Entrepreneurs should be aware of the burden of sales levels on capital investment and operational expenses.

WARNING SIGNS OF BANKRUPTCY

Entrepreneurs should be sensitive to signals in the business and the environment that may be early warning signs of trouble. Often, the entrepreneur is not aware of what is going on or is not willing to accept the inevitable. Table 15.4 lists some of the key early warning signs of bankruptcy. Generally, they are interrelated, and one can often lead to another.

For example, when management of the financial affairs becomes lax, there is a tendency to do anything to generate cash, such as reducing prices, cutting back on supplies to meet orders, or releasing important personnel such as sales representatives. A new office furniture business catering to small or medium-sized businesses illustrates how this can happen. Top management of the firm decided that moving merchandise was its top priority. Sales representatives earned standard commission on each sale and were free to reduce prices where necessary to make the sale. Hence, without any cost or break-even awareness, sales representatives often reduced prices below direct costs. They still received their commissions when the price charged was below cost. Thus, the venture eventually lost substantial amounts of money and had to declare bankruptcy.

When an entrepreneur sees any of the warning signs in Table 15.4, he or she should immediately seek the advice of a CPA or an attorney. It may be possible to prevent bankruptcy by making immediate changes in the operation to improve the cash flow and profitability of the business. Turnaround strategies are discussed later in this chapter.

STARTING OVER

Bankruptcy and liquidation do not have to be the end for the entrepreneur. History is full of examples of entrepreneurs who have failed many times before finally succeeding.

Gail Borden's tombstone reads, "I tried and failed, and I tried again and succeeded." One of his first inventions was the Terraqueous Wagon, which was designed to travel on land or water. The invention sank on its first try. Borden also had three other inventions that failed to get patents. A fourth invention was patented but eventually wiped him out because of lack of capital and poor sales. However, Borden was persistent and convinced that his vacuum condensation process, giving milk a long shelf life, would be successful. At 56, Borden had his first success with condensed milk.

Over the years, other famous entrepreneurs have also endured many failures before finally achieving success. Rowland Hussey Macy (of Macy's retail stores), Ron Berger (of National Video), and Thomas Edison are other examples of struggling entrepreneurs who lived through many failures.

The characteristics of entrepreneurs were discussed in Chapter 3. From that chapter we know that entrepreneurs are likely to continue starting new ventures even after failing. There is evidence that they learn from their mistakes, and investors often look favorably on someone who has failed previously, assuming that he or she will not make the same mistake again.[18]

Generally, entrepreneurs who have failed in their endeavors tend to have a better understanding and appreciation for the need for market research, more initial capitalization, and stronger business skills. Unfortunately, not all entrepreneurs learn these skills from their experiences; many tend to fail over and over again.

However, business failure does not have to be a stigma when it comes time to seek venture capital. Past records will be revealed during subsequent start-ups, but the careful entrepreneur can explain why the failure occurred and how he or she will prevent it in the future, restoring investors' confidence. As discussed in Chapter 7, the business plan will help sell the business concept to investors. It is in the business plan that the entrepreneur, even after many failures, can illustrate how *this* venture will be successful.

THE REALITY OF FAILURE

Unfortunately, failure does happen, but it isn't necessarily the end. Many entrepreneurs are able to successfully turn failure into success. It is one of the important historical characteristics of entrepreneurs that we have continually identified throughout this text. Since failure can happen, there are also some important considerations that should be mentioned if it should occur.

First and foremost, the entrepreneur should consult with his or her family. As difficult as it is for the entrepreneur to deal with bankruptcy, it is even more so for spouses. Problems occur because the spouse usually has no control over the venture's operations unless it is a family-operated business. As a result, he or she may not even be aware of any bankruptcy threats. Thus, the first thing the entrepreneur should do is sit down with his or her spouse and explain what is happening. This discussion will also help alleviate some of the stress of dealing with bankruptcy.

Second, the entrepreneur should seek outside assistance from professionals, friends, and business associates. Although not all of these people may be sympathetic, it is usually not difficult to find individuals among these groups who will be supportive. Professional support is also available from the Small Business Administration (SBA), universities, the Senior Corps of Retired Executives (SCORE), and small-business development centers.

Third, it is important to not try to hang on to a venture that will continually drain resources if the end is inevitable. It is better to consider the time spent trying to save a dying business as an opportunity cost. The time spent could be more effectively and profitably used to either start over or do something else. If a turnaround is considered possible (see the following discussion), it is wise to set a time frame and, if it is not accomplished in that time frame, to simply end the venture.

BUSINESS TURNAROUNDS

We have discussed a number of turnaround examples throughout this chapter, such as the opening profile on Kabloom, Bankrate, and the Cork and Olive Store. All were faced with declining sales and earnings that either resulted in bankruptcy or threatened bankruptcy. What we have learned from successful examples of turnarounds is summarized and discussed in the next few paragraphs.[19]

During a business's life cycle it is likely that an entrepreneur will face adversity, perhaps because of external factors (the economy; competition; changes in consumer needs; technology; or unpredictable acts such as war, terrorism, or weather); or the adversity may be self-inflicted (that is, due to poor management). The severity of the adversity can result in bankruptcy or in a need to refocus the business and strive for a turnaround. The process of turnaround can take many directions, but there are some basic principles and support that can be considered to help the entrepreneur.

First and foremost it is important for the entrepreneur to recognize the warning signs of bankruptcy discussed earlier and listed in Table 15.4. However, recognition of the warning signs does not solve the problem; instead, it is the point at which the principles discussed next should be considered. If the entrepreneur feels inadequate in dealing with any of these warning signs, then it is recommended that he or she consult with a CPA or an attorney. There are also a number of turnaround management consulting firms that support businesses of all sizes. They can be identified with a simple search on the Internet. The Business Finance and Turnaround Association can also provide support in this situation.

The first principle in any successful turnaround (reflected in all our earlier examples) is aggressive hands-on management. Leadership in all these cases focused initial efforts on getting out among, meeting, and communicating with all employees. This high-visibility strategy is significant to identify the roots of any issues that are contributing to the threat of bankruptcy or to the need to successfully resurface from bankruptcy. The entrepreneur needs to keep all the employees energized and focused on bringing the company back to a position of market and financial stability and then, it is hoped, moving it toward managed growth. The entrepreneur needs to be honest and up-front with all the employees regarding the situation to get them involved in identifying the issues that need to be addressed. Historically, at this stage neither an absentee management nor a bunker mentality in which management works long hours is sufficient.

The second principle is that management must have a plan. We've discussed many times in this text that there are three questions that need to be addressed in any planning process (see Chapter 8). The same questions are applicable here as part of a turnaround plan. Step 1 in this plan is getting out into the business and trying to understand the problem, as described in the preceding paragraph. This addresses the situation analysis, or the question, "Where are we now?" The second question in any plan is, "Where are we going?" This is when the plan becomes important, since goals and objectives will need to be developed to get the company turned around. Again it is important to get everyone in the organization involved in looking for opportunities to improve the company's existing market and financial position by cutting costs, increasing efficiencies, and improving customer service and loyalty, as well as by pursuing strategies to increase sales.

The third and last step, or principle, in the turnaround process is action. This relates to the third question in the planning process, which is, "How do we get there?" The plan should involve aggressive corrective action. Time is of the essence here, either to avoid bankruptcy or to prove to the creditors or the bankruptcy court that you can get the company back on track. At this point, a turnaround consultant may be called in to support these actions if the entrepreneur feels inadequate.

IN REVIEW

SUMMARY

This chapter of the textbook deals with exit strategies that the entrepreneur will need to consider. These decisions can involve finding a successor to the venture, selling the business either totally or partially, or ending the venture because of bankruptcy. All of these likely scenarios are real and common among small businesses. Thus, to be prepared the entrepreneur should understand each of these issues and be prepared with an exit plan before it is too late. One of the venture-ending decisions that an entrepreneur may face is succession of the business. If the business is family owned, the entrepreneur would likely seek a family member to succeed. Other options, if no family member is available or interested, include transferring some or all of the business to an employee or outsider or hiring an external person to manage the business. Direct sale of the business, employee stock option plans, and management buyouts are alternatives for the entrepreneur in selling the venture. These are all exit strategy options for the entrepreneur and need to be planned for early so that crises are minimized.

Even though the intent of all entrepreneurs is to establish a business for a long time, many problems can cause these plans to fail. Since about one-half of all new ventures fail in their first four years of business, it is important for the entrepreneur to understand the options for either ending or salvaging a venture.

Bankruptcy offers three options for the entrepreneur. Under Chapter 11 of the Bankruptcy Act of 1978 (amended in 1984 and again in 2005), the venture will be reorganized under a plan approved by the courts. With this plan the entrepreneur strives to revitalize the financial condition of the venture and return to the market with new strategies.

Chapter 13 of the Bankruptcy Act provides for an extended time payment plan to cover outstanding debts. The 2005 amendment to the Bankruptcy Act has made this particular choice a more likely first option—and an option that must be exhausted before the entrepreneur is allowed to file for Chapter 7 liquidation. The courts feel that individuals should be required to pay back some of their debt, and therefore this amendment makes it more difficult to file for Chapter 7 liquidation. If the individual is unable to make extended payments, then liquidation, either voluntarily or involuntarily, is the final option.

Keeping the business going is the primary intent of all entrepreneurs. Avoiding excessive optimism, preparing good marketing plans, making good cash projections, keeping familiar with the market, and being sensitive to stress points in the business can help keep the business operating.

Entrepreneurs can also be sensitive to key warning signs of potential problems. Lax management of finances, discounting to generate cash, loss of key personnel, lack of raw materials, nonpayment of payroll taxes, demands of suppliers to be paid in cash, and increased customer complaints about service and product quality are some of the key warning signs that a firm is headed for bankruptcy. If the business does fail, however, the entrepreneur should always consider starting over. Failure can be a learning process, as evidenced by the many famous inventors who succeeded after many failures.

RESEARCH TASKS

1. Find three accounts by entrepreneurs in which they describe their experience with poorly performing firms and the process of going through bankruptcy. In what ways were their experiences similar? In what ways were they different? Did emotions play a role? Did the entrepreneurs learn from the experience?
2. Interview a member of a family business and gain a deeper understanding of the issues surrounding the management of such a business, especially those related to succession.
3. Write an account of the emotions that you felt when someone or something close to you was lost forever (you will not be required to present this to the class). How did these emotions impact your ability to perform other tasks? How did you overcome these negative emotions? To what extent do you believe that entrepreneurs go through a similar process when their businesses fail?

CLASS DISCUSSION

1. If your family had a highly successful business, would succession to the next generation (you and/or your siblings) likely be smooth, or would there be the potential for conflict and hurt feelings? What would be a "fair" way to set up succession?
2. Do you believe the laws should be changed to make it easier for entrepreneurs to go into, and recover from, bankruptcy? What are the implications of your answer for the entrepreneur, creditors, and the national economy?
3. What are the issues facing an entrepreneur in deciding whether or not the business needs to be put into bankruptcy today?
4. The following role-plays require you to think and act as if you were the person being described in each situation.
   a. *Role-play 1.* One student prepares and presents a speech as if she or he is an entrepreneur informing employees that her or his business has failed and will not be operating from tomorrow on. The rest of the class can respond and ask questions as if they are devoted employees upset about losing their jobs.
   b. *Role-play 2.* In small groups, role-play the interchange between an entrepreneur of a failed business expressing his or her negative emotions and a friend providing advice on how to best cope with the situation.

SELECTED READINGS

Driscoll, Suzanne. (Spring 2011). Ten Ways Your Succession Plan Can Go Wrong. *Family Business*, vol. 22, issue 2, pp. 16–19.

This article identifies ten important factors that can cause problems with a succession plan. Advice is offered as to how to avoid these issues. Some of the issues identified were failure to consider the viewpoint of all parties, failure to give control to successor, automatic designation of son or daughter as successor, and failure to consult family members.

Finnell, Kelly. (July 2011). The ESOP Boom in Succession Planning. *Employee Benefit Advisor,* vol. 9, issue 7, pp. 50–56.

This article explains how an ESOP operates, how stocks are handled, and what tax advantages might exist now that the U.S. Congress is creating new tax incentives for businesses who use the plan.

Gerlach, Christopher S. (2011). Reorganize or Liquidate? An Empirical Investigation of Post-Bankruptcy Reform Law. *Retail Property Insights,* vol. 18, issue 1, pp. 1–5.

Critics argue that the new bankruptcy law of 2005 has led to more liquidations rather than reorganizations. Supporters of the law indicate that there are other factors leading to this trend. The research reported in this article includes data from 29 countries spanning 19 years and finds that lenient and friendly bankruptcy laws are significantly correlated with the level of entrepreneurship development.

Grove, Hugh; and Tom Cook. (July 2011). Whitetrack Design, Inc. *Entrepreneurship Theory and Practice,* vol. 35, issue 4, pp. 831–48.

This is an interesting case of owners of a snowshoe manufacturing business that are contemplating selling. Their dilemma relates to whether the business should be sold now or should be operated for a while longer in order to enhance its value. The case focuses on valuation and provides some ways to assist in the valuation of a business.

Heggde, Githa; and Sunitha Vilakshan Panikar. (March 2011). Causes of Sickness and Turnaround Strategies in Public and Private Sector Organizations. *The XIMB Journal of Management,* vol. 7, issue 3, pp. 53–70.

The authors of this paper argue that there is a need to identify the cause of industrial sickness that is pervasive in both developed and developing countries. With this organizations would then be able to formulate turnaround strategies. Research examined turnaround strategy in public and private sector organizations and found that a major cause of this sickness was the external and internal organization structure.

Klein, Karen E. (April 18, 2011). Succeeding in Business after Bankruptcy. *Business-Week.com,* p. 1.

This article presents an interview with a recent scholar at the American Enterprise Institute. She indicates that the original notion of bankruptcy was to provide a fresh start. In the interview she points out how the bankruptcy laws can have a positive effect on entrepreneurship.

Knowlton, John. (January 2010). Building a Successful Succession Plan for a Financial Service Practice. *Journal of Financial Service Professionals,* vol. 64, issue 1, pp. 60–65.

There are important elements to consider in order to have a successful transition from one financial advisor to a successor. These elements are also beneficial to any entrepreneur thinking about a succession strategy, particularly in the service sector where clients are involved. The author maintains the importance of selection of the successor, implementing an effective transition, and even allowing the retiring person to maintain some equity.

Mercer, Christopher Z. (June 2011). Buy-Sell Agreements. *CPA Journal,* vol. 81, issue 6, pp. 62–67.

Buy-sell agreements for privately owned businesses with two or more owners are discussed in this article. It explores the importance of these agreements and discusses topics that trigger the need for these agreements such as death or departure of one or more owners. Recommendations for valuation are also discussed.

Nunes, Paul; and Tim Breene. (January/February 2011). Reinvent Your Business Before It Is Too Late. *Harvard Business Review,* vol. 89, issue 1/2, pp. 80–87.

To survive over the long term a business needs to reinvent itself periodically, moving from one business performance curve to another. Very few firms make this leap successfully, mainly because they start the process too late. The authors report on an extensive longitudinal study that looks at the differences between companies that have successfully reinvented themselves and those that failed.

Shepherd, Dean A.; and Andrew Zackarakis. (2000). Structuring Family Business Succession: An Analysis of the Future Leader's Decision Making. *Entrepreneurship: Theory and Practice,* vol. 24, no. 4, pp. 25–39.

This article examines the perception of potential family business leaders from a behavioral economics theory perspective. The authors argue that founders should structure succession so that the future leader incurs both financial and behavioral sunk costs as well as hold the future leader to stringent performance requirements prior to the succession.

Wood, Robert W. (April 2011). Can't Find a Buyer? Create an ESOP. *M & A Tax Report,* vol. 19, issue 9, pp. 5–6.

In order to facilitate the sale of a business the author advises owners to create an employee stock ownership plan (ESOP). The firm can claim a tax deduction for its ESOP contributions providing significant tax savings. There may also be tax deductions for certain kinds of dividends depending on how they are distributed.

END NOTES

1. See www.kabloom.com; Chris Reidy, "The Balloon That May Save Kabloom," *The Boston Globe,* July 19, 2010, pp. B5, B7; www.foxvideo.foxbusiness.com; Eve Tahmincioglu, "Small Business: How to Grow Without a Lot of Capital," *The New York Times,* January 8, 2004, p. B1; and Chris Reidy, "Flower Power Kabloom Says It Aims to Be Floral World's Starbucks," *The Boston Globe,* October 19, 2002, p. D1.
2. Emily Osbun Bermes, "Succession Planning for the Small Business," *Business People* (February 2011), p. 60.
3. www.ffi.org.
4. Jennifer Alsever and Adam Bluestein, "What Not to Do When You Decide It's Time to Step Aside," *INC* (October 2011), p. 67.
5. John Knowlton, "Building a Successful Succession Plan for a Financial Service Practice," *Journal of Financial Service Professionals* (January 2010), pp. 60–65.
6. Clyde E. Witt, "Plan Ahead, Stay Ahead," *Material Handling Management* (January 2006), pp. 33–35.
7. See Arik Hesseldahl, Olga Kharif, Douglas MacMillan, and Rachael King, "Best Young Tech Entrepreneurs 2010: The Finalists," April 20, 2010, www.bloombergbusinessweek.com; and Ari Levy and Cory Johnson, "RadiumOne Raises $21 Million Backers Led by Crosslink," March 10, 2011, www.bloombergbusinessweek.com.
8. The ESOP Association, www.esopassociation.org.
9. See American Bankruptcy Institute's Web site, www.abiworld.org; and www.uscourts.gov/bankruptcystats.
10. Steve Barclay, "Electric Car Maker THINK Resets for a New Start," *Automotive Industries* (July 2011), p. 9.
11. Carlye Adler, "The Grand Rebound," *Fortune Small Business* (February 2005), pp. 56–60; and "Ground Round Franchise Group to Become Debt Free Later This Month," *Associated Press Newswire,* April 16, 2011.

12. www.bankrate.com.

13. David Twomey and Marianne Jennings, *Anderson's Business Law and the Legal Environment, Standard Volume,* 21st ed. (Mason, OH: South-Western Cengage Learning, 2011), pp. 765–86.

14. Erin Ailworth, "Clean-tech Firms Lose Luster," *The Boston Globe,* November 13, 2011.

15. Karen Klein, "Succeeding in Business after Bankruptcy," April 18, 2011, www.businessweek.com.

16. www.mbeans.com; and Nichole L. Torres, "Underdog Days," *Entrepreneur* (April 2008), p. 94.

17. Jason Daley, "A Franchisor Bankruptcy," *Entrepreneur* (January 2010), p. 106.

18. L. M. Lament, "What Entrepreneurs Learn from Experience," *Journal of Small Business Management* (1972), p. 36.

19. See Paul Nunes and Tim Breene, "Reinvent Your Business Before It's Too Late," *Harvard Business Review* (January/February 2011), pp. 80–87; and Jonathan Byrnes, "How to Manage a Profitability Turnaround," *MWorld* (Spring 2011), pp. 32–35.

6

CASES

CASE 12

Mayu LLC

CASE 13

Nature Bros. Ltd.

CASE 14

Amy's Bread

CASE 15

Supply Dynamics

CASE 16

Datavantage Corporation

CASE 17

Tire Valet: A Mobile Tire Company

CASE 1
TURNER TEST PREP CO.

INTRODUCTION

In the Spring of 2003, Jessica Turner felt that she had come to a crossroads with her business. As the founder and CEO of Turner Test Prep, a California company specializing in preparing people for the Certified Public Accountant (CPA) exam, she felt that she was not achieving market share and growing in the right direction. After three years of providing prep classes to both students and professionals, Turner had about 10 percent of the market and was facing fierce competition from her primary rival, National Testing Services. Uncertain about which growth direction to take, Jessica contemplated several options.

BACKGROUND

Jessica Turner started Turner Test Prep in the summer of 1997 after graduating from Case Western Reserve University's Weatherhead School of Management with a master's degree in accounting. She passed the CPA exam and began applying to Big Six accounting firms. Frustrated after receiving several rejections, Jessica began to consider other employment options. Her undergraduate degree was in business, and after graduation, Jessica worked for several years in the business office of a small test prep company based in San Francisco. The company prepared students who wanted to take primarily the SAT, GRE, GMAT, MCAT, and LSAT. Although her job was to manage the company's business affairs, she also began teaching math to students several nights a week. Jessica received training from the company in teaching basic testing skills, and she applied those skills toward teaching the math portion of the exams. She received positive feedback from her students as a conscientious and innovative teacher.

Jessica felt that her experience as a teacher for the test prep company helped her when she began studying for the CPA exam. She knew how to study efficiently, how to organize her notes, and how to practice for the various sections. Jessica was one of the 25 percent of students who passed all sections of the CPA exam on the first try.[1]

When contemplating what to do next, Jessica was struck by the fact that so many of her colleagues were

Source: This case study was prepared by Michael P. Peters with the intention of providing a basis for class discussion.

unable to pass the exam. Convinced that she was not only skilled in the accounting and finance principles but also in knowing how to study effectively, she decided to start her own test prep business teaching specifically to the CPA exam. She was confident that students and professionals wishing to become CPAs would benefit from a full-service program that gave students full classes and individualized attention so that they could pass the exam.

Jessica returned to California, put together a business plan, and secured financing from a local venture capital firm specializing in small start-ups. She decided to focus her business and marketing efforts in the San Francisco Bay area. On the basis of her research and the Bay area's concentration of different types of businesses, Jessica estimated that there was a market of about 1,000 students a year.

THE CPA EXAM

Although people with undergraduate or graduate degrees in accounting or business may do accounting work for a company, becoming a CPA provides an additional certification that employers prefer. Becoming a CPA can increase an accountant's salary by 10 to 15 percent[2] and is typically necessary to secure upper-level positions. In order to be certified to become a CPA, people must fulfill the following requirements:

- Have a college or master's degree with 24 semester units dedicated to business-related subjects, and at least 24 credits in accounting (a minimum of three credits), auditing (a minimum of three credits), business law, finance, and tax subjects;
- Pass the CPA exam;
- Have two years of work experience with a bachelor's degree or one year of work experience with 150 course credits.[3]

The exam is offered two times a year, in May and November. It is a grueling two-day, 15-hour event comprised of multiple choice, essay questions, and problem sets. The subjects tested are: Business Law and Professional Responsibility, Auditing, Accounting and Reporting, and Financial Accounting and Reporting.

CPA EXAM PREP SERVICES

The CPA exam varies only slightly from state to state. In order to study for the exam, people typically purchase books, software, or an online course to help them prepare.

The materials usually provide an overview of the tested material, study guides, and practice questions. The online tutorials often provide more practice questions and give students timed exams so that they can simulate actual testing conditions. Due to the amount of material covered on the exam as well as its level of difficulty, students are advised to give themselves four months to study.

In the San Francisco Bay area, several community colleges offer one-week review classes to help students prepare. These classes give students a starting point, after which they could use supplemental materials to study on their own.

NATIONAL TESTING SERVICES

National Testing Centers (NTC) is Turner's primary competition. NTC is a national test preparation company that has been in existence since 1962. The company focuses on virtually every standardized test that is offered and has programs for high school students taking the SAT, undergraduate students taking graduate school entrance tests (such as the GMAT, LSAT, GRE, and MCAT), and graduate students taking certification tests like the bar and CPA exams. In addition, the company has a program designed for international students taking the Test of English as a Foreign Language (TOEFL) exam.

NTC is a full-service program that offers a variety of options for students taking any of these exams. Most courses offer the opportunity to have classroom lectures, home-study videotapes, books, software, online tests, or a combination of any of these options.

The CPA course does not offer live classroom sessions but gives students the option of books, software, and online testing for one or all of the areas covered on the exam. Students also have a toll-free number that they can call if they have questions as well as online chats with NTC instructors to answer questions. NTC offers students a free repeat course if they do not pass the CPA exam and boasts a 75 percent pass rate. The course is priced from $1,000 to $1,500, depending on which of the services the student chooses. Many of NTC's students are repeaters who initially chose to study on their own and use a book or software package. Such students are dedicated to passing the second time they take the exam and want the structure that the courses provide. NTC provides a study schedule, study techniques, and information about how to take the exam that, it boasts, can not be found in any other course on the market.

Many of NTC's students have also taken an NTC course for a previous entrance exam. NTC boasts a higher overall pass rate for all its courses than any other test prep center in the country. People who had taken a course for the GMAT and had passed, for example, felt confident that they would be equally prepared for passing the CPA exam. In a survey of undergraduate students who had taken NTC for the SAT, 85 percent said they would take another NTC course to prepare them for a graduate school entrance exam.

THE TURNER TESTING ADVANTAGE

Despite NTC's success, Jessica knew that with a pass rate of only 25 percent for first-time takers, there was a need to provide a comprehensive program to students so that they could pass on their first try. She devised a full-service program that lasted for six weeks and was three to six hours per day. She worked with accounting, finance, and law professors to design a curriculum to give students a comprehensive approach to studying for the exam. She hired the professors to give three live, one-hour lectures per day, and she taught the test-taking techniques and organizing skills necessary to easily assimilate the mountains of information that students needed to know. Jessica also provided audiotapes for students so that they could review the lectures at home and suggested that they listen to them in their cars to maximize the use of their time. The course also included several timed minitests for each topic and four practice essay questions, which Jessica and her professors graded. The responses to essays included many comments and much feedback to give students guidance on areas to improve.

Jessica also made herself completely available to her students. She felt that one-on-one attention was critical to their success, and she held biweekly meetings with each student to gauge progress and answer questions. In addition to the meetings, students could call Jessica or e-mail her with questions, and she promised to get back to them within 24 hours.

Jessica held two sessions a year in March and September, three months prior to the exams, allowing students to continue to study on their own before the exams. She also made herself available to students after the course to answer their questions and help them in any way she could. Pricing her course at $1,100 per student, she felt that she was providing her students with more of an advantage and better preparation than any of the NTC options. She also offered a guarantee, allowing students to repeat the course if they did not pass the exam.

Jessica had taken a year to develop the materials and create a marketing plan for her company. She

EXHIBIT 1	Operating Costs for Turner Testing Services
Professor salaries (about 1,200 hours per year)	$75 per hour
Office space	$2,000 per month
Utilities and insurance	$1,000 per month
Materials	$ 600 per student
Printing	$ 500 per month
Marketing	$ 400 per month
Travel	$ 200 per month

decided to place ads in Bay area business schools to attract students contemplating taking the exam after graduation. She also created flyers to be placed in the schools and asked the school administrations if she could place them in students' mailboxes. She introduced herself to local businesses and tried to alert them to her program so that up-and-coming accountants would be encouraged to take her class if they wanted to take the CPA exam.

The first year that she ran the program she had 10 students. Despite the small class size, students felt that they had been well prepared for the exam and appreciated the individual attention they received. All students passed the exam. The second course had 45 students, 70 percent of whom passed. The last session that she held had 105 students, and 80 percent of those students passed. Jessica did not feel comfortable advertising her pass rate, however, because many of her students had taken the CPA exam one or two times before and failed. She wasn't sure whether they passed after taking her course because of the quality of the program or because they were bound to pass it at some point. Jessica did some cost and revenue estimates indicated in Exhibit 1.

SPRING 2003

By the spring of 2003, Jessica had finished teaching the course for the May exam and was looking forward to the September class. Although she was pleased that the number of students in each session was rising, she felt concerned that she was not making enough of an impact in the market. With only 10 percent of the market tapped, Jessica wanted to know how to improve her marketing and gain market share. She also wondered if she needed to format the course differently to attract students who did not want to attend live lectures. She had initially believed that students would benefit from

a structured program that kept them on track, but now she was not so sure. Many times students did not come to class but opted to listen to the tapes at home. Finally, Jessica realized that in her zeal to get her business up and running she had neglected to calculate her break-even point. How many students did Jessica need to break even, and at what point could she recognize a profit? She realized that these were all critical questions that needed answers to ensure the future success of her business.

END NOTES

1. www.micromash.net.
2. www.cpazone.org.
3. www.picpa.org.

CASE 2
JIM BOOTHE, INVENTOR

Jim Boothe has invented dozens of different products in his 25 years as an engineer to a large research and development lab. For some time, he has been thinking of leaving his current company and starting his own but has never seemed to have the nerve to do so. Jim feels that with his children grown up and on their own, now would be a good time to start his own business.

Having been an avid bicyclist for many years, Jim had invented an automatic derailleur for a 15-speed bike. This derailleur can be easily attached to any bicycle. The user does no shifting as the bicycle shifts the gears of the bicycle automatically (depending on terrain) much like the automatic transmission on an automobile. Jim feels that this invention has significant market potential, particularly since he has observed a rapid growth in the bicycling industry. This growth has been related to Lance Armstrong's success in the Tour de France, increased interest in physical fitness, and technological improvements in bicycles allowing for off-road travel as well as more comfort for longer-distance riding. In his cycling club alone, the membership has doubled in the past two years and to his knowledge is consistent with a national trend.

Jim feels that all he needs to do is to write a business plan and submit it to his bank to obtain the estimated

Source: This case study was prepared by Michael P. Peters with the intention of providing a basis for class discussion.

$100,000 needed to get started. He is willing to support this by taking out a second mortgage as collateral. Jim feels that he can subcontract the manufacturing of the derailleur and the bicycle separately; then upon receiving the items, he can complete the final installation and fabrication functions before shipping to customers.

Jim's wife Nora is a little skeptical about him leaving a good job for the purpose of fulfilling one of his many fantasies or lifelong dreams. She is the more practical of the two and is concerned about their financial future and the commitment that will be required of Jim in the first few months of the start-up. Taking a second mortgage on the house makes her uncomfortable. She is also not sure Jim is the entrepreneurial type.

In spite of all the concerns, Jim has prepared a business plan that he expects to submit to his banker in the next few days. The business plan consists of six parts: a one-page summary of the plan, a detailed description of his invention, forecasts of growth for the bicycle market, a one-year profit and loss statement, a plan for the manufacturing and final fabrication of the derailleur and bicycle, and an appendix which contains surveys with some of his friends who own ten-speed bikes.

CASE 3
A. MONROE LOCK AND SECURITY SYSTEMS

Ray Monroe was sitting back in his chair in his home office trying to understand why the new venture had not made him the rich man he thought he would be. A. Monroe Lock and Security Systems (AMLSS) had been established about two years ago and offered lock-smithing services to residential and commercial customers as well as automobile owners in the greater Boston area. These services included lock rekeying, lock and deadbolt installation and repair, master key systems, emergency residential lockouts, foreign and domestic automobile lockouts, and window security locks. In addition, AMLSS was certified by the Commonwealth of Massachusetts to perform alarm installation and offered a full range of alarm products.

Financial results have been relatively poor, with losses of $6,500 in the first year and a profit of only about

Source: This case study was prepared by Michael P. Peters with the intention of providing a basis for class discussion.

$3,500 in year 2. Currently, AMLSS's target market is three local communities in the Boston area with similar demographics (see Exhibit 1).

BACKGROUND

Ray Monroe is the only child of parents who were both successful entrepreneurs. His parents are now deceased, and Monroe received a substantial inheritance that would satisfy any of his financial needs for the rest of his life. Ray had been educated at a local private high school and then at a small liberal arts college in Vermont. He was not a great student but always seemed to get by. His summers were usually spent at the college, taking summer courses.

Upon graduation, his father had helped him get a job with a friend who owned a security and alarm manufacturing business in the western part of the state. Ray worked in various areas of the business learning a great deal about alarms and locks. After two years there, Ray decided that he'd prefer to be his own boss and, using some of his inheritance, entered a special program to learn more about the locksmith business. His intent upon completion of the program was to start his own lock and security business. He felt from his experience and education that this market offered tremendous opportunities. Increased crime and residential house sales that often required new locks offered many opportunities to succeed in this business.

Ray did not want to offer alarm installations as part of his new venture since he felt that they were bothersome to install. He also knew that there were many large competitors already in the alarm market that would be able to offer products and service at much lower prices.

INDUSTRY STRUCTURE/COMPETITION

The locksmith industry was dominated by small operators, 60 percent of which consisted of an owner and one employee. Only about 20 percent of these firms had five or more employees.

Because of the low entry barriers, the number of small operators had grown dramatically in the past few years. These businesses were often operated out of the home with no storefront and concentrated mainly on the residential market. There were also a large number of family-owned businesses that usually had a retail store serving their communities for several generations of family members. The larger operators were the most sophisticated in terms of service and products and relied primarily on commercial accounts.

EXHIBIT 1   Demographic Profile of Present Market

Demographics	Newton	Needham	Wellesley
Total population	83,829	28,911	26,613
Total number of households	31,201	19,612	8,594
Percent family	66.7	73.3	76.0
Percent nonfamily	34.3	26.8	24.0
Total number of families	20,486	7,782	6,537
Number of married-couple families	17,209	6,887	5,772
Number of female householder families	2,500	728	607
Average household income	$86,025	$88,079	$113,686
Education			
Percent high school educated	94.5	96.4	97.6%
Percent college or higher educated	68.0	64.9	75.9%
Labor force			
Percent total population employed	66.1	64.9	63.0%
Percent female population employed	62.4	56.4	53.9%
Disability			
Percent with mobility or self-care disability (21–64)	10.4	9.0	6.4%
Percent with mobility or self-care disability (65+)	31.5	28.8	21.8%
Total number of housing units	32,112	10,846	8,861
Median number of rooms	6.4	6.9	7.6
Total number of owner-occupied housing units	21,692	8,587	7,139
Total number of renter-occupied housing units	9,509	2,025	1,455
Retail industry—number of establishments (2000)	595	168	187
Service industry—number of establishments (2000)	1,077	336	1,580

The Boston area was densely populated, with 160 locksmiths all advertising in the area yellow pages. In the three communities on which AMLSS concentrated, there were 37 other locksmiths.

PRESENT STRATEGY

Excluding alarms, Ray offered just about every locksmith service. His company van was used to store these products and any necessary tools for servicing his clients. This company van was 10 years old with a few minor dents, but it ran quite well.

Ray had a beeper system and a cellular phone in order to respond to customer requests. After 5 p.m., however, Ray turned off the system and refused to take calls. During his operating hours he was able to respond to all requests fairly quickly even if he was not in the office,

primarily because of the beeper and cellular phone. He had tried using an answering machine, but it did not allow him to respond to a customer fast enough, especially if he was at a job that kept him out of the office for a number of hours. He also knew that many job requests were emergencies and required a quick response.

During the past year, Ray had decided to advertise in the yellow pages. He felt that with all the locksmiths listed in the yellow pages he needed to be at the top of the list, so he decided to use his middle name initial (for Arthur) to form A. Monroe Locksmith and Security Systems. The yellow pages ad seemed to help business and contributed to the $4,000 profit (see Exhibits 2 and 3 for billing and expenses).

Ray spent a lot of his time in the office thinking of ways to increase his business, yet to this point nothing had been very successful. His understanding was that many

EXHIBIT 2	A. Monroe Monthly Billings for Year Two	
January	$	1,200.01
February		2,260.85
March		2,777.26
April		1,748.62
May		922.20
June		1,414.12
July		1,595.18
August		1,652.37
September		2,264.64
October		2,602.19
November		4,087.37
December		1,905.80
Total		$24,430.61

EXHIBIT 3	Year Two Expenses	
Business expenses		
Selling expenses		$ 9,454
Memberships (chambers of commerce and Associated Locksmiths of America)		2,490
Telephone (includes beeper and cellular)		1,920
Office expenses (materials/supplies)		1,775
Yellow pages		4,200
Other promotional expenses		600
Total expenses		$20,439

of his competitors had found that the yellow pages were the most likely place for customers to find a locksmith. His ad identified the three communities, the services he offered, and a telephone number. In addition, he included that he was bonded and insured and a member of the Massachusetts Locksmith Association. Competitors typically stressed products and services, 24-hour emergency service, follow-up guarantee service, being bonded and insured, and membership in the locksmith association.

Time was running out for Ray, and he was trying to think of other businesses that he could start up. He would often question his decision to enter the locksmith business, but then he would quickly decide that since he didn't really need the money, it wasn't a big deal. However, at some point he felt he should try to

establish himself so he could settle down to a more routine life.

CASE 4
BEIJING SAMMIES

When Sam Goodman opened a new Sammies café in Beijing's Motorola Building, he cut prices by 50 percent for the first three months in order to attract customers. The initial period was very successful, but when he returned prices to normal, sales dropped dramatically and fell short of targets. The local store manager, when presenting the figures, suggested that Goodman simply lower the sales targets. Goodman was frustrated; the manager had failed to address any of the issues that were keeping customers from returning. There were countless orders that went out with missing utensils, in the wrong bag, or [with items] simply left out. Delivery orders were being sent hours late or to the wrong location. This typified Goodman's early experience; the market was showing interest in Beijing Sammies's products but he knew that without exceptional service, good food would not be enough. Goodman questioned whether he could find employees who were thinkers and problem solvers and he wondered how to improve upon the business in order to turn Beijing Sammies into a sustainable and profitable enterprise.

According to Goodman, face and money were the two most important subjects. With experience as a student and businessman in China, he knew one must observe the cultural beliefs:

> Face is a huge issue here, and as the economy develops, so is money. If one is not relevant, the other is. Once you recognize this is crucial, it was not hard to learn. The difficult part is incorporating it into the business. We need to offer a superior experience in order for customers to justify paying more. This means providing a quality product with excellent service. It sounds easy, but in China the concept of service is not the same as in

Source: This case was prepared by Christopher Ferrarone under the supervision of Boston College Professor Gregory L. Stoller as the basis for class discussion rather than to illustrate either effective or ineffective handling of an administrative situation.

the West. I just can't seem to get my employees to understand that there is a way to serve the customer while also keeping the company's interest at heart. It is an, "all for us" or "all for them" mentality here.

Throughout the company's initial years Goodman sought to teach a service-oriented approach to his employees. In doing so, he ironically learned that face was as much of an important issue for Beijing Sammies's customers as it was for its employees.

BEIJING SAMMIES

Canadian native, Sam Goodman, started Beijing Sammies[1] in 1997. Aside from producing food for the everyday, walk-in customer, Sammies provided fare for company meetings, presentations, picnics, and gifts. Sammies was open for breakfast, lunch, and dinner and delivered all products to its customers. The menu included a selection of sandwiches, salads, bagels, brownies, cookies, coffee, soda, and tea (Exhibit 1).

Goodman started the company with personal savings and money borrowed from family. He opened his first café at the Beijing Language and Culture University with the goal of providing people with a place to "hang out" and enjoy homemade western food.

By 2003 Beijing Sammies had five outlets [composed] of four "deli-style" cafés and one kiosk. The stores were traditional in terms of layout and size for fast food restaurants. Two Sammies cafés were 1,200 square feet, and the other two were roughly 800 square feet each, while the kiosk was a stand-alone structure with open seating inside the lobby of a corporate building. All of the café locations had enclosed seating that was maximized, as there was no need for self-contained kitchens.

The Central Kitchen

Goodman found that revenues of the first café were driven as much by corporate delivery orders as they were by the local walk-in customers. This motivated Goodman to open more cafés and a centralized kitchen in 1998. Located in Beijing's Chao Yang District, the kitchen ran from 10 p.m. to 5:30 a.m. each day making the sandwiches and baked goods for all of Sammies's locations. Between 5:30 and 6 a.m., trucks delivered the goods from the kitchen to each Sammies outlet. No cooking was done at any of the Sammies locations. Every sandwich, cookie, and muffin was prepared, baked, and packaged centrally. Only coffee and smoothies were prepared onsite at individual retail cafés.

While the central kitchen created a number of efficiencies for Beijing Sammies, what Goodman liked even more was the quality control that it provided:

It is much easier for me to teach the kitchen staff how to make the food correctly than it is to teach all of the employees at each location. At the kitchen I can make sure that the product going out to all of the stores is consistent. In the end that's what I am striving for, to offer a consistently great product with superior service. Only having one kitchen to manage makes this task much easier.

The central kitchen not only provided Beijing Sammies with efficiencies with ingredients, machines, and manpower, but also allowed for larger customer capacity at each café location and enabled the employees to uniquely focus on customer service.

THE SAMMIE

The idea behind Beijing Sammies originated from Goodman. Moving to Hong Kong after college and subsequently moving to Beijing to attend Beijing Language and Culture University, Goodman yearned for a place to hang out and eat a traditional sandwich or "sammie" that reminded him of home. Three years later Beijing Sammies was named Beijing's #1 western food delivery service by *City Weekend* magazine.

Modeled after Goodman's version of a New York deli, Beijing Sammies's staple is the "sammie." Each sammie started with homemade bread made every night at Sammies's kitchen. Customers could order from a menu of standard sammies or could create their own. Goodman found the pre-set menu best for the local customers, while many foreigners frequently customized their sandwich:

Having a menu of pre-crafted sandwiches is a necessity. Many of the Chinese customers simply do not know how to order. They do not understand the notion of selecting different types of deli meats and condiments for a sandwich. I didn't even think about this at first. Personally, I know exactly what goes with roast beef and what goes with turkey.

When we opened our first location many people came in and left without ordering. They didn't know how, and did not want to look foolish ordering something inappropriate. Many times, and this still happens, people come in and just order whatever the person in front of them ordered. Putting complete sandwiches together allows the inexperienced customer to come in and feel more comfortable about ordering.

Creating pre-made selections of sandwiches worked so well for Sammies that Goodman put together an

EXHIBIT 1

Ordering Information

Min Order:

PEAK HOURS: 100rmb	(Mon–Fri:10:30–13:30)
OTHER HOURS: 50rmb	

Orders under 50 rmb: add 20 rmb service charge

Free delivery within Chao Yang CBD

Delivery takes 30–45 minutes during rush hours

For large orders or special time deliveries please call 1 day in advance

Save Your Company Time & Money

Sammies Corporate Accounts

Convenience & Flexibility in Payment, Ordering & Delivery

Sammies is a healthy alternative for your

Meetings ○ Seminars ○ Training Sessions

We provide menu suggestions.

For more information, special requests or comments please call Customer Service: English and Chinese service

6506 8838
www.beijingsammies.com

All prices subject to change.

Ingredients may change due to availability and freshness

Where East Eats West

CORPORATE DELIVERY

Monday – Friday:	8:00 a.m.–9:00 p.m.
Saturday – Sunday:	9:00 a.m.–7:00 p.m.

TEL: 6506 8838   FAX: 6503 2688

Online Ordering: www.beijingsammies.com

Breakfast & Lunch Meetings ○ Training Sessions

Where East Eats West

(Continued)

EXHIBIT 1 (Continued)

Bakery Bundles

Sammies selection of freshly baked goods, great for any occasion: meetings, boosting staff morale, customer gifts, picnics or parties. Guaranteed to bring a smile to anyone's face.

Muffin Madness A satisfying breakfast or afternoon treat! Includes all 6 varieties of Sammies' original recipe muffins. 18 small ···· 55

Cookie Monster Sammies' freshly baked, original recipe cookies! Includes Chocolate Chunk, Double Chocolate and Oatmeal Raisin. 18 regular ····· 55

The Bagel Bag Baked fresh everyday. Plain, Sesame & Cinnamon Raisin (2 of each) whole or cut in half, served with cream cheese (140g), strawberry preserves (70g) and butter ····· 40

W.O.F.E (Warm Oven Fresh Eats) For meetings, after lunch, or anytime of the day, this box suits all tastes! Includes 2 Brownies(cut into 1/4), 8 mini-muffins, 6 regular cookies and 2 Biscottis ····· 65

Box Lunches

Great for meetings, bus tours, travelling, picnics and parties !

Classic Box ····· 40
Your choice of sammie
Potato Chips
Lg. Chocolate Chunk Cookie

Health Box ····· 40
Your choice of sammie
Veggies & Dip
Lg. Oatmeal Raisin Cookie

Sammie Packs

When ease and efficiency are the names of the game, these packs hit the spot. No need to ask everyone what they want, variety will take care of that. Sammies are cut into 1/4's for convenience.

GOOD FOR 6~8 PERSONS, EACH PACK COMES WITH VEGGIES N' DIP.

Predator Pack
For meat lovers with healthy appetites! Dante's Inferno, Classic Grilled Chicken and Frankenstein. (2 of each) ····· 160

Classic Favorites
Deliciously simple and filling! Classic Turkey, Ham n' Cheese and Poseidon's Pleasure. (2 of each) ····· 160

The Conglomerate
An assortment to suit all! Classic Roast Beef, Funky Chicken, Turkey Shoot, Homestead, Poseidon's Pleasure, Garden Special ····· 160

Vegetarian
Healthy and loaded with taste! Poseidon's Pleasure, Early Bird, and Veggies n' Cheese (2 of each) ····· 150

EXHIBIT 2 Beijing Sammies Introductory E-mail

OUR NEW SILK ALLEY SAMMIES CAFE IS ALSO OPEN!

Drop on by to enjoy some of your Sammies favorites . . . and more!

- Enjoy our wider breakfast selection
- Choose from café beverages and goodies
- Select from smoothies, espresso, cappuccinos, and our selection of baked goods
- Warm, inviting café atmosphere—whether you're networking, on a date, getting a meal-to-go or getting social, Sammies Xiu Shui Jie café is the place to be!

Located at the Silk Alley/Xiu Shui Jie south entrance on Chang An Jie, in the Chaoyang District; open every day from 07:30 to 24:00.

WHERE EAST EATS WEST

---

*THANKS FOR REGISTERING! NOW YOU CAN ORDER ALL YOUR SAMMIES FAVORITES THROUGH THE WEB!

Browse online and order our delicious Sammies sandwiches, salads, baked goods including muffins, cookies, brownies, biscotti, and bagels. Great for business meetings, social events, breakfast, lunch, or dinner! Registration allows you to enjoy the following:

SAVE TIME

One-time registration of delivery information—no need to re-explain your contact info at every order. Just log in, order, and then submit for successful delivery every time you come to the Web site.

SAVE MONEY

Bonus points for future discounts—sign up and receive bonus points based on every RMB you order, which you can redeem for future discounts and Sammies products.

IMPROVED EFFICIENCY

Online ordering and delivery—order directly from our Web site menu and we'll deliver to you!

CUSTOM-MADE ORDERS

Customize your Sammies, and track your orders with our new menu and online ordering interface.

RE-ORDER YOUR FAVORITES

Quick ordering of your favorite Sammies items—registered users can re-order from a recorded list of past favorite orders.

ORDER 24 HOURS A DAY

Order hours or days in advance.

Questions? Please e-mail our helpful customer service staff at beijingsammies@yahoo.com. Tell a friend to visit us at www.beijingsammies.com.

"Ordering Tips" section on the menu. The section not only suggested what types of products to order for breakfast and what products to buy for lunch, but also provided a guide for corporate clients to ensure correct portions and variety for meetings. In addition, Sammies trained sales clerks to act as customer service representatives who could assist both the walk-in client and a growing base of corporate delivery clients with their orders.

Corporate Clients and Sammies Rewards

As Beijing Sammies realized a growing corporate delivery base, Goodman adapted the model to provide the business client with as much flexibility and customization as possible. Sammies set up corporate accounts, online ordering, flexible payment options, and a rewards program.

Corporate customers who registered with Beijing Sammies could choose weekly or monthly payment

EXHIBIT 3   Corporate Clients

- Nokia China Investment
- U.S.A. Embassy
- Canada Embassy
- Intel PRC, Corp.
- Boeing
- AEA SOS
- American Chamber of Commerce
- Agilent
- Andersen Consulting
- Australia Embassy
- APCO Associates Inc.
- Benz
- Ford Foundation
- Henkel
- Hewlett-Packard
- IBM China Ltd.
- Motorola China Electronics, Ltd.
- Western Academy of Beijing
- Reuters

terms whereby Beijing Sammies would send out itemized statements and invoices. Clients could choose to set up a debit account as well. Under the debit account, clients prepaid a certain amount (usually a minimum of RMB1000*) that was credited to an account and deducted each time an order was placed.

Along with the flexible payment options, corporate customers could become enrolled in the Bonus Points program, which offered credits based on the frequency and size of orders. Customers who spent between RMB500 and 750 received an RMB50 credit, orders between RMB750 and 1000 an RMB75 credit, and orders over RMB1000 are given an RMB100 credit. Furthermore, each time a client cumulatively spent over RMB5000, they were rewarded with an RMB500 credit. All of this could be done over the Beijing Sammies Web site, www.beijingsammies.com, where customers could log in and manage their account (Exhibit 2).

The Bonus Points program was offered to the walk-in customer as well. Customers who registered with Beijing Sammies online could become enrolled in the program. Every registered customer received a point for each RMB

*Note: Conversion rate is: RMB8.3 = $1.

they spent. Every 10 points could be redeemed for 1 RMB off the next order. Extra points could be received for filling out surveys, referring new customers, or attending selected special events. The point system was well received by Beijing Sammies's customers and contributed to a solid base of returning foreign clients (Exhibit 3).

Charity Sponsorship

Beijing Sammies served large numbers of foreigners, and consequently, Goodman felt a strong responsibility to sponsor charity, youth, and community events focused around the ex-pat community in Beijing:

> The Canadian community in Beijing and around China in general is pretty strong. As a foreign student here I really appreciated the sense of kinship that I felt even though I was far away from home. In addition, the foreign businesses and tourists have been very supporting of Beijing Sammies so I really enjoy and feel compelled to participate in the community's events.

Along with providing snacks and food, Beijing Sammies helped certain organizations by allowing promotional and ticket sale efforts to be staged from Sammies's locations. Sammies's sponsorship events included:

- Special Olympics
- Canadian Day and Independence Day
- Sporting and school events held by the Western Academy of Beijing and The International School of Beijing
- Annual Terry Fox Run for Cancer
- ACBC Baseball Events

SAMMIES'S EVOLUTION

Starting out with $25,000 borrowed from friends and family back in Canada, Goodman opened Beijing's first sandwich shop. In order to more easily get past the bureaucracy involved with opening the café, Goodman located a Chinese partner. After an initial four months of business, Beijing Sammies was a hit. The store was so successful that the new partner attempted to strong-arm Goodman out of the company by locking him out. In response, Goodman rallied some friends and broke into the shop one night and removed the appliances and supplies. The partner agreed to be bought out.

Soon after Goodman regained control, his landlord disappeared. The government demanded the tenants cover his back taxes. When they could not, it demolished

EXHIBIT 4

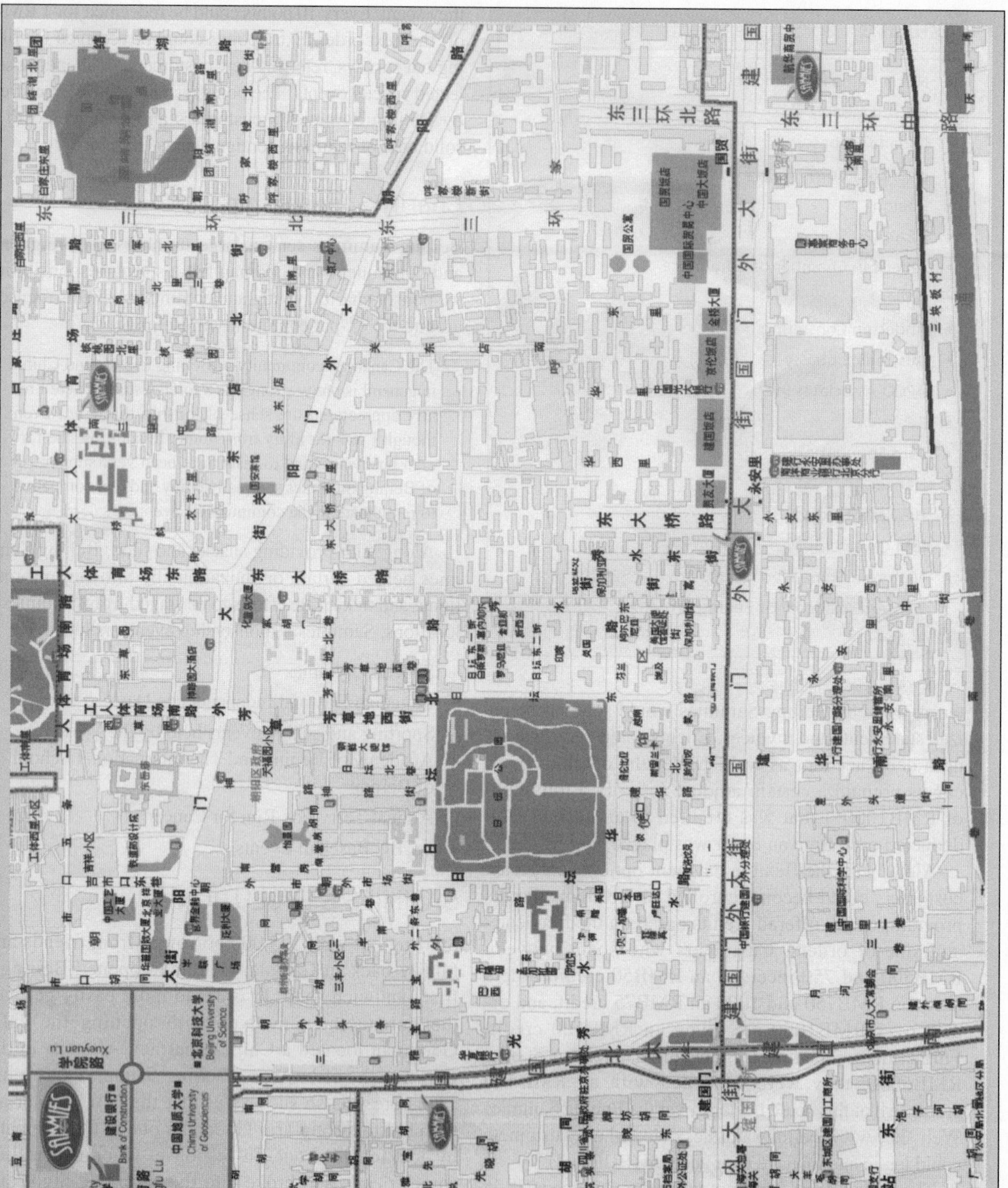
Beijing Languages and Culture University
北京语言文化大学
成府路
Chengfu Lu
学院路
Xueyuan Lu
建设银行
Bank of Construction
中国地质大学
China University of Geosciences
北京科技大学
Beijing University of Science
N

the whole row and left the tenants with the bricks. Goodman was able to sell them for $25.

Goodman responded by opening a café at the Beijing Language and Culture University. Again, Sammies opened to a steady stream of customers, particularly from foreign students and local corporations.

In 1998, after realizing success with the first café in its newfound location, Goodman found another business partner. Together they planned to invest $350,000 more into Beijing Sammies. The next step was to build a centralized kitchen and add more café locations. Soon after construction started, however, the funds supposedly coming from the newfound business partner quickly dried up and Goodman was left financing the new kitchen on his own.

At the end of 1998, Sammies had a central kitchen with great capacity but no new store locations to deliver to. Goodman was able to generate yet another round of financing. With some western investment and all of the profits from his previous two years in business, Goodman was able to put $150,000 together and open three new cafés.

In addition to the first café located at Beijing Language and Culture University, Sammies cafés were opened between 1998 and 2001 at the Silk Alley Market, 1/F Exchange Beijing, and The Motorola Building. A Sammies kiosk was also opened at the China Resource Building (Exhibit 4). The expansion allowed Goodman to more adequately serve the Beijing area while also firmly establishing Beijing Sammies in an increasingly competitive environment:

> Overall, I see the expansion into multiple cafés as a success. Two of the cafés are doing well while the two others have not met sales targets yet. The kiosk, because of less rent, is doing moderately well but is still not as busy as I'd like it to be. 2002 looks to be our best year to date with a revenue increase of 54%, and an operating profit of $20,000. However, due to the fact that the central kitchen is its own cost center, we will record a $24,000 loss (including depreciation). 2003 should show our first profits.

By the end of 2001, Beijing Sammies was recording monthly revenues over RMB500,000 and by 2003, the company had recorded positive net income in certain months (Exhibit 5).

COMPETITION

The economic expansion of the late 1990s dramatically changed dining in Beijing. Private establishments that catered to China's emerging middle class replaced old state-run restaurants. Most traditional meals were under $5 per person. Peking duck and other local specialties were the most popular, but new restaurants opened that offered regional tastes from all around Asia. Additionally, the number of western-style restaurants targeting tourists, expatriates, and younger, trendy Chinese customers increased.

Sam Goodman viewed all restaurants physically close to Sammies as competitors:

> As far as I'm concerned, everyone in Beijing who orders lunch is a potential customer and every restaurant serving it is a competitor. There are those who stick to the traditional Chinese meal, but who is to say that they will never try Sammies?
>
> I do not want to restrict Sammies to serving just western businesses or students. We are delivering not only to western businesses but to traditional Chinese companies as well. While we rely on western students for our walk-in business, we do have Chinese customers who come to Sammies every day. There are others who only come once in a while. These people go to the Chinese restaurants when they don't come here, so I must think broadly in terms of whom my customers are and who my competition is. Of course the western restaurants like McDonald's, Subway, Schlotzskys, and Starbucks are the most obvious competitors. Competition in this business is day-to-day as people rarely eat lunch at the same location each afternoon.

Like most major cities, Beijing had an array of restaurant choices ranging from traditional Chinese to Mexican, German, Scandinavian, Italian, Swiss, and English Continental.

THE GREAT WALL OF CHINA

As Beijing Sammies adapted to the competitive environment, Goodman increasingly turned to the delivery business for revenue. But the model did not work as planned, due to the lack of experience Goodman had in delivery logistics. Corporate clients were more demanding and lunch delivery complicated. Goodman states:

> We started out delivering from a central source. At first, things did not go as planned. Quite frankly, I was an inexperienced manager and made quite a few mistakes. The delivery model here in China is very different from the West. Clients have no understanding of what goes on behind the scenes, and they do not understand that it is nearly impossible for us to take a large delivery order for a corporate luncheon and bring it to them ten minutes later. I didn't plan for all of the possible problems

EXHIBIT 5   Income Statement

Beijing Sammies	Kitchen Office	Kitchen Production	Kitchen Delivery	Kitchen Café
Revenue			2,007,921.19	
Cost of Goods Sold	17,886.73		641,106.51	
Gross Profit	−17,886.73		1,366,814.68	
Gross Margin			68.07%	
Taxes	8,983.00		99,884.24	
Salary	583,260.12	308,911.56	267,225.53	
Insurance	57,067.01	24,131.97		
Rent Related	185,246.10	102,917.10	82,331.60	41,165.80
Utilities	38,075.39	41,237.04	22,891.23	2,531.10
Office Expenses	131,989.31	445.38	5,750.55	
Marketing/Advertising	29,687.74		25,129.00	
Transportation	37,798.57	256.75	20,545.85	
Maintenance	68,965.65	6,357.00	1,560.00	
Entertainment	16,660.54	1,033.50	2,388.10	
Law & Other Expenses	47,623.29			
Bank Charges	−91.60			
Others	1,238.08	5,987.22	10,414.69	
HR	8,580.00			
Legal/Gov't Charge	33,566.00			
Low-Cost and Short-Lived Articles	14,581.58	21,594.56	4,869.28	
CK Service Fee	−327,302.43		100,396.06	
Total Expenses	935,928.34	512,872.07	643,386.13	43,696.90
Gross Income	−953,815.07	−512,872.07	723,428.55	−43,696.90
Amortization Pre-Operating Costs	154,683.52			
Amortization-Renovations	71,500.00			
Depreciation Expense	49,392.72	144,283.10	2,296.71	
Total	275,576.24	144,283.10	2,296.71	0.00
Net Income	−1,229,391.31	−657,155.17	721,131.84	−43,696.90

*Note: Exhibit 5 amounts are in Chinese Renminbi.

that a different culture would bring. I should have put more effort and time into educating the customer about the product. This definitely had a negative impact on the business at first.

In addition to overcoming the existing perceptions and expectations of the customer, Goodman learned about the prevailing attitude of the employees. One of his biggest challenges was not securing the hard-to-come-by ingredients, dealing with the local government, or raising capital, but rather teaching his employees the concept of service. For many of Beijing Sammies's employees, service was little

BY Café	SA Café	CR Café	EB Café	2002YTD		
				RMB	USD	
					0.120479942	conversion factor
1,562,707.90	2,413,590.26	253,667.83	308,161.39	6,546,048.56	788,667.55	
458,643.00	660,387.10	85,284.58	116,182.07	1,979,489.98	238,488.84	
1,104,064.90	1,753,203.15	168,383.25	191,979.32	4,566,558.58	550,178.71	
70.65%	72.64%	66.38%	62.30%	69.76%	69.76%	
26,129.18	126,258.34	8,716.06	15,408.20	285,379.02	34,382.45	
295,125.60	280,945.80	43,670.25	90,302.94	1,869,441.80	225,230.24	
12,160.29	6,641.12	2,151.96	0.00	102,152.34	12,307.31	
104,000.00	585,000.00	28,199.80	85,322.84	1,214,183.23	146,284.73	
45,492.79	7,103.90	7,587.91	6,598.31	171,517.66	20,664.44	
4,298.84	14,296.32	3,451.76	17,737.90	177,970.07	21,441.82	
18,306.60	41,151.07	17,203.88	43,155.50	174,633.78	21,039.87	
4,286.23	743.60	0.00	237.90	63,868.90	7,694.92	
12,139.01	21,128.90	1,843.40	1,625.00	113,618.96	13,688.81	
6,477.25	1,123.20	0.00	789.10	28,471.69	3,430.27	
	0.00	0.00	0.00	47,623.29	5,737.65	
	−103.48	7.15	39.00	−148.93	−17.94	
6,236.88	4,112.19	250.76	43.63	28,283.44	3,407.59	
	0.00	0.00	0.00	8,580.00	1,033.72	
	533.00	0.00	0.00	34,099.00	4,108.25	
5,411.90	2,859.58	0.00	13,277.94	62,594.84	7,541.42	
78,135.40	120,679.51	12,683.40	15,408.07	0.00	0.00	
618,199.96	1,212,473.04	125,766.30	289,946.32	4,382,269.07	527,975.52	
485,864.94	540,730.11	42,616.95	−97,967.00	184,289.51	22,203.19	
			15,468.34	154,683.36	18,636.24	
			16,300.87	92,852.02	11,186.81	
16,088.84	10,502.70	11,881.35	24,125.41	241,254.13	29,066.28	
16,088.84	10,502.70	11,881.35	55,894.62	488,789.51	58,889.33	
469,776.10	530,227.41	30,735.60	−153,861.62	−304,500.00	−36,686.14	

more than opening the store in the morning and closing it at night. To Goodman, service was much more. It was what he believed would differentiate Beijing Sammies from the other western food establishments, and what would cause the traditional Chinese consumer to pay more money for lunch. Service was not only delivering the product on time, with the correct number of forks and knives, but was also helping the customer to understand the product. According to Goodman:

> For most of my employees it doesn't matter "how" you get things done—it just matters that you get the end result. The concept of face for them manifests itself with the feeling that appearance is much more important than the service or quality of the product. While for the customer, the service provided by us is part of the final product.

EXHIBIT 5   Income Statement (Continued)

Beijing Sammies	Jan-02	Feb-02	Mar-02	Apr-02	May-02	Jun-02
Revenue	474,490.19	340,345.07	633,584.38	636,305.41	714,801.13	768,954.55
Cost of Goods Sold	116,310.43	112,891.03	209,662.56	221,218.57	185,420.17	221,374.62
Gross Profit	358,179.76	227,454.05	423,921.82	415,086.84	529,380.96	547,579.93
Gross Margin	75.49%	66.83%	66.91%	65.23%	74.06%	71.21%
Taxes	21,449.26	15,003.20	21,514.52	21,744.06	31,754.91	24,373.65
Salary	195,127.49	200,044.95	179,709.69	197,527.25	172,055.86	208,886.93
Insurance	9,027.64	8,697.01	10,910.74	10,991.92	7,642.39	10,484.72
Rent Related	118,045.59	118,045.53	118,045.66	118,045.92	118,046.11	112,665.80
Utilities	14,993.68	20,974.36	13,872.64	13,989.55	14,436.11	18,413.58
Office Expenses	7,002.19	9,775.81	10,184.63	15,715.78	23,112.66	15,346.73
Marketing/Advertising	2,080.00	8,476.00	5,473.00	7,670.00	17,500.60	24,986.00
Transportation	3,458.00	1,738.10	4,951.70	3,695.64	4,497.74	11,303.50
Maintenance	7,800.00	5,281.25	309.40	4,564.30	6,630.00	38,958.40
Entertainment	3,216.20	6,073.60	3,313.70	2,471.30	852.80	4,378.14
Law & Other Expenses	1,798.33	1,798.33	6,998.33	1,798.33	14,798.33	1,798.33
Bank Charges	104.00	78.00	−379.54	−13.17	163.15	−425.63
Others	845.00	234.00	7,179.64	4,312.10	0.00	3,208.14
HR	650.00	975.00	4,615.00	0.00	975.00	0.00
Legal/Gov't Charge	1,950.00	1,950.00	16,016.00	1,950.00	1,950.00	2,483.00
Low-Cost and Short-Lived Articles	2,171.00	1,295.84	3,055.00	10,031.27	10,522.07	5,995.31
Total Expenses	389,718.38	400,440.96	405,770.11	414,494.24	424,937.72	482,856.60
Gross Income	−31,538.62	−172,986.92	18,151.72	592.60	104,443.24	64,723.33
Amortization Pre-Operating Costs	15,468.34	15,468.34	15,468.34	15,468.34	15,468.34	15,468.34
Amortization-Renovations	7,150.00	7,150.00	7,150.00	7,150.00	7,150.00	7,150.00
Depreciation Expense	24,125.41	24,125.41	24,125.41	24,125.41	24,125.41	24,125.41
Total	46,743.75	46,743.75	46,743.75	46,743.75	46,743.75	46,743.75
Net Income	−78,282.37	−219,730.67	−28,592.03	−46,151.14	57,699.49	17,979.58
Cumulative Net Income	−78,282.37	−298,013.04	−326,605.07	−372,756.22	−315,056.73	−297,077.14

Jul-02	Aug-02	Sep-02	Oct-02	2002YTD	
				RMB	USD
					0.120479942 conversion factor
819,787.15	743,912.26	659,126.31	754,742.12	6,546,048.56	788,667.55
271,224.40	216,298.58	210,682.54	214,407.10	1,979,489.98	238,488.84
548,562.76	527,613.68	448,443.78	540,335.02	4,566,558.58	550,178.71
66.92%	70.92%	68.04%	71.59%	69.76%	69.76%
42,118.17	32,275.32	25,169.18	49,976.76	285,379.02	34,382.45
151,037.11	172,597.30	181,573.80	210,881.44	1,869,441.80	225,230.24
12,577.94	10,606.44	10,606.44	10,607.09	102,152.34	12,307.31
99,665.80	124,581.20	142,870.82	144,170.82	1,214,183.23	146,284.73
16,504.80	14,210.99	19,398.47	24,723.49	171,517.66	20,664.44
21,650.58	29,671.43	33,736.55	11,773.71	177,970.07	21,441.82
23,403.09	33,382.75	24,166.45	27,495.88	174,633.78	21,039.87
5,270.98	18,112.15	5,557.37	5,283.72	63,868.90	7,694.92
26,887.90	9,034.61	7,272.20	6,880.90	113,618.96	13,688.81
546.00	461.50	4,406.35	2,752.10	28,471.69	3,430.27
8,038.33	6,998.33	1,798.33	1,798.33	47,623.29	5,737.65
176.80	117.00	9.36	21.10	−148.93	−17.94
3,867.12	3,606.10	1,757.47	3,273.87	28,283.44	3,407.59
0.00	0.00	0.00	1,365.00	8,580.00	1,033.72
1,950.00	1,950.00	1,950.00	1,950.00	34,099.00	4,108.25
3,622.32	20,954.62	3,919.89	1,027.00	62,594.32	7,541.36
417,316.94	478,559.73	464,192.68	503,981.21	4,382,268.55	527,975.46
131,245.82	49,053.95	−15,748.90	36,353.61	184,290.03	22,203.25
15,468.34	15,468.34	15,468.34	15,468.34	154,683.36	18,636.24
7,150.00	16,300.87	13,250.58	13,250.58	92,852.02	11,186.81
24,125.41	24,125.41	24,125.41	24,125.41	241,254.13	29,066.28
46,743.75	55,894.62	52,844.32	52,844.32	488,789.51	58,889.33
84,502.07	−6,840.67	−68,593.23	−16,490.51	−304,499.48	−36,686.08
−212,575.08	−219,415.74	−288,008.97	−304,499.48		

EXHIBIT 5   Income Statement (Continued)

2001–2002 Comparison

Beijing Sammies		Jan	Feb	Mar	Apr	May	Jun	Jul	Aug	Sep
Revenues-Total										
	2002	474,490	340,345	633,584	636,305	714,801	768,955	819,787	743,912	659,126
	2001	195,360	221,729	273,194	322,826	360,585	487,627	485,567	479,232	495,706
Revenues-CD										
	2002	125,663	101,290	209,557	173,213	226,170	269,890	360,783	338,797	92,303
	2001	118,331	167,267	157,382	190,320	164,654	161,971	153,994	142,709	136,926
Revenues-BY										
	2002	150,800	55,375	173,870	202,190	213,181	245,040	86,393	20,944	191,542
	2001	77,029	54,462	115,812	132,506	122,457	161,166	130,244	112,095	136,210
Revenues-SA										
	2002	171,306	166,733	221,391	231,774	255,840	229,739	286,696	260,326	273,640
	2001	0	0	0	0	73,473	164,492	172,101	197,597	197,532
Revenues-CR										
	2002	26,722	16,949	28,768	29,128	19,612	24,287	28,860	26,354	27,414
	2001	0	0	0	0	0	0	29,229	26,832	23,036
Gross Profit										
	2002	358,180	227,454	423,922	415,087	529,381	547,580	548,563	527,614	448,444
	2001	136,161	155,046	181,279	216,507	243,420	334,135	340,288	353,393	340,074
Total Expenses										
	2002	389,718	400,442	405,770	414,495	424,938	482,856	415,874	478,560	439,563
	2001	199,170	212,702	203,262	204,741	292,468	293,136	271,625	318,711	367,199
Salary										
	2002	195,127	200,045	179,710	197,527	172,056	208,887	151,037	172,597	181,574
	2001	130,803	135,100	123,547	123,572	136,526	141,993	143,111	165,208	161,795
Rent Related										
	2002	118,046	118,046	118,046	118,046	118,046	112,666	99,666	124,581	142,871
	2001	36,833	36,833	36,833	36,833	93,180	93,180	71,500	71,500	112,666
Insurance										
	2002	9,028	8,697	10,911	10,992	7,642	10,485	12,578	10,606	10,606
	2001	0	0	0	260	0	3,894	5,203	6,003	4,694
Utilities										
	2002	14,994	20,974	13,873	13,990	14,436	18,414	16,505	14,211	19,398
	2001	11,239	13,459	7,232	8,932	11,063	11,041	13,607	16,717	24,505
Office Expenses										
	2002	7,002	9,776	10,185	15,716	23,113	15,347	21,651	29,671	33,737
	2001	5,437	4,486	5,652	7,899	9,877	9,994	8,281	12,463	9,611
Marketing/Advertising										
	2002	2,080	8,476	5,473	7,670	17,501	24,986	23,403	33,383	24,166
	2001	1,950	7,150	2,842	3,900	19,682	17,508	6,838	14,598	9,460
Transportation										
	2002	3,458	1,738	4,952	3,696	4,498	11,304	5,271	18,112	5,557
	2001	1,158	1,131	2,298	2,662	2,989	1,219	2,428	2,522	2,510
Maintenance										
	2002	7,800	5,281	309	4,564	6,630	38,958	26,888	9,035	7,272
	2001	735	371	3,785	1,707	98	1,110	1,365	1,754	1,252
Entertainment										
	2002	3,216	6,074	3,314	2,471	853	4,378	546	462	4,406
	2001	0	520	4,976	5,881	2,896	0	1,123	255	12,332
Law & Other Expenses										
	2002	3,748	3,748	23,014	3,748	16,748	4,281	9,988	8,948	3,748
	2001	3,613	6,500	6,500	2,665	3,848	0	867	4,767	6,136
Taxes										
	2002	21,384	15,003	21,515	21,744	31,755	24,374	42,119	32,275	25,169
	2001	6,871	5,950	8,639	8,813	6,360	6,163	13,657	15,219	16,592

	Oct	Nov	Dec	Total	Average	%	Total USD	Average USD	
									0.12048 conversion factor
	754,742	0	0	6,546,049	654,605	32.94%	788,668	78,867	
	501,579	565,923	534,743	4,924,071	410,339		593,252	49,438	
	110,257	0	0	2,007,923	200,792	12.52%	241,914	24,191	
	111,007	146,241	131,628	1,784,429	148,702		214,988	17,916	
	223,374	0	0	1,562,708	156,271	1.18%	188,275	18,827	
	155,964	173,991	172,487	1,544,423	128,702		186,072	15,506	
	316,147	0	0	2,413,592	241,359	66.65%	290,789	29,079	
	216,702	221,035	205,347	1,448,279	193,104		174,489	23,265	
	25,579	0	0	253,672	25,367	72.63%	30,562	3,056	
	17,908	24,656	25,284	146,944	24,491		17,704	2,951	
	540,335	0	0	4,566,559	456,656	33.45%	550,179	55,018	
	360,762	406,459	354,387	3,421,909	285,159		412,271	34,356	
	503,981	0	0	4,356,196	435,620	25.44%	524,834	52,483	
	358,769	367,961	383,097	3,472,840	289,403		418,408	34,567	
	210,881	0	0	1,869,442	186,944	5.67%	225,230	22,523	
	163,081	169,485	174,984	1,769,204	147,434		213,154	17,763	
	144,171	0	0	1,214,183	121,418	28.69%	146,285	14,628	
	118,045	118,048	118,047	943,497	78,625		113,672	9,473	
	10,507	0	0	102,152	10,215	174.55%	12,307	1,231	
	6,516	5,049	5,589	37,207	3,101		4,483	374	
	24,723	0	0	171,518	17,152	−0.10%	20,664	2,066	
	18,764	17,195	17,936	171,690	14,307		20,685	1,724	
	11,774	0	0	177,970	17,797	63.35%	21,442	2,144	
	10,245	10,773	14,229	108,948	9,079		13,126	1,094	
	27,496	0	0	174,634	17,463	42.87%	21,040	2,104	
	9,494	17,076	11,736	122,234	10,186		14,727	1,227	
	5,284	0	0	63,869	6,387	149.15%	7,695	769	
	2,626	1,651	2,439	25,635	2,136		3,088	257	
	6,881	0	0	113,619	11,362	588.67%	13,689	1,369	
	1,273	681	2,366	16,498	1,375		1,988	166	
	2,752	0	0	28,472	2,847	−13.33%	3,430	343	
	372	759	3,738	32,852	2,738		3,958	330	
	3,748	0	0	81,718	8,172	123.09%	9,845	985	
	867	867	0	36,630	3,053		4,413	368	
	49,977	0	0	285,315	28,531	83.43%	34,375	3,437	
	25,346	16,892	25,046	155,546	12,962		18,740	1,562	

EXHIBIT 5 Income Statement *(Continued)*

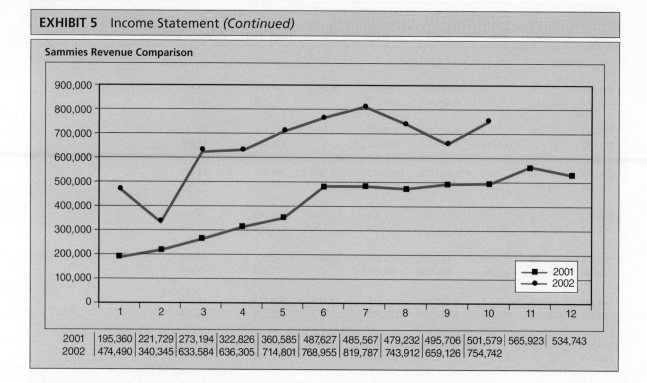

Sammies Revenue Comparison

2001	195,360	221,729	273,194	322,826	360,585	487,627	485,567	479,232	495,706	501,579	565,923	534,743
2002	474,490	340,345	633,584	636,305	714,801	768,955	819,787	743,912	659,126	754,742		

Just as the client base did not understand the wait for a delivery, the employee did not understand the product that Beijing Sammies was trying to sell:

> The staff does not understand the urgency needed in running a service-oriented business. The whole concept of service is new in China. The business traditions are very strong here. I don't know if it's because of the issue of face and pride, the political history, or something else, but our employees have a very difficult time understanding how we need to deliver service as much as we need to deliver a sandwich.

For Sam Goodman, the initial years of operation proved that Beijing Sammies could hold a niche. While he was pleased to see Beijing Sammies growing toward profitability, he was concerned about whether it could ever become cash-flow positive, and if so, whether he could sustain it. In addition, Goodman was no closer to finding the type of employee who would adopt his concept of service than he was when he started and wondered if the answer lay in increased automation, training, or somewhere else.

END NOTES

1. Beijing Sammies is the name of the entire company, while "a Sammies" is a particular café.

CASE 5
INTELLIGENT LEISURE SOLUTIONS

INTRODUCTION

Intelligent Leisure Solutions (ILS) is a group of five companies based in Brazil working to create, implement, and manage intelligent solutions. As a completely technology-based solutions company, ILS is unique in its approach to travel, real estate, technology, and sustainable tourism. With high growth in the tourism industry, Intelligent Leisure Solutions' founding entrepreneur, Robert Phillips, is working to find the most appropriate, innovative growth strategy for expansion and sustainability of the business.

GEOGRAPHIC BACKGROUND

Brazil is located on the Atlantic Coast of South America with a slightly smaller geographic area than the United States (see Exhibit 1). With the fifth largest country

Source: This case study was prepared by Robert D. Hisrich and Cristina Ricaurte with the intention of providing a basis for class discussion. It was previously published in Robert D. Hisrich, *International Entrepreneurship,* 2nd edition, SAGE, 2013, pp 255–276.

EXHIBIT 1 Map of Brazil

Source: CIA (2010).

population in the world, it is home to more than 200 million people. Brazil's economy is larger than that of all other South American countries, characterized by developed mining, manufacturing, agricultural, and service sectors, and is increasing its presence in world markets. After the global recession in 2008, Brazil was one of the first emerging markets to begin recovering with about a 5 percent growth in 2010 (Central Intelligence Agency [CIA], 2010).

Brazil's economy is now the eighth largest in the world. It has recently acquired a temporary seat on the United Nations Security Council until the end of 2011 and is seeking a growing international role and geopo-litical influence (Economist Intelligence Unit, 2010a). Brazil's government, led by Dilma Rousseff of the Worker's Party, welcomes private sector concessions, although bureaucracy still impairs efficiency. Foreign direct investment is welcomed, although domestic investors receive priority in certain areas, especially in the oil and energy sectors. Development of the export industry continues to be a priority and trade barriers are expected to be lowered. Brazil's tax system is poorly structured and tax evasion is widespread while the tax breaks applied to lessen the burden of the financial crisis of 2008 are scheduled to be lifted; yet, the overall tax burden will continue to be high. Both foreign and

EXHIBIT 2 Brazil's Consumer Segmentation, 2010–2020 (in thousands)

	2010	2015	2020	Growth (%)
Babies/Infants (0–2 years)	9,084	8,070	7,656	−15.7
Kids (3–8 years)	20,236	17,859	16,005	−20.9
Tweenagers (9–12 years)	13,928	13,490	11,865	−14.8
Teens (13–19 years)	23,347	24,104	23,627	1.2
People in their twenties	35,258	33,749	33,335	−5.5
People in their thirties	29,875	33,207	34,611	15.9
Middle-aged adults (40–64 years)	50,359	56,508	62,662	24.4
Older population (65+ years)	13,335	15,877	19,290	44.6

Source: Euromonitor International (2010).

national companies spend considerable resources toward managing their tax issues. Compliance with environmental law is a new crucial aspect of doing business in Brazil, and intellectual property rights must be respected (Economist Intelligence Unit, 2010b). The looming 2014 World Cup and 2016 Olympics are expected to bring an increase in public–private partnerships (Economist Intelligence Unit, 2010a).

Brazil's middle class is expanding due to the prosperity brought about by sound macroeconomic policies since 2000 (Euromonitor International, 2010). For the first time in Brazil's history, 50 percent of its citizens, more than 94 million people, belong to the middle class. Many low-income Brazilians have benefitted from new opportunities for stable jobs in the past decade. Because more people are being hired in the formal economy, access to working benefits such as health care, transportation, and food has increased. The real average monthly income grew 2.3 percent between 2008 and 2009 (Euromonitor International, 2010); this new middle class has access to certain products and services for the first time in their lives and are demanding more products and higher quality of service.

Lower fertility rates are also contributing to higher disposable incomes. Brazil's fertility rate of 1.9 children per woman in 2009 has allowed parents to spend more on consumer goods and services (Euromonitor International, 2010). This has also resulted in a rise in demand for travel services, as families are increasingly able to afford vacations.

Brazil has a very young population, with 33.2 percent of its population in its twenties and thirties (see Exhibit 2). This segment of the population is technology savvy with financial independence and the means

EXHIBIT 3 Annual Disposable Income Per Household, 2010–2020

	2010	2015	2020	Growth (%)
Above US$500	55,224	60,306	65,374	18.4
Above US$1,000	54,662	59,873	65,026	19.0
Above US$5,000	45,673	52,420	58,709	28.5
Above US$10,000	32,705	40,290	47,466	45.1
Above US$25,000	11,969	16,801	22,052	84.3
Above US$45,000	4,535	6,696	9,238	103.7
Above US$75,000	1,790	2,654	3,697	106.6
Above US$150,000	569	798	1,069	87.9

Source: Euromonitor International (2010).
Note: Constant value at 2009 prices.

to travel (Euromonitor International, 2010). They tend to travel to different regions of Brazil and to other countries over the holidays, and are looking for comfort and efficiency in their services. The annual disposable income will increase by 2020 (see Exhibit 3). The number of families in the US$75,000 income bracket will more than double from 1.7 million households in 2010 to 3.6 million in 2020 (Euromonitor International, 2010).

The tourism industry in Brazil grew 22 percent from 2003 to 2007, almost 3 percent more than the overall Brazilian economy during that time (Euromonitor International, 2010). Leisure and recreation spending is expected to grow by 65 percent by 2020 (see Exhibit 4) with more Brazilians traveling during Carnival, Christmas, and other vacation times. Many Brazilians are starting to buy vacation packages

EXHIBIT 4 Consumer Expenditure by Broad Category (in billions of reals), 2010–2020

Product	2010	2015	2020	Growth (%)	CAGRa (%)
Food and nonalcoholic beverages	527	678	839	59.3	4.8
Alcoholic beverages and tobacco	40	50	61	51.2	4.2
Clothing and footwear	68	80	90	31.5	2.8
Housing	313	397	492	57.4	4.6
Household goods and services	107	135	163	52.8	4.3
Health goods and medical services	95	126	160	68.9	5.4
Transport	281	372	469	67.1	5.3
Communications	118	160	209	77.8	5.9
Leisure and recreation	72	95	119	65.1	5.1
Education	153	204	259	69.6	5.4
Hotels and catering	56	68	79	40.5	3.5
Miscellaneous goods and services	296	390	487	64.6	5.1
TOTAL	**2,124**	**2,755**	**3,426**	**61.3**	**4.9**

Source: Euromonitor International (2010).
Note: Constant value at 2009 prices.
aCAGR = compound annual growth rate.

EXHIBIT 5 Consumer Expenditure on Package Holidays (in millions of reals), 2005–2009

Product	2005	2006	2007	2008	2009	Growth (%)
Package holidays	3,976	4,301	4,635	4,941	5,071	27.5

Source: Euromonitor International (2010).
Note: Constant value at 2009 prices.

through travel agencies and airlines that can be paid for in installments; the amount spent in this area grew 27.5 percent from 2005 to $5 billion Brazilian reals in 2009 (see Exhibit 5) (Euromonitor International, 2010). People in the upper and upper-middle classes are the primary customers for these packages.

HISTORY OF THE ENTREPRENEUR AND COMPANY

Robert Phillips, founder and CEO of Intelligent Leisure Solutions, has a BS in electrical engineering and an MS in space power. He worked in space power and in oil exploration in the United States and received an MBA from Thunderbird School of Global Management in 1994. He is a U.S. citizen who spent most of his child-hood living in South America, specifically in Brazil, Bolivia, and Colombia (Guthry, 2010).

Phillips began Intelligent Leisure Solutions in 1998 while working at Odebrecht, the largest engineering, construction, chemical, and petrochemical company in Latin America. As an internal consultant for tourism, tourism development, and real estate projects in Brazil, Phillips acted as a liaison between McKinsey and Ernst & Young, two large consulting firms in the United States, who were hired to evaluate tourism industry possibilities for Odebrecht. When Odebrecht decided not to invest in the tourism sector, Phillips saw a market opportunity and developed a Web-based travel company to sell Brazil to the world. Focused completely on Internet marketing, the company was unique among travel companies in Brazil in its innovative marketing strategy. In

> **EXHIBIT 6** Awards and Honors Won by Intelligent Leisure Solutions Companies
>
> - Winner – 2008 UN World Tourism Org Ulysses Award for Innovation in Tourism Enterprises
> - Nominee – 2009 and 2010 World Travel Award as World's Leading Travel Agency
> - Nominee – 2010 World Travel Award as World's Leading Travel Management Company
> - Winner – 2009 and 2010 World Travel Award as S. America's Leading Travel Agency
> - Winner – 2008, 2009, and 2010 World Travel Award as S. America's Leading Travel Management Company
> - Winner – 2008 and 2010 World Travel Award as Central America's Leading Travel Agency
> - Robert Phillips, managing partner, elected President of American Society of Travel Agents (ASTA), Brazil Chapter
> - Selected as an Affiliate Member of the UN World Tourism Organization by Brazilian Ministry of Tourism

2003, Phillips left Odebrecht to start DiscoverBrazil.com, a self-funded, Web-based travel company (now Intelligent Travel Solutions, or ITS), with the help of two partners, both colleagues from Odebrecht.

DiscoverBrazil.com began selling travel from Phillips' home office, and expanded to offer Central and South American luxury vacation packages, growing to 11 travel consultants, four websites, and monthly sales of US$300,000. The team acquired expert knowledge in Internet marketing and technology through their application of solely Internet marketing during their first few years of operations, allowing them to attain first-place results in Google's and Yahoo's search engine results pages (SERPs) for their business keywords.

Phillips and the team began setting up websites for Brazilian companies using the Internet marketing techniques they had developed for the Discover Brazil sites. Within weeks, these sites attained first placements in SERPs, something that usually took at least 3 to 6 months to achieve in the travel sector in English. In 2007, Intelligent Web Solutions (IWS) was created out of these results, and soon after, Intelligent Content Solutions (ICS) was created when Phillips partnered with another entrepreneur with translation experience. The result was an award-winning, integrated service that included Web marketing, Web business services, Web content creation, and translation service (see Exhibit 6).

ORGANIZATIONAL STRUCTURE

Intelligent Leisure Solutions Consulting (ILSC) is an efficient outsourcing service, with a broad network of specialized partners for each outsourced service.

Demand is identified, and innovative, intelligent solutions are created, turning this demand into business opportunities. ILSC started with two employees. In 2007, the company had 26 employees. The company was restructured because of the financial crisis of 2008 and foreign exchange debt to 12 employees, which then grew again to 16 employees in 2009 (Guthry, 2010).

Throughout the creation of IWS, ICS, ITS, and IRES (Intelligent Real Estate Solutions), Phillips continued his work with ILSC, which helped fund new projects. In 2009, Phillips brought three new partners into ILSC who helped Discover Brazil evolve into a group of five companies. Due to tax structure requirements in Brazil, companies need to be kept separate to qualify for certain tax incentives.

The group has incorporated Internet technology into the horizontally integrated leisure chain. The companies in the group offer a range of services from leisure development to the marketing and distribution of products. It is able to use shared knowledge between the five companies resulting in a strategic advantage. The group considers itself unique in that it has its own business laboratory (ITS) where it is able to test and develop its integrated services and Web techniques.

Intelligent Leisure Solutions is made up of five companies, each focusing on its own market niche:

Intelligent Leisure Solutions Consulting (ILSC) is a leisure, real estate, travel, tourism, and entertainment development consulting company with customers ranging from independent project owners, banks, investment funds, universities, and municipal, state, and federal governments. The company has a strong international and multicultural team located within

Brazil. Its strategic advantage is its knowledge of the entire travel real estate and its all-in-one solutions comprising tourism consulting, Web marketing, real estate brokerage, and travel consulting. With rapidly growing tourism and real estate industries in Brazil, ILSC hopes to capitalize on increased foreign investors in the next decade. Sample clients include the Ministry of Tourism of Brazil, the Secretariat of Tourism of Bahia, the World Bank, the Inter-American Development Bank, the CERT Foundation, Sapiens Park, and Zank Boutique Hotel. ILSC is also the exclusive representative for Odebrecht and Gehry Technology in Brazil and has recently won the bid to provide services for the Panama Metro and the Olympics and World Cup arenas in Brazil.

Intelligent Real Estate Solutions (IRES) offers complete real estate brokerage solutions in Brazil with clients such as international investors, banks, and funds investing in real estate and real estate projects in Brazil. This member company also has a cross-cultural and multilingual team that is able to provide foreign investors with services in their own languages. Because most ILSC clients need real estate consulting and brokerage services, IRES is able to offer these additional services as part of an integrated solution.

Intelligent Web Solutions (IWS) offers Internet marketing and business plan consulting and development, specializing in both search engine optimization and search engine marketing. Customers of IWS want a presence online and include small, medium, and large companies, artists, banks, universities and governments. Since few companies in the tourism sector offer content creation solutions, IWS offers this combined with project management and global services knowledge.

IWS believes it will be able to grow efficiently because of the lower costs of Internet marketing compared to traditional marketing, offering cost savings up to 90 percent. Internet marketing can reach anyone around the world with access to the Internet. Since any company interested in using Internet marketing is a potential IWS client, the firm capitalized on this by holding its second Internet Marketing Road Show in 2010. Through this, Intelligent Leisure Solutions entered the European market in 2009 with two new large clients.

Sample clients include in Spain—Universitat Oberta de Catalunya (www.uoc.edu) and Costa Brava of Girona (www.costabrava.org); in Argentina—Festival de Verão and Pepsi (www.sociallize.com.br), and Finca don Otaviano (www.FincadonOtaviano.com.ar); in Brazil—Carlinhos Brown (www.CarlinhosBrown.com.br),

Physio Pilates (www.PhysioPilates.com), and Odebrecht Real Estate and Tourism projects, including Reserva do Paiva (www.reservadopaiva.com), Hangar Business Park (www.hangarsalvador.com.br), Boulevard Side (www.boulevardside.com.br), Quintas Private (www.quintasprivate.com.br), Mitchell (www.mitchell.com.br), and The Planet Fashion Wear (www.theplanet.com.br).

Intelligent Content Solutions (ICS) provides full service Web content creation and translation to both individuals and companies needing translations and Web copywriting services. The company offers Web site translation into any language through its international team working within Brazil and its consultants located around the world. Only techniques that have been tested in the business laboratory (ITS) are offered to clients. Since companies increasingly want to sell their products globally, ICS has many opportunities for growth.

Intelligent Travel Solutions (ITS) offers personalized luxury travel solutions in Central and South America to individual travelers, travel agencies, tour operators, schools, universities, churches, other institutions, companies from diverse sectors, and countries offering incentive trips. All ITS's employees are multicultural and multilingual consultants, not travel agents, who apply in-house Web marketing techniques to establish the image of Central and South America as luxury travel destinations.

ITS is the first Web-based tour operator in Brazil and it promotes local development of sustainable tourist activity through excellence in its services. Opportunities for growth can be seen in applying this low-cost model to smaller regional and specialty travel websites.

OBSTACLES FACED

- **2008 Economic Crisis**—This represented a significant challenge to Intelligent Leisure Solutions as the decrease in demand led to a loss in revenue for the business. This was addressed by restructuring the business to travel consultants working from home instead of from corporate office space. This allowed the company to cut costs and implement a differentiated commission structure (Guthry, 2010).

- **Human Resources**—In Phillips' words, "What I have found to be one of the primary obstacles is human resources and human resource selection. If I were hiring a lawyer or a finance guy, that's all pretty standard. But when you go to set up an Internet-based travel company, who do you use as your foundation?" Phillips identified capable staff and implemented quality training, procedures, and a business culture appropriate for each company.

- **Lack of Understanding of the Need for the Products**—Since IWS offers an integrated travel solution, something not currently seen on the market, many prospective clients need to be educated about the company's products. The sales strategy for Intelligent Leisure Solutions was designed to first educate consumers about the product, overcome skepticism of the Web-based approach, and effectively present the quality of its products. A network of past clients was then built to demonstrate credibility and generate new clients.

- **Project Management Standards**—These standards, not yet developed in the industry, were developed by the group through trial and error.

FINANCIAL INFORMATION

Intelligent Leisure Solutions was initially self-funded by Phillips until 2005, when it received investments from two individuals. It has been funded periodically by investments throughout the life of the business. The business is currently being funded by the group's operations (see Exhibit 7).

INDUSTRY OVERVIEWS
Marketing Consulting Industry Overview

The management and marketing consultancy market in the United States had a value of $106.9 billion in 2009 (Exhibits 8 and 9), with a compound annual growth rate (CAGR) of 4.4 percent between 2005 and 2009 (Datamonitor, 2010d). This market has experienced steady growth, and is forecasted to reach $161.2 billion in 2014, an increase of 50.7 percent since 2009, representing a CAGR of 8.6 percent between 2009 and 2014 (Exhibit 10). The largest segment of the management and marketing consultancy market in the United States is corporate strategy with 27.8 percent of the total market, while the operations management segment accounts for 26.5 percent (Exhibit 11). The United States represents 39.3 percent of the global market value (Datamonitor, 2010d).

The size of this market is the total revenues received from corporate strategy services, operations management services, information technology solutions, human resource management services, and outsourcing services. Since management and marketing consultancies provide objective external advice to improve business performance, this service involves specific professional knowledge, which can be costly.

Strong brand reputations are important in this industry, as evidenced by the success of large global organizations such as PriceWaterhouseCoopers and Deloitte. The time

EXHIBIT 7 Intelligent Leisure Solutions' Estimated Net Operational Profit, 2005–2009 (in U.S. dollars)

	2005	2006	2007	2008	2009
Estimated Operational Profit (net)	$120,000	$360,000	$480,000	$390,000	$640,000

Source: Guthry (2010).

EXHIBIT 8 U.S. Management and Marketing Consultancy Market Value, 2005–2009

Year	Dollars (in billions)	Euros (in billions)	Growth (%)
2005	90.0	64.7	—
2006	99.7	71.7	10.8
2007	108.4	78.0	8.8
2008	113.6	81.7	4.8
2009	106.9	76.9	5.9
Cagar 2005–2009			**4.4**

Source: Datamonitor (2010d).

EXHIBIT 9   U.S. Management and Marketing Consultancy Market Value, 2005–2009

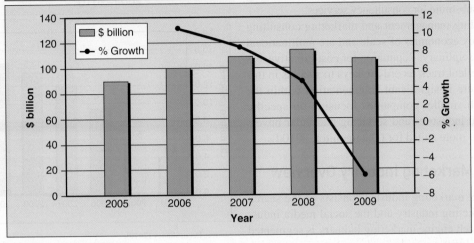

Source: Datamonitor (2010d).

EXHIBIT 10   U.S. Management and Marketing Consultancy Market Value Forecast, 2009–2014

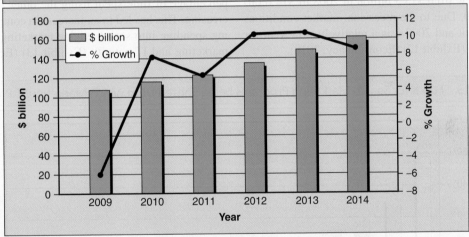

Source: Datamonitor (2010d).

EXHIBIT 11   U.S. Management and Marketing Consultancy Market Segmentation

Category	Share (%)
Corporate Strategy	27.8
Operations Management	26.5
Human Resources Management	10.6
Information Technology	8.8
Other	26.3
Total	**100**

Source: Datamonitor (2010d).

and experience required to build this reputation presents a strong barrier to entry in this industry. Also, many large organizations employ in-house analysts and marketing teams as a substitute for consultancy services.

The leading management and marketing consulting firms employ economies of scale and are multinational and multidisciplinary. Reputation for cost-effectiveness and an excellent track record are keys to success in this market. There is significant fragmentation within the market with smaller companies focusing on specific markets and industries and servicing particular buyers that they are more suited for (Datamonitor, 2010d).

Internet Marketing Industry Overview

The Internet marketing industry consists of the search engine marketing industry and the social media industry. The search engine marketing industry is segmented into money spent on paid search marketing and search engine optimization (SEO), as well as spending on search engine marketing technology (Econsultancy, 2010). The North American search engine marketing industry grew from $13.5 billion in 2008 to $14.6 billion in 2009. Due to the recession, market conditions were difficult and 2009 was a relatively slow year for the industry (Exhibit 12) (Econsultancy, 2010).

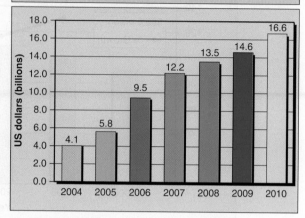

EXHIBIT 12 Value of North American Search Engine Marketing Industry, 2004–2010

Source: Econsultancy (2010).

Of the four media forms—Internet/social media, newspaper, magazine, and TV—only the percentage of time spent using Internet/media is on the rise, while the percentage of time spent using the other forms is decreasing. This has led to an increase in companies shifting spending into search engine marketing from other marketing and IT activity (Exhibit 13) (Econsultancy,

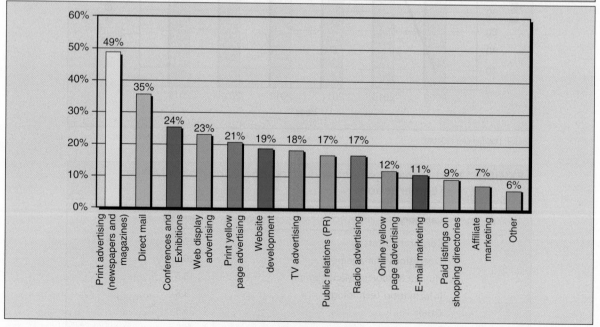

EXHIBIT 13 Funds for Search Marketing Programs being Shifted from which Marketing/IT Programs?

Source: Econsultancy (2010).

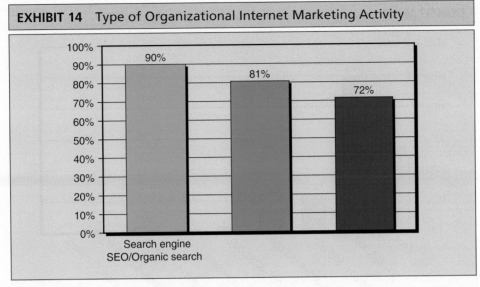

EXHIBIT 14 Type of Organizational Internet Marketing Activity

Source: Econsultancy (2010).

2010). In 2009, there were 1.8 billion global Internet users, a 13 percent increase from 2008, with just under half (46 percent) from five countries: Brazil, China, India, Russia, and the United States. In the United States alone, there were 240 million users, a 4 percent increase from 2008, indicating a 76 percent penetration rate per 100 inhabitants. In Brazil, there were 76 million users, up 17 percent from 2008, indicating a 39 percent penetration rate (Meeker, Devitt, & Wu, 2010).

According to a survey done by Econsultancy of 1,500 client-side advertisers and agency respondents, the number of companies using SEO has remained at 90 percent since 2007, while paid search marketing has increased from 78 percent in 2009 to 81 percent in 2010 (Exhibit 14). More than half of companies surveyed expected to spend more on paid search and SEO in 2010 than they did in 2009, anticipating an average increase in spending of 37 percent and 43 percent, respectively (Econsultancy, 2010).

One fifth of companies surveyed spent over $1 million on paid search in 2009, compared to a modest budget of less than $25,000 for social media marketing for 73 percent of companies (Exhibit 15). This includes 23 percent of companies reporting a budget of zero for social media marketing (Econsultancy, 2010). Yet the use of social marketing is on the rise. Fifty-nine percent of companies say their budgets for social media marketing will increase in 2010 (Econsultancy, 2010).

With 1.5 billion visits to social networks every day (Parker & Thomas, 2010), 74 percent and 73 percent of companies report using Facebook and Twitter, respectively, to promote their brand (Exhibit 16) (Econsultancy, 2010). Facebook is the largest social network in English-speaking countries with 620 million global visitors in 2009, while Twitter boasts 102 million users (Meeker et al., 2010).

Google's dominance as a search engine is clear. Ninety-seven percent of companies are paying to advertise on Google AdWords, and 71 percent are paying to advertise on Google search network, with 56 percent using the Google content network (Exhibit 17). Only 50 percent of respondents used Yahoo! Search in 2010, a drop from 68 percent in 2009 and 86 percent in 2008 (Econsultancy, 2010).

For many marketers, the measurement of return on investment (ROI) for paid search, social media marketing and SEO is a particular challenge. Forty-three percent of respondents report ROI measurement for paid search as one of their top three challenges, while 42 percent say the same for both social media marketing and SEO (Econsultancy, 2010).

Global Real Estate Management and Development Industry Overview

The size of the global real estate management and development industry is $461 billion, a decrease of 8 percent since 2009. It had a compound rate of change of −0.3 percent since 2005. No growth was expected in 2010, but steady growth was expected in 2011 and was

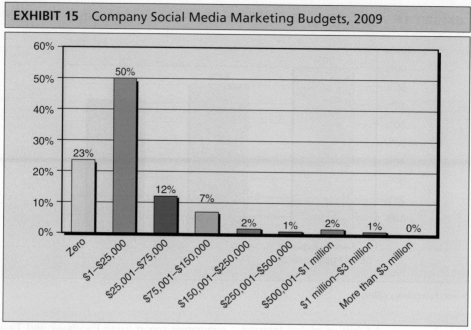

EXHIBIT 15 Company Social Media Marketing Budgets, 2009

Source: Econsultancy (2010).

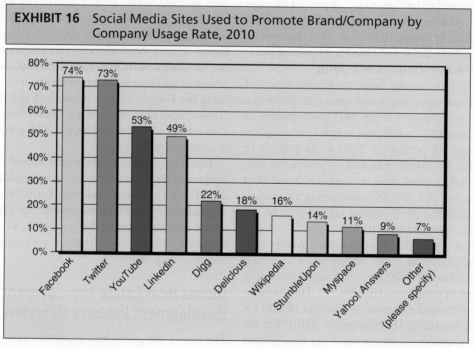

EXHIBIT 16 Social Media Sites Used to Promote Brand/Company by Company Usage Rate, 2010

Source: Econsultancy (2010).

EXHIBIT 17 Percentage of Companies Paying to Advertise on Each Search Engine

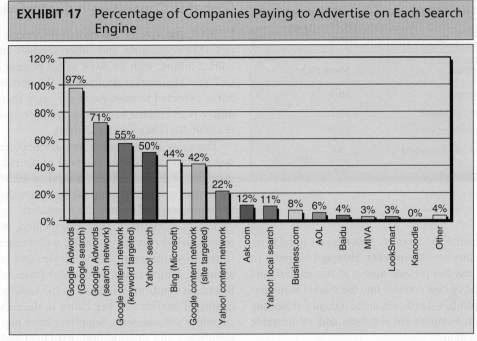

Source: Econsultancy (2010).

EXHIBIT 18 Global Real Estate Management and Development Industry Value Forecast, 2009–2014

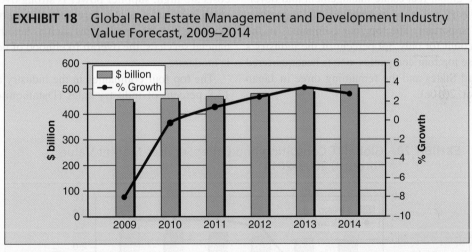

Source: Datamonitor (2010c).

forecasted to increase to $511 billion by 2014, with an expected CAGR of 2.1 percent for the period 2009–2014 (Exhibit 18) (Datamonitor, 2010c).

The residential segment of the industry accounts for 56.7 percent of the industry with the nonresidential segment being 43.3 percent. The leading companies in the industry are in Europe and the United States, accounting for 36.3 percent and 33.7 percent, respectively (Exhibit 19) (Datamonitor, 2010c).

Buyers within the industry range in size and financial strength so large buyer power is mitigated by strong financial strength and ability to negotiate with key players, keeping buyer power moderate. Supplier power is moderate, with a large number of construction contractors

EXHIBIT 19   Global Real Estate Management and Development Industry Segmentation, 2009

Region	Share (%)
Europe	36.3
United States	33.7
Asia-Pacific	20.9
Rest of the world	9.1
Total	100

Source: Datamonitor (2010c).

offering essential key services. Substantial capital is required for entry into the market, although business or mortgage loans can provide access to this capital, and the likelihood of new entrants into the market is moderate. Competition is significant in the industry, reflecting the uncertain business environment and an unstable financial situation.

Players in the market try to differentiate themselves by the types of property or services, such as brokerage offered. The global real estate management and development industry is highly fragmented, and name recognition is important. The top four companies in the industry account for only 3.9 percent of the industry's size. Of these top four companies, one is headquartered in the United States and the remaining three in Japan (Datamonitor, 2010c).

Global IT Consulting Industry Overview

In 2009, the size of the global information technology (IT) consulting and other services market was $498.2 billion, with a CAGR of 5.1 percent from 2005 to 2009. The market declined by 0.6 percent in 2009, but is expected to increase in the years ahead. The industry is forecasted to grow to $561.5 billion by 2014 (Exhibit 20) (Datamonitor, 2010b).

The sales of integration and development services was the most significant segment of the industry, with revenues of $246.7 billion, a total of 49.5 percent of the market's value. The top markets were the Americas (51.9 percent) and Europe (27.8 percent).

The industry is highly fragmented, with large, multinational players operating with numerous small firms. Key customers are businesses and government agencies, which range in size and financial strength. Brand recognition is crucial to the industry because quality IT service is a key factor in the success of the customer's businesses. Suppliers have highly skilled employees and provide both hardware and software. Because customers are dependent on being provided dependable service from their suppliers and switching costs are high, supplier power is strong overall. While small companies can differentiate themselves by specializing in certain industries such as health care or financial services, the overall likelihood of new entrants is moderate.

The top four companies in the industry account for 13.8 percent of industry sales (Datamonitor, 2010b).

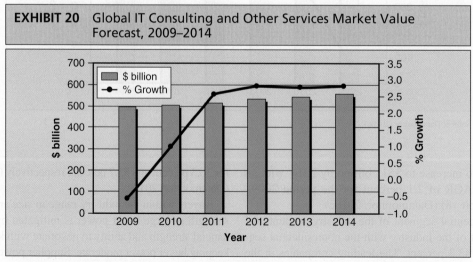

EXHIBIT 20   Global IT Consulting and Other Services Market Value Forecast, 2009–2014

Source: Datamonitor (2010b).

Competition is intense as the key companies continue to grow, and have focused on diversification to lessen the degree of competition.

Global Internet Software and Services Industry Overview

This industry is composed of companies developing and marketing Internet software and/or providing Internet services, including online databases and interactive services, Web address registration services, database construction, and Internet design services (Datamonitor, 2010a). The size of this industry is $893.7 billion (Exhibit 21), an increase of 9.1 percent in 2009, representing a CAGR of 14.7 percent (Datamonitor, 2010a). It is forecast to increase 75.4 percent to $1,567.7 billion by 2014 (Exhibit 22).

The industry is split into two segments—the broadband segment, by far the largest (74.4 percent of the industry's overall size), and the narrowband segment

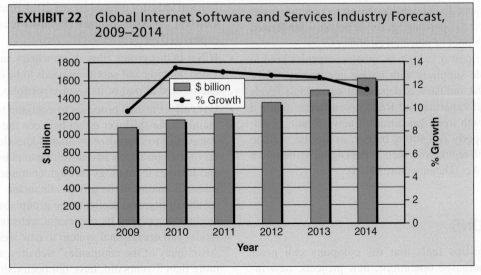

EXHIBIT 21 Global Internet Software and Services Industry Value, 2005–2009

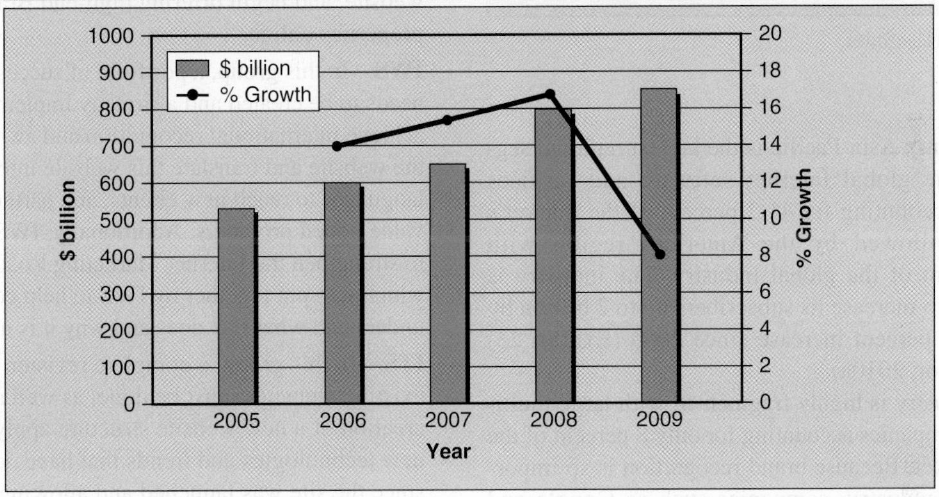

Source: Datamonitor (2010a).

EXHIBIT 22 Global Internet Software and Services Industry Forecast, 2009–2014

Source: Datamonitor (2010a).

EXHIBIT 23 Global Internet Software and Services Industry Forecast, 2009–2014

Year	Subscribers (billions)	Growth (%)
2009	1.3	11.6
2010	1.4	11.0
2011	1.6	9.7
2012	1.7	9.1
2013	1.9	8.5
2014	2.0	7.9
CAGR: 2009–2014		9.2

Source: Datamonitor (2010c).

(25.6 percent). Asia-Pacific is the largest regional segment of the global Internet software and services industry, accounting for 41.2 percent of the market's volume, followed by the Americas region with 33.2 percent of the global industry. The industry is forecasted to increase its subscribers up to 2 billion by 2014, a 55 percent increase since 2009 (Exhibit 23) (Datamonitor, 2010a).

The industry is highly fragmented with large multinational companies accounting for only 8 percent of the global market. Because brand recognition is so important in the industry, companies such as Google and Yahoo! have global recognition and buyers such as individual consumers tend to frequent the brand. Commercial buyers do not consider brand recognition a significant factor in purchasing. Buyer power is moderated by the large pool of potential customers.

Supplier power is high, as many companies tend to rely on sole suppliers with strong negotiating skills. Entry in the industry is dependent upon high levels of technical expertise and R&D investments. While a strong growth trend has attracted new entrants, intellectual property is a strong barrier, as are the costs to comply with regulations such as the Digital Millennium Copyright Act (Datamonitor, 2010a).

SOLUTIONS

Robert Phillips feels that the company can grow through increased operations, new projects, new investors, and increased consulting. To do this, Phillips proposes the following for each of the group's companies (Guthry, 2010).

- **ILSC**—To capitalize on opportunities provided by the 2014 Brazil World Cup and the 2016 Summer Olympics, Phillips proposes solidifying the relationships the company has with other international companies, such as Advanced Leisure Services of Spain, Target Euro of Italy, and Gehry Technology of the United States. Additionally, a new website should be created for ILSC using the company's innovative Web marketing techniques.

- **IRES**—In this group, a leader needs to be identified to step in and grow the business, finish the IRES website, and begin offering high-end Brazilian properties online.

- **IWS**—In this group, a portfolio of success stories needs to be created and a strategy implemented to achieve international recognition and awards, update the website and translate this website into multiple languages to reach new clients, and partner with value-added providers. Additionally, IWS will work to strengthen the Internet Marketing Roadshow, which was put together by IWS to help companies understand what ILS does and why it is needed.

- **ITS**—In this group, a complete revision of ITS's existing websites must be done, as well as the creation of a new website structure applying new technologies and trends that have developed since the site was launched and allowing for rapid expansion into new destination areas and markets by replication. Also, opportunities in the Brazilian tourism industry offered by the 2014 Brazil World Cup and the 2016 Summer Olympics must be capitalized on.

- **ICS**—In this group, film, documentary, and training video dubbing and subtitling needs to be developed and offered as part of its service portfolio.

- **Overall**—Phillips proposes to continue to maintain the spillover effect between the companies to capitalize on shared knowledge, be up-to-date on trends and developments in tourism and Internet technology through continuous research, maintain the group's financial sustainability, and replicate the group's success stories by applying its successful website business model and operational system to new websites. Also, many of the companies' websites, some more than 8 years old, have not been redone since their initial creation and will be updated shortly.

REFERENCES

Central Intelligence Agency. (2010). *The world factbook.* Retrieved from https://www.cia.gov/library/publications/the-world-factbook/index.html

Datamonitor. (2010a). *Global Internet software & services: Industry profile.* Retrieved from http://www.marketresearch.com/Datamonitor-v72/Global-Internet-Software-Services-6445589/

Datamonitor. (2010b). *Global IT consulting & other services.* Retrieved from http://www.datamonitor.com/store/Product/global_it_consulting_other_services?productid=D3F44101-8292-4FBE-9614-1C6ED508C2CA

Datamonitor. (2010c). *Global real estate management & development.* Retrieved from http://www.companiesandmarkets.com/Market-Report/global-real-estate-management-development-market-report-624768.asp

Datamonitor. (2010d). *Management & marketing consultancy in the United States: Industry profile.* Retrieved from http://www.amazon.com/Management-Marketing-Consultancy-United-States/dp/B004FFWN4W

Economist Intelligence Unit. (2010a). *Country forecast Brazil.* Retrieved from http://www.eiu.com/index.asp?layout=displayIssue&publication_id=490003649

Economist Intelligence Unit. (2010b). *Country report Brazil.* Retrieved from http://www.eiu.com/index.asp?layout=displayIssue&publication_id=1720000972

Econsultancy. (2010). *State of search engine marketing report 2010.* Retrieved from http://econsultancy.com/us/reports/sempo-state-of-search-2010

Euromonitor International. (2010). *Consumer lifestyles in Brazil.* Retrieved from http://www.euromonitor.com/consumer-lifestyles-in-brazil/report

Guthry, D. (2010). *Thunderbird 2010 Alumni Entrepreneur of the Year nomination: Robert Phillips.* Glendale, AZ: Walker Center for Global Entrepreneurship.

Meeker, M., Devitt, S., & Wu, L. (2010, November 16). *Ten questions Internet execs should ask & answer.* San Francisco: Morgan Stanley. Retrieved from http://www.morganstanley.com/institutional/techresearch/pdfs/tenquestions_web2.pdf

Parker, G., & Thomas, L. (2010). *The socialisation of brands:* Wave 5. New York: Universal McCann. Retrieved from http://www.umww.com/global/knowledge/download?id=1791&hash=F1C9F17E9E5CB4A2681D74 4A9AD018B3413C00BFad20708460e44685b4e8a7cb5612c496&fileName=Wave%205%20-%20The%20 Socialisation%20Of%20Brands.pdf

CASE 6
THE BEACH CARRIER

Mary Ricci has a new product concept, The Beach Carrier, that she is ready to bring to market. Ricci is creative, optimistic, enthusiastic, flexible, and motivated. She is willing to put substantial time into developing and bringing The Beach Carrier to market. Although she lacks capital, Ricci is unwilling to license or sell the pattern to a manufacturer; she is determined to maintain control and ownership of the product throughout the introduction and market penetration phases. Ricci believes there is a significant amount of money to be made and refuses to sell her product concept for a flat fee.

THE PRODUCT

The Beach Carrier is a bag large enough to carry everything needed for a day at the beach, including a chair. When empty, the bag can be folded down to a 12-inch by 12-inch square for easy storage. The bag's 36-inch by 36-inch size, adjustable padded shoulder strap, and various-sized pockets make it ideal for use in carrying chairs and other items to the beach or other outdoor activities, such as concerts, picnics, and barbecues. The bag can also be used to transport items, such as ski boots, that are difficult to carry. Manufactured in a lightweight, tear-resistant, fade-proof fabric that dries quickly, the bag will be available in a variety of fluorescent as well as conservative colors.

COMPETITION

Currently there are two competitive products sold online that Ricci felt would compete with The Beach Carrier. The first one, found at www.shadeusa.com, is the "Caddy Sack" and is advertised as a backpack-type

Source: This case study was prepared by Michael P. Peters with the intention of providing a basis for class discussion.

product that can hold a beach chair, an umbrella, a boogie board, and even a small collapsing table. There is also an outside pocket for a towel, a snorkel, or fins. It is available in three colors and is priced at $16.95. Ricci purchased one of these and felt that it would not hold all the items advertised at one time. The chair had to be very small, and room for extra beach accessories was very limited. This item was ideal for someone biking or walking to the beach with gear for only himself or herself.

The second item is called the "Wonder Wheeler" and can be found at www.4thebeach.com. It looks similar to a two-wheel shopping cart that might be used to carry purchased groceries while walking home from the store. This product is advertised as having oversized wheels; it weighs less than 10 lbs. and folds up easily. It can hold a significant amount of beach gear, such as multiple chairs, an umbrella, a cooler, beach towels, and toys. It has a list price of $59.99, and Ricci felt that even with the advertised oversized wheels it would be cumbersome to maneuver on the sand. Its high price was also felt to be a negative for many consumers.

MARKETING RESEARCH

Ricci commissioned a consulting company to perform a feasibility study for the product, which included a demographic profile, cost estimates, packaging recommendations, and a patent search. The patent search revealed the above-mentioned products and a chair that could be folded and carried as a small tote bag that could also hold a few small beach items. None of these were felt to be a threat to Ricci's product, and she was optimistic that a patent could be obtained.

A focus group was used to determine potential consumer response. Results of the focus group indicated that several features of the product should be modified. For example, the material was perceived as durable; however, the fluorescent color was see-through and considered "trendy," lessening the perceived quality of the

bag. The size also represented an issue, as the bag was perceived as much larger than necessary.

MARKET POTENTIAL

People who use suntan and sunscreen products have been identified as the primary target market for The Beach Carrier. Research indicates that 43.9 percent of the adult U.S. population, or 77,293,000 people, use suntan and sunscreen products. Of these, 57.8 percent are female. Assuming that women are the primary purchasers of beach bags, the potential market is estimated at 44,675,000. Beach bags are replaced every three years. The primary market for suntan and sunscreen products is described in Exhibit 1. The marketing share objectives for the first year of The Beach Carrier's sales have been determined based on the following assumptions:

- People who use suntan and sunscreen products represent the market for The Beach Carrier.
- Most men do not buy beach bags; consider women only (57.8 percent of population).
- Women buy new beach bags every three years on average; that is, one-third will buy a new bag this year.

Based on these assumptions, the unit sales needed to achieve market share objectives of 1 percent, 2 percent, and 5 percent of the total market during the first year of The Beach Carrier's sales are shown in Exhibit 2. Ricci is targeting 1 percent of this potential market. Regional market share objectives can be developed from the same data as seen in Exhibits 3A and 3B.

STRATEGY

Ricci investigated several methods of marketing The Beach Carrier, including selling it in upscale (i.e., Bloomingdale's) or discount (i.e., Wal-Mart) stores, licensing the product concept to a manufacturer, selling the idea for a flat fee, selling the bag to corporations for

EXHIBIT 1

Segment	Percentage of Total Users of Suntan/Sunscreen Products
Ages 18–44	66.9
High school graduate	40.2
Employed full time	60.5
No child in household	54.5
Household income of $30,000+	55.3

EXHIBIT 2

	Population	Sunscreen Users	Replace Bag This Year
Total adults	176,251,000	77,293,000	25,764,333
Females	92,184,000	44,671,000	14,890,333
	Market Share		
	1%	2%	5%
Total adults	257,643	515,287	1,288,217
Females	148,903	297,807	744,517

EXHIBIT 3A

	Population	Sunscreen Users	Women	Replace Bag This Year
Northeast	37,366,000	17,165,000	9,921,370	3,307,123
Midwest	43,426,000	19,630,000	11,346,140	3,782,047
South	60,402,000	23,980,000	13,860,440	4,620,147
West	35,057,000	16,518,000	9,547,404	3,182,468
Total	176,251,000	77,293,000	44,675,354	14,891,785

EXHIBIT 3B

	Market Share		
	1%	2%	5%
Northeast	33,071	66,142	165,356
Midwest	37,820	75,641	189,102
South	46,201	92,403	231,007
West	31,825	63,649	159,123
Total	148,917	297,835	744,588

use as a promotional item, selling it on the Internet, and setting up a mail-order operation. Ricci believes that the mail-order option, while requiring the most effort, will provide higher margins, lower risk, and the overall best fit with Ricci's strengths and weaknesses, her market penetration objectives, and her limited financial resources. The Internet could also create opportunities, but Ricci was unsure of this option.

The mail-order sales strategy will be implemented nationally using a regional rollout and following a seasonal demand pattern. With three-month intervals between rollout phases, national market exposure will be achieved within 12 months. Ricci is also exploring how to set up a Web site with a local university team of student consultants.

PROMOTION

The product initially will be promoted in novelty and general interest mail-order catalogs and special interest magazines that appeal to beachgoers and boat owners.

PRICING

The costs of manufacturing have been estimated at $6.50 per unit for material, zippers, Velcro, and so on. The costs for assembly and packaging have been estimated at $3.50 per unit, bringing the total manufacturing cost to $10.00. After analysis of competitive products and focus group results, a mail-order price in the $12.99 to $14.99 range has been established.

EXHIBIT 4

	Unit Variable	Cost per Unit	Price Contribution
Materials	$6.50	$12.99	$2.99
Assembly	3.00	$13.99	$3.99
Packaging	0.50	$14.99	$4.99
Total unit VC	$10.00		

Fixed Costs

	Northeast	Midwest	South	West	Total
Advertising	$25,000	$25,000	$25,000	$25,000	$100,000
Warehousing	266	305	372	256	1,199
General S&A	2,500	2,500	2,500	2,500	10,000
Total fixed costs	$27,766	$27,805	$27,872	$27,756	$111,199

Break-Even Units

	Northeast	Midwest	South	West	Total
$12.99	9,286	9,299	9,322	9,283	37,190
Percent of total market	0.28	0.25	0.20	0.29	0.25
$13.99	6,959	6,969	6,985	6,956	27,869
Percent of total market	0.21	0.18	0.15	0.22	0.19
$14.99	5,564	5,572	5,586	5,562	22,284
Percent of total market	0.17	0.15	0.12	0.17	0.15

DISTRIBUTION

The product will be manufactured at a local New England factory, drop-shipped to a storage facility, and shipped via UPS to the consumer. Initially, inventory can be carried at no cost in Ricci's house or garage. This same process could also be used if the Web site is developed.

FINANCING

A $30,000 small-business loan is the minimum amount Ricci needs to fund her fixed costs for the first phase of the rollout for the mail-order program. Marketing the product through traditional retail channels would require approximately $250,000 for advertising and other selling costs associated with a new product introduction.

BREAK-EVEN ANALYSIS

Break-even analysis was performed at three mail-order prices, as seen in Exhibit 4. On the basis of this analysis, Ricci must meet only one-fourth of her target sales goal, or one-quarter of 1 percent of the total market, in order to break even in the first year.

CASE 7
GOURMET TO GO

INTRODUCTION

Today, many households have two incomes. At the end of the day the questions arise, "Who will cook?" or "What do I cook?" Time is limited. After a long day at work, few people want to face the lines at the grocery store. Often the choice is to eat out. But the expense of dining out or the boredom of fast food soon becomes unappealing. Pizza or fast-food delivery solves the problem of going out but does not always satisfy the need for nutritious, high-quality meals. Some people prefer a home-cooked meal, especially without the hassle of grocery shopping, menu planning, and time-consuming preparation.

Jan Jones is one of those people. She is a hardworking professional who would like to come home to a home-cooked meal. She would not mind fixing it herself but, once at home, making an extra trip to the store is a major hassle.

Source: This case study was prepared by Robert D. Hisrich with the intention of providing a basis for class discussion.

Jones thought it would be great to have the meal planned and all the ingredients at her fingertips. She thought of other people in her situation and realized there might be a market need for this kind of service. After thinking about the types of meals that could be marketed, Jones discussed the plan with her colleagues at work. The enthusiastic response led her to believe she had a good idea. After months of marketing research, menu planning, and financial projections, Jones was ready to launch her new business. The following is the business plan for Gourmet to Go.

EXECUTIVE SUMMARY

Gourmet to Go is a new concept in grocery marketing. The product is a combination of menu planning and grocery delivery; a complete package of groceries and recipes for a week's meals is delivered to a customer's door. The target market consists of young urban professionals living in two-income households in which individuals have limited leisure time, high disposable income, and a willingness to pay for services.

The objective is to develop a customer base of 400 households by the end of the third year after start-up. This level of operation will produce a new income of about $120,000 per year and provide a solid base for market penetration in the future.

The objective will be achieved by creating an awareness of the product through an intense promotional campaign at start-up and by providing customers with first-class service and premium-quality goods.

The capital required to achieve objectives is $258,000. Jones will invest $183,000 and will manage and own the business. The remainder of the capital will be financed through bank loans.

PRODUCT

The product consists of meal-planning and grocery shopping services. It offers a limited selection of preplanned five-dinner packages delivered directly to the customer.

The criteria for the meal packages will be balanced nutrition, easy preparation, and premium quality. To ensure the nutritional requirements, Gourmet to Go will hire a nutritionist as a consultant. Nutritional information will be included with each order. The most efficient method for preparing the overall meal will be presented. Meals will be limited to recipes requiring no more than 20 minutes to prepare. Premium-quality ingredients will be a selling feature. The customer should feel that he or she is getting better-quality ingredients than could be obtained from the grocery store.

MANUFACTURING AND PACKAGING

Since the customer will not be shopping on the premises, Gourmet to Go will require only a warehouse-type space for the groceries. The store location or decor will be unimportant in attracting business. There will be fewer inventory expenses since the customer will not be choosing among various brands. Only premium brands will be offered.

It will be important to establish a reliable connection with a distributor for high-quality produce and to maintain freshness for delivery to the customer.

As orders are processed, the dinners will be assembled. Meats will be wrapped and ready for the home freezer. All ingredients will be labeled according to the dinner to which they belong. The groceries will be sorted and bagged according to storage requirements: freezer, refrigerator, and shelf. Everything possible will be done to minimize the customer's task. Included in the packaging will be the nutritional information and preparation instructions.

Customers will be given the option of selecting their own meals from the monthly menu list or opting for a weekly selection from the company.

FUTURE GROWTH

Various options will be explored in order to expand the business. Some customers may prefer a three- or four-meal plan if they eat out more often or travel frequently. Another possibility might be the "last-minute gourmet"; that is, they can call any evening for one meal only.

Increasing the customer base will increase future sales. Expansion of Gourmet to Go can include branches in other locations or even future franchising in other cities. With expansion and success, Gourmet to Go might be a prime target for a larger food company to buy out.

INDUSTRY

The Gourmet to Go concept is a new idea with its own market niche. The closest competitors would be grocery stores and restaurants with delivery services.

Of the 660 grocery stores in the Tulsa/Tulsa County region, only two offer delivery service. They are higher-priced stores and will deliver for $4, regardless of order size. However, they offer no assistance in meal planning.

A number of pizza chains will deliver pizza as well as fried chicken. There is also a new service that will pick up and deliver orders from various restaurants. However,

Gourmet to Go would not be in direct competition with these services because the meals available from them are either of a fast-food type or far more expensive than a Gourmet to Go meal.

SALES PREDICTION

The market segment will be households with an income of at least $65,000 per year. In Tulsa/Tulsa County, this will cover an area including over 16,600 households that meet the target requirements of income

with an age range of 24 to 50 years. By the end of the third year, a customer base of 400 households will be developed (2.3 percent of the target market). At a growth rate of 2.73 percent a year, the target market of households should increase over three years to 18,000.

FINANCIAL

Various financial statements are included in Exhibits 1 through 8.

EXHIBIT 1 Start-Up Expenses

Ad campaign		
Ad agency*	$3,000	
Brochures†	7,000	
Radio spots‡	8,000	
Newspaper ads§	7,000	
Total		$25,000
Pre-start-up salaries**		16,000
Nutritionist consulting		6,000
Miscellaneous consulting (legal, etc.)		1,500
Pre-start-up rent and deposits		4,000
Pre-start-up utilities and miscellaneous supplies		2,000
		$54,500

*40 hrs. @ $75/hr.
†20,000 brochures; printing, development, etc. @ $0.35/ea.
‡4-week intense campaign: 20 spots/week (30 seconds); $100/spot.
§50 ads at an average of $100/ad.
**Jan Jones @ 3 months; clerks, two @ 2 weeks.

EXHIBIT 2 Capital Equipment List

Computers:		
Apple, Macintosh Office System		
3 Mac systems	$3,000	
Laser printer HP2300 series	1,000	
Networking	2,000	
Software	3,000	
Total		$ 9,000
Delivery vans, Chevrolet Astro		66,000
Food lockers and freezers		15,000
Phone system (AT&T)		1,500
Furniture and fixtures		3,500
		$95,000

EXHIBIT 3 Pro Forma Income Statement

	Year 1											
	Mo. 1	Mo. 2	Mo. 3	Mo. 4	Mo. 5	Mo. 6	Mo. 7	Mo. 8	Mo. 9	Mo. 10	Mo. 11	Mo. 12
Sales[1]	2,600	3,900	6,500	13,000	19,500	23,400	26,000	28,600	31,200	33,800	36,400	39,000
Less: Cost of goods sold[2]	1,700	2,550	4,250	8,500	12,750	15,300	17,000	18,700	20,400	22,100	23,800	25,500
Gross profit	900	1,350	2,250	4,500	6,750	8,100	9,000	9,900	10,800	11,700	12,600	13,500
Less: Operating expenses												
Salaries and wages[3]	7,400	7,400	7,400	7,400	7,400	7,400	9,800	9,800	9,800	9,800	9,800	9,800
Operating supplies	300	300	300	300	300	300	300	300	300	300	300	300
Repairs and maintenance	250	250	250	250	250	250	250	250	250	250	250	250
Advertising and promotion[4]	130	195	325	650	975	1,170	1,300	1,430	1,560	1,690	1,820	1,950
Bad debts	100	100	100	100	100	100	100	100	100	100	100	100
Rent[5]	1,667	1,667	1,667	1,667	1,667	1,667	1,667	1,667	1,667	1,667	1,667	1,667
Utilities	1,000	1,000	1,000	1,000	1,000	1,000	1,000	1,000	1,000	1,000	1,000	1,000
Insurance	600	600	600	600	600	600	600	600	600	600	600	600
General office	150	150	150	150	150	150	150	150	150	150	150	150
Licenses	200	0	0	0	0	0	0	0	0	0	0	0
Interest[6]	310	310	310	310	310	310	530	530	530	530	530	530
Depreciation[7]	1,271	1,271	1,271	1,271	1,271	1,271	1,271	1,271	1,271	1,271	1,271	1,271
Total operating expenses	13,378	13,243	13,373	13,698	14,023	14,218	16,968	17,098	17,228	17,358	17,488	17,618
Profit (loss) before taxes	(12,478)	(11,893)	(11,123)	(9,198)	(7,273)	(6,118)	(7,968)	(7,198)	(6,428)	(5,658)	(4,888)	(4,118)
Less: Taxes	0	0	0	0	0	0	0	0	0	0	0	0
Net profit (loss)	(12,478)	(11,893)	(11,123)	(9,198)	(7,273)	(6,118)	(7,968)	(7,198)	(6,428)	(5,658)	(4,888)	(4,118)

[1] Average unit sale for groceries is about $43.00, plus $10.00 per week for delivery (Exhibit 1), making the monthly unit sales per household (2 people) about $212.00.

[2] Cost of goods sold—80 percent of retail grocery price, or $32.00 per household per week ($170.00/month household). (80 percent an average margin on groceries.)

[3] Salaries and wages—Ms. Jones's salary will be $5,000/month. Order clerks will be paid $1,300/month, and delivery clerks will be paid $1,100/month. One additional order clerk and delivery clerk each will be added once sales reach 100 households, and again at 200 households. Salaries will escalate at 6 percent/year.

[4] Advertising and promotion—The grocery industry standard is 1 percent of sales. However, Gourmet to Go, being a new business, will require more than that level; 5 percent of sales is used in this plan. (Special pre-start-up advertising is covered with other start-up expenses.)

[5] Rent—2,000/ft.^{2} @ $10.00/ft.^{2}; $1,667/month; escalate at 6 percent/year.

[6] Interest—Loans on computer ($10,000) and delivery vehicles ($22,000 ea.) at 12.0 percent/year. (Delivery vehicles will be added with delivery clerks.) (Debt service—based on three-year amortization of loans with payments of ⅓ at the end of each of three years.)

[7] Depreciation—All equipment will be depreciated per ACRS schedules: vehicles and computers—3 years; furniture and fixtures—10 years.

EXHIBIT 4 Pro Forma Income Statement

	Year 2				Year 3			
	Q1	Q2	Q3	Q4	Q1	Q2	Q3	Q4
Sales[1]	136,500	156,000	194,698	234,000	253,500	273,000	292,500	312,000
Less: Cost of goods sold[2]	89,250	102,000	127,302	153,000	165,750	178,500	191,250	204,000
Gross profit	47,250	54,000	67,395	81,000	87,750	94,500	101,250	108,000
Less: Operating expenses								
Salaries and wages[3]	31,164	38,796	38,796	38,796	41,124	41,124	41,124	41,124
Operating supplies	900	900	900	900	900	900	900	900
Repairs and maintenance	750	750	750	750	750	750	750	750
Advertising and promotion[4]	6,825	7,800	9,735	11,700	12,675	13,650	14,625	15,600
Bad debts	300	300	300	300	300	300	300	300
Rent[5]	5,301	5,301	5,301	5,301	5,619	5,619	5,619	5,619
Utilities	3,000	3,000	3,000	3,000	3,000	3,000	3,000	3,000
Insurance	1,800	1,800	1,800	1,800	1,800	1,800	1,800	1,800
General office	450	450	450	450	450	450	450	450
Interest[6]	1,280	1,940	1,720	1,720	1,410	1,190	970	970
Depreciation[7]	6,910	6,910	6,910	6,910	7,493	7,493	7,493	7,493
Total operating expenses	58,680	67,947	69,662	71,627	75,520	76,275	77,030	78,005
Profit (loss) before taxes	(11,430)	(13,947)	(2,267)	9,373	12,230	18,225	24,220	29,995
Less: Taxes	0							
Net profit (loss)	(11,430)	(13,947)	(2,267)	9,373	12,230	18,225	24,220	29,995

[1]Average unit sale for groceries is about $43.00, plus $10.00 per week for delivery (Exhibit 1), making the monthly unit sales per household (2 people) about $212.00.

[2]Cost of goods sold—80 percent of retail grocery price, or $32.00 per household per week ($138.00/month household). (80 percent an average margin on groceries—*Progressive Grocer;* April 1984; p. 94.)

[3]Salaries and wages—Ms. Jones's salary will be $5,000/month. Order clerks will be paid $1,300/month, and delivery clerks will be paid $1,100/month. One additional order clerk and delivery clerk each will be added once sales reach 100 households, and again at 200 households. Salaries will escalate at 6 percent/year.

[4]Advertising and promotion—The grocery industry standard is 1 percent of sales. However, Gourmet to Go, being a new business, will require more than that level; 5 percent of sales is used in this plan. (Special pre-start-up advertising is covered with other start-up expenses.)

[5]Rent—2,000/ft.² @ $8.00/ft.²; 1,333 $1/month; escalate at 6 percent/year.

[6]Interest—Loans on computer ($10,000) and delivery vehicles ($12,000 ea.) at 12.5 percent year. (Delivery vehicles will be added with delivery clerks.) (Debt service—based on three-year amortization of loans with payments of ⅓ at the end of each of three years.)

[7]Depreciation—All equipment will be depreciated per ACRS schedules: vehicles and computers—3 years; furniture and fixtures—10 years.

EXHIBIT 5 Pro Forma Cash Flow Statement

							Year 1						
	Mo. 1	Mo. 2	Mo. 3	Mo. 4	Mo. 5	Mo. 6	Mo. 7	Mo. 8	Mo. 9	Mo. 10	Mo. 11	Mo. 12	Total
Cash receipts													
Sales	2,600	3,900	6,500	13,000	19,500	23,400	26,000	28,600	31,200	33,800	36,400	39,000	263,900
Other													
Total cash receipts	2,600	3,900	6,500	13,000	19,500	23,400	26,000	28,600	31,200	33,800	36,400	39,000	263,900
Cash disbursements													
Cost of goods sold	1,700	2,550	4,250	8,500	12,750	15,300	17,000	18,700	20,400	22,100	23,800	25,500	172,550
Salaries and wages	7,400	7,400	7,400	7,400	7,400	7,400	9,800	9,800	9,800	9,800	9,800	9,800	103,200
Operating supplies	300	300	300	300	300	300	300	300	300	300	300	300	3,600
Repairs and maintenance	250	250	250	250	250	250	250	250	250	250	250	250	3,000
Advertising and promotion	130	195	325	650	975	1,170	1,300	1,430	1,560	1,690	1,820	1,950	13,195
Bad debts	100	100	100	100	100	100	100	100	100	100	100	100	1,200
Rent	1,667	1,667	1,667	1,667	1,667	1,667	1,667	1,667	1,667	1,667	1,667	1,667	20,004
Utilities	1,000	1,000	1,000	1,000	1,000	1,000	1,000	1,000	1,000	1,000	1,000	1,000	12,000
Insurance	600	600	600	600	600	600	600	600	600	600	600	600	7,200
General office	150	150	150	150	150	150	150	150	150	150	150	150	1,800
Licenses	200	0	0	0	0	0	0	0	0	0	0	0	200
Interest	310	310	310	310	310	310	530	530	530	530	530	530	5,040
Debt service (principal)										10,333		10,333
Total cash disbursements	13,807	14,522	16,352	20,927	25,502	28,247	32,697	34,527	36,357	38,187	40,017	52,180	353,322
Net cash flow	(11,207)	(10,622)	(9,852)	(7,927)	(6,002)	(4,847)	(6,697)	(5,927)	(5,157)	(4,387)	(3,617)	(13,180)	(89,422)

EXHIBIT 6 Pro Forma Cash Flow Statement

	Year 2				Year 3			
	Q1	Q2	Q3	Q4	Q1	Q2	Q3	Q4
Cash receipts								
Sales	136,500	156,000	194,698	234,000	253,500	273,000	292,500	312,000
Other								
Total cash receipts	136,500	156,000	194,698	234,000	253,500	273,000	292,500	312,000
Cash disbursements								
Cost of goods sold	89,250	102,000	127,302	153,000	165,750	178,500	191,250	204,000
Salaries and wages	31,164	38,796	38,796	38,796	41,124	41,124	41,124	41,124
Operating supplies	900	900	900	900	900	900	900	900
Repairs and maintenance	750	750	750	750	750	750	750	750
Advertising and promotion	6,825	7,800	9,735	11,700	12,675	13,650	14,625	15,600
Bad debts	300	300	300	300	300	300	300	300
Rent	5,301	5,301	5,301	5,301	5,619	5,619	5,619	5,619
Utilities	3,000	3,000	3,000	3,000	3,000	3,000	3,000	3,000
Insurance	1,800	1,800	1,800	1,800	1,800	1,800	1,800	1,800
General office	450	450	450	450	450	450	450	450
Licenses	0	0	0	0	0	0	0	0
Interest	1,280	1,940	1,720	1,720	1,410	1,190	970	970
Debt service (principal)		7,333		10,333	7,333	7,333		10,333
Total cash disbursements	141,020	170,370	190,054	228,050	241,111	254,616	260,788	284,846
Net cash flow	(4,520)	(14,370)	4,643	5,950	12,389	18,384	31,712	27,154

EXHIBIT 7 Pro Forma Balance Sheets

End of:	Year 1	Year 2	Year 3		Year 1	Year 2	Year 3
Assets				**Liabilities**			
Current assets				Accounts payable	12,750	21,217	31,875
Cash	3,000	5,000	7,000	Notes payable	0	0	0
Accounts receivable	19,500	32,450	48,750	Total current liabilities	12,750	21,217	31,875
Inventory	12,750	21,217	31,875	Long-term liabilities			
Supplies	300	300	300	Bank loans payable	42,667	47,000	22,000
Prepaid expenses	1,667	1,767	1,873	Personal loans payable	0	0	0
Total current assets	37,217	60,734	89,798	Total long-term liabilities	42,667	47,000	22,000
Fixed assets				Total liabilities	55,417	68,217	53,875
Furniture and fixtures	18,000	16,000	14,000	Owner's equity			
Vehicles	33,000	32,780	8,140	Paid-in capital	133,889	62,897	28,068
Equipment	6,750	3,330	0	Retained earnings	(94,339)	(18,271)	29,995
Total fixed assets	57,750	52,110	22,140	Total owner's equity	39,550	44,627	58,063
Total assets	94,967	112,844	111,938	Total liabilities and equity	94,967	112,844	111,938

EXHIBIT 8   Sources and Uses of Funds

Sources of Funds	
Jan Jones (personal funds)	$182,913
Bank loans for computer and vehicles	75,000
Total sources	$257,913
Uses of Funds	
Computer, peripherals, and software	$9,000
Food lockers and freezers	15,000
Delivery vehicles*	66,000
Phone system	1,500
Miscellaneous furniture and fixtures	3,500
Start-up expenses	54,600
Working capital†	108,313
Total uses‡	$257,913

*See detail, following.

†To cover negative cash flow over first 1½ years of operation. (See pro forma cash flow statements.)

‡Total for initial 3-year period. Computer and one delivery van will be acquired prior to start-up, one delivery van will be added 6 months after startup, and another will be added 15 months after start-up. Financing will be handled simultaneously with procurement.

MARKETING
Distribution

The product will be delivered directly to the customer.

Sales Strategy

Advertising will include newspaper ads, radio spots, an Internet Web page, and direct-mail brochures. All four will be used during normal operations, but an intense campaign will precede start-up. A series of "teaser" newspaper ads will be run prior to start-up, announcing a revolution in grocery shopping. At start-up, the newspaper ads will have evolved into actually introducing the product, and radio spots will begin as well. A heavy advertising schedule will be used during the first four weeks of business. After start-up, a direct mailing will detail the description of the service and a menu plan.

Newspaper ads aimed at the target markets will be placed in entertainment and business sections. Radio spots will be geared to stations most appealing to the target market. Since the product is new, it may be possible to do interviews with newspapers and obtain free publicity.

Sales promotions will offer large discounts to first-time customers. These promotions will continue for the first six months of operations.

The service will be priced at $10 per week for delivery and planning, with the groceries priced at full retail level. According to the phone survey, most people who were interested in the service would be willing to pay the weekly service charge.

MANAGEMENT

The management will consist of the owner/manager. Other employees will be delivery clerks and order clerks. It is anticipated that after the business grows, an operations manager might be added to supervise the employees.

CASE 8A
INTERVELA D.O.O. KOPER— VICTORY SAILMAKERS, PART A

Zvonko and Zeljko stepped through the glass door of the sail loft they started a decade ago and paused on the blue iron stairs. Their glances drifted out to the sea, shimmering in the evening sunshine. The ships in the Bay of Koper were set on a southerly course. The sailboats in the marina were quietly moored as if patiently waiting for the helmsmen and crews to finally untie them and unfurl their sails. Grey clouds coming in from the southwest did not disturb their thoughts; they were already thinking past dinner to the next day, when time limits would again be pressuring them. Their most successful business year was now behind them and several new options were emerging.

SAILING

Zvonko Bezic and Zeljko Perovic, both born in 1962, met each other in the early 1970s when they both started sailing with the Galeb Sailing Club in Rijeka, Croatia. As students, they sailed together in the Flying

Source: The case was written by Bostjan Antoncic, Faculty of Management at the University of Primorska. Copyright 2001 of the author. Published with the author's permission.

The case is intended as a basis for class discussion rather than to illustrate either effective or ineffective handling of management situations.

Dutchman Class. At that time they were already modifying their racing sails, primarily of foreign make, adjusting them to their weight and style of sailing. They finished their university studies in the late 1980s (Zvonko Bezic with a degree in pedagogy and Zeljko Perovic in maritime traffic engineering).

In 1988, they were both employed, Zvonko Bezic as a journalist and editor for the Rijeka region with the Trade Union paper "Radnicke novine," and Zeljko Perovic (who usually goes by his sailing nickname, Huck) as a sailing coach in Galeb. Zeljko Perovic occasionally worked with Mr. Grego, who was making sails. It was here that Zeljko learned how to make sails for large sailboats; this involved knowing how much curve is needed for each horizontal panel and how to make the sail's final cut. In addition, he read English books dealing with this topic, which he found extremely interesting. In 1988, Zvonko Bezic and Zeljko Perovic started making sails on their own, at first only for the smallest optimist-class sailboats. They made their first design for these sails by taking apart a sail produced by Green, the most renowned sail manufacturer among sailors and coaches in the optimist class at that time. The same sail was also usable for larger sailboats, which was particularly important. The first set of sails for the sailing school in Rijeka was a direct copy of such a sail.

THE AFFABLE ESTABLISHMENT OF A COMPANY

At that time a friend from Rijeka, who himself was already a well-established and experienced tradesman, persuaded Zvonko Bezic to start his own business. He even suggested the type of business (chemicals) and a partner, but in the end they did not go into that field. Instead, together with Zeljko Perovic, they decided to establish a sail loft business. The above-mentioned friend offered them a loan of SFR 2,000 under the following conditions: should their enterprise survive for two years, they would not have to pay back the loan, but should they go bankrupt and not be successful, they would have to repay the loan together with accrued interest. They accepted the offer. Their friend also provided them with business cards and promotional material.

In 1989, the two started manufacturing regatta sails for the youth Optimist Class. They adapted the basic design and cut of the panels from the disassembled Green sail to the needs of lighter sails. Zeljko

Perovic said that "they began to play with the form of sails." They simultaneously started to manufacture sails for larger sailboats and yachts. The sails were cut in the school gym they rented on weekends; on weekdays the sails were sewed at home together with Zeljko Perovic's grandmother. He remembers: ". . . we occupied a part of her house, first a small room and then an entire floor and even the garage." In the manufacturing of sails for larger sailboats the know-how and information acquired from Mr. Grego helped them extensively.

In 1990, the two decided to go into the sail business full time. They studied books and magazines and gathered a great deal of information on: (1) the materials used for sailmaking, (2) the manufacturing process itself, its history and developmental trends, and (3) other sail manufacturers. They learned about computer-aided sail cutting, and were also able to obtain information directly from sail manufacturers, particularly those from Slovenia and northern Italy. In the then relatively large factory for the mass production of sails in Forli, Italy, where the pair offered to sell the Italian firm's sails in the former Yugoslavia, they learned how the factory organized sail production and what equipment they used. "They employed an expert from New Zealand and used a computer program. In Forli we primarily tried to learn what they do and how they do it," relates Zeljko Perovic. They also learned a great deal during their visit to the newly opened sail loft of the largest global manufacturer, North, in Monfalcone, Italy, accompanying Dusan Puh who was then ordering sails for "Elan Team," of which Zvonko Bezic was a member, and for the Elan sailboat then called "Packa." They got useful information about the equipment they used and about where it could be ordered. While looking for a sail loft on Sardegna to have his torn sails repaired, Zeljko Perovic by chance found himself in a sail loft manufacturing Fois sails. He saw how simply they finish some details on the sail (e.g., edges and reinforcements) and how they have adapted their machines for this process.

The two decided to purchase a computer program for cutting the sails. For half a year they gathered data on which program to buy and tested five different demo programs. At the end of 1990, they bought a personal computer and Sailmaker Software (SMSW) from Autometrix, USA. While they knew that renowned sail manufacturers were also using plotters and cutters in addition to computers, they could not afford them. They also had difficulties financing production and covering fixed costs, since they had rented manufacturing facilities in Rijeka.

STANDSTILL AND A NEW START

In 1991 they accepted positions as hired sailors in Italy in order to raise some money. Concurrently, the market for sails in Croatia and Slovenia shrank that year, resulting in their not manufacturing sails but only maintaining some resale business. As there was practically no market in Croatia, they started looking for a new location for their sail loft—somewhere closer to Italy. They were about to decide on either Portorose, Slovenia, or Ravenna, Italy, when Mr. J. Kosmina offered them the opportunity to take over the sail repair service during the Match Race in Koper, Slovenia. They decided to stay in Koper and rented premises in the Koper Marina to start making sails again. At the beginning of 1992 they used their savings to buy a second-hand Autometrix plotter. "We were among the first in the local market (i.e., Slovenia, Croatia, and northern Italy) to start applying computer technology in the manufacturing of sails; in the whole of Italy, only the leading manufacturer—North—availed itself of computer technology," explains Zeljko Perovic.

In 1992, while they were making sails in Koper, they launched an additional activity—making advertising signs. As they started to plot the letters, they learned from other sign makers what programs to use, how they read the sketches and transfer them to the plotter (in terms of size and form). They used this know-how also in the computer aided design of reinforcements. The company was becoming known in this local market and could more easily establish contacts and exchange information with other local sailmakers. At the end of 1992, the company moved into larger premises in the marina and modernized their manufacturing process with the purchase of additional new sewing machines.

MARKETING STRATEGY

In 1993, sales increased and the company was obtaining customers from Italy, Germany, and Austria. At that time, the main local competitors of Intervela (their company) were: Olimpic Trieste, Italy (with sales of about USD 900,000 in 1993), Ulmer Kolius Lignano, Italy (USD 600,000), North Monfalcone, Italy (USD 180,000), Seaway Portorose, Slovenia (USD 180,000), and Zadro Trieste, Italy (USD

90,000). At the end of that year a sailor from Koper who had the status of junior researcher at the Faculty of Economics of the University of Ljubljana, Slovenia, prepared, in cooperation with both proprietors, a marketing plan for Intervela, which had hitherto only haphazardly planned a marketing strategy. Based on an analysis of the current demand and the competition, an increase in sales of 58 percent over the next three years (1994–1996) was established as the main goal, along with: a gradual increase in market share, the promotion of the company and its products to potential customers, and an improvement in the internal efficiency of the company and the quality of its products. The strengths (price and quality, including the finishing of sails and a two-year warranty), weaknesses (marketing communication, standardization, design), opportunities (selling larger series to companies, manufacturing sails for larger yachts), and threats (market contraction, poor advertising for sails, essential technological changes) were also established for sails—the key product of the company.

Development and market penetration were the primary focus of the company's business plan. The marketing strategy was formulated: product (standardization, design improvements, the transfer of improvements from racing sails to other sails, following trends closely, the introduction and improvement of after-sale services—i.e., the tuning of sails and instructing customers); price (competitive prices with regard to individual customers); place (the extension of the distribution network); and promotion (promotion by means of a first-class sailboat—*Gaia Cube*—in races, personal contacts, the distribution of promotional material to sailboat owners, and advertising in the Slovenian nautical magazine "Val"). They focused on the promotion of the Victory sail trademark.

In 1993, Intervela was the first to introduce a novelty in the production of larger sails: double batten pockets. This concept had previously only been applied to smaller Olympic sailboats and mentioned in professional journals. Some local rivals soon copied this idea.

Despite the shrinkage of the Italian market, the company consistently enjoyed increasing sales throughout 1994. The quality of their sails and the good publicity gained when the *Gaia Cube* sailboat won races contributed much to the sales results. In that year, Mr. Vencato, a rival from Trieste and the manufacturer of Ullman sails, proposed cooperation in part to learn what computer program and plotter they were using and how they worked. Soon afterwards, Mr. Vencato bought an

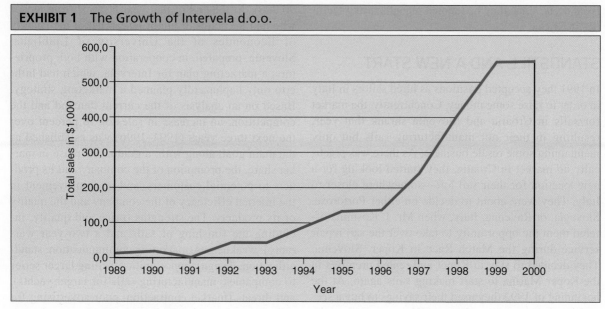

EXHIBIT 1 The Growth of Intervela d.o.o.

Source: Data from the company and the annual accounts of Intervela d.o.o.

improved version of the same software and plotter that at the same time worked as a cutter.

A DECISION ON THE CUTTER AND THE SITUATION IN 1995

In 1995, after another successful business year (a further increase in sales to USD 128,300—see Exhibit 1), the owner-managers of Intervela decided, among other new investments, to purchase a new plotter-cutter to cut sailcloth material. They also visited Mr. DeMartisu of the Olimpic sail loft in Trieste, who had purchased a new plotter-cutter that year. In 1995 more competitors visited Intervela than in the year before.

Intervela d.o.o. Koper is a relatively small limited liability company wholly owned by Zvonko Bezic and Zeljko Perovic. In 1995, the company primarily manufactured sails for racing sailboats and keelboats.[1] Sales under the brand name Victory accounted for 90 percent of total sales in 1995 (of which 65 percent were regatta sails), while sail repairs, advertising-sign making, and the manufacture of canvas covers, bags, and trapezes for sailboats accounted for the remaining 10 percent. Intervela in 1994 had USD 86,300 in sales revenue and six full-time staff (including owners) and USD 128,300 in sales revenue with five full-time employees in 1995. Zvonko Bezic is primarily responsible for marketing, while Zeljko Perovic is in charge of production.

THE PURCHASE OF A CUTTER

In 1995, Intervela purchased a sailcloth material cutter and two software packages for planning and designing sails, resulting in the use of three different software packages: SMSW, ProSail, and Crain. The American ProSail software program is, as one of the sail loft owners says, rather easy to use particularly for the designs for the cruising sails. The American SMSW and the French Crain software packages are more complex and require more time to design sails and are appropriate for the more demanding sails used in racing. The company started using SMSW in the first half of the nineties.

THE ACQUISITION OF THE KUTIN SAIL LOFT WORKSHOP

Due to the rapidly increasing demand for Victory sails, the two partners looked for additional workspace and staff in 1996. When the Kutin sail loft in Rijeka declared bankruptcy, the company acquired the workshop and moved their old plotter to Rijeka. The new location in Croatia began operations in May 2000.

ELAN

Prior to the bankruptcy, Kutin made sails for Elan, the biggest producer of sailboats in Slovenia. The Kutin-Elan relationship had difficulties due to quality problems and customer complaints. One of the Intervela owners explained that about 60 percent of the complaints received by Elan at that time concerned sails produced by Kutin, causing Elan to look for a new supplier.

Elan desired to have an inland supplier. Elan tried to have Rado Pelajic manufacture sails for small Zeta class sailboats, but that cooperation did not last. Elan then contacted Intervela and Zvonko and Zeljko prepared a contract. Because Victory sails were of higher quality than those produced by Kutin, a higher price was quoted, above Kutin's delivery price to Elan. Through negotiations a slightly lower price was agreed to in the final contract.

Zvonko and Zeljko thought that "this would be some business to fill in the gaps—in winter time when the market is flat." It involved the rather simple mass production of sails. A regular customer would also "provide a certain degree of security." However, in dealing with such a big customer as Elan, payment difficulties occurred. In spite of the agreed 60-day payment term, payment was received after 120 days or later. In 1998 a sailboat was received in compensation for unpaid invoices. In 2000 that sailboat, an Elan 36, captained by Franci Stres, sunk in a storm along the Croatian coast. In a second compensation deal in 1999, an Elan 333 Cruising boat was received as payment. In that year, Elan "faced bankruptcy."

Elan sent to Intervela a proposal for writing off such receivable claims, but Zvonko and Zeljko did not agree to it. Negotiations on the allocation of bankruptcy assets dragged on into mid-2001. "Since we were among the more important suppliers, they retained us as suppliers and did not write off our receivables," stated Zvonko Bezic. In 2001, Intervela continued to do business with Elan, but required pre-payment for the sails supplied. Orders from Elan increased. From 60 sailboats per year, sales of Elan sailboats (and Victory sails) increased to about 110 sailboats in the year 2000 and a planned 150 sailboats in 2001. Sales to Elan accounted for about one-fourth (about USD 137,500) of the total sales (about USD 550,000) of Intervela in 2000.

THE *GAIA CUBE* PROJECT

Intervela made their first sails for the racing boat *Gaia Cube* (subsequently the *Gaia Legend*) Consortium in 1995. In the period 1995–1997 they were also members of the crew and won races at the famous sailing event Barcolana in the bay of Trieste. Later, in 1998, the Kosmina family, which played the leading role in the

consortium, decided to use sails made by the Trieste-based Olimpic. Olimpic, being the strongest local company at that time, offered some very low prices. The company made money by selling sails for smaller sailboats, which made it important to enter into this project regardless of the low price.

PENETRATING THE GLOBAL MARKET WITH FINN CLASS SAILS

At the end of 1997 and at the beginning of 1998 Intervela started to manufacture sails for the Olympic one-man Finn sailboat. Karlo Kuret, a renowned Croatian sailor in the class, asked them to make him a sail, because in his Olympic program the cost of sails was very high. He proposed they make him a copy of the Sobstadt sail, but Zvonko and Zeljko decided to develop a completely new sail. This new sail was a great international success. Using the Victory sail, Kuret won the Olympic Week race in Athens in February 1998.

Olympic champion Mateusz Kusnierewicz from Poland wanted to test the new sail at the pre-Olympic regatta in Medemblik, Netherlands. The sail was sewn by Intervela overnight. The next day Kusnierewicz was racing with his sail. At the next pre-Olympic regatta, in Kiel, Germany, Kusnierewicz won seven out of nine races. From 1999 to 2001, using the Victory sail, he was the number one sailor in the world—his worst result was second place in the World and European championships (World Champion 1999 in Greece and 2000 in England); he took fourth place at the Olympic Games in Sydney.

When Intervela started to produce the Finn class sails, they also started to cooperate with the University of Zagreb, Croatia, where the first analyses of sailcloth were done. A comparison of various materials was made by analyzing 26 parameters. This analysis helps the company determine the quality of materials and the appropriateness of a material for their products.

Zvonko and Zeljko believe that, in addition to the development of a new product, the securing of top sailors in the Finn class having good results, and the application of new materials, the following three factors were important in their penetration into the Finn sails market:

- *Development of sails.* Victory sail representatives visit regattas, watch the races, and collect information and comments; Intervela has composed a team of top-level sailors (four of them were among the top ten in the world ranking in 2000 as well as of mid-2001) and offers them special conditions such as adjusting the sails to their specific needs.

- *Novelty in sail design technology.* Intervela used sophisticated computer software in designing and constructing the sails for "one-design" types of sailboats, such as the Finn.
- *Analysis of sail quality.* The company tests sails by attaching sensors to the sail and a camera to the top of the mast to record sail performance during sailing; they then improve the sails based on an analysis of their performance.

Intervela was growing into a globally renowned company with the Victory brand name. At the Olympics in Sydney, 18 of the 25 sailors in the Finn class used Victory sails. The sails are now being sold all over the world: Canada, USA, Brazil, Australia, New Zealand, Republic of South Africa, China, Japan, Sweden, Denmark, Poland, Russia, Belarus, Ukraine, Lithuania, Germany, Great Britain, Belgium, France, Spain, Italy, Ireland, Austria, Croatia, Slovenia, Hungary, Greece, and Turkey.

EUROPE CLASS

The company also succeeded in penetrating the European Dinghy class market. In 1999 the company's sails dominated the Slovene, Croatian, and Italian market and realized some sales even in Poland and Belarus. At the 2000 Olympics, female representatives of the USA, Italy, Belarus, and Poland raced with Victory sails.

THE OPTIMIST CLASS

In 2001, Intervela started developing a sail for the Optimist youth dinghy. In February and March 2001 the new sail was completed. They employed Karel Kuret, a top-sailor and an authority among Croatian sailors, who helped them with the development of the sail.

The company entered into an agreement with Sime Fantella, the 2000 World Champion, and with his father who was also his coach, that he would test their sail during the preparation stage (from February to April 2001), even though he had been racing with sails made by Olimpic of Trieste. Sime and his father were satisfied with the sail and soon other members of the Croatian team started to use Victory sails in races. In April 2001, Fantella won the South American Championship. The second Croatian competitor took third place; and in the women's competition, first place was won by a Croatian sailor. The Croatian team also won the team competition. In spite of the fact that in mid-2001 Olimpic enjoyed a market share of 50 percent, followed by North, Denmark and Toni Tio from Spain, the company established an objective of having 50 percent of the Croatian market within two years.

Even before manufacturing sails for the Optimist class, the company had encountered some competitive problems. After making a sail for an Italian, who finished very high in a regatta, an Olimpic representative gave the Italian one of their sails as a gift. Similarly, when the company tried to cooperate with Milan Morgan, who makes Optimist dinghies in Portorose, Slovenia, Intervela gave him some promotional sails. Milan used these sails as the basis for negotiating with Olimpic. Because of these and other unpleasant experiences, Intervela decided to proceed in a different way in Croatia. "Our first goal is the Croatian market—and we will not give up; we will attain this goal by September (2001). If you do not control your domestic market, you cannot control foreign ones," stated Zvonko Bezic. In 2001, there were already too many potential sales agents in Croatia and the company was receiving calls from agents from Peru, Brazil, Sweden, England, and the United States.

CLASS 470

Another goal established was to make it to the top in the 470 Olympic class. They started to develop the sails in cooperation with the coach of Russia's female sailors. In Slovenia they started to cooperate with the Olympian Vesna Dekleva, and in Croatia with Bulaja, who had participated in the Olympic Games in Sydney.

SAILS FOR CRUISING & RACING YACHTS

In addition to sails for smaller one-design dinghies, such as the Finn, Europe, Optimist, and 470, which in mid-2001 accounted for around 30 percent of Intervela's sales, and sails produced for Elan, which accounted for about 30 percent of sales revenue, the company was continually evaluating new market opportunities. The entrepreneurs were always evaluating their rivals' products and how they were producing sails. At the end of the twentieth century, independent computer aided development and design of sails became important. The main markets for their sails were Slovenia and Croatia, and to a lesser extent Italy.

PROMOTION AND MARKETING IN 2000 AND 2001

At the beginning Intervela relied primarily on word of mouth advertising (satisfied owners of sails told other sailors about their experiences). The company did more formalized promotion and advertising in 2000 and 2001. They participated in nautical fairs in Slovenia and Croatia. They advertised in specialized nautical journals, such as "Val" and "Navtika" in Slovenia and "More" in Croatia, as well as in the specialized magazines of international sailing classes such as Finnfare and Optimist Dinghy. They also promoted their sails in newspaper articles which they wrote themselves or were written by journalists. Articles on sailors' preparations and their cooperation with Intervela, the success of Victory sails and the Intervela company appeared particularly in the Slovene newspapers "Primorske novice" and "Slovenske novice," in the Croatian "Novi list," and in the Italian journals "Fare Vela" and "Giornale della vela."

In 1998 the Web site of the company was designed. They increased the number of "hits" or visits by publishing news from regattas and by reporting the results online. At the same time, sailing clubs, organizers of races, and sailing associations started using the Internet for the real-time online reporting of race results.

The company made the sail covers and packaging (particularly the sail bags) uniform. They enlarged the Victory logo and decided on a red-white combination for the brand and background, because red made the logo very visible.

The company also created a clearer identity for the Victory brand name by using special material. They contracted with one of the factories to have a special sailcloth made exclusively for Victory sails. The material is Kevlar and the usual black thread in the cloth was exchanged for a red one. In this way, with no additional costs, easier and clearer recognition of their sails occurred. When they first introduced this novelty in the Finn class, many sailors believed that it was a completely new type of sail, not just a new material.

The two started doing more lectures and presentations in sailing clubs and during sailing races. In sailing clubs, they discussed, in particular, how sails operate and are trimmed. After having returned from the United States in the fall 2000, they presented to the organizer of the Europe class regatta the material used during that day's racing. Digital photos were shown and their presentation focused on sails and technical advice on trimming the mast. After establishing the cooperation with Karlo Kuret Intervela decided to organize training camps for the best coaches and sailors in the class.

VISIT TO THE USA IN AUTUMN 2000

In the fall 2000, Zvonko Bezic and Zeljko Perovic went to visit some of the most important factories producing sailcloth material on the East Coast of the United States. "When we started, we could not even talk to or visit such factories or talk to sailcloth material sales representatives. . . . Today sales representatives visit us at least every three months," explained Zvonko Bezic.

When they arrived at the biggest sailcloth producer in the world, Bainbridge International, the general manager spent the entire day with them. A PowerPoint presentation, containing a section on cooperation between Bainbridge International and Intervela, and a "slide" showing the logos of both brand names and a link between them demonstrating future cooperation between the two companies occurred. They were guests of Bainbridge International for three days and it was there they got the idea to start using sales presentations to promote their sails.

MAIN CHANGES IN THE MARKET

In ten years of existence, Intervela has grown and become an important factor in the sail market. They have grown faster than their competition and reached and surpassed most. In 2001 the nautical market was still growing. "There is no recession, many people are buying yachts, sails. . . . The market is growing. . . . And Intervela is growing even faster," Zvonko Bezic commented.

STAFF, OUTSOURCING, AND REORGANIZATION

By mid-2001, Intervela had 15 regularly employed individuals working on contracts in Slovenia and 5 individuals in Croatia. Since the company did not have sufficient production space, they started to outsource the manufacturing of some parts, such as bags and reinforcements, to suppliers in Koper. A subcontractor was given two sewing machines and started sewing for Intervela in his garage.

The company introduced the special position of plotter operator, in order to use their facilities more efficiently. This person's job was to operate the computer or some other operation of the plotter. "We are looking for new people all the time. We also employ through the Employment Agency of Slovenia. But the number employed through the Agency is actually very low," commented Zvonko Bezic.

The friend who first helped Zvonko Bezic and Zeljko Perovic in the start-up of their company, decided—after the bankruptcy of his relatively large company in Croatia—to help establish production standards and improve the organization of the workshop. He analyzed how much a worker can do per hour, how much time is needed for each element of the production process, and the capabilities of workers. Zvonko Bezic said: "an experienced entrepreneur entered our workshop and found a hundred mistakes. . . . We are burdened with complicated issues. . . . Regarding simpler issues, such as the proper laying of material, however, improvements can also be found in the details, which add up to a lot in the end."

INTERNATIONAL PRODUCTION

Having taken over the workshop in Rijeka, Croatia, the company began production there as well. From this production facility the company covered the Croatian market and also produced Optimist sails. Two main possibilities are available for establishing production facilities in Italy.

The company first considered a location in Gorizia—in the International Business Center (a business incubator in Trieste with a branch office in Gorizia). The incubator offered assistance such as: sales staff with 50 percent of the pay subsidized, Internet services at minimum rates, assistance in getting loans and other forms of financing, and lower rent for business premises.

In 2001 the company considered purchasing the company of a local Italian sailor who had machines and workers but was not successful and had no desire to continue in the business. With the intention to expand their activities in Italy, they began training an Italian in their sail loft in Koper so he could then manage the work in Italy.

OTHER PLANS FOR THE FUTURE AND OPTIONS

In 2001, Intervela was planning to expand their 450 square meter facilities in Croatia. "Particularly for cruising sails . . . charter business is on the increase: 120 percent more tourists, 300 percent more than in 1999. . . . We shall have to invest here too," Zvonko Bezic reasoned. They began to search for a new location with about 1,000 square meters of space.

The company was also considering the possibility of using the brand name Victory on garments (jackets, T-shirts, etc.). This would promote the brand name on the one hand and bring in additional income. They

started to look for partners who manufacture sportswear who would be willing and able to carry out such a project. In 1999, the company negotiated with a potential partner, but the potential partner withdrew from the project. In 2001, Intervela was still opposed to pushing the project forward without finding a good partner who was very interested.

At this same time, the company had contact with some major sailmakers, mainly in the United States. They started discussing a possible merger or at least joining an already established group. The two main conditions needed were money and less operational work. Right now Zvonko Bezic and Zeljko Perovic are in a dilemma regarding the following three alternatives:

- Develop a foreign trade name and work as a member of a group;
- Merge with a foreign company; or
- Sell the company—find a potential partner with money who would acquire a part or the entire company.

END NOTE

1. Keelboats are medium-sized and larger sailing boats that now prevail in all marinas in the world. They shall be distinguished from smaller dinghies that, in most cases, are single-type sport sailboats made according to strictly defined international rules in order to avoid, as much as possible, any differences within the same class (e.g., class: 470, Finn, Laser, Europe, Optimist, etc.).

CASE 8B
INTERVELA VICTORY SAILMAKERS, PART B

The year was 2011, and Zeljko Perovic was driving on that familiar highway between Materija and the Bay of Koper. He was using this weekend to catch up on his beloved hobby—sailing. As he watched the Slovenian countryside pass by him, he thought about how sailing had defined so much of his life, both personally and professionally. His mind wandered over the past ten years which had seemed to go by so quickly. He thought of how Intervela began as a small-scale project with his friend Zvonko and had become something much larger than either of them could have imagined. When Zeljko finally reached the bay and felt the cool sea air on his face, he still could not fully leave the thoughts about his business behind. He continued to reminisce about Intervela over the past ten years, a decade full of some considerable gains—and some very big losses.

DECISION ABOUT THE NEW SAIL LOFT

As business continued to expand after 2001, Zvonko and Zeljko felt that they were outgrowing their current space at the Koper marina. In addition to the inadequate size of the Koper sail loft, the marina had started to demand their own slice of the Victory Sails pie by increasing rent costs to the two entrepreneurs, and the two needed a cheaper place to produce their sails. In the past year Zvonko and Zeljko had been planning on buying a sail loft in Italy and had even been training an Italian to manage the new loft. When it became apparent that Slovenia would join the European Union in 2004, however, Zvonko and Zeljko saw no more need for a concrete presence in Italy. It would be better to take advantage of the new single EU market and centralize their production. The two then began to search for new premises within Slovenia.

They found an interesting offer in the Slovenian town of Materija, roughly 32 km inland from Koper, and a 30–45 minute drive to Rijeka, Croatia, and Trieste, Italy. A textile plant had recently gone bankrupt, and the municipal authorities of Materija were looking to solve a twofold problem with one stroke. First, the city simply wanted to find a company that could employ the laid-off textile workers. The second problem had to do with a nightclub on the premises that the previous owner had rented out as a source of additional revenue. The nightclub was reportedly engaging in questionable activity, and the city wanted to find a buyer for the land who would agree to expel the business. With the city so eager to see new owners for the property, the two entrepreneurs considered the Materija plant with much optimism.

Zvonko and Zeljko saw the move to Materija as a prime opportunity for several reasons. Being inland from the coast, the price was right, which would certainly add to the bottom line. They were dealing with a very supportive town government instead of the Bay of Koper authorities, who had become too demanding and were cutting into profits. Size would also be very important for the new production facility. The Materija plant was about 2500m^2—much larger than their space in Koper. They could even continue to rent space to a kindergarten on the premises as a source of revenue. Materija was closer to their other production facility in Rijeka, Croatia, making coordination between the two facilities much easier. Almost providentially, the sewing skills of the textile workers were directly transferable to sailmaking. Finally, Zvonko and Zeljko were ready to get out of the marina environment; there was too much pressure in the spring and summer seasons to meet sailors' constant demands for immediate sail repairs, and they felt they could better focus on the business from a quieter area. The two decided to purchase the Materija plant, and were able to finance their new purchase through their excess cash flows and a bank loan. They moved their plotters, cutters, and other production equipment to Materija and set up a significantly larger production floor for the manufacture of much larger sails. Victory Sails headquarters were officially moved to Materija in 2003.

SMOOTH SAILING

The move to Materija proved to be a great success. Zvonko and Zeljko were quite happy with their new headquarters and enjoyed both their quieter surroundings and their larger production floor. They were now able to increase their production as well as start producing some sails for larger boats.

The two entrepreneurs continued many aspects of their marketing strategy (advertising in nautical trade journals, attending nautical fairs, and supporting contestants using Victory Sails at regattas) but began to expand their reach geographically. In an effort to increase the international presence of the Victory sails brand, Zvonko began visiting some of the top regattas in Europe. He traveled to competitions in Hyeres, France, Medimblick in Holland, and Kiel, Germany—the top three regattas in Europe. He attended the continental and world championships to promote the Finn class of sails in various locations. As more and more sailors won races using Victory Sails, Intervela's international prestige grew.

Zvonko also won more notice within Slovenia when he began working with the Slovenian sailing team. He became the selector for the sailing federation of Slovenia and it was his responsibility to determine who would

Source: This case study was prepared by Alan Grisanti and Bostjan Antoncic with the intention of providing a basis for class discussion.

represent Slovenia in major regattas. Beyond Slovenia, they focused greatly on the Croatian market. They promoted the Optimist class heavily and collaborated with Sime Fantela, the Croatian Optimist champion. They also collaborated with Karlo Kuret, an Olympic Finn class sailor for Croatia (who continues his partnership with Intervela by helping them with sales and promotion to this day).

As they expanded their promotion and advertising, Intervela enjoyed increasing revenues. Except for their single corporate customer Elan (a sailboat manufacturer), Zvonko and Zeljko continued to custom-make their sails for each individual sailor on an on-demand basis. As business continued to grow in the mid-2000s, Zvonko and Zeljko began to delegate some of the operational and managerial work to some other employees and took advantage of their new free time. They even bought motorbikes for themselves to enjoy in their new-found free time. Although business was going well at the time, the smooth sailing would not last for long.

6:00 PM, 06-06-2006

On the evening of June 6, 2006, Zvonko Bezich was enjoying a ride on his new bike on the Croatian peninsula of Istria when, at approximately 6:00 PM, tragedy struck. Zvonko, heartbreakingly, was in a serious crash and did not survive. Zvonko's passing of course meant Intervela had lost one of its leaders, but this was nothing compared to Zeljko's loss of his best friend. Despite his pain, Zeljko had no choice but to continue the business he had founded with his late friend.

THE ONE SAILS DECISION

Zeljko Perovic was now not only in charge of sail production and development, but of Zvonko's previous marketing and distribution responsibilities as well. Using work as an outlet for his grief, Zeljko worked diligently and was able to keep Intervela on its successful course of profit and growth. Standing alone in competitive sails market, however, had already begun to take its toll on business.

Before Zvonko's passing, the two entrepreneurs had begun to consider two options for the future of the business: (1) expand the plant and begin producing some materials themselves, such as canvas and cloth; or (2) partner with other sailmakers in the form of a business group. Each option had certain benefits and drawbacks. Expanding the production plant and beginning to integrate vertically would allow Intervela to extend the reach of its brand name and would allow Zeljko more autonomy

in running the company. This course of action also entailed much risk and a considerable amount of stressful work. Joining a group, on the other hand, would mean that the Victory sails brand name would be replaced with the group's name and trademark, and Zeljko would have less of a say in the marketing of Intervela products. The benefits of joining a group were increased international awareness, increased purchasing power relative to suppliers, and minimized costs for each member individually for promotion and advertising. Weighing the pros and cons of each option, Zeljko decided to join the ONE sails group. ONE sails brought together fifteen, mostly Italian, sailmakers. Zeljko was confident in his decision to join the ONE group for several reasons. Although Intervela and Victory Sails had gained international recognition on their own, ONE sails took international visibility of his sails a step further. Intervela sails now benefited from the well-known ONE trademark and were able to penetrate more markets. Due to the ONE sails group's size and purchasing volume, Zeljko was now able to obtain materials at lower prices. Zeljko also found that outsourcing much of the marketing and promotion work allowed him to focus on sail development and production, his area of expertise.

THE PERFECT STORM

Zeljko was happy with his decision to join the ONE sails group. His business seemed to benefit from the new capabilities of the ONE sails network—cloth prices were down and Intervela gained access to an even more international market. Zeljko was also grateful that the majority of the marketing responsibilities were carried out by others who could devote more time to it.

Then the financial crisis hit. The worldwide economic downturn of 2008 did not spare the sails market. Revenues for Intervela had grown to 2.6 million dollars in 2008 before the crisis, but had fallen to 1.4 million by 2010 (see Exhibit 1). Not only was the demand from individual sailors down, but Intervela's largest corporate customer, Elan, found itself in financial hardship as well. Because of the crisis, payments to Intervela were coming in late or not at all. In some cases Intervela was paid with sailboats—a nice gesture perhaps, but such nonliquid assets were of little help to Intervela's business needs. The persistence of the global recession only made matters worse and ensured continued hardship for the sails market and for Intervela.

INTERVELA IN 2011

Intervela is still fully operational, and Zeljko Perovic continues to manage the Materija sails loft. Zeljko has

EXHIBIT 1   Intervela d.o.o. Total Revenue (2005–2010)

Year	Total Revenue ($)
2005	1,434,121
2006	1,762,463
2007	2,198,522
2008	2,615,625
2009	2,192,241
2010	1,422,547

Source: iBon 2005–2010.

had several ideas for new projects and expansions, but banks are still reeling from the financial crisis and are less willing to lend their money. The banks' conservative lending policies mean that, unlike in years past, future cash flow projections are little help when securing a loan and collateral is preferred. Despite the inconvenience, Intervela has been forced to finance some operations with short-term loans because of continued late payments by some customers. Given these hardships, how can Intervela return to and exceed their pre-crisis revenues, and how can Zeljko put Intervela on a long-term course for growth?

CASE 9
THE GRIL-KLEEN CORPORATION

"Well, where do I begin?" Warren Ryan wondered as he surveyed the chaos before him. Boxes and bottles were piled all over the place, invoices and order forms cluttered the desktop and filled the drawers, and he couldn't seem to locate anything resembling an orderly set of books.

It was spring of 2001, and just a few days earlier Ryan had quit his job with a large management consulting firm to assume the presidency of Gril-Kleen Corporation and help get the young company off the ground.

The company's efforts to market its innovative product, a liquid restaurant grill cleaner, had been extremely successful. Ryan felt that with a professional marketing approach, the product could capture a sizable share of a national market.

The product, a chemical solution which could be applied directly to a working grill and would clean off burnt-on food and accumulated grease in a matter of

Source: This case study was prepared by Michael P. Peters with the intention of providing a basis for class discussion.

minutes, represented a significant departure from the existing methods of cleaning restaurant grills. It appeared to have several major advantages over competing products, and initially it had generated such enthusiastic response from users that the product had practically sold itself.

PRODUCT EVOLUTION

Gril-Kleen had been developed for their own use by two brothers who owned a small, busy restaurant in Eastern Massachusetts. The restaurant's grill needed cleaning several times a day, especially during busy periods, and the brothers were disturbed by the amount of time and effort it took to clean the grill. They were also bothered by the orders they lost while the grill was being cleaned.

Most grill-cleaning products then available could not be used on a hot grill, and the time required to cool, clean, and then reheat the grill varied from about 20 minutes to almost an hour, depending on the method being used and the condition of the grill.

Two of the most popular methods of cleaning grills used a carborundum "stone" or a wire mesh screen to scrub the grill clean. Though inexpensive, they required a great deal of physical labor and both products tended to wear, with some danger of stone chips or metal particles ending up in food cooked on the grill.

Spray foam oven-cleaner type products, similar to those sold for home use, were easier to use but considerably more expensive. Most had critical effective temperatures of around 160°–200° Fahrenheit, compared to normal grill operating temperatures of around 350°, and often had objectionable odors, which restricted their use in small or poorly ventilated restaurants.

Dissatisfied with the products then on the market, the two brothers decided to develop their own grill cleaner. They sought the advice of one of their customers in the chemical business, and from him they learned of some chemicals and began to experiment with different combinations in various proportions.

The cleaner they sought would clean grills quickly, easily, and at normal operating temperature. It had to be economical, easy to mix, and have no discernible odor or taste, and it would have to pass safety requirements (i.e., be both nontoxic for use on food preparation surfaces and noncaustic to the user's skin). In addition, it had to leave the grill "seasoned" so that food wouldn't stick to the grill after it had been cleaned.

After experimenting and modifying the solution for a couple of years, the brothers finally arrived at a mixture having all the desired properties. It would work on both hot and cold grills, and the grill operator could clean a grill in less than five minutes by simply pouring the solution on, allowing it to dry, and then rinsing the grill with water. After a light seasoning with cooking oil, the grill was ready for use again.

Soon, friends in the restaurant business heard about the product and began asking for samples, then coming back for more. As demand increased, the brothers started to sell the product by the gallon, charging whatever they felt the market would bear.

THE GRIL-KLEEN CORPORATION

The product appeared to be so successful that the brothers began to think about marketing it on a larger scale. One of the restaurant's customers, a line foreman for the Boston Edison Company, was impressed by the demand for the product, and urged the brothers to consider manufacturing and selling it on a regular basis. In early 1997, the three of them formed the Gril-Kleen Corporation.

Working out of the basement of the restaurant, the three new partners bottled and sold Gril-Kleen in their spare time and on their days off. The chemicals were mixed in a large plastic tub with a spigot, then transferred to gallon-size plastic bottles labeled "Gril-Kleen."

On Tuesdays, when the restaurant was closed, the two brothers made sales calls to other restaurants, leaving behind samples of the product. Even with this minimal sales effort, orders began to increase to the point where larger facilities were needed to bottle and store the product. Less than a year after its incorporation, the Gril-Kleen Corporation moved to a new and larger headquarters in a nearby industrial park.

The new plant was a 1,500-square-foot cinderblock building, and the equipment consisted of a large stainless steel tub, formerly used for pasteurizing milk and capable of producing 450 gallons of Gril-Kleen per day. The company hired one part-time employee to mix the chemicals and fill the bottles.

After one unfortunate experience with a traveling salesman who offered to sell the product and instead, sold several phony "exclusive distributorships" for Gril-Kleen throughout New England before he disappeared, the company established relationships with half a dozen bona fide distributors of restaurant and cleaning supplies in New England.

As sales volume grew, the need for a full-time manager became increasingly apparent. Orders and invoices were piling up, billing was haphazard, records were disorganized and incomplete. With no regular system of record-keeping, orders often went unfilled, or customers were never billed for orders that had been shipped.

Recognizing that the company had grown too large to continue operating on a one-day-per-week basis, the owners hired a local politically ambitious individual to run the company, and offered him a 25 percent interest in the business. The new partner was well known locally, had a number of important connections, and the company owners felt that his name would lend some prestige to the operation.

As it turned out, he devoted little of his time and attention to running the business and most of it to campaigning for re-election, even charging some of his campaign expenses to the company. After more than a year, with company sales declining, the other three partners bought him out, paid his bills, and returned to running the business on their days off.

WARREN RYAN

At this point, Warren Ryan, a management consultant working on an assignment nearby, began patronizing the restaurant and became friendly with the owners. When he learned of the situation at Gril-Kleen, he suggested that the company hire his consulting firm to do a market study and map out an operating and marketing plan for the company. He also recommended that they utilize his firm's Executive Search service to find a new president for Gril-Kleen.

Reluctant to deal with a large consulting firm or to hire anyone they didn't know to run the company, the brothers asked Ryan if he would take over the job himself. Ryan, an MBA with extensive experience in marketing, advertising, and industrial management, was intrigued by the idea. He had grown up in a household with a small, family-owned business, and had long been interested in applying his management and marketing skills to running a company. He agreed to consider the offer, and then began to research the product and its market. From library sources, he estimated the national restaurant cleaning market at about $80 million a year, and learned that no single company held a dominant share of the market.

From experience with the product and interviews with current users of Gril-Kleen, he became convinced of Gril-Kleen's performance superiority over competing products. Moreover, he was impressed by the apparent success of the company despite the lack of good planning, and concluded that the product could be developed successfully. After serious consideration and considerable research, he decided to accept the offer, and in April of 2001 became the new president of the Gril-Kleen Corporation.

THE SITUATION IN EARLY 2001

When Ryan took over, he found the product being manufactured in the small, one-story cinderblock plant in Hingham. The company's one part-time employee could mix and bottle up to 200 gallons a day to meet orders, and plant capacity could easily be increased by buying a larger mixing tank and hiring more labor. It was also possible to rent additional floor space if necessary. The product was packaged in cases of four (4) one-gallon-size plastic containers. It was sold for $28 a case retail, $18 a case wholesale, F.O.B. the wholesaler's warehouse. Included with each case was a 16-ounce squeeze-type plastic applicator bottle.

Sales volume at the time was approximately $35,000 a year. The average usage rate was approximately one case per month. The company's primary customers were six wholesale distributors in Massachusetts: the Gantlin Company, a supplier of chemicals to restaurants and institutions; the Downer Company, a paper products distributor; the Bay State Restaurant Equipment and Supply Company; Alden Sales Corporation, which supplies cleaning products to small restaurants; the Janitor Supply Company, selling to hotels and motels; and Theatres, Inc., a distributor of food products and supplies to theatres and drive-ins.

Ryan found few records, little financial data, and no regular flow of paperwork within the company. Prices were based on those charged for a competitive product, with no regard for or knowledge of actual costs or profit margins.

To apply for a working capital loan, Ryan had to develop a marketing plan for the next 12 months and projected cash flow statements for the next three years and then present his marketing plan and cash requirements to a bank.

ADDITIONAL PRODUCT USES

Before he could develop a marketing plan, Ryan had to decide which markets to approach and determine realistic market-share goals for Gril-Kleen. There was considerable evidence that the product could do much more than just clean restaurant grills. Preliminary tests had indicated that the product was effective in cleaning stainless steel, ceramic tile, formica, vinyl, plastic, chrome, machine tools, clothing, and fiberglass. The last use suggested a possible application in cleaning boat hulls, a market which strongly appealed to the owners of Gril-Kleen. (See Exhibit 3.) The product also appeared to be effective as a rust remover and preventative, suggesting a wide variety of possible industrial uses.

Ryan had to determine which markets to develop, which product lines to offer, and what degree of market penetration could be achieved in each market segment before he could set profit targets and schedules. The restaurant, marine, and industrial markets required different selling methods and different channels of distribution and posed different pricing, packaging, promotion, and selling requirements.

Before deciding which markets to pursue, Ryan needed additional information on the requirements of each market segment and the dollar and volume potential for each. Within each market, he had to decide whether to segment the market by uses, type of customer, or geographical territory.

Ryan wondered whether market testing would be useful in analyzing market need, product potential, and the habit patterns of users in the various markets, and if so, whether market testing should be accomplished by field product testing, field interviews, or mail or telephone surveys.

It was felt by Warren Ryan that Gril-Kleen could significantly increase its share in this market. Current sales of $35,000 a year represented a little less than half of 1 percent of the potential market for restaurant cleaning products in the New England area alone. However, the product appeared to fill a particular need in this market, while there was considerable competition from similar products in the other markets under consideration (marine, industrial, consumer).

PRICING

To help determine standard costs, break-even volumes over a range of possible product prices, and profit margins, Ryan collected the cost data in Exhibit 1.

Ryan needed to determine a pricing strategy, set profit targets, determine the volume necessary to meet those targets, and establish a policy on trade discounts, allowances, and credit terms. He also needed further information on price elasticity (one dealer had tripled his sales from 4 to 13 cases a month by lowering the retail price from $28 a case to $24).

Checking the reorder rates, Ryan calculated the rate of usage of the product to be approximately one case every month in a small, one-grill restaurant. Approximately 97 percent of end-users who had tried Gril-Kleen continued to order it.

DISTRIBUTION

Among the distribution decisions to be made were whether to (1) hire a sales force (and if so, how large),

EXHIBIT 1   Cost Data for Gril-Kleen

Materials:

1 ounce = $.0028

1 batch = 32 cases = 1,120 lbs. = $45.32 (83 percent water)

Bottles (cost per thousand):

	Number of Units (dollar amount is cost per 1,000)			
Size	1,000	5,000	10,000	25,000
16 oz.	$ 90	$ 85	$ 78	$ 60.75
32 oz.	155	135	125	97.30
64 oz.	220	195	154.75	147.25
128 oz.*	245	202.75	184.75	178.95
Caps				
28 mm	$ 12			$ 10
33 mm	15			12
38 mm	20			15
Printing				
16 oz.	$ 17.50	$ 15	$ 12.50	$ 12.50
32 oz.	20	17.50	15	15
64 oz.	25	20	20	20
128 oz.	30	30	30	30

Sprayer: (bought separately by customer)

for 28 mm cap $.48 ea. $.43 ea. $.39 ea. $.38 ea. for 15,000 or more

* = 1 gallon

Shipping Costs: $6.00 per hundredweight, or about $1.50 per case

Approximate Fixed Costs (per month)		Labor
Rent	$1,000	32 oz.: $.046 per bottle
Travel	400	128 oz.: .057 per bottle
Telephone	80	
Gas heat	450	Sales costs estimated at
Insurance	200	400 percent of labor,
Accounting	300	G & A at 250 percent of labor.
Depreciation	300	
Office	500	

(2) use manufacturer's representatives (and if so, how many and with what commissions), (3) sell exclusively to wholesalers, (4) sell directly to restaurants and large chain operations, and (5) grant exclusive privileges to any dealers, distributors, or representatives (and if so, what demands to make upon the holders of such exclusive rights).

Other decisions related to distribution included questions on consignment sales, volume discounts, and shipping costs. Ryan also had to decide whether to expand his distribution network geographically or to concentrate on getting a larger share of the New England market.

EXHIBIT 2 Sample Catalog Sheet

TECHNICAL DATA FOR OVEN CLEANER AND DEGREASER

General Description—DUBOIS OVEN CLEANER and DEGREASER is a light tan alkaline liquid which is highly effective for the removal of baked-on fats, greases, and carbon deposits normally found in baking ovens. Also recommended for grills, deep fryers, and undersides of range hoods or canopies, where grease and carbon accumulate. OVEN CLEANER is nonflammable and USDA acceptable in meat and poultry plants.

PROPERTIES—Chemical Composition....	Caustic, soil suspending agents and foam boosting surfactants
Biodegradable	Yes, all surfactants
Caustic...............	Present
pH 1% Solution........	11.7
Metal Safety	Safe on iron, steel, stainless steel, nickel, porcelain, and glass. May be used on enamel and paint (when diluted). It may etch aluminum and will tarnish copper, brass, zinc, and tin, and galvanize on long contact.

USING PROCEDURE—Oven & Equipment—For first-time cleaning of heavy carbon and grease, use UNDILUTED. Thereafter, use 1:1 to 1:3 with water.

For best results, use on a warm oven (160°–200°). Spray on with Trigger Spray Unit, direct from gallon bottle of solution. Foaming action allows product to cling to walls and top side of oven: thus, cleaner works harder. Allow cleaner to penetrate for five minutes. For heavy carbon, use oven brush, or Scotch Bright brand applicator on a handle. Rinse with wet sponge to remove all grease and carbon residue. Can be applied with good results on cold oven when cleaner is allowed to set 15 to 20 minutes. Heavily encrusted ovens may require a second application. One application will be adequate for periodically cleaned ovens.

Grills—use 1:1 to 1:3 with water

Hoods—use 1:4 with water

Fryers—use 1:15 with water

Steak Platter—use 1:1 with water

PACKAGING—Four 1 gal. plastic bottles per case (35# net weight)

6 gal. cans (53# net weight)

30 gal. drums (264# net weight)

CAUTION—ALKALINE. Do not take internally. Do not get in eyes or on skin. In case of contact, flush skin with plenty of water; for eyes, flush with plenty of water for at least 15 minutes and get medical attention. If swallowed drink a large quantity of water, followed by whites of eggs or mineral oil, and call physician.

DUBOIS CHEMICALS DIVISION W. R. GRACE & COMPANY

DuBois Technical Representatives are located throughout the U.S., Canada, the United Kingdom, Latin America, Germany, France, Japan, and Africa.

PROMOTION

To successfully promote the product, Ryan had to determine which media to employ, how much to spend on advertising, and how to push or pull the product through to the ultimate user. In addition, he had to design some catalog sheets and fact sheets for Gril-Kleen similar to those in Exhibits 2 and 3. In designing these, he had to decide which product features to stress: price, convenience, effectiveness, safety, etc.

EXHIBIT 3 Sample Fact Sheet		

FANTASTIK BOAT CLEANER—MARINE WHOLESALE FACT SHEET

PRODUCT: Fantastik Boat Cleaner

MANUFACTURER: Texize Chemicals, Inc., P.O. Box 368, Greenville, SC 29602

PACKS:	32 oz. Spray Gun	64 oz. Refill
Code	#298	#299
Case pack	12	6
Case weight	31 lbs.	30 lbs.
UNIT RETAIL:	$2.59	$3.29
CASE RETAIL:	$31.08	$19.74
WHOLESALE DISCOUNT:	50%–10%	
WHOLESALE COST:	$13.99	$8.88
TERMS:	2%/10 Days	Net 30 Days

WHOLESALE INTRODUCTORY OFFER:

Texize Offers One Case Free with Each Five Cases Purchased on All Orders

BILLING: Free Goods to Be Invoiced at No Charge

SALESPERSON INCENTIVE OFFER:

Texize to Pay $1.00 per Case to Salesperson for Each Case Sold to Retail Outlets
PAYMENT: Payment to Be Made on a Count and Recount Basis by Texize Representative
Monies to Be Paid Directly to Individual Salesperson at the Close of Each Month

WHOLESALE EXCLUSIVE:

Fantastik Boat Cleaner Will Be Offered for Sale Only through Bonified Wholesale

Distributors

Shipments Will Not Be Made Directly to Any Exclusively Retail Accounts

SALES GUARANTEE:

Texize Guarantees the Sale of This Product When Adequately Displayed at Retail Sales Point

ADVERTISING:

Fantastik Boat Cleaner Will Be Advertised with Full- and Half-Page Spreads in the Following
Publications: BOATING, MOTOR BOATING, RUDDER, YACHTING, LAKELAND BOATING, BOAT
BUYER'S GUIDE, BOATING INDUSTRY, MARINE PRODUCTS, and MARINE MERCHANDISING.

(Plus: The Bonus of a Multi-Million Dollar Campaign That Is Making the Fantastik Name a
Household By-Word)

SHIPPING POINTS: Texize Plant or Warehouse

PRODUCT LIABILITY INSURANCE: Yes

PATENT AND TRADEMARK

Ryan also wondered whether he should try to patent the product. He didn't know if it was patentable, if it infringed upon any existing patents, or if he could obtain a trademark on the name Gril-Kleen and/or on the product logo he planned to design.

He wasn't sure that a patent would be valuable to the company, or even necessary, or whether it was worth all the trouble and expense required for a patent application. Legal costs alone, whether the patent were granted or not, could amount to about $4,000 or more and would afford doubtful protection from imitators. The company would have the right to sue if it discovered anyone else using its formula, but patent litigation would be too time-consuming and expensive for a company of Gril-Kleen's size.

COMPETITION

The most common grill cleaning products then in use, especially in smaller restaurants, were the "stone" and the "screen." The stone is a block of carborundum (hard soapstone) about the size of a brick, which was used to scrub the grill and remove grease and food residue. The screen was a wire mesh screen placed in a device similar to a sandpaper holder which was used to scour the grill much like home scouring pads. Both were inexpensive but required a great deal of effort to use, took about an hour to clean a fairly dirty grill, and could not be used on a hot grill. In addition, the stone especially tended to wear and chip, with some danger that stone chips might end up in food cooked on the grill.

There were also several chemical liquid and spray foam oven-cleaner-type products on the market that could be used to clean grills. Most of these were fairly expensive and had critical effective temperatures of around 160° to 200°F. These competitive products were generally marketed by fairly large companies, with large advertising budgets and wide distribution networks. Among these were Swell, DuBois, Easy-Off, and Jifoam. Colgate-Palmolive and Lever Brothers also had plans to introduce new chemical oven cleaner products.

DuBois liquid oven cleaner (see Exhibit 2) was sold in four-gallon cases for $28.00 a case retail and employed its own sales force to sell directly to retailers. Swell was marketed via wholesale distributors for $7.00 a gallon or $26.50 a case retail and used its own sales force to sell to wholesalers.

DEVELOPING A MARKETING PLAN

To develop a sound marketing plan, it was necessary to determine the size of the potential market in units and dollars, estimate the market share that Gril-Kleen could expect to attain, and then develop sales projections over a 12-month period.

They needed to find out who and where the distributors of restaurant cleaning products in New England were and determine the best means of selling to them. They also had to calculate potential sales volumes at various prices and price the product to maximize profits (or volume). They would need to construct volume discount schedules and determine the effects of any increase or decrease in price on demand and on profits.

They should consider whether any market or product testing is necessary, and if so, what type and how much. These decisions would form the basis for Gril-Kleen's marketing plan, from which Warren Ryan could develop projected cash flow statements and estimate his working capital needs over the next 12 months.

CASE 10
MASI TECHNOLOGY

U.S. FISH INDUSTRY

The U.S. fishing industry is a large, highly fragmented business, characterized by dwindling resources and extremely poor regulatory oversight. It is comprised of equal amounts of "finfish"[1] and "shellfish,"[2] with an aggregate "landed" value of approximately $8.5 billion, consisting of 19 billion lbs. of product.

The U.S. industry is comprised of a domestic component supplied by the 25,000 U.S. registered vessels operating within the 200 mile federal territory known as the EEZ, and an imported component from such locations as Mexico, Chile, Equador, South Africa, the Phillipines, and Sri Lanka, to mention a few.

It is estimated that the domestic business generates about $4 billion in income and 12 billion lbs. in landed weight. This amount is estimated to be equally divided between finfish and shellfish. About 98 percent of this total comes from within the EEZ. There are also 55,000 registered domestic sports fishing vessels that are estimated to catch somewhere in the range of 10–15 million lbs. of fish per year. Because the vast majority of this product does not move through U.S. processing/distribution facilities, it is impossible to generate reliable numbers. The imported component, which is growing due to severely "over-fished" U.S. sites, represents about $4.5 billion in retail value, but only about 7 billion in weight because the vast majority is imported in "loined" form. Approximately 20 percent is flown in as "fresh," and 80 percent arrives by boat as "flash frozen" or frozen product. None of these figures include "farmed" product or canned tuna.

Source: This case study was prepared by Michael P. Peters with the intention of providing a basis for class discussion.

MERCURY (METHYL MERCURY) CONCERNS

Mercury in fish is a pervasive and extremely serious concern. It can cause serious neurological and physical problems, particularly in children and pregnant women. The vast majority of people have no idea what causes mercury contamination in fish. Mercury is the effluent from coal-burning facilities (examples include power generation, brick manufacturing, and paper mills) around the world. The common denominator is soft coal. The byproduct (ash) from the manufacturing ovens goes up the stacks and directly into the local environment or the jet stream, which may carry the mercury thousands of miles, where it is deposited on the world's waterways.

Acid rain, which may be more familiar to the average person, is similarly caused by chemicals released into the air from these fossil fuel plants as well as from gas-burning vehicles. These chemicals mix and react with water, oxygen, and other chemicals to form acidic pollutants that affect our crops, water, and forests.

In the case of mercury, the ash is deposited on an ocean or lake surface where it is converted into methyl mercury that is absorbed by plankton, the primary food supply for most small fish. The chemical can also be assimilated through the fish's gill structure. The net result is that the smaller fish ingest methyl mercury and in turn are eaten by larger predator fish. The fish contain some mercury, but the concentrations are relatively insignificant for all except the larger predator fish at the end of the food chain. Thus swordfish, tuna, marlin, shark, mackerel, or large halibut, grouper, and black cod fall into the category of fish that are likely to contain high levels of mercury. While the presence of mercury depends largely on size, location is also often a factor. For example, swordfish from Mexico generally contain significantly higher concentrations of mercury than do the swordfish caught in the Philippines. As a rule of thumb, blue fin tuna, the large (>120 lb.) sushi grade tuna, have a significantly higher level of mercury than the smaller big-eye or yellow fin variety. When it comes to canned tuna, "light" tuna or albacore tuna are the best varieties. While most (nonpredator) finfish are usually okay, we do occasionally find bass, lungcod, spak, halibut, grouper, flounder, and even salmon with unacceptable mercury levels, which speaks to the need for broad testing of a significant part of the fish population.

In 2004 the EPA and FDA released an advisory regarding the consumption of fish. Although it recognized that the consumption of fish and shellfish are an important part of a healthy diet, they recommended that high risk individuals such as children, infants, pregnant woman, and nursing mothers reduce their intake and exposure to the harmful effects of mercury. A summary of these recommendations is found in Exhibit 1. However, more recently the FDA took a step back and revoked its warning about mercury in fish. The announcement stated that the consumption of mercury-contaminated fish no longer represented a health threat to children, pregnant women, nursing mothers and infants. It suggested in the announcement that the nutritional benefits of eating fish far outweighed the risks. On the other hand the EPA quickly responded that the basis of this new announcement was based on poorly conducted and flawed scientific research. The media has also been outspoken that the FDA was making this announcement primarily to protect its position that mercury dental fillings were safe. Whatever one believes it is clear that the threat of mercury exposure is real and that consumers must take precautions in planning their diet.[3]

With all of the uncertainties associated with the consumption of fish, the consumer is often unsure of what to do. Typically the FDA and other agencies that oversee regulation have suggested that consumers use moderation in consuming any high risk fish. For example, a trip to the sushi counter for tuna is okay once a month. It is also recommended that sushi lovers focus on yellow tail and salmon, which are likely to contain much less mercury levels. Tuna sandwich lovers are recommended to use the light varieties rather than blue fin.

A more significant issue may be how to find a way to stop the migration of mercury to our waterways. One solution would be to place scrubbers on top of the offending smokestacks. However, at a cost of $3–$5 million per stack that option is probably not of interest to many emerging economies where the vast majority of the mercury contamination originates. A second option would be to move to alternative forms of energy such as nuclear, solar, wind, and gasified coal. China, one of the past major offenders of soft coal production, has begun production of eighteen nuclear energy plants.

FINDING A SOLUTION/DEVELOPING A PROTOTYPE

In the year 2000, Mal Wittenberg, a patent attorney with an engineering background, and an affinity for tuna sandwiches, decided to try to invent a simple test for mercury in

EXHIBIT 1 FDA and EPA Summary of Recommendations for Consumption of Fish and Shellfish by High-Risk Individuals

Message to Consumers:

- Fish and shellfish are important parts of a healthy and balanced diet. They are good sources of high quality protein and other nutrients. However, depending on the amount and type of fish you consume it may be prudent to modify your diet if you are: planning to become pregnant; pregnant; nursing; or a young child. With a few simple adjustments, you can continue to enjoy these foods in a manner that is healthy and beneficial and reduce your unborn or young child's exposure to the harmful effects of mercury at the same time.

Key Parts of the Advisory:

- Fish and shellfish are an important part of a healthy diet. Fish and shellfish contain high quality protein and other essential nutrients, are low in saturated fat and contain omega-3 fatty acids. A well balanced diet that includes a variety of fish and shellfish can contribute to heart health and children's proper growth and development. Thus, women and young children in particular should include fish or shellfish in their diets due to the many nutritional benefits.

- By following these 3 recommendations for selecting and eating fish or shellfish, women and young children will receive the benefits of eating fish and shellfish and be confident that they have reduced their exposure to the harmful effects of mercury.
    1. Do not eat Shark, Swordfish, King Mackerel, or Tilefish because they contain high levels of mercury.
    2. Eat up to 12 ounces (2 average meals) a week of a variety of fish and shellfish that are lower in mercury.
        - Five of the most commonly eaten fish that are low in mercury are shrimp, canned light tuna, salmon, pollock, and catfish.
        - Another commonly eaten fish, albacore ("white") tuna has more mercury than canned light tuna. So, when choosing your two meals of fish and shellfish, you may eat up to 6 ounces (one average meal) of albacore tuna per week.
    3. Check local advisories about the safety of fish caught by family and friends in your local lakes, rivers, and coastal areas. If no advice is available, eat up to 6 ounces (one average meal) per week of fish you catch from local waters, but don't consume any other fish during that week.

- Follow these same recommendations when feeding fish and shellfish to your young child, but serve smaller portions.

fish. He made a variety of home test kits, recognizing that nobody wanted to use chemicals in their kitchen, and more importantly, no one wanted to dispose of any failed fish after it had been purchased. His objective therefore was to develop a machine that could reliably test fish in a short period of time. The prevailing methodology was and remains today to send a fish sample to an outside laboratory and if fortunate get a response within a two-week time period. In addition, if you sent the same fish to three distinctly different labs you were almost guaranteed to get three different responses.

By 2003 Mal had established his company Masi Technologies and had developed a reliable machine that could function in a domestic processing plant for two shifts a day. Needing a more commercial-ready machine Mal began working in a friend's lab on a commercial quality prototype machine that would be cost effective. After a period of five years, testing at least five different prototypes, thousands of trials on fish, and millions of dollars in investments, Masi Technologies had a viable machine. The outcome was a commercial quality machine that could test a fish in 40 seconds and more importantly replicate the results (statistically accurate) over and over again.

Once the machine was ready for commercialization the more difficult questions remained: Who was the primary customer? How should the machine be marketed? What should be the price to the user? These were a few of the major questions that needed to be resolved in a business plan.

As Masi Technologies proceeded with their plan there were a number of known facts that had to be taken into consideration as the strategy was developed. First, the final machine that was developed was extremely sophisticated and very expensive to replicate. The estimated cost to produce one machine was $60,000 with an additional need to maintain an inventory of $15,000 in spare parts. In order to sell this machine to a customer it would be necessary to charge a final price of about $150,000. There was much concern as to whether a fish processor/distributor would be willing to expend this amount on a machine. In addition there was the risk that if a machine was sold it could be easily reverse-engineered and duplicated. Patents had been explored but the sense was that the patents could be easily circumvented and would only provide limited protection for a finite period.

Another important consideration was the actual operator of the machine. This person needed extensive training to be able to operate the machine effectively. Masi Technologies could provide training for a buyer's employees as part of the packaging cost. On the other hand there was consideration of leasing the machine and providing a Masi-trained employee to conduct the testing to avoid the above explained issue with imitation. This might also enhance marketing opportunities. For example, if the company decided to lease the machine with a Masi-employed operator it could charge a fee based on the number of lbs. of fish tested. At a fee of $.20/lb. a 100 lb. tuna could generate $20 in the 40 seconds it took to conduct the test. The machine is also capable of testing at least 500 lbs. of fish during an eight hour work shift generating about $10,000 in revenue.

The possible leasing of the machine raised other issues that needed to be considered. Where would the machine be located? Would it make sense to locate the machinery at the point of origin or where the fish is taken off the boat or would it make more sense to locate the machine at the processing plants? The fish to be tested would need to be tagged with a permanent record maintained of vessel, location of catch, hand line or long line catch, and the amount of mercury involved. This decision is complicated by other considerations that are discussed below. It appears that each strategic option contained problems that needed to be weighed as the final strategic decisions were made.

COMPLICATIONS IN STRATEGIC DECISION MAKING

The FDA is the agency responsible for monitoring and setting safe limits on mercury for imported as well as domestic fish. For example, the FDA ruled that tuna containing less than 1.0 parts per million (ppm) was safe to eat. Canada and Europe, however, decided that they would reject any in-coming tuna that contained more than .5 ppm of mercury. Japan initially set a standard of .3 ppm for tuna but has since rescinded this requirement because it resulted in failure of 90 percent of the tuna that could be imported. The problem with these different standards is that if a fisherman in Chile catches a load of tuna with a mercury count of .4 ppm it would very likely be shipped to Canada or Europe rather than the U.S.

In response to all of these different requirements Masi Technologies decided to develop its own set of standards and a certification process called Safe Harbors Certification. This certification standard is significantly more demanding than prevailing FDA standards. (See Exhibits 2, 3, and 4 for a comparison of FDA and Safe Harbor Certification standards.) This data also illustrates which species have the highest and lowest levels of mercury based on FDA testing. Masi Technology's primary long-term objective with this certification will be to test all the fish offered at any retail location so that the consumer can buy with confidence anytime he or she sees the Safe Harbor Certification.

SAFE HARBOR TARGET MARKET

Exhibit 5 summarizes the world aquaculture by species providing an effective means for estimating the market for fish testing. As an example, the largest species is shrimps and prawns at 6.9 billion lbs. with an estimated dollar value of about $12.5 billion.

Masi Technologies would thus have a potential market of $627 million in just this species. Exhibit 5 also summarizes the aquaculture market for all other species with a total of $34.7 billion or about 18.5 billion lbs. The total fish and shellfish world market is thus about $100 billion or about 12 billion pounds. However, it should be noted that many of the species included in the other category would have to be batch tested and are not initially regarded as the primary market for Safe Harbor Certification.

It is clear that the potential revenue that can be earned is significant. The real issues facing the company will be to decide on an effective strategy to be

EXHIBIT 2   Fish and Shellfish with Highest Levels of Mercury

Species	Mercury Concentration (PPM)		
	Mean	Max	Safe Harbor Standard[a]
Shark	0.99	4.54	0.80
Tilefish (Gulf of Mexico)	1.45	3.73	NA
Swordfish	0.98	3.22	0.80
Mackerel, King	0.73	1.67	NA
Bass, Chilean	0.39	2.18	0.30
Mackerel (Gulf of Mexico)	0.45	1.56	NA
Halibut	0.25	1.52	0.50
Snapper	0.19	1.37	0.40
Scorpionfish	0.29	1.35	NA
Lobster (Northern American)	0.31	1.31	0.10
Tuna (Fresh/Frozen)	0.38	1.30	0.40
Grouper (All Species)	0.47	1.21	0.50
Tuna (Fresh/Frozen, Yellowfin)	0.33	1.08	0.40
Tuna (Fresh/Frozen, Bigeye)	0.64	1.04	0.40
Monkfish	0.18	1.02	0.20
Bass (Saltwater, Black, Striped)	0.22	0.96	0.50
Marlin	0.49	0.92	0.80
Orange Roughy	0.55	0.86	NA
Tuna (Canned, Albacore)	0.36	0.85	0.40
Tuna (Fresh/Frozen, Albacore)	0.36	0.82	NA
Sea Trout	0.26	0.74	NA
Mackerel (Spanish-South Atlantic)	0.18	0.73	NA
Sablefish	0.22	0.70	NA
Bluefish	0.34	0.63	NA
Sheepshead	0.13	0.63	NA
Tilefish (Atlantic)	0.14	0.53	NA
Buffalofish	0.19	0.43	NA
Croaker White (Pacific)	0.29	0.41	NA
Skate	0.14	0.36	NA
Perch (Freshwater)	0.14	0.31	NA
Lobster (Species Unknown)	0.17	0.31	NA
Carp	0.14	0.27	NA
Tuna (Fresh/Frozen, Skipjack)	0.21	0.26	NA

Note: FDA Standard for mercury in all seafood is 1.0 ppm.

[a]Some species are naturally low in mercury or are always too high to warrant a Safe Harbor Standard.

Source: www.fda.gov/food/foodsafety/.

EXHIBIT 3 Fish and Shellfish with Lowest Levels of Mercury

Species	Mercury Concentration (PPM)	
	Mean	Max
Clam	No data	No data
Salmon (canned)	No data	No data
Whiting	No data	No data
Tuna (canned, light)	0.22	0.85
Pollock	0.04	0.78
Trout (freshwater)	0.07	0.68
Crab	0.06	0.61
Jacksmelt	0.11	0.50
Cod	0.10	0.42
Squid	0.07	0.40
Butterfish	0.06	0.36
Anchovies	0.04	0.34
Catfish	0.05	0.31
Whitefish	0.07	0.31
Lobster (spiny)	0.01	0.27
Oyster	0.01	0.25
Scallop	0.05	0.22
Shad American	0.07	0.22
Mackeral Chub (Pacific)	0.09	0.19
Salmon (fresh/frozen)	0.01	0.19
Flatfish	0.05	0.18
Mackeral (North Atlantic)	0.05	0.16
Croaker (Atlantic)	0.07	0.15
Herring	0.04	0.14
Mullet	0.05	0.13
Tilapia	0.01	0.07
Crawfish	0.03	0.05
Shrimp	No data	0.05
Hake	0.01	0.05
Haddock (Atlantic)	0.03	0.04
Sardine	0.02	0.04
Perch (ocean)	No data	0.03

Note: FDA standard for mercury in all seafood is 1.0 ppm.

Source: www.fda.gov/food/foodsafety/.

EXHIBIT 4   Safe Harbor Certification Standards

SAFE HARBOR CERTIFICATION—Safe Harbor standards identify the maximum level of mercury concentration allowed in each species of fish sold with the Safe Harbor seal. Safe Harbor certification standards vary by species since each species contains different average levels of mercury. Our standards are reported in parts per million (ppm) which is how the government measures the mercury concentration in fish. The FDA action level for mercury in all seafood is 1.0 ppm.

Individually Tested Fish Species	Safe Harbor Mercury Standard (ppm)	Batch Tested Fish Species	Safe Harbor Mercury Standard (ppm)
Bass, Black	0.50	Arctic Char	0.20
Bass, Bluenose Sea	0.30	Barramundi	0.10
Bass, Chilean Sea	0.30	Bass (Swal)	0.10
Bass, White California Sea	0.30	Catfish	0.10
Bass, Wild Striped	0.50	Cod (Alaska Cod)	0.20
Corvina	0.30	Cod (True Cod)	0.20
Escolar	0.50	Crab	0.20
Grouper	0.50	Dory, John	0.30
Halibut	0.50	Eel	0.30
Lingcod	0.40	Lobster	0.10
Marlin	0.80	Mussels	0.10
Monkfish	0.20	Opakapaka	0.20
Mahi-Mahi	0.40	Prawns	0.10
Wahoo	0.40	Rockfish	0.30
Opah	0.70	Salmon, Atlantic	0.10
Black Cod	0.50	Salmon, Coho	0.10
Salmon, King	0.20	Salmon, Sockeye	0.10
Shark, Thresher	0.80	Scallops	0.10
Snapper, Thai	0.40	Shrimp	0.10
Swordfish	0.80	Snapper, Red	0.40
Tuna, Albacore (Tombo)	0.40	Sole, Dover	0.30
Tuna, Yellowfin	0.40	Sole, English	0.20
Whitefish	0.20	Sole, Petrala	0.20
Yellowtale (Hamachi)	0.40	Sole, Rex	0.30
		Squid	0.10
		Steelhead	0.10
		Tilapia	0.10
		Trout	0.10

Source: www.fda.goc/food/foodsafety.

EXHIBIT 5 World Aquaculture by Species: Safe Harbor Target Market

Species	$ U.S. (000s)	Lbs. (000s)	Safe Harbor Testing Price	$ Potential Market (000s)
Tunas, Bonitaos, Bullfishes	163,256	32,245	0.25	8,062
Lobster	322,118	86,552	0.19	16,445
Misc. Demersal[a]	202,970	61,769	0.16	9,883
Misc. Pelagic[b]	1,405,366	438,760	0.16	70,202
Flounders, Halibuts, and Soles	708,778	279,107	0.13	36,284
Salmon, Trout, and Smelt	9,893,798	4,725,913	0.10	47,259
Freshwater Crustaceans	4,714, 823	2,350,067	0.10	235,007
River Eels	1,100,321	587,269	0.09	52,824
Shrimps, Prawns	12,485,834	6,977,467	0.09	627,972
Cods, Hakes, and Haddocks	50,667	29,269	0.09	2,634
Crabs, Sea spiders	656,718	495,684	0.07	34,698
Misc. Coastal Fish	3,083,345	2,410,499	0.06	144,630
Total	**$34,787,994**	**18,474,601**		
Percent of Market	**34.79%**	**6.16%**		
Other Fish and Shellfish	65,214,017	281,525,400		
Percent of Market	**65.21%**	**93.84%**		

Total world fish market is approximately $100 billion and about 300 billion lbs.

U.S. market is about 4 percent or approximately 12,000,000,000 lbs.

[a]Demersal fish live on or near the bottom of the sea or lakes.

[b]Pelagic fish live in the water columns, but not on the bottom of sea or lake.

EXHIBIT 6 Actual and Projected Monthly Revenue and Expenses ($000s): August, Year 1–December, Year 2

	Actual			Forecasted														
	AUG	SEPT	OCT	NOV	DEC	JAN	FEB	MAR	APR	MAY	JUN	JUL	AUG	SEPT	OCT	NOV	DEC
Revenue	45	48	51	65	68.6	104.6	120	150	152	192	197	217	257	257	254	327	325
G & A	38	33	43	33	33.0	39.0	39	60	57	57	57	62	62	62	87	67	67
Salary, Taxes, and Medical	57	56	59	61	60.6	62.6	71.9	73.5	86.9	88.9	89.2	90.2	92.2	92.2	92.0	109.7	109.6
Profit/Loss	(50)	(41)	(51)	(29)	(25)	3.0	9.1	16.7	8.1	46.1	50.8	64.8	102.8	102.8	75.0	150.3	148.4

able to maximize the revenue potential. Exhibit 6 summarizes the early revenue and cost data for the firm. It is anticipated that the firm will be profitable in its first year of operation. Most of this revenue has been accumulated by taking the machine to specific sites where fish is tested as it is removed from the boat. Partnerships with major food distributors and retailers have been the initial focus for reaching these revenue goals.

The company now seems to be at a crossroads. It has proven that it can test large amounts of fish at a low cost. It must now consider long-term marketing issues and strategies for reaching higher levels of revenues to satisfy the initial investors in the company.

END NOTES

1. Examples of finfish would be cod, pollock, salmon, and halibut.
2. Examples of shellfish would be shrimp, lobster, scallops, oysters, clams, and crab.
3. Mike Adams, "FDA Stuns Scientists, Declares Mercury in Fish to be Safe for Infants, Children, Expectant Mothers," December 17, 2008, www.naturalnews.com/news_000622_mercury_FDA_fish.html; and Sharon Begley, "Smackdown! EPA, FDA and Mercury in Fish," April 24, 2009, http://blog.newsweek.com/blogs/labnotes/archive/2009/04/24/smackdown-epa-fda-and-mercury-in-fish.aspx.

CASE 11
NEOMED TECHNOLOGIES

Marc Umeno, president and founder of NeoMed Technologies, and George Coleman, chief operating officer and vice president of business development and marketing, arrived back at NeoMed headquarters after a frustrating and disheartening meeting with venture capital investors. Now late into August of 2002, after months of revising the company strategy, continuously improving the technology and product design, and meeting with investors still not willing to commit their capital, the company had finally run out of cash. Such brutal reality made Marc and George wonder what they could possibly be doing wrong. There was no doubt in their mind[s] that NeoMed had the right people and an outstanding technology. They were convinced that NeoMed's device had the potential for helping people in a way that other alternatives could not. This dedication has sustained the company to this point. However, despite the great commercial opportunity of its innovation, the company had walked a tight rope between technical development and business and financing issues. Though each team member is convinced that the capital that the company needs to prove the technology is available, the existing financing environment had investors becoming cautious and risk averse. In light of the present situation, NeoMed was at a decision point

Source: This case study was prepared by Amanda Holland, Nadya Tolshchikova, Jeff Glass, and Robert Hisrich, with the intention of providing a basis for class discussion.

as to what actions to take to finally close a deal with investors and avoid dissolving the company.

COMPANY HISTORY AND FOUNDERS

Marc Umeno, one of the founders of NeoMed Technologies, developed the initial concept for NeoMed during graduate work in the Physics Entrepreneurship Program, a partnership between the Physics Department and the Weatherhead School of Management at Case Western Reserve University (CWRU) in Cleveland, Ohio. Before starting the program, Marc, in collaboration with a radiologist from West Virginia University, created patents for a technology that had been introduced to him earlier that year by a scientist looking to commercialize his ideas. Marc conducted preliminary research and evaluated the market opportunities for the technology while participating in the program at CWRU. As a result, in the spring of 2001, NeoMed was officially formed with the purpose of commercializing a novel radionuclide imaging technology for cardiac testing, developed based on research conducted over the past three decades in experimental particle physics detector technology at the Department of Energy National Laboratories and in nuclear cardiology imaging at UCLA. It was decided to locate the new company in Cleveland, Ohio, a region that supported world-class research in the area of medical imaging. This allowed NeoMed to have access to top-notch engineering services, software partners, and industry suppliers. Major players in the diagnostic imaging market, such as GE Medical and Philips, have also been historically located in this region. From the very beginning NeoMed was thought to have a bright future due to the very promising commercial potential of the market for cardiac testing. This was based on the fact that in the United States, as well as other industrialized nations, CAD[1] is a leading cause of fatalities, with the first symptom of this disease often being death. Given this sobering reality, it is not surprising that NeoMed's vision is as follows:

> NeoMed Technologies is committed to establishing its technology as the standard of care for initial diagnosis of coronary artery disease and will be instrumental in saving millions of lives.

Marc Umeno, Stan Majewski, and Harry Bishop were the three original founders of NeoMed. After searching for recommendations for someone with industry experience who would work well in the start-up environment, Marc was introduced to George Coleman. George joined the company

EXHIBIT 1 Principals/Management Team Board of Directors*

Management Team

Marc Umeno, PhD, President and Founder

Dr. Umeno is currently developing NeoMed full-time. He received his BS in Physics at Harvey Mudd College and his PhD in Physics at American University while doing Neuroscience research at the National Institutes of Health. Dr. Umeno has served as a Nuclear Medical Science Officer in the U.S. Army, where he led a multi-agency team of experts to develop critical nuclear weapons standards, was the U.S. representative for three NATO committees, chaired three Department of Defense–wide groups, and was involved in FDA approval of a military pharmaceutical. Prior to his work with NeoMed, Dr. Umeno was a project manager at Veridian, where he managed multiple projects with over $2 million annual budget and led the commercialization of a medical software tool.

George Coleman, Chief Operating Officer and Vice President of Business Development and Marketing

Mr. Coleman is a full-time member of the NeoMed team. He has over 25 years of experience in the medical, biotechnology, and specialty chemical industries. He has start-up experience as General Manager and V.P. of Sales and Marketing for an innovative medical engineering firm that produced image processing and micro-endoscope systems, surgical instruments, and MEMS components. Mr. Coleman also has experience as managing director at Federal Process, new business development manager of biotechnology at British Petroleum, and sales, sales management and marketing management for a division of Merck, where he was awarded Merck's highest management award for performance.

Walt Bieganski, Chief Financial Officer and General Counsel

Mr. Bieganski is a full-time member of the NeoMed team. He has 16 years of financial and tax advisory experience with Ernst & Young LLP, including 9 years of experience building and managing a multi-million-dollar specialty practice where he serviced clients in various industries, including financial services, distribution, manufacturing, natural resources, and power generation. He also spent two years as a co-leader of the firm's e-business initiatives in the region. Mr. Bieganski is a CPA and has an MBA in Finance from Cleveland State University and a JD from Ohio State University.

Stan Majewski, PhD, Chief Scientific Officer and Founder

Dr. Majewski is head of the detector group at the Thomas Jefferson National Accelerator Facility. He received his educational degrees in Experimental Particle and High Energy Physics from the University of Warsaw in Poland. Dr. Majewski's career has included significant work under two Nobel Prize winners at the European Center for Particle Research (CERN) and the Fermi National Accelerator Laboratory. Dr. Majewski has developed many similar devices involving breast cancer detection, surgical probes, and small animal imaging, and has consulted for NIH, NASA, and UCLA. He also has start-up company experience with a device that successfully gained FDA approval and has launched a small technology start-up. At Jefferson Lab, Dr. Majewski led the development of novel biomedical imagers, co-authored over 100 publications, and invented or co-invented eight patents.

Harry Bishop, MD, Medical Advisor and Founder

Dr. Bishop, inventor of the NeoMed cardiac screening test, is an adjunct associate professor of radiology at West Virginia University. He serves as a medical advisor to the company. He has over 40 years of medical experience, specializing in radiology and nuclear medicine. Dr. Bishop received his BA in Physics from UC Berkeley and his MD from

---

as COO shortly thereafter, and Walt Bieganski joined subsequently as the chief financial officer (Exhibit 1). As a part of the company formation process, the Board of Directors was initiated early on in NeoMed's existence, and from the very beginning, played a significant role in the company's strategic positioning. By 2002, the carefully selected Board consisted of five members (Exhibit 1).

CORONARY ARTERY DISEASE (CAD)

CAD is the leading cause of death in the U.S. and throughout the world. It caused more than 1 out of

every 5 deaths in the United States in 2000, claiming the lives of 681,000 people. In 2003 an estimated 650,000 people in the U.S. alone will have a first coronary attack and 450,000 a recurring attack.[2] For example, in the U.S. approximately every 29 seconds a person will suffer a coronary event, and nearly every minute someone will die from it. Nearly 47 percent of coronary events are fatal, of which 250,000 occur without previous symptoms of the disease. Coronary artery disease takes place when one or more of the coronary arteries are narrowed down or blocked resulting in decreased blood supply to

EXHIBIT 1 Principals/Management Team Board of Directors* (continued)

UC San Francisco. He was the first physician in the U.S. to perform coronary angiography and was awarded the Picker Fellowship to study cardiac physiology. Dr. Bishop is also an expert in nuclear cardiology and PET for breast cancer imaging. He is a Fellow of the American College of Radiology and has numerous publications.

Allen Goode, MS

Mr. Goode has committed his availability to coordinate clinical trials and to participate in software development as a consultant. Mr. Goode is coordinator for five multicenter cardiovascular-related trials in the Division of Nuclear Cardiology at the University of Virginia. Mr. Goode is also board certified as a nuclear medicine technologist.

Norm Yager

Mr. Yager is currently assisting NeoMed with the FDA approval process. He has written 11 successful FDA 510(k) applications as a regulatory manager for Picker International (now Marconi Medical, a subsidiary of Philips) and was previously at Johnson & Johnson.

Board of Directors

Paul Amazeen, PhD

Dr. Amazeen has been a senior executive developing medical imaging products for more than 20 years, including Raytheon, General Electric, Rohe Scientific Corporation, and Sound Imaging. Dr. Amazeen received his BSEE from the University of New Hampshire and his MS and PhD from Worcester Polytechnic Institute. He has received the Ford Foundation Faculty Fellowship at MIT and has a patent for a real-time ultrasonic image display.

Robert D. Hisrich, PhD

Dr. Hisrich is Professor of Entrepreneurial Studies at Case Western Reserve University's Weatherhead School of Management. He has had extensive experience in starting and growing companies and is presently on the Board of Directors of two publicly traded companies. Dr. Hisrich has been an entrepreneurship professor at the University of Tulsa and MIT and also has held Fulbright Professorships in Hungary and Ireland. He received his BA from DePauw University and his MBA and PhD degrees from the University of Cincinnati.

Mark Lowdermilk, MBA

Mr. Lowdermilk is currently CEO of a network infrastructure start-up company. He has 28 years of management experience, including 10 years with medical device components and nuclear medicine. Mr. Lowdermilk was formerly with Saint-Gobain Crystals and Detectors serving as Business Manager of Nuclear Medicine. He received his BS in Business Administration from Kent State University and his MBA from the Weatherhead School of Management at Case Western Reserve University.

Alan Markowitz, MD

Dr. Markowitz is currently Chief of Cardiothoracic Surgery at University Hospitals of Cleveland. He received his MD from the Albany Medical School of Union College. Along with his distinguished clinical record, Dr. Markowitz has been a consultant for many companies such as Medtronic and Johnson & Johnson, involved in clinical trials for their cardiac products.

*NeoMed Business Plan, March 2002.

the heart, which can be fatal. It is believed that the addition of this plaque to the heart blood vessels is a detectable process that can be estimated indirectly through the measurement of coronary circulation.

In 1997 there were about 700,000 outpatient surgical procedures performed on the cardiovascular system, 1,200,000 inpatient cardiac catheterizations, and 607,000 coronary bypass surgeries. This level of surgical intervention not only presents high risk for both patients and physicians, but uses a very large share of

the nation's health care resources. For example, the average cost of coronary artery surgery in 1995 was $44,820. In 1996, for anyone under the age of 65, the average cost of a coronary event from admission to discharge was $22,720, with the average length of stay 4.3 days.[3] Furthermore, in 1998, Medicare paid $10.6 billion to its beneficiaries for hospital expenses due to coronary heart disease (CHD)[4] [$10,428 per discharge for acute myocardial infarction (MI);[5] $11,399 per discharge for coronary atherosclerosis; and

$3,617 per discharge for other CHDs].[6] Moreover, the problem of an aging population is more likely to escalate these costs as a result of increased incidence of coronary artery disease in older people. According to the U.S. Census, there will be 40 million Americans age 65 and older in 2010. In addition, an increase in the prevalence of obesity and type 2 diabetes also amplifies the risk of heart disease. Given the costs and increase in scope of this health problem, early identification and nonsurgical treatment and prevention of CAD are becoming more important than ever.

CAD DIAGNOSTIC PROCEDURES

Normally, patients are screened for CAD during routine office visits, even if the patient doesn't have any symptoms of CAD. Frequently detection occurs when the patient arrives at the emergency room with a myocardial infarction (heart attack). Typically though, CAD detection starts with a thorough physical exam and careful documentation of family, personal history, lifestyle habits, and other factors. Blood cholesterol tests and blood pressure measurements are also used to screen for CAD. Recently, the U.S. government recommended new guidelines of CAD testing that increase the likelihood of disease detection with the following test methods actively used to screen patients.

Chest X-ray produces images of the heart and the surrounding areas showing the size and shape of the coronary system. This technology enables detection of misshaped or enlarged hearts as well as abnormal calcification in the main blood vessels.

Electrocardiogram (ECG or EKG) is a graphical record of the electrical activity of the heart. Typically, a normal ECG rules out the presence of heart disease while an abnormal ECG has been relatively good at indicating the existence of the disease.

Stress Test involves taking ECG before, during, and after the exercise on the treadmill. Although widely accepted by health care professionals and reimbursement organizations due to its low cost, ease of use, and 50–80 percent accuracy, it has some major drawbacks such as relatively low accuracy, ineligibility of some patients due to the high risk of heart attack during the performance of the test, and insurance reimbursement problems for asymptomatic patients.

A preliminary test using *Fast/Multi-Slice CT Scan* with ECG is a relatively new noninvasive method of heart and coronary artery imaging. It is often used as an alternative for invasive catheterization to determine calcium deposits in the coronaries and stenoses (narrowing of arteries) that can eventually lead to a heart attack.

EBCT,[7] when it was first introduced to the market, attracted attention in the medical community due to its ability to screen asymptomatic patients for CAD. Although it was proven that a negative EBCT scan is highly accurate at excluding CAD, it is not certain whether the levels of coronary calcification that EBCT detects can be translated into high CAD risk.

NUCLEAR DIAGNOSTIC IMAGING

Nuclear medicine uses radioactive material that is injected into the patient to diagnose disease or assess a patient's condition. Nuclear imaging is different from regular imaging in several important ways: (1) the source of rays is internal to the patient versus external, (2) the radioactivity is attached to biochemically active agents injected into the patient's body so that an organ's functionality is observed rather than simply viewing the image of an organ.

Equipment for nuclear imaging typically contains several common components. One of these components is the sodium iodide detector, which consists of a crystal that scintillates with blue light, a photomultiplier to convert the light into a proportional electrical signal, and support electronics to intensify and shape the electric signal into a readable form.

Early nuclear imaging devices used scanning procedures to record information from the patient. More recent devices are the gamma cameras that are simultaneously sensitive to the entire radioactivity within a large field of view and do not require scanning. These cameras are advantageous because they can measure changes in the radioactive distribution as a function of time. In general, nuclear images have a fundamental resolution that is about 1 percent of the image dimension, and the images are fairly simple to investigate quantitatively.[8]

NEOMED NUCLEAR DIAGNOSTIC IMAGING

During the initial research, NeoMed considered several applications for its proprietary technology. Founders recognized that it could be used for the in vivo analysis of animals in drug studies, allowing researchers to conduct long-term drug experiments on animals and analyze the results without sacrificing the animals' lives, thus significantly reducing laboratory costs. In addition, NeoMed could apply its technology to screening drug candidates, drug delivery applications, or perhaps even to detecting cancer. Furthermore, Marc and his team were convinced that the core set of technologies could be applied in Homeland Defense for detection of nuclear weapons or "dirty bombs."

However, despite the numerous possible applications for the technology, it was decided to focus on cardiac testing for several reasons. Primary among these was the ability of this technology to fill the largest market need and address a very real problem in society. It was estimated that based on a high cholesterol level, 36 million people in the U.S. are at risk of CAD, of which 11.3 million visit cardiologists each year. If each CAD diagnostic test is estimated to be between $200 and $400 a test, the overall market potential is projected to be between $7.2 and $14.4 billion.

Taking into consideration the above reasoning, NeoMed has developed a device to monitor coronary artery function that combines 75 years of expertise in the fields of detector physics and nuclear cardiology and is unique in its sensors, data acquisition electronics, and analytical software. Recent developments in scintillation technology make the NeoMed device possible, allowing for small, compact, and inexpensive gamma detectors that can measure high rates of activity while still maintaining excellent resolution. In addition, NeoMed's proprietary state-of-the-art software allows detailed analysis of the CTI measurements. This powerful functional package is based on proven technology applied in a new way, thereby avoiding technological risks and supplier challenges inherent in a less mature technology.

NeoMed's diagnostic system provides medical personnel with the ability to detect coronary artery disease (CAD) with a quick and painless noninvasive test. In the process of testing, the patient while at rest is injected with a radioactive tracer, the passage of which is dynamically measured as it flows through the heart. As a result, Coronary Transit Index (CTI) is generated, which allows determination of the performance of the heart system. The radiation dose used in this test is much lower than in standard diagnostic imaging procedures involving CT, fluoroscopy, or traditional nuclear cardiology. Furthermore, the NeoMed test has a much higher degree of accuracy than conventional methods of detection, as illustrated in Exhibit 2. The NeoMed test is expected to be less expensive, will last less than five minutes, and the results will be obtainable immediately after the completion of the test. NeoMed's objectives for its state-of-the-art technology are to provide quick and accurate cardiac testing of patients at risk for CAD and to monitor patients who have had an acute myocardial infarction or stent surgery.

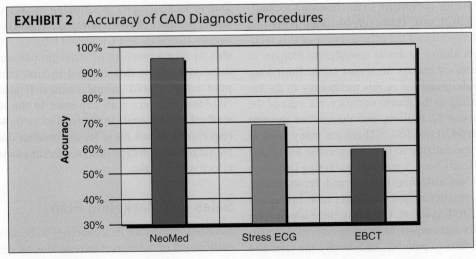

EXHIBIT 2 Accuracy of CAD Diagnostic Procedures

Source: NeoMed Business Plan, March 2002.

COMPETITION

The main competition for any new nuclear diagnostic imaging equipment is most likely to come from the alternative methods rather than in the form of direct competition from other manufacturers. NeoMed decided early on to focus on functional testing, which acts as a preliminary "gate" test for more detailed and expensive diagnostic procedures such as nuclear perfusion, electron beam tests, and angiography, which are used at later stages of the diagnostic process. Although not all CAD diagnostic methods directly compete with NeoMed's technology, overcoming ECG Stress Test's and EBCT's popularity in the current health care system presents a significant barrier to entry for NeoMed.

ECG stress test is a current industry standard that has been on the market for a few decades and is well received and accepted by both medical professionals and Medicare reimbursement agents. Although the technological shortcomings of this test are well known, the ease of use, low cost, and although not necessarily high, but consistent, predictive accuracy rate of 50–80 percent have established the ECG stress test as an industry standard. Some of the drawbacks of this test, where NeoMed saw an opportunity for its technology, were absence of ECG test Medicare Reimbursement for patients with no symptoms, and a risk of performing the test on certain patients with severe symptoms of CAD. One in 10,000 people will die, and 2–3 in 10,000 will have a major myocardial infarction while performing a physical exercise as a part of this test.[9]

Another major competitor to the NeoMed technology is the EBCT test. However, NeoMed feels that the controversy around the effectiveness of this technology in its ability to detect noncalcium plaques in coronary arteries and its high cost could limit long term and widespread use of this technology in the future. According to the recent statistics, the cost of the device is about $2 million, and the cost of the test ranges from $420 to $500.[10] There are many smaller companies specializing in EBCT screening tests. One of them is HeartCheck, a national marketing firm with 7 locations in California, Illinois, and Pennsylvania that targets smaller regional markets with low penetration of EBCT systems. Currently there are around 100 hospitals and outpatient imaging centers that provide EBCT tests to patients, and despite the cost and technology shortcomings, their number is expected to rapidly increase.

NEOMED BUSINESS MODEL

According to NeoMed's current business model, revenue will be generated through license arrangements with outpatient imaging centers, cardiology groups, and hospitals. When the test is administered by the diagnostics provider, a $233 reimbursement fee will be collected from insurance companies, of which NeoMed will receive $133. This arrangement allows for a 20 percent profit margin for the service providers and a 70 percent gross margin for NeoMed. The price of the NeoMed test will be set at $400, taking into consideration the pricing for compatible CAD screening tests ranging from $300 to $700.

Distribution

The first facilities licensed to perform the NeoMed procedure commercially are expected to be the sites used to conduct the clinical trials. Using the contacts at these facilities, NeoMed can further expand its customer base. Another possible distribution channel is through mobile nuclear medicine firms who service rural areas. Also, the international market holds considerable potential for NeoMed technology and could possibly be tapped through strategic partnerships. Using these existing sales and distribution channels would allow NeoMed to establish a broad market presence more rapidly than building its own.

Strategic Partnerships

Due to its geographic positioning in an area with the strong presence of two renowned medical centers (University Hospitals and Cleveland Clinic), NeoMed was able to take advantage of strategic partnerships with these institutions that enabled in-kind clinical trials, pilot projects, and animal studies. It also provided NeoMed founders with exposure to the world class medical professionals in the field of cardiology and an opportunity to test ideas for the product during multiple stages of prototype design, market assessment, and effectiveness trials.

Sales and Marketing Plan

NeoMed expects for its technology to be adopted in the early stages of the market introduction by cardiologists,

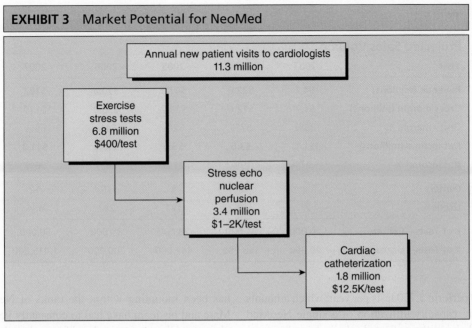

EXHIBIT 3   Market Potential for NeoMed

Annual new patient visits to cardiologists
11.3 million

Exercise
stress tests
6.8 million
$400/test

Stress echo
nuclear
perfusion
3.4 million
$1–2K/test

Cardiac
catheterization
1.8 million
$12.5K/test

Source: NeoMed Business Plan, March 2002.

whom NeoMed chose to target as a primary audience. After an extensive analysis of various market segments, the company decided to focus its entry strategy on two niche markets that have no current solutions:

• Patients who cannot be stressed (3.5 million patients per year)

• Monitoring CAD treatment progress (1.5 million patients per year)

Traditional exercise ECG stress tests cannot be administered to 1/3 of patients due to their physical disability, heart attack risk, or other physical factors. Also, a large percentage of patients that have undergone surgical treatments for CAD experience a reversal of their treatment. For instance, approximately 20 percent of coronary artery stents will undergo rejection within two months and 80 percent within 5 years. These patients have no reliable noninvasive means of detecting recurring problems. Therefore, NeoMed expects that its diagnostic method will serve both of these market segments, which together represent a market potential of $1.2 billion (Exhibit 3). However, when it comes to marketing the product, as with most pharmaceutical products and medical device systems, NeoMed must primarily market its

technology not to the patients, but instead to the cardiologists who are the main decision makers in the choice of the diagnostic testing procedures. NeoMed estimated that there were close to 19,623 cardiologists in the United States, including 4,500 nuclear cardiologists.

NeoMed is planning on penetrating the market through initially targeting cardiologist opinion leaders and establishing positive working relationships with such organizations as the American Heart Association, American College of Cardiology, and others, hoping to receive their endorsements when the product is ready to be launched. NeoMed expects to create product awareness among the rest of the nation's cardiologists through active participation in trade shows, publications in professional journals, and through sales representatives.

The company anticipates its revenue to increase over 5 years reaching $182 million in 2007. To achieve these sales, NeoMed's technology will need to capture 4 percent of the U.S. target market. This revenue is projected based on the assumption that out of 49 patients a cardiologist sees each week, 15 are nonstress patients.[11] If taking an average of 5 cardiologists per facility working an average of 50 weeks per year, one facility is

TABLE 1

Projected Sales Volume

Year	2003	2004	2005	2006	2007
Revenue (millions)	$4.7	$22.0	$47.1	$90.6	$182
Gross margin (millions)	$1.7	$12.6	$29.2	$58.0	$119
Gross margin %	36%	57%	62%	64%	65%
Net income (millions)	($1.1)	$3.6	$8.6	$18.6	$41.0
Net income %	−27%	19%	21%	24%	26%
Centers	4	6	8	10	12
Licenses	21	61	121	242	484
# of Tests—Centers	10,000	21,000	28,000	35,000	50,000
# of Tests—Licensees	29,000	156,000	342,000	700,000	1,415,000

estimated to perform 3,750 tests per year, which amounts to 75 percent capacity utilization of a single NeoMed unit. Table 1 shows the projected sales volume for years 2003 through 2007.

COMPANY SITUATION

As of August 2002, NeoMed has built an initial prototype of its nuclear imaging device suitable for use in research-level patient testing. It has also been approved for use in preclinical trials at West Virginia University. In addition, NeoMed was invited to participate in clinical trials at University Hospitals in Cleveland, Ohio. Further, an advanced prototype was constructed to be used for clinical testing, FDA approval, and product development. In January 2002, animal studies were performed at the University of Virginia, resulting in strong evidence supporting the CTI procedure. Pilot clinical studies are planned and will be directed by Dr. George Beller, a leading nuclear cardiologist at the university, as soon as the additional financing is obtained. For the complete outline of NeoMed milestones refer to Exhibit 4.

There are numerous challenges that the management team at NeoMed is facing. First of all, the company seriously lacks the financing that is needed to keep the company solvent and to continue the process of validating the technology. This requires that clinical studies be performed, and due to external factors such as the struggling economy and weak venture capital environment, NeoMed has had a difficult time securing the funds to conduct these trials. While seemingly close to proving that their technology will beat the competition, frustration

has been mounting within the ranks of NeoMed, and Marc and his team have had to constantly keep the people around them motivated and focused on the long-term vision of the company. While always maintaining a belief in their technology, Marc and his colleagues have been forced to reanalyze their business strategy to determine the reasons for not getting the financing they need.

NeoMed has also been faced with an ongoing issue of "how good is good enough," an issue faced by many companies in product development situations. While the NeoMed technology is better than many competing alternatives, and its accuracy has been proven in animal studies, the possibility exists that the device can be further improved to make it easier for technicians to operate, and thus increase the likelihood of an accurate reading. The company is faced with two options: (1) keep the technology as it is and proceed with clinical trials, with the likelihood of overall trial success, but at a lower degree of accuracy, or (2) take four to five months and the remaining capital to make improvements in the device, assuring a better quality product, but assuming the risk of not having sufficient funds at a later date to validate the improved technology. While Stan Majewski, the renowned physicist on the team, suggests that the company needs to "do it right" and go for the better product, some members of the team, including the CFO Walt Bieganski and Marc Umeno himself, see no need to take higher risks from the capital standpoint if the technology is already sufficient. Each month of delay is costing $30,000, and as has been stated before, NeoMed is simply out of cash. The old saying "perfection is the enemy of completion" comes to mind.

EXHIBIT 4*   Projected Timeline

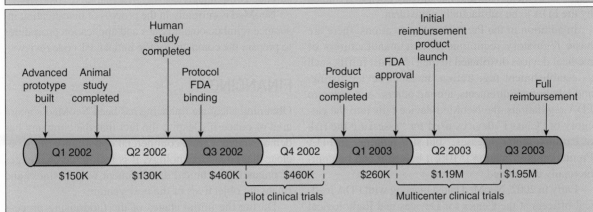

Description of Milestones for the Timeline Graph:

1. Animal Study. This study will confirm the physiological basis of the NeoMed technology and clinical application.

2. Human Study. 5– to 10–subject human study to further establish the link between coronary vascular blood flow and the NeoMed exam.

3. Protocol/FDA Binding.

4. Pilot Clinical Trials. A pilot clinical trial involving 80–120 patients is planned to compare the NeoMed technology with coronary catheterization. Positive results from the clinical trials will be leveraged to assure market adoption of the NeoMed technology.

5. Product Development. The commercial design and development of the product will be finalized based on feedback from clinical trials and in-house assessments at NeoMed.

6. FDA Approval.

7. Multicenter Clinical Trials. Multicenter clinical trials are planned involving examination of 400–500 patients to verify the results from the pilot clinical trial.

8. Product Launch. Establishing operations at targeted hospitals and geographic locations through use of personal relationships with clinicians involved with the trials.

9. Reimbursement. Widespread reimbursement approval from the Center for Medicare and Medicaid Services and the private insurance industry as a result of leveraging successful outcomes from the clinical trials.

*The costs detailed [here] include allocations of general and administrative expenses.

In addition to the challenges mentioned above, there are two main contingencies that affect the success of NeoMed's diagnostic system: FDA approval and insurance reimbursement.

FDA Approval

NeoMed, as any medical equipment manufacturer and distributor, faces an FDA approval process. FDA's Center for Devices and Radiological Health (CDRH) is responsible for regulating firms who manufacture, repackage, relabel, and/or import medical devices sold in the United States. In addition, CDRH regulates radiation-emitting electronic products (medical and nonmedical) such as lasers, x-ray systems, ultrasound equipment, and many

household electronic items. Medical devices usually fall into Class I, II, or III category under FDA classification, with regulatory control significantly increasing from Class I to Class III. The device classification regulation defines the level of regulatory requirements and the stage of market introduction at which device approval or notification becomes necessary. Most Class I devices are exempt from Premarket Notification 510(k); most Class II devices require Premarket Notification 510(k); and most Class III devices require Premarket Approval. If the device requires the submission of a Premarket Notification 510(k), the manufacturer cannot commercially distribute the device until the "letter of substantial equivalence" from the FDA is received. This letter states that the device is substantially equivalent to the device that received authorization to be legally commercialized in the United States or to the device that has already been determined by the FDA to be substantially equivalent.

In addition to the Premarket Notifications, there are basic regulatory requirements that manufacturers of medical devices distributed in the U.S. must fulfill, such as establishment registration, medical device listing, and labeling requirements, among others. According to FDA regulations, the NeoMed device falls into the category of "Class I" devices used for "assessing the risk of cardiovascular diseases," but still requires an FDA Premarket Notification [510(k)] before it can be commercially distributed.

Early in 2002, NeoMed had a meeting with FDA medical officers at the Center for Devices and Radiological Health (CDRH), at which representatives of the cardiology and nuclear medicine divisions presented recommendations to NeoMed on several issues that the company needed to consider for FDA approval. Some of the topics covered included evidence of CTI efficiency in diagnosing CAD, explanation of the physiology underlying the CTI procedure using previous clinical data and animal studies, and estimation of correct patient population size.

NeoMed was planning to submit an FDA application by the end of 2002, which would allow the company to obtain 510(k) approval for its CAD diagnostic probe system in early 2003, since the approval process typically takes 3–6 months from the date of submission of the application. However, given the financial situation the company is currently facing, it is difficult for Marc and his team to predict if NeoMed will be able to stick to its original timeline with an FDA approval process and submit the application in the next three to four months.

Insurance Reimbursement

In order to get insurance reimbursement from any company in the health care field, the given procedure must receive an approval from the American Medical Association (AMA). In the initial stages of this process, most companies typically hire consultants who help them to determine whether their procedure falls under one of the AMA's reimbursement Current Procedure Terminology (CPT) codes. If existing codes are identified, the company files the description of the procedure with the AMA, along with a Physicians Procedure Report explaining how the test will be administered. Once the approval, which typically takes two to three months, is granted, the procedure can be reimbursed by Medicare and Medicaid. This is perceived as an important step in the product commercialization, since it opens up a

likelihood of procedure reimbursement by private insurance companies.

NeoMed is currently in the process of investigating insurance reimbursement issues and application procedures to prepare the company for the initial CPT code reviews.

FINANCING

Obtaining adequate financing has been NeoMed's major area of concern. Despite the fact that the company has demonstrated a great commercial opportunity of its nuclear diagnostic technology, it is facing the challenges of balancing technical development with business and financing objectives of the new venture.

During the initial stages of the fundraising process that started in early 2001, NeoMed was able to generate $85,000 in financing through various sources. In February 2001 the company received a $20,000 grant from the National Collegiate Inventors and Innovators Alliance (NCIIA). Since one of the founders, Marc Umeno, was in the process of completing his graduate degree at Case Western Reserve University in Cleveland, the company was able to participate in the Case Western Reserve University Business Launch Competition in May of 2001, winning an additional $35,000. Another $30,000 came from the company's founders. Using this capital, NeoMed was able to construct the initial prototype and begin preclinical tests. However, the company continued to actively seek additional capital. The efforts paid off in October of 2001 when NeoMed was able to secure an additional $200,000 in private equity, which was used to build an advanced prototype, conduct animal studies, and file additional patent applications.

The next step for the company is to raise further capital to conduct a human clinical study of 5–10 subjects and develop the clinical protocol for FDA approval. The founders estimated that they would need around $130,000. Simultaneously, NeoMed is planning two future rounds of equity financing. In the Series A round, the company will be seeking $2 million to perform clinical testing using the advanced prototype, complete product development, and obtain FDA approval. In the Series B round, the company is expecting to obtain $10 million to begin the development of the commercially applicable device and its market introduction. This would involve approval of insurance reimbursement from Medicare and Medicaid, as well as private insurance companies, and also active product endorsement strategies involving the American Heart Association and American College of Cardiology. Exhibit 5 illustrates the sources and uses of the Series A plus the preseed and seed investments. Unfortunately, the venture

EXHIBIT 5 Sources and Uses of Funds*

Sources of Funds	
Entrepreneurs	$ 85,000
Seed investors	330,000
Series A investors	2,000,000
Total	$2,415,000
Application of Funds	
Legal/IP/planning	$ 135,000
Clinical studies	640,000
FDA approval	570,000
Product development	640,000
Reserve for contingencies	430,000
Total	$2,415,000

*[This] table . . . summarizes the sources and uses of the Series A plus the pre-seed and seed investments.

capital industry climate and overall financing environment have affected NeoMed's ability to obtain financing, in ways Marc and his partners could not have foreseen when they started the company less than two years ago.

VENTURE CAPITAL FINANCING

The economic downturn, equity market decline, and increased overall political and national uncertainty in 2002 took its toll on venture capital (VC) investments.

After an unprecedented rise in 2000, VC investment continued to decline and by the third quarter of 2002, the VC investment in entrepreneurial firms amounted to only $4.5 billion invested over 671 companies. In 2002 the total venture capital investment was a modest $21.2 billion compared to $43.1 billion invested in 2001. Many believed this downturn was simply a return to normalcy after the bubble of the late 90s, but either way, it severely affected the prospects for NeoMed.

Venture Capital Firms

As many expected, venture capital funds experienced a significant decline in 2002 due to fewer high quality investment opportunities, lower private company valuations, and increased economic uncertainty. An additional factor that contributed to the situation was the high level of capital already committed to venture capital funds, but not yet invested. Such surplus of investment capital coupled with the shortage of feasible investment opportunities created an unprecedented situation in the entire venture capital industry. As a result, in 2002, 108 venture funds raised only $6.9 billion, compared to 331 funds in 2001 raising $40.7 billion. The situation did not seem to be improving. A breakdown of number of funds and amounts raised in 2002 further illustrates this downward trend[12] (Exhibit 6).

EXHIBIT 6 Funds Raised by VC Firms, 2000–2002

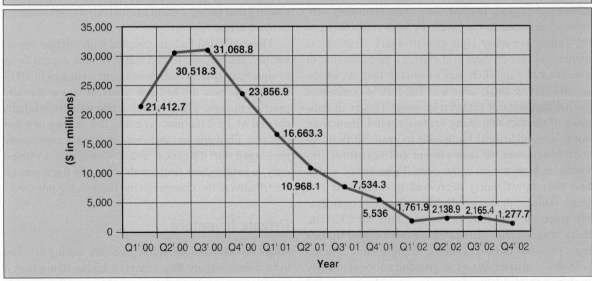

Source: PricewaterhouseCoopers/Thomson Venture Economics/National Venture Capital Association MoneyTree™ Survey; http://www.pwcmoneytree.com/moneytree/index.jsp.

EXHIBIT 7   Venture Capital Investments by State in 2002 (Number of Deals)

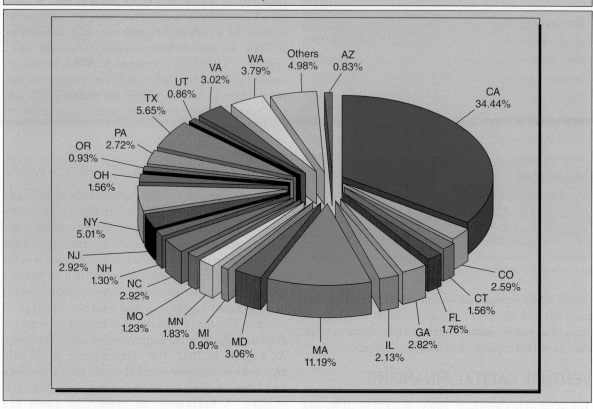

Source: PricewaterhouseCoopers/Thomson Venture Economics/National Venture Capital Association. MoneyTree™ Survey 2002 by State and by Quarter, http://www.pwcmoneytree.com/moneytree/index.jsp.

There are several factors that could explain this situation. First, many large funds were not raising any additional capital. Instead, they were returning substantial amounts to the investors who contributed to the funds in earlier high growth years. Second, as mentioned earlier, there still existed a large amount of noninvested capital. It was estimated that, as of the second half of 2002, there was $80 billion committed capital that had not yet been invested. This is an indicator of the fact that many venture capital firms were not raising additional funds, due to availability of resources to cover the then-current and near-future investment opportunities, the overall number of which had also significantly decreased over the last two years. Third, company valuations dropped considerably since the downturn in the economy. In addition, there was a clear shift in investment opportunities from previous industry sectors, to those more aligned with the industrial sectors of growing national priority such as homeland security, military applications, and

protection from various biological and chemical threats. For example, in 2002, there were funds in the country that raised capital exclusively for investments in these areas.

These external factors, coupled with internal opportunities and threats, forced many venture capital firms to significantly alter their investment strategies in 2002. Previously, over the last few years, it was a standard practice to close a fund within a few months, while by the end of 2002 the process could last as long as a few quarters. Furthermore, increased budgetary constraints, prolonged due diligence, and a willingness to invest only in established firms with a proven track record, contributed to the changes in the fundraising process.[13]

Private Investors

Angel investors are individuals who are willing to invest in businesses where they can get a higher return than if investing into traditional ventures. Many of these people are entrepreneurs themselves, who have started successful businesses and would like to help other entrepreneurs succeed. Although, due to the privacy of information, it is difficult to approximate how much angels invest, it is estimated by the Small Business Administration that there are about 250,000 angel investors active in the United States, funding about 30,000 ventures each year with amounts ranging from $150,000 to $1.5 million. It is estimated that the total angel investment is anywhere from $20 to $50 billion a year, compared to the $3 to $5 billion a year that a formal venture capital community invests. See Chapter 12 for a description of a typical angel investor.

Most angel investors have clear expectations for the businesses in which they choose to invest. Although each investor has his or her own criteria, most of them expect a board seat or at least a consulting position, and anywhere from a 5 to 25 percent stake in the business, an internal rate of return of five times the investment in a period of five years, and the right of first refusal in the next round of financing.[14]

Venture Capital and Private Investors in Ohio

The fact that NeoMed chose to start its business in Ohio presents the company with certain challenges. Typically this part of the country has not provided companies with an abundance of financing opportunities. As Exhibits 7 and 8 indicate, historically, venture capital investments in Ohio have not represented more than 2 percent of venture capital investments in the country. The current overall venture capital creates even greater financing difficulties for companies in Ohio as they are dealing with a certain level of conservatism of Ohio investors in addition to the naturally low level of available funding.

Although, as Exhibit 9 indicates, financing in the biotechnology arena has been affected less than many other industries, start-up/seed investments, which were already low compared to other stages of financing, have declined greatly, starting in 2000 (Exhibit 10). Ohio was

---

EXHIBIT 8   Venture Capital Investments by State in 2002 ($ Amount)

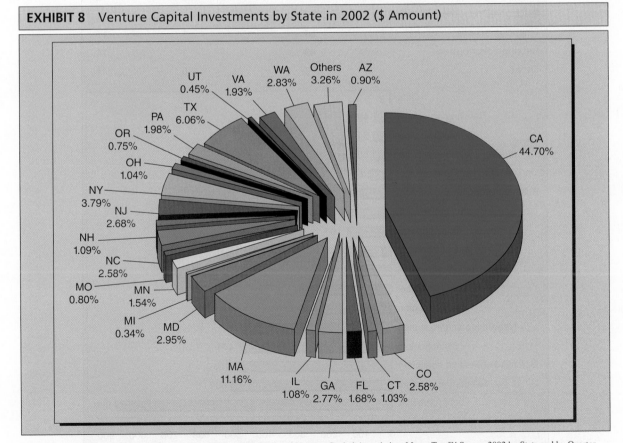

Source: PricewaterhouseCoopers/Thomson Venture Economics/National Venture Capital Association. MoneyTree™ Survey 2002 by State and by Quarter, http://www.pwcmoneytree.com/moneytree/index.jsp.

EXHIBIT 9 Investments by Industry in the 4th Quarter 2002

Industries Defined	Total $ Invested	Average $ Per Deal	Deals
	$4,081,008,000	$5,923,088	689
	Amount in $ millions	% of Total	Deals
Software	869	21	183
Telecommunications	502	12	78
Medical devices and equipment	486	12	57
Biotechnology	474	12	61
Networking and equipment	467	11	47
Semiconductors	243	6	28
IT services	218	5	33
Media and entertainment	142	3	32
Industrial/energy	140	3	37
Computers and peripherals	134	3	26
Health care services	98	2	17
Business products and services	94	2	29
Consumer products and services	68	2	18
Electronics/instrumentation	53	1	11
Financial services	54	1	17
Retailing/distribution	49	1	14
Other	2	0	1

Source: PricewaterhouseCoopers/Thomson Venture Economics/National Venture Capital Association MoneyTree™ Survey 2002.

EXHIBIT 10   PricewaterhouseCoopers/Thomson Venture Economics/National Venture Capital Association MoneyTree™ Survey

	Start-Up/Seed Stage		Early Stage		Expansion Stage		Later Stage	
Year–Qtr	($ in millions)	Deals	($ in millions)	Deals	($ in millions)	Deals	($ in millions)	Deals
1995–1	20,418,000	2	10,349,000	5	8,841,000	5	300,000	1
1995–2	1,491,000	2	7,076,000	5	6,525,000	4	1,266,000	1
1995–3	147,000	1	3,886,000	2	2,300,000	1	0	1
1996–1	6,157,000	3	5,206,000	3	3,173,000	5	750,000	1
1996–2	10,262,000	6	3,250,000	2	6,193,000	3	6,000,000	1
1997–1	2,514,000	2	8,953,000	1	11,846,000	5	18,953,000	2
1997–2	6,395,000	3	22,103,000	2	53,250,000	6	10,900,000	2
1997–4	15,000,000	1	12,132,000	5	22,719,000	9	200,000	1
1998–1	4,550,000	3	11,500,000	1	50,223,000	17	3,700,000	3
1998–2	6,500,000	2	26,700,000	5	21,891,000	7	3,282,000	3
1998–3	3,750,000	2	46,724,000	3	63,815,000	6	1,299,000	1
1999–2	3,825,000	2	27,125,000	5	13,374,000	6	6,500,000	1
2000–2	1,000,000	1	20,532,000	6	231,637,000	15	2,700,000	1
2002–3	3,000,000	1	11,500,000	3	7,300,000	4	365,000	1

Source: PricewaterhouseCoopers/Thomson Venture Economics/National Venture Capital Association MoneyTree™ Survey 2002.

not an exception in this respect, with a steady decline in start-up/seed capital financing over the last two years. These factors made obtaining financing for NeoMed extremely difficult. After many months of VC presentations to various Ohio-based VC firms and follow-up meetings with discouraging results, NeoMed's founders wondered what was keeping them from obtaining capital. As 2002 progressed, NeoMed was quickly running out of cash. While the level of frustration and disappointment increased with every venture capital meeting, Marc and his team wondered if their company would ever make it to the next important strategic milestone of clinical trials—a stage that Marc saw as a true chance to test the technology that he was convinced could save the lives of many people.

CONCLUSION

Now that the situation is more critical than ever, NeoMed must re-analyze what steps to take in order to obtain the desperately needed financing. It is clear to the team that investors are not yet comfortable with investing in NeoMed. While every meeting with venture capitalists seemed encouraging, the follow-up consisted of multiple requests to make certain changes to the concept,

product, positioning strategy, or some other aspect of NeoMed's business concept. As the team brainstormed possible strategic solutions, a number of ideas were brought up, among which were to completely redefine marketing strategy (pursue other markets and/or segments); change some aspects of the business model; obtain additional expertise on the team and the board; pursue other applications of the core technology; relocate the company to an area with more financing opportunities; delay operations until the overall environment becomes more favorable; or finally quit and move on to something else. Marc and his colleagues obviously opposed the last option, but without any injection of new capital, NeoMed might be left with no other alternative if drastic measures are not taken soon.

END NOTES

1. Coronary artery disease.
2. Heart Disease and Stroke Statistics—2003 Update, American Heart Association.
3. www.nicore.com/economicfacts.htm.
4. Includes heart attack, angina pectoris (chest pain), or both.

5. Myocardial infarction (heart attack).
6. Heart Disease and Stroke Statistics—2003 Update, American Heart Association.
7. http://imaginis.com/heart-disease/cad_screen.asp?mode51.
8. John G. Webster, *Medical Instrumentation: Application and Design,* 3rd edition, pp. 555–561.
9. "Clinical Exercise Stress Testing—Safety and Performance Guidelines," *MJA The Cardiac Society of Australia and New Zealand,* 164 (1996), pp. 282–84.
10. Robert Roos, "Noninvasive Detection of Coronary Artery Disease. Can the New Imaging Techniques Help?" *The Physician and Sportsmedicine,* vol. 28, no. 1, January 2000.
11. 1998 Socioeconomic Monitoring System survey of nonfederal patient care physicians; cited in "Overview of the Physician Market," American Medical Association.
12. National Venture Capital Association, February 10, 2003.
13. Ibid.
14. "Angel Investors," Small Business Notes, www.smallbusinessnotes.com/financing/.

CASE 12
MAYU LLC

INTRODUCTION

After graduating from college with a BS in business administration, Kate Robertson was not seeking a traditional office job. Instead, she was looking for an adventure, one that would fulfill her never-ending wanderlust and allow her to unleash her entrepreneurial spirit. She joined the Peace Corps as a Small Business Development Volunteer and was sent to a rural community high in the Andes Mountains of Peru. During the 2½ years that Kate lived in Peru, she became enamored with the country. After months of teary-eyed goodbyes, she returned to Chicago in early 2010 with an idea. Kate would create Mayu LLC, a company that would sell hand-knit fashion accessories made with pure Peruvian alpaca fiber by the artisans with

Source: This case study was prepared by Kate Robertson with the intention of providing a basis for class discussion. It was previously published in Robert D. Hisrich, *International Entrepreneurship, 2nd edition,* SAGE, 2013, pp. 299-310.

whom Kate worked in the Peace Corps. Kate believed that by establishing this small social enterprise, she could remain connected to her Peace Corps community. The company would not only provide additional income to Peruvian women, but also fulfill a market need for knitwear that was both one-of-a-kind and stylish.

To test the waters, Kate returned from the Peace Corps with two giant rice sacks full of alpaca shawls, scarves, and blankets. Seeing the positive reactions of friends and family, Kate decided that starting Mayu was indeed an excellent idea. As the demand was there and the weather was cold, she dove in head first without creating a formal business plan. One year later, as Mayu was growing, Kate was faced with a number of challenges and realized she had better answer a couple of questions before moving ahead.

1. Assuming demand continued to grow, how would she scale operations in Peru? She had already accepted a full-time job in Chicago and would be working on Mayu on a part-time basis.
2. How would she take Mayu from an in-person, event-based company to a successful online store if people could not see and feel the alpaca fiber? She needed an online marketing strategy.
3. Admitting that finance was not her strong suit, Kate worried that the pro forma financial data she had calculated were missing something. She was looking for feedback on what she had done.
4. What fraction of equity would need to be given up assuming outside capital would be sought for expansion?
5. Should she partner with several individuals who had asked her to help them also import knitwear from Peru? She wanted to protect her "trade secret"—the artisans who she had worked hard to train.

COMPANY AND PRODUCT

Mayu, which means river in Quechua, the native language of Mayu's Peruvian artisans, imports and sells alpaca accessories including hand-knit scarves, hats, shawls, wraps, gloves, and blankets. Mayu's pro bono attorney incorporated the company as an LLC and Mayu is now a registered trademark. Kate developed the following mission for the company:

Mayu strives to be the industry leader in the sale of high-quality, one-of-a-kind, ultra-classic alpaca accessories. Mayu offers social value by increasing the livelihood and contributing to the personal and professional development of their female producers in Peru. At the same time, Mayu transparently and honestly educates American consumers about the origins of Mayu's ethical fashion accessories. Superb customer service, mutual-respect, and triple bottom line initiatives (people, planet, profit) are the elements guiding Mayu's business activities.

After many shopping excursions in Lima's markets and Internet research on alpaca accessories currently offered in the market, Kate defined the unique selling propositions of Mayu's products. The exclusive, stylish designs were handmade with eco-friendly alpaca fiber, were fairly traded (Mayu is a member of the Fair Trade Federation), and were of the highest quality, lasting a lifetime. This product offering was different from the mass-produced, machine made accessories found in brick-and-mortar and Internet-based shops in Peru and the United States. Kate also noticed that most of these products were not actually knit with pure alpaca yarn. Instead, they were typically a combination of alpaca and other wools of lesser quality. Another uniqueness was that Mayu's products used purely Peruvian materials and labor and had an interesting story behind them. The story reflected Kate's Peace Corps experience and direct relationship with the artisans.

INDUSTRY AND CURRENT TRENDS

Clothing and Accessories

Kate's research indicated that the demand for clothing and accessories was driven by personal income and fashion trends and that women purchased approximately 64 items of clothing per year. According to 2010 IBISWorld Clothing & Accessories stores industry forecasts, the industry was valued at $7.0 billion with profits of $772.8 million and of all the accessory products sold, 18 percent involved neckwear, scarves, and hats. The accessories market had seen annual growth of 5.1 percent over the previous 5 years and was expected to reach 7 percent annual growth from 2010 to 2015. The market size of the women's outerwear and clothing industry had consistent growth between 2003 and 2008. Although the recent economic downturn had impacted the accessories market as the consumer sentiments index fell by 4.1 percent during the preceding years, the index was expected to rise by 13.6 percent in 2010. Per capita disposable income in the U.S. was also on the rise from its lowest values in 2008. As a result, Kate thought that her target market would not be severely impacted. Studies showed that even in times of economic downturn, consumers shifted buying behavior to more classic, forever pieces, which is precisely what Mayu offered.

E-Commerce

The e-commerce industry was growing steadily, having annual growth of 6.6 percent from 2005 to 2010 and annual revenues over $93.8 billion. Fortunately, online sales were expected to continue growing at an even faster rate of 10.5 percent from 2010 to 2015. Looking at these statistics, it was clear that online retailing was a growing medium for the purchase of specialty items such as those knit by Mayu's artisans in Peru. Of all online businesses in 2010, 15 percent were clothing and accessories retailers. Due to increased connectivity, positive perceptions of online security, and ease of conducting transactions, online companies such as Mayu could be expected to benefit from this growth.

Trends

Kate knew that growing awareness of fair trade and ethical fashion and the recent signs of a "green revolution" would be beneficial to Mayu. There was no doubt that consumers were becoming more responsible shoppers, and Mayu offered a solution to the market's increasing demand for products that offered social value. With that, the consumer market was developing a need for transparency and traceability throughout supply chains, especially for products from the developing world. The implementation of corporate social responsibility programs and establishment of not-for-profit advocacy organizations was proof that the 21st-century business environment was changing, and companies would be unable to survive without considering the consequences of their behaviors. The Mayu website contained information about the Mayu product life cycle, and Kate intended to further expand the site to allow for even greater transparency.

According to surveys administered by the Fair Trade Federation, the trend toward fair trade shopping in the United Sates was growing quickly. By 2010, 71.4 percent of American consumers knew about fair trade and 88 percent considered themselves conscious consumers. In 2009, fair trade organizations averaged annual sales of $517,384, compared to $499,892 in 2006, and 72.4 percent of these organizations were for-profit entities, showing that social, mission-driven businesses were valid substitutes for the traditional "charity-based" not-for-profits. Established fair trade companies were growing with increasing numbers of employees and volunteers and increasing impact in the countries where the production of their goods took place.

As for consumer trends, A.T. Kearney indicated that in 2009, the market for sustainable products was estimated at $118 billion, while, according to the Boston Consulting Group, firms with a "true commitment to sustainability" outperformed industry peers, especially in the retail sector. These trends reiterate American society's desire to create positive change through purchasing habits.

The concept of ethical fashion was also gaining momentum, which would also benefit Mayu's eco-friendly products. The 2009 Cone Consumer Environmental Survey, which was conducted by Opinion Research Corporation, indicated that 34 percent of American consumers were likely to buy environmentally responsible products and 25 percent more Americans had greater interest in the environment today than they did one year ago. As a result, there was an increased expectation for companies to produce and sell environmentally conscious products. Seventy percent of Americans indicated that they were paying attention to what companies were doing with regard to the environment. This interest indicates that the "green revolution" is more than just a passing trend.

A 2008 study by Conscious Innovation claimed that products and services that help customers live a sustainable life and fulfill their "help me to be a conscious consumer" desire would also thrive. Consumer behaviors for purchasing clothing and gifts have changed from previous years and are expected to continue being influenced by conscious choices.

Competition

A broad range of competition existed in the industry including both online and brick-and-mortar shops selling accessories, and while some items were handmade, most were machine made. All were available in a variety of raw materials, including alpaca, cashmere, wool, and cotton.

Kate defined direct competition as online retail stores selling alpaca accessories and clothing. There were a number of e-commerce sites selling alpaca accessories but none of them sold products as unique as Mayu's. The following websites were good examples of the competition:

- Peruvian Connection—www.peruvianconnection.com
- Alpaca Direct—www.alpacadirect.com

- Purely Alpaca—www.purelyalpaca.com
- Alpaca Boutique—www.alpacaboutique.com

Mayu differentiated itself from this primary competition because of the quality and uniqueness of its products. Kate thought that the Mayu website was a higher caliber and appealed to a more fashion-forward and conscious clientele. Once customers landed on the Mayu site, they were attracted to the stylishness, sleekness, and simplicity. The site was professional, personalized, aesthetically pleasing, and most important, up-to-date with current social media and "green" shopping trends. While Mayu's prices were comparable to the competition, customers received greater value when purchasing from Mayu. Mayu provided excellent and timely customer service and a personalized touch to potential and past customers. Ease of communication with Mayu created a positive shopping experience, despite the online nature of the business.

Kate defined secondary competition as online and brick-and-mortar retail stores selling knitwear made from raw materials such as cotton, cashmere, silk, or wool. Most of these companies have an advantage over Mayu in that they are more established and therefore, had greater brand awareness and Internet presence. These larger companies have excess capital and budgets to spend on marketing and other business development activities. Mayu differentiated itself through its personal story and social mission. Kate wanted Mayu to appeal to shoppers interested in supporting independent and local companies as opposed to those who purchased from "big-box" retailers who often lacked transparency, originality, personality, and ethical behavior. The following companies are among those considered secondary competition:

- Anthropologie—www.anthropologie.com
- Nordstrom—www.nordstrom.com
- Neiman Marcus—www.neimanmarcus.com

Marketing

Target Market Based on her research, Kate planned to target educated women between the ages of 32 and 62, who make up 67 percent of the accessories market. This range allowed Mayu to target a majority of women aged 15 to 65, who represent 90 percent of total consumer spending. Kate expected that this market would be more socially aware and understanding of global issues and would be consumers that were more responsible. It was shown that luxury shoppers, defined as consumers who earn over $100,000 per year, are more educated and demanding so workmanship, longevity, and artistry play a large role in their purchasing behaviors.

Because Mayu is striving to become an Internet business, it has access to the entire world. In order to narrow its online marketing, Kate thought she should focus on three Standard Metropolitan Statistical Areas (SMSAs)—Chicago, New York City, and San Francisco. The reasons for choosing these particular cities are that they have appropriate weather and large populations of educated and affluent female consumers. Chicago was a natural starting point, as it is Mayu's home base with existing relationships. San Francisco has a high concentration of socially conscious female consumers and New York City's inhabitants are fashion forward and the country's trendsetters.

Price Mayu's pricing structure is cost-based pricing. Kate used the traditional industry markup of between 200 percent and 250 percent to calculate both wholesale and retail prices. The base price that Mayu pays its artisans in Peru covers labor, raw materials, and transportation in Peru. Once the products arrive in the United States, Kate added on international shipping from Peru and customs duties to generate the total cost of each item (cost of goods sold). In some instances, however, Mayu receives slightly lower or slightly higher margins than the industry standard, depending on the product and what she thought the market could pay for each item.

Distribution

Distribution will be discussed in terms of in-personal events, online, and wholesale.

In-Person Events Until now, Mayu's greatest source of revenue had been from high-end, in-person weekend holiday events. Mayu had been invited to at least 10 such events and sales ranged from $0 to $2,500 per event. Participation fees were usually 10 percent of revenues. Because Kate worked full time, one of her family members or her future part-time employee would staff weekday events in the fall and spring. Mayu would make itself available for private "shopping parties" throughout the Chicago area. During a party like this, the host would invite friends over for an evening of Mayu shopping. To entice hosts to have a party, items would be offered at a 10 percent discount from online prices and hosts would be compensated with a generous Mayu gift card.

Online Although the majority of Mayu's sales took place during holiday shopping events, Kate's goal was to increase online sales and decrease her reliance on labor intensive and sometimes "hit-or-miss" events. She knew it would be a challenge to sell high-end products through a website, especially without a well-established brand. The beauty of the alpaca was most apparent when customers could touch the materials and try on the products. She did offer swatches of the alpaca to interested consumers but overall, the biggest problem was driving customers to her website with a limited marketing budget and convincing them that the higher-priced items were worth the investment.

Kate purchased a social media platform at $1,000 per year. Through the platform, Mayu could efficiently target numerous social media websites with the click of a button. This was an excellent strategy to build links and increase an online presence. Kate also managed a blog, which was part of the Mayu website. There, she blogged about topics related to Peru, alpaca, fair trade, and the Mayu story; photos, videos, articles, and other prose made up the content. In addition, Kate knew that Google AdWords would provide direction in terms of online marketing. She paid $250 per month on a seasonal basis to a group of professionals who would create an AdWords account and she would have to start with a $500 monthly budget for the actual pay-per-click ads.

Kate planned to buy certain advertising banners on websites during the winter months and especially before the holidays. The cost of such ads would be about $100 per month; this was for second-tier publications that had some type of an eco-fashionista following. She budgeted $500 per month for the ads.

Kate already had a functioning website created at a very reasonable price of $1,000, including six months of site adjustments and modifications. Website logistics such as domain names, security encryption, payment services, and other related costs were low and thus led to very low start-up costs. These monthly costs totaled about $50.

Wholesale Kate received inquiries from retailers who were interested in stocking Mayu products, but during the first year, the orders were small and margins were even smaller. The minimum order was $500 and lead time was typically no more than 6 weeks, depending on the time of year. By slightly changing her prices, Kate believed she could increase wholesale orders and therefore benefit from sales volume. The question remained though whether the artisans would be able to keep up with the increased demand. The chance of decreasing the price she paid the knitters in Peru was slim so costs savings had to be found elsewhere on the value chain.

To increase wholesale accounts, Mayu planned to hire three sales representatives, one to cover the West Coast, another for the East Coast, and one for the Midwest. Research indicated that the sales representatives would be compensated at least 10 percent of total sales. She had heard nightmarish stories from her friends about their experiences with sales representatives, so it was important to find the perfect ones who would best represent the Mayu line. An additional middleman would decrease Mayu's profits further but to gain brand recognition, get the products distributed, and start striving for volume, the investment in a team of sales reps was necessary, especially because Kate could not "pound the pavement" on her own.

Mayu would also continue to open drop-ship arrangements (affiliate marketing) with online boutiques that posted Mayu's products on their sites. When a product is sold, Mayu ships the item from the Chicago warehouse and is compensated a defined price, generally 55 percent to 60 percent of the retail sales price. These drop-ship relationships are convenient, risk free, and without cost to Mayu.

Eventually, Kate planned to participate in trade shows such as Chicago's StyleMax to place Mayu's alpaca accessories in front of thousands of retailers. These events cost at least $5,000 for 4 days and profitability is not guaranteed. Kate decided to wait on these events for the first couple of years unless she could partner with a similar small business to share a booth and costs.

Promotion   During its short life, Mayu had received free publicity, which directly boosted sales. The company was mentioned on reputable blogs and in print publications, and was covered in local magazines. Publicists seemed to enjoy the Mayu story and readers were intrigued by what Kate had accomplished in the Peace Corps. The publicity did lead to additional sales but on a small scale. Kate considered hiring her friend, a PR specialist. The rate for the season would be $3,000 with the objective to get Mayu featured in fashion publications' holiday gift guides. There was, of course, no guarantee that editors would choose to feature the Mayu brand.

Mayu implemented a referral program to help spread needed word-of-mouth sales. Past Mayu customers were given a $25 Mayu gift card each time they referred someone who purchased something from Mayu.

Operations

Peru   Kate knew that it would be difficult to manage Mayu from her home base in Chicago without frequent visits to Peru. Fortunately, she was able to communicate with the producers via telephone and occasionally by e-mail. The fact that the artisans were not computer literate and did not have consistent access to cellular phones (not to mention the frequent power outages) made communication a challenge. By living in Peru, Kate had learned to be both flexible and adaptable to the Peruvian operating environment. She placed orders and dealt with logistical issues with the designated group leader, Maria Rosemberg de Huerta. Another obstacle Kate faced was ensuring that the products had a certain level of quality and consistency. The Peruvians were less demanding and had different ideas of what constituted high quality. In addition, the artisans were frequently dishonest, claiming certain products would arrive on a certain date, when in reality, they had not even been knit yet.

The nearest regional city is 3 hours by bus and Lima, the capital of Peru, is an 8-hour trip from the village where the knitters reside. This means that Mayu's artisans have to travel long hours to access their bank accounts and to send shipments to Kate from the Federal Express office. They are always faced with the risk that large quantities of cash or finished products could be stolen during the journey. Similarly, raw materials have to be ordered via the Internet and delivered to the community by overnight bus from Lima. The cost of the raw material ranges from US$27 to $30 per kilogram for pure alpaca wool and is paid for by the artisan group. The price variation depends on whether the fiber is dyed or natural and prices are slightly susceptible to general economic conditions in Peru. Kate and the artisans jointly decide the pricing structure of the products and Kate compensates the artisans per unit produced. This price includes labor and material costs. Kate pays the artisans via wire transfer at a rate of US$11 to $85 per item knit. Typically, Kate would pay for the products up front so the artisans would be able to purchase the raw materials.

When it became necessary to scale, Kate knew that quality control, logistics, and creating a solid organizational structure would be the biggest challenges. She thought she could hire a part-time employee who would work 5 months out of the year and be compensated $1,750 for the duration of the position.

United States   Kate was responsible for operations in the United States and overseeing production in Peru.

EXHIBIT 1 Mayu's Projected 3-Year Income Statement (in Dollars)

	Year 1	Year 2	Year 3
Net Sales	32,000	44,800	58,240
Cost of Goods Sold	6,400	8,960	11,648
Gross Income	**25,600**	**35,840**	**46,592**
Operating Expenses			
Advertising (*5mo.)	2,500	2,500	2,500
Marketing & Promotion			
(AdWords *5 mo. & PR)	6,750	6,750	6,750
Social Media Platform	1,000	1,000	1,000
Dues & Subscription (FTF etc.)	300	300	300
Payroll Expenses			
Part-Time Employee Peru	1,750	1,750	1,750
Part-Time Employee USA	3,600	3,600	3,600
Product Design Fees	5,000	5,000	5,000
Administrative Expenses			
Website Logistics & Design	600	700	800
Travel to Peru	1,000	1,000	1,000
Office Expenses	500	700	900
Total Operating Expenses	**23,000**	**23,300**	**23,600**
Operating Income	**2,600**	**12,540**	**22,992**
Income Before Taxes	2,600	12,540	22,992
Net Income	**2,600**	**12,540**	**22,992**

From her home, she managed the website, online content, social media, marketing, and customer service aspects of Mayu and also attended sales events. She created an internship program and began employing students on an unpaid, 10 to 15 hour per week basis. Although time consuming, Kate felt that the use of interns could be a mutually beneficial experience and that "two heads were better than one." Once products arrived from Peru, Kate's mother was responsible for counting, ironing, and tagging inventory and outbound logistics such as shipping and handling. Kate knew that her mother would continue doing this forever so she planned to hire seasonal help for three months (November through January). The part-time help would be paid about $1,200 per month.

Team

Although Kate was receiving advice from a number of individuals, she did not have a formal advisory board. Her father provided her with legal advice, her uncle was a CPA, and her Web designer guided her on all aspects of managing a website. Kate wanted to widen her support network and started thinking about contracting a product designer who excelled in knitwear, a professional photographer, and a clothing model as well as a team that could optimize her website. She knew that it was not in her budget to hire anyone on a full-time basis so she decided she could hire the necessary help on a per-project basis. Kate is a good networker and excels in finding high-quality help at minimum prices.

Mayu's Short Term Plan

To take Mayu to the next level, Kate plans to hire a fashion designer and is already in contact with a woman who specializes in knitwear. The design fees per collection will be about $5,000 and include arrangements with a professional photographer, model, and hair and makeup team. The designer will take care of the creative vision behind Mayu. Kate will travel to Peru periodically to work with the artisans to create new collections. Each trip to Peru will cost about US$700 to $1,000.

Financials

The financial statements for the company include a 3-year pro forma income statement (Exhibit 1); the first-year pro forma income statement by month (Exhibit 2); and a 3-year pro forma cash flow statement (Exhibit 3).

EXHIBIT 2   Mayu's Projected First-Year Income Statement by Month (in Dollars)

	Q1			Q2			Q3			Q4			Year 1
	January	February	March	April	May	June	July	August	September	October	November	December	
Net Sales	3,500	3,000	2,000	500	500	0	0	500	1,000	3,000	10,000	8,000	32,000
Cost of Goods Sold	700	600	400	100	100	0	0	101	200	600	2,000	1,600	6,400
Gross Income	**2,800**	**2,400**	**1,600**	**400**	**400**	**0**	**0**	**400**	**800**	**2,400**	**8,000**	**6,400**	**24,600**
Operating Expenses													
Advertising (*5mo.)	500	500	0	0	0	0	0	0	0	500	500	500	2,500
Marketing & Promotion													
(AdWords *5 mo. & PR)	1,350	1,350	0	0	0	0	0	0	0	1,350	1,350	1,350	6,750
Social Media Platform	1,000	0	0	0	0	0	0	0	0	0	0	0	1,000
Dues & Subscription (FTF etc.)	300	0	0	0	0	0	0	0	0	0	0	0	300
Payroll Expenses													
Part-Time Employee Peru	583	0	0	0	0	0	0	0	0	0	583	583	1,750
Part-Time Employee USA	1,200	0	0	0	0	0	0	0	0	0	1,200	1,200	3,600
Product Design Fees	0	0	0	0	0	0	2,500	2,500	0	0	0	0	5,000
Administrative Expenses													
Website Logistics & Design	600	0	0	0	0	0	0	0	0	0	0	0	600
Travel to Peru	0	0	0	0	0	0	1,000	0	0	0	0	0	1,000
Office Expenses	500	0	0	0	0	0	0	0	0	0	0	0	500
Total Operating Expenses	**6,033**	**1,850**	**0**	**0**	**0**	**0**	**3,500**	**2,500**	**0**	**1,850**	**3,633**	**3,633**	**23,000**
Operating Income	**(3,233)**	**550**	**1,600**	**400**	**400**	**0**	**(3,500)**	**(2,100)**	**800**	**550**	**4,867**	**3,267**	**2,600**
Income Before Taxes	(3,233)	550	1,600	400	400	0	(3,500)	(2,100)	800	550	4,867	3,267	2,600
Net Income	**(3,233)**	**550**	**1,600**	**400**	**400**	**0**	**(3,500)**	**(2,100)**	**800**	**550**	**4,867**	**3,267**	**2,600**

EXHIBIT 3   Mayu's Projected 3-Year Cash Flows (in Dollars)

	Year 1	Year 2	Year 3
Cash In			
Cash Sales	32,000	44,800	58,240
Total Cash In	32,000	44,800	58,240
Total Cash Available	32,000	44,800	58,240
Cash Out			
Inventory	6,400	8,960	11,648
Operating Expenses			
Advertising (*5mo.)	2,500	2,500	2,500
Marketing & Promotion (AdWords *5 mo. & PR)	6,750	6,750	6,750
Social Media Platform	1,000	1,000	1,000
Dues & Subscription (FTF etc.)	300	300	300
Payroll Expenses			
Part-Time Employee Peru	1,750	1,750	1,750
Part-Time Employee USA	3,600	3,600	3,600
Product Design Fees	5,000	5,000	5,000
Administrative Expenses			
Website Logistics	600	700	800
Travel to Peru	1,000	1,000	1,000
Office Expenses (tag etc.)	500	700	900
Estimated Income Tax Payment	0	0	0
Total Cash Out	29,400	32,260	35,248
Beginning Cash Balance	500	3,100	15,640
Ending Cash Balance	3,100	15,640	38,632

CASE 13
NATURE BROS. LTD.

BACKGROUND

Thanksgiving Day 1993 is the day that Dale Morris remembers as the "public debut" of his creation, a new seasoned salt mix. Although he was a salesman by temperament and career, his hobby was cooking. Having experimented with both traditional home cooking and more exotic gourmet cooking, Morris had developed an appreciation for many herbs and spices. He had also done a lot of reading about the health hazards of the typical American diet. When his mother learned that she had high blood pressure, Morris decided it was time for some action. He created a low-salt seasoning mix, based on a nutritive yeast extract, that could be used to replace salt in most cases. This Thanksgiving dinner, prepared for 25 family members and friends, would be his final testing ground. He used his mix in all the recipes except

the pumpkin pie—everything from the turkey and dressing to the vegetables and even the rolls. As the meal progressed, the verdict was unanimously in favor of his secret ingredient, although he had a hard time convincing them that it was his invention and was only 10 percent salt. Everyone wanted a sample to try at home.

Over the next two years, Morris perfected his product. Experiments in new uses led to "tasting parties" for friends and neighbors, and the holiday season found the Morris kitchen transformed into a miniature assembly line producing gift-wrapped bottles of the mix. Morris

Source: This case was modified by Sergey Anokhin of the Weatherhead School of Management, Case Western Reserve University, as a basis for classroom discussion rather than to illustrate either effective or ineffective handling of an administrative situation. The name of the company and the names of its officers have been disguised. Support for the development of this case was provided by the Centre for International Business Studies, University of Manitoba, Canada.

*Market size estimates are based on two decades of average growth rate for the human nutrition salt market, with some corrections to reflect the growing share of salt substitutes in total consumption of salt-like substances.

became something of a celebrity in his small town, but it wasn't until the Ladies' Mission Society at his church approached him with the idea of allowing them to sell his mix as a fund-raiser that he realized the possibilities of his creation. His kitchen-scale operation could support the sales effort of the church women for a short time, but if he wanted to take advantage of a truly marketable product, he would have to make other arrangements.

Morris agreed to "test-market" his product through the church group while he looked for ways to expand and commercialize his operation. The charity sale was a huge success (the best the women had ever experienced), and, based on this success, Morris moved to create his own company. Naming his product "Nature Bros. Old Fashioned Seasoning," he incorporated the company in 1995 as Nature Bros. Ltd. Morris used most of his savings to develop and register the trademarks, for packaging, and for product displays. He researched the cost of manufacturing and bottling his product in large quantities and concluded that he just didn't have the cash to get started. His first attempts to raise money, in the form of a personal bank loan, were unsuccessful, and he was forced to abandon the project.

For several years he concentrated on his career, becoming a regional vice president of the insurance company he worked for. He continued to make "Nature Bros. Seasoning" in small batches, mainly for his mother and business associates. These users eventually enabled Morris to get financial support for his company. To raise $65,000 to lease manufacturing equipment and building space, he sold stock to his mother and to two other regional vice presidents of the insurance company. For their contributions, each became the owner of 15 percent of Nature Bros. Ltd. The process of getting the product to the retail market began in August 2002, and the first grocery store sales started in March 2003. The initial marketing plan was fairly simple—to get the product in the hands of the consumer. Morris personally visited the managers of individual supermarkets, both chains and independents, and convinced many to allow a tasting demonstration booth to be set up in their stores. These demonstrations proved as popular as the first Thanksgiving dinner trial nearly 10 years earlier. Dale Morris's product was a hit, and in a short time he was able to contract with food brokerage firms to place his product in stores in a 10-state region.

PRESENT SITUATION

As indicated in the balance sheet (see Exhibit 1), more capital is needed to support the current markets and expand both markets and products. Two new products are being developed: a salt-free version of the original product and an MSG-based flavor enhancer that will compete with Accent. Morris worked with a business consultant in drawing up a business plan to describe his company, its future growth, and its capital needs.

OVERALL PROJECTIONS

The first section discusses the objectives and sales projections for 2004 and 2005 (Exhibits 2 and 3). The resulting pro forma income statements for 2004 to 2005 are in Exhibits 4 and 5.

2004 OBJECTIVES

The company's objectives for 2004 are to stabilize its existing markets and to achieve a 5 percent market share in the category of seasoned salt, a 10 percent market share in salt substitutes, and a 5 percent market share in MSG products. Although the original product contains less than 10 percent salt, the company has developed a salt-free product to compete with other such products. The dollar volume for the seasoned salt category in the seven markets the company is in will amount to $7,931,889 in 2004. In 2003, sales of the company in the Oklahoma market were 5.5 percent of the total sales for that market for the eight-month period that the company was operational. Since these sales were accomplished with absolutely no advertising, the company can be even more successful in the future in all seven current markets with a fully developed and funded advertising campaign. The marketing approach will include advertisements in the print media, with ads on "food day" offering cents-off coupons. This program will take place in all seven markets, while stores will continue to use floor displays for demonstrations. Nearly 100 percent warehouse penetration should be achieved in 2004 in these markets.

The goal for the category of salt substitutes for 2004 is 10 percent of the market share. This larger market share can be achieved since there are only a few competitors, Mrs. Dash, AMBI Inc. with Cordia Salt Alternative, and RCN with No Salt. The company's product is superior in all respects and has a retail price advantage of 10 to 20 cents per can. In addition, the company's product is much more versatile than competitors' products. Aggressive marketing and advertising will emphasize the tremendous versatility of usage as well as the great taste and health benefits of the product. The informal consumer surveys at

EXHIBIT 1

NATURE BROS. LTD.
Balance Sheet
As of September 30, 2003

Unaudited

Current assets

110 Cash—American Bank	$ 527.11
112 Cash—Bank of Okla-Pryor	31.86
115 Cash on hand	24.95
120 Accounts receivable	21,512.75
125 Employee advances	327.37
140 Inventory—Shipping	940.43
141 Inventory—Raw materials	1,082.29
142 Inventory—Work-in-progress	803.70
143 Inventory—Packaging	4,548.41
144 Inventory—Promotional	2,114.95
Total current assets	**$31,913.82**

Fixed assets

160 Leasehold improvements	$ 2,402.25
165 Fixtures and furniture	1,222.46
167 Equipment	18,768.21
169 Office equipment	.00
170 1986 Lincoln Town Car	15,000.00
180 Less: Accumulated depreciation	(7,800.01)
181 Less: Amortization	(502.50)
Total fixed assets	**$29,090.41**

Other assets

193 Organizational cost	$ 4,083.36
194 Prepaid interest	2,849.69
195 Utility deposits	.00
Total fixed and other assets	**$36,023.46**
Total assets	**$67,937.28**

Current liabilities

205 Accounts payable	$15,239.41
210 Note payable-premium finances	88.26
220 Federal tax withheld	150.00
225 FICA tax withheld	937.92
230 State tax withheld	266.49
231 State and federal employment taxes	230.92
Total current liabilities	**$16,913.00**

Long-term liabilities

245 Note payable—All fill	$ 2,734.86
246 Note payable—American Bank	23,740.00
247 Note payable—Sikeston Leasing	15,126.66
Total long-term liabilities	**$41,601.52**
Total liabilities	**$58,514.52**

Capital account

290 Original capital stock	$ 1,000.00
291 Additional paid-in capital	41,580.00
292 Treasury stock	(70.00)
295 Retained earnings	(3,819.71)
298 Net profit or loss	(29,267.53)
Total owner's equity account	**$ 9,422.76**
Total liabilities and equity	**$67,937.28**

EXHIBIT 2 2004 Sales Projection			
Category	Seasoned Salt	Salt Substitute	MSG
Our Product	**Old Fashioned Seasoning**	**Salt-Free Old Fashioned Seasoning**	**Enhance**
Existing markets #1			
Oklahoma	$1,101,844	$ 715,638	$ 237,778
Nebraska	799,260	605,538	201,916
Springfield, MO	508,620	385,432	128,034
Arkansas	435,960	330,294	109,742
Houston	1,671,180	1,266,128	420,684
Dallas	2,325,120	1,761,570	585,298
Albuquerque	1,089,900	825,736	274,358
	$7,931,884	$5,890,246	$1,957,090
Market share (%)	×5%	×10%	×5%
1st year sales	$ 396,594	$ 589,024	$ 97,854
		396,594	
		589,024	
		97,854	
Total 1st year sales volume		$1,083,472	

demonstrations indicated that consumers prefer Nature Bros. to competitors' products by a wide margin.

A new product, which is already developed, will be added during this time. Called "Enhance," it too is a dry-mixed, noncooked, low-overhead, high-profit food product. Its category of MSG products has a dollar volume of $1,957,090 in these markets. This category includes only one main competitor, Accent, made by Pet Inc. Accent has not been heavily advertised, and it is a one-line product with little initial name recognition. The company's new product will have a 10- to 20-cent per can retail price advantage to help achieve a 5 percent share of this category. In summary, 2004 will be spent solidifying the company's present market positions.

2005 OBJECTIVES

The company intends to open eight new markets in 2005 that include Los Angeles, Phoenix, Portland, Sacramento, Salt Lake City, San Francisco, Seattle, and Spokane. These new markets make up 17.1 percent of grocery store sales, according to the *Progressive Grocer's Marketing Guidebook,* the industry standard. In the

category of seasoned salt, these markets have a dollar volume of $15,218,886 a year. Salt substitutes sell at a volume of $10,064,028, and the MSG category $3,285,528. With proper advertising, the company's shares forecast in our current markets will also be realized.

A 5 percent penetration of the seasoned salt category is a very conservative projection considering the strong health consciousness of the West Coast. The products will be introduced in shippers, used in store demonstrations, and supported with media advertising to achieve at least a 5 percent market share. This would result in sales of $760,943 in that category.

A 10 percent penetration is targeted in the salt-free category. Using aggressive marketing, price advantage at retail, and better packaging, the company will be well positioned against the lower-quality products of our competitors. With the dollar volume of this category at $10,064,028, a conservative estimate of our share would be $1,006,420. In the category of MSG, a 5 percent share will be achieved. The main competitor in this category does very little advertising. Again,

EXHIBIT 3   2005 Sales Projection

Category	Seasoned Salt	Salt Substitute	MSG
Our Product	Old Fashioned Seasoning	Salt-Free Old Fashioned Seasoning	Enhance
Existing markets #1			
Oklahoma	$ 1,156,936	$ 751,418	$ 249,778
Nebraska	978,946	635,816	211,350
Springfield, MO	622,966	404,610	134,496
Arkansas	533,970	346,808	115,282
Houston	2,046,886	1,329,432	441,914
Dallas	2,847,842	1,885,644	614,838
Albuquerque	1,334,926	867,020	288,206
Existing markets total	$ 9,522,472	$ 6,220,748	$2,055,864
Market share	×7.5%	×12.5%	×7.5%
Existing markets $ volume	$ 714,185	$ 775,593	$ 154,189
New markets:			
Los Angeles	$ 5,784,678	$ 3,757,088	$1,248,888
Phoenix	1,245,930	809,218	268,990
Portland	1,157,294	751,418	249,776
Sacramento	1,690,906	1,098,226	365,060
Salt Lake City	1,157,294	751,416	249,776
San Francisco	2,313,870	1,502,838	499,554
Seattle	1,157,294	751,416	249,776
Spokane	711,960	462,412	153,708
New markets total	$15,218,886	$10,064,028	$3,285,528
Market share	×5%	×10%	×5%
New markets $ volume	$760,943	$ 1,006,420	$164,276
New markets $ total	760,943	1,006,420	164,276
Existing markets $ total +	714,185	777,593	154,189
Total volume	$ 1,475,128	$ 1,784,013	$ 318,465
Old Fashioned Seasoning sales		$1,475,128	
Salt-Free Old Fashioned Seasoning sales		1,784,013	
Enhance sales (a new product)		318,465	
Total 2005 sales		$3,557,606	

attractive packaging, aggressive marketing, high quality, and a retail price advantage of 30 to 40 cents per unit will enable the company to realize a 5 percent market penetration. This share of the West Coast markets will generate sales of $164,276. Total sales of all three products in these eight new markets will be around

$1,931,639. The company plans to continue to solidify the markets previously established through the use of coupons, co-op advertising, quality promotions, and word-of-mouth advertising. Market share in these original markets should increase by another 2.5 percent in 2005. The dollar volume of the seasoned salt category

EXHIBIT 4   2004 Pro Forma Totals

	2004	Percent
Sales	$1,083,472	100
Cost of goods		
Packaging	129,444	11.9
Ingredients	175,668	16.2
Plant labor	35,580	3.2
Freight in	24,036	2.2
Shipping materials	924	.08
Total cost of goods sold	$ 365,004	33.68
Gross profit	718,468	66.31
Operating expenses		
President's salary	43,200	
Sales manager	30,000	
Secretary	14,400	
Employee benefits	2,400	
Insurance	1,992	
Rent	3,000	
Utilities	1,800	
Phone	7,200	
Office supplies	1,200	
Postage	1,200	
Car lease	5,640	
Professional services	3,000	
Travel and entertainment	24,000	
Freight out	59,088	5.4
Advertising	216,684	20.0
Promotion	12,036	1.1
Brokerage	54,168	5.0
Incentives	7,500	.6
Cash discounts	21,660	2.0
Total expenses	$ 510,168	47.0
Cash flow		
Taxes	207,648	19.1
Net profit before debt service	155,736	14.3

in 2005 should be around $9,522,472, and our market share at 7.5 percent would amount to $714,185. The dollar volume for the salt substitute category would be $6,220,748, giving sales at 12.5 percent of $775,593. In the MSG category, a 7.5 percent market share of the $2,055,864 volume would give sales of $154,189. The company's total sales for the existing markets in 2005 will be in excess of $1,643,967. The totals for 2005 sales of Nature Bros. Old Fashioned Seasoning will be $1,475,128. Nature Bros. Salt-Free volume should be

EXHIBIT 5

NATURE BROS. LTD.
Pro Forma Income Statement
2005–2008

	2005	2006	2007	2008
Sales	$3,557,606	$6,136,224	$10,089,863	$18,506,302
Cost of goods				
Packaging	423,355	730,210	1,200,693	2,202,249
Ingredients	572,774	987,932	1,624,467	2,979,514
Plant labor	37,359	48,826	60,867	63,910
Freight in	72,930	125,793	206,842	379,379
Shipping materials	2,960	4,908	8,071	14,805
Total cost of goods sold	$1,106,575	$1,897,618	$ 3,100,240	$ 5,639,858
Percent of sales	31.36%	31.41%	30.90%	30.65%
Gross profit	2,451,031	4,238,606	6,988,923	12,866,444
Operating expenses				
President's salary	43,200	51,840	62,208	74,649
Sales manager	30,000	36,000	39,000	45,000
Sales rep	25,000	30,000	34,000	38,000
Sales rep		25,000	30,000	34,000
Sales rep			26,000	30,000
Sales rep				28,000
Secretary	16,000	18,000	20,000	22,000
Secretary				15,000
Employee benefits	2,400	4,000	10,000	15,000
Insurance	3,000	4,000	5,000	5,000
Rent	3,600	3,600	3,600	3,600
Utilities	2,400	3,000	3,500	4,500
Phone	12,000	14,000	15,000	18,000
Office supplies	2,000	2,500	3,000	5,000
Postage	2,000	2,500	3,000	4,000
Car lease	5,640	5,640	5,640	5,640
Car lease	3,600	3,600	4,000	4,000
Car lease		3,600	3,600	4,000
Car lease			4,000	4,000
Professional services	6,000	8,000	8,000	10,000
Travel and entertainment	48,000	72,000	96,000	120,000
New equipment	4,000	14,000	14,000	24,000
Freight out	197,269	334,424	549,897	1,000,859
Advertising	711,521	1,227,244	2,017,972	3,701,260
Promotion	40,000	68,112	111,997	205,419
Brokerage	177,880	306,811	504,493	925,315
Incentives	24,547	42,399	69,680	205,419
Cash discounts	71,152	122,724	201,792	370,126
Total expenses	$1,431,209	$2,402,994	$ 3,845,192	$ 6,921,787
Cash flow before taxes	1,019,822	1,835,612	3,845,192	6,921,787
Taxes	209,063	458,903	785,932	1,486,164
Net profit before debt service	$ 810,759	$1,376,709	$ 2,357,799	$ 4,458,493
Percent of sales	22.78%	22.43%	23.36%	24.09%

$1,784,013. The sales of Enhance, our MSG product, should be $318,465. This will give us a total sales volume of $3,557,606 for all three products in 2005.

FINANCIAL NEEDS AND PROJECTIONS

In this plan, Morris indicated a need for $100,000 equity infusion to expand sales, increase markets, and add new products. The money would be used to secure warehouse stocking space, do cooperative print advertising, give point-of-purchase display allowances, and pay operating expenses.

NEW PRODUCT DEVELOPMENT

The company plans to continue an ongoing research and development program to introduce new and winning products. Four products are already developed that will be highly marketable and easily produced. Personnel are dedicated to building a large and profitable company and attracting quality brokers. The next new product targets a different market segment but can be brought online for about $25,000 by using our existing machinery, types of containers, and display pieces. A highly respected broker felt that the product would be a big success. The broker previously represented the only major producer of a similar product, Pet Inc., which had sales of $4.36 million in 1985. The company can achieve at least a 5 percent market share with this product in the first year. The company's product will be at least equal in quality and offer a 17 percent price advantage to the consumer, while still making an excellent profit.

Another new product would require slightly different equipment. This product would be initially produced by a private-label manufacturer. The product would be established before any major machinery was purchased. Many large companies use private-label manufacturers, or co-packers, as they are called in the trade. Consumer tests at demonstrations and food shows have indicated that each of these products will be strong.

PLANT AND EQUIPMENT

The company's plant is located in a nearly new metal building in Rose, Oklahoma. The lease on the building limits payments to no more than $300 per month for the next seven years. The new computer-controlled filling equipment will be paid off in two months, and the seaming equipment is leased from the company's container manufacturer for only $1 per year. The com-

pany has the capability of producing about 300,000 units a month with an additional $15,000 investment for an automatic conveyer system and a bigger product mixer. This production level would require two additional plant personnel, working one shift with no overtime. The company could double this production if needed with the addition of another shift. One of the main advantages of the company's business is the very small overhead required to produce the products. The company can generate enough product to reach sales of approximately $4 million a year while maintaining a production payroll of only $37,000 a year.

To meet the previously outlined production goals, the company will need to purchase another filling machine in 2005. This machine will be capable of filling two cans at once with an overall speed of 75 cans per minute, which would increase capacity to 720,000 units a month. A higher-speed seaming machine will also need to be purchased. The filling machine would cost approximately $22,000; a rebuilt seamer would cost $25,000, while a new one would cost $50,000. With the addition of these two machines, the company would have a capacity of 1,020,000 units per month on one shift.

By 2006, the company will have to decide whether to continue the lease or buy the property where located and expand the facilities. The property has plenty of land for expansion for the next five years. The company has the flexibility to produce other types of products with the same equipment and can react quickly to changes in customer preferences and modify its production line to meet such demands as needed.

CASE 14
AMY'S BREAD

Amy glanced at the clock and moaned. It was 3:30 A.M., time to get up and head to her Manhattan bakery, but she hadn't slept all night. She had a big decision to make. "No," she muttered to herself; she had a multitude of big decisions to make.

Amy muttered to herself, "There are already so many days when I feel stretched past the breaking point. There are so many demands." Amy mentally ticked them off: Ensuring consistent quality, scheduling and training

Source: This case study was reprinted by permission from the Case Research Journal. Copyright 2001 by Paula S. Weber, Cathleen S. Burns, James E. Weber, and the North American Case Research Association. All rights reserved.

staff, ordering supplies, developing new recipes, contacting potential customers, collecting from slow-paying clients . . . the list was truly endless. Amy wondered, "If I decide to expand, can I do it successfully? Can I find another trustworthy manager, like Toy Kim Dupree, to help me manage the staff and maintain bread quality? Can I find expansion space in Manhattan? Should I close our current location and expand to a much larger space, thus eliminating the need to manage two locations? Should I look for a location for my wholesale production, or a space that would provide both retail and wholesale opportunities?" There was so much to decide. Right now though, Amy's dough starters were waiting, as were her employees. She had to get up and face another busy day at her bakery.

Amy's Bread, founded in 1992, served about 50 wholesale customers, including some of the finest restaurants, hotels, and gourmet food shops in Manhattan. Amy's Bread also had a waiting list of more than 30 wholesale customers from other quality restaurants, hotels, and shops.

Amy thought, "I really want to meet their needs and accept their business, but any further production expansion in my existing space is impossible. I know I can't produce one more loaf without hurting bread quality, which is absolutely unthinkable! We are already working three shifts, and there is no more room for additional equipment."

Amy and her assistant manager, Toy Kim Dupree, had commiserated: "The bakery is stretched to the limits. Dough production ranges from 1,800 to 3,000 lbs. of bread per day, well over capacity for just 1,300 square feet." As Toy described, "We are like sardines making bread. Surviving in these close quarters is so difficult. Not only do we produce all of the wholesale and retail bread in this one location, but we also store ingredients and have a small office."

Amy worried that some of the customers on her long waiting list were on the brink of turning away. But, Amy thought, "Am I really ready to tackle a major expansion? On the one hand, I have worked so hard to make my dreams a reality, I can't imagine stopping now. But, can I handle an expansion and larger ongoing operations? Financially? Mentally? Physically?" Amy remembered Toy's recent comment: "Amy's Bread is finally turning a profit." The thought of an expansion and additional debt was very scary.

AMY'S PERSONAL HISTORY

Amy was born and raised in Minnesota, where her father was a high-level executive for Pillsbury and her mother was a gourmet cook with a family reputation for baking fresh breads. As a child, Amy remembered coming home from school to the smell of her mother's homemade breads wafting from the kitchen. After high school, Amy earned a degree in economics and psychology. She then moved to New York in 1984 to try her luck in the Big Apple.

Amy soon found that an office job was not for her, and that she longed to pursue a more creative career. She talked endlessly to her managers and coworkers about her dream of opening her own business. It was then that Amy began to solicit support and promises of financial backing if she were ever to start her own business. After 3 years, Amy left her white-collar marketing position to pursue her dream. She decided to attend the New York Restaurant School for culinary training. After graduating from their program, Amy landed a job as a chef for one of New York's most highly acclaimed French restaurants. After 2 years of very challenging work and longer hours than her marketing job, Amy escaped to Europe. Amy said, "It was there I discovered my true passion: bread baking." She backpacked around England and Italy and eventually settled in France, where there are strong traditions of bread baking. Amy worked at French bakeries in three different towns, spending a month at each. "When I returned to New York in 1989, I was brimming with ideas and excitement about opening my own bakery," Amy recalled.

Amy spent the next 2 years as a pastry chef and bread baker for another top New York eatery. As Amy worked, she simultaneously developed recipes and business plans. Amy dreamed that someday soon she would be working for herself.

HISTORY OF AMY'S BREAD

Amy knew that opening a bakery in New York would be extremely challenging. First, it was a highly competitive industry with low wholesale profit margins. Second, space in New York was always at a premium, and renting a desirable location was going to be extremely expensive. Third, she discovered that banks would not loan her money. Banks viewed bakeries as restaurants—far too risky an investment without a prior proven track record. Amy remained undaunted. She was determined to achieve her goal of running her own business, one that sold a million dollars worth of beautiful breads each year made by employees who took pride in their work and were rewarded for their efforts. Amy had clear goals: "I wanted to be famous for making a great product and for creating a good place to work. I did not care a lot about being rich. I just want to sell beautiful breads from a cute, cozy place."

In 1992, armed with some savings, a loan from her parents, private loans from her former colleagues in the marketing profession, a good business mind, and a very determined spirit, Amy took the big step. She quit her restaurant job and opened Amy's Bread on Ninth Avenue in a tough area of Manhattan known as Hell's Kitchen. The space she found was an old storefront that had been a fish market and had been empty for 5 years. Although only 650 square feet, it was still expensive, but it was the most affordable space she could find. With the help of family and friends, it still took 6 months to renovate the space, including plastering and painting. Amy installed equipment, hired and trained staff, developed a customer list, and began production.

CURRENT OPERATIONS OF AMY'S BREAD

Personnel

Amy's Bread started with a staff of six dedicated employees who scrubbed up used equipment, built shelves, and lent a hand as needed. Amy recalled, "I taught them bread making techniques, and then, with little idea of what was to come, we opened for business." Amy's Bread sometimes used newspaper advertisements for attracting employees, but most responded to a "Now Hiring" sign in the bakery's window. Assistant manager, Toy Kim Dupree, described reasons employees came to work for Amy's Bread. "Some were interested in bread baking, but many came because we offered a 5-day workweek while many bakeries and restaurants have a 6-day workweek. We also worked hard to create a happy, open, and friendly environment. It's what we wanted for ourselves and what we hoped to create for our employees. Our aim was to have a perfect product, but we recognized that we were dealing with human beings. Anyone who is too intense does not fit in well here. We don't have any room for prima donnas. We also tend to pay more than our competitors."

A typical employee would begin in the shaping area, working to form the bread loaves. From there, they can move to baking the bread and, finally, to the mixing of the dough. Toy described a key management challenge as "helping employees to beat the boredom of their repetitive work." Toy said, "Our most successful employees have a positive outlook, are dependable and

conscientious, think on their feet, and interact well with their coworkers. We have no cubicles here!" Employees suggested solutions to management issues, with Amy having the final say. As Toy described, "We all put our heads together, bringing in our separate areas of expertise. Our goals were to produce very high-quality breads by hand, pay our employees a decent living wage, and ensure that our customers get good value for their money."

Over the years, Amy's Bread had experienced very low turnover. Retail staff started at $8.00 an hour and baking staff at $10.00. In fact, Amy's Bread's lowest paid employees were the cleaning staff, and they started at $7.50 an hour, well above minimum wage. Benefits were available to employees who worked more than 20 hours a week, and employees who were with the company longer than a year were eligible for a 401k plan. The majority of her employees (88 percent) were minorities for whom English was a second language. Training was often done by demonstration. Payroll expenses were extremely high, representing over 50 percent of sales. With a handmade product, it was difficult to attain any economy of scale concerning labor. New sales led to additional payroll expense.

Amy reminisced, "The first year was by far the toughest. We learned to handle dough in stifling hot weather. We had to keep going on only a few hours of sleep a day and get by without money when our customers were slow to pay. Our space was so narrow and cramped that we struggled to get racks of dough through it. However, sales were good, and sometimes all the bread was sold by noon!"

Bread Production

Amy surmised that "practice and patience were the keys to perfect bread, and all successful bread started with quality ingredients." Amy explained, "Dough batters are very challenging. They can be too dry, too wet, not rising quickly enough, or rising too quickly. Many external elements can affect the dough, including the air temperature, the temperature of the water, the timing of each step." One of the most critical aspects of the success of Amy's Bread was her devotion to sourdough starters. The starters are essentially flour, yeast, and water. Amy quipped, "The starters are the miracle ingredient that gives life to the bread."

Amy mused, "A baker's work is really never done. The demands are constant. The dough keeps rising and must be carefully watched throughout the process. The bakery operates 24 hours a day, 7 days a week. Wholesale customers want bread every day. On weekends and holidays, their orders double!" Amy's Bread had a staff of 32 bread mixers, shapers, and bakers by 1998.

At about 5:00 A.M., the mixing began. Amy described the process: "We fill a large mixer with flour, water, the all-important sourdough starter, salt, and yeast. Before long, the mixer's fork kneader pulls and stretches a mass of supple dough. The dough is put aside to rest and rise slowly at a cool temperature and then divided into portions to be shaped and baked."

Every step was physically demanding, and workers got sore arms and shoulders and very, very tired legs and feet. At noon, the shaping of the loaves for the next day's orders began. Racks of rising dough were cut and formed. This was a totally manual process, as each loaf must be hand-shaped. The bread was then left to rise again at a cool temperature so it can ferment. Finally, the loaves were baked in the early hours of the morning. After the bread was baked, it was cooled and packed for delivery by an Amy's Bread truck. Amy commented, "Smelling the bread as it comes out of the oven, seeing its golden color, feeling its texture, and enjoying its delicious flavor certainly contribute to job satisfaction!"

Customers

Amy's original business plans called for providing breads wholesale to restaurants and hotels. She had a loyal customer in a former employer and a list of interested customers. Her location was really not the best for retail traffic. Retail business would simply be a sideline—she would sell excess loaves to people who wandered in to check out the bakery.

Slowly, but surely, Amy began earning a city-wide reputation for high-quality, innovative yet consistent products. Her signature bread, semolina with golden raisins and fennel, brought Amy's Bread lots of attention. By 1996, her wholesale customer list had grown to almost 40 customers, and she was preparing about 600 lbs. of dough a day just for her semolina, golden raisin, fennel bread. Her product line included approximately 50 items made from 15 different doughs. Amy's best-selling products included her semolina bread, walnut scallion bread, black olive twists, apple walnut raisin rings, and organic whole wheat bread with toasted seeds.

As Amy's business grew, she discovered a growing retail interest. The area around Amy's Bread was improving, and new restaurants and coffee shops were opening. She began to bake rolls and single-serving loaves specifically for retail customers. She eventually hired counter help to service the retail customers and began selling not only breakfast breads, like muffins and scones, but sandwiches to customers as well. She set up attractive window displays and added a few small tables in the front of her shop. Amy's retail business gradually grew until it represented about 25 percent of sales. Best-selling items for retail traffic included focaccia with rosemary, bread twists, sourdough baguettes, and country sourdough loaves. Amy noted that her staff "took great pride in serving retail customers." They told Amy, "We enjoyed hearing directly from the customers how much they enjoy the bread."

Amy commented that "wholesale is my mainstay and where the greatest volume of sales exist. However, the profit margin on retail is better than on wholesale." Amy remarked, "A critical part of my expansion decision is deciding whether the expansion should be solely for wholesale space, a combination of retail and wholesale, or purely retail." Amy felt this was a crucial issue because the use of the space really drove the location decision. Amy knew, "If I were to expand to meet my waiting list of wholesale customers only, then the facility needed to have good access to major streets with an ample truck dock for loading baked loaves and unloading supplies and ingredients. It also could be located in a less "desirable" neighborhood. However, if retail were to be the emphasis, then I needed to find an attractive space with lots of foot traffic in a neighborhood where many people lived and worked."

Competitors

When Amy's Bread opened, bread baking appeared to be a growth industry, boosted by healthful eating trends. The U.S. Department of Commerce reported that per capita consumption of specialty breads increased 12 percent from 1988 to 1993. A 1992 article in *Bakery Production and Marketing* stated that key trends predicted for supermarkets in the 1990s would be the expansion of in-store bakeries as a key aspect of enhancing their outreach to customers.

In 1993, per capita consumption of specialty breads was 23.28 lbs. which represented 30 percent of all bread consumption. A Gallup Poll in January 1995 showed that 71 percent of adults prefer bread to all other grain-based foods. Ninety percent indicated that grain-based foods were convenient, and 63 percent thought bread was low fat. New bread chains and franchise locations were springing up every day, including Stone Mill Bread

Company, Panere, La Madeleine, and the original, Au Bon Pain. Perhaps the biggest of the franchise chains was the Great Harvest Bread Company, founded in 1976. In 1995, Great Harvest had 87 stores with 15 more under development, sporting a 30 percent annual growth rate.

Closer to home, Amy's Bread had several primary competitors for specialty breads, including the Tom Cat Bakery in Queens (one of New York's other boroughs), Ecce Panis, and Eli's Bread. They were well-established and larger than Amy's Bread. They supported a client list that included famous restaurants such as the Union Square Café, Balducci's, and Dean & Deluca. These bakeries tended to be more mechanized than Amy's Bread, utilizing equipment for dough shaping and baking.

Some of the larger commercial bakeries had folded due to competitive pressures but, at the same time, more and more small bakeries featuring specialty varieties were opened in Manhattan and the surrounding area. These microbakeries, like Amy's Bread, catered to upscale restaurants and gourmet shops that wanted to pamper their customers with the best of fresh, creative breads. Amy felt that "the secret to financial success in the bakery business was to differentiate your breads, rather than copying what everyone else made." Amy maintained, "The keys to getting and maintaining wholesale customers are innovative and consistently high-quality breads. One of the ways I ensure high quality is by the hand-shaping and individual baking of the bread. The retail customers also want consistent quality, but they are looking for convenient locations and prompt service, too. I don't focus on what my competitors charge. Occasionally, I see their price lists, but I basically charge what I feel I must to cover my expenses and overhead. In fact, many of our prices have not changed since we first opened for business."

Financial Results

Shortly after her 1992 opening, Amy discovered what many entrepreneurs find to be a major roadblock: cash flow. As new entrepreneurial businesses began to flourish, more and more up-front money was needed for equipment, supplies, and staff. Typically, the customer base had not grown large enough to cover all the expenses, nor were customer accounts as current as desired, and sometimes products were not priced correctly. Amy remarked, "Soon after opening, I discovered that even if I sold every loaf I could make, my revenue would not be high enough to cover my high monthly lease

and equipment rental expenses." Amy was very lucky though, when adjoining space opened up in December, and although she could not easily afford to lease the space, she also knew that she could not continue to exist without expanding. Quickly, Amy was able to borrow enough additional funds from family and friends to lease the adjoining open space. By January 1993, she was in full production in her newly expanded space.

Though the beginning months proved to be quite a struggle, Amy's Bread gradually grew. The 1998 income statement and accompanying schedules for Amy's Bread highlight her sales and profitability. Amy remarked, "Since payroll expenses rise with sales, the real profits only come from economies of scale reached with fixed expenses like rent and utilities." Amy further noted, "Given the low unemployment rate, there often is a shortage of good staff available at the salaries my business could afford to pay." Amy's contribution margin on retail operations was 47 percent; it was only 35 percent for wholesale operations. Other bakeries that were more mechanized experienced higher profit margins. In order to ensure the highest quality of product, Amy's Bread hand-shaped all their breads; therefore, labor costs were much higher than other bakeries. For example, a "mechanized" bakery with sales revenue similar to Amy's Bread had only five employees; Amy's Bread needed 20 employees to produce the same amount of sales.

In analyzing other expenses, Amy commented, "Food cost changes usually come from flour, nuts, dairy products, and olive oil. Prices for those products are quite volatile while prices for other ingredients remain quite stable." In the mid-1990s the baking industry experienced a steep rise in the price of flour. However, industry reports showed that bakeries were only able to raise their prices 5 percent over the same time period. In addition, restaurants, overwhelmed with sources of bread providers, were resistant to bakery industry pressures for price hikes. For quality reasons, though, Amy rejected using "quick-bread" mixes where you only add eggs and oil, preferring more expensive fresh, organic ingredients and sourdough starters.

Marketing Techniques

Amy said her most successful marketing technique was to "keep current customers happy." She noted, "Word of mouth is very powerful in the New York restaurant business." Another way that Amy had obtained new customers was by being very available to the press. Amy emphasized, "Whenever someone calls for an interview, I make the time to meet with them and make every effort to make them feel welcome. I invariably discuss what is unique about my breads and, of course, everyone receives free bread samples. The fact that I am a woman in a male-dominated industry helps ensure that my business is an interesting story." Amy also determined that "whenever there was a mention of my business in a local paper, business increased a great deal for the next 2 to 3 weeks, and some of the new customers continued to return. A positive review by an outsider is better than any ad I could write." However, limited advertising was used for special events or seasonal product promotion.

Amy's Bread has been recognized by *The New York Times, New York Magazine, Modern Baking, Gourmet,* and *Food & Wine,* just to mention a few. Excerpts from these articles include the following.

"At her tiny, charming storefront in what used to be known as Hell's Kitchen, Amy Scherber turns out a dozen and a half sublime varieties that are anything but conventional white bread. Amy's is the candy store of bread bakeries." *New York Magazine,* June 1994. "Armed with a gentle manner, modest business plan and a genuine love for baking bread, Amy Scherber, 34, has managed, in less than 2 years, to position her bakery in the highly competitive, sometimes cutthroat, specialty wholesale bread market of New York City." *Modern Baking,* November 1994.

Amy had other successes as well. The 1996 *Zagat Marketplace Survey* ranked Amy's bread third out of 27 New York bread bakeries. "The best thing to happen to Ninth Avenue" say admirers of this "charming" bread shop filled with the aroma of "home baking"; it offers "imaginative breads to build meals around" and "consoling sticky buns"; the breads are also sold in food specialty shops around Manhattan; owner, Amy Scherber (the "Streisand of bakers") and her "friendly" staff "revere bread and it shows in every loaf." *Zagat,* 1996.

Other marketing techniques pursued by Amy's Bread included decorating the shop windows for every holiday. One could find large decorated heart cookies on Valentine's Day and big baskets of specialty breads on Easter. Amy regularly sent free samples of her breads to influential chefs. She donated bread to charities, taught baking classes, and appeared on television Food Network shows. In addition, the Amy's Bread delivery truck helped spread the word as it circled Manhattan delivering bread.

Amy was not one to rest on her laurels. With her assistant manager, Toy Kim Dupree, Amy developed a cookbook that was published in 1996. This effort consumed countless hours to carefully modify recipes meant for huge batches of dough down to the one loaf size. It also involved having the recipes tested by untrained bakers and editing and improving the instructions. Amy had to explain her techniques so that the novice baker could understand them. Amy noted, "The cookbook project took way more of my time than I could have ever anticipated." The cookbook was a hit with bakers everywhere. Reviews of the book, as well as glowing customer comments, were posted at the Amazon.com Web site.

To add to her challenges, Amy's long-time exposure to bread and yeast had made her allergic to many basic bread ingredients. Amy said, "I have learned that if I spend too much time around the mixing of the dough, I get an itchy nose, watery eyes, and a cough. I also have to be careful to eat bread in moderation."

Because of the popularity of her Manhattan bakery and her cookbook, Amy was contacted to consult with bakeries across the country. She also made a videotape appearance on the Oprah Winfrey show featuring successful young entrepreneurs.

Amy was also in the process of developing an Amy's Bread Web site designed primarily for marketing and public relations purposes. Although they would accept on-line orders, Amy noted that, "bread is about freshness, impulse buying, and temptation. We do not expect much mail-order business, and truthfully, shipping expenses can often be higher than the cost of the bread."

Future Opportunities

Armed with 6 years of continuing success, Amy was facing a critical decision. Should she expand or stand pat? She had a waiting list of wholesale customers, but could she stretch herself and her resources enough to expand successfully? Despite the popularity of Amy's Bread, Amy was still working long hours and earning only a modest income. Amy had managed to put away a good-sized nest egg, but it wasn't nearly enough for expansion. Armed with sales and financial projections, she began by looking for additional wholesale production space in Manhattan. Amy was looking for about 3,000 to 4,000 square feet that would essentially triple her current space. She based this requirement on her growing waiting list of potential customers, analyses of optimal production layouts, and associated projections for sales and expenses.

Amy eventually found a 6,000-square-foot building on 31st Street that she felt she could afford. She also succeeded in getting a bank to agree to a $150,000 loan for her business plan. Unlike her 1992 application for a loan, Amy now had a proven track record and was interested in borrowing funds to purchase a hard asset, a building. However, her estimated budget for purchasing the building and making needed improvements was approximately $300,000. Amy's personal savings as well as the bakery business savings were not enough to make up the difference. Creative finances would be required to expand . . . but Amy declared, "I have managed before and will again."

While pursuing this plan, a developer contacted Amy with a new option. A lease was available on a 7,500-square-foot space that was part of a block-long warehouse renovation on 15th Street. The developer's idea was to fill the space with a variety of food producers with small retail shops who sold their products at slightly reduced prices directly from the production source. The proposed market would include a fresh produce shop, flower shop, and pastry shop. This space was essentially an empty shell with no wiring, ventilation, plumbing, or interior walls. Amy would need to make all the leasehold improvements, but she could also choose how things were to be designed and constructed. Amy estimated that it would take 4 months to construct her store at a cost of approximately $500,000. This rental space had retail potential; the 31st Street building she could purchase was essentially a production facility only and was located in a desolate area. Amy was faced with a decision to lease space that would service both retail and wholesale customers, or to buy a space that would serve wholesale customers only.

Amy commented, "Although retail is profitable, you need many locations to reach more customers and increase retail volume. Wholesale business volume can be increased from just one location." Amy's gross sales were approximately 75 percent wholesale and 25 percent retail. The wholesale business was much more stable with advance bread orders for large, fixed amounts. Retail business depended on individual consumer buying decisions for much smaller quantities. However, an item that sold for $1.10 wholesale would retail at $1.75. This represented a price increase of 59 percent contrasted with an additional retail cost of only about 14 percent (for counter staff, table space, and so forth) resulting in a projected per item net retail gross profit margin increase of 45 percent. And, retail sales were for cash only.

Amy said, "I am sure the answer lies in careful financial projections for sales and associated costs, a bit of luck, and a lot of passion and hard work." It was time to complete some detailed financial analysis, including cash flows to help decide the best course of action. Amy stated, "Deciding not to expand would be the only "sure" bet. But, I'm not sure I am ready to sit back and be satisfied with what I have already accomplished. I have worked so hard to get this far, I am not sure I can turn hard-earned customers away. And, what if my business slumps because I can't meet increasing demand? Can I keep interest in my bread high if I am turning away potential customers? Should I rely on my personal insights and awareness of New York City trends?"

What should Amy do? Expand or stand pat? If expand, should it be a wholesale operation only? Wholesale and retail? Retail only? Two locations or one?

CASE 15
SUPPLY DYNAMICS

INTRODUCTION

Trevor Stansbury gazed at the frozen winter landscape outside of his office window, absorbed in thoughts of the future. As the founder of Supply Dynamics, a manufacturing consulting practice, he should have been celebrating their acquisition by O'Neal Steel, but the entrepreneur in him was busy analyzing new business opportunities and the implications of suddenly being part of the largest privately held metals service center in the United States. Stansbury knew that he could replicate the Supply Dynamics' business model in other industries and within the sectors the firm currently served. Due to the fact that Supply Dynamics' proprietary aggregation process was in its infancy, he could see the potential untapped opportunities on the horizon. While Supply Dynamics started out primarily aggregating bar, sheet, and plate materials, opportunities to do the same for fasteners, carbon steel structural items (i.e., I-beams, channel, angle), and even certain plastics and composites were equally promising. The question was, how could he do this without losing focus or spreading resources too thin? How would his new affiliation with a major distributor alter the existing business model? How would the relationships with nine other O'Neal-owned affiliates translate into operational synergies for Supply Dynamics?

Source: This case study was prepared by Tiffany Tirres with the intention of providing a basis for class discussion.

SUPPLY DYNAMICS

Supply Dynamics was created in 2001 after Trevor Stansbury resigned as a Director of Honeywell's International Purchasing organization and moved his family to Loveland, Ohio. The move was prompted by an opportunity to launch a niche consulting practice with the owners of Aerospace International Materials (AIM), a medium-sized, Ohio-based distributor of specialty metals. The new venture would address a specific facet of international sourcing and AIM would serve as the incubator. The primary object of Supply Dynamics was to assist major Original Equipment Manufacturers (OEMs) with the challenges that arose from managing large globally extended supply chains that required the supply of common raw materials and other material-inputs, including sheet metal, plastics, electronic components, and fasteners. Since then, Supply Dynamics has pioneered an innovative approach to the way large multinational companies manage material-input related interactions across their business, inclusive of outside suppliers, mill distributors, and even customers. Thus, Supply Dynamics was started as an innovation center of sorts, incubated within AIM.

INCUBATION AND SPIN-OFF

AIM's core business focused on the distribution of metals for the aerospace industry, whereas Stanbury's business focused on managing the entire material-input supply chain, of which distribution was but one part. While Stansbury managed the day-to-day operations of his as-yet unnamed and incubated consulting practice, his partners, Kennard and Bucher, spent the majority of their time running AIM. In 2003, the combination of the 9/11 trauma, economic recession, and the SARS outbreak in Asia dealt a severe blow to the aviation industry and, by association, to AIM's distribution business. In the midst of these difficulties, Supply Dynamics secured its first multimillion-dollar contract to aggregate nickel and cobalt sheet metal requirements for General Electric and was able to steer this distribution business to AIM. Simultaneously, Supply Dynamics was generating hundreds of thousands of dollars in consulting fees for various global sourcing and offset-related activities. While this could not have come at a better time for AIM, Stansbury was concerned that Supply Dynamics' interests would forever be subordinated to those of the company incubating his new business. Stansbury and his partners had not officially incorporated the new business and by mid-2003, Stansbury's patience and enthusiasm had begun to wane.

After being incubated for three years within AIM, it was time for Supply Dynamics to spin off on its own.

In October of 2003, Supply Dynamics was incorporated as a limited liability company (LLC). Without the financial benefits of being located in an "incubator" environment, Stansbury remained conscious of keeping costs to a minimum. He outsourced company payroll, accounting, and HR services to AIM and arranged to have Supply Dynamics offices relocated to a renovated schoolhouse. Up until its incorporation, Supply Dynamics did not have a single, definitive service that it provided. Rather, Stansbury (and his three other employees) had simply dabbled in various experimental consulting services ranging from the deployment of a "standard part transition process" for migrating manufacturing work to low-cost regions to offset fulfillment–related activities. Although modestly profitable, Stansbury determined that to succeed and truly grow, a more focused approach that provided significant value to his customers was needed. While there were a variety of services that Supply Dynamics offered at the time, one outshined all of the others in its audacious potential to provide step change improvements in OEM performance. The service was called "Material Demand Aggregation."

MATERIAL DEMAND AGGREGATION

Over the past 20 years, most Original Equipment Manufacturers (OEMs) have outsourced a majority of parts that go into their finished products. This has resulted in a variety of unintended consequences—including the fact that outside suppliers often purchase (independently) the same raw materials in sub-optimized quantities from multiple sources at premium prices.

Stansbury and Kennard recognized this inefficiency and envisioned a business process and service that would allow an OEM to regain exposure to the raw materials that went into its parts and to use that visibility to influence cost and service levels. "It's about visibility and control," Stansbury stated. "We give our customers visibility into something many of them can't see, and we then help them to use that information to control things they have never been able to control."

Material Demand Aggregation (MDA) is a proprietary software–enabled process that provides OEMs with real time visibility and control over the cost and service levels associated with the metals and other "material-inputs" that go into their finished parts. In the production of OEM finished parts, "material-inputs" are inputs such as bar stock, sheet metal, casting forgings, plastics, electronic components, and fasteners. Collectively, these items contribute as much as 30 to 60 percent of the cost of an OEM's final product, irrespective of who makes the parts. The MDA process entails the identification, analysis, tracking and leveraging of all of those common material inputs to secure the very best price and service levels for the OEM and its outside suppliers. It also involves integration of the discrete bills-of-material (BOM) for thousands of part numbers into a web-based (multi-enterprise) application that "connects the dots" between all the parties in an extended raw material supply chain. With such a decision support system in place, OEMs can forecast and manage the procurement and on-time delivery of consolidated raw material requirements to itself and its outside suppliers.

SUPPLY DYNAMICS' BUSINESS MODEL: UNPRECEDENTED TRANSPARENCY THROUGH BOM CHARACTERIZATION

Material Demand Aggregation can potentially save an OEM millions of dollars. However, due to its complexity, and the necessity of a sophisticated multi-enterprise platform to proverbially "connect the dots," the OEM's option of performing MDA on its own is fraught with risk and is generally not cost effective.

Due to the fact that you cannot control what you cannot see, OEMs hire Supply Dynamics to restore the Bills of Material (BOMs) visibility. In those instances when the detailed BOMs associated with outsourced parts are not available to the OEM (which is most of the time), Supply Dynamics offers a BOM Characterization and validation service. To do this, Supply Dynamics utilizes a sophisticated technology solution, perfected over the last eight years, and an army of retired manufacturing engineers to translate physical or electronic blueprints into a multi-echelon BOM. Detailed BOMs are then electronically associated with individual finished part numbers and linked to OEM finished part forecasts to produce a detailed aggregate view of common materials across multiple OEM sites and sometimes hundreds of outside vendors. This information is then updated dynamically and in real-time without requiring the OEM to change or replace any of its existing internal IT or MRP/ERP systems.

In the next phase of an MDA program, Supply Dynamics licenses a sophisticated IT solution called OASIS to the OEM, which is provided in a hosted,

SaaS model. OASIS allows the OEM to view and analyze aggregate material demand in real-time, and then negotiates large, consolidated material-input contracts for and on behalf of its outside vendors—often at prices that are 7–25 percent better than prevailing market prices, depending on the commodity. The OEM then directs those outside vendors to procure common materials through an OEM's designated "aggregation source." As a result, everyone wins—the OEM, the sub-tier supplier and whichever distributor and/or mill is selected to furnish the material-inputs. Unlike similar failed consortium buying approaches, OASIS allows the OEM to monitor and, where necessary, enforce program compliance.

For the average OEM, the MDA benefits can be summarized as follows:

- Visibility into total consolidated demand for material-inputs across the OEM supply chain, according to alloy, grade, specification, size, and quality and/or safety requirements.
- Cost savings due to leveraged volume.
- Cost savings due to the elimination of uncertainty about order sizes and quantities at the mill or distributor.
- Optimization of purchases (across the OEM supply chain) that qualify for quantity discounts (often referred to as "mill minimum" discounts).
- Introduction of a decision support system that enables the OEM to proactively expedite the timely purchase and supply of material-inputs to outside part manufacturers—effectively eliminating one of the most common reasons for delays in the production process.
- No need to replace or modify existing MRP/ERP or IT systems.
- Identification of material-input standardization opportunities.
- Opportunities to use consolidated bill of material information and demand data to eliminate sole sources of supply.
- Improved predictability and continuity of supply.
- Improved traceability and control of the materials that go into parts.

SUPPLY DYNAMICS' GROWTH

In June of 2004, Stansbury and his partners sold a quarter of the company to an angel investor for a seven figure cash investment. This deal was significant for three reasons: it redistributed ownership equally among the four partners, it transferred the intellectual property rights of the proprietary software, and it established a value for the company. The redistributed ownership was important because it created a healthier balance on the Board of Directors, making it less likely that Supply Dynamics' interests would be subordinated to those of AIM. Furthermore, Supply Dynamics now owned all of the intellectual property rights of the company's proprietary software. Lastly, the effective establishment of a valuation for the company would prove fortunate a few years later, when Supply Dynamics was the target of an acquisition by two major metal distribution companies. With its newfound independence, Stansbury concentrated his efforts on the development of the OASIS multi-enterprise platform. He increased the number of developers working on OASIS as well as the functionality of the software with the goal of one day being able to commercially license it to external customers. Prior to 2008, the majority of Supply Dynamics' revenue was derived from a combination of BOM characterization fees and large (traditional) consulting retainers that Supply Dynamics would charge for essentially managing the entire aggregation process on behalf of an OEM customer, inclusive of program roll-out and mill/distributor selection. Beginning in 2008, however, Supply Dynamics succeeded in licensing OASIS for the first time, enabling it to offer OEMs the option of implementing aggregation on their own, utilizing Supply Dynamics processes and systems.

The company's sustained investment in the OASIS software solution has resulted in a product that has become an integral part of the value proposition, a major differentiator for Supply Dynamics, and a formidable barrier to potential competitiors. Additionally, Supply Dynamics' ability to keep costs low and avoid significant debt, coupled with a simple and clear value proposition, has attributed to its growth.

KEY FACTORS OF SUCCESS FOR SUPPLY DYNAMICS

Oasis Software

OASIS software provides OEMs with visibility and control over the cost and service levels associated with the material inputs that go into their finished parts. Additionally, it allows OEMs to proactively monitor and enforce outside supplier participation in an aggregation program. An adequate monitoring and enforcement

mechanism is essential not only for the OEM and its suppliers, but also for the mills, manufacturers, and/or distributors selected to furnish aggregate material input requirements. Furthermore, any attempt to consolidate common materials in an ever-changing environment, across dozens and sometimes hundreds of outside suppliers, would be nearly impossible without a robust multi-enterprise system like OASIS.

Simplicity

The concept of MDA is new and unique. Developing an effective approach to what is an entirely new market segment is challenging and requires a focus on convincing prospective clients that they have a problem, before you can help them understand how to fix it. A combination of web conferences, viral marketing media, and a simple, straight-forward return-on-investment analysis is used to educate and engage customers.

Talent and Retention

Stansbury understood the need for hiring and retaining the right people within his organization and creating a healthy and engaging work environment. He is dedicated to the task of assisting his employees in understanding how to align their individual talents and goals with those of the company. He espouses company values rather than rules and cultivates an open, honest, and respectful work environment. Supply Dynamics offers above average compensation, generous bonus incentives, and, most importantly, the opportunity for employees to contribute their ideas and to become leaders within the organization, irrespective of title or position. Stansbury often calls himself the "chief barrier buster" and welcomes the opportunity to assist employees in finding creative solutions to problems. At the same time, Stansbury tries to introduce flexibility and a bit of levity by allowing flex time, and at least once a month, arranging for a "theme Friday," which has included events such as "Fake a Workplace Injury Friday" and the annual "Office Olympics." As a result, Supply Dynamics has enjoyed high levels of employee retention and consistent increases in productivity.

THE ACQUISITION BY O'NEAL STEEL

In early 2006, AIM was put up for sale and issued a prospectus soliciting buyers through a well-known broker. Ironically, the prospectus attributed much of

AIM's recent success and the majority of future earnings potential to MDA Programs. The fact that AIM's success had been so directly attributed to Supply Dynamics' activities resulted in prospective AIM buyers also becoming interested in Supply Dynamics. The symbiotic relationship between the material aggregator (Supply Dynamics) and the material distributor (AIM) made for an attractive acquisition synergy, particularly if the acquiring company could leverage the Supply Dynamics value proposition to generate business not only for the materials distributed by AIM, but also for other raw material products in the acquiring company's portfolio. On November 20, 2006, both AIM and Supply Dynamics were purchased by O'Neal Steel, the largest privately held metals distribution operation in the United States, for more than $30 M. Supply Dynamics now operates as a wholly-owned subsidiary of O'Neal Industries.

SUPPLY DYNAMICS, A SUBSIDIARY OF O'NEAL STEEL

As part of an agreement associated with the acquisition, Stansbury agreed to stay on as president and operate Supply Dynamics as a wholly-owned subsidiary, reporting directly to the chairman of O'Neal. Consistent with the O'Neal culture of investing in new companies and allowing them to operate independently, Supply Dynamics has retained considerable autonomy over the past three years. The acquisition has opened doors for a number of potential customers due to the existing relationships of various O'Neal sister companies, and vice versa. Additionally, the acquisition has allowed Supply Dynamics to eliminate most up-front consulting fees and shorten their sales cycle from an average of 12–14 months to an average 4–6 months. Another benefit of the acquisition has been O'Neal's willingness to sustain a level of R&D investment in Supply Dynamics that has averaged $1.5 M/year. This has allowed Supply Dynamics to increase head count, further refine its software and branch out into a number of other complementary industries, including nuclear, automotive, and medical.

POSSIBLE NEXT STEPS: A STRATEGIC DECISION MUST BE MADE

Stansbury knows this unique business model can be replicated in other industries and for other commodities within the sectors they currently serve. For example, there are potentially large, untapped opportunities to

aggregate materials in such markets as nuclear, medical, semiconductor, and consumer electronics. The challenge, as Stansbury characterizes it, is to do so without losing focus or spreading resources too thin. This challenge is formidable because of the unknown differences between the aerospace sector and those that Stansbury sees as potential new markets. Such differences could include different levels and supply of specific experts needed for sector-specific BOM characterizations. Also, although Stansbury and Supply Dynamics presently enjoy the competitive advantage of being the founder and incumbent in its own niche market, they could face competition from "home-grown" imitators. For example, it may well be that Stansbury's counterparts in these other sectors, i.e., former supply chain or international sourcing directors in the nuclear or medical sectors, look to Supply Dynamics as a model, imitate it on a general level, but tailor it to the specifications of their own industries.

More enticing to Stansbury are the opportunities to monetize the information Supply Dynamics possesses regarding who uses what materials, in what quantities over what period of time. This information has the potential (when combined across OEMs and the 1,400+ sub-tier suppliers in OASIS) to be of enormous value to the investment banking industry, mills, and other parties invested in metal demand and related commodity prices and trends. Supply Dynamics is currently exploring various options for combining data, potentially in a strategic alliance with various other companies, in order to develop a metals benchmarking tool and/or generic metals outlook/forecast for sale to the financial industry and possibly to other mills/distributors for use with hedging or investment strategies.

Stansbury is determined to expand Supply Dynamics' BOM characterization activities and OASIS license fees, and to continue to generate metal distribution opportunities for his sister companies. He also recognizes the need to keep one eye on the ever changing future and the need to constantly adapt to that changing landscape. In an increasingly transparent and hyper-connected world, Stansbury believes that Supply Dynamics can help transform O'Neal's traditional distribution business into the largest metals distribution business in North America in 5 to 10 years.

APPENDIX 1: THE FOUNDER'S BACKGROUND

Stansbury began his formal education at Lynchburg College in Virginia, where he earned a BA in International Relations with a minor in economics and graduated with high honors. In 1992, he received his MBA from the Thunderbird School of Global Management in Glendale, Arizona. During his time as a full-time graduate student, Stansbury obtained a part-time internship with McDonnell Douglas (now Boeing) Helicopter Company and had the opportunity to test his entrepreneurial inclinations. Stansbury wrote a business plan for a trading company called Ecotech International, which he believed would serve as a more efficient vehicle for fulfilling the global countertrade and offset obligations of his employer. Lacking the funds to launch the venture, Stansbury applied and won a Department of Commerce grant created to promote bilateral trade between the newly independent states of the former Soviet Union and the United States. This "first experiment" as an entrepreneur was a profoundly influential precursor to his later efforts at Supply Dynamics.

Between 1992 and 1996, Ecotech conducted business as a trading company loosely affiliated with McDonnell Douglas, and joined the Arizona Technology Incubator. During this "incubation period," Ecotech established four joint venture operations in the United Arab Emirates, opened a fully staffed trading company in Moscow, Russia, and succeeded in exporting hundreds of thousands of dollars of oil spill clean-up technology to Russia and Taiwan. Then, in 1997, Boeing purchased McDonnell Douglas. As a result, Stansbury and all of his U.S. employees were effectively absorbed into Boeing Helicopter's countertrade and offset organization, with Stansbury briefly assuming responsibility for reciprocal trade obligations in the Middle East.

After working for Boeing, Stansbury was recruited by Allied Signal (which later became Honeywell) to serve as their Director of International Programs. During his five-year tenure at Honeywell, Stansbury orchestrated the acquisition of a Czech company that has subsequently become Honeywell's largest low-cost manufacturer of fabricated components in the world. In 2001, after rumors of a GE merger with Allied Signal, Stansbury began to assess his career prospects and options, including an unsolicited offer made by Cessna Aircraft Company. While evaluating these choices, he was approached by Tom Kennard, owner of an Ohio-based metals distribution company, Aerospace International Materials (AIM). Kennard was interested in Stansbury's knowledge of Honeywell's procurement processes and wanted to combine forces to fulfill both GE's and Honeywell's sheet metal purchases through AIM. Together, Stansbury and Kennard hatched an idea to partner up and launch a boutique consulting firm specializing in global sourcing and materials management. Stansbury did not enter into a deal with Kennard on behalf of GE and/or Honeywell. Instead, he resigned his position at Honeywell, persuaded Cessna to hire him as a consultant rather than an employee, and teamed up with Kennard and Barry Bucher at AIM to launch what would eventually become Supply Dynamics.

APPENDIX 2: REVENUE HISTORY

	Non-Product Revenue (license fees, BOM characterization fees, retainers, etc.)	MDA-related Product Revenue to Affiliates (material-input sales)
2010	$560,000	$15,000,000.00
2009	$510,000	$13,100,000.00
2008	$540,000	$10,000,000.00
2007	$900,000	$6,900,000.00
2006	$1,200,000	$5,500,000.00
2005	$900,000	$4,000,000.00
2004	$250,000	$2,000,000.00
Total	**$4,480,000**	**$40,400,000.00**

Note: All figures are rounded estimates, rounded to the nearest $500.

CASE 16
DATAVANTAGE CORPORATION
... CONTINUING THE ENTREPRENEURIAL SPIRIT

Christopher Columbus set the foundation for the entrepreneurial spirit in America, by pursuing at great risk his vision of a different world. This spirit has evolved from that early point in American history to become the cornerstone of today's business innovation and growth. Those embodying the spirit look beyond current business practices and processes to question their

Source: This case study was prepared by Michael Harriston, Nadya Tolshchikova, Michael Walsh, and Sean Wenger of the Weatherhead School of Management, Case Western Reserve University, with the intention of providing a basis for class discussion.

most fundamental beliefs and corporate structures. They seek not merely to satisfy market demands, but to anticipate and create markets that have not yet been conceived. They invent a vibrant corporate culture and elicit the dynamic leadership needed to bring it into action. They rewrite the rules and take on seemingly impossible tasks. And, they invest in a future so bold it redefines not only an organization, but an entire industry.[1]

It was a brisk fall day outside in Cleveland, Ohio, where Chaz Napoli, president of Datavantage, and Marvin Lader, CEO of Datavantage, were having lunch at a new restaurant that had just opened near their office. As the anxious restaurant owner came by to check on their meal, the restaurateur's concern for his business immediately reminded them of their concern regarding the looming decisions they were faced with regarding their own organization. During Chaz and Marvin's discussion of the situation at hand, they remarked how much their business had evolved.

After having initially started out in 1988 as a reseller of third-party software to small distribution businesses and corporate systems for retail home offices, Datavantage made a conscious strategic decision in 1994 to better control its own destiny and internally develop its own point-of-sale software products. Even though Datavantage's financial performance was healthy at that time as a distributor of third-party software, the two owners knew that the transition to become a developer would be best for the long-term success of the company. Now, they were faced with another decision that could potentially change the company—they were in the final stages of negotiation to acquire XBR Track, which was a small loss prevention software company based in Boston, Massachusetts. Chaz and Marvin discussed many related issues regarding the XBR acquisition— was loss prevention going to become a viable new market for the retail industry to justify the price of XBR? What would be the internal implications of this new product line on the company's culture, financial and organizational structure, as well as sales and marketing capabilities? Would it be complementary to Datavantage's current business model? As the two finished their meal, they began to discuss the options that lay ahead.

DATAVANTAGE—BACKGROUND

Datavantage was founded in 1988 by Marvin Lader, an IBM veteran and a serial entrepreneur from Cleveland, Ohio. Marvin's background in sales and application software/system engineering, gained after many years

at IBM, allowed him to collect extensive knowledge of business applications that ranged from sales to feeder distributors to large retail chain applications. Exposure to the retail industry, coupled with the experience of starting two other companies prior to Datavantage, one of which went public, allowed him by 1993 to grow Datavantage to 16 employees and $1.5 million in sales with only $50,000 of external financing. The company was a reseller of business application software to small distribution businesses and corporate systems for the retailers' home offices as well as a provider of legacy COBOL Systems for Distributors (SFD). Only a few programs were written internally and, by 1993, Datavantage was slowly transforming itself into a consulting company. Despite relative success, it wasn't exactly what Marvin envisioned to be an exciting entrepreneurial opportunity and [he] was ready to get out of the business. A radical change was needed in order for Marvin to consider staying and growing the company.

The opportunity arrived in 1994 when Datavantage acquired the retail services division of LDI that was up for sale at an affordable price. LDI was a reseller of products for store systems and provided a complementary foundation for Datavantage's further development. LDI's business was centered on [the] niche, specialty retail market segment, providing Datavantage with a base for future company growth. This acquisition dramatically changed Marvin's perception of Datavantage's overall future potential.

Soon after the acquisition was complete, Chaz, who originally started at LDI and stayed with the company after Datavantage took over, decided to completely redefine the company's product strategy under Marvin's guidance. Chaz's knowledge of the industry came from his background in retail marketing and extensive consulting experience with retail stores. The blend of Marvin's technical background and entrepreneurial skills with Chaz's retail experience resulted in a shift of Datavantage's strategic direction. Not surprisingly, both Marvin and Chaz see this period as the real beginning of Datavantage. (The balance sheet and statement of operations for the company are indicated in Exhibits 2 and 3.)

DATAVANTAGE SOLUTIONS

As a part of the new strategy, Datavantage moved from a pure reseller to a software developer and point-of-sale solution provider. Both Marvin and Chaz felt that this would build the value of the company and allow it to control its own destiny. Furthermore, it was decided not to outsource the product development for two main reasons: (1) it was very rare that companies outsourced product development at that time, making Datavantage somewhat uncertain about the benefits of the yet unproven strategy, and (2) Datavantage had limited time and resources to get the initial product to market. Under these circumstances Chaz and Marvin felt that the development should be kept in-house, which would allow Datavantage to better deal with the pressures of new product introduction. Therefore, the next step was to execute the strategy by defining the market, developing the product, and creating a feasible business model supported by a strong organizational infrastructure.

Target Market

Looking back on that period of time, Chaz and Marvin realize that they did not consciously identify the market segment that Datavantage decided to target; instead, it happened by default. Since LDI had already built substantial expertise and credibility in the niche specialty retail segment, Datavantage decided to initially target this particular area of the retail industry. Specialty retailers concentrate on a single product category niche such as apparel, sporting goods, jewelry, and others. Although grocery stores, mass-merchandising (Wal-Mart), food service and hospitality (hotels, cruise ships), and [convenience] stores (BP, Shell) were also potentially large and profitable segments, specialty retail seemed to be the most attractive retail category. Despite the slow growth in the overall retail industry, the specialty retail segment was experiencing significant expansion with many new start-up retailers opening their stores all over the country.

INDUSTRY/COMPETITION

Point-of-sale [POS] software is a relatively young, fragmented part of the software industry that in the last few years has started undergoing rapid consolidation. A wave of mergers and acquisitions has transformed the industry, such that it is now dominated by a few large players. This shift has been supported by the fast advances in technology, changing point-of-sale systems from being glorified calculators to sophisticated POS software solutions. Such technology/product shift occurs about every 10 years, bringing new innovations to existing systems. In light of these industry transformations, the Datavantage founders knew that there would emerge only a few highly successful companies in this industry and (they) were determined to have Datavantage be one of this elite group.

Store 21

Having evaluated various point-of-sale packages that were on the market at that time, Datavantage founders were not able to identify a single product that they felt had a true competitive advantage. Therefore, they saw a real market opportunity and decided to launch the development of their own product that could run on Windows technology, a relatively new operating system at the time. This was a very critical decision since at the time POS systems still ran on the DOS platforms. The goal was to develop one product and one user interface that could run all store operations such as register, inventory management, production, internal fraud, employee scheduling, and others. Based on clients' requests, consultants' input, and Chaz's and Marvin's personal industry experiences, the two major requirements for the new product were functionality and simplicity.

When Store 21 was developed and introduced to the market in 1996, it was a complete store management system based on full transaction point-of-sale (POS) applications software that ran on Windows. The system combined point-of-service features, such as deal pricing and item location, with several back office functions including labor management and scheduling, inventory shipping/receiving, productivity goals, and clientelling.[2]

The software also performed as a state-of-the-art connectivity package that linked individual stores with the home office via secure Internet/Intranet communications. This feature was called the "chatterbox" module, which gave the retailer real-time access to centralized intelligence or enterprise sales reporting. The centralized communication capability allowed for faster credit, debit, and check authorizations which significantly increased productivity of store transaction data streams.

RETAIL INDUSTRY'S CURRENT NEEDS

Despite the presence of the state-of-the-art POS software in many retail stores, most retailers were still struggling to reduce store shrinkage problems. Retailers in the U.S. were losing an average of 2 percent of sales due to retail theft or shrinkage each year. The losses due to shrinkage directly affected the bottom line of the retailer in the form of a pure profit loss. It was estimated that retail employees account for 55 percent to 75 percent of lost revenue because of various fraudulent transactions. Transaction fraud ranged from improper cash refunds and price overrides, to employee discount abuse and fraudulent credit card activity, amounting to $13.2 billion in retail losses annually.

On the basis of a preliminary market study to identify where inventory shrinkage occurs, Datavantage determined that employee theft and shoplifting combined accounted for the largest source of property crime committed annually in the United States[3] with the following classifications:

- Employee Theft 44.5 percent
  - Average financial loss caused by the typical dishonest employee theft is $1,023.
  - A dishonest employee typically works for his or her employer an average of nine months.
- Shoplifting 32.7 percent
  - The average value of merchandise taken by the typical shoplifter is $128.
- Administrative Error 17.5 percent
- Vendor Fraud 5.1 percent

Additionally, the following retail segments were determined to have higher than average shrink rates as a percent of sales:

- Gifts   2.91%
- Toys & Hobbies   2.81%
- Optical   2.59%
- Discount Stores   2.01%
- Sporting Goods   1.91%
- Department Stores 1.89%

Retailers were looking for new technology and techniques to help them become more proactive in identifying problem cashiers or employees at their stores, as well as providing real-time validation that certain employees were in fact committing crimes. Historically, retailers' loss prevention technology had been ineffective due to its highly manual characteristics. Retailers were also hampered by a lack of technical resources available for loss prevention initiatives.

The techniques that existed to specifically link an employee to a theft were not user friendly to a company's loss prevention manager. Transaction logs (t-logs) had to be manually sorted to provide concrete evidence of a specific employee theft. Employees' schedules also needed to be verified with the dates and times of the transactions to make a stronger case to the court system.

The volume of data generated by point-of-sale (POS) key t-logs made it difficult, if not impossible, to sort through transaction activity looking for trends that would identify employee theft. A secondary drawback to existing loss prevention software was the length of

time, typically several days, required to alert a retailer of a suspicious transaction. The lack of timeliness in identifying shrinkage limited the effectiveness of an investigation, confrontation, and the ultimate resolution of a theft.

XBR LOSS PREVENTION SOFTWARE

The XBR Loss Prevention software application that Datavantage is considering acquiring is based on "by exception" reporting methods that are determined by the specialty retail store. The main reason for Datavantage's interest in this software is the groundbreaking solution it can bring to the retail stores. Just as Store 21 is considered to be "best in class" point-of-sale application software, Marvin and Chaz know that XBR has the same potential in the loss prevention segment of the technical solution market for the retail industry. The system is designed to quickly identify, track, and manage potentially fraudulent transactions. An exception history for an associate or store is developed by establishing control points that sift through transactions to identify and analyze trends. The control point feature of XBR also allows for comparisons to other employees and stores in the same risk transaction areas.

In addition, the software has the capability to perform digital register surveillance, which is used to "mark" high risk transactions. A loss prevention officer is then able to retrieve the digital video clip of a specific transaction to verify and resolve employee theft.

The XBR Track software has the potential to substantially reduce employee fraud if it could be optimized to search t-logs for defined exceptions. While Store 21 can give the home office real-time POS transaction data and employee scheduling, it was not designed to scan for fraud. Chaz considers that the combination of the two applications would increase a store's productivity and reduce shrinkage, while creating value for both customers and Datavantage. A number of Datavantage's customers have already successfully integrated XBR Track with Store 21, which allows them to be proactive in dealing with employee fraud through predetermined "by exception" features.

In addition to the technical benefits, Datavantage expects to use XBR as the main instrument to initiate relationships with new customers. Chaz calls it "get into the castle" strategy, which ultimately means establishing a relationship with a customer through a relatively low-cost project that would create the necessary level of trust to commit to larger projects in the future. To Datavantage, XBR is just that instrument due to its relatively low cost and almost guaranteed return on investment. Moreover, the concept of XBR is fairly straightforward compared to the other complex solutions Datavantage is developing, which would make it easier for the sales people to sell XBR to the new Datavantage customers. Finally, both Chaz and Marvin are convinced that if they do not purchase XBR, someone else will, creating a potential to significantly change competitive dynamics, not in Datavantage's favor.

DATAVANTAGE—CUSTOMERS

Early in its existence Datavantage set a goal to differentiate itself by keeping its products and services simple, continuously improving through innovation, excelling at the delivery of the highest quality products and services, and developing stable technology and an unmatched level of customer care.

The company experienced multiple challenges when going through a rapid growth stage. By 1997 it was able to obtain 5 percent market share in the U.S. specialty retail market, which was a significant accomplishment in the fragmented market that retail systems data management represented at that time. Despite extensive product development beginning in 1994, Datavantage did not launch Store 21 until 1996. At that time, the software was introduced to its then two largest customers, Lids and The Finish Line, which [composed] a significant portion of the company's total revenue.

Although, during the early stages of the company's development, having a few customers account for a substantial portion of annual revenue was an acceptable arrangement, Datavantage recognized that it had to quickly grow its customer base in order to minimize the risk of dependence on a few larger customers. A stated goal was not to allow a single customer to comprise more than a few percent of the revenue base. By 1997, Datavantage had each customer representing between 10 and 20 percent of the total company revenue, with the largest customer varying from year to year.

Further, Chaz and Marvin realized that they had to target only certain types of customers in order to maximize profitability. Accordingly, Datavantage used the following customer selection criteria:

- The client had to be a relatively large retailer operating a minimum of 30 stores; or

EXHIBIT 1 Datavantage's Largest Customers in 1997

Sunglass Hut	Things Remembered
S&K Menswear	Piercing Pagoda Jewelers
Casual Male	Genesco
Footaction	Lids
The Athlete's Foot	Tradehome Shoes
The Finish Line	

- The client's minimum revenue had to be at least $200 million.

Datavantage mainly concentrated on niche retailers that had stores at shopping malls and outlet shopping centers, operated on average from 400 to 1,000 stores, or earned gross revenue anywhere between $200 million and $1 billion.

As of 1997, Datavantage had about 20 customers, many of which were large nationwide retail chains. See Exhibit 1 for the list of Datavantage's largest retail customers in 1997.

Along with growing its client base, Datavantage sought to provide additional solutions to customers. Even though the majority of Datavantage's revenue was driven by Store 21, both Marvin and Chaz understood that the acquisition of XBR Track could provide further growth of the already successful Store 21 product, which had been on the market for a year. Although XBR Track was projected to account for only about 15 percent of Datavantage's revenue, it would further strengthen its business by providing Datavantage's customers with the ability to control shrinkage through an integrated suite of applications. Additionally, it would provide customers with remarkable savings of about 2 percent of revenue, which was currently being lost on internal and external shrinkage. The combined benefits of Store 21 and XBR would result in a potentially significant financial savings to the customer, and consequently, a quick return on their investment in the XBR Track product.

DATAVANTAGE—SALES AND MARKETING

The primary methods utilized by Datavantage to sell its products and services are direct marketing, trade shows, and existing client testimonials. After developing Store 21, Chaz and Marvin realized that the existing reseller sales and marketing staff were not capable of selling the new product. The necessary level of knowledge and motivation was simply not there. This resulted in nearly an entire turnover of the sales and marketing staff.

Following this complete turnover, Datavantage was able to create a strong sales and marketing team that followed a very precise and thorough marketing strategy. Instead of using a traditional marketing campaign targeting retailers in general, the company concentrates heavily on what Chaz refers to as "personal marketing and referential selling." This involves using existing client testimonials and case studies (with Datavantage products at the center of the solution) which are featured in the company's publications and regularly mailed to targeted new and prospective customers. However, this approach has its own drawbacks, which include an increase in the sales cycle period that consequently requires a higher level of persistence and customer relationship building on the part of the sales people.

The company also actively participates in the major retail trade shows and leverages its strong sales force to gain contacts that are often converted into valuable customer relationships. As one Datavantage customer mentioned:

> One of the company's strengths is its very well thought through marketing strategy. They always try to be in the right place at the right time.

Another important strategy that the company incorporated into its standard selling and marketing practice is the "Annual User Conference" organized each year in Cleveland, Ohio, where all Datavantage clients are invited to attend. It is a three-day event full of presentations on new products or updates, Q&A sessions, and entertainment activities. Customers are able to interact in an informal setting with other Datavantage customers, as well as employees, and share their experiences.

In order to support its active sales and marketing efforts, Datavantage implemented an extensive hiring and training program for its sales representatives. This program focuses on good work ethics, honesty, integrity, and the development of close relationships with existing and potential clients. As a result, Datavantage sales people are able to close over 90 percent of sales during the final product presentation round during which customers travel to Cleveland to Datavantage headquarters. When asked for the reason for such success, Chaz responded:

> We hire people with the same grass roots who are concerned with good work.

Convinced that proper sales and marketing techniques significantly contribute to the company's success, Chaz continually encourages the sales people to sell the *benefits* rather than features of Datavantage's products. This strategy is based on the company's "Guiding Principles," which are as follows:

1. Invest in Products "Best in Class."
2. Invest in Infrastructure and Operations.
3. Superior Sales & Marketing: Position Itself as a Retail Company Selling Technology vs. a Technology Company Selling Retail Systems.
4. Product, Service, and Sales Are Three Key Areas of Main Focus.

HELP DESK/CALL CENTER

Business application software for the retail industry, such as Datavantage's, requires real-time customer support through a call center or help desk, which was established early in the development of Store 21. Although one of the company's goals was to provide the best level of service to its customers, things did not always go as anticipated. The company's strategy to quickly acquire new customers led to an unintentional decrease in the level of service provided to existing long-term customers.

While not losing a single customer due to these shortcomings, Datavantage nevertheless recognized it as a major issue to be addressed. Over time the improvement in the Help Desk area allowed Datavantage to handle most of the problems over the phone, with major problems being solved by sending a specialist on site. Due to its responsiveness and strong drive for customer satisfaction, Datavantage soon was able to build a reputation of being one of the top vendors among clients' large pool of suppliers. Surveyed clients attributed their high level of satisfaction to the dedication of Datavantage personnel, their honesty and openness about issues, customer driven internal culture, and continuous drive for improvement.

As stated by one of the clients, "With Datavantage I never feel that my problems are being put on the corporate agenda when it takes a while to solve a problem. Datavantage always accepts responsibility and if something can't be done right away because of lack of resources or for any other reason, admits it." According to another customer: "They have passion for what they do and get done what needs to get done." Yet one more customer confessed: "They make me feel that they really care about my business."

Chaz and Marvin think the reason for such a high level of customer satisfaction is the very candid way in which the company operates. In fact, Chaz constantly reminds his employees that they are a direct extension of the client's staff, to the extent that their paychecks should not have the Datavantage name on them because the checks entirely come from the client's business.

With Datavantage personnel being carefully selected and capable of providing a high level of service, reflecting on the turnover in sales and marketing personnel related to Store 21, Chaz and Marvin wondered whether the acquisition of XBR would put the company through another hiring and firing turmoil that could threaten the company's strong position with its customers.

DATAVANTAGE—BUSINESS MODEL

Chaz and Marvin continued to develop Datavantage away from a reseller of third-party software, into a business applications technology company that develops its own proprietary business-to-business software for specialty retailers. The company developed a revenue model that incorporated *both* product and service revenue streams that were generated from the following five distinct and standalone profit centers.

The first profit center, Software Licenses & Royalties, generated product-related revenue that accounted for 17 percent of the total sales revenue in 1997, and was forecasted to further increase as a percentage of sales. This profit center was comprised of the Store 21 product line. When XBR is in fact acquired, the associated revenue would be part of this classification.

The second profit center, Hardware & Equipment, generated product-related revenue that accounted for 50 percent of the total sales revenue in 1997, and was forecasted to decrease as a percentage of sales.

The third profit center, Professional Services, generated service-related revenue that accounted for 19 percent of the total sales revenue in 1997, and was forecasted to increase as a percentage of sales. This service component of the company's business model included Datacomm Services, Handling/Restocking, Staging Fees, Professional Services Training, and Consulting.

The fourth profit center, Software Maintenance & Development, generated service-related revenue that accounted for 11 percent of the total sales revenue in 1997, and was forecasted to increase as a percentage of sales. This service component of the company's business model included SMA[4] Fees, Chatterbox, and Custom Software Modifications.

The final profit center of Datavantage was its Help Desk/Call Center Operations.

The strategy behind using these five specific profit centers was to match revenue to key similar functional areas, and allow associated categories of revenue to be pooled together. For example, anything related to hardware procurement had its own revenue category; all the software licensing revenue was grouped in a category; anything to do with a nonprogramming professional service, such as consulting, training, staging systems, technical support, etc., had a revenue category; anything having to do with computer programming, both ongoing software maintenance fees and any custom programming, was in a separate category; and finally the call center services were also in a standalone revenue category.

This categorization allowed for accountability of the company's main services by keeping clean lines of ownership in the profit centers, so that appropriate business plans and goals could be established and monitored on a moving forward basis.

DATAVANTAGE—FINANCING

The company financed its entire operations and growth primarily through retained earnings, as a result of solid cash management. A critical success factor in its cash management has been Datavantage's ability to aggressively control its accounts receivable, an especially difficult task in the retail industry. This strong cash position allowed the company to consider all possibilities in negotiating the purchase price for XBR. The issue still remained, though, how best to finance the transaction. Should the company purchase the software outright and pay all cash, structure the purchase as an all royalty deal, or come up with some combination of cash and royalties? An all cash purchase would significantly increase the consequences of a situation where the loss prevention market did not develop as hoped. If Datavantage incorporates a royalty scenario, and the loss prevention market is successful, Datavantage may not realize as much return on its investment as would otherwise be possible from an all cash deal. As a result, Datavantage wondered what would be the best way to structure the XBR Track deal, so as to provide protection against downside risk as well as maximize the upside potential.

Both Chaz and Marvin agreed that the combination of cash and royalties seemed to be the best acquisition financing option. Datavantage planned to structure the deal with an initial $300,000 payment for the right to use the product and royalties of 5 percent of gross revenue resulting from the product sales. A buyout clause was expected to be incorporated into the agreement, which would allow Datavantage to buy out the remaining royalty payments. This option was perceived as a relatively low risk and low upfront cash deal that would provide high expected return on investment.

The company's strong cash position allowed for sustained growth that did not require any equity financing. As a result, Datavantage management and employees maintained 100 percent equity ownership of the company. However, taking into account the trade-offs of external equity financing, Chaz and Marvin wondered if outside financing should be considered to purchase XBR Track, or to possibly pursue future opportunities.

DATAVANTAGE—MANAGEMENT CULTURE

Datavantage has experienced constant evolution over the life of the organization. In early 1994, when the company consisted of 25–30 employees with Marvin and Chaz as the only senior level managers, the two founders made the majority of critical decisions, including sales presentations to new customers. Chaz still feels that in a small company start-up environment this type of top-down organizational structure was necessary to keep control over the company's limited resources and carefully protect the company's emerging image because every strategic decision had a potential of significantly affecting the future success of the organization.

By the time Datavantage reached about $10 million in revenue, Chaz realized that the company needed a well-defined infrastructure and a capable management team. Consequently, Datavantage significantly decentralized its decision making by creating a more distributive culture where each manager had authority to make critical decisions in their area of responsibility. As a direct result of the decision to create an empowered environment, members of the senior management team received authority to contribute input toward the strategic direction of the company. This shift allowed Chaz and Marvin to move away from initiating and following through with each strategic move. Now they mostly review the proposals brought to them by the team of executive managers in the organization.

However, as Datavantage became less centralized, the founders wondered what effect it would have on the entrepreneurial small-company environment that dominated the company internally from the very beginning

and significantly contributed to its success. As a result, Chaz and Marvin identified main aspects of the entrepreneurial culture and put strong emphasis on instilling these into Datavantage's rapidly evolving internal organizational structure.

Major elements of entrepreneurial culture:

- Stability of the management team
- Commitment to empowerment
- Limited bureaucracy
- Clearly defined reward and compensation system that involves bonuses and equity
- Clear lines of responsibility
- Working management culture—"hands on" management style

In addition to its entrepreneurial culture, the key characteristic of Datavantage's success is its ability to take calculated risks. While not a risk averse organization, Datavantage put mechanisms in place to help mitigate it. Every important decision, such as an acquisition or new product launch, is first explored in a formal business plan. Team leaders have control over the development of business plans and are expected to execute the plans they create.

Therefore, Chaz and Marvin were able to form an empowered organization measured with a set of controls to oversee the performance of each decision-maker within the organization. Chaz calls this approach "management by exception" and Datavantage's overall organizational culture "decentralized and empowered culture with right controls."

Effective communication, as another key to the success of any small organization going through an active growth and transformation period, was embodied in Datavantage's daily operations. In fact, from the early years of organizational growth, Datavantage made it a rule not to penalize employees for making mistakes as long as a mistake or a shortcoming is immediately reported before it turns into a major problem. To emphasize the importance of communication, twice a year Chaz presents the "*State of the Company*" address to all the employees and senior management. The major objective of this communication tool is to highlight the progress of each department, identify key goals and objectives for the upcoming year, and also restate Datavantage's guiding principles that ensure the company's success.

Similarly to many successful start-ups, Datavantage shared equity with its key managers in order to

EXHIBIT 2 Datavantage Corporation Balance Sheets

	December 31		
	1995 (Unaudited)	1996 (Unaudited)	1997 (Unaudited)
Assets			
Current assets:			
Cash and cash equivalents	$ 501,875	$ 362,286	$ 319,885
Accounts receivable	970,836	842,234	1,675,554
Prepaid expenses	97,716	44,961	94,541
Refundable income taxes	—	—	—
Deferred tax asset	—	—	—
Inventory	860,769	84,163	—
Total current assets	2,431,196	1,333,644	2,089,980
Fixed assets:			
Computers and office equipment	458,357	606,613	688,045
Furniture and fixtures	161,776	245,373	241,590
Leasehold improvements	29,787	97,867	106,284
Other	39,480	6,732	34,122
	689,400	956,585	1,070,041
Less allowance for depreciation	(370,280)	(521,293)	(423,215)
	319,120	435,292	646,826
Purchased and licensed software, net	—	—	359,512
Deferred loan costs, net			
Software development costs, net	—	—	—
	—	—	359,512
Deferred tax asset	—	—	—
Other assets	11,233	17,519	12,456
Total assets	$2,761,549	$1,786,455	$3,108,774
Liabilities and Shareholders' Equity			
Current liabilities:			
Bank term loan	$ —	$ —	$ 166,667
Supplier note payable	—	—	—
Notes payable to employees	—	—	—
Current portion of obligation under capital leases	—	—	16,883
Deferred revenue	1,218,086	332,512	1,087,103
Accrued expenses	336,475	426,924	759,291
Income/Franchise tax payable	—	—	—
Salaries, wages, taxes and commissions payable	87,000	6,950	231,032
Accounts payable	355,768	278,487	426,796
Total current liabilities	1,997,329	1,044,873	2,687,772
Long-term obligations:			
Bank term loan & line of credit	—	—	291,667
Subordinated notes payable	—	—	—
Supplier note payable	—	—	—
Obligations under capital leases	—	—	9,802
Total long-term obligations	—	—	301,469
Shareholders' equity:			
Common stock	7,620	7,800	5,578
Treasury stock	—	—	(1,145,043)
Additional capital	115,151	132,971	207,847
Retained earnings	641,449	600,811	1,051,151
Total shareholders' equity	764,220	741,582	119,533
Total liabilities and shareholders' equity	$2,761,549	$1,786,455	$3,108,774

EXHIBIT 3   Datavantage Corporation Statements of Operations

	Actual for the Years Ended December 31					
	1995 (Unaudited)	%	1996 (Unaudited)	%	1997 (Unaudited)	%
Revenue						
Point-of-sale equipment	$5,058,561	64%	$4,887,461	54%	$6,333,718	50%
Software licenses	432,778	5%	489,352	5%	2,180,104	17%
Professional services	1,522,417	19%	2,301,031	25%	2,444,015	19%
Software maintenance & development	840,033	11%	1,181,135	13%	1,379,602	11%
Operating system software	—	0%	69,566	1%	48,084	0%
Other	103,437	1%	155,756	2%	326,867	3%
Total revenue	7,957,226	100%	9,084,301	100%	12,712,390	100%
Operating Costs and Expenses						
Cost of equipment sold	3,851,672	48%	3,689,238	41%	4,967,024	39%
Salaries, wages, and benefits	1,870,324	24%	2,613,105	29%	3,923,645	31%
Professional fees	428,885	5%	712,991	8%	628,093	5%
Selling, general, and administrative	359,346	5%	367,759	4%	437,808	3%
Research and development	339,384	4%	389,777	4%	820,920	6%
Cost of system software sold	—	0%	55,653	1%	35,033	0%
Travel	99,191	1%	137,203	2%	241,173	2%
Depreciation and amortization	137,511	2%	146,788	2%	104,630	1%
Telephone	127,059	2%	287,168	3%	289,346	2%
Purchase of stock option rights	—	0%	—	0%	—	0%
Total operating expenses	7,213,372	91%	8,399,682	92%	11,447,672	90%
Income from operations	743,854	9%	684,619	8%	1,264,718	10%
Other Income (Expense)						
Interest income	33,935	0%	18,603	0%	6,441	0%
Interest expense	—	0%	—	0%	(20,008)	0%
Total other income (expense)	33,935	0%	18,603	0%	(13,567)	0%
Income taxes	—	0%	—	0%	—	0%
Net income	$ 777,789	10%	$ 703,222	8%	$1,251,151	10%
EBITDA	$ 881,365	11%	$ 850,010	9%	$1,375,789	11%

maintain employees' existing level of commitment to the organization and its future. It did not only allow the company to maintain its successful approach to business, but kept employees from making decisions that sacrificed future growth for immediate results. However, Marvin and Chaz realized that

there is significant risk associated with this strategy because giving someone equity does not mean that they would align their performance and the vision for the company with their status. Therefore, since equity stake in business is the most expensive and therefore valuable compensation that the company can offer to an employee, both Marvin and Chaz created a culture where people see the value of this compensation and are willing to perform accordingly by aligning their actions with the organizational goals and objectives.

MERGING OF TWO CULTURES

After deciding to acquire XBR, Marvin and Chaz had to create a strategy to merge the two different organizations. Both founders recall the acquisition of LDI where most of the LDI employees had to be let go. Although this was less likely to be the case with XBR, both Chaz and Marvin knew that the growth and long-term success of the company was directly correlated to the level of its employees' competency. Reflecting on the LDI acquisition, Chaz thought:

> As we grew into a tier one company, we put increasingly high efforts on continuously upgrading our staff.

The acquisition had several factors for the entrepreneurs to consider. The most important issue was integration of the two cultures into one. Marvin and Chaz wondered whether the XBR acquisition would affect Datavantage's well-organized internal structure, which fosters the company's present entrepreneurial environment. Would XBR management buy into Datavantage's rules and principles of internal organization and relationships with external partners? Although XBR had only 12 employees, Datavantage believed that the company had a strong management team in place. Therefore, when considering making a decision regarding the fate of these employees, Chaz believed the two companies had a good chance of success:

> One of the keys to our enthusiasm for their management team is the similarity in cultures. Both cultures are hard working and very customer service oriented.

Location was another issue. Since XBR was headquartered in Boston, several hundred miles away from Cleveland, Datavantage had to decide whether relocation and physical integration of the two companies in Datavantage's headquarters in Cleveland, Ohio, was a feasible option. An alternative would be to have XBR remain in Boston and operate as a standalone division of Datavantage.

The success of this acquisition could bring significant competitive advantage to Datavantage. However, if some of the important factors discussed above are not taken into consideration, the acquisition and postacquisition integration could negatively affect the very factors that allowed Datavantage's success in the first place, inhibiting long-term company performance.

END NOTES

1. Modified from the Web site of Legacy Consulting.
2. Clientelling is the process of gathering data about an individual customer's buying habits and preferences during interactions in the store, typically applied in high-end or luxury retail stores.
3. 2000 National Retail Security Survey.
4. SMA stands for software maintenance, which is a recurring annual fee that virtually all clients pay for that provides the right to any bug corrections at no additional charge, as well as the right to receive upgrades to the software as new and improved versions are released. The typical fee is 15 percent of all license fees and customization fees paid to Datavantage; therefore, this amount can increase as the client purchases more licenses or pays for more customization.

CASE 17
TIRE VALET: A MOBILE TIRE COMPANY

Any part of the day during the week you may see a white box truck in the high income neighborhoods of the Boston suburbs working on a resident's automobile, SUV, or truck. The driver of the truck who is also an auto mechanic may be changing the tires on a vehicle or performing some mechanical service. Inside the truck you can find machinery to change, balance, and repair tires, or tools and parts to repair brakes, change oil, or perform other basic repair functions.

After about an hour and a half, the owner of the vehicle may be seen paying the driver with a credit card or check the $600 plus it cost to replace four new tires on her SUV. This service was performed right in her driveway and saved her a few hours of precious time that it would have taken to drive to a tire service facility and then to wait to have the four new tires installed. The customer in this instance appreciates the fact that

Source: This case study was prepared by Michael P. Peters with the intention of providing a basis for class discussion.

the cost of this service will be slightly higher than what a retailer would charge but is well worth it given the time saved and convenience of having this service performed right in her driveway, even during cold weather months.

The company, Tire Valet—A Tire Changing Service, is based in Waltham, Massachusetts (a Boston suburb), and is a recent start-up launched last spring. The owner of this start-up is Jack Welch and according to his research his is the only company performing this service in the Boston area. He discovered that there were many mobile tire service companies in other states, particularly in warmer climates, but none based in the Northeast. Welch's inspiration for this start-up occurred after two events: the first was having a damaged windshield replaced in his driveway in January and the second was when he had four new tires installed on his SUV for which he had to wait more than two hours. His frustration at having to wait so long for the tire installation perhaps inspired his realization that if windshields could be replaced any time of the year, the same could be said for changing tires at a customer's home or where they worked. He also found that many small mobile tire companies in Florida and California were beginning to sell franchises of their operations. This indicated to him that these companies were experiencing enough growth to warrant the decision to franchise their operations.

Welch decided to launch his version of a mobile tire company during the spring. He started with one truck that was purchased used from a large truck rental company. He also found machinery for changing, repairing, and balancing tires from a GMC dealership that was closing down. He was thus able to buy the truck and then outfit the truck with all the necessary equipment for less than $40,000. Convenience and time savings at a reasonable cost would be the central selling points for the Tire Valet.

Welch's is a classic example of an entrepreneur's having been successful as well as a failure in previous entrepreneurial endeavors. As a high school student he had sold T-shirts and had his own landscaping company with two other friends. His landscaping business was very successful in his sophomore and junior years of high school but during his senior year his friends became more involved in other activities and lost interest in the business forcing him to end the endeavor. After graduating from college in 1995 he started collecting antiques while working for an industrial cleaning products company. He found that antiques were much more interesting than his job as a purchasing agent for this company so he decided in 2001 to leave his job and become an antiques dealer. At first he bought space at antiques flea markets, also continuing to collect and buy wherever he found an opportunity. Estate sales, auctions, and flea markets were his best sources of finding quality antiques. His specialty was carpets and furniture, which took up too much space in his converted garage and basement, so he eventually opened his own retail store in an upscale Boston suburb. His success with the one shop eventually led him to open a second antiques store in another community. After eight successful years of business and significant changes in his personal life with the birth of two children, Jack became tired of the constant traveling to auctions, sales, and shows and thus decided to sell his business. This was about the time that he realized that there might be an opportunity to start a mobile tire changing company.

In January, Welch started testing the idea, driving around to office buildings, walking in to companies at random, and offering to do tire changes for the employees who worked there. He'd remove a customer's wheels, throw them into his SUV, take them to a nearby service station to have the tires replaced, and bring them back. "I tested the market demand that way for two months before I decided to buy the truck," he explains. It was at this time he noted that there were other companies like this in other parts of the country but none in the Northeast. He also wondered why none of the major national auto-service chains such as Goodyear, National Tire and Battery, and Sears had attempted to enter this market. He thought that perhaps the major resistance was because of the climate in the Northeast. Most of the existing firms providing this service were located in warmer climates such as Florida, Arizona, and California. As mentioned, he reflected that many of them were also beginning to sell franchises, which indicated to him that the opportunities were great. He felt that if the glass replacement companies could provide their services year round despite the cold climate, why not mobile tire changing?

Welch's marketing pitch is simple and focuses on the fact that most people are busy and do not enjoy spending precious time at a tire store waiting around for the service to be performed. His initial marketing communications strategy was to print fliers that stressed the time saving and convenience of his service. He would come to your home or where you worked and would perform the service. The fliers were left in coffee shops and anywhere else that Welch could persuade to display his fliers. He recently developed a web site with the assistance of one of his college classmates. In addition he bought a yellow pages ad (1/8 of a page in size). He was willing to make cold calls and even visit local companies during his free time. At this time he has utilized no other marketing strategy but plans on budgeting more money for promotion in the future.

Most customers aren't particular about the brand of tires that he supplies; Welch buys tires for each job from a local distributor. Most people just want tires that are reliable but there are occasions where a customer specifies a brand of tire which Welch can satisfy by a special order from his distributor. The average invoice for service on passenger cars and SUVs for the tires and labor has been about $600 (this reflects an average service call, which may include 1–4 tires). He has been averaging about six service calls per week in the first two months of operation. However, he projects that he will average about 10 service calls per week in month three of operation. Eventu-

ally, Welch says, he may offer brake pad and rotor replacement, too, which would enable the company to charge another $400 or so. Welch claims that each job he does is profitable but that the bottom line could be improved significantly by offering the same customer more than just tire service.

Welch estimates that he has spent about $10,000 on marketing to this point but he realizes that he needs to refine his marketing strategy as well as come up with other more effective strategies to grow the business. He has considered offering discounts or a one-time payment to customers who would provide him with referrals. However, he is not sure how this would be accepted. It is important to consider a more structured strategy at this point if he wants to grow his business. His goal is to add trucks and continue to expand his geographic coverage of his market. Right now he focuses on three communities (households and businesses): Waltham, Wellesley, and Framingham (see Exhibit 1 for demographics of these communities). His office right now is in his home but he sees the need to find office space by the beginning of the second quarter.

EXHIBIT 1   Demographic Profile of Present Market

Demographics	Waltham	Wellesley	Framingham	Total State
Population	59,226	26,613	66,910	6.4 million
Households	23,207	8,594	26,153	2.44 million
Percent with children under 18	20.3	39.9	29.1	
Percent with married couples	41.3	67.2	50.0	
Percent with single parent	8.9	7.1	10.2	
Percent nonfamily	46.3	23.9	36.6	
Median income–households	$60,434	$125,814	$54,288	$50,502
Median income–family	$79,877	$155,539	$67,420	
Registered vehicles per capita is 0.56	33,100	14,900	37,400	3.58 million
Registered vehicles-Massachusetts				
Private & commercial[a]				3.6 million
Registered trucks, Massachusetts				
Private & commercial				1.8 million

[a]Includes taxis.

EXHIBIT 2   Sales Projections for Year 1: Number of Customers per Month

	Month											
	1	**2**	**3**	**4**	**5**	**6**	**7**	**8[a]**	**9**	**10**	**11**	**12**
# of Customers	5	7	10	13	17	21	25	30	33	37	42	48

[a]Second truck added for $40,000 investment.

EXHIBIT 3   Financial Projections for Next 12 Months

QUARTER	Q1	Q2	Q3[a]	Q4	Total
SALES REVENUE	$52,000	$120,400	$205,200	$300,000	$677,600
COGS (40%)	20,800	48,160	82,080	120,000	271,040
GROSS PROFIT	31,200	72,240	123,120	180,000	406,560
OPERATING EXPENSES					
Salaries	00	26,400[b]	31,200	36,000	93,600
Insurance	4,500	5,500	9,000	9,000	28,000
Utilities	1,000	3,000	3,500	3,500	11,000
Rent	00	4,500	4,500	4,500	13,500
Travel costs	1,200	1,600	2,200	2,800	7,800
Advertising	10,000	3,000	3,000	3,500	19,500
Office Supplies	500	1,200	1,500	1,700	3,900
Legal Fees	10,000	1,000	5,000	1,000	17,000
Maintenance	1,000	1,000	1,600	2,000	5,600
Depreciation	2,600	2,600	5,200	5,600	16,000
Taxes	00	2,600	3,100	3,600	9,300
Misc.	1,500	1,500	1,500	1,500	6,000
TOTAL EXPENSES	32,300	53,900	71,300	74,700	232,200
NET PROFIT BEFORE TAXES	(1,100)	18,340	51,820	105,300	174,360
TAXES (30%)	000	5,500	15,560	31,590	52,650
NET PROFIT	(1,100)	12,838	36,260	73,710	121,710

[a]Second truck and part time driver added.
[b]Add full-time driver at $20/hr, secretary at $2,400/mo, and Welch begins drawing a salary of $3,200/mo.

Exhibit 2 presents the sales projections for year 1. Welch feels that in the first month he will average about one customer per day. The average invoice per customer has been about $600. In the second month and subsequent months he has projected increases in the number of customers. In the eighth month he expects to add a second truck with a similar cost of $40,000. In the first three months Welch will perform the entire tire changing services himself but he is planning on hiring a driver/mechanic at the beginning

of the fourth month at a salary of $20/hour. He also will hire a secretary at the same time so that he can focus more of his time on marketing and strategies for future growth. Welch also feels he could draw a salary beginning the fourth month given the revenue that he has been able to generate so far. Exhibit 3 illustrates the projected revenues and expenses for the operation over the next 12 months. Given his prediction of success in the next 12 months Welch feels that he will need to seek investment monies to

EXHIBIT 4   Pricing and Cost Information

Labor $60/hr (minimum charge is one hour).

Tire prices for passenger cars at wholesale range from $45 to $150 for BF Goodrich, Cooper, or Falken tires to over $350 for certain truck tires. Large SUV tires ranged from $120 to $200 per tire depending on the brand. Bridgestone, Firestone, and Michelin tires were about 10 to 20 percent higher in price. An average price for tires for a passenger car was about $75 to $80 per tire. Markup typically for these tires was to double the wholesale price to cover overhead and profit.

Truck drivers and mechanics earned about $18 to $20/hour for an 8-hour day or 40 hour week.

(See Exhibit 3 for more financial projections.)

continue to grow the company. He will also need to prepare a more comprehensive business plan to submit to potential investors. Exhibit 4 presents some of the costs of tires as well as the labor rate that he will charge his customers with a minimum of one hour of labor for every job.

In addition to needing assistance with the preparation of a business plan Welch also needs to address some of the following issues: Is there a growing need for this service? What conditions in the economy and market would support growth for this service? Who are his major competitors? What would be their major strengths and weaknesses? What changes in the environment could negatively affect any future opportunities for this venture? What should be the target market for this venture? Are there other specific markets besides people at work or at home that might need this service?

What additional information do you think you would need in order to complete a quality business plan? How can he grow his business? Is this a business that he should think about franchising? Why or why not? Do you think that it is possible to add other services to the tire service? Why or why not?

INDEX

Page numbers followed by n indicate notes.